*Applied Regression Analysis
for Business and Economics*

Applied Regression Analysis

for Business and Economics

Second Edition

Terry E. Dielman

M. J. Neeley School of Business
Texas Christian University

Duxbury Press
An Imprint of Wadsworth Publishing Company
An International Thomson Publishing Company

I(T)P®

Belmont • Albany • Bonn • Boston • Cincinnati • Detroit • London • Madrid • Melbourne
Mexico City • New York • Paris • San Francisco • Singapore • Tokyo • Toronto • Washington

Editor: Curt Hinrichs
Editorial Assistant: Cynthia Mazow
Production: Greg Hubit Bookworks
Print Buyer: Barbara Britton
Permissions Editor: Peggy Meehan
Copy Editor: Lura Harrison
Text Designer: Cloyce Wall
Cover Designer: Stuart Paterson / Image House
Compositor: Techsetters, Inc.
Printer: R. R. Donnelly & Sons, Crawfordsville

This text is printed on acid-free recycled paper.

For more information, contact Wadsworth Publishing Company:

Wadsworth Publishing Company
10 Davis Drive
Belmont, California 94002, USA

International Thomson Publishing Europe
Berkshire House 168-173
High Holborn
London, WC1V 7AA, England

Thomas Nelson Australia
102 Dodds Street
South Melbourne 3205
Victoria, Australia

Nelson Canada
1120 Birchmount Road
Scarborough, Ontario
Canada M1K 5G4

International Thomson Editores
Campos Eliseos 385, Piso 7
Col. Polanco
11560 Mexico D.F. Mexico

International Thomson Publishing GmbH
Königswinterer Strasse 418
53227 Bonn, Germany

International Thomson Publishing Asia
221 Henderson Road
#05-10 Henderson Building
Singapore 0315

International Thomson Publishing Japan
Hirakawacho Kyowa Building, 3F
2-2-1 Hirakawacho
Chiyoda-ku, Tokyo 102, Japan

Library of Congress Cataloging-in-Publication Data

Dielman, Terry E.
   Applied regression analysis for business and economics / Terry E.
Dielman. — 2nd ed.
      p. cm.
   Includes bibliographical references and index.
   ISBN 0-534-26586-3
   1. Economics—Statistical methods.   2. Commercial statistics.
3. Regression analysis.   I.   Title.
HB137.D54 1996
330'.01'519536—dc20   95-24036

Contents

Preface

*A*pplied Regression Analysis for Business and Economics is designed for a one-semester course in regression analysis for business and economics undergraduates and MBAs. The goal of the text is to present regression concepts and techniques in a way that avoids unnecessary mathematical rigor. The emphasis is on understanding the assumptions of the regression model, knowing how to validate a selected model for these assumptions, knowing when and how regression might be useful in a business setting, and understanding and interpreting computer output from commonly encountered statistical packages. The text presents output from the statistical packages SAS and MINITAB. And brief introductions to both are presented in Appendix C. Other statistical packages containing regression procedures can also be easily used with the text.

Level and Prerequisites

To use the text, little mathematical expertise beyond basic college algebra is necessary. No knowledge of linear algebra is assumed in the text. Appendix D does provide a summary of matrices and matrix operations and a brief introduction to the use of matrices in presenting the least squares method for the interested reader. An introductory (or first semester) course in statistics is assumed. Chapter 2 does, however, contain a brief review of most of the concepts covered in an introductory statistics course.

It is assumed throughout the text that students have access to a computer and statistical software. The text concentrates on using the computer to do the calculations, while the student is responsible for knowing what to do with the resulting computer output. Although the text could be used without computer access, the author believes that actually analyzing data is an important component of the learning process.

Real Data

Actual data drawn from various sources are used throughout the book in the examples and exercises. When data are simulated, an attempt has been made to provide realistic data and situations in which these data might occur. In this way, the relevance of the techniques being presented is highlighted for students.

Data sets for the exercises in this text are available on a data disk accompanying each new copy of this book. The data are formatted in ASCII, MINITAB, SAS, Microsoft Excel, and STATA form and are accessible to any statistical software package. File names needed to read the data when using MINITAB or SAS are shown with each exercise.

Organization and Coverage

Chapter 2 provides a quick review of most concepts covered in a first-semester statistics course. Chapters 3 through 7, covered sequentially, provide the material on linear regression. Chapter 3 introduces simple linear regression, including MINITAB and SAS regression outputs. Chapter 4 provides the extension to multiple linear regression. Chapter 5 discusses the implications of violations of assumptions of the regression model, presents ways to recognize possible violations, and suggests corrections for violations. In Chapter 6, the use of indicator and interaction variables is described. Chapter 7 discusses several techniques used to aid in selecting explanatory variables for the regression.

Chapters 8 and 9 can be viewed as optional in a course on linear regression. Chapter 8 presents a brief introduction to analysis of variance. One-way analysis of variance and its relationship to regression with indicator variables is discussed. The chapter concludes with an examination of randomized block designs and two-way complete factorial designs. Chapter 9 introduces two procedures that can be used when qualitative dependent variables are encountered: discriminant analysis and logistic regression. The chapter concentrates on the two-group case.

Changes to the Second Edition

There are a number of changes in this text from the first edition. The major changes include:

■ Most of the data sets in the text have been updated. Some additional problems and examples involving "real" data have been added to the text. Some of these data sets come from actual business settings, while others are taken from journals and popular publications.

■ Time-series topics have been integrated into the text chapters. Comments received on the first edition suggested students believed that time-series regression must be a lot harder than the other topics in the book since it was covered in the last chapter. As a result, students often avoided time-series data when choosing topics for projects, and so on. Given the current emphasis on analysis of processes in business settings and the frequency with which time-series data are encountered in actual applications, it seems appropriate to introduce these concepts at an earlier stage. Fitting a trend line is in Chapter 3 (Simple Regression Analysis). Using lagged variables in time-series regression is discussed in Chapter 4 (Multiple Regression Analysis). Testing for autocorrelation and corrections for autocorrelation are discussed in Chapter 5 (Assessing the Assumptions of the Regression Model), and using indicator variables to model seasonal variation is included in Chapter 6 (Using Indicator and Interaction Variables). All of the time-series regression topics previously covered are still in the text. They are simply reordered.

■ Analysis of variance (ANOVA) topics have been moved to a separate chapter (Chapter 8) instead of including them in the chapter on indicator variables. This should prevent any interruption in the flow of regression topics and should make it easy for instructors who choose not to cover ANOVA.

■ A new chapter (Chapter 9) has been added that includes a brief introduction to discriminant analysis and logistic regression. Since 0/1 dependent variables are encountered frequently in business applications, the student should be aware that linear regression is not optimal for this situation, but that there are techniques that are specifically designed for qualitative dependent variables. The presentation in this chapter is intentionally brief.

■ A new section, Using the Computer, has been added at the end of each chapter. The MINITAB and SAS commands used to generate outputs in each chapter have been placed in these new sections.

Acknowledgments

I would like to thank those who reviewed the manuscript at various stages of the revision of this text: Jamie Eng, San Francisco State University; Michael Parzen, University of Chicago; Darrell Radson, University of Wisconsin–Milwaukee; Elizabeth Rose, University of Southern California; Richard A. Scott, University of Arizona; Vivek Shah, Southwest Texas State University; and Martin Wells, Cornell University.

I would also like to express my appreciation to the staff and associates of Duxbury, especially Curt Hinrichs, Jennie Burger, Clair Masson, Greg Hubit, and Cynthia Mazow.

Thanks also to my graduate assistant, Sarah Luke, for reading the text and solutions and providing comments from the students' point of view.

Finally, thanks to my wife Karen for her support, patience, and input throughout this process.

Terry E. Dielman
Fort Worth

An Introduction to Regression Analysis

Computers and telecommunications equipment have buried the present-day manager under a mountain of data. Although the purpose of these data is to assist the manager in the decision-making process, the corporate executive who faces the task of juggling data on many variables may find himself or herself at a loss when attempting to make sense of such information. The decision-making process is further complicated by the dynamic elements in the business environment and the complex interrelationships among these elements.

This text has been prepared to give the manager (or future manager) a tool for examining possible relationships between two or more variables. For example, sales and advertising are two variables commonly thought to be related. When a soft drink company increases advertising expenditures by paying professional athletes millions of dollars to do its advertisements, it expects that this outlay will increase sales. In general, when decisions on advertising expenditures of millions of dollars are involved, it would be comforting to have some evidence that, in the past, increased advertising expenditures indeed led to increased sales.

Another example is the relationship between the selling price of a house and its square footage. When a new house is to be listed for sale, how should the price be determined? Is a 4000-square-foot house worth twice as much as a 2000-square-foot house? What other factors might be involved in the pricing of houses and how should these factors be included in the determination of the price?

In a study of absenteeism at a large manufacturing plant, management may feel that several variables have an impact. These variables might include job complexity, base pay, the number of years a worker has been with the plant, and the age of that worker. If absenteeism can cost the company thousands of dollars, then the importance of identifying its associated factors becomes clear.

Perhaps the most important analytic tool for examining the relationships between two or more variables is regression analysis. *Regression analysis* is a statistical technique for developing an equation describing the relationship between two or more variables. One variable is specified to be the *dependent* variable or the variable to be explained. The other one or more variables are called the *independent* or explanatory variables. Using the previous examples, the soft drink firm would identify sales as the dependent variable and advertising expenditures as the explanatory variable. The real estate firm would choose selling price as the dependent variable and size as the independent variable to explain variations in selling prices from house to house.

There are several reasons why business researchers might want to know how certain variables are related. The retail firm may want to know how much advertising is necessary to achieve a certain level of sales. An equation expressing the relationship between sales and advertising would be useful in answering this question. For the real estate firm, the relationship might be used in assigning prices to houses coming onto the market. The management of the manufacturing firm would like to know what variables are most highly related to absenteeism to try to lower the absenteeism rate. Reasons for wanting to develop an equation relating two or more variables can be classified as follows: (1) to describe the relationship, (2) for control purposes (what value of the explanatory variable is needed to produce a certain level of the dependent variable) or (3) for prediction.

Much statistical analysis is a multistage process of trial and error. A good deal of exploratory work must be done to select appropriate variables for study and to determine the relationships between or among them. This requires that a variety of statistical tests and other procedures be performed and sound judgments made before one arrives at a satisfactory choice of dependent and explanatory variables. The emphasis in this text will be on this multistage process rather than on the computations themselves or an in-depth study of the theory behind the techniques presented. In this sense, the text is directed at the applied researcher or the user of statistics.

Except for a few preparatory examples, we will assume that a computer is available to the reader to perform the actual computations. Statistical software frees the user to concentrate on the multistage "model-building" process.

Most examples will use illustrative computer output to present the results. The two statistical software packages used will be MINITAB and SAS. The mainframe version 6.07 of SAS and the PC version 10.2 (Windows) of MINITAB have been used to develop the materials. Both packages are available in PC and mainframe versions. The output from these two packages is fairly standard and easily understood. Many of the exercises at the end of the chapters are intended to be done with the aid of a computer. Any statistical software package with a regression routine can be used for this purpose. Some of the options available in MINITAB and SAS may not be present in other packages, but this should not create a problem in completing the exercises.

A disk has been provided with the data sets used in most of the analyses in this text. In each problem where data sets are provided, the MINITAB and SAS commands to read the data will be given. In the commands to read the data files, no disk drive has been specified; only the file name is used. A disk drive may need to be indicated on the commands.

A section is included at the end of each chapter called "Using the Computer." Commands from MINITAB and SAS are provided for statistical procedures used in the chapter. Also, menu categories for menu-driven versions of MINITAB are provided. In addition, Appendix C provides a discussion of the use of MINITAB and SAS.

This book, however, is not intended to provide full information on the use of these statistical packages. For further information on MINITAB and SAS, the interested reader is referred to one of the following references:

Miller, R. *MINITAB Handbook for Business and Economics*. Boston: PWS-Kent Publishing Co., 1988.

MINITAB Reference Manual, Release 10 for Windows. Minitab, Inc., July 1994.

MINITAB Reference Manual, Release 8, PC Version. Minitab, Inc., November 1991.

Ryan, B., and Joiner, B. *MINITAB Handbook*. 3d ed. Belmont, CA: Duxbury Press, 1994.

SAS Introductory Guide. 3d ed. Cary, NC: SAS Institute Inc., 1985.

SAS/STAT User's Guide: Vols. 1 and 2, Version 6. 4th ed. Cary, NC: SAS Institute Inc., 1990.

2

Review of Basic Statistical Concepts

2.1
Introduction

The purpose of this chapter is to summarize and review many of the basic statistical concepts taught in an introductory statistics course. For the most part, introductory courses in statistics deal with three main areas of interest: descriptive statistics, probability, and statistical inference.

Typically, the problem in statistics is one of studying a particular population. A *population*, for purposes of this text, may be defined as the collection of all items of interest to a researcher. The researcher may want to study the sales figures for firms in a particular industry, the rates of return on public utility firms, or the lifetimes of a new brand of automobile tires. But because of time limitations, cost, or the destructive nature of testing, not all elements in a population can be examined. Instead, a subset of the population, called a *sample*, is chosen and the characteristic of interest is determined for the items in the sample.

Descriptive statistics is that area of statistics that summarizes the information contained in a sample. This summarization may be achieved by condensing the information and presenting it in tabular form. For example, frequency distributions are one way to summarize data in a table. Graphical methods of summarizing the data also may be used. The types of graphs discussed in introductory statistics courses often include histograms, ogives, and stem-and-leaf plots.

Data also may be summarized by numerical values. For example, to describe the center of a data set, the mean or median is often suggested. To describe variability, the variance, standard deviation, or interquartile range might be used. Each of the numerical values is a single number computed from the data and describes a certain characteristic of a sample.

Describing the information contained in a sample is only a first step for most statistical studies. If the study of a population's characteristics is the researcher's goal, then he or she would like to be able to use the information obtained from the sample to make statements about the population. The process of generalizing from characteristics of a sample to those of a population is called *statistical inference*. The bridge leading from descriptive measures computed for a sample to inferences made about population characteristics is the field of probability.

Statistical sampling is an additional topic discussed in introductory statistics. By choosing the elements of a sample in a particular manner, objective evaluations can be made of the quality of the inferences concerning population characteristics. Without proper choice of a sample, inferences can be made, but there is no way to evaluate these generalizations objectively. Thus, the manner in which the sample is chosen is important.

The most common type of sampling procedure discussed in introductory statistics is simple random sampling. Suppose a sample of n items is desired. To qualify as a *simple random sample* (SRS), the items in the sample are selected so that each possible sample of size n is equally likely to be chosen. In other words, each possible sample has an equal probability of being the one actually chosen. This is one of the pieces of the bridge that probability builds between descriptive statistics and statistical inference. Another piece of the bridge is a description of the behavior of certain of the numerical summaries that are computed as descriptive statistics.

Any numerical summary computed from a sample is called a *statistic*. A researcher will compute a single statistic from one sample chosen from the population of interest and use the numerical value of this statistic to make a statement about the value of some population characteristic. For example, suppose a particular brand of tires is to be studied to determine the average life of these tires. If the average life were known, the tire company might use this information to establish guarantees for its tires. An SRS of tires is chosen and tested to determine the individual lifetimes of the tires. Then the *sample average lifetime* is computed. This sample average can be used as an estimate of the population average lifetime of these tires.

The statistic computed, however, is the sample average lifetime for one particular sample of tires chosen. If a different set of n tires had been chosen, a different sample average would have resulted because of individual variation in the tires' lifetimes. Thus, the sample means themselves vary depending on which set of n tires is chosen as the sample. If this variation in the sample means was without any pattern, then there would be no way to relate the value of the sample mean obtained to the unknown value of the population mean. Fortunately, the behavior of the sample means (and other statistics) from random samples is not without a pattern. This behavior is described by a concept called a *sampling distribution*. Probability again enters the picture because sampling distributions are simply probability distributions. Through knowledge of the sampling distribution of a statistic, procedures can be developed to objectively evaluate the quality of sample statistics used to approximate population characteristics.

In this chapter many of the concepts mentioned previously will be reviewed. These include descriptive statistics, random variables and probability distributions, sampling distributions, and statistical inference. Because most or all of these topics are covered in an introductory course in statistics, the coverage here will be brief.

For detailed references on introductory statistics, the interested reader is referred to texts such as:

Hildebrand, D. K., and Ott, L. *Statistical Thinking for Managers.* 3d ed. Belmont, CA: Duxbury Press, 1991.

Mendenhall, W., and Beaver, R. J. *A Course in Business Statistics.* 3d ed. Belmont, CA: Duxbury Press, 1992.

Shiffler, R. E., and Adams, A. J. *Introductory Business Statistics with Computer Applications.* 2d ed. Belmont, CA: Duxbury Press, 1995.

2.2
Descriptive Statistics

Table 2.1 shows the three-year return as of 1 January 1994 for a random sample of 26 mutual funds. All of these funds involve a load (a type of sales charge). Examining the 26 numbers in this list provides little information of use. Just looking at a list of numbers is confusing even when the sample size is only 26. For larger samples, the confusion would be even greater.

The field of descriptive statistics provides ways to summarize the information in a data set. Summaries can be tabular, graphical, or numerical. One common tabular method of summarizing data is the *frequency distribution*. Intervals covering the range of the data are constructed and the number of observations in each interval is then tabulated and recorded.

A graphical representation of a frequency distribution is called a *histogram*. From the frequency distribution or the histogram, one can obtain a quick picture of certain characteristics of the data. For example, the center of the data and how much variability is present can be observed. The data have been summarized so that these characteristics are more obvious.

Most statistical software packages provide various tabular and graphical methods of summarizing data. Figure 2.1 shows the histogram constructed by MINITAB for the mutual-fund-return data.

The histogram shows that the returns for these funds vary from a low of about 5.5% (the lower boundary of the first interval) to a high of about 35% (the upper boundary of the last interval). Most of the returns are in the classes with midpoints of 13% and 18%. Very high returns (above 20% or so) are more rare than returns in these central classes.

Numerical summaries are single numbers computed from a sample to describe some characteristic of the data set. Some common numerical summaries are *sample mean*, *sample median*, *sample variance*, and *sample standard deviation*. The sample mean and sample median are measures of the center or central tendency of the data. The sample mean is just the average of all observations in the data set:

T A B L E **2.1**

Three-Year-Return Data for Load Mutual Funds

Fund Name	Three-Year Return
Dean Witter Equity Income	8.0
Dean Witter Utilities	13.4
Fidelity Select Leisure	29.2
First Investors Global	11.0
Flag Investors Quality Growth	8.6
G. T. America Growth	19.4
Heritage Capital Appreciation	20.6
J. Hancock Growth	19.4
Kemper Blue Chip	14.0
Kemper International	12.1
Mainstay Capital Appreciation	28.7
Merrill Lynch Fund for Tomorrow A	16.1
Metlife-State St. Cap. Apprec.	32.7
Metlife-State St. Equity-Inc.	17.8
Mutual Benefit	15.2
Nationwide	12.7
Pioneer	16.8
Prudential Growth B	11.5
Rightime Blue Chip	11.2
Rodney Square International Equity	9.8
Smith Barney Income & Growth	16.4
Stagecoach Growth & Income	15.4
United International Growth	20.0
United Retirement Shares	15.7
United Science & Energy	18.4
Van Eck World Trends	8.0

SOURCE: From *Kiplinger's Mutual Funds '94* (©Kiplinger Washington Editors, Inc.).

$$\bar{y} = \frac{\sum\limits_{i=1}^{n} y_i}{n},$$

where y_i represents the ith observation in the data set. (See Appendix A for an explanation of summation notation.) The sample median is the midpoint of the data after the data have been ordered. If n, the number of observations, is even, then the median is the average of the two middle observations after the observations have been ordered from smallest to largest. If n is odd, the unique middle value in the ordered data set is the median.

F I G U R E 2.1

Histogram of Three-Year Returns for Load Mutual Funds

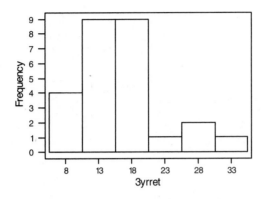

F I G U R E 2.2

MINITAB Numerical Summaries for the Three-Year-Return Data*

Variable	N	Mean	Median	TrMean	StDev	SEMean
3yrret	26	16.23	15.55	15.89	6.36	1.25

Variable	Min	Max	Q1	Q3
3yrret	8.00	32.70	11.43	19.40

*The summaries computed include the number of observations (N), the sample mean (Mean), sample median (Median), the 5% trimmed mean (TrMean), the standard deviation (StDev), the standard error of the mean (SEMean), the minimum (Min), the maximum (Max), the first quartile (Q1), and the third quartile (Q3).

The sample variance and sample standard deviation are measures of the data's variability. The sample variance is computed as

$$s^2 = \frac{\sum_{i=1}^{n}(y_i - \bar{y})^2}{n-1}$$

This is the average squared distance of each data point, y_i, from the center of the data, $\bar{y}$. The divisor, $n-1$, is used rather than n to provide an unbiased estimator (one which neither consistently overestimates or underestimates the true parameter) of the population variance. Because s^2 expresses variability in squared units, an intuitively more appealing measure is the sample standard deviation, s, which is simply the square root of s^2. Although many other numerical summaries exist, they will not be discussed in this review.

Figure 2.2 shows the results of using MINITAB to compute several descriptive measures for the mutual-fund-return data, including the sample mean, sample median, sample variance, and sample standard deviation.

Exercises

1   The highway mileages of 146 cars are available on the data disk. These cars are all 1994 models and were all listed in the *Road & Track Complete '94 Car Buyer's Guide*. Find the mean, standard deviation, and median for the mileages. Also, construct a histogram of the data. These data can be read in MINITAB using the command

```
READ 'CARS2' C1
```

or in SAS from the file CARS2.DAT using the command

```
INPUT HWYMPG;
```

The data are listed in Table 2.2.

T A B L E *2.2*

Highway Mileages for 146 Cars

Name of Car	Highway Mileage	Name of Car	Highway Mileage
Acura Integra	31	Chevrolet Caprice	26
Acura Legend	26	Chevrolet Cavalier	37
Acura NSX	24	Chevrolet Corsica	31
Acura Vigor	26	Chevrolet Corvette	25
Alfa Romeo 164	24	Chevrolet Lumina	29
Alfa Romeo Spider	30	Chrysler NY 5th Ave	25
Audi 90	26	Chrysler Condorde	28
Audi 100	26	Chrysler Le Baron Conv.	28
Audi V8	20	Chrysler Le Baron Sedan	27
BMW 3-Series	30	Chrysler NY & LHS	26
BMW 5-Series	25	Dodge (Plymouth) Colt	40
BMW 7-Series	22	Dodge Intrepid	28
Buick Century	34	Dodge Shadow (P Sundance)	32
Buick Le Sabre	29	Dodge Spirit (P Acclaim)	28
Buick Park Avenue	28	Dodge Stealth	24
Buick Regal	29	Dodge Viper RT/10	21
Buick Riviera	25	Eagle Summit	40
Buick Roadmaster Wagon	25	Eagle Summit Wagon	29
Buick Skylark	31	Eagle Talon (P Laser)	32
Cadillac De Ville	25	Eagle Vision	28
Cadillac Eldorado	25	Ferrari 348	19
Cadillac Fleetwood	25	Ferrari 512 TR	16
Cadillac Seville & STS	25	Ford Crown Victoria	23
Chevrolet Beretta	34	Ford Escort	31
Chevrolet Camaro	28	Ford Probe	33

T A B L E *2.2* (*Cont.*)
Highway Mileages for 146 Cars

Name of Car	Highway Mileage	Name of Car	Highway Mileage
Ford Taurus	29	Mercury Capri	31
Ford Tempo	33	Mercury Cougar XR7	27
Ford Thunderbird	27	Mercury Grand Marquis	24
Geo Metro	50	Mercury Sable	29
Geo Prizm	33	Mercury Topaz	33
Honda Accord	31	Mercury Tracer	37
Honda Civic	40	Mitsubishi Diamante	25
Honda Civic del Sol	41	Mitsubishi Eclipse	32
Honda Prelude	29	Mitsubishi Expo and LRV	28
Hyundai Elantra	29	Mitsubishi Galant	30
Hyundai Excel	33	Mitsubishi Mirage	39
Hyundai Scoupe	35	Mitsubishi 3000 GT	24
Hyundai Sonata	27	Nissan Altima	30
Infiniti G20	32	Nissan Maxima	26
Infiniti J30	23	Nissan Sentra	37
Infiniti Q45	22	Nissan 240SX Convertible	26
Jaguar XJS	23	Nissan 300 ZX	24
Jaguar XJ6	24	Oldsmobile Achieva	31
KIA Sephia	33	Oldsmobile Aurora	25
Lamborghini Diablo	14	Oldsmobile Cutlass Ciera	32
Lexus ES300	24	Oldsmobile Cutlass Supreme	28
Lexus GS300	23	Oldsmobile 88 Royale	28
Lexus LS400	23	Oldsmobile 98	27
Lexus SC300 & SC400	23	Pontiac Bonneville	28
Lincoln Continental	26	Pontiac Firebird	28
Lincoln Mark VII	25	Pontiac Grand Am	32
Lincoln Town Car	23	Pontiac Grand Prix	28
Lotus Esprit S4	27	Pontiac Sunbird	35
Mazda MX-3	37	Porsche 911	25
Mazda MX-5 Miata	27	Porsche 928 GTS	19
Mazda MX-6	34	Porsche 968	26
Mazda Protege	37	Saab 900	28
Mazda RX-7	25	Saab 9000	27
Mazda 323	37	Saturn Sports Coupe	37
Mazda 626	34	Saturn Sedan	37
Mazda 929	24	Saturn Wagon	37
Mercedes-Benz C-Class	28	Subaru Impreza	31
Mercedes-Benz E-Class	25	Subaru Justy	37
Mercedes-Benz S-Class	24	Subaru Legacy	31
Mercedes-Benz SL-Class	24	Subaru Loyale Wagon	29

T A B L E 2.2 *(Cont.)*
Highway Mileages for 146 Cars

Name of Car	Highway Mileage	Name of Car	Highway Mileage
Subaru SVX	25	Toyota Tercel	36
Suzuki Swift	43	Volkswagen Corrado	25
Toyota Camry	30	Volkswagen Golf	32
Toyota Celica	34	Volkswagen Jetta	30
Toyota Corolla	34	Volkswagen Passat	24
Toyota MR2	29	Volvo 850	29
Toyota Paseo	34	Volvo 940	28
Toyota Supra	23	Volvo 960	26

2   The National Collegiate Athletic Association (NCAA) is concerned with the graduation rate of student athletes. Part of an effort to increase graduation rates for student athletes involved implementing Proposition 48, beginning with the 1986–87 school year. Proposition 48 mandated that student athletes obtain a 700 SAT or a 15 ACT test score. Table 2.3 shows the graduation rates (percentages) for several groups of students: all students entering freshman classes in 1983–84 through 1985–86 (AS83), student athletes from freshman classes entering in those same years (SA83), all students entering in 1986–87 (AS86), and student athletes entering in 1986–87 (SA86). All Division I schools with complete data for all four groups are represented. [The data were obtained from the *Fort Worth Star-Telegram* (2 July, 1993 and 20 May, 1993 issues).]

T A B L E 2.3
Graduation Rates for All Students Entering 1983–84 Through 1985–86 (AS83) and 1986–87 (AS86), and for Student Athletes Entering 1983–84 Through 1985–86 (SA83) and 1986–87 (SA86)

Name of School	AS83	SA83	AS86	SA86	Name of School	AS83	SA83	AS86	SA86
Akron	42	63	41	58	Auburn	64	53	65	58
Ala.-Birmingham	36	28	31	33	Austin Peay	29	31	32	29
Alabama	52	36	55	57	Ball St.	48	61	48	68
Alabama St.	18	29	55	57	Baylor	69	63	71	66
American	66	64	67	60	Bethune-Cookman	37	32	36	57
Appalachian St.	54	55	59	58	Boise St.	19	36	18	27
Arizona	46	46	49	54	Boston College	85	86	88	94
Arizona St.	30	27	45	52	Boston Univ.	63	75	67	77
Arkansas	35	41	18	52	Bowling Green	54	54	63	61
Arkansas St.	30	27	29	37	Bradley	64	67	64	52

T A B L E **2.3** *(Cont.)*

Graduation Rates for All Students Entering 1983–84 Through 1985–86 (AS83) and 1986–87 (AS86), and for Student Athletes Entering 1983–84 Through 1985–86 (SA83) and 1986–87 (SA86)

Name of School	AS83	SA83	AS86	SA86	Name of School	AS83	SA83	AS86	SA86
Brigham Young	39	41	48	42	E. Michigan	34	44	38	47
Bucknell	90	93	94	97	E. Washington	35	39	38	42
Butler	58	72	66	80	Evansville	52	61	59	55
Cal-Berkeley	73	67	77	61	Fairfield	82	76	86	69
Cal-Irvine	58	58	65	57	Fairleigh Dickinson	39	37	39	53
Cal-S. Barbara	64	66	66	67	Florida	56	45	61	52
Cal St.-Fresno	47	36	50	49	Florida A&M	35	28	33	41
Cal St.-Fullerton	41	29	45	38	Florida Int.	56	47	55	50
Cal St.-Long Beach	33	20	36	37	Florida St.	53	43	50	50
Cal St.-Northridge	29	20	31	30	Fordham	77	87	77	84
Cal St.-Sacramento	38	34	34	32	Furman	73	74	81	82
Campbell	41	53	47	40	George Mason	41	54	46	63
Canisius	55	58	59	76	George Washington	67	79	70	76
Centenary	46	61	57	58	Georgetown	89	86	92	95
Cent. Florida	43	40	49	56	Georgia	59	43	61	58
Central Michigan	53	63	56	60	Georgia Tech	66	60	68	57
Charleston So.	18	33	33	31	Georgia So.	38	48	36	45
Chicago St.	11	20	8	25	Georgia St.	32	31	40	52
Cincinnati	46	51	47	42	Gonzaga	55	58	61	62
The Citadel	71	67	66	63	Grambling St.	49	47	45	35
Clemson	70	50	70	47	Hartford	56	80	51	65
Cleveland St.	34	33	34	48	Hawaii	81	75	78	78
Coastal Carolina	31	47	34	62	Hofstra	57	59	58	55
Colgate	89	84	91	84	Holy Cross	88	86	91	93
Colorado	60	56	66	58	Howard	41	41	45	49
Colorado St.	55	60	57	55	Idaho	44	41	43	47
Connecticut	68	55	68	70	Idaho St.	46	41	59	36
Creighton	66	53	65	31	Illinois	78	66	78	74
Davidson	88	81	91	66	Ill.-Chicago	33	48	32	55
Dayton	70	78	72	90	Illinois St.	49	49	53	62
Delaware	69	61	71	57	Indiana St.	37	44	36	49
Delaware St.	30	41	26	38	Indiana	56	61	65	62
DePaul	61	69	61	81	Iona	61	66	56	38
Detroit Mercy	47	49	54	68	Iowa	60	63	59	63
Drake	55	56	60	56	Iowa St.	60	51	64	67
Drexel	65	76	54	64	Jackson St.	19	37	34	43
Duke	92	91	94	89	Jacksonville	39	41	50	56
Duquesne	69	78	71	72	James Madison	79	68	82	69
East Carolina	46	56	50	52	Kansas	54	48	55	56
E. Tenn. St.	34	49	34	58	Kansas St.	48	46	48	66
E. Illinois	54	59	61	53	Kent St.	42	51	43	48
E. Kentucky	33	43	30	61	Kentucky	45	56	50	59

T A B L E **2.3** (*Cont.*)

Graduation Rates for All Students Entering 1983–84 Through 1985–86 (AS83) and 1986–87 (AS86), and for Student Athletes Entering 1983–84 Through 1985–86 (SA83) and 1986–87 (SA86)

Name of School	AS83	SA83	AS86	SA86	Name of School	AS83	SA83	AS86	SA86
LaSalle	66	79	63	94	Nevada	36	40	32	47
Lafayette	87	84	89	82	New Hampshire	67	72	74	75
Lamar	18	15	25	36	New Mexico	67	72	33	47
Lehigh	87	83	87	89	New Mexico St.	37	41	38	51
Liberty	26	48	35	49	New Orleans	18	25	19	21
Long Island	32	43	28	44	Niagara	55	78	56	82
Louisiana St.	34	30	37	36	Nicholls St.	19	28	22	35
Louisiana Tech	39	41	36	59	N.C.-Asheville	34	43	35	47
Louisville	28	42	31	54	N. Carolina	78	74	82	67
Loyola (Md.)	69	82	74	71	N.C.-Charlotte	49	50	49	64
Loyola Marymount	67	42	68	68	N.C.-Wilmington	42	67	46	67
Loyola (Ill.)	59	87	63	77	N.C. A&T	38	40	37	44
Maine	49	53	56	59	North Texas	32	29	34	42
Manhattan	70	83	70	100	NE Louisiana	27	36	32	43
Marist	60	50	63	67	Northeastern	47	67	46	60
Marquette	74	83	74	70	N. Illinois	52	52	52	57
Marshall	39	39	39	51	Northern Iowa	56	61	62	58
Maryland-Balt.	36	61	35	66	Northwestern St.	14	30	22	32
Maryland	56	58	64	54	Northwestern	87	82	89	77
Md.-Eastern Shore	19	23	21	25	Notre Dame	92	83	94	84
Massachusetts	63	66	68	73	Ohio St.	52	60	54	69
McNeese St.	27	29	28	33	Ohio University	53	69	61	70
Memphis St.	34	37	33	64	Oklahoma	43	39	42	46
Mercer	40	54	40	59	Oklahoma St.	43	27	44	30
Miami (Fla.)	56	48	55	52	Old Dominion	47	44	45	38
Miami (Ohio)	75	65	83	75	Oregon	47	47	54	66
Michigan	82	65	85	79	Oregon St.	50	54	52	47
Michigan St.	66	64	69	62	Pacific	62	65	62	63
Middle Tenn. St.	33	31	36	44	Penn St.	74	67	77	78
Minnesota	34	47	42	53	Pepperdine	59	42	68	50
Mississippi	48	48	49	57	Pittsburgh	61	55	62	56
Mississippi St.	51	52	52	53	Portland	55	48	60	59
Miss. Valley St.	31	42	43	44	Providence	83	84	95	93
Missouri	55	53	55	54	Purdue	68	60	70	65
Monmouth (N.J.)	48	48	52	48	Radford	52	67	54	68
Montana	28	35	28	38	Rhode Island	58	62	62	67
Morehead St.	38	44	44	69	Rice	86	69	87	78
Morgan St.	38	46	16	40	Richmond	82	75	81	73
Mount St. Mary's	71	70	73	70	Rider	62	60	63	74
Murray St.	39	47	43	40	Robert Morris	55	57	48	80
Nebraska	48	48	50	64	Rutgers	73	69	76	69
Nev.-Las Vegas	27	34	27	40	St. Bonaventure	68	76	70	83

T A B L E *2.3* (*Cont.*)

Graduation Rates for All Students Entering 1983–84 Through 1985–86 (AS83) and 1986–87 (AS86), and for Student Athletes Entering 1983–84 Through 1985–86 (SA83) and 1986–87 (SA86)

Name of School	AS83	SA83	AS86	SA86	Name of School	AS83	SA83	AS86	SA86
St. Francis (N.Y.)	34	57	34	27	UT-Pan Am	11	21	19	38
St. Francis (Pa.)	55	61	64	80	UT-San Antonio	21	32	22	26
St. John's	64	78	62	73	Texas A&M	67	38	66	53
St. Joseph's	71	78	73	88	TCU	61	54	62	57
St. Louis	63	81	65	92	Texas Southern	9	13	10	24
St. Mary's	65	63	66	100	Texas Tech	41	35	40	45
St. Peter's	47	57	49	59	Toledo	39	45	47	52
San Diego	53	72	60	81	Tulane	68	57	70	62
San Diego St.	37	31	41	40	Tulsa	47	49	44	51
San Francisco	56	61	58	100	UCLA	70	60	74	60
San Jose St.	30	33	39	36	Utah	33	49	34	50
Santa Clara	78	77	81	81	Utah St.	47	33	46	32
Seton Hall	59	59	61	71	Valparaiso	69	67	74	75
Siena	79	67	81	75	Vanderbilt	78	71	81	82
South Alabama	25	33	23	48	Vermont	76	79	77	79
S. Carolina	59	56	61	49	Villanova	83	83	86	76
S. Carolina St.	50	43	51	59	Virginia	80	81	92	88
S. Florida	38	46	46	54	Va. Commonwealth	41	58	46	55
SE Missouri St.	34	33	34	48	Va. Military	65	61	66	67
Southeastern La.	19	35	22	33	Va. Tech.	71	46	72	55
Southern Ca.	64	51	66	69	Wagner	36	57	48	50
Southern Illinois	43	56	20	61	Wake Forest	78	62	84	71
SMU	69	48	68	71	Washington	60	53	63	61
Southern Miss.	40	41	40	43	Washington St.	52	48	55	49
Southern	24	26	25	30	Weber St.	20	27	43	31
SW Missouri St.	37	52	43	62	West Virginia	54	62	55	66
SW Texas St.	29	33	30	44	Western Carolina	42	44	45	62
Southwestern La.	29	24	30	39	Western Illinois	40	52	43	58
Stanford	92	84	92	86	W. Kentucky	39	47	37	38
Stephen F. Austin	40	41	40	58	W. Michigan	46	50	54	49
Stetson	58	59	58	48	Wichita St.	45	27	44	33
Syracuse	62	61	64	69	William & Mary	84	83	89	85
Temple	44	56	43	57	Winthrop	51	44	50	49
Tenn-Chatt.	28	38	33	33	Wisc.-Green Bay	32	53	37	67
Tennessee	52	48	50	49	Wisconsin	66	63	70	69
Tenn.-Martin	22	27	29	38	Wright St.	30	46	33	54
Tenn.-Tech.	45	58	41	53	Wyoming	41	44	44	42
UT-Arlington	28	23	28	30	Xavier (Ohio)	66	78	65	77
Texas	59	43	63	55	Youngstown St.	38	59	40	60
UT-El Paso	25	23	26	38					

These data may be read into MINITAB from the data disk using

```
READ 'GRADRAT2' C1-C4
```

where C1 is AS83, C2 is SA83, C3 is AS86, and C4 is SA86.

In SAS, the data may be read from the file GRADRAT2.DAT using the command

```
INPUT AS83 SA83 AS86 SA86;
```

Examine the four groups by finding the mean and median graduation rates for each. Also, construct a histogram for each set of graduation rates.

2.3
Discrete Random Variables and Probability Distributions

A *random variable* can be defined as a rule that assigns a number to every possible outcome of an experiment. A *discrete* random variable is one with a definite distance between each of its possible values. For example, consider the toss of a coin. The two possible outcomes are head (H) and tail (T). A random variable of interest could be defined as

$$X = \text{ number of heads on a single coin toss}$$

Then X will assign the number 1 to the outcome H and the number 0 to outcome T.

As another example, suppose two cards are randomly drawn successively and without replacement from a deck of 52 cards. Let

$$Y = \text{ number of kings on two draws}$$

Then Y will assign the number 0, 1, or 2 to each possible outcome of the experiment.

In each of these examples, the outcome of the experiment will be determined by chance. Probabilities can be assigned to the outcomes of the experiment and thus to the values of the random variables. A table listing the values of a random variable and the probabilities associated with each value is called a *probability distribution* for the random variable.

For the coin toss, the probability distribution of X would be

x	$P(x)$
0	1/2
1	1/2

Here the notation $P(x)$ means "the probability that the random variable X has the value x" or $P(x) = P(X = x)$. The function $P(x)$ is called the *probability mass function* (pmf) of X.

For the card-drawing experiment, the probability distribution of Y would be

y	$P(y)$
0	188/221
1	32/221
2	1/221

Note that the probabilities $P(x)$ must satisfy the following conditions:

1 They must be between 0 and 1.

$$0 \leq P(x) \leq 1$$

2 They must sum to 1.

$$\sum P(x) = 1$$

When we discussed a sample of observations drawn from a population in the previous section, certain characteristics were of interest, primarily center and variability. Numerical summaries were used to measure these characteristics. Describing the center and the variation in a probability distribution also is often useful. The measures most often used to do this are the mean and variance (or standard deviation) of the random variable.

As an example, consider two random variables X and Y, representing the profit from two different investments. Suppose the two probability distributions have been set up as follows:

x	$P(x)$	y	$P(y)$
− 2000	.05	0	.40
−1000	.10	1000	.20
1000	.10	2000	.20
2000	.25	3000	.10
5000	.50	4000	.10

If only one of the investments can be chosen, some methods to compare the two would be useful. As can be seen, chances of a loss are greater for investment X than for investment Y, although the chances for a large profit are also greater for investment X.

One way to compare the investments might be to use the expected value, or mean, of the random variables representing the outcomes of the investments. The *expected value* of a discrete random variable X is defined as the sum of each value of X times the probability associated with that value:

$$E(X) = \mu_X = \sum x P(x)$$

The subscript X on μ_X often is dropped if it is clear which random variable is being discussed. The computation of the expected values of X and Y is shown in Table 2.4. The expected value of X is greater than the expected value of Y. Thus, on the basis of maximizing expected values, investment X would be chosen.

T A B L E 2.4

Computation of $E(X)$ and $E(Y)$

x	$P(x)$	$xP(x)$	y	$P(y)$	$yP(y)$
−2000	.05	−100	0	.40	0
−1000	.10	−100	1000	.20	200
1000	.10	100	2000	.20	400
2000	.25	500	3000	.10	300
5000	.50	2500	4000	.10	400
		$\sum xP(x) = 2900$			$\sum yP(y) = 1300$
		$E(X) = 2900$			$E(Y) = 1300$

The expected value of a random variable deserves some additional explanation at this point. Consider again the coin toss experiment with X equal to the "number of heads" and probability distribution

x	$P(x)$
0	1/2
1	1/2

Computing the expected value of X gives

$$E(X) = \frac{1}{2}$$

Obviously, if a coin is tossed, either the outcome 0 (tail) or 1 (head) will appear. The expected value of X represents the average that will be obtained over a large number of trials. If the coin were tossed a large number of times and zeros were recorded for tails and ones for heads, then the average of these zeros and ones would be close to $\frac{1}{2}$. The same interpretation can be made for the case of the investments. The expected outcomes represent the averages obtained over a large number of trials rather than a single trial. Thus, in the long run, investment X will provide a higher average profit than investment Y.

There are, of course, other criteria for choosing between investments than simply maximizing the expected returns. A measure of each investment's risk also might be important. The variability of the outcomes is sometimes used as a measure of such risk. One measure of a random variable's variation is the *variance*, defined for a discrete random variable, X, as

$$\text{Var}(X) = \sigma_X^2 = \Sigma(x - \mu)^2 P(x) = \Sigma x^2 P(x) - \mu^2$$

To compute $\text{Var}(X)$, the mean is subtracted from each possible value of X, and the differences are squared and then multiplied times the probability of the value of X occurring. The resulting sum is the variance, which represents an average squared

TABLE 2.5

Computation of σ_X^2 and σ_Y^2

x	$P(x)$	$xP(x)$	$x - \mu_X$	$(x - \mu_X)^2$	$(x - \mu_X)^2 P(x)$
-2000	.05	-100	-4900	24,010,000	1,200,500
-1000	.10	-100	-3900	15,210,000	1,521,000
1000	.10	100	-1900	3,610,000	361,000
2000	.25	500	-900	810,000	202,500
5000	.50	2500	2100	4,410,000	2,205,000
		$\mu_X = 2900$			5,490,000

y	$P(y)$	$yP(y)$	$y - \mu_Y$	$(y - \mu_Y)^2$	$(y - \mu_Y)^2 P(y)$
0	.4	0	-1300	1,690,000	676,000
1000	.2	200	-300	90,000	18,000
2000	.2	400	700	490,000	98,000
3000	.1	300	1700	2,890,000	289,000
4000	.1	400	2700	7,290,000	729,000
		$\mu_Y = 1300$			1,810,000

distance of each value of X to the center of the probability distribution. Note that no division is used in computing this "average." The division used to compute a sample variance has been replaced by the weighting of each outcome by its probability. The variances of X and Y are computed in Table 2.5.

The variances are

$$\sigma_X^2 = 5,490,000 \quad \text{and} \quad \sigma_Y^2 = 1,810,000$$

Obviously, investment X is more variable than investment Y. The variances are somewhat difficult to interpret, however, because they measure variability in squared units (squared dollars for the investments). To return to the original units of the problem, the square root of the variance, called the *standard deviation*, may be used:

$$\sigma_X = 2343.07 \quad \text{and} \quad \sigma_Y = 1345.36$$

The standard deviations are expressed in the original units of the problem.

All of the random variables discussed so far have been *discrete* random variables. A *continuous* random variable is one whose values are measured on a continuous scale. It is measured over a range of values with all numbers within that range as possible values (at least in theory). Examples of quantities that might be represented by continuous random variables are temperature, gas mileage, or stock prices. In the next section, a very useful continuous random variable in statistics, the normal random variable, will be introduced.

Exercises

3   Consider the roll of a single die. Construct the probability distribution of the random variable $X =$ "number of dots showing on the die." Find the expected value and standard deviation of X. How would you interpret the number obtained for the expected value?

4   Let X be a random variable defined as

$$X = 1 \text{ if an even number of dots appears on the roll of a single die}$$
$$= 0 \text{ if an odd number of dots appears on the roll of a single die}$$

Construct the probability distribution of X. Find the expected value and standard deviation of X. How would you interpret the number obtained for the expected value?

5   Consider the roll of two dice. Let X be a random variable representing the sum of the number of dots appearing on each of the dice. The probabilities of each possible value of X are shown in the following table:

x	$P(x)$
2	1/36
3	2/36
4	3/36
5	4/36
6	5/36
7	6/36
8	5/36
9	4/36
10	3/36
11	2/36
12	1/36

Determine the expected value and standard deviation of X.

6   The game of craps deals with rolling a pair of fair dice. In one version of the game, a field bet is a one-roll bet and is based on the outcome of the pair of dice. For every $1 bet, you lose $1 if the sum is 5, 6, 7, or 8; you win $1 if the sum is 3, 4, 9, 10, or 11; or you win $2 if the sum is 2 or 12.

   a   Using the information in Exercise 5, construct the probability distribution of the different outcomes available in a field bet.

   b   Determine the expected value of this probability distribution. How would you interpret this number?

7   The number of defective parts per shipment is to be modeled as a random variable X. The random variable is assumed to have the following distribution:

x	$P(x)$
0	.55
1	.15
2	.10
3	.10
4	.05
5	.05

a What is the expected number of defectives per shipment?

b If each defective costs the company $100 in rework costs, what is the expected cost per shipment?

c What is the probability that a shipment will have more than two defectives?

2.4
The Normal Distribution

A *continuous random variable* is a random variable that can take any value over a given range. An example that is important in statistical inference is the *normal random variable*. The probability distribution of the normal random variable, called the *normal distribution*, is often depicted as a bell-shaped symmetric curve as shown in Figure 2.3. The normal distribution is centered at the mean, μ. Variation in the distribution is described by the variance σ^2 or the standard deviation σ. Figure 2.4 shows two normal distributions with different means but equal standard deviations, while Figure 2.5 shows two distributions with the same mean but different standard deviations. Although the location of the distribution is determined by the mean, the spread of the distribution (how tall or flat the distribution appears) is determined by the standard deviation.

For a continuous distribution such as the normal distribution, the probability that the random variable takes on a value within a certain range can be determined by computing the area under the curve that defines the probability distribution between the limits of the range. To determine the probability that a normal random variable will be between 0 and 1, the area under the normal curve between these values must be computed. This computation is a fairly difficult task if done from scratch. Fortunately, a table of certain areas or probabilities under the normal curve is available to simplify these computations considerably.

Table 1 of Appendix B lists probabilities between certain values of the standard normal distribution. The standard normal distribution has a mean of $\mu = 0$ and a standard deviation of $\sigma = 1$. Throughout this text, the standard normal random variable will be denoted by the letter Z. This table is set up to show the probability that the normal random variable is between 0 and some number z written

$$P(0 \le Z \le z)$$

The z numbers are given by the values in the far left-hand column of the table to one decimal place. A second decimal place is provided by using the values in the top row

F I G U R E 2.3
The Normal Distribution with Mean μ and Standard Deviation σ

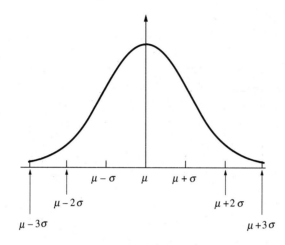

F I G U R E 2.4
Normal Distributions with Equal Standard Deviations but Different Means

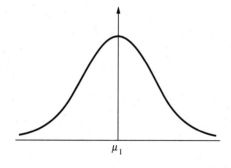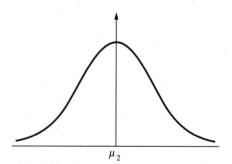

of the table. For example, to find the probability that Z is between 0 and 1, the value 1.0 is located in the left-hand column and the probability is read from the .00 column of the table:

$$P(0 \leq Z \leq 1.0) = .3413$$

This area is illustrated by the shaded region in Figure 2.6.

Similarly, the probability between 0 and 2.3 is

$$P(0 \leq Z \leq 2.3) = .4893$$

To compute the probability between 0 and 1.96, first find 1.9 in the left-hand column. The probability is then read from the .06 column of the table as

FIGURE **2.5**

Normal Distributions with Equal Means but Different Standard Deviations

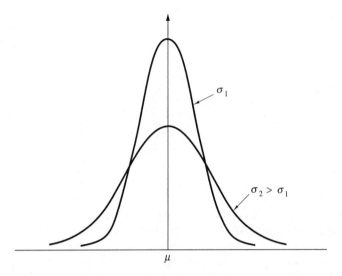

FIGURE **2.6**

Area or Probability under the Standard Normal Curve Between 0 and 1.0

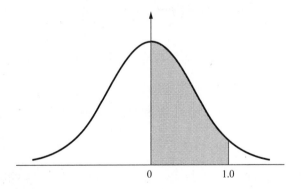

$$P(0 \leq Z \leq 1.96) = .4750$$

Because the standard normal curve has a mean of 0, the numbers to the right of the mean are positive as illustrated in the examples thus far. The numbers to the left of the mean would be negative. How is the table used to find the probability that Z is between, say, -1.0 and 1.0? There are no negative z values in the table. But the fact that the curve is symmetric can be used to determine the probabilities for numbers to the left of the mean.

F I G U R E 2.7

Area or Probability under the Standard Normal Curve Between −1.0 and 1.0

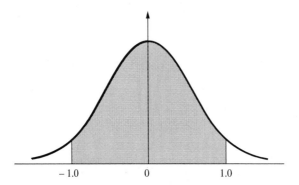

The probability between 0 and 1.0 already has been determined to be .3413. Because the curve is symmetric, the half of the curve to the left of the mean is a mirror image of the half to the right. Thus, in an interval between 0 and −1.0 there will be exactly the same probability as in the interval between 0 and 1.0, because these regions are mirror images of each other. So,

$$P(-1.0 \leq Z \leq 1.0) = .3413 + .3413 = .6826$$

This probability is illustrated in Figure 2.7.

Now, consider finding the following probability:

$$P(Z > 1.7)$$

The area between 0 and 1.7 can be found from Table 1 in Appendix B as

$$P(0 \leq Z \leq 1.7) = .4554$$

The desired area is to the right of 1.7, however. Here we use the facts that the total area under the curve must be 1.0 and that the curve is symmetric. The total area under the standard normal curve must be 1.0 since this area represents probability and probability must sum to 1. Because the curve is symmetric, the area to the right of the mean (0) must be .5. In Figure 2.8, if the unshaded area between 0 and 1.7 is subtracted from the total area to the right of 0, the remainder is the area in the shaded region:

$$P(Z > 1.7) = .5 - .4554 = .0446$$

The probabilities in the standard normal table also can be used to find probabilities for normal distributions other than the standard normal. For example, suppose X is a normal random variable with mean $\mu = 10$ and standard deviation $\sigma = 2$. Find the probability that X is between 10 and 12:

$$P(10 \leq X \leq 12)$$

F I G U R E **2.8**

Area or Probability under the Standard Normal Curve Between 0 and 1.7 and above 1.7

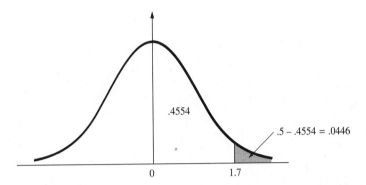

.4554

.5 – .4554 = .0446

0   1.7

The standard normal table cannot be used to find this probability as it is currently stated. But the problem can be solved by translating it into standardized units. Referring to Figure 2.9, first recognize that 10 is the mean of the normal distribution represented by X. Because $\sigma = 2$, 12 is one standard deviation above the mean. Then, in standardized units (or units of standard deviation away from the mean), the problem becomes

$$P(10 \leq X \leq 12) = P(0 \leq Z \leq 1)$$

The area between 10 and 12 under the normal curve with $\mu = 10$ and $\sigma = 2$ is the same as the area between 0 and 1 under the standard normal curve. By translating the original units into standardized units, any probability can be determined from the standard normal table. The general transformation is given by the formula

$$Z = \frac{x - \mu_X}{\sigma_X}$$

To translate a number, x, into standardized units, Z, simply subtract the mean and divide by the standard deviation. The following examples should help to further illustrate.

E X A M P L E **2.1**

Suppose X is a normal random variable with $\mu = 50$ and $\sigma = 10$. What is $P(30 \leq X \leq 60)$?

　Answer:

$$P(30 \leq X \leq 60) = P\left(\frac{30 - 50}{10} \leq Z \leq \frac{60 - 50}{10}\right)$$
$$= P(-2 \leq Z \leq 1)$$
$$= .4772 + .3413 = .8185$$

The solution is illustrated in Figure 2.10. ∎

F I G U R E 2.9

Finding $P(10 \leq X \leq 12)$ When X Is a Normal Random Variable with $\mu = 10$ and $\sigma = 2$

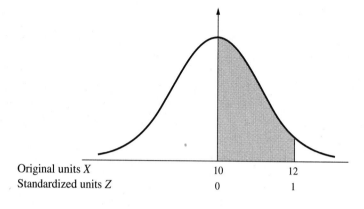

| Original units X | | 10 | 12 |
| Standardized units Z | | 0 | 1 |

F I G U R E 2.10

Finding $P(30 \leq X \leq 60)$ When X Is a Normal Random Variable with $\mu = 50$ and $\sigma = 10$

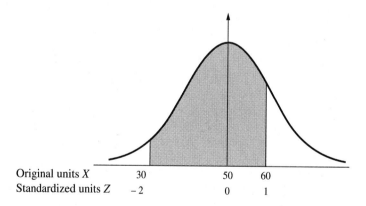

| Original units X | 30 | | 50 | 60 |
| Standardized units Z | -2 | | 0 | 1 |

E X A M P L E 2.2

A large firm has accounts receivable that are assumed to be normally distributed with mean $\mu = \$281$ and standard deviation $\sigma = \$35$.

1   What proportion of accounts have balances greater than $316?

Answer:

$$P(X > 316) = P\left(Z > \frac{316 - 281}{35}\right)$$
$$= P(Z > 1) = 0.5 - .3413$$
$$= .1587$$

F I G U R E 2.11

Finding $P(X > 316)$ When X Is a Normal Random Variable with $\mu = 281$ and $\sigma = 35$

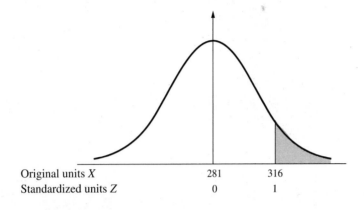

Original units X 281   316
Standardized units Z 0   1

F I G U R E 2.12

Above What Value Will 13.57% of All Accounts Lie When $\mu = 281$ and $\sigma = 35$?

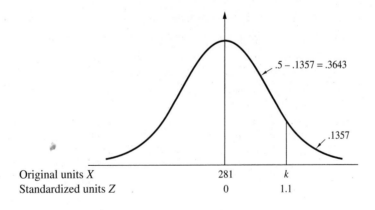

.5 – .1357 = .3643

.1357

Original units X 281 k
Standardized units Z 0   1.1

So, .1587 or 15.87% of all accounts have balances greater than $316. The solution is illustrated in Figure 2.11.

2   Above what value will 13.57% of all account balances lie?

Answer: Figure 2.12 illustrates the problem to be solved. Find an account balance, call it k, such that the probability above k is .1357. This means the probability between the mean and k must be $.5 - .1357 = .3643$. Looking up .3643 in the standard normal table, k has a z value of 1.1, so k is 1.1 standard deviations above the mean:

$$k = \mu + 1.1\sigma = 281 + (1.1)(35) = \$319.50 \quad \blacksquare$$

Exercises

8   Calculate the following probabilities using the standard normal distribution:

   a $P(0.0 \leq Z \leq 1.2)$

   b $P(-0.9 \leq Z \leq 0.0)$

   c $P(0.0 \leq Z \leq 1.45)$

   d $P(0.3 \leq Z \leq 1.56)$

   e $P(-2.03 \leq Z \leq -1.71)$

   f $P(-0.02 \leq Z \leq 3.54)$

   g $P(Z \geq 2.50)$

   h $P(Z \leq 1.66)$

   i $P(Z \geq 5)$

   j $P(Z \geq -6)$

9   All applicants at a large university are required to take a special entrance exam before they will be admitted. The exam scores are known to be normally distributed with a mean of 800 and a standard deviation of 100. Applicants must score 700 or more on the exam before they are admitted.

   a   What proportion of all applicants will be granted admission?

   b   What proportion of all applicants will score 1000 or more on the exam?

   c   For the coming academic year, 2500 applicants have registered to take the exam. How many would we expect to be admitted to the university?

10   A manufacturer wishes to produce bearings with diameters that are required to be 1.2 centimeters (cm). Because of variability in the production process, not all bearings have the same diameter. The diameters have a normal distribution with mean of 1.2 cm and standard deviation of 0.01 cm. The manufacturer has determined that diameters in the range of 1.18 to 1.22 cm are acceptable. What proportion of all bearings fall in the acceptable range?

11   Find the value of Z from the standard normal table such that the probability between Z and $-Z$ is

   a   .9544

   b   .9010

   c   .9802

   d   .9902

12   A large manufacturing plant uses light bulbs with lifetimes that are normally distributed with mean $\mu = 1000$ hours (hr) and standard deviation $\sigma = 50$ hr. To minimize the number of bulbs that burn out during operating hours, all bulbs are replaced at once. How often should the bulbs be replaced so that no more than 1% burn out between replacement periods?

2.5
Populations, Samples, and Sampling Distributions

Statistics is concerned with the use of sample information to make generalizations or inferences about a *population*, which is simply the group to be studied. A population may consist of people, households, firms, automobile tires, and so on. A *sample* is a subset of a population. In other words, a sample is a group of items chosen from the population.

Typically, the study of every item in a population is not feasible. It may be too time-consuming or too expensive to examine every item. As an alternative, a few items are chosen from the population studied. From the information provided by this sample, we hope to make reliable generalizations about characteristics of the population.

In this section, we assume that the items of the sample are randomly chosen from the population. By choosing the sample in this way, it is possible to objectively evaluate the quality of the generalizations made about the population characteristics of interest.

As discussed in Section 2.1, many possible random samples can be chosen from a particular population. In practice, of course, only one such sample is chosen and examined. But to understand the processes that govern how inferences should be made, it is necessary to imagine all possible random samples of a given sample size n chosen from a particular population. Suppose the characteristic of interest for this population is the mean, μ. To estimate the population mean, the statistic most often used is the sample mean, $\bar{y}$; each possible random sample has an associated value of $\bar{y}$. Thus, the sample mean acts just like a random variable: It assigns a number (the value of the sample mean for each sample) to each of the possible outcomes of an experiment. The experiment, in this instance, is the process of choosing samples of size n from the population. Because the samples are chosen randomly, each one has an equal probability of being chosen. So, each value of $\bar{y}$ has a probability associated with it.

Because the sample mean $\bar{y}$ can be viewed as a random variable, it has a probability distribution. This probability distribution is called the *sampling distribution* of the sample mean. In this section, some of the properties of the sampling distribution of the sample mean will be reviewed. These are discussed in more detail in most introductory statistics courses.

First, suppose the population of interest has a mean μ and variance σ^2. The mean of the sampling distribution of $\bar{y}$, written $\mu_{\bar{y}}$, will be equal to the population mean:

$$\mu_{\bar{y}} = \mu$$

The variance of the sampling distribution of $\bar{y}$, written $\sigma_{\bar{y}}^2$, will be

$$\sigma_{\bar{y}}^2 = \frac{\sigma^2}{n}$$

Or the standard deviation of the sampling distribution of $\bar{y}$, $\sigma_{\bar{y}}$, could be written

$$\sigma_{\bar{y}} = \frac{\sigma}{\sqrt{n}}.$$

Thus, if all possible sample means for samples of size n could be collected, the average of the sample means would be the same as the average of all the individual population values. The sample mean values, however, would be less spread out than the individual population values because $\sigma_{\bar{y}}$ is always less than σ.

If the original population from which the samples were drawn is a normal distribution, then the sampling distribution of sample means also will be a normal distribution for any sample size n. Thus, if μ and σ were known, and the population to be sampled were normal, probability statements could be made about the sample mean $\bar{y}$. Consider the following example.

E X A M P L E 2.3

In a certain manufacturing process, the standard diameter of a part produced is 40 cm on average, although it varies somewhat from part to part. This variation is thought to be well represented by a normal distribution with a standard deviation of 0.2 cm. If a random sample of 16 parts is chosen, what is the probability that the sample mean will be greater than 40.1 cm?

Answer: Because the population is normal, the sampling distribution of sample means also will be normal with mean $\mu_{\bar{y}} = 40$ and standard deviation

$$\sigma_{\bar{y}} = \frac{0.2}{\sqrt{16}} = 0.05$$

So,

$$P(\bar{y} > 40.1) = P\left(Z > \frac{40.1 - 40}{0.05}\right) = P(Z > 2) = .5 - .4772 = .0228 \quad \blacksquare$$

Knowledge of the sampling distribution provides information about how sample means from a particular population should behave. But what if the population does not have a normal distribution, or what if the actual distribution of the population is unclear? In this case, there is an important result in statistics called the *Central Limit Theorem* (CLT), which states:

As long as the sample size is large, the sampling distribution of the sample means will be approximately normal, regardless of the population distribution.

The CLT states that probabilities still can be computed concerning sample means, even though the population does not have a normal distribution, as long as the sample size used is large enough. How large is "large enough" varies somewhat from one population distribution to another, but a generally accepted rule is to treat a sample size of 30 or more as large.

The next example illustrates the use of the CLT.

E X A M P L E 2.4

A cereal manufacturer claims that boxes of its cereal weigh 20 ounces (oz) on average with a population standard deviation of 0.5 oz. The manufacturer does not know whether the population distribution is normal. A random sample of 100 boxes is selected. What is the probability that the sample mean is between 19.9 and 20.1 oz?

Answer: Because the sample size is large ($n = 100$), the sampling distribution will be approximately normal even though the population distribution may be nonnormal. The mean and standard deviation of the sampling distribution are

$$\mu_{\bar{y}} = 20 \text{ and } \sigma_{\bar{y}} = \frac{.5}{\sqrt{100}} = 0.05$$

So,

$$P(19.9 \le \bar{y} \le 20.1) =$$
$$P\left(\frac{19.9 - 20}{0.05} \le Z \le \frac{20.1 - 20}{0.05}\right) =$$
$$P(-2 \le Z \le 2) = .4772 + .4772 = .9544 \quad \blacksquare$$

Exercises

13 The daily receipts of a fast food franchise are normally distributed with a mean of $1200 per day and a standard deviation of $50. A random sample of 25 days' receipts is chosen for an audit.

    a What is the probability that the sample mean will be larger than $1220?

    b What is the probability that the sample mean will differ from the true population mean by more than ± $10?

14 The accounts receivable of a large department store are normally distributed with mean $250 and standard deviation $80. If a random sample of 225 accounts is chosen, what is the probability that the mean of the sample will be between $232 and $268?

15 In a certain manufacturing process, the standard length of a machine part is 200 cm. When the process is correctly adjusted, this measurement actually is a random variable with a mean of 200 cm and a standard deviation of 0.1 cm. The individual measurements are normally distributed.

    a What is the probability that an individual part will be longer than 200.2 cm?

    b Suppose a sample of 25 parts is chosen randomly. What is the probability that the mean of the sample will be bigger than 200.2 cm?

16   Suppose we have a large population of houses in a community. The average annual heating expense for each house is $400 with a population standard deviation of $25. A random sample of 25 houses had a sample mean of $380 and a sample standard deviation of $35.

   a   What is the mean of the sampling distribution of sample means for samples of size 25 chosen from the population of all homes?

   b   What is the standard deviation of the sampling distribution of sample means for samples of size 25 chosen from the population of all homes?

17   The average time to complete a certain production-line task is assumed to be normally distributed with a standard deviation of 5 minutes (min). A random sample of 16 workers' times is selected to estimate the average time taken to complete the task. What is the probability that the sample mean will be within ±1 min of the population's true mean time?

2.6
Estimating a Population Mean

Two types of estimates can be constructed for any population parameter: point estimates and interval estimates. *Point estimates* are single numbers used as an estimate of a parameter. To estimate the population mean, μ, the sample mean, $\bar{y}$, typically is used. An *interval estimate* is a range of values used as an estimate of a population parameter.

The width of the interval provides a sense of the accuracy of the point estimate. The interval tells us the likely values of the population mean.

Assuming the population standard deviation, σ, is known, a confidence interval for the population mean, μ, can be constructed as

$$\left(\bar{y} - z_{\alpha/2}\frac{\sigma}{\sqrt{n}},\ \bar{y} + z_{\alpha/2}\frac{\sigma}{\sqrt{n}}\right)$$

where $z_{\alpha/2}$ is a standard normal value chosen so that the probability above $z_{\alpha/2}$ is $\alpha/2$. Thus, between $z_{\alpha/2}$ and $-z_{\alpha/2}$ there is a probability of $1 - \alpha$ (see Figure 2.13). For this reason, the confidence interval written in its general form will be referred to as a $(1 - \alpha)100\%$ (read "one minus alpha times 100 percent") confidence interval estimate of μ. By replacing $z_{\alpha/2}$ by the appropriate standard normal value, the desired level of confidence can be achieved. For example, to achieve 95% confidence, use $z_{.025} = 1.96$ because the probability under the standard normal curve between -1.96 and 1.96 will be .95. Note that lowercase z's are used here to represent the specific values chosen from the standard normal distribution as opposed to the uppercase Z's, which represent the standard normal random variable.

The term "95% confidence interval" means that, if repeated samples of size n are taken from the same population, and a confidence interval is constructed in the manner just described for each sample, 95% of those intervals will contain the population mean.

F I G U R E 2.13
Choosing z Values for a $(1 - \alpha)100\%$ Confidence Interval

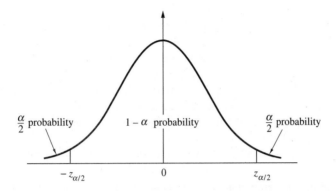

The use of the interval assuming that σ is known is justified for any sample size if the population is normal. In this case, the sampling distribution of sample means is known to be normal, which is the basis for the construction of the interval. If the distribution of the population is unknown or if it is known to be nonnormal, the interval still can be used as long as the sample size is large (generally $n \geq 30$) because the Central Limit Theorem guarantees that the sampling distribution of sample means will be approximately normal.

E X A M P L E 2.5

The management of Newman-Markups Department Stores want a 90% confidence interval estimate of the current average balance of its charge customers. With a random sample of 100 accounts, sample mean of $245, and population standard deviation of $45, what is the 90% interval estimate of the true average balance?

Answer: The 90% confidence interval estimate of the true average balance is

$$\left(245 - 1.65 \left(\frac{45}{\sqrt{100}} \right), 245 + 1.65 \left(\frac{45}{\sqrt{100}} \right) \right) \quad \text{or ($237.58, $252.43)} \quad \blacksquare$$

In Example 2.5, the population standard deviation σ was assumed to be known. In many instances, however, this will not be true. In this case, σ can be estimated by the sample standard deviation.

$$s = \sqrt{\frac{\sum_{i=1}^{n}(y_i - \bar{y})^2}{n - 1}}$$

Replacing σ by s in the previous interval and $z_{\alpha/2}$ by $t_{\alpha/2,n-1}$ gives

$$\left(\bar{y} - t_{\alpha/2,n-1} \frac{s}{\sqrt{n}}, \ \bar{y} + t_{\alpha/2,n-1} \frac{s}{\sqrt{n}} \right)$$

Changing $z_{\alpha/2}$ to $t_{\alpha/2,n-1}$ reflects the fact that an estimator of σ, s, is being used to construct a confidence interval estimate for μ. The value of $t_{\alpha/2,n-1}$ is chosen from Table 2 of Appendix B. The t value chosen depends on the number of *degrees of freedom* (df) and on the confidence level desired. The number of degrees of freedom for estimating μ is $n - 1$. These values are listed on the left-hand side of the t table. The confidence levels are reflected through the upper-tail areas at the top of the table. Note that the .025 column would be used for a 95% level of confidence ($\alpha/2 = .025$).

The shape of the t distribution depends on the number of degrees of freedom. The t distribution has fatter tails than the normal distribution, and thus, has greater probability in its tails. The t value for a given level of confidence will therefore be larger than the standard normal values, producing wider confidence intervals (less precise estimates) because s rather than σ is being used to construct the interval estimate.

Also, as the number of degrees of freedom increases, the t distribution begins to look more like the normal distribution. In the last row of the t table, the ∞ degree of freedom row, the z values corresponding to the given upper-tail areas are shown. This indicates that for a very large sample, the t and Z distribution would be identical.

When the number of degrees of freedom is 30 or more, the t values often will be replaced by z values because there is little difference between the two in these cases. Although using t values is more correct in all cases when σ is unknown, replacing the t values by z values for large degrees of freedom is often adopted simply for convenience.

In small samples ($n < 30$) the population should be normal, or close to a normal distribution, before the interval is used. If the population is nonnormal and small samples are used, nonparametric methods may be appropriate. These methods are discussed in most introductory statistics texts (for example, see Chapter 19 of *Statistics for Management and Economics* by Mendenhall, Reinmuth, and Beaver). When the sample size is large, the assumption of a normal population is not necessary. The flowchart in Figure 2.14 describes the interval choices when σ is unknown. The σ known case is not shown because it rarely occurs in practice.

E X A M P L E 2.6

A manufacturer wants to estimate the average life of an expensive electrical component. Because the test to be used destroys the component, a small sample is desired. The lifetimes of five randomly selected components in hours are

92, 110, 115, 103, 98

F I G U R E **2.14**

Estimating μ Assuming σ Is Unknown

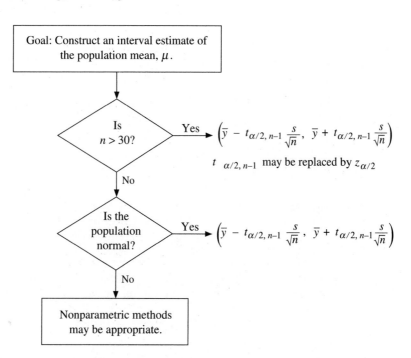

What are a point estimate and a 95% confidence interval estimate of the population average lifetime of the components? The population of lifetimes is assumed to be normal.

Answer: Because σ is unknown, the interval to be used is

$$\left(\bar{y} - t_{.025,4} \frac{s}{\sqrt{n}}, \ \bar{y} + t_{.025,4} \frac{s}{\sqrt{n}} \right)$$

The quantities needed to construct the interval are

$$\bar{y} = \frac{\sum_{i=1}^{n} y_i}{n} = 103.6$$

$$s = \sqrt{\frac{\sum_{i=1}^{n} (y_i - \bar{y})^2}{n-1}} = 9.18$$

$$t_{.025,4} = 2.776$$

The interval estimate of μ is

$$\left[103.6 - 2.776 \left(\frac{9.18}{\sqrt{5}} \right), \ 103.6 + 2.776 \left(\frac{9.18}{\sqrt{5}} \right) \right] \text{ or } (92.2, 115.0)$$

F I G U R E 2.15

Using MINITAB to Construct Confidence Intervals

```
MTB > tint 90 c1

Variable     N      Mean     StDev   SE Mean        90.0 % C.I.
lifetime     5     103.60     9.18     4.11    (   94.84,  112.36)

MTB > tint 95 c1

Variable     N      Mean     StDev   SE Mean        95.0 % C.I.
lifetime     5     103.60     9.18     4.11    (   92.20,  115.00)

MTB > tint 99 c1

Variable     N      Mean     StDev   SE Mean        99.0 % C.I.
lifetime     5     103.60     9.18     4.11    (   84.70,  122.50)
```

The point estimate of μ is

$$\bar{y} = 103.6 \quad \blacksquare$$

Computer packages such as MINITAB and SAS also can be used to construct confidence intervals. Figure 2.15 shows the MINITAB output for requests for 90%, 95%, and 99% confidence intervals using the data from Example 2.6.

Exercises

18 A local department store wants to determine the average age of the adults in its existing marketing area to help target its advertising. A random sample of 40 adults is selected. The sample mean age is found to be 35 years with a sample standard deviation of 3 years. Construct a 95% confidence interval estimate of the population average age of the adults in the area.

19 The management of a large manufacturing plant is studying the number of times employees in a large population are absent. A random sample of 25 employees is chosen, and the average number of absences in the sample is found to be 6. The sample standard deviation is 0.6. Assuming the population of absences is normally distributed, construct a 99% confidence interval estimate of the population average number of absences.

20 A quality control inspector is concerned with the average amount of weight that can be held by a type of steel beam. A random sample of five beams is tested with the following amounts of weight added (in thousands of pounds):

$$9, \ 11, \ 10, \ 10, \ 8$$

Assuming that the population of weights is normally distributed, construct a 95% confidence interval estimate of the population average weight that can be held.

21   Table 2.2 shows the highway mileage figures for 146 different model cars for 1994. Find a 95% confidence interval estimate for the population mean miles per gallon. See Exercise 1 for information on reading these data.

22   The 1993 one-year returns for a random sample of 26 mutual funds with a load were obtained. The returns are shown in Table 2.6. Find a 95% confidence interval estimate for the population mean 1993 return. You may assume this sample is from a population of returns that is approximately normal.

T A B L E **2.6**

1993 One-Year-Return Data for Load Mutual Funds

Fund Name	1993 One-Year Return
Dean Witter Equity Income	−3.5
Dean Witter Utilities	12.8
Fidelity Select Leisure	39.6
First Investors Global	23.0
Flag Investors Quality Growth	−5.6
G. T. America Growth	8.3
Heritage Capital Appreciation	18.4
J. Hancock Growth	13.2
Kemper Blue Chip	3.8
Kemper International	35.7
Mainstay Capital Appreciation	14.0
Merrill Lynch Fund for Tomorrow A	11.4
Metlife-State St. Cap. Apprec.	22.9
Metlife-State St. Equity-Inc.	22.8
Mutual Benefit	8.7
Nationwide	6.8
Pioneer	14.2
Prudential Growth B	8.5
Rightime Blue Chip	7.3
Rodney Square International	35.1
Smith Barney Income & Growth	16.3
Stagecoach Growth & Income	8.5
United International Growth	46.6
United Retirement Shares	12.7
United Science & Energy	8.5
Van Eck World Trends	22.3

SOURCE: *Kiplinger's Mutual Funds '94* (©Kiplinger Washington Editors, Inc.).

These data may be read into MINITAB from the data disk using

```
READ 'LOAD2' C1
```

and into SAS from the file LOAD2.DAT using the command

```
INPUT RET1LOAD;
```

2.1

Hypothesis Tests about a Population Mean

In Section 2.6, estimation of a population mean was discussed. Estimation was the first of our two main topics of statistical inference. In this section, we will discuss the second topic—hypothesis tests. Again, the population mean will be used to demonstrate tests of hypotheses.

The following definitions will be useful in testing hypotheses:

Null Hypothesis, H_0: The null hypothesis states the hypothesis to be tested.

Alternative Hypothesis, H_a: The alternative hypothesis includes possible values of the population parameter not included in the null hypothesis.

Test Statistic: A number computed from sample information.

Decision Rule: A rule used in conjunction with the test statistic to determine whether the null hypothesis should be accepted or rejected.

In setting up a hypothesis test, the null hypothesis is initially assumed to be true. Under this assumption, a decision rule is constructed, based on the sampling distribution of the test statistic. The decision rule states a range of values for the test statistic that would be plausible if H_0 is true and a range of values for the test statistic that seem implausible if H_0 is true. Depending on the test statistic value, a statistical decision is made to either accept H_0 (the test statistic falls in the plausible range) or to reject H_0 (the test statistic falls in the implausible range).

Because the decision is based on sample information, it is not possible to be certain that the correct decision has been made. A statistical decision does not prove or disprove the null hypothesis with certainty, although it does present support for one or the other of the two hypotheses. In a business environment, decisions are typically made on the basis of limited information. Hypothesis-testing results provide support for alternative possible courses of action based on such limited (sample) information.

Two types of errors are possible in hypothesis testing. These are illustrated in Figure 2.16. On the left-hand side of the table are the two possible states of nature: Either H_0 is true or H_0 is false. The statistical decisions, accept H_0 or reject H_0, are listed at the top of the table. If H_0 is true and the sample information says to accept H_0, a correct decision has been made. Also, if H_0 is false and the sample information says reject H_0, the decision is correct. If H_0 is true, however, and the sample information says to reject H_0, the decision is incorrect. Rejecting the null

F I G U R E 2.16
The Risks of Hypothesis Testing

		Decision	
		Accept H_0	Reject H_0
State of Nature	H_0 True	Correct Decision	Type I Error
	H_0 False	Type II Error	Correct Decision

hypothesis when it is true is called a *Type I error*. A *Type II error* occurs if the null hypothesis is actually false but the sample information says to accept H_0.

Note that the decision made is always stated with reference to the null hypothesis: Either reject H_0 or accept H_0. Also note that, because only two possibilities are considered (either H_0 or H_a), rejecting H_0 would imply agreement with H_a.

Some texts suggest using the expression "fail to reject H_0" rather than "accept H_0." When the data suggest that we should not reject H_0, this is not proof that H_0 is true. This is a statistical decision and may imply simply that we do not have enough evidence to reject H_0. The expression "accept H_0" is sometimes viewed as too strong in suggesting that H_0 has been proven true. In this text "accept H_0" will be used, but be sure to recognize that just because the null hypothesis is accepted, this is not proof of its truth. Our sample may simply not provide enough evidence to reject.

When testing any hypothesis, it is desirable to keep the chances of error occurring as small as possible. Typically, when setting up the test, a desired level for the probability of a Type I error is established. By specifying a small probability, control can be exercised over the chances of making such an error. The probability of a Type I error is called the *level of significance* of the test and is denoted α.

To illustrate, suppose the following hypotheses are to be tested:

$$H_0: \mu = 10$$
$$H_a: \mu \neq 10$$

Also, assume that the population standard deviation is known to be 2. This assumption will be relaxed later. The sample to be drawn will consist of 100 items, and the desired level of significance will be $\alpha = 0.05$, or a 5% chance of making a Type I error.

The hypotheses have now been set up and a level of significance chosen. The next step is to establish the decision rule for the test. To do this, consider the sampling distribution of sample means as shown in Figure 2.17.

If the null hypothesis is true ($\mu = 10$), then a region can be determined in which 95% of all sample means will fall. The upper bound of this region is denoted C_1 and the lower bound C_2. Above and below these bounds there is a combined probability of only 0.05 of obtaining a sample mean. The decision rule for the test can be set up as:

F I G U R E   2.17

Sampling Distribution of Sample Means Assuming H_0: $\mu = 10$ Is True

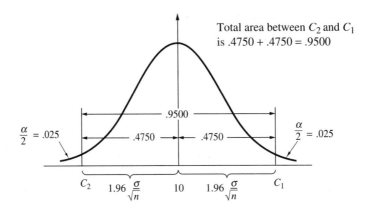

Reject H_0 if $\bar{y} > C_1$ or $\bar{y} < C_2$,

Accept H_0 if $C_2 \leq \bar{y} \leq C_1$

If the null hypothesis is true, 95% of all sample means will fall between C_1 and C_2. Thus, there is only a 5% chance of obtaining a sample mean that falls in the rejection region. In other words, there is a 5% chance of rejecting H_0 if H_0 is true. Thus, the desired level of significance for the test has been achieved.

The critical values C_1 and C_2 in the decision rule can be determined because the sampling distribution is normal (because the sample size is large). Between C_1 and C_2, there is to be a probability of 0.95, so the associated z value for these numbers is 1.96. The upper critical value is

$$C_1 = 10 + 1.96 \left(\frac{2}{\sqrt{100}} \right) = 10.392$$

and the lower critical value is

$$C_2 = 10 - 1.96 \left(\frac{2}{\sqrt{100}} \right) = 9.608$$

The decision rule would become:

Reject H_0 if $\bar{y} > 10.392$ or $\bar{y} < 9.608$

Accept H_0 if $9.608 \leq \bar{y} \leq 10.392$

Now suppose a sample of size 100 is randomly selected and the sample mean computed is $\bar{y} = 11.2$. Based on this value of the sample mean, the null hypothesis is not supported. A sample mean of 11.2 is too extreme to believe it came from a population with mean $\mu = 10$. So the null hypothesis would be rejected. Note that the null hypothesis has not been proved false. There is simply contradictory evidence and so a statistical decision to reject was made. The alternative hypothesis, $\mu \neq 10$, seems more plausible given the evidence obtained.

The previous hypothesis-testing problem was set up in terms of the sampling distribution of the sample means. An alternative and more typical way of performing hypothesis tests is with a standardized test statistic. The basic philosophy and structure of the test are the same. The only difference is that the test statistic is standardized and compared directly with the z value. For example, the standardized test statistic for testing hypotheses about the population mean is

$$z = \frac{\bar{y} - \mu_0}{\sigma / \sqrt{n}},$$

where μ_0 is the hypothesized value of the population mean. For the previous example, the decision rule is:

Reject H_0 if $\dfrac{\bar{y} - \mu_0}{\sigma / \sqrt{n}} > 1.96$ or $\dfrac{\bar{y} - \mu_0}{\sigma / \sqrt{n}} < -1.96$

Accept H_0 if $-1.96 \leq \dfrac{\bar{y} - \mu_0}{\sigma / \sqrt{n}} \leq 1.96$

The standardized test statistic value is

$$\frac{\bar{y} - \mu_0}{\sigma / \sqrt{n}} = \frac{11.2 - 10}{2 / \sqrt{100}} = 6$$

Because the test statistic value falls in the rejection region, the null hypothesis is rejected.

Whether the standardized or unstandardized form of the test is used, the decision made (accept H_0 or reject H_0) will always be the same. Throughout this text, the standardized form will be used unless otherwise noted. This is consistent with computer packages that typically print out standardized test statistic values.

The hypothesis structure previously discussed is called a *two-tailed test* because rejection occurs in both the upper and lower tails of the sampling distribution. Two other hypothesis structures need to be considered: upper-tailed and lower-tailed tests. Both of these involve rejection in only one tail of the sampling distribution and are therefore referred to as one-tailed tests.

If σ is unknown, the same procedure is used as with confidence intervals. The unknown population standard deviation, σ, is replaced by an estimate, s, and the z value is replaced by the t value with $n - 1$ degrees of freedom. The hypothesis structures, test statistic, and decision rules for the case when σ is unknown are shown in Table 2.7. The σ known case is omitted because it is rarely encountered in practice.

As was the case for confidence intervals, the t tests are constructed with the assumption that the population is normally distributed. The population should be normal (or nearly so) before tests are used with small samples ($n < 30$), or nonparametric methods may be appropriate. When the sample size is large, the assumption of a normal population is unnecessary.

T A B L E   2.7

Hypotheses, Test Statistics, and Decision Rules for Testing Hypotheses about Population Means

Hypotheses	Test Statistic	Decision Rules
$H_0: \mu = \mu_0$ $H_a: \mu \neq \mu_0$	$t = \dfrac{\bar{y} - \mu_0}{s/\sqrt{n}}$	Reject H_0 if $t > t_{\alpha/2, n-1}$ or if $t < -t_{\alpha/2, n-1}$ Accept H_0 if $-t_{\alpha/2, n-1} \leq t \leq t_{\alpha/2, n-1}$
$H_0: \mu \leq \mu_0$ $H_a: \mu > \mu_0$	$t = \dfrac{\bar{y} - \mu_0}{s/\sqrt{n}}$	Reject H_0 if $t > t_{\alpha, n-1}$ Accept H_0 if $t \leq t_{\alpha, n-1}$
$H_0: \mu \geq \mu_0$ $H_a: \mu < \mu_0$	$t = \dfrac{\bar{y} - \mu_0}{s/\sqrt{n}}$	Reject H_0 if $t < -t_{\alpha, n-1}$ Accept H_0 if $t \geq -t_{\alpha, n-1}$

The following examples should help to illustrate hypothesis-testing techniques.

E X A M P L E   2.7

Consider again the manufacturer of electrical components in Example 2.6. Suppose the manufacturer wishes to test whether the population average life of the components is 110 hr or more. If it is less than 110 hr, the components do not meet specifications and the production process must be adjusted to raise the average lifetimes.

As in Example 2.6, five components are randomly selected and the lifetimes, in hours, for these components are determined to be

$$92, \ 110, \ 115, \ 103, \ 98$$

Assume the population of lifetimes is known to be normally distributed. The hypotheses to be tested are

$$H_0: \mu \geq 110$$
$$H_a: \mu < 110$$

Using a 5% level of significance, the decision rule for the test is:

$$\text{Reject } H_0 \quad \text{if} \quad t < -t_{.05,4} = -2.132$$
$$\text{Accept } H_0 \quad \text{if} \quad t \geq -t_{.05,4} = -2.132$$

The sample mean and standard deviation are

$$\bar{y} = 103.6, \quad s = 9.18$$

and the test statistic, t, is

$$t = \frac{\bar{y} - \mu_0}{s/\sqrt{n}} = \frac{103.6 - 110}{9.18/\sqrt{5}} = -1.56,$$

resulting in a decision to accept the null hypothesis. ■

E X A M P L E **2.8**

A company that manufactures rulers would like to ensure that the average length of its rulers is 12 inches (for obvious reasons). From each production run a random sample of 25 rulers is selected and their lengths determined by very accurate measuring instruments. On one particular run, the average length of the 25 rulers is determined to be 12.02 in. with a sample standard deviation of .02 in.

Using a 1% level of significance, is the average length of the rulers produced by this manufacturer equal to 12 in.?

Answer: The hypotheses to be tested are

$$H_0: \mu = 12$$
$$H_a: \mu \neq 12$$

Using a 1% level of significance, the decision rule for the test is:

Reject H_0 if $t > t_{.005, 24} = 2.797$

or if $t < -t_{.005, 24} = -2.797$

Accept H_0 if $-2.797 \leq t \leq 2.797$

From the sample information,

$$t = \frac{\bar{y} - \mu_0}{s/\sqrt{n}} = \frac{12.02 - 12}{.02/\sqrt{25}} = 5.0$$

resulting in a decision to reject the null hypothesis. This decision suggests that the average length of rulers is not 12 in. Some adjustment to the production process is necessary. ■

Most statistical software packages will perform tests of hypotheses. Instead of reporting a reject or accept decision, however, the output will often include a number called a p value. By comparing the p value to the level of significance, α, for the test, an alternative decision rule can be constructed:

Reject H_0 if p value $< \alpha$

Accept H_0 if p value $\geq \alpha$

The p value is the computed area under the curve representing the sampling distribution at or beyond the value of the test statistic obtained from the sample. That

FIGURE 2.18
Computation of *p* Value

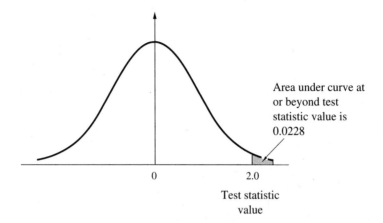

Area under curve at
or beyond test
statistic value is
0.0228

0   2.0

Test statistic
value

is, it is the probability of observing a *t* value or *z* value as extreme as or more than the sample test statistic. For example, suppose the hypotheses to be tested are

$$H_0: \mu \leq 10$$
$$H_a: \mu > 10$$

A sample size of 100 is to be used and σ is known to be 10 (again, merely for illustrative purposes). From the random sample of 100 items a sample mean of $\bar{y} = 12$ is obtained. The standardized test statistic is

$$z = \frac{12 - 10}{10/\sqrt{100}} = 2.0$$

In Figure 2.18 the standard normal distribution is shown and the position of the test statistic has been located. The *p* value for this test is

$$p \text{ value } = P(z \geq 2.0) = .5 - .4772 = .0228$$

Regardless of which approach to hypothesis testing is chosen (unstandardized or standardized test statistic or *p* value), the decision made will be identical for a given level of significance.

EXAMPLE 2.9

Figure 2.19 shows the MINITAB output for testing the hypothesis discussed in Example 2.7. The output shows $\bar{y} = 103.60$, $s = 9.18$, $s/\sqrt{n} = 4.11$, $t = -1.56$, and the *p* value $= 0.097$. Using the *p*-value decision rule, note that the null hypothesis would be accepted with levels of

F I G U R E 2.19

MINITAB Output for Test of Hypothesis in Example 2.7

```
Test of mu = 110.00 vs mu < 110.00

Variable     N      Mean    StDev   SE Mean        T    P-Value
C1           5    103.60     9.18      4.11    -1.56      0.097
```

significance of 1% or 5% but would be rejected at 10%. Reporting the p value is somewhat more informative in a case such as this than simply reporting a reject or accept decision. ▪

Exercises

23 If any null hypothesis is rejected at the 5% level of significance, what decision would have been made at the 10% level? Why?

24 To investigate an alleged unfair trade practice, the Federal Trade Commission takes a random sample of sixteen "5-ounce" candy bars from a large shipment. The mean of the sample weights is 4.85 oz and the sample standard deviation is 0.1 oz. Test the hypotheses

$$H_0: \mu \geq 5$$
$$H_a: \mu < 5$$

at the 5% level of significance. Assume the population of candy bar weights is approximately normally distributed. Based on the results of the test, does the FTC have grounds to proceed against the manufacturer for the unfair practice of short-weight selling? State the decision rule, the test statistic, and your decision.

25 A quality inspector is interested in the time spent replacing defective parts in one of the company's products. The average time spent should be at most 20 minutes (min) per day according to company standards. The following hypotheses are set up to examine whether the standards are being met:

$$H_0: \mu \leq 20$$
$$H_a: \mu > 20,$$

where μ represents the population average time spent replacing defective parts. To conduct the test, a random sample of 16 employees is chosen. The average time spent replacing defective parts for the sample was 20.5 min with a sample standard deviation of 4 min. Perform the test at a 5% level of significance. Assume the population of service times is approximately normally distributed. State the decision rule, the test statistic, and your decision. Are company standards being met?

26 Consider again the mileage figures for 146 cars for 1994 shown in Table 2.2. Suppose we wish to examine whether average mileage is at least 20 miles per gallon. The following hypotheses will be tested:

$$H_0: \mu \geq 20$$
$$H_a: \mu < 20,$$

where μ is the population average gas mileage for all 1994 cars. Use a 5% level of significance. State the decision rule, the test statistic, and your decision. What is your conclusion regarding the average mileage of 1994 cars? (See Exercise 1 for information on reading these data.)

27   The 1993 one-year returns for a random sample of 26 load mutual funds were obtained. The returns are shown in Table 2.6. Test to see if there is evidence that the average 1993 one-year return for the population is less than zero. You may assume this sample is from a population of returns that is approximately normal.

Use a 5% level of significance. State the hypotheses to be tested, the decision rule, the test statistic, and your decision. What is your conclusion regarding the average 1993 return for load funds? (See Exercise 22 for information on reading these data.)

2.8
Estimating the Difference Between Two Population Means

The comparison of two separate populations often is of more concern than the estimation of the parameters of a single population as discussed in Section 2.6. In many cases the comparison is between the means of the two populations. In this section, point and interval estimates of the difference between these means will be discussed.

Throughout this section we will assume that two populations with parameters μ_1, σ_1 and μ_2, σ_2 are to be studied. Random samples are to be drawn independently from the two populations. Summary statistics from the two samples are

	Sample 1	Sample 2
Sample size	n_1	n_2
Sample mean	$\bar{y}_1$	$\bar{y}_2$
Sample standard deviation	s_1	s_2

A point estimate of the difference between the two populations means, $\mu_1 - \mu_2$, is given by the difference between the two sample means, $\bar{y}_1 - \bar{y}_2$.

If σ_1 and σ_2 were known, the standard deviation of the sampling distribution of $\bar{y}_1 - \bar{y}_2$ would be written as

$$\sqrt{\frac{\sigma_1^2}{n_1} + \frac{\sigma_2^2}{n_2}}$$

In addition, the sampling distribution of $\bar{y}_1 - \bar{y}_2$ can be shown to be normally distributed if each of the populations is normal. The sampling distribution will be approximately normal if both sample sizes are large ($n_1 \geq 30$ and $n_2 \geq 30$) even if the populations are not normal. A $(1 - \alpha)100\%$ confidence interval for $\mu_1 - \mu_2$ would be

$$\bar{y}_1 - \bar{y}_2 \pm z_{\alpha/2}\sqrt{\frac{\sigma_1^2}{n_1} + \frac{\sigma_2^2}{n_2}}$$

As in the previous situations we discussed, it is unlikely that the population variances, σ_1^2 and σ_2^2, will be known in practice. They must be estimated by the sample variances, s_1^2 and s_2^2. These estimates are substituted into the formula for the standard deviation of the sampling distribution of $\bar{y}_1 - \bar{y}_2$, which results in

$$\sqrt{\frac{s_1^2}{n_1} + \frac{s_2^2}{n_2}}$$

An approximate $(1 - \alpha)100\%$ confidence interval for $\mu_1 - \mu_2$ would then be

$$\bar{y}_1 - \bar{y}_2 \pm t_{\alpha/2,\Delta}\sqrt{\frac{s_1^2}{n_1} + \frac{s_2^2}{n_2}}$$

The interval is approximate because the population variances may differ. When $\sigma_1^2 \neq \sigma_2^2$, an exact interval cannot be constructed. In statistics this is known as the Behrens–Fischer problem. This interval will be referred to as the *approximate* interval.

The approximate degrees of freedom for the sampling distribution of $\bar{y}_1 - \bar{y}_2$ are given by

$$\Delta = \frac{(s_1^2/n_1 + s_2^2/n_2)^2}{[(s_1^2/n_1)^2/(n_1 - 1)] + [(s_2^2/n_2)^2/(n_2 - 1)]}$$

If the population variances can be assumed equal, $\sigma_1^2 = \sigma_2^2$, then an exact interval can be constructed. Because $\sigma_1^2 = \sigma_2^2$, it is no longer necessary to provide separate estimates of the two variances. The information in both samples can be combined, or pooled, to estimate the common variance. The *pooled estimator* of the population variance is

$$s_p^2 = \frac{(n_1 - 1)s_1^2 + (n_2 - 1)s_2^2}{n_1 + n_2 - 2}$$

The $(1 - \alpha)100\%$ confidence interval is given by

$$\bar{y}_1 - \bar{y}_2 \pm t_{\alpha/2,n_1+n_2-2}\sqrt{s_p^2\left(\frac{1}{n_1} + \frac{1}{n_2}\right)}$$

This interval will be referred to as the *exact* interval.

Which of these intervals, exact or approximate, should be used in practice? The answer depends on what we know about the population variances, σ_1^2 and σ_2^2. If σ_1^2 and σ_2^2 are known to be equal, choose the exact interval. If σ_1^2 and σ_2^2 are known to be unequal, choose the approximate interval. But what is we have no information on whether or not the variances are equal? In this case, current research recommends using the approximate interval.[1]

---

[1] We could test for equality of the variances and choose an approach based on the test result but this procedure has been shown to be less powerful than simply using the approximate interval. See for example, "Homogeneity of Variance in the Two-Sample Means Test" by Moser and Stevens in *The American Statistician* 46(1992): 19–21.

T A B L E   **2.8**

Three-Year-Return Data for No-Load Mutual Funds

Name	3yrret
API Growth	20.7
Blanchard Global Growth	11.6
Bull & Bear Special Equities	28.0
Eclipse Equity	22.4
Fidelity Real Estate	23.2
GIT Equity Special Growth	15.5
IAI International	15.3
Managers International Equity	19.4
T. Rowe Price New Horizons	27.1
Scudder Capital Growth	22.5
Steinroe Prime Equities	18.0
USAA Balanced	11.0
USAA Income Stock	15.3
Weitz Series Value	20.3

SOURCE: *Kiplinger's Mutual Funds '94* (©Kiplinger Washington Editors, Inc.).

E X A M P L E   **2.10**

Table 2.1 listed the three-year returns for a random sample of 26 load mutual funds. Table 2.8 shows the return figures (also as of 1 January 1994) for a random sample of 14 no-load funds.

Construct a 95% confidence interval estimate of the difference between the population average three-year returns for load and no-load funds.

The MINITAB output shown in Figure 2.20 can be used to obtain the confidence interval. As will be discussed in Section 2.9, this output also can be used to test hypotheses about the difference between the two population means.

In Panel A of Figure 2.20, the results correspond to the approximate interval (assuming $\sigma_1^2 \neq \sigma_2^2$). Panel B shows the results for the exact interval (assuming $\sigma_1^2 = \sigma_2^2$).

Which interval is appropriate in this problem? Since we really have no information on the population variances, the approximate interval would probably be the better choice. In this case, there is little difference between the two intervals, but sizable differences can occur that can produce misleading conclusions if the exact interval is used in an inappropriate situation. The approximate interval will provide a conservative result when the population variances are equal but also provides protection against the case when the variances are not equal.

The interval produced by the approximate method is $(-6.9\%, 0.7\%)$. This result suggests that we can be 95% confident that the difference in population average three-year returns for load and no-load funds ($\mu_{LOAD} - \mu_{NOLOAD}$) is between -6.9% and 0.7%. What does this result suggest to you regarding the two types of funds? ■

FIGURE 2.20
MINITAB Output for Examples 2.10 and 2.11

Panel A

```
Twosample T for 3yrload vs 3yrno
              N      Mean    StDev    SEMean
3yrload      26     16.23     6.36       1.2
3yrno        14     19.31     5.20       1.4


95% C.I. for mu 3yrload - mu 3yrno: ( -6.9,  0.7)
T-Test mu 3yrload = mu 3yrno (vs not =): T=-1.65  P=0.11  DF=31
```

Panel B

```
Twosample T for 3yrload vs 3yrno
              N      Mean    StDev    SEMean
3yrload      26     16.23     6.36       1.2
3yrno        14     19.31     5.20       1.4

95% C.I. for mu 3yrload - mu 3yrno: ( -7.1,  0.9)
T-Test mu 3yrload = mu 3yrno (vs not =): T=-1.55  P=0.13  DF=38
Both use Pooled StDev = 5.99
```

Exercises

28 A graduate school of business is interested in estimating the difference between mean GMAT scores for applicants with and without work experience. Independent random samples of 50 applicants with and 50 applicants without work experience are chosen. The following results were obtained:

With Work Experience	Without Work Experience
$n = 50$	$n = 50$
$\bar{y} = 545$	$\bar{y} = 510$
$s = 104$	$s = 95$

Construct a 95% confidence interval estimate of the difference between the mean GMAT scores for the two groups.

29   Two suppliers are being considered by a manufacturer. Independent random samples of 10 parts from shipments from each supplier are selected, and the lifetime in hours for each part is determined for each sample. Use the information below to construct a 98% confidence interval estimate of the difference in the population average lifetimes. Assume that the population variances are equal and the populations normally distributed.

Supplier 1	Supplier 2
$n = 10$	$n = 10$
$\bar{y} = 15$	$\bar{y} = 11$
$s = 1.5$	$s = 1.0$

30   To help validate a new employee-rating form, a company administers it to independent random samples of employees in two different divisions. The following information is obtained from the scores on the forms:

Division 1	Division 2
$n = 15$	$n = 15$
$\bar{y} = 82$	$\bar{y} = 78$
$s = 3$	$s = 2.5$

Use the information to construct a 95% confidence interval estimate of the difference in mean scores between the two divisions. Assume that the population variances are equal and the populations normally distributed.

31   The 1993 one-year returns for a random sample of 26 load mutual funds and 14 no-load funds were obtained. The returns for the load funds are shown in Table 2.6 and for the no-load funds in Table 2.9. Construct a 95% confidence interval estimate of the difference between the population mean returns. Assume that the populations are approximately normally distributed.

These data are available on the data disk and can be read in MINITAB using

```
READ 'FUNDS2' C1,C2
```

where C1 is the load-fund data and C2 is the no-load data.

32   Table 2.10 shows the city mileage and the type of transmission for a sample of cars. The transmissions variable is coded 1 for automatic and 0 for manual. Construct a 99% confidence interval estimate for the difference between population average city mileage for cars with manual and automatic transmissions.

These data are available on the data disk and can be read in MINITAB using

```
READ 'TRANS2' C1-C2
```

and in SAS from the file TRANS2.DAT using the command

```
INPUT CITYMPG AUTO;
```

Note that the data for both samples is contained in the first column. The second column indicates to which sample (automatic = 1, manual = 0) each value in column 1 belongs.

T A B L E **2.9**
One-Year-Return Data for No-Load Mutual Funds

Name	1990ret
API Growth	18.3
Blanchard Global Growth	24.5
Bull & Bear Special Equities	16.4
Eclipse Equity	17.1
Fidelity Real Estate	12.5
GIT Equity Special Growth	14.9
IAI International	40.2
Managers International Equity	38.2
T. Rowe Price New Horizons	22.0
Scudder Capital Growth	20.1
Steinroe Prime Equities	12.9
USAA Balanced	13.7
USAA Income Stock	11.6
Weitz Series Value	20.0

SOURCE: *Kiplinger's Mutual Funds '94* (©Kiplinger Washington Editors, Inc.).

T A B L E **2.10**
Data on City Mileage for Automatic (1) and Manual (0) Transmission Cars

Name of Car	City Mileage	Type of Transmission	Name of Car	City Mileage	Type of Transmission
Acura Integra	25	0	Buick Roadmaster Wagon	17	1
Acura Legend	18	0	Buick Skylark	23	1
Acura NSX	19	0	Cadillac De Ville	16	1
Acura Vigor	20	0	Cadillac Eldorado	16	1
Alfa Romeo 164	17	0	Cadillac Fleetwood	16	1
Alfa Romeo Spider	22	0	Cadillac Seville & STS	16	1
Audi 90	20	0	Chevrolet Beretta	25	0
Audi 100	19	0	Chevrolet Camaro	19	1
Audi V8	14	1	Chevrolet Caprice	18	0
BMW 3-Series	22	0	Chevrolet Cavalier	26	1
BMW 5-Series	17	0	Chevrolet Corsica	25	1
BMW 7-Series	16	1	Chevrolet Corvette	17	0
Buick Century	24	1	Chevrolet Lumina	19	1
Buick Le Sabre	19	1	Chrysler Concorde	20	1
Buick Park Avenue	19	1	Chrysler Le Baron Conv.	21	1
Buick Regal	19	1	Chrysler Le Baron Sedan	20	1
Buick Riviera	16	1	Chrysler NY & LHS	18	1

T A B L E **2.10** *(Cont.)*

Data on City Mileage for Automatic (1) and Manual (0) Transmission Cars

Name of Car	City Mileage	Type of Transmission	Name of Car	City Mileage	Type of Transmission
Dodge (Plymouth) Colt	32	0	Lincoln Town Car	17	1
Dodge Intrepid	20	1	Lotus Esprit S4	17	0
Dodge Shadow (P Sundance)	27	0	Mazda MX-3	29	0
Dodge Spirit (P Acclaim)	23	1	Mazda MX-5 Miata	22	0
Dodge Stealth	18	0	Mazda MX-6	26	0
Dodge Viper RT/10	13	0	Mazda Protege	30	0
Eagle Summit	32	0	Mazda RX-7	17	0
Eagle Summit Wagon	23	0	Mazda 323	29	0
Eagle Talon (P Laser)	23	0	Mazda 626	26	0
Eagle Vision	20	1	Mazda 929	19	1
Ferrari 348	13	0	Mercedes-Benz C-Class	21	1
Ferrari 512 TR	11	0	Mercedes-Benz E-Class	19	1
Ford Crown Victoria	17	1	Mercedes-Benz S-Class	17	1
Ford Escort	26	0	Mercedes-Benz SL-Class	17	1
Ford Probe	26	1	Mercury Capri	25	0
Ford Taurus	20	1	Mercury Cougar XR7	20	1
Ford Tempo	24	0	Mercury Grand Marquis	18	1
Ford Thunderbird	20	0	Mercury Sable	20	1
Geo Metro	46	0	Mercury Topaz	23	0
Geo Prizm	28	0	Mercury Tracer	30	0
Honda Accord	25	0	Mitsubishi Diamante	18	1
Honda Civic	34	0	Mitsubishi Eclipse	23	0
Honda Civic del Sol	35	0	Mitsubishi Expo and LRV	21	0
Honda Prelude	23	0	Mitsubishi Galant	23	0
Hyundai Elantra	22	0	Mitsubishi Mirage	31	0
Hyundai Excel	29	0	Mitsubishi 3000 GT	18	0
Hyundai Scoupe	27	0	Nissan Altima	24	0
Hyundai Sonata	20	0	Nissan Maxima	19	0
Infiniti G20	24	0	Nissan Sentra	29	0
Infiniti J30	18	1	Nissan 240SX Convertible	21	1
Infiniti Q45	17	1	Nissan 300 ZX	18	0
Jaguar XJS	17	1	Oldsmobile Achieva	24	0
Jaguar XJ6	17	1	Oldsmobile Aurora	16	0
KIA Sephia	28	0	Oldsmobile Cutlass Ciera	24	1
Lamborghini Diablo	9	0	Oldsmobile Cutlass Supreme	19	0
Lexus ES300	18	1	Oldsmobile 88 Royale	19	1
Lexus GS300	18	1	Oldsmobile 98	19	1
Lexus LS400	18	1	Pontiac Bonneville	19	1
Lexus SC300 & SC400	18	1	Pontiac Firebird	19	0
Lincoln Continental	18	1	Pontiac Grand Am	22	1
Lincoln Mark VII	18	1	Pontiac Grand Prix	19	1

T A B L E **2.10** *(Cont.)*
Data on City Mileage for Automatic (1) and Manual (0) Transmission Cars

Name of Car	City Mileage	Type of Transmission	Name of Car	City Mileage	Type of Transmission
Pontiac Sunbird	25	0	Toyota Camry	22	1
Porsche 911	17	0	Toyota Celica	27	0
Porsche 928 GTS	12	0	Toyota Corolla	27	0
Porsche 968	17	0	Toyota MR2	22	0
Saab 900	20	0	Toyota Paseo	28	0
Saab 9000	19	0	Toyota Supra	18	0
Saturn Sports Coupe	28	0	Toyota Tercel	32	0
Saturn Sedan	28	0	Volkswagen Corrado	18	0
Saturn Wagon	28	0	Volkswagen Golf	24	0
Subaru Impreza	25	0	Volkswagen Jetta	23	0
Subaru Justy	33	0	Volkswagen Passat	17	0
Subaru Legacy	23	0	Volvo 850	23	0
Subaru Loyale Wagon	24	0	Volvo 940	20	1
Subaru SVX	17	1	Volvo 960	18	1
Suzuki Swift	39	0			

2.9
Hypothesis Tests about the Difference Between Two Population Means

We may be interested in testing hypotheses about the difference between two population means rather than estimating that difference. The most common hypotheses tested in comparing two populations are

$$H_0: \quad \mu_1 = \mu_2$$
$$H_a: \quad \mu_1 \neq \mu_2$$

The null hypothesis states that the means of the two populations are equal, while the alternate states that the two population means differ. These hypotheses can be restated in terms of the difference between two means as

$$H_0: \quad \mu_1 - \mu_2 = 0$$
$$H_a: \quad \mu_1 - \mu_2 \neq 0$$

The decision rule for the test is:

Reject H_0 if $t > t_{\alpha/2}$ or $t < -t_{\alpha/2}$
Accept H_0 if $-t_{\alpha/2} \leq t \leq t_{\alpha/2}$

The construction of the test statistic, t, depends on whether the population variances can be assumed equal.

If $\sigma_1^2 = \sigma_2^2$, then

$$t = \frac{\bar{y}_1 - \bar{y}_2}{\sqrt{s_p^2 \left(\dfrac{1}{n_1} + \dfrac{1}{n_2} \right)}}$$

and the critical value, $t_{\alpha/2}$, is chosen with $n_1 + n_2 - 2$ degrees of freedom. The pooled estimate of the population variance, s_p^2, is used in computing the standard deviation of the sampling distribution.

If $\sigma_1^2 \neq \sigma_2^2$, then

$$t = \frac{\bar{y}_1 - \bar{y}_2}{\sqrt{\dfrac{s_1^2}{n_1} + \dfrac{s_2^2}{n_2}}},$$

and the approximate critical value is chosen with

$$\Delta = \frac{(s_1^2/n_1 + s_2^2/n_2)^2}{[(s_1^2/n_1)^2/(n_1 - 1)] + [(s_2^2/n_2)^2/(n_2 - 1)]}$$

degrees of freedom.

The justification for using two different standard errors in constructing the test statistics is the same as that for constructing the confidence intervals in the previous section.

Table 2.11 shows the three possible hypothesis structures, the test statistic to be used, and the decision rules for the case when $\sigma_1^2 = \sigma_2^2$. Table 2.12 presents similar information for $\sigma_1^2 \neq \sigma_2^2$.

E X A M P L E **2.11**

In Section 2.2, a random sample of 26 load mutual funds was examined. These funds and their three-year returns were shown in Table 2.1. In Table 2.8, the three-year returns for a random sample of 14 no-load funds were shown.

Let μ_L represent the population mean three-year return for load funds and μ_N represent the population mean three-year return for no-load funds. Then the hypotheses

$$H_0: \quad \mu_L - \mu_N = 0$$
$$H_a: \quad \mu_L - \mu_N \neq 0$$

can be tested to determine any differences between the average returns for these two groups.

Figure 2.20 shows the MINITAB output for testing the hypotheses. Assuming that the population variances are unequal (or that we have no information about the variances) the Panel A output is appropriate. Using this output the null hypothesis would be accepted. The t

T A B L E **2.11**

Hypotheses, Test Statistics, and Decision Rules for Testing Hypotheses about Differences Between Population Means When $\sigma_1^2 = \sigma_2^2$

Hypotheses	Test Statistics	Decision Rules
H_0: $\mu_1 - \mu_2 = 0$ H_a: $\mu_1 - \mu_2 \neq 0$	$t = \dfrac{\bar{y}_1 - \bar{y}_2}{\sqrt{s_p^2 \left(\dfrac{1}{n_1} + \dfrac{1}{n_2} \right)}}$	Reject H_0 if $t > t_{\alpha/2, n_1+n_2-2}$ or if $t < -t_{\alpha/2, n_1+n_2-2}$ Accept H_0 if $-t_{\alpha/2, n_1+n_2-2} \leq t \leq t_{\alpha/2, n_1+n_2-2}$
H_0: $\mu_1 - \mu_2 \geq 0$ H_a: $\mu_1 - \mu_2 < 0$	$t = \dfrac{\bar{y}_1 - \bar{y}_2}{\sqrt{s_p^2 \left(\dfrac{1}{n_1} + \dfrac{1}{n_2} \right)}}$	Reject H_0 if $t < -t_{\alpha, n_1+n_2-2}$ Accept H_0 if $t \geq -t_{\alpha, n_1+n_2-2}$
H_0: $\mu_1 - \mu_2 \leq 0$ H_a: $\mu_1 - \mu_2 > 0$	$t = \dfrac{\bar{y}_1 - \bar{y}_2}{\sqrt{s_p^2 \left(\dfrac{1}{n_1} + \dfrac{1}{n_2} \right)}}$	Reject H_0 if $t > t_{\alpha, n_1+n_2-2}$ Accept H_0 if $t \leq t_{\alpha, n_1+n_2-2}$

T A B L E **2.12**

Hypotheses, Test Statistics, and Decision Rules for Testing Hypotheses about Differences Between Population Means When $\sigma_1^2 \neq \sigma_2^2$

Hypotheses	Test Statistics	Decision Rules
H_0: $\mu_1 - \mu_2 = 0$ H_a: $\mu_1 - \mu_2 \neq 0$	$t = \dfrac{\bar{y}_1 - \bar{y}_2}{\sqrt{\dfrac{s_1^2}{n_1} + \dfrac{s_2^2}{n_2}}}$	Reject H_0 if $t > t_{\alpha/2, \Delta}$ or if $t < -t_{\alpha/2, \Delta}$ Accept H_0 if $-t_{\alpha/2, \Delta} \leq t \leq t_{\alpha/2, \Delta}$
H_0: $\mu_1 - \mu_2 \geq 0$ H_a: $\mu_1 - \mu_2 < 0$	$t = \dfrac{\bar{y}_1 - \bar{y}_2}{\sqrt{\dfrac{s_1^2}{n_1} + \dfrac{s_2^2}{n_2}}}$	Reject H_0 if $t < -t_{\alpha, \Delta}$ Accept H_0 if $t \geq -t_{\alpha, \Delta}$
H_0: $\mu_1 - \mu_2 \leq 0$ H_a: $\mu_1 - \mu_2 > 0$	$t = \dfrac{\bar{y}_1 - \bar{y}_2}{\sqrt{\dfrac{s_1^2}{n_1} + \dfrac{s_2^2}{n_2}}}$	Reject H_0 if $t > t_{\alpha, \Delta}$ Accept H_0 if $t \leq t_{\alpha, \Delta}$

statistic or the p value can be used to come to this decision. If the t statistic is used the decision rule would be:

$$\text{Reject } H_0 \text{ if } t > 2.042 \text{ or } t < -2.042$$
$$\text{Accept } H_0 \text{ if } -2.042 \leq t \leq 2.042$$

where $t_{.025,30} = 2.042$. Note that 30 degrees of freedom were used since the t value for 31 degrees of freedom is not in the table. The z value of 1.96 could also have been used in this case since the degrees of freedom is over 30. Using the t value with 30 degrees of freedom provides a somewhat more conservative test. The test statistic value is $t = -1.65$.

If the p value is used the decision rule would be:

$$\text{Reject } H_0 \text{ if } p \text{ value } < 0.05$$
$$\text{Accept } H_0 \text{ if } p \text{ value } \geq 0.05$$

where the test statistic is, in this case, p value $= 0.11$. As always, both procedures lead to the same decision.

The statistical decision is to accept the null hypothesis, so we conclude that there is no difference between the average three-year returns for load and no-load mutual funds. ∎

Exercises

33 Consider again Exercise 28 in Section 2.8. Two independent random samples of applicants to business schools who had and did not have work experience were chosen. Each sample contained 50 applicants.

To determine whether there is a difference in the population average test scores, the following hypotheses should be tested:

$$H_0: \quad \mu_1 - \mu_2 = 0$$
$$H_a: \quad \mu_1 - \mu_2 \neq 0$$

Use a 5% level of significance. State the decision rule, test statistic, and your decision. What implication do these test results have for admissions officers in MBA programs?

34 Use the information in Exercise 29. Suppose that the manufacturer currently uses supplier 2. A change to supplier 1 will be made only if the average lifetime of parts for supplier 1 is greater than the average for supplier 2. Using a 1% level of significance, conduct the appropriate test. State the hypotheses to be tested, the decision rule, test statistic, and your decision. Assume the population variances are equal and the populations normally distributed. On the basis of the test result, which supplier will the manufacturer choose?

35 Use the information in Exercise 30. Is there a difference in population mean rating scores for the two divisions? State the hypotheses to be tested, the decision rule, the test statistic, and your decision. Assume the population variances are equal and the populations normally distributed. Use a 5% level of significance.

36 The 1993 one-year returns for a random sample of 26 load mutual funds and 14 no-load funds were obtained. The returns for the load funds are shown in Table 2.6 and for the no-load funds in Table 2.9. Test to see if there is any difference between the population average 1993 one-year returns for load and no-load funds. Assume that the populations are approximately normally distributed. Use a 5% level of significance. State the decision rule, test statistic, and your decision. Is there a difference in the population averages? Based on the test results, what conclusions would you draw concerning investment in load versus no-load funds? (See Exercise 31 for information on reading the data.)

37 Use the data from Exercise 32 of Section 2.8. Let μ_0 = the population average city mileage for cars with manual transmissions and μ_1 = the population average for cars with automatic transmissions. Suppose that a claim is made that the cars with manual transmissions have better (higher) city gas mileage, on average, than cars with automatic transmissions. Examine the claim by testing the following hypotheses:

$$H_0: \quad \mu_0 - \mu_1 \leq 0$$
$$H_a: \quad \mu_0 - \mu_1 > 0$$

Use a 5% level of significance. State the decision rule, the test statistic, and your decision. Is the claim supported? (See Exercise 32 for information on reading the data.)

2.10
Using the Computer

Output from the computer packages MINITAB and SAS will be used throughout this text to illustrate various statistical procedures. In the final section of each chapter the commands used to generate the output are illustrated. For more on MINITAB and SAS commands, see Appendix C.

Note that the MINITAB output in the text was generated from the Windows version. The Windows version does not require commands since it is fully menu-driven. Commands can be used, however, and most of the commands listed in the sections at the end of each chapter will work in the Windows version. The command sections at the end of each chapter are included for those users without a menu-driven version of MINITAB or those who prefer commands to menus. The menu headings and subheadings used to access the commands will also be noted in parentheses next to the commands.

2.10.1 MINITAB

Descriptive Statistics

```
HISTOGRAM C1      (GRAPH: HISTOGRAM)
```

generates a histogram for the data in C1.

```
DESCRIBE C1     (STAT: BASIC STATISTICS: DESCRIPTIVE STATISTICS)
```

generates a variety of descriptive statistics (see Figure 2.2).

Confidence Interval Estimate of μ

```
TINT C1
    (STAT: BASIC STATISTICS: 1-SAMPLE T: CONFIDENCE INTERVALS)
```

constructs a 95% confidence interval estimate of the population mean, μ, using data in C1. Other levels of confidence can be requested. For example, TINT 90 C1 requests a 90% confidence interval.

Hypothesis Tests about μ

```
TTEST OF MU=k C1
    (STAT: BASIC STATISTICS: 1-SAMPLE T: TEST MEAN)
```

produces the output necessary to test the hypotheses:

$$H_0: \quad \mu = k$$
$$H_a: \quad \mu \neq k,$$

where some number needs to be substituted for the letter k on the command line. The value for k represents the hypothesized value in the problem.

To do an upper-tailed test of $H_0: \mu \leq k$ versus $H_a: \mu > k$, a subcommand is necessary:

```
TTEST OF MU=k C1;
ALT = 1.
```

To do a lower-tailed test of $H_0: \mu \geq k$ versus $H_a: \mu < k$, use

```
TTEST of MU=k C1;
ALT = -1.
```

Confidence Interval Estimate of $\mu_1 - \mu_2$

```
TWOSAMPLE C1 C2        (STAT: BASIC STATISTICS: 2-SAMPLE T)
```

constructs a 95% confidence interval estimate of the difference between two population means, $\mu_1 - \mu_2$. The data in C1 are a sample from the population with mean μ_1 and the data in column two are a sample from the population with mean μ_2.

To include the assumption that the population variances (or standard deviations) are equal, use the following sequence:

```
TWOSAMPLE C1 C2;
POOLED.
```

The subcommand POOLED tells MINITAB to assume the population variances are equal.

```
TWOT C1,C2
    (STAT: BASIC STATISTICS: 2-SAMPLE T: SAMPLES IN ONE COLUMN)
```

performs the same analysis as TWOSAMPLE C1 C2. However, TWOT assumes the data are arranged differently. TWOSAMPLE requires the two samples to be placed in two separate columns. TWOT requires that all data be placed in the first column (C1 in this example). The second column (C2 in this example) must indicate to which sample each of the elements in the first column belongs. This is done by assigning an integer to each element and listing this integer in the second column. For example, the integers 0 and 1 could be used to distinguish between the elements of the two samples. The choice between whether to use TWOSAMPLE or TWOT is based purely on how your data are arranged. Otherwise, TWOT operates exactly as does TWOSAMPLE.

Hypothesis Tests about $\mu_1 - \mu_2$

```
TWOSAMPLE C1 C2
```

produces the output necessary to test

$$H_0: \quad \mu_1 - \mu_2 = 0$$
$$H_a: \quad \mu_1 - \mu_2 \neq 0$$

The ALT= subcommand can be used to request upper- or lower-tailed tests in the same way as with the TTEST command.

The subcommand POOLED can be used when the assumption that population variances are equal is warranted.

```
TWOT C1 C2
```

As with confidence intervals, TWOT can be used instead of TWOSAMPLE if the data are all contained in one column (C1) and the second column (C2) is an indicator to tell MINITAB to which sample each data element belongs.

2.10.2 SAS

Hypothesis Tests about $\mu_1 - \mu_2$

```
PROC TTEST;
 CLASS V1;
 VAR V2;
```

produces output to conduct a test of the difference between two population means. V1 is a variable used to separate the observations of the variable V2 into two groups. The two group means can be called μ_1 and μ_2. The t statistic produced can be used to conduct either a one- or two-tailed test. The p values in the PROB > $|T|$ column are designed specifically for two-tailed tests.

Two versions of the test statistic are produced, the variances-equal version and the variances-unequal version. The appropriate statistic depends on the assumptions deemed correct for the population variances.

Additional Exercises

38   A university wants to examine starting salaries for its finance and marketing graduates. Independent random samples of 12 finance graduates and 12 marketing graduates are selected from the files of last year's graduates. The following starting salaries are obtained from these people:

Salaries	
Finance	**Marketing**
1850	1675
2150	1275
1700	1800
1500	2100
2200	2200
1650	2250
2100	1950
2140	1850
1790	2000
1650	1800
2300	2100
2000	2150

The data are available on the data disk and can be read in MINITAB using

```
READ 'SALARY2' C1,C2
```

Finance salaries will be read into C1 and marketing salaries into C2.
    In SAS, the data can be read from the file SALARY2.DAT using

```
INPUT FINANCE MARKET;
```

where FINANCE represents the salary variable for finance and MARKET represents the marketing salaries.
    Use these data to determine the following:

a   Find the sample mean starting salaries for finance graduates and marketing graduates (separately).

b   Construct a histogram for starting salaries in both finance and marketing.

c   Construct a 95% confidence interval estimate of the population mean starting salary for finance majors. Do the same for marketing majors. Assume the populations of starting salaries for both groups are normally distributed.

39 Consider again the finance and marketing starting salaries in Exercise 38.

a Conduct a test to determine whether the population mean starting salaries for the two majors are equal. State the hypotheses to be tested, the decision rule, the test statistic, and your decision. Use a 5% level of significance.

b What conclusion can be drawn from the result in (a)?

[*Note:* In SAS, the data for conducting this test can be read from the file SALARY2.SAS using

```
INPUT SALARY MAJOR;
```

The TTEST command can be used with MAJOR as a classification variable (1 = finance and 2 = marketing).

In MINITAB, the data can be read as in Exercise 38.]

40 In selling magazine subscriptions door-to-door, two different sales approaches are tried. Two independent random samples of 20 salespeople each are selected to use either approach 1 or 2 for the same period and for the same number of household contacts. The sales data (number of subscriptions sold per period) are given here.

Approach 1	Approach 2
12	8
15	10
28	24
14	14
18	10
10	20
15	20
20	15
5	0
4	7
12	10
10	16
24	17
16	20
13	12
14	4
18	12
22	18
6	3
12	16

a Is there a difference in average sales produced by the two approaches? Assume that the populations are normally distributed. State the hypotheses to be tested, the decision rule, the test statistic, and your decision. Use a 10% level of significance.

b What does the result in (a) suggest to a sales division manager?

In MINITAB, these data can be read using

```
READ 'SALES2' C1, C2
```

with C1 containing the approach 1 data and C2 containing the approach 2 data.

In SAS, the data should be read from the file SALES2.SAS using

```
INPUT SALES APPROACH;
```

where APPROACH is a classification variable (coded 1 or 2) and SALES is a variable with sales figures for both approaches.

41   Table 2.13 shows 1977 starting salary data for 93 employees of Harris Bank of Chicago. The column of data denoted "MALE" indicates whether the employees were MALE (1) or FEMALE (0). These data were obtained from a 1987 article by Daniel W. Schafer, "Measurement-Error Diagnostics and the Sex Discrimination Problem," which appeared in *Journal of Business and Economic Statistics* 5 (1987): 529–537.

These data can be read for a MINITAB analysis using

```
READ 'HARRIS2' C1, C2
```

where C1 represents salaries and C2 is the classification variable (male = 1, female = 0).

In SAS, the data can be read from the file HARRIS2.DAT using the command

```
INPUT SALARIES MALE;
```

Let μ_0 = average starting salary for females and μ_1 = average starting salary for males.

a   Set up and test hypotheses to determine whether there is evidence of wage discrimination for the Harris Bank employees. Use a 5% level of significance. Note that discrimination is represented by an average wage for females that is less than the average wage for males. Set up the hypotheses accordingly.

b   What implications do your test results have for Harris Bank?

c   Are there other factors that might need to be considered in this analysis? If so, state them and why you feel they are important.

42   Refer to Exercise 2. The NCAA has asked for your input concerning the effect of Proposition 48 on graduation rates. Using any of the techniques studied in this chapter, what would you report to the NCAA based on the data you have been given?

T A B L E **2.13**

Starting Salaries for Harris Bank Employees

SALARY	MALE	SALARY	MALE	SALARY	MALE	SALARY	MALE
3900	0	5100	0	5520	0	5400	1
4020	0	5100	0	5520	0	5700	1
4290	0	5100	0	5580	0	6000	1
4380	0	5100	0	5640	0	6000	1
4380	0	5100	0	5700	0	6000	1
4380	0	5160	0	5700	0	6000	1
4380	0	5220	0	5700	0	6000	1
4380	0	5220	0	5700	0	6000	1
4440	0	5280	0	5700	0	6000	1
4500	0	5280	0	6000	0	6000	1
4500	0	5280	0	6000	0	6000	1
4620	0	5400	0	6120	0	6000	1
4800	0	5400	0	6300	0	6000	1
4800	0	5400	0	6300	0	6000	1
4800	0	5400	0	4620	1	6000	1
4800	0	5400	0	5040	1	6300	1
4800	0	5400	0	5100	1	6600	1
4800	0	5400	0	5100	1	6600	1
4800	0	5400	0	5220	1	6600	1
4800	0	5400	0	5400	1	6840	1
4800	0	5400	0	5400	1	6900	1
4800	0	5400	0	5400	1	6900	1
4980	0	5400	0	5400	1	8100	1
5100	0						

3

Simple Regression Analysis

3.1
Using Regression Analysis to Describe a Linear Relationship

Regression analysis is a statistical technique used to describe relationships among variables. A relationship is expressed in the form of an equation. The simplest case to examine is the one in which a variable y, referred to as the dependent variable, may be related to another variable x, called an independent, explanatory, or predictor variable. If the relationship between y and x is believed linear, then the equation expressing this relationship will be the equation for a line:

$$y = b_0 + b_1 x$$

If a graph of all the (x, y) pairs is constructed, then b_0 represents the point where the line crosses the vertical (y) axis and b_1 represents the slope of the line.

Consider the data shown in Table 3.1. A graph of the (x, y) pairs would appear as shown in Figure 3.1. Regression analysis is not needed to obtain the linear relationship between these two variables. In equation form:

$$y = 1 + 2x$$

This is an *exact* or *deterministic* linear relationship.

Exact linear relationships are sometimes encountered in business environments. For example, from accounting:

$$\text{assets} = \text{liabilities} + \text{owner equity}$$
$$\text{total costs} = \text{fixed costs} + \text{variable costs}$$

T A B L E **3.1**
Example Data

x	1	2	3	4	5	6
y	3	5	7	9	11	13

FIGURE 3.1
Graph of an Exact or Deterministic Linear Relationship

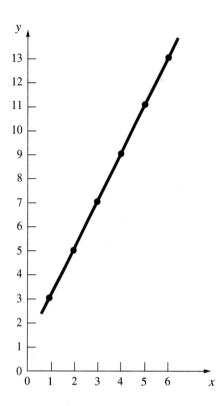

Other exact relationships may be encountered in various science courses. In the social sciences (for example, psychology or sociology) and in business and economics, exact linear relationships are the exception rather than the rule. Data encountered in a business environment would be more likely to appear as in Table 3.2. These data graph as shown in Figure 3.2.

It appears that x and y may be linearly related, but it is not an exact relationship. Still, it may be desirable to describe the relationship in equation form. This can be done by drawing what appears to be the "best" fitting line through the points and

TABLE 3.2
Example Data

x	1	2	3	4	5	6
y	3	2	8	8	11	13

F I G U R E   **3.2**

Graph of a Relationship That Is Not Deterministic

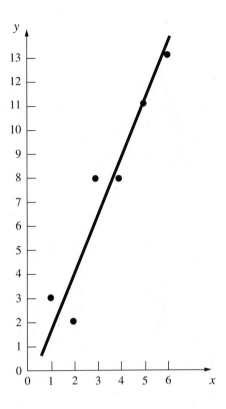

estimating (guessing) what the values of b_0 and b_1 are for this line. This has been done in Figure 3.2. For the line drawn, a good guess might be the following equation:

$$y = -1 + 2.5x$$

The drawbacks to this method of fitting the line should be clear. For example, if the (x, y) pairs graphed in Figure 3.2 were given to two people, each would probably guess different values for the intercept and slope of the "best-fitting" line. Furthermore, there is no way to assess who would be more correct. To make line fitting more precise, a definition of what it means for a line to be the "best" is needed. The criterion for a best-fitting line that we will use might be called the "minimum-sum-of-squared-errors" criterion or, as it is more commonly known, the *least squares criterion*.

In Figure 3.3, the (x, y) pairs from Table 3.2 have been plotted and an arbitrary line drawn through the points. Consider the pair of values denoted (x^*, y^*). The actual y value is indicated as y^*; the value that would be predicted to be associated with x^* if the line shown were used is indicated as $\hat{y}^*$. The difference between the

F I G U R E **3.3**

Motivation for the Least Squares Regression Line

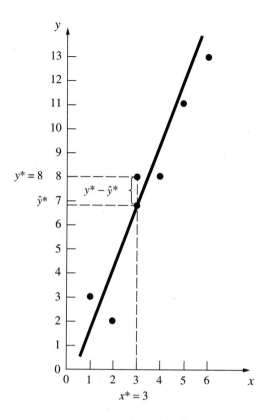

actual y value and the predicted y value at the point x^* is called the *residual* and represents the "error" involved. This is denoted $y^* - \hat{y}^*$. If the line is to "fit" the data points as accurately as possible, these errors should be minimized. This should be done not just for the single point (x^*, y^*), but for all the points on the graph. There are several possible ways to approach this task.

1   Use the line that minimizes the sum of the errors, $\sum_{i=1}^{n}(y_i - \hat{y}_i)$. The problem with this approach is that for *any* line that passes through the point $(\bar{x}, \bar{y})$

$$\sum_{i=1}^{n}(y_i - \hat{y}_i) = 0,$$

so there will be an infinite number of lines satisfying this criterion, some of which obviously do not fit the data well. For example, in Figure 3.4, lines A

F I G U R E   3.4

Lines A and B Both Satisfy the Criterion $\sum\limits_{i=1}^{n}(y_i - \hat{y}_i) = 0$

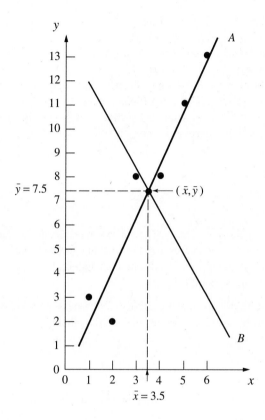

and B have both been constructed so that

$$\sum_{i=1}^{n}(y_i - \hat{y}_i) = 0$$

But, line A obviously "fits" the data better than line B; that is, it keeps the $y_i - \hat{y}_i$ distances small.

As mentioned previously, any line that passes through the point represented by the means of x and y $(\bar{x}, \bar{y})$ will have errors that sum to zero. The line passes through the points in such a way that positive and negative errors cancel each other out. Because a criterion that simply makes the errors small, regardless of whether they are positive or negative, is desired, some method of removing negative signs is required. One such method uses absolute values of the errors; another squares the errors. Each method provides another possible criterion.

2   Use the line that minimizes the sum of the absolute values of errors,

$$\sum_{i=1}^{n} |y_i - \hat{y}_i|$$

This is called the *minimum-sum-of-absolute-errors* criterion. The resulting line is called the *least absolute value* (LAV) regression line. Although use of this criterion is gaining popularity in many situations, it is not the one that we will use in this text. Finding the line that satisfies the minimum-sum-of-absolute-errors criterion requires solving a fairly complex problem by a technique called *linear programming*. This is a difficult process by hand, and the LAV procedure is not available in most statistical software packages. Furthermore, there may be no *unique* LAV regression line.

3   Use the line that minimizes the sum of the squared errors,

$$\sum_{i=1}^{n} (y_i - \hat{y}_i)^2$$

Applying the *least squares* (LS) criterion results in a unique least squares regression line. Its advantages over the LAV line include computational simplicity and the wide availability of statistical packages that contain easily implemented least squares regression routines.

Now that a criterion has been established, the next question is: Can convenient computational formulas for the values of b_0 and b_1 that minimize

$$\sum_{i=1}^{n} (y_i - \hat{y}_i)^2 \tag{3.1}$$

be developed? The answer is "yes" and the resulting equations are

$$b_1 = \frac{\sum_{i=1}^{n} (x_i - \bar{x})(y_i - \bar{y})}{\sum_{i=1}^{n} (x_i - \bar{x})^2} \tag{3.2}$$

$$b_0 = \bar{y} - b_1 \bar{x} \tag{3.3}$$

A computationally simpler form of Equation (3.2) is

$$b_1 = \frac{\sum_{i=1}^{n} x_i y_i - 1/n \sum_{i=1}^{n} x_i \sum_{i=1}^{n} y_i}{\sum_{i=1}^{n} x_i^2 - 1/n \left(\sum x_i\right)^2} \tag{3.4}$$

T A B L E **3.3**

Computations for Finding b_0 and b_1

i	x_i	y_i	$x_i y_i$	x_i^2
1	1	3	3	1
2	2	2	4	4
3	3	8	24	9
4	4	8	32	16
5	5	11	55	25
6	6	13	78	36
Sums	21	45	196	91

E X A M P L E **3.1**

As an example of the use of these formulas, consider again the data in Table 3.2. The intermediate computations necessary for finding b_0 and b_1 are shown in Table 3.3. The slope, b_1, can now be computed using the formula in Equation (3.4):

$$b_1 = \frac{196 - (1/6)(21)(45)}{91 - (1/6)(21)^2} = \frac{38.5}{17.5} = 2.2$$

The intercept, b_0, is computed as in Equation (3.3):

$$b_0 = 7.5 - 2.2\,(3.5) = -0.2$$

because

$$\bar{x} = \frac{21}{6} = 3.5 \quad \text{and} \quad \bar{y} = \frac{45}{6} = 7.5$$

The least squares regression line for these data is

$$\hat{y} = -0.2 + 2.2x$$

There is no longer any guesswork associated with computing the best-fitting line once a criterion has been stated that defines "best." Using the criterion of minimum sum of squared errors, the regression line we computed best describes the relationship between the variables x and y. Any other values used for b_0 and b_1 will result in a larger sum of squared errors. For example, Table 3.4(a) shows the computation of the sum of squared errors, $\sum_{i=1}^{n}(y_i - \hat{y}_i)^2$, for the original "guessed" line $y = -1 + 2.5x$ and (b) shows the same computation for the least squares line $y = -0.2 + 2.2x$.   ■

T A B L E **3.4**

(a) Computation of Sum of Squared Errors (Line: $y = -1 + 2.5x$)

x	y	$\hat{y}$	$y - \hat{y}$	$(y - \hat{y})^2$
1	3	1.5	1.5	2.25
2	2	4.0	−2.0	4.00
3	8	6.5	1.5	2.25
4	8	9.0	−1.0	1.00
5	11	11.5	−0.5	0.25
6	13	14.0	−1.0	1.00
$\sum_{i=1}^{n}(y_i - \hat{y}_i)^2 = 10.75$				

T A B L E **3.4**

(b) Computation of Sum of Squared Errors (Line: $y = -0.2 + 2.2x$)

x	y	$\hat{y}$	$y - \hat{y}$	$(y - \hat{y})^2$
1	3	2.0	1.0	1.00
2	2	4.2	−2.2	4.84
3	8	6.4	1.6	2.56
4	8	8.6	−0.6	0.36
5	11	10.8	0.2	0.04
6	13	13.0	0.0	0.00
$\sum_{i=1}^{n}(y_i - \hat{y}_i)^2 = 8.8$				

Exercises

Exercises 1 and 2 should be done by hand.

1   **Flexible Budgeting**   A budget is an expression of management's expectations and goals concerning future revenues and costs. To increase their effectiveness, many budgets are flexible, including allowances for the effect of variation in uncontrolled variables. For example, the costs and revenues of many production plants are greatly affected by the number of units produced by the plant during the budget period, and this may be beyond a plant manager's control. Standard cost-accounting procedures can be used to adjust the direct cost parts of the budget for the level of production, but it is often more difficult to handle overhead. In many cases, statistical methods are used to estimate the relationship between overhead (y) and the level of production (x) using historical data. As a simple example, the following table gives historical data for a certain plant:

Production (in 10,000) units:	5	6	7	8	9	10	11
Overhead costs (in $1000):	12	11.5	14	15	15.4	15.3	17.5

a   Construct a scatterplot of *y* versus *x*.

b   Find the least squares line relating overhead costs to production.

c   Graph the regression line on the scatterplot.

2   **Central Company**   The Central Company manufactures a certain speciality item once a month in a batch production run. The number of items produced in each run varies from month to month as demand fluctuates. The company is interested in the relationship between the size of the production run (x) and the number of hours of labor (y) required for the run. The company has collected the following data for the 10 most recent runs:

Number of items:	40	30	70	90	50	60	70	40	80	70
Labor (hours):	83	60	138	180	97	118	140	75	159	144

a   Construct a scatterplot of *y* versus *x*.

b   Find the least squares line relating hours of labor to number of items produced.

c   Graph the regression line on the scatterplot.

3.2
Examples of Regression as a Descriptive Technique

E X A M P L E   3.2   **Estimating Residential Real Estate Values**

The Tarrant County Appraisal District must appraise properties for all of the county. The appraisal district uses data such as square footage of the individual houses as well as location, depreciation, and physical condition of an entire neighborhood to derive individual appraisal values on each house. This avoids labor intensive reinspection each year.

Regression can be used to establish the weight assigned to various factors used in assessing values. For example, Table 3.5 shows the current value and size in square feet for a sample of 100 Tarrant County homes (in 1990). A scatterplot of current value (y) versus size (x) is shown in Figure 3.5.

Using a statistical package such as MINITAB or SAS, the equation relating value to size can be determined as

$$\text{VALUE} = -50{,}035 + 72.8\text{SIZE}$$

If size were the only factor thought to be of importance in determining value, this equation could be used by the appraisal district. Obviously, there are other factors that need to be considered. Developing an equation that includes more than one important factor (explanatory variable) will be discussed in Chapter 4.   ∎

E X A M P L E   3.3   **Pricing Communications Nodes**

In recent years the growth of data communications networks has been amazing. The convenience and capabilities afforded by such networks is appealing to businesses with locations

T A B L E **3.5**

VALUE and SIZE for Residential Real Estate Value Example

VALUE	SIZE	VALUE	SIZE	VALUE	SIZE
23,974	1442	12,001	783	21,536	1404
24,087	1426	37,650	1874	24,147	1676
16,781	1632	27,930	1242	17,867	1131
29,061	910	16,066	772	21,583	1397
37,982	972	20,411	908	15,482	888
29,433	912	23,672	1155	24,857	1448
33,624	1400	24,215	1004	17,716	1022
27,032	1087	22,020	958	224,182	2251
28,653	1139	52,863	1828	182,012	1126
33,075	1386	41,822	1146	201,597	2617
17,474	756	45,104	1368	49,683	966
33,852	1044	28,154	1392	60,647	1469
29,046	1032	20,943	1058	49,024	1322
20,715	720	17,851	1375	52,092	1509
19,461	734	16,616	648	55,645	1724
21,377	720	38,752	1313	51,919	1559
52,881	1635	44,377	1780	55,174	2133
43,889	1381	43,566	1148	48,760	1233
45,134	1372	38,950	1363	45,906	1323
47,655	1349	44,633	1262	52,013	1733
53,088	1599	12,372	840	56,612	1357
38,923	1171	12,148	840	69,197	1234
57,870	1966	19,852	839	84,416	1434
30,489	1504	20,012	852	60,962	1384
29,207	1296	20,314	852	47,359	995
44,919	1356	22,814	974	56,302	1372
48,090	1553	24,696	1135	88,285	1774
40,521	1142	23,443	1170	91,862	1903
43,403	1268	35,904	960	242,690	3581
38,112	1008	21,799	1052	296,251	4343
27,710	1120	28,212	1296	107,132	1861
27,621	960	27,553	1282	77,797	1542
22,258	920	15,826	916		
29,064	1259	18,660	864		

scattered throughout the United States or the world. Using networks allows centralization of a main computer with access through personal computers at remote locations.

The cost of adding a new communications node at a location not currently included on the network was of concern for a major Fort Worth manufacturing company. To try to predict the price of new communications nodes, data were obtained on a sample of existing nodes. The

F I G U R E 3.5

Scatterplot of VALUE versus SIZE for Example 3.2

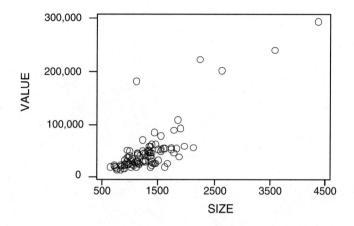

T A B L E 3.6

Cost and Number of Ports for the Communications Node Example*

Cost	Number of Ports
52,388	68
51,761	52
50,221	44
36,095	32
27,500	16
57,088	56
54,475	56
33,969	28
31,309	24
23,444	24
24,269	12
53,479	52
33,543	20
33,056	24

*Note: These data have been modified as requested by the company to provide confidentiality.

installation cost and the number of ports available for access in each existing node were readily available information. These data are shown in Table 3.6 and a scatterplot of cost (y) versus number of ports (x) is shown in Figure 3.6.

F I G U R E   **3.6**

Scatterplot of Cost Versus Number of Ports for Example 3.3

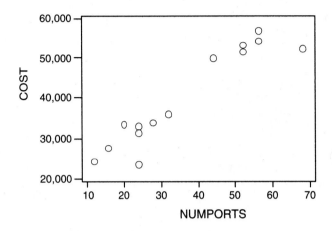

Again, using a statistical package, the equation relating the price of the new communications node to the number of access ports to be included at the node is

$$COST = 16,594 + 650NUMPORTS,$$

where NUMPORTS represents the number of ports. This equation could be used to help predict the cost of installing a new communications node based on the number of access ports to be included.   ∎

E X A M P L E   **3.4**   **Forecasting Housing Starts**

Forecasts of various economic measures are important to the U.S. government and to various industries throughout the United States. The construction industry is concerned with the number of housing starts in a given year. Accurate forecasts can help with plans for expansion or cutbacks within the industry.

Table 3.7 shows data on the number of housing starts for the years 1963 to 1991. Also shown are data on home mortgage rates for new home purchases (U.S. average) for the same years. A scatterplot of housing starts (y) versus mortgage rates (x) is shown in Figure 3.7. Note that the relationship appears to be considerably "weaker" than in the other scatterplots presented in this section. Intuitively, we might expect the relationship between housing starts and mortgage rates to be a strong one. But, from the data, this does not appear to be the case. Perhaps there are other variables that might be more strongly related to housing starts that could be used to provide accurate forecasts for future years. From viewing the scatterplot, mortgage rates alone do not appear to be particularly helpful.

T A B L E 3.7

Annual Housing Starts and Mortgage Rates for 1963–1991

Year	STARTS	RATES
1963	1603.2	5.80
1964	1528.8	5.75
1965	1472.8	5.74
1966	1164.9	6.14
1967	1291.6	6.33
1968	1507.6	6.83
1969	1466.8	7.66
1970	1433.6	8.27
1971	2052.2	7.59
1972	2356.6	7.45
1973	2045.3	7.78
1974	1337.7	8.71
1975	1160.4	8.75
1976	1537.5	8.77
1977	1987.1	8.80
1978	2020.3	9.33
1979	1745.1	10.49
1980	1292.2	12.26
1981	1084.2	14.13
1982	1062.2	14.49
1983	1703.0	12.11
1984	1749.5	11.88
1985	1741.8	11.09
1986	1805.4	9.74
1987	1620.5	8.94
1988	1488.1	8.83
1989	1376.1	9.77
1990	1192.7	9.68
1991	1014.5	9.01

The data examined in this example are called *time-series data* because they are gathered over a time sequence (years in this case). There are certain special techniques available when working with time-series data that may be helpful in developing forecasts. These techniques will be discussed throughout subsequent chapters where appropriate.

Cross-sectional data are gathered on a number of different individual units at approximately the same point in time. Examples 3.2 and 3.3 can be considered cross-sectional data. Most of the techniques discussed in this and subsequent chapters can be applied to either time-series or cross-sectional data. When special techniques apply to only one type of data, this will be mentioned. ∎

F I G U R E **3.7**

Scatterplot of Housing Starts Versus Mortgage Rates for Example 3.4

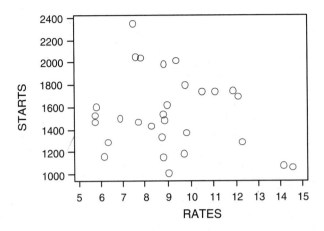

Exercises

3   The data from each of the examples in this section are available on the data disk. For each of these data sets, use a computer to read the data, graph a scatterplot of *y* versus *x*, and produce the regression output relating *y* to *x*. The commands in MINITAB and SAS to read each of the data sets are shown here:

a   Estimating Residential Real Estate Values

```
MINITAB: READ 'REALEST3' C1,C2
```

where C1 is VALUE and C2 is SIZE.
SAS: Read the data from the file REALEST3.DAT using

```
INPUT VALUE SIZE;
```

b   Pricing Communications Nodes

```
MINITAB: READ 'COMNODE3' C1,C2
```

where C1 is COST and C2 is NUMPORTS.
SAS: Read the data from the file COMNODE3.DAT using

```
INPUT COST NUMPORTS;
```

    c Forecasting Housing Starts

```
MINITAB: READ 'HSTARTS3' C1,C2
```

    where C1 is STARTS and C2 is RATES.

    SAS: Read the data from the file HSTARTS3.DAT using

```
INPUT STARTS RATES;
```

3.3
Inferences from a Simple Regression Analysis

3.3.1 Assumptions Concerning the Population Regression Line

Thus far, regression analysis has been viewed as a way to *describe* the relationship between two variables. The regression equation obtained can be viewed in this manner simply as a descriptive statistic. But, the power of the technique of least squares regression is not in its use as a descriptive measure for one particular sample, but in its ability to draw inferences or generalizations about the relationship for the entire population of values for the variables x and y.

To draw inferences from a sample regression equation, we must make some assumptions about how x and y are related in the population. These initial assumptions will describe an "ideal" situation. Later, each of these assumptions will be relaxed and we will demonstrate modifications to the basic least squares approach that will provide a model that is still suitable for statistical inference.

Assume that the relationship between the variables x and y is represented by a population regression line. The equation of this line is written as

$$\mu_{y|x} = \beta_0 + \beta_1 x, \tag{3.5}$$

where $\mu_{y|x}$ is called the *conditional mean* of y given a value of x, β_0 is the y-intercept for the population regression line, and β_1 is the slope of the population regression line. Examples of possible relationships are shown in Figure 3.8.

The use of $\mu_{y|x}$ requires some additional explanation. Suppose the y variable represents the cost of installing a new communications node as discussed in Example 3.3, and x represents the number of access ports (NUMPORTS) to be included. It is possible that these two variables are related. Now consider all possible communications nodes with 30 access ports. If the costs were known, the average value for all communications nodes with 30 access ports could be calculated. This is the conditional mean of y given $x = 30$:

$$\mu_{y|x=30}$$

F I G U R E 3.8

Examples of Possible Population Regression Lines

(a) A direct relationship ($\beta_1 > 0$)

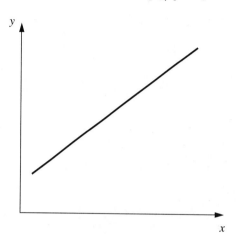

(b) An inverse relationship ($\beta_1 < 0$)

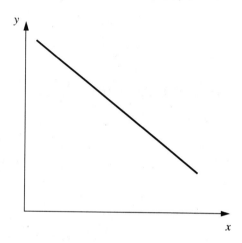

(c) No linear relationship ($\beta_1 = 0$)

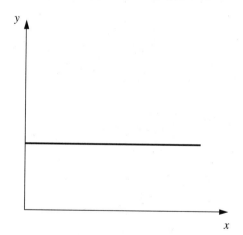

(d) A curvilinear relationship

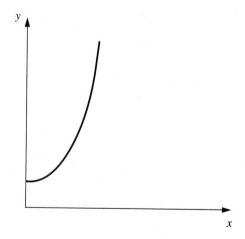

Suppose this computation could be done for a number of *x* values and the resulting conditional means plotted as in Figure 3.9. The population regression line is the line passing through the conditional means. The relationship between *y* and *x* is linear if all of the conditional means lie on a straight line (or nearly so).

For a given number of ports, say 30, costs will vary; that is, not every communications node will have a cost equal to the mean of *y* given *x* = 30. The actual cost

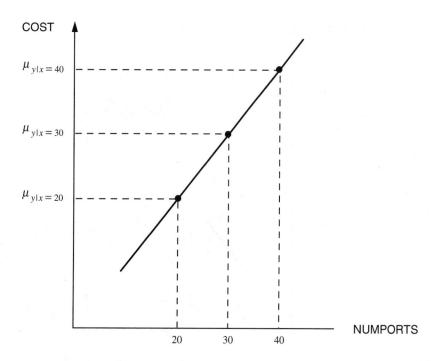

F I G U R E **3.9**

The Population Regression Line Passes Through the Conditional Means

will be distributed around the point $\mu_{y|x=30}$, or around the regression line. Thus, in a sample of communications nodes with 30 ports, the costs would be expected to differ (see Figure 3.10).

Because of this variation of the y values around the regression line, it is convenient to rewrite the equation representing an individual response as

$$y_i = \beta_0 + \beta_1 x_i + e_i, \tag{3.6}$$

where β_0 and β_1 have the same interpretation as they did in Equation (3.5). The term e_i represents the difference between the true cost for communications node i and the conditional mean of all costs for nodes with that number of ports:

$$e_i = \text{COST}_i - \mu_{y|x}$$
$$= y_i - (\beta_0 + \beta_1 x_i)$$

The e_i's are called disturbances. These disturbances keep the relationship from being an exact one. If the e_i's were all equal to zero, then there would be an exact linear relationship between all COSTs and all NUMPORTS. The effects of all unknown factors influencing COSTs are included in the disturbances. To allow statistical

F I G U R E **3.10**

Distribution of Costs Around the Regression Line

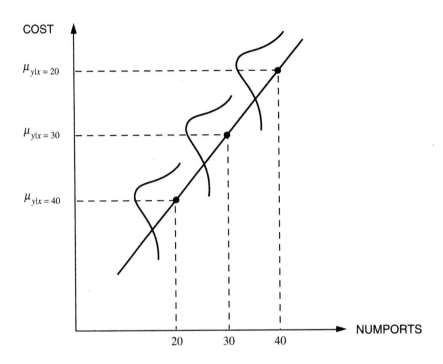

inference from a sample to the population, some assumptions about these disturbances are necessary.

1 Assume that the e_i's are normally distributed random variables. The individual response, y_i, is then the sum of a constant component and a normal random variable:

$$y_i = \underbrace{\beta_0 + \beta_1 x_i}_{\text{constant}} + \underbrace{e_i}_{\text{normal random variable}}$$

Thus, the y_i's are normally distributed around the regression line conditional on the values of x.

2 The e_i's have an expected value (or mean) of zero:

$$E(e_i) = 0$$

where $E(\cdot)$ denotes mean or expected value of a random variable.

3 The variance of each e_i is equal to σ_e^2. Referring to Figure 3.10, this assumption means that each of the distributions along the regression line has the same variance regardless of the value of x.

4   The e_i's are independent. This is an assumption that is most important when data are gathered over time. When the data are cross-sectional (i.e., gathered at the same point in time for different individual units), this is typically not an assumption of concern.

These assumptions allow inferences to be made about the population regression line from a sample regression line. The first inferences considered will be those made about β_0 and β_1, the intercept and slope, respectively, of the population regression line.

The previous assumptions define an ideal case for linear regression. In Chapters 3 and 4 we examine regression procedures designed for this ideal case. We do not, however, assume that these assumptions will automatically be met in all situations. In Chapter 5, we examine how violations of each of the assumptions might be detected and how corrections for these violations can be made.

3.3.2   Inferences about β_0 and β_1

The point estimates of β_0 and β_1 were previously justified by saying that b_0 and b_1 will minimize the sum of squared errors for the sample. With the assumptions made concerning the random disturbances of the model, additional justification of the use of b_0 and b_1 can be made by stating certain properties these estimators possess. To fully discuss these properties, some characteristics of the sampling distributions of b_0 and b_1 must first be established.

Recall that a statistic is any value calculated from a sample. Thus, b_0 and b_1 are statistics. Because statistics are random variables, they have probability distributions called *sampling distributions*. Some characteristics of the sampling distributions of b_0 and b_1 are given here:

Sampling Distribution of b_0

1 $E(b_0) = \beta_0$ $\hfill (3.7)$

2 $\mathrm{Var}\,(b_0) = \sigma_e^2 \left(\dfrac{1}{n} + \dfrac{\bar{x}^2}{\displaystyle\sum_{i=1}^{n}(x_i - \bar{x})^2} \right) = \sigma_e^2 \left(\dfrac{1}{n} + \dfrac{\bar{x}^2}{(n-1)s_x^2} \right),$ $\hfill (3.8)$

where $s_x^2 = \displaystyle\sum_{i=1}^{n}(x_i - \bar{x})^2/(n-1)$ is the sample variance of the x values.

3   The sampling distribution of b_0 is normally distributed.

Sampling Distribution of b_1

1 $E(b_1) = \beta_1$ $\hfill (3.9)$

2 $$\text{Var}\,(b_1) = \frac{\sigma_e^2}{\displaystyle\sum_{i=1}^{n}(x_i - \bar{x})^2} = \frac{\sigma_e^2}{(n-1)s_x^2} \qquad (3.10)$$

3   The sampling distribution of b_1 is normally distributed.

The sampling distributions of both b_0 and b_1 are centered at the true parameter values β_0 and β_1, respectively. Because the means of the sampling distributions are equal to the parameter values to be estimated, b_0 and b_1 are called *unbiased estimators* of β_0 and β_1 (see Figure 3.11(a)). The variances of the sampling distributions are given in Equations (3.8) and (3.10). The standard deviations of the sampling distributions are obtained by taking the square roots of the variances:

$$\sigma_{b_0} = \sigma_e \sqrt{\frac{1}{n} + \frac{\bar{x}^2}{(n-1)s_x^2}} \qquad (3.11)$$

$$\sigma_{b_1} = \sigma_e \sqrt{\frac{1}{(n-1)s_x^2}} \qquad (3.12)$$

With the assumption that the disturbances are normally distributed, the sampling distributions of b_0 and b_1 also will be normally distributed regardless of the sample size used.

The estimators b_0 and b_1 also possess certain other properties that make them desirable as estimators of β_0 and β_1. Although these properties do not have a direct bearing on the work in this text, they are stated here for completeness. Each estimator is a consistent estimator of its population counterpart. Using b_1 as an example, this means that as sample size increases, the probability increases that b_1 will be "close" to β_1. Another way to view this property is by considering the standard deviation of the sampling distribution of b_1. As the sample size increases, the standard deviation of the sampling distribution decreases (as it did for the sample mean when viewed as an estimator of the population mean in Chapter 2). When this happens, the probability under the curve representing the sampling distribution becomes more concentrated near the center, β_1, and less concentrated in the extreme tails (see Figure 3.11(b)).

A final property of both b_0 and b_1 can be illustrated by considering all other possible estimators of β_0 and β_1 that are unbiased. The standard deviations of the sampling distributions of b_0 and b_1 will be smaller than those of any of the other unbiased estimators. This minimum variance property can be restated by saying that b_0 and b_1 will have smaller sampling errors than any other unbiased estimator. Of course, this says nothing about estimators that are biased. It does specify that the least squares estimators are best within a certain class of estimators (see Figure 3.11(c)).

Using the properties of the sampling distributions of b_0 and b_1, inferences about the population parameters β_0 and β_1 can be made. This is analogous to what was done in Chapter 2 when properties of the sampling distribution of the sample mean, $\bar{x}$, were used to make inferences about the population mean, μ.

F I G U R E **3.11**

Properties of b_0 and b_1 as Estimators of β_0 and β_1 (illustrated for b_1)

(a) *Unbiased Estimators:* The mean of the sampling distribution is equal to the population parameter being estimated.

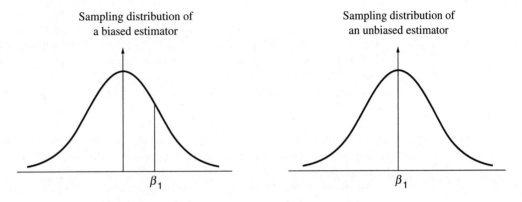

(b) *Consistent Estimators:* As *n* increases, the probability that the estimator will be close to the true parameter increases.

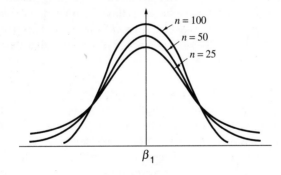

(c) *Minimum Variance Estimators:* The varaiance of b_1 is smaller than the variance of any other linear unbiased estimator of β_1, say b_1^*.

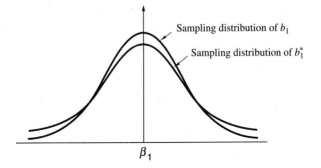

First, however, an estimate of one other unknown parameter in the regression model is needed: an estimate of σ_e^2, the variance around the regression line. This estimate of σ_e^2 is given by

$$s_e^2 = \frac{\sum_{i=1}^{n}(y_i - \hat{y}_i)^2}{n-2} = \frac{SSE}{n-2} = MSE,$$

where $\hat{y}_i = b_0 + b_1 x_i$. The term s_e^2 represents an estimate of the variance round the regression line. Recall that in Figure 3.3, $y_i - \hat{y}_i$ represented the distance from the ith sample y value to the point on the regression line associated with the ith sample x value. The sum of the squares of these distances (SSE) adjusted for (or divided by) degrees of freedom $(n-2)$ is used as an estimator of the variance around the regression line. *MSE* stands for mean squared error. A *mean square* is any sum of squares divided by its degrees of freedom. In any regression problem, the number of degrees of freedom is n, the sample size, minus the number of regression coefficients to be estimated. In simple regression, there are two regression coefficients, β_0 and β_1, so the degrees of freedom is $n-2$.

The square root of s_e^2, denoted s_e, is an estimate of the standard deviation around the regression line. It is often referred to as the *standard error of the regression*.

Now it is possible to discuss inferences about the population regression coefficients. Point estimates of β_0 and β_1 are simply the least squares estimates b_0 and b_1. Point estimates are single numbers. Often it is more desirable to state a range of values in which the parameter is thought to lie rather than a single number. These ranges are called *confidence interval estimates*. They are less precise than point estimates because they cover a range of values rather than a single number. There is a trade-off, however, between the precision of an estimate and confidence in it.

Think back to Chapter 2 and the construction of estimates for the population mean, μ. A point estimate of μ was given by the sample mean, say $\bar{x} = 40$. This is a very precise estimate, but the population mean would not equal 40. This value was obtained from one of a large number of possible samples, each of which would have a different sample mean. The chances of one of these sample means being exactly equal to the population mean was so small that a 0% level of confidence would be assigned to the possibility that μ was exactly 40. When constructing a confidence interval estimate of μ, however, the situation changes. For example, using the fact that the sampling distribution of $\bar{x}$ was normal (or approximately normal), 95% error bounds could be determined using a value from the standard normal table times the standard deviation of the sampling distribution. Putting these numbers into interval form, a 95% confidence interval for the population mean would be

$$\left(\bar{x} - 1.96\frac{\sigma}{\sqrt{n}}, \quad \bar{x} + 1.96\frac{\sigma}{\sqrt{n}}\right)$$

Although the interval estimate is less precise, confidence that the true population mean would be between the interval limits is considerably increased. In constructing interval estimates, a high level of confidence in the estimates is desired (90%, 95%, or 99% are commonly used), but the interval also should be precise enough to be practically useful. Telling the boss "I'm 90% confident that sales next month will be between $1000 and $1500" is probably better than "I'm 100% confident sales will be between $0 and $100,000." These same considerations in constructing interval estimates of the population mean also apply to interval estimates of population regression coefficients.

To construct a confidence interval estimate for β_1, the slope of the regression line, an estimate of the standard deviation of the sampling distribution is needed. This estimate is obtained by substituting s_e for σ_e in Equation (3.12):

$$s_{b_1} = s_e \sqrt{\frac{1}{(n-1)s_x^2}}$$

When sample sizes are small (say $n \leq 30$), the t distribution is used to construct the interval estimate. A $(1 - \alpha)100\%$ confidence interval for β_1 is given by

$$(b_1 - t_{\alpha/2}s_{b_1}, \quad b_1 + t_{\alpha/2}s_{b_1})$$

The value $t_{\alpha/2}$ is a number chosen from the t table to ensure the appropriate level of confidence. For example, for a 90% confidence interval estimate, $\alpha = .10$, so that $(1 - \alpha)100\% = 90\%$, and a t value with $\alpha/2 = .05$ probability in each tail of the t distribution with $n - 2$ degrees of freedom would be used.

For β_0, the $(1 - \alpha)100\%$ confidence interval is

$$(b_0 - t_{\alpha/2}s_{b_0}, \quad b_0 + t_{\alpha/2}s_{b_0}),$$

where

$$s_{b_0} = s_e \sqrt{\frac{1}{n} + \frac{\bar{x}^2}{(n-1)s_x^2}}$$

The estimated standard deviations of the sampling distributions of b_0 and b_1 are sometimes referred to as *standard errors of the coefficients* or *estimated standard deviations of the coefficients*. Thus, s_{b_0} is the standard error of b_0 and s_{b_1} is the standard error of b_1.

Hypothesis tests about β_0 and β_1 also can be performed. The most common hypothesis test in simple regression is

$$H_0: \quad \beta_1 = 0$$
$$H_a: \quad \beta_1 \neq 0,$$

where H_0 represents the null hypothesis and H_a the alternative hypothesis. The null hypothesis states that the slope of the population regression line is zero. This would mean that there is no linear relationship between y and x and that knowledge of x would not help in explaining the variation in y. The alternative hypothesis states that the slope of the population regression line is not equal to zero; that is, x and y are linearly related. Knowledge of the value of x *does* provide information concerning the associated value of y.

To test this hypothesis, a t statistic with $n - 2$ degrees of freedom is used:

$$t = \frac{b_1}{s_{b_1}}$$

If the null hypothesis is true, then the t statistic will have a t distribution with $n - 2$ degrees of freedom, and it should be small in absolute value. If the null hypothesis is false, then the t statistic should be large in absolute value.

To decide whether to accept or reject the null hypothesis, a level of significance, α, must first be chosen. The level of significance is the probability of a Type I error; that is, α is equal to the probability of rejecting the null hypothesis if the null hypothesis is really true. Typical α values used are .01, .05, and .10. The decision rule for the test can be stated as:

$$\text{Reject} \quad H_0 \quad \text{if} \quad t > t_{\alpha/2} \quad \text{or} \quad t < -t_{\alpha/2}$$
$$\text{Accept} \quad H_0 \quad \text{if} \quad -t_{\alpha/2} \leq t \leq t_{\alpha/2}$$

The value $t_{\alpha/2}$ is called a critical value and is chosen from the t table to ensure that the test is performed with the stated level of significance. A t value with $\alpha/2$ probability in each tail of the t distribution with $n - 2$ degrees of freedom is used.

Although the test of the null hypothesis H_0: $\beta_1 = 0$ is the most common and important test in simple regression analysis, tests of whether β_1 is equal to any value are possible. The general hypotheses can be stated as

$$H_0: \quad \beta_1 = \beta_1^*$$
$$H_a: \quad \beta_1 \neq \beta_1^*,$$

where β_1^* is any number chosen as the hypothesized value. The decision rule is:

$$\text{Reject} \quad H_0 \quad \text{if} \quad t > t_{\alpha/2} \quad \text{or} \quad t < -t_{\alpha/2}$$
$$\text{Accept} \quad H_0 \quad \text{if} \quad -t_{\alpha/2} \leq t \leq t_{\alpha/2}$$

and the test statistic is

$$t = \frac{b_1 - \beta_1^*}{s_{b_1}}$$

When the null hypothesis is true, t should be small in absolute value because the estimate of β_1, b_1, should be close to β_1^*, making the numerator, $b_1 - \beta_1^*$, close to zero. When the null hypothesis is false, b_1 should be different in value from the hypothesized value β_1^*, and the difference $b_1 - \beta_1^*$ should be large in absolute value, resulting in a large absolute value for the t statistic.

Tests for hypotheses about β_0 proceed in a similar fashion. To test

$$H_0: \quad \beta_0 = \beta_0^*$$
$$H_a: \quad \beta_0 \neq \beta_0^*,$$

the test statistic is

$$t = \frac{b_0 - \beta_0^*}{s_{b_0}},$$

where β_0^* is any hypothesized value. The decision rule for the test is:

Reject H_0 if $t > t_{\alpha/2}$ or $t < -t_{\alpha/2}$

Accept H_0 if $-t_{\alpha/2} \leq t \leq t_{\alpha/2}$

An alternative method of reporting hypothesis-testing results also is available in many computer software packages. Consider again the hypotheses

$$H_0: \quad \beta_1 = 0$$
$$H_a: \quad \beta_1 \neq 0$$

The test statistic used is

$$t = \frac{b_1}{s_{b_1}}$$

Some computerized regression software routines will perform this computation and then report the p value associated with the computed test statistic. The p value is the probability of obtaining a value of t at least as extreme as the actual computed value if the null hypothesis is true. Suppose a simple regression analysis is performed on a sample of 25 observations and the computed t value is 2.50. The p value for the two-tailed test of $H_0: \beta_1 = 0$ would be p value = probability $(t > 2.5 \text{ or } t < -2.5) = .02$ from the t table because there is a probability of .01 above 2.5 and .01 below -2.5 in the t distribution with $n - 2 = 23$ degrees of freedom.

The p value can be viewed as the minimum level of significance, α, that can be chosen for the test and result in rejection of the null hypothesis. Thus, a decision rule using p values can be stated as:

Reject H_0 if p value $< \alpha$

Accept H_0 if p value $\geq \alpha$

For a given level of significance, the same decision will result regardless of which test procedure is used.

Using the previous example, the decision would be to reject H_0 if $\alpha = .05$, but to accept H_0 if $\alpha = .01$. Reporting p values associated with hypothesis tests provides additional information beyond simply reporting that the null hypothesis was rejected or accepted at a single level of significance. Readers then can make their own decisions about the strength of the relationship by comparing the p value to any desired significance level.

Figure 3.12(a) shows the structure of the initial portion of the MINITAB output for a regression analysis. The estimated regression coefficients b_0 and b_1 are given along with the standard errors of the coefficients, s_{b_0} and s_{b_1}, and the t ratios for testing either $\beta_0 = 0$ or $\beta_1 = 0$. The last column reports the p values associated with the two-tailed tests of the hypotheses $H_0: \beta_0 = 0$ and $H_0: \beta_1 = 0$. Note that the t ratios can be

F I G U R E **3.12**

Illustration of MINITAB and SAS Regression Outputs

(a) MINITAB

Predictor	Coef	Stdev	t-ratio	p
Constant	b_0	s_{b_0}	b_0/s_{b_0}	p value
x1 variable name	b_1	s_{b_1}	b_1/s_{b_1}	p value

(b) SAS

Parameter Estimates

Variable	DF	Parameter Estimate	Standard Error	T for H0: Parameter $=0$	Prob $>$ |T|
INTERCEPT	1	b_0	s_{b_0}	b_0/s_{b_0}	p value
X1 VARIABLE NAME	1	b_1	s_{b_1}	b_1/s_{b_1}	p value

used for performing either one- or two-tailed tests as long as the hypothesized value is zero. The one-tailed tests simply require an adjustment in the decision rules. These are shown in Table 3.8 for the more general hypothesis structures. The MINITAB t ratios are still appropriate when β_0^* and β_1^* (the hypothesized values) are zero.

Figure 3.12(b) shows the structure of the equivalent SAS output. Again, the parameter estimates, standard errors, t ratios, and p values are reported. An additional column, DF, indicates that 1 degree of freedom is used up for each parameter estimated. The DF values will always be 1 for cases considered in this text.

The p values for both MINITAB and SAS represent the appropriate values for a two-tailed test. Both the MINITAB and SAS outputs will be fully illustrated in Example 3.6.

T A B L E **3.8**

Hypothesis Structures and Their Associated Decision Rules for Hypotheses about β_0 and β_1

Hypotheses			Decision Rule	
H_0: $\beta_1 = \beta_1^*$	or	H_0: $\beta_0 = \beta_0^*$	Reject H_0 if $t > t_{\alpha/2,n-2}$ or $t < -t_{\alpha/2,n-2}$	
H_a: $\beta_1 \neq \beta_1^*$		H_a: $\beta_0 \neq \beta_0^*$	Accept H_0 if $-t_{\alpha/2,n-2} \leq t \leq t_{\alpha/2,n-2}$	
H_0: $\beta_1 \geq \beta_1^*$	or	H_0: $\beta_0 \geq \beta_0^*$	Reject H_0 if $t < -t_{\alpha,n-2}$	
H_a: $\beta_1 < \beta_1^*$		H_a: $\beta_0 < \beta_0^*$	Accept H_0 if $t \geq -t_{\alpha,n-2}$	
H_0: $\beta_1 \leq \beta_1^*$	or	H_0: $\beta_0 \leq \beta_0^*$	Reject H_0 if $t > t_{\alpha,n-2}$	
H_a: $\beta_1 > \beta_1^*$		H_a: $\beta_0 > \beta_0^*$	Accept H_0 if $t \leq t_{\alpha,n-2}$	

E X A M P L E **3.5**

Consider the data in Table 3.2 and the computations required to obtain the least squares estimates in Table 3.3. To compute s_{b_0} and s_{b_1}, the following quantities are needed:

$$n = 6$$

$$\bar{x}^2 = \left(\sum x_i/n\right)^2 = \left(\frac{21}{6}\right)^2 = 12.25$$

and

$$(n - 1)s_x^2 = \sum x_i^2 - \frac{1}{n}\left(\sum x_i\right)^2 = 91 - \frac{1}{6}(21)^2 = 17.5,$$

which can be determined using the sums obtained in Table 3.3. In addition, the standard error of the regression must be computed:

$$s_e = \sqrt{\frac{\sum(y_i - \hat{y}_i)^2}{(n - 2)}}$$

$$= \sqrt{\frac{8.8}{4}}$$

$$= 1.48$$

The error sum of squares, $\Sigma(y_i - \hat{y}_i)^2$, was computed in Table 3.4.
    Using this information:

$$s_{b_0} = s_e\sqrt{\frac{1}{n} + \frac{\bar{x}^2}{(n - 1)s_x^2}}$$

$$= 1.48\sqrt{\frac{1}{6} + \frac{12.25}{17.5}} = 1.38$$

and

$$s_{b_1} = s_e\sqrt{\frac{1}{(n - 1)s_x^2}}$$

$$= 1.48\sqrt{\frac{1}{17.5}} = 0.35$$

The 95% confidence interval estimates for β_0 and β_1 now can be constructed.

For β_0: $[-0.2 - 2.776(1.38),\quad -0.2 + 2.776(1.38)]$

$$\text{or } (-4.03,\ 3.63)$$

For β_1: $[2.2 - 2.776(0.35),\quad 2.2 + 2.776(0.35)]$

$$\text{or } (1.23,\ 3.17) \quad \blacksquare$$

F I G U R E **3.13**

MINITAB Regression Output for Examples 3.3 and 3.6

```
The regression equation is
cost = 16594 + 650 numports

Predictor         Coef      Stdev    t-ratio        p
Constant         16594       2687       6.18    0.000
numports        650.17      66.91       9.72    0.000

s = 4307        R-sq = 88.7%    R-sq(adj) = 87.8%

Analysis of Variance

SOURCE        DF          SS          MS         F        p
Regression     1  1751268352  1751268352     94.41    0.000
Error         12   222594144    18549512
Total         13  1973862528

Unusual Observations
Obs. numports       cost      Fit  Stdev.Fit   Residual   St.Resid
   1     68.0       52388    60805       2414      -8417     -2.36R
  10     24.0       23444    32198       1414      -8754     -2.15R

R denotes an obs. with a large st. resid.
```

E X A M P L E **3.6** **Pricing Communications Nodes (continued)**

Table 3.6 shows the cost of installing a sample of communications nodes for a large manufacturing firm whose headquarters is based in Fort Worth, Texas, with branches throughout the United States. The number of access ports at each of the sampled nodes is also shown. The administrator of the network would like to develop an equation that would be helpful in pricing the installation of new communications nodes on the network.

Figure 3.6 shows the MINITAB scatterplot of cost versus number of nodes. The MINITAB regression output is shown in Figure 3.13. Figures 3.14 and 3.15 show the same information using SAS. Use the outputs to answer the following questions:

1. What is the sample regression equation relating NUMPORTS to COST?

Answer:

$$COST = 16,594 + 650 NUMPORTS$$

2. Is there sufficient evidence to conclude that a linear relationship exists between COST and NUMPORTS?

Answer:

(a) To answer this question, the hypotheses

$$H_0: \quad \beta_1 = 0$$
$$H_a: \quad \beta_1 \neq 0$$

should be tested. Choosing a 5% level of significance, the decision rule for the test is:

$$\text{Reject} \quad H_0 \quad \text{if} \quad t > 2.179 \text{ or } t < -2.179$$
$$\text{Accept} \quad H_0 \quad \text{if} \quad -2.179 \leq t \leq 2.179$$

F I G U R E **3.14**

SAS Scatterplot of Cost versus Number of Ports for Examples 3.3 and 3.6

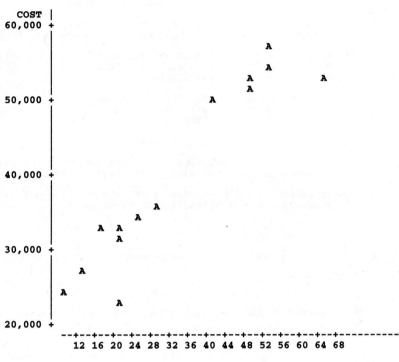

```
    Plot of COST*NUMPORTS.   Legend: A = 1 obs, B = 2 obs, etc.

  COST |
60,000 +
       |                                          A
       |                                        A
       |                                  A
       |                                  A               A
50,000 +                            A
       |
       |
       |
40,000 +
       |
       |                      A
       |                    A
       |              A  A
30,000 +              A
       |
       |        A
       |     A
       |        A
20,000 +
         --+--+--+--+--+--+--+--+--+--+--+--+--+--+----------
           12 16 20 24 28 32 36 40 44 48 52 56 60 64 68

                                                    NUMPORTS
```

The test statistic from either Figure 3.13 or 3.15 is

$$t = 9.72,$$

so the decision is to reject H_0. There is sufficient evidence to conclude that a linear relationship between COST and NUMPORTS does exist.

Answer:

(b) The p value also could be used as a test statistic to test the hypotheses. The decision rule is:

Reject H_0 if p value $< .05$

Accept H_0 if p value $\geq .05$

The test statistic is

$$p \text{ value } = 0.000,$$

so because 0.000 is less than .05, the decision is to reject H_0.

F I G U R E **3.15**

SAS Regression Output for Examples 3.3 and 3.6

Dependent Variable: COST

Analysis of Variance

Source	DF	Sum of Squares	Mean Square	F Value	Prob>F
Model	1	1751268375.7	1751268375.7	94.410	0.0001
Error	12	222594145.79	18549512.149		
C Total	13	1973862521.5			

Root MSE	4306.91446	R-square	0.8872	
Dep Mean	40185.50000	Adj R-sq	0.8778	
C.V.	10.71758			

Parameter Estimates

Variable	DF	Parameter Estimate	Standard Error	T for H0: Parameter=0	Prob > |T|
INTERCEP	1	16594	2687.0499985	6.175	0.0001
NUMPORTS	1	650.169172	66.91388832	9.717	0.0001

3. Find a 95% confidence interval estimate of β_1.

Answer:

$$650.17 \pm 2.179(66.91) \quad \text{or} \quad 650.17 \pm 145.80$$

Our point estimate of the change in cost, on average, for each additional port is $650.17. The confidence interval provides an error bound for this estimate, $145.80. We can now construct a range of values that can be used as an estimate of the average change in cost for each additional port. The range is $650.17 ± $145.80 or $504.37 to $795.97. We can be 95% confident that the true average change will fall within this range.

4. Test whether there is a direct (positive) relationship between COST and NUMPORTS.

Answer:

To answer this question, the hypotheses

$$H_0: \quad \beta_1 \leq 0$$
$$H_a: \quad \beta_1 > 0$$

should be tested. The null hypothesis states that the slope of the population regression line is either zero (no relationship) or negative (an inverse relationship). The alternate hypothesis states that the slope of the population regression line is positive (a direct relationship). Choosing a 5% level of significance, the decision rule for the test is:

$$\text{Reject } H_0 \quad \text{if} \quad t > 1.782$$
$$\text{Accept } H_0 \quad \text{if} \quad t \leq 1.782$$

The test statistic from either Figure 3.13 or 3.15 is

$$t = 9.72,$$

so the decision is to reject H_0. There is sufficient evidence to conclude that a direct (positive) linear relationship between COST and NUMPORTS does exist.

If the null hypothesis had been accepted, the conclusion would be that either there is an inverse relationship or there is no relationship. The relationship is not direct, but acceptance would not imply that no linear relationship existed as in the case of the two-tailed test. Care must be taken in interpreting the results of one-tailed tests.

5. A claim is made that each new access port adds at least \$1000 to the installation of a communications node. To examine this claim we test the hypotheses

$$H_0: \quad \beta_1 \geq 1000$$
$$H_a: \quad \beta_1 < 1000$$

using a 5% level of significance.

Answer:
The decision rule is:

$$\text{Reject } H_0 \quad \text{if} \quad t < -1.782$$
$$\text{Accept } H_0 \quad \text{if} \quad t \geq -1.782$$

The test statistic is
$$t = \frac{b_1 - \beta_1^*}{s_{b_1}} = \frac{650.17 - 1000}{66.91} = -5.23,$$

so the decision is to reject H_0. The slope of the line is not 1000 or more. In practical terms, there is no evidence to support the claim that each port adds at least \$1000 to the cost of installing a new communications node.

The previous problems illustrate the aspects of greatest interest in the communications node example. Simply for illustrative purposes, here are two problems showing how the techniques discussed for the intercept term in the equation could be used.

6. Find a 95% confidence interval estimate of β_0.

Answer:
$16,594 \pm 2.179(2687)$ or $16,594 \pm 5854.97$

7. Test the hypotheses
$$H_0: \quad \beta_0 = 0$$
$$H_a: \quad \beta_0 \neq 0$$

using a 5% level of significance.

Answer:
(a) Decision rule:

$$\text{Reject } H_0 \quad \text{if} \quad t > 2.179 \text{ or } t < -2.179$$
$$\text{Accept } H_0 \quad \text{if} \quad -2.179 \leq t \leq 2.179$$

Test statistic: $t = 6.18$
Decision: Reject H_0.
Conclusion: The population intercept is not equal to zero.
Note: This test has no practical significance in this problem and is performed merely to illustrate tests for the intercept. Note, however, that rejection of the null hypothesis $H_0: \beta_0 = 0$

does *not* mean that x and y are related. It merely makes a statement about the intercept of the population regression line.

(b) Decision rule (Using the p value):

$$\text{Reject } H_0 \quad \text{if} \quad p \text{ value } < .05$$
$$\text{Accept } H_0 \quad \text{if} \quad p \text{ value } \geq .05$$

Test statistic: p value $= 0.000$

Decision: Because $0.000 < .05$, reject H_0. ∎

Exercises

Exercises 4 and 5 should be done by hand.

4   Flexible Budgeting (continued)   Refer to Exercise 1.

    a   Test the hypotheses H_0: $\beta_1 = 0$ versus H_a: $\beta_1 \neq 0$ at the 5% level of significance. State the decision rule, test statistic value, and decision.

    b   From the result in (a), are production and overhead costs linearly related?

    c   Test the hypotheses H_0: $\beta_1 = 1$ versus H_a: $\beta_1 \neq 1$ at the 5% level of significance. State the decision rule, test statistic value, and decision.

    d   From the result in (c), what can be concluded?

5   Central Company (continued)   Refer to Exercise 2.

    a   Test the hypotheses H_0: $\beta_1 = 0$ versus H_a: $\beta_1 \neq 0$ at the 5% level of significance. State the decision rule, test statistic value, and decision.

    b   From the result in (a), are hours of labor and number of items produced linearly related?

    c   Test the hypotheses H_0: $\beta_0 = 0$ versus H_a: $\beta_0 \neq 0$ at the 5% level of significance. State the decision rule, test statistic value, and decision.

    d   From the result in (c), what can be concluded?

6   Dividends   A random sample of 50 firms was chosen from the June 1994 *Standard and Poor's Security Owners' Stock Guide*.[1] The indicated dividend yield for May 1994 (DIVYIELD) and the earnings per share for the last 12 months (EPS) were recorded for these 50 firms.

    Using DIVYIELD as the dependent variable and EPS as the independent variable, a regression was run. Use the output to answer the questions. The list of firms and the accompanying data are shown in Table 3.9. The MINITAB scatterplot and regression output are in Figures 3.16 and 3.17, respectively. The SAS regression output is in Figure 3.18.

---

[1] *Standard and Poor's Security Owner's Stock Guide.* ©1994 Standard and Poor's, a division of McGraw-Hill Inc.

T A B L E **3.9**
Dividend Yield and EPS Data for Dividends Exercise

Firm Name	DIVYIELD	EPS	Firm Name	DIVYIELD	EPS
Bristol-Myers Squibb	5.3	3.83	Tandy	1.6	1.26
Intel	0.4	5.36	Cyprus Amax Minerals	2.8	1.86
Fansteel Inc.	5.5	0.10	Betz Laboratories	3.1	2.04
Waterhouse Investor Svc.	1.1	1.95	Owens & Minor	1.2	0.98
Schering-Plough	3.1	4.41	Wendy's International	1.4	0.79
Weyerhaeuser	2.9	2.33	General Signal	2.9	1.57
PNC Bank	4.2	3.22	Kansas City Southern Inds.	0.7	2.28
Marion Merrell Dow	5.7	1.35	New Plan Realty Trust	6.0	0.96
Park Electrochemical	1.2	2.02	Ohio Casualty	5.4	2.12
United Mobile Homes	4.8	0.29	Maybelline Inc.	1.0	1.30
Burlington Resources	1.3	1.98	Tidewater	1.9	0.67
Consolidated Papers	3.3	1.41	Brooklyn Union Gas	5.7	1.75
AMRESCO Inc.	2.9	2.01	Stone & Webster	1.8	0.91
Consolidated Natural Gas	5.1	2.08	Wilmington Trust	4.2	2.29
Louisiana-Pacific	1.5	2.29	Idaho Power	8.0	2.03
Wheelabrator Technologies	0.5	0.89	BIC	2.8	1.92
Baker Hughes	2.3	0.57	PacifiCorp	6.1	1.60
McGraw-Hill	3.5	0.22	Millipore	1.1	1.87
Clorox	3.5	3.84	Masco Corp.	2.5	1.51
Nalco Chemical	2.9	2.02	Central Maine Power	8.0	1.31
Pioneer Hi-Bred Int'l	1.6	1.82	Lance Inc.	5.3	0.95
TJX	2.3	1.58	Sealright Co.	3.3	0.95
Loral	1.6	2.72	Health Equity Prop.	10.1	0.78
DPL	5.9	1.45	Jones Medical Indus.	0.9	0.71
Johnson Controls	2.9	3.43	Diamond Shamrock	2.1	1.25

a What is the sample regression equation relating dividends to EPS?

b Is there a linear relationship between dividends paid and EPS? Use $\alpha = .05$. State the hypotheses to be tested, the decision rule, the test statistic, and your decision.

c What conclusion can be drawn from the test result?

d Construct a 95% confidence interval estimate of β_1.

e Construct a 95% confidence interval estimate of β_0.

These data are available on the data disk for further analysis. In MINITAB, they can be read using

```
READ 'DIV3' C1,C2
```

where C1 will contain DIVYIELD and C2 will contain EPS.

In SAS, the data can be read from the file DIV3.DAT using

```
INPUT DIVYIELD EPS;
```

F I G U R E **3.16**

MINITAB Scatterplot for Dividends Exercise

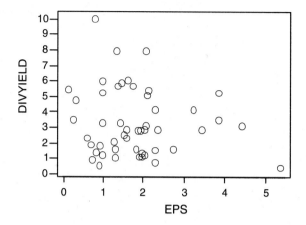

F I G U R E **3.17**

MINITAB Regression Output for Dividends Exercise

```
The regression equation is
divyield = 3.78 - 0.267 eps

Predictor        Coef        Stdev      t-ratio          p
Constant       3.7775       0.6050         6.24      0.000
eps           -0.2665       0.2935        -0.91      0.368

s = 2.171        R-sq = 1.7%      R-sq(adj) = 0.0%

Analysis of Variance

SOURCE         DF           SS           MS         F           p
Regression      1        3.886        3.886      0.82      0.368
Error          48      226.133        4.711
Total          49      230.019

Unusual Observations
Obs.      eps   divyield        Fit  Stdev.Fit   Residual    St.Resid
   2     5.36      0.400      2.349      1.096     -1.949      -1.04 X
   5     4.41      3.100      2.602      0.832      0.498       0.25 X
  40     2.03      8.000      3.236      0.316      4.764       2.22R
  45     1.31      8.000      3.428      0.336      4.572       2.13R
  48     0.78     10.100      3.570      0.424      6.530       3.07R

R denotes an obs. with a large st. resid.
X denotes an obs. whose X value gives it large influence.
```

7   **Sales/Advertising**   The vice-president of marketing for a large firm is concerned about the effectiveness of advertising in generating sales of the firm's major product. To investigate the relationship between advertising and sales, data on the two variables were gathered from a random sample of 20 sales districts. The data are shown in Table 3.10.

F I G U R E 3.18

SAS Regression Output for Dividends Exercise

Dependent Variable: DIVYIELD

Analysis of Variance

Source	DF	Sum of Squares	Mean Square	F Value	Prob>F
Model	1	3.88588	3.88588	0.825	0.3683
Error	48	226.13332	4.71111		
C Total	49	230.01920			

Root MSE	2.17051	R-square	0.0169	
Dep Mean	3.30400	Adj R-sq	-0.0036	
C.V.	65.69338			

Parameter Estimates

Variable	DF	Parameter Estimate	Standard Error	T for H0: Parameter=0	Prob > |T|
INTERCEP	1	3.777524	0.60503291	6.244	0.0001
EPS	1	-0.266534	0.29347364	-0.908	0.3683

T A B L E 3.10

Sales and Advertising Data

District	Sales (in $100)	Advertising Expenditures (in $100)
1	4250	235
2	3700	210
3	2000	160
4	5800	345
5	6200	325
6	6500	365
7	7000	400
8	4900	370
9	6100	350
10	2900	200
11	3200	200
12	3500	210
13	4000	230
14	5175	210
15	5450	300
16	5900	325
17	7110	390
18	6500	375
19	7400	415
20	6600	380

F I G U R E **3.19**

MINITAB Regression Output for Sales/Advertising Exercise

```
The regression equation is
sales = - 57 + 17.6 adv

Predictor        Coef       Stdev     t-ratio       p
Constant        -57.3       509.8      -0.11      0.912
adv            17.570       1.642      10.70      0.000

s = 594.8       R-sq = 86.4%     R-sq(adj) = 85.7%

Analysis of Variance

SOURCE        DF         SS           MS         F         p
Regression     1     40523672     40523672    114.54     0.000
Error         18      6368342       353797
Total         19     46892016

Unusual Observations
Obs.      adv      sales        Fit   Stdev.Fit   Residual   St.Resid
  8       370      4900        6444       176       -1544      -2.72R
 14       210      5175        3632       198        1543       2.75R

R denotes an obs. with a large st. resid.
```

F I G U R E **3.20**

SAS Regression Output for Sales/Advertising Exercise

```
Dependent Variable: SALES

                        Analysis of Variance

                     Sum of          Mean
Source        DF     Squares         Square      F Value    Prob>F

Model          1 40523671.367 40523671.367      114.539    0.0001
Error         18 6368342.3828 353796.79904
C Total       19 46892013.75

        Root MSE       594.80820    R-square       0.8642
        Dep Mean      5209.25000    Adj R-sq       0.8566
        C.V.            11.41831

                        Parameter Estimates

              Parameter      Standard     T for H0:
Variable  DF   Estimate        Error    Parameter=0   Prob > |T|

INTERCEP   1  -57.280921   509.75030157    -0.112       0.9118
ADV        1   17.569745     1.64167810    10.702       0.0001
```

The MINITAB and SAS outputs for the regression of sales (SALES) on advertising (ADV) are shown in Figures 3.19 and 3.20, respectively. The scatterplot is in Figure 3.21. Using the outputs, answer the following questions:

FIGURE 3.21

MINITAB Scatterplot for Sales/Advertising Exercise

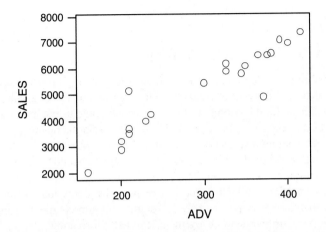

a Is there a linear relationship between sales and advertising? Use $\alpha = .05$. State the hypotheses to be tested, the decision rule, the test statistic, and your decision.

b What implications does this test result have for the firm?

c What is the sample regression equation relating sales to advertising?

d Construct a 90% confidence interval estimate of β_0.

e Construct a 95% confidence interval estimate of β_1.

f Test the hypotheses

$$H_0: \quad \beta_1 = 20$$
$$H_a: \quad \beta_1 \neq 20$$

using a 5% level of significance. State the decision rule, the test statistic, and your decision.

g What conclusion can be drawn from the result of the test in (f)?

These data are available on the data disk for further analysis. In MINITAB, they can be read using

```
READ 'SALESAD3' C1,C2
```

where C1 will contain SALES and C2 will contain ADV.

In SAS, the data can be read from the file SALESAD3.DAT using

```
INPUT SALES ADV;
```

3.4
Assessing the Fit of the Regression Line

3.4.1 The ANOVA Table

In Example 3.6 (communications nodes) the goal might be to obtain the best possible prediction of the cost of a new node to be installed. Using a sample of n previously installed nodes the sample mean of the n costs could be computed and used to predict the cost of any future node. But additional information on the number of access ports at each communications node might be used to obtain "better" predictions. When predicting, the goal in fitting a regression equation would be to obtain a more accurate prediction of a node's cost. This improvement in accuracy can be measured in terms of how much better the predictions are using the regression line instead of simply the mean of the y variable. If there is a significant improvement in prediction accuracy, then it is worthwhile to utilize the additional information.

In Figure 3.22, suppose that x^* represents the number of access ports at a particular communications node and y^* is the true cost of that node. If $\bar{y}$ is used to predict the cost of this node, then the prediction error is

$$y^* - \bar{y}$$

But if the regression equation is used the error is

$$y^* - \hat{y},$$

thus reducing the error by

$$\hat{y} - \bar{y}$$

Note that the error in using the sample mean to predict, $y^* - \bar{y}$, is equal to the error produced by using the regression line, $y^* - \hat{y}$, plus the improvement over using the mean, $\hat{y} - \bar{y}$:

$$y^* - \bar{y} = (y^* - \hat{y}) + (\hat{y} - \bar{y}) \tag{3.13}$$

Squaring both sides of (3.13) gives

$$(y^* - \bar{y})^2 = [(y^* - \hat{y}) + (\hat{y} - \bar{y})]^2$$

or, expanding the right-hand side,

$$(y^* - \bar{y})^2 = (y^* - \hat{y})^2 + 2(\hat{y} - \bar{y})(y^* - \hat{y}) + (\hat{y} - \bar{y})^2 \tag{3.14}$$

The terms on either side of (3.14) can be summed for all the individuals in the sample to obtain

$$\sum_{i=1}^{n}(y_i - \bar{y})^2 = \sum_{i=1}^{n}(y_i - \hat{y}_i)^2 + 2\sum_{i=1}^{n}(\hat{y}_i - \bar{y})(y_i - \hat{y}_i) + \sum_{i=1}^{n}(\hat{y}_i - \bar{y})^2$$

F I G U R E 3.22

Partitioning the Variation in *y*

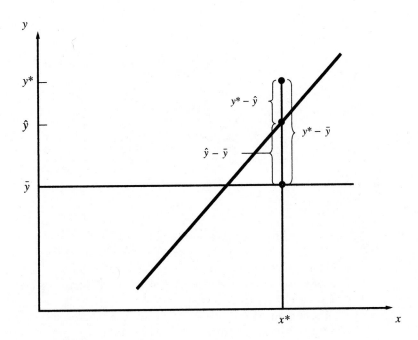

The term $\sum_{i=1}^{n}(\hat{y}_i - \bar{y})(y_i - \hat{y}_i)$ can be shown to equal zero, so that

$$\sum_{i=1}^{n}(y_i - \bar{y})^2 = \sum_{i=1}^{n}(y_i - \hat{y}_i)^2 + \sum_{i=1}^{n}(\hat{y}_i - \bar{y})^2 \qquad (3.15)$$

Each term in (3.15) is a sum of squares and has a special interpretation in regression analysis. The term on the left-hand side of the equality,

$$SST = \sum_{i=1}^{n}(y_i - \bar{y})^2,$$

is called the *total sum of squares (SST)*. This is the numerator of the fraction used to compute the sample variance of *y* and is interpreted as the total variation in *y*.

On the right-hand side of the equation are two additional sums of squares:

$$SSE = \sum_{i=1}^{n}(y_i - \hat{y}_i)^2,$$

called the *error sum of squares (SSE)*, and

$$SSR = \sum_{i=1}^{n}(\hat{y}_i - \bar{y})^2,$$

called the *regression sum of squares (SSR)*.

F I G U R E 3.23

Analysis of Variance Tables from MINITAB and SAS Regressions

(a) MINITAB

SOURCE	DF	SS	MS	F	p
REGRESSION	1	SSR	MSR = SSR/1	F = MSR/MSE	p value
ERROR	n − 2	SSE	MSE = SSE/(n − 2)		
Total	n − 1	SST			

(b) SAS

Source	DF	Sum of Squares	Mean Square	F Value	Prob > F
MODEL	1	SSR	MSR = SSR/1	F = MSR/MSE	p value
ERROR	n − 2	SSE	MSE = SSE/(n − 2)		
C Total	n − 1	SST			

The terms in *SSE*, $y_i - \hat{y}_i$, are the prediction errors for the sample—that is, the differences between the true *y* values and the values predicted by using the regression line. *SSE* is often referred to as the "unexplained" sum of squares or as a measure of "unexplained" variation in *y*.

The terms in *SSR*, $\hat{y}_i - \bar{y}$, are measures of the improvement in using the regression line rather than the sample mean to predict. *SSR* often is referred to as the "explained" sum of squares or as a measure of "explained" variation in *y*. The "explaining" is done through the use of the variable *x*.

The terms *explained* and *unexplained* should be interpreted with some caution. Explained does not mean that *x* causes *y*. It means that the variation in *y* around the regression line is smaller than the variation around the sample mean, $\bar{y}$. This caveat will be explored in more detail in Section 3.7.

Figure 3.23 shows how MINITAB and SAS report certain of the quantities discussed in this section. The tables shown are called *analysis of variance* (ANOVA) tables in both software packages. This name refers to the partitioning of the total variation in the dependent variable into the regression and error sums of squares. These tables are typical of ANOVA tables presented in most statistical packages.

In the MINITAB ANOVA table in 3.23(a), the three sources of variation in *y* are denoted Regression, Error, and Total as in this text. In the SAS ANOVA table in 3.23(b), the equivalent names used are Model, Error, and C Total. The quantities *SSR*, *SSE*, and *SST* will be found in the SS column in MINITAB and the Sum of Squares column in SAS in the appropriate row of the ANOVA tables. In addition, the DF column reports the degrees of freedom associated with each of these sums of squares. *SSR* has 1 degree of freedom, *SSE* has $n - 2$ degrees of freedom, and *SST* has $n - 1$ degrees of freedom. Just as $SSR + SSE = SST$, it is also true that the regression and error degrees of freedom always add up to the total degrees of freedom:

$$1 + (n - 2) = n - 1$$

The MS column in MINITAB and the Mean Square column in SAS show the values of *SSR* and *SSE* divided by their respective degrees of freedom:

$$MSR = \frac{SSR}{1}$$

$$MSE = \frac{SSE}{n - 2}$$

MSR is referred to as the *mean square due to regression* (or to the model), and *MSE* is the *mean square due to error* (or, more simply, "mean square regression" and "mean square error"). Note that *MSR* always will equal *SSR* because the divisor always will be 1. This holds true in the case of simple regression, but, it will differ when multiple regression is discussed in the next chapter. *MSE* was used earlier in this chapter and can be written as

$$MSE = \frac{SSE}{n - 2},$$

which also was denoted s_e^2 to represent an estimate of the variance around the regression line. The square root of the *MSE*, denoted s_e, was called the standard deviation around the regression line or the standard error of the regression.

The remaining columns in the ANOVA tables and further uses of *MSR* and *MSE* will be discussed in the next section.

3.4.2 The Coefficient of Determination and the Correlation Coefficient

In an exact or deterministic relationship, $SSR = SST$ and $SSE = 0$. A line could be drawn that passed through every sample point. This will not be the case in most practical business situations. A measure of how well the regression line fits the data is needed. In other words, "What proportion of the total variation has been explained?" This measure is provided through a statistic called the *coefficient of determination*, denoted R^2 (this is read "R squared"):

$$R^2 = \frac{SSR}{SST}$$

The value R^2 is computed by dividing the explained sum of squares by the total sum of squares. The result is the proportion of variation in y explained by the regression. R^2 will be between 0 and 1. The closer to 1 the value of R^2 is, the better the "fit" of the regression line to the data. An alternative formula for computing R^2 is to compute the proportion of variation unexplained by the regression and subtract this proportion from 1:

$$R^2 = 1 - \frac{SSE}{SST}$$

Most computerized regression routines report R^2, and some also report another quantity called the *correlation coefficient*, which is the square root of R^2 with an appropriate sign attached:

$$R = \pm\sqrt{R^2}$$

Note that this relationship will hold in the case of simple regression, but not for multiple regression (discussed in Chapter 4).

The sign of R will be positive if the relationship is direct ($b_1 > 0$, or an upward sloping line) and negative if the relationship is inverse ($b_1 < 0$, or a downward sloping line). R will range between -1 and 1.

Note that R^2 is referred to as a measure of fit of the regression line. It is not interpreted as a measure of the predictive quality of the regression equation even though the ANOVA decomposition was motivated using the concept of improved predictions. R^2 will generally overstate the regression equation's predictive ability. This fact will be discussed further in Section 3.5 and an alternative measure of the regression's predictive ability will be suggested. R^2 will continue to be referred to as a measure of fit.

3.4.3 The F Statistic

An additional measure of how well the regression line fits the data is provided by the F statistic, which tests whether the equation $\hat{y} = b_0 + b_1 x$ provides a better fit to the data than the equation $\hat{y} = \bar{y}$. It is computed as

$$F = \frac{MSR}{MSE}$$

MSR is the mean square due to the regression, or the regression sum of squares divided by its degree of freedom. *MSE* is the mean square due to error, or the error sum of squares divided by its degrees of freedom, so $MSE = SSE/(n - 2)$. If the regression line fits the data well—that is, if the variation around the regression line is small relative to the variation around the sample mean $\bar{y}$—then *MSR* should be large relative to *MSE*. If the regression line does not fit well, then *MSR* will be small relative to *MSE*. Thus, large values of F support the use of the regression line, while small values suggest that x is of little use in explaining the variation in y.

To formalize the use of the F statistic, consider again the hypotheses

$$H_0: \quad \beta_1 = 0$$
$$H_a: \quad \beta_1 \neq 0$$

The F statistic can be used to perform this test. The decision rule is:

$$\text{Reject } H_0 \quad \text{if} \quad F > F(\alpha; \quad 1, n - 2)$$
$$\text{Accept } H_0 \quad \text{if} \quad F \leq F(\alpha; \quad 1, n - 2)$$

F I G U R E **3.24**

Additional Statistics Provided in MINITAB and SAS Regression Outputs

(a) MINITAB

$s = s_e$ R-sq = R^2 R-sq(adj) = R^2_{ADJ}

(b) SAS

Root MSE	s_e	R-Square	R^2
DEP MEAN	$\bar{y}$	ADJ R-Sq	R^2_{ADJ}
CV	$100 \times (s_e / \bar{y})$		

where $F(\alpha; \quad 1, n-2)$ is a critical value chosen from the F table for level of significance α. The F statistic has degrees of freedom associated with both the numerator and denominator sums of squares used in its computation. For a simple regression, there is 1 numerator degree of freedom and $n-2$ denominator degrees of freedom. These are the degrees of freedom associated with *SSR* and *SSE*, respectively. F tables are provided in Appendix B.

If the null hypothesis $H_0: \beta_1 = 0$ is rejected, then the conclusion is that x and y are linearly related. In other words, the line $\hat{y} = b_0 + b_1 x$ fits the data better than $\hat{y} = \bar{y}$.

The hypotheses tested by the F statistic also can be tested using the t test previously discussed. The decision made using either test will be exactly the same. This is because the F statistic is equal to the square of the t statistic. Also, the $F(\alpha; \quad 1, n-2)$ critical value is the square of the $t_{\alpha/2}$ critical value for the t distribution with $n-2$ degrees of freedom:

$$F = \frac{MSR}{MSE} = t^2$$

and

$$F(\alpha; \quad 1, n-2) = t^2_{\alpha/2, n-2}$$

Because the two test procedures yield exactly the same decision, it does not matter which is used when testing $H_0: \beta_1 = 0$ versus $H_a: \beta_1 \neq 0$ (when testing $H_0: \beta_1 \leq 0$ vs. $H_a: \beta_1 > 0$ or $H_0: \beta_1 \geq 0$ vs. $H_a: \beta_1 < 0$ or any tests where $\beta_1^* \neq 0$, the t and F tests are *not* equivalent). The importance of the F statistic in multiple regression, however, makes it necessary to learn how to use this test. When there are two or more explanatory variables, the F test can be used to test hypotheses that cannot be tested using the t test.

Figure 3.24 shows the additional statistics provided by both MINITAB (3.24(a)) and SAS (3.24(b)). In MINITAB, these statistics will appear as shown directly above the ANOVA table. In SAS, the statistics will appear as shown directly below the ANOVA table. Figure 3.25 shows a representation of the complete MINITAB and SAS outputs. The bracketed sections will be discussed in later chapters.

F I G U R E **3.25**

Complete Regression Outputs for MINITAB and SAS

(a) MINITAB

The regression equation is
$y = b_0 + b_1 x$

Predictor	Coef	Stdev	t-ratio	p
Constant	b_0	s_{b_0}	b_0/s_{b_0}	p value
x1 Variable name	b_1	s_{b_1}	b_1/s_{b_1}	p value

$s = s_e$ R-sq $= R^2$ $[\text{R-sq(adj)} = R^2_{ADJ}]$

Analysis of Variance

SOURCE	DF	SS	MS	F	p
Regression	1	SSR	MSR	MSR/MSE	p value
Error	$n-2$	SSE	MSE		
Total	$n-1$	SST			

Unusual Observations						
Obs.		X1	Y	Fit	Stdev.Fit	Residual	St.Resid
Obs. No.	Value of X1	Value of y	$\hat{y}$		s_m	$y - \hat{y}$	—

R denotes an obs. with a large st. resid.
X denotes an obs. whose X value gives it large influence.

(b) SAS

Analysis of Variance

Source	DF	Sum of Squares	Mean Square	F Value	Prob > F
Model	1	SSR	MSR	MSR/MSE	p value
Error	$n-2$	SSE	MSE		
C Total	$n-1$	SST			

Root MSE $= s_e$ R-square $= R^2$
Dep Mean $= \bar{y}$ $[\text{R-sq(adj)} = R^2_{ADJ}]$
C.V. $= (100) \times s_e/\bar{y}$

Parameter Estimates

Variable	DF	Parameter Estimate	Standard Error	T for H0: PARAMETER = 0	Prob > |T|
INTERCEPT	1	b_0	s_{b_0}	b_0/s_{b_0}	p value
VARIABLE NAME	1	b_1	s_{b_1}	b_1/s_{b_1}	p value

   In the MINITAB output, s is the standard deviation around the regression line. This was denoted s_e in the text. Also, R-sq is the R^2 value. The SAS output labels s_e as Root MSE, which comes from the fact that the square root of *MSE* is equal to s_e. The R^2 value is labeled R-square. In addition, SAS shows the mean of the dependent variable, Dep Mean, and a quantity labeled C.V., for coefficient of variation.

The C.V. expresses the standard deviation around the regression line in units of the mean of the dependent variable. The multiplication by 100 is merely a rescaling. C.V. is a number representing variability around the regression line and expresses this variation in unitless values. Thus, the C.V.'s for two different regressions could be compared more readily than the standard deviations because the influence of the units of the data has been removed.

E X A M P L E **3.7**

To compute the R^2 for the data in Table 3.2, the quantities SSE and SST must be computed.

$$R^2 = 1 - \frac{SSE}{SST}$$

$$= 1 - \frac{\Sigma(y_i - \hat{y}_i)^2}{\Sigma(y_i - \bar{y})^2}$$

SSE was computed in Table 3.4 as $SSE = 8.8$. SST can be computed by the formula

$$\Sigma y_i^2 - \frac{1}{n}(\Sigma y_i)^2 = 431 - \frac{1}{6}(45)^2 = 93.5$$

The coefficient of determination or R^2 is

$$1 - \frac{8.8}{93.5} = .91,$$

so 91% of the variation in y has been explained by the regression.

Note that the formula

$$R^2 = \frac{SSR}{SST}$$

could have been used here. But because SSE already had been computed and SSR had not, the alternative formula was used. If it were desired to compute SSR, this could be done by recalling that

$$SSR = SST - SSE = 93.5 - 8.8 = 84.7$$

The F statistic is computed as

$$F = \frac{MSR}{MSE}$$

$$= \frac{SSR/1}{SSE/(n-2)}$$

$$= \frac{84.7}{8.8/4} = 38.5$$

The hypotheses

$$H_0: \quad \beta_1 = 0$$

$$H_a: \quad \beta_1 \neq 0$$

can be tested using the F statistic. Using a 5% level of significance, the decision rule is:

$$\text{Reject } H_0 \quad \text{if} \quad F > F(.05; \quad 1, 4) = 7.71$$
$$\text{Accept } H_0 \quad \text{if} \quad F \le F(.05; \quad 1, 4) = 7.71$$

The test statistic was computed as $F = 38.5$, which results in a decision to reject H_0. In this case, the conclusion is that β_1 is not equal to zero and that the two variables x and y are linearly related.   ■

E X A M P L E   3.8   **Pricing Communications Nodes (continued)**

Refer to Example 3.6 to complete the following problems, using the regression output in Figure 3.13 or 3.15.

1   What percentage of the variation in COST is explained by the regression?

   Answer: Using the R^2 value, 88.7% of the variation in COST has been explained by the regression.

2   Use the F test and a 5% level of significance to test the hypotheses

$$H_0: \quad \beta_1 = 0$$
$$H_a: \quad \beta_1 \neq 0$$

   Answer: (a) Decision rule:

$$\text{Reject } H_0 \quad \text{if} \quad F > 4.75$$
$$\text{Accept } H_0 \quad \text{if} \quad F \le 4.75$$

Test statistic: $F = 94.41$
Decision: Reject H_0.
Conclusion: There is evidence to conclude that COST and NUMPORTS are linearly related.

(b) Decision rule:

$$\text{Reject } H_0 \quad \text{if} \quad p \text{ value } < .05$$
$$\text{Accept } H_0 \quad \text{if} \quad p \text{ value } \ge .05$$

Test statistic: p-value = 0.000
Decision: Reject H_0.   ■

Exercises

Exercises 8 and 9 should be done by hand.

8   **Flexible Budgeting (continued)**   Refer to Exercise 1.

   a   Compute the coefficient of determination (R^2) for the regression of overhead costs on production.

    b What percentage of the variation in overhead costs has been explained by the regression?

    c Use the F test to test the hypotheses H_0: $\beta_1 = 0$ versus H_a: $\beta_1 \neq 0$ at the 5% level of significance. Be sure to state the decision rule, test statistic value, and decision.

    d From the result in (c), are production and overhead costs linearly related?

9 **Central Company (continued)** Refer to Exercise 2.

    a Compute the coefficient of determination (R^2) for the regression of number of labor hours on number of items produced.

    b What percentage of the variation in hours of labor has been explained by the regression?

    c Use the F test to test the hypotheses H_0: $\beta_1 = 0$ versus H_a: $\beta_1 \neq 0$ at the 5% level of significance. Be sure to state the decision rule, test statistic value, and decision.

    d From the result in (c), are hours of labor and number of items produced linearly related?

10 **Dividends (continued)** Use the output in Figure 3.17 or 3.18 to help answer the questions.

    a What percentage of the variation in dividend yield has been explained by the regression?

    b Use the F test to test the hypotheses H_0: $\beta_1 = 0$ versus H_a: $\beta_1 \neq 0$ at the 5% level of significance. Be sure to state the decision rule, test statistic value, and decision.

11 **Sales/Advertising (continued)** Use the output in Figure 3.19 or 3.20 to help answer the questions.

    a What percentage of the variation in sales has been explained by the regression?

    b Use the F test to test the hypotheses H_0: $\beta_1 = 0$ versus H_a: $\beta_1 \neq 0$ at the 5% level of significance. Be sure to state the decision rule, test statistic value, and decision.

3.5
Prediction or Forecasting with a Simple Linear Regression Equation

One of the possible goals for fitting a regression line to data, as stated in Chapter 1, is to be able to use the regression equation to predict or forecast values of the dependent variable y. Given that a value of x has been observed, what is the best prediction of the response value, y? To discuss how to best predict y and how to make inferences using predictions based on a random sample, two cases that may arise in practice are considered.

3.5.1 Estimating the Conditional Mean of y Given x

In Example 3.6, suppose that the network administrator wants to consider all possible nodes with 40 communications ports. The question to be answered is, "What will the cost be, on average, for nodes with 40 ports?"

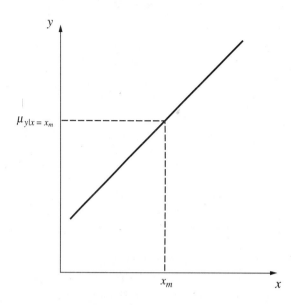

The average cost of all nodes with 40 communications ports is to be estimated. Thus, an estimate of the conditional mean cost given $x = 40$, or an estimate of $\mu_{y|x=40}$, is required (see Figure 3.26). If a relationship between y and x does exist, the best estimate of this point on the population regression line is given by

$$\hat{y}_m = b_0 + b_1 x_m,$$

where b_0 and b_1 are the least squares estimates of β_0 and β_1, x_m is the number of ports for which an estimate is desired, and $\hat{y}_m$ is the estimate of the conditional mean cost. In this case, $\hat{y}_m$ represents the estimate of the point on the regression line corresponding to (or conditional on) $x = x_m$. Thus, it is the estimate of a population mean. The variance of this estimate can be shown to equal

$$\sigma_m^2 = \sigma_e^2 \left(\frac{1}{n} + \frac{(x_m - \bar{x})^2}{(n-1)s_x^2} \right) \tag{3.16}$$

Because σ_e^2 is unknown, s_e^2 is substituted to obtain an estimate of σ_m^2:

$$s_m^2 = s_e^2 \left(\frac{1}{n} + \frac{(x_m - \bar{x})^2}{(n-1)s_x^2} \right) \tag{3.17}$$

The standard deviation or standard error of the estimate, s_m, is simply the square root of s_m^2.

F I G U R E   3.27

Effect on $\hat{y}_m$ of Variation in b_1 from Sample to Sample

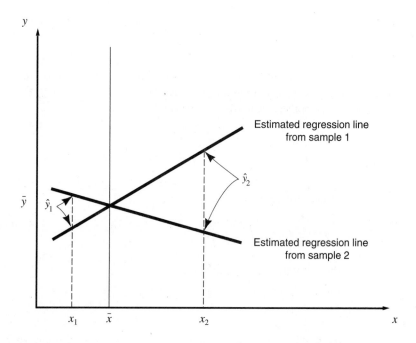

The variance or standard error of the estimate of the point on the regression line is affected by the distance of the value x_m from the sample mean $\bar{x}$. The closer the value of x_m to the mean of all the sample x values, the closer the term $(x_m - \bar{x})^2$ will be to zero. If $x_m = \bar{x}$, the term $(x_m - \bar{x})^2/(n-1)s_x^2$ will equal zero, and the standard error will equal $s_e/\sqrt{n}$. Thus, the closer the value x_m is to the sample mean $\bar{x}$, the smaller the standard error will be or the more accurate the estimate is expected to be.

The reason for this is illustrated in Figure 3.27. Because all least squares lines pass through the point $(\bar{x}, \bar{y})$, two least squares lines, A and B, have been drawn intersecting at the point $(\bar{x}, \bar{y})$. The two lines could represent least squares lines fitted to two independent random samples taken from the same population. It is assumed that the two samples have means $\bar{x}$ and $\bar{y}$. Even though both lines will pass through a common point, the slopes of the two estimated lines could be quite different, as illustrated. Thus, there is more certainty as to the value of a point on the regression line near the value $\bar{x}$ than at the extreme values of x. When estimating a point on the regression line for an extreme value of x, the greater uncertainty is reflected through a larger standard error.

It was previously stated that when the term $(x_m - \bar{x})^2/(n-1)s_x^2$ is zero, the standard error will be $s_m = s_e/\sqrt{n}$. This will happen when $x_m = \bar{x}$. The quantity $s_e/\sqrt{n}$ is very much like the standard error associated with the sample mean, $\bar{y}$, when it is used to estimate the (unconditional) population mean of the y values. A population mean is being estimated in the case of regression, so this is to be expected. The difference is that the mean in regression is conditional on the value of x, $\mu_{y|x}$, rather than being unconditional.

Confidence intervals can be constructed for forecasts using

$$(\hat{y}_m - t_{\alpha/2}s_m, \quad \hat{y}_m + t_{\alpha/2}s_m), \tag{3.18}$$

where $\hat{y}_m$ is the point estimate and $t_{\alpha/2}$ is chosen from the t distribution with $n - 2$ degrees of freedom in the usual fashion.

Hypothesis tests also can be conducted. To test

$$H_0: \quad \mu_{y|x_m} = \mu^*_{y|x_m}$$
$$H_a: \quad \mu_{y|x_m} \neq \mu^*_{y|x_m},$$

where $\mu^*_{y|x_m}$ is a hypothesized value for the point on the population regression line, the decision rule is:

Reject H_0 if $t > t_{\alpha/2}$ or $t < -t_{\alpha/2}$
Accept H_0 if $-t_{\alpha/2} \leq t \leq t_{\alpha/2}$

The test statistic, t, is computed as

$$t = \frac{\hat{y}_m - \mu^*_{y|x_m}}{s_m}$$

and will have a t distribution with $n - 2$ degrees of freedom when H_0 is true.

One-tailed tests also can be performed provided the usual modifications are made in constructing the decision rule.

3.5.2 Predicting an Individual Value of y Given x

Now suppose the network administrator is interested in a single communications node in a plant in Kansas City, Missouri, which will have 40 access ports. Predict the cost of installation for this particular node.

With $x_p = 40$ access ports, the best prediction of the cost of this node is

$$\hat{y}_p = b_0 + b_1 x_p,$$

which is exactly the same number that would be used to estimate the average cost for all nodes with 40 access ports. One can do no better in predicting cost for an individual node than to use the estimate of average cost for all nodes with the same number of access ports. This is because there is no additional information used in the regression that would distinguish this one node from all the others (see Figure 3.28).

The prediction for an individual value, however, would not be as accurate as the estimate of a population mean for all individuals in a certain category. The variance

F I G U R E 3.28

Predicting an Individual y Value

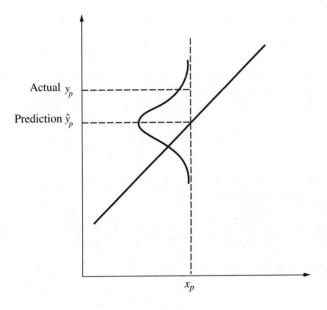

of the prediction for an individual is

$$\sigma_p^2 = \sigma_e^2 \left[1 + \frac{1}{n} + \frac{(x_p - \bar{x})^2}{(n-1)s_x^2} \right], \tag{3.19}$$

which can be estimated by replacing σ_e^2 with s_e^2:

$$s_p^2 = s_e^2 \left[1 + \frac{1}{n} + \frac{(x_p - \bar{x})^2}{(n-1)s_x^2} \right] \tag{3.20}$$

To compare s_p^2 to the variance of the estimate of a conditional mean, write the prediction variance as

$$s_p^2 = s_e^2 + s_m^2$$

The variance of the prediction for an individual value is equal to the variance from estimating the point on the regression line for $x = x_p$, s_e^2, plus the estimate of the variation of the individual y values around the regression line, s_m^2. Even if the exact position of $\mu_{y|x_p}$ were known, y_p still would not be known. The individual y values are distributed around $\mu_{y|x_p}$ with standard deviation σ_e. Because $\mu_{y|x_p}$ is actually unknown, there is uncertainty associated with the estimation of this value (reflected in s_m or s_m^2) plus the uncertainty in predicting an individual value (reflected in s_e or s_e^2).

Interval estimation of y_p is accomplished by constructing prediction intervals. The term *prediction interval* is used rather than *confidence interval* because a population

F I G U R E **3.29**

Confidence Interval Limits versus Prediction Interval Limits

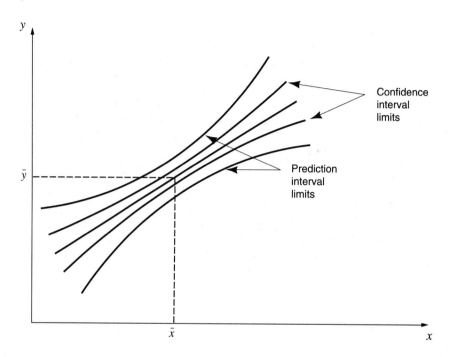

parameter is not being estimated in this case; instead, the response or performance of a single individual in the population is being predicted.

A $(1 - \alpha)100\%$ prediction interval for y_p is

$$(\hat{y}_p - t_{\alpha/2}s_p, \quad \hat{y}_p + t_{\alpha/2}s_p), \tag{3.21}$$

where $\hat{y}_p$ is the predicted value and $t_{\alpha/2}$ is chosen from the t distribution with $n - 2$ degrees of freedom.

Figure 3.29 illustrates the difference between the confidence interval estimate of $\mu_{y|x}$ and the prediction interval for an individual. Both the confidence interval in equation (3.18) and the prediction interval in equation (3.21) are narrower, more precise, near $x = \bar{x}$, and wider at the extreme values of x. The prediction interval always will be wider than the confidence interval because of the added uncertainty involved in predicting an individual response.

3.5.3 Assessing Quality of Prediction

As noted in Section 3.4, the R^2 of the regression is a measure of the fit of the regression to the sample data. It is not generally considered an adequate measure of the regression equation's ability to estimate $\mu_{y|x}$ or to predict new responses. The standard R^2 will overestimate the quality of future (or nonsample) predictions.

Two possible means of assessing prediction quality will be presented in this section. The first is called *data splitting*. In this method, partition the data set into two groups. One group of n_1 data points is used to estimate or fit possible equations used for forecasting. The second group of n_2 data points, called a *holdout sample* or *validation sample*, is used to assess predictive ability of the models estimated using the fitting sample. Any models that are considered possible candidates are estimated using the fitting sample. Predictions, $\hat{y}$, then are computed for these models using the explanatory variable values in the validation sample. For each candidate model, prediction errors, $y_i - \hat{y}_i$, are computed for all n_2 observations in the validation sample. A measure of forecast accuracy based on the forecast errors then can be computed. For example, the mean square forecast error

$$\frac{\sum_{i=1}^{n_2}(y_i - \hat{y}_i)^2}{n_2}$$

and the mean absolute forecast error

$$\frac{\sum_{i=1}^{n_2}|y_i - \hat{y}_i|^2}{n_2}$$

are two commonly computed measures.

Models with smaller mean square forecast errors or mean absolute forecast errors would be better for prediction purposes. The advantage of using this approach is that the models are tested on data that were not used in the fitting or model estimation process. This provides an independent assessment of the models' predictive ability.

After an appropriate model has been chosen, the entire data set can be used to estimate the model parameters. This model then would be used to produce future predictions.

A second means of assessing prediction quality is to use the *PRESS* statistic. *PRESS* stands for Prediction Sum of Squares and is defined as

$$PRESS = \sum_{i=1}^{n}(y_i - \hat{y}_{i,-1})^2$$

In this formula, $\hat{y}_{i,-1}$ represents the prediction obtained from a model estimated with one of the sample observations deleted. If there are n observations in the sample, there will be n different predictions, $\hat{y}_{i,-1}$. The prediction $\hat{y}_{i,-1}$ is obtained by evaluating the regression equation at x_i, but the data point (x_i, y_i) is not used in obtaining the estimated regression equation. Thus, as with use of a validation sample, predictions are obtained from data that are not used to fit the model.

The quantities $y_i - \hat{y}_{i,-1}$ often are called *PRESS* residuals because they are similar to the actual regression residuals, $y_i - \hat{y}_i$. The prediction sum of squares also is similar to the error sum of squares, *SSE*. This suggests construction of an R^2-like statistic that might be called the prediction R^2:

$$R^2_{\text{PRED}} = 1 - \frac{PRESS}{SST}$$

Larger values of R^2_{PRED} (or smaller values of *PRESS*) suggest models of greater predictive ability.

E X A M P L E 3.9

1   Again, refer to the data in Table 3.2.

Using the least squares regression equation

$$\hat{y} = -0.2 + 2.2x,$$

an estimate of the point on the regression line when $x = 6$ is

$$\hat{y} = -0.2 + 2.2(6) = 13,$$

and the prediction of an individual y value when $x = 6$ also is 13.

The standard deviation of the estimate of the point on the regression line is

$$s_m = s_e \sqrt{\frac{1}{n} + \frac{(x_m - \bar{x})^2}{(n-1)s_x^2}}$$

$$= 1.48 \sqrt{\frac{1}{6} + \frac{(6 - 3.5)^2}{17.5}} = 1.07$$

(For computation of s_e, $\bar{x}$, and $(n-1)s_x^2$, see Example 3.5 (page 91).)

2   The standard deviation of the prediction is

$$s_p = s_e \sqrt{1 + \frac{1}{n} + \frac{(x_p - \bar{x})^2}{(n-1)s_x^2}}$$

$$= 1.48 \sqrt{1 + \frac{1}{6} + \frac{(6 - 3.5)^2}{17.5}} = 1.83$$

The 95% confidence and prediction intervals are, respectively,

$$[13 - 2.776(1.07), \quad 13 + 2.776(1.07)] \quad \text{or} \quad (10.03, \quad 15.97)$$

and

$$[13 - 2.776(1.83), \quad 13 + 2.776(1.83)] \quad \text{or} \quad (7.92, \quad 18.08) \quad \blacksquare$$

E X A M P L E 3.10 **Pricing Communications Nodes (continued)**

1   On average, how much would we expect communications nodes to cost if there were to be 40 access ports.

F I G U R E 3.30

MINITAB Regression Output Using PREDICT for Example 3.10

```
The regression equation is
cost = 16594 + 650 numports

Predictor        Coef        Stdev     t-ratio        p
Constant        16594         2687        6.18    0.000
numports       650.17        66.91        9.72    0.000

s = 4307        R-sq = 88.7%      R-sq(adj) = 87.8%

Analysis of Variance

SOURCE         DF          SS          MS         F        p
Regression      1  1751268352  1751268352     94.41    0.000
Error          12   222594144    18549512
Total          13  1973862528

Unusual Observations
Obs. numports        cost       Fit  Stdev.Fit   Residual   St.Resid
  1      68.0       52388     60805       2414      -8417     -2.36R
 10      24.0       23444     32198       1414      -8754     -2.15R

R denotes an obs. with a large st. resid.

   Fit   Stdev.Fit      95.0% C.I.           95.0% P.I.
 42600       1178   (  40034,   45167)   (  32870,   52331)
```

Answer: Figure 3.30 shows the MINITAB regression output using the PREDICT option and the value 40. The resulting output (at the bottom) can be used to answer the question. A point estimate of cost for all nodes with 40 access ports is $42,600. A 95% confidence interval estimate is given by ($40,034, $45,167). Thus, we can say with 95% confidence, the average cost of all nodes with 40 access ports is expected to be between $40,034 and $45,167.

2   For an individual node with 40 access ports, find a prediction of cost.

Answer: The point prediction would again be $42,600. A 95% prediction interval for the individual node would be ($32,870, $52,331). Note that the prediction interval is considerably wider than the confidence interval, reflecting the additional uncertainty of predicting for an individual (as opposed to estimating an average). ∎

Exercises

Exercises 12 and 13 should be done by hand.

12   **Flexible Budgeting (continued)**   Refer to Exercise 1.

   a   Find a point estimate of the overhead costs, on average, for production runs of 80,000 units.

   b   Find a 95% confidence interval estimate of overhead costs, on average, for production runs of 80,000 units.

F I G U R E 3.31

MINITAB Regression Output for Exercise 15(a)

```
The regression equation is
sales = - 57 + 17.6 adv

Predictor         Coef       Stdev     t-ratio       p
Constant         -57.3       509.8       -0.11     0.912
adv             17.570       1.642       10.70     0.000

s = 594.8       R-sq = 86.4%      R-sq(adj) = 85.7%

Analysis of Variance

SOURCE         DF          SS          MS          F       p
Regression      1     40523672    40523672     114.54   0.000
Error          18      6368342      353797
Total          19     46892016

Unusual Observations
Obs.       adv       sales      Fit   Stdev.Fit   Residual   St.Resid
  8        370        4900      6444        176      -1544      -2.72R
 14        210        5175      3632        198       1543       2.75R

R denotes an obs. with a large st. resid.

   Fit   Stdev.Fit        95.0% C.I.           95.0% P.I.
  4335         156    (   4007,     4663)  (   3043,     5627)
```

    c Find a point prediction of the overhead costs for a single run of 80,000 units.

    d Find a 95% prediction interval for overhead costs for a single production run of 80,000 units.

    e State why the prediction interval is wider than the confidence interval.

13   **Central Company (continued)**   Refer to Exercise 2.

    a Find a point estimate of the number of hours of labor required, on average, when 60 units are to be produced.

    b Find a 95% confidence interval estimate of hours of labor required, on average, when 60 units are to be produced.

    c Find a point prediction of the number of hours of labor required for one run producing 60 units.

    d Find a 95% prediction interval for the number of hours of labor required for one run producing 60 units.

14   **Dividends (continued)**   Consider the dividend yield problem in Exercise 6 and the associated computer output in either Figure 3.17 or 3.18. An analyst wants an estimate of dividend yield for all firms with earnings per share of $3. Will the equation developed provide a more accurate estimate than simply using the sample mean dividend yield for all 50 firms examined? State why or why not.

15   **Sales/Advertising (continued)**   Use the output in Figure 3.31 or 3.32 to help answer the questions.

F I G U R E **3.32**
MINITAB Regression Output for Exercise 15(b)

```
The regression equation is
sales = - 57 + 17.6 adv

Predictor        Coef      Stdev     t-ratio        p
Constant        -57.3      509.8      -0.11      0.912
adv            17.570      1.642      10.70      0.000

s = 594.8       R-sq = 86.4%      R-sq(adj) = 85.7%

Analysis of Variance

SOURCE         DF         SS         MS         F         p
Regression      1    40523672   40523672    114.54     0.000
Error          18     6368342     353797
Total          19    46892016

Unusual Observations
Obs.       adv      sales       Fit   Stdev.Fit    Residual    St.Resid
  8        370       4900      6444        176        -1544       -2.72R
 14        210       5175      3632        198         1543        2.75R

R denotes an obs. with a large st. resid.

   Fit   Stdev.Fit        95.0% C.I.             95.0% P.I.
  3457       211      (   3013,    3900)    (   2130,    4783)
  4335       156      (   4007,    4663)    (   3043,    5627)
  5214       133      (   4934,    5493)    (   3933,    6494)
  6092       157      (   5763,    6421)    (   4800,    7385)
```

a Find an estimate of average sales for all sales districts with advertising expenditures of $25,000. Find a point estimate and a 95% confidence interval estimate. The output in Figure 3.31 was obtained from MINITAB using the PREDICT option, requesting a prediction with $x = 250$ (for $25,000).

b Predict sales for individual districts having advertising expenditures of $20,000, $25,000, $30,000, and $35,000. Find point predictions as well as 95% prediction intervals. The output in Figure 3.32 was obtained from MINITAB using the PRE-DICT option, requesting a prediction for $x = 200$, 250, 300, and 350, respectively (for $20,000, $25,000, $30,000, and $35,000).

3.6
Fitting a Linear Trend to Time-Series Data

Data gathered on individuals at the same point in time are called cross-sectional data. *Time-series data* are data gathered on a single individual (person, firm, and so on) over a sequence of time periods, which may be days, weeks, months, quarters, years, or virtually any other measure of time. In a given problem, however, it will be assumed that the data are gathered over only one interval of time (daily and weekly data will not be combined, for example).

When dealing with time-series data, the primary goal often is to be able to produce forecasts of the dependent variable for future time periods. Two separate approaches to this problem can be identified. On one hand, a researcher may identify variables that are related to the dependent variable in a causal manner and use these in developing a causal regression model. For example, when trying to forecast sales for a particular product, causal variables might include advertising expenditures and competitor's market share. Changes in these variables are felt to produce or cause changes in sales. Thus, the term *causal regression model* is used.

The researcher may, on the other hand, identify patterns of movement in past values of the dependent variable and extrapolate these patterns into the future using an *extrapolative regression model.* An extrapolative model uses explanatory variables, although they are not related to the dependent variable in a causal manner. They simply describe the past movements of the dependent variable so that these movements can be extended into future time periods. Variables that represent trend and seasonal components often are included in extrapolative models.

Both causal and extrapolative models have their benefits and drawbacks. Causal models require the identification of variables that are related to the dependent variable in a causal manner. Then data must be gathered on these explanatory variables to use the model. Furthermore, when forecasting for future time periods, the values of the explanatory variables in these periods must be known. In extrapolative models, only past values of the dependent variable are required, and thus variable selection and data gathering are much simpler processes.

Whether a causal or extrapolative model performs better is determined to some extent by how far into the future the forecast refers. Forecasts often are classified as short-term (0 to 3 months), medium-term (3 months to 2 years), or long-term (2 years and longer). Extrapolative models tend to perform best in the short term, but they can be reasonably accurate for medium-term forecasts. Causal models often outperform extrapolative models when medium-term or long-term forecasts are desired. Extrapolative models appear to be just as effective as causal models in the short term, however, and are often easier to develop and use.

The success of extrapolative models depends on the stability of the behavior of the time series. If past time-series movement patterns are expected to continue into the future, then an extrapolative model should be relatively successful in making accurate forecasts. If these past patterns are altered for some reason, and future movements differ in general from past movements, then extrapolative models will not perform well. Thus, an assumption when using an extrapolative model for forecasting is that past patterns of movement of the data are reflective of future patterns.

Causal models can respond, to some extent, to more drastic changes in patterns. Changes in the explanatory variables caused by changes in economic or market conditions should produce relatively accurate forecasts of changes in the dependent variable. Of course, this assumes that the changes in the explanatory variables will be known for future time periods. In addition, if the model itself changes—that is, if the way the variables are related changes in the future—the causal model will not be capable of making accurate forecasts.

In this section, the use of a *linear trend model* for time-series data will be examined. The linear trend model is a type of extrapolative model that may be useful in certain time-series applications. In subsequent chapters, other techniques useful in building extrapolative time-series models will be examined.

A *trend* in time-series data is a tendency for the series to move upward or downward over many time periods. This movement may follow a straight line or a curvilinear pattern. Regression analysis can be used to model certain trends and to extrapolate these trends into future time periods.

The simplest form of a trend over time is a *linear* trend. The linear trend model can be written

$$y_i = \beta_0 + \beta_1 t + e_i$$

The explanatory variable simply indicates the time period ($x_i = t$). Usually, the variable t is constructed by using the integers, 1, 2, 3, . . . to indicate the time period. This is preferred to using the actual year (1980, 1981, 1982, . . .) because it reduces computational problems.

Forecasts are simple to compute when the linear trend model is used. Simply insert the appropriate value for the time period to be forecast into the equation. The time period T forecast can be written as

$$\hat{y}_T = \beta_0 + \beta_1(T)$$

Many other types of trends can be modeled using regression. Some examples, including the linear trend, are shown in Figure 3.33. Note that the other types of trends are represented by curves. Equations to represent curvilinear trends will be discussed in Chapter 5.

E X A M P L E   **3.11**   **ABX Company Sales**

The ABX Company sells winter sports merchandise including skis, ice skates, sleds, and so on. Quarterly sales (in thousands of dollars) for the ABX Company are shown in Table 3.11. The time period represented starts in the first quarter of 1985 and ends in the fourth quarter of 1994.

A MINITAB time-series plot of the sales figures is shown in Figure 3.34. The time-series plot suggests a strong linear trend in the sales figures. The regression with the linear trend variable was estimated and the resulting output is shown in Figure 3.35 for MINITAB and Figure 3.36 for SAS. The linear trend model estimated is

$$y_i = \beta_0 + \beta_1 t + e_i$$

To test whether the linear trend component is useful in explaining the variation in sales, the following hypotheses should be tested:

$$H_0: \quad \beta_1 = 0$$
$$H_a: \quad \beta_1 \neq 0$$

F I G U R E 3.33
Examples of Types of Trends

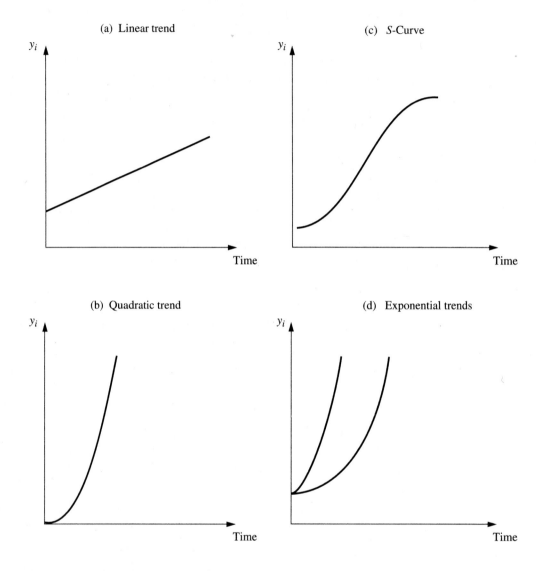

Using a 5% level of significance, the decision rule is:

$$\text{Reject } H_0 \quad \text{if} \quad t > 1.96 \quad \text{or} \quad t < -1.96$$

$$\text{Accept } H_0 \quad \text{if} \quad -1.96 \leq t \leq 1.96$$

The z value of 1.96 is used as a critical value because the number of degrees of freedom is large (38).

T A B L E 3.11

Data for ABX Company Sales Example

Year/Qtr	Sales	Trend	Year/Qtr	Sales	Trend
1985.1	221.0	1	1990.1	260.5	21
1985.2	203.5	2	1990.2	244.0	22
1985.3	190.0	3	1990.3	256.0	23
1985.4	225.5	4	1990.4	276.5	24
1986.1	223.0	5	1991.1	291.0	25
1986.2	190.0	6	1991.2	255.5	26
1986.3	206.0	7	1991.3	244.0	27
1986.4	226.5	8	1991.4	291.0	28
1987.1	236.0	9	1992.1	296.0	29
1987.2	214.0	10	1992.2	260.0	30
1987.3	210.5	11	1992.3	271.5	31
1987.4	237.0	12	1992.4	299.5	32
1988.1	245.5	13	1993.1	297.0	33
1988.2	201.0	14	1993.2	271.0	34
1988.3	230.0	15	1993.3	270.0	35
1988.4	254.5	16	1993.4	300.0	36
1989.1	257.0	17	1994.1	306.5	37
1989.2	238.0	18	1994.2	283.5	38
1989.3	228.0	19	1994.3	283.5	39
1989.4	255.0	20	1994.4	307.5	40

F I G U R E 3.34

MINITAB Time-Series Plot of ABX Company Sales

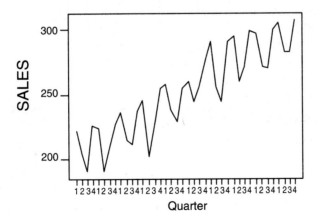

F I G U R E 3.35

MINITAB Regression Output for Regression of ABX Company Sales on the Linear Trend Variable

```
The regression equation is
sales = 199 + 2.56 trend

Predictor        Coef       Stdev     t-ratio        p
Constant      199.017       5.128       38.81    0.000
trend          2.5559      0.2180       11.73    0.000

s = 15.91       R-sq = 78.3%     R-sq(adj) = 77.8%

Analysis of Variance

SOURCE        DF          SS          MS         F        p
Regression     1       34818       34818    137.50    0.000
Error         38        9622         253
Total         39       44440

Unusual Observations
Obs.     trend       sales       Fit   Stdev.Fit    Residual    St.Resid
  14      14.0      201.00    234.80        2.89      -33.80      -2.16R

R denotes an obs. with a large st. resid.
```

F I G U R E 3.36

SAS Regression Output for the Regression of ABX Company Sales on the Linear Trend Variable

```
Dependent Variable: SALES

                      Analysis of Variance

                         Sum of        Mean
Source          DF      Squares      Square     F Value     Prob>F

Model            1   34817.88322  34817.88322   137.505     0.0001
Error           38    9622.06053    253.21212
C Total         39   44439.94375

         Root MSE       15.91264     R-square      0.7835
         Dep Mean      251.41250     Adj R-sq      0.7778
         C.V.            6.32930

                     Parameter Estimates

                   Parameter      Standard     T for H0:
Variable   DF       Estimate         Error   Parameter=0    Prob > |T|

INTERCEP    1     199.017308    5.12787526        38.811        0.0001
TREND       1       2.555863    0.21796092        11.726        0.0001
```

The test statistic is $t = 11.73$, so the null hypothesis is rejected. The linear trend component should be included in the model. ∎

F I G U R E 3.37

MINITAB Regression Output to Obtain the Next Four Periods' Forecasts

```
The regression equation is
sales = 199 + 2.56 trend

Predictor        Coef        Stdev     t-ratio        p
Constant      199.017        5.128       38.81    0.000
trend          2.5559       0.2180       11.73    0.000

s = 15.91       R-sq = 78.3%     R-sq(adj) = 77.8%

Analysis of Variance

SOURCE          DF          SS          MS         F        p
Regression       1       34818       34818    137.50    0.000
Error           38        9622         253
Total           39       44440

Unusual Observations
Obs.    trend      sales       Fit  Stdev.Fit   Residual   St.Resid
 14     14.0      201.00    234.80       2.89     -33.80     -2.16R

R denotes an obs. with a large st. resid.

     Fit  Stdev.Fit       95.0% C.I.              95.0% P.I.
  303.81       5.13   ( 293.42,  314.19)   ( 269.96,  337.66)
  306.36       5.32   ( 295.59,  317.13)   ( 272.39,  340.34)
  308.92       5.51   ( 297.76,  320.08)   ( 274.82,  343.02)
  311.48       5.71   ( 299.92,  323.03)   ( 277.25,  345.71)
```

When using time-series data for forecasting, it is generally true that prediction intervals are more appropriate than confidence intervals for representing the uncertainty in predictions for future time periods. Figure 3.37 shows the MINITAB output for the next four periods' forecasts. Using the linear trend equation estimated by MINITAB, the point forecasts are determined by substituting values of the trend variable for the appropriate time period into the equation:

$$1995.1 \text{ sales} = 199.017 + 2.5559(41) = 303.81$$
$$1995.2 \text{ sales} = 199.017 + 2.5559(42) = 306.36$$
$$1995.3 \text{ sales} = 199.017 + 2.5559(43) = 308.92$$
$$1995.4 \text{ sales} = 199.017 + 2.5559(44) = 311.48$$

The prediction intervals in the output would be used as our interval predictions of sales in each of the four quarters. Thus, our interval prediction for sales in the first quarter of 1995 would be $269,960 to $337,660.

If you look closely again at the time-series plot of sales in Figure 3.34 you may notice a pattern other than the trend. Note that the sales figures for the first and fourth quarters tend to be higher than the figures for the second and third quarters. This systematic variation among time periods from year to year is called *seasonal variation*. In Chapter 6, methods to account for seasonal variation will be discussed.

Exercises

16   Fort Worth Water Department   The city of Fort Worth, Texas, is interested in maintaining a high level of water purity. One aspect helpful in maintaining water purity is monitoring the quality of water at storm drains that pour into the Trinity River. This river supplies drinking water for Fort Worth. Even though water from the river is filtered later, preventing contaminants from entering the river from storm drains is helpful in maintaining purity. Table 3.12 shows five of the variables the city monitors to test water purity entering the river from storm drains. These are monthly data from January 1986 through December 1989. In all cases, lower numbers are better. The variables are

odor: determined by a sensory test
color: no color is best—determined by comparing to a standard water sample
scum: floatable solids
hydrocarbon sheen: hydrocarbon (oil) sheen on surface of water
sewage bacteria: filamentous sewage bacteria

Your job is to use time-series plots and linear trend regression to examine the performance of the city's water department in improving the quality of storm drain water entering the Trinity River. Which of the variables show a significant decrease? Are there areas where the city might concentrate their efforts to achieve future improvements? Use a 5% level of significance in any tests.

These data are on the data disk and can be read in MINITAB using

```
READ 'WATER3' C1-C5
```

where C1 is odor, C2 is color, C3 is scum, C4 is hydrocarbon sheen, and C5 is sewage bacteria.

In SAS, the data can be read from the file WATER3.DAT using

```
INPUT ODOR COLOR SCUM SHEEN BACTERIA;
```

T A B L E **3.12**

Variables Used to Describe Water Purity

Odor	Color	Scum	Hydrocarbon Sheen	Sewage Bacteria
11	9	8	7	2
12	5	4	6	3
9	2	6	6	3
9	3	2	5	4
8	6	6	3	1
10	4	2	5	4
8	1	5	7	2
7	6	4	6	2
6	2	5	4	1

T A B L E 3.12 (*Cont.*)
Variables Used to Describe Water Purity

Odor	Color	Scum	Hydrocarbon Sheen	Sewage Bacteria
7	4	3	6	1
4	2	6	5	1
8	6	2	10	2
5	3	4	4	3
7	4	4	4	2
2	2	6	3	2
6	7	9	3	1
4	7	2	5	3
5	0	3	3	0
7	4	6	4	2
3	7	4	6	3
2	4	4	6	3
3	4	4	9	2
4	0	1	7	2
2	2	3	7	2
3	5	3	5	4
1	6	2	3	2
3	2	1	10	2
6	1	5	1	2
3	1	3	2	1
2	3	3	3	0
2	1	6	4	0
2	1	4	1	0
1	0	5	3	1
0	2	2	5	0
0	2	4	3	0
0	1	4	1	0
3	4	4	2	0
1	1	5	3	1
2	0	7	0	0
2	1	7	1	1
1	0	6	1	0
3	0	4	0	1
1	0	5	1	0
1	0	6	0	1
1	0	9	0	0
1	0	2	1	1
4	1	1	0	1
2	0	6	0	1

3.7
Some Cautions in Interpreting Regression Results

3.7.1 Association versus Causality

A common mistake made when using regression analysis is to assume that a strong fit (high R^2) of a regression of y on x automatically means that "x causes y." This will not necessarily be true.

Some alternative explanations for the good fit would include:

1   The reverse is true; y causes x. Linear regression computations pay no attention to the direction of causality. If x and y are highly correlated, a high R^2 value will result even if the causal order of the variables is reversed.

2   There may be a third variable related to both x and y. It may be that neither x causes y nor y causes x. Both variables may be related to some third common cause. As an example, consider the price and gasoline mileage of automobiles. These two variables are inversely related. As mileage rises, price goes down (on average). But it is not the rise in mileage that "causes" the price to drop. A third variable, size of car, may be influencing both of the other two variables. As size increases, price increases and mileage drops.

To infer that x causes y requires that additional conditions be satisfied. A high R^2 for a regression of y on x might be considered supporting evidence for causality, but on its own this is not enough to ensure that x causes y.

Note that the absence of causality is not necessarily a drawback in regression analysis. An equation showing a relationship between x and y can be important and useful even if it is recognized that x does not cause y.

3.7.2 Forecasting Outside the Range of the Explanatory Variable

When using an estimated regression equation to construct estimates of $\mu_{y|x}$ or to predict individual values of the dependent variable, some caution must be used if forecasts are outside the range of the x variable. Consider the communications nodes example. The explanatory variable was NUMPORTS, the number of access ports. The sample values ranged from 12 to 68. The estimated regression model can be expected to be reliable over this range of the x variable. If, however, a node is to be installed with 100 ports, there is some question as to how reliable the model will be. The relationship that holds over the range from 12 to 68 may differ from the relationship outside this range. Estimates of $\mu_{y|x}$ or predictions outside the range of the x variable require some caution for this reason.

There are often occasions where forecasts outside the range of the x variable must be made. One common example is when time-series data are used and forecasts for future time periods are desired. It may be that the values of the explanatory variables in future time periods are outside the range observed in the past, as, for example, when the linear trend model is used. In such cases, it must be recognized that the quality of the forecasts depends on whether the estimated relationship still holds for values of the explanatory variables that are outside the observed range.

Exercises

17 **Sales/Advertising (continued)**   Use the output in Figure 3.19 or 3.20 to help answer the questions.

   a Find a point estimate of average sales for all sales districts with advertising expenditures of $60,000. Are there any cautions that should be exercised regarding this estimate?

   b A district sales manager examines the model developed. The manager points out that $0 advertising expenditure will result in sales of −$5700, which is impossible. She suggests that this means the model is of no use. Do you agree or disagree with her assessment? Explain why.

3.8
Using the Computer

3.8.1 MINITAB

Plotting Data

```
PLOT C1 VS C2      (GRAPH: PLOT)
```

Plots the data in column 1 on the vertical axis and the data in column 2 on the horizontal axis to create a scatterplot.

Some of the newer versions of MINITAB use PLOT C1*C2 instead of PLOT C1 VS C2 and the newest versions of MINITAB are menu-driven.

```
TSPLOT [K] C1      (GRAPH: TIME-SERIES PLOT)
```

Plots the data in column 1 in time sequence. MINITAB assumes the data are entered in column 1 with the most recent time period as the last entry in the column. The K in the command is optional but useful in identifying the time period if data are quarterly or monthly. If data are quarterly, use $K = 4$

and the points on the graph will be numbered 1, 2, 3, 4 for each quarter. For monthly data use $K = 12$. Points on the graph will be numbered 1 through 9 and 0, A, B with each month having a unique value.

In new versions of MINITAB, the month indicators appear on the horizontal axis. The use of month, quarter, and so on is chosen by menu or, if the TSPLOT command is used, can be directly indicated as a subcommand (simply type in MONTH, QUARTER, and so on, as appropriate, on the subcommand).

Regression

```
REGR C1 1 C2      (STAT: REGRESSION: REGRESSION)
```

The dependent (y) variable data values are listed in column 1 and the independent variable (x) data values are listed in column 2. The 1 in the command tells MINITAB that just one independent variable is to be used.

With new versions of MINITAB, choice of dependent and independent variables is requested by menu, in which case the number of independent variables need not be specified.

Forecasting with the Regression Equation

```
REGR C1 1 C2;
PRED K.
```

The PREDICT (PRED) subcommand is used to generate confidence intervals for estimating a conditional mean and prediction intervals for predicting individual values. The value K in the PREDICT subcommand is used for the independent variable. K can be either a single number or a column of numbers if forecasts for several different values of the x variable are desired. Put each value into a column (say C3) and then use the subcommand PRED C3.

For example, to generate the forecasts in Figure 3.37 the following sequence of commands could be used:

```
SET IN C3
41 42 43 44
END.
REGR C1 1 C2;
PREDICT C3.
```

New versions of MINITAB work in a similar manner, with choices made through menus.

Creating a Trend Variable   (CALC: SET PATTERNED DATA)

In MINITAB, to create a trend variable for the linear trend model use a patterned set command:

```
SET IN C1
1:n
END.
```

where *n* is the total number of time periods. This patterned set command will put the integers 1 through *n* into column C1.

3.8.2 SAS

Plotting Data

Plots in SAS are generated using the following command sequence:

```
PROC PLOT;
  PLOT COST*NUMPORTS;
```

The variable to be plotted on the vertical axis (COST) is listed first, with the variable to be plotted on the horizontal axis (NUMPORTS) second.

This sequence will generate the scatterplot in Figure 3.14.

Regression

The following command sequence will produce the regression results in Figure 3.15:

```
PROC REG;
  MODEL COST=NUMPORTS;
```

The dependent variable (COST) is listed first; the independent variable (NUMPORTS) is listed second.

Forecasting with the Regression Equation

Forecasts in SAS are generated using an "appended" data set. To the values of the independent variable in the original data set, add the values for which predictions are desired. Then to the values of the dependent variable add '.' (SAS for missing data), since we do not know those values. Now rerun the regression as follows:

```
PROC REG;
  MODEL COST=NUMPORTS/P CLM CLI;
```

The option P requests forecasts (or predicted values), CLM requests upper and lower confidence interval limits for the estimate of the conditional mean, and CLI requests upper and lower prediction interval limits for an individual prediction.

Creating a Trend Variable

In the data input phase in SAS use the command

```
TREND=_N_;
```

to create a trend variable. The command TREND=_N_ will set the variable TREND equal to the integers 1 through n, where n is the total number of observations in the data set. To do a time-series plot of a dependent variable SALES use the commands

```
PROC PLOT;
  PLOT SALES*TREND;
```

To fit the linear trend model use the commands

```
PROC REG;
  MODEL SALES=TREND;
```

Additional Exercises

18 Indicate whether the following statements are true or false.

a If the hypothesis H_0: $\beta_1 = 0$ is rejected, then it can be safely concluded that x causes y.

b Suppose a regression of y on x is run and the t statistic for testing H_0: $\beta_1 = 0$ versus H_a: $\beta_1 \neq 0$ has a p value of 0.0295 associated with it. Using a 5% level of significance, the null hypothesis should be rejected.

c If the correlation between y and x is 0.9, then the R^2 value for a regression of y on x will be 90%.

d As long as the R^2 value is high for an estimated regression equation, it is safe to use the equation to predict for any value of x.

e If the R^2 value for a regression of y on x is 75%, then the R^2 value for a regression of x on y will also be 75%.

19 Suppose a regression analysis provides the following results:

$$b_0 = 1.0, \quad b_1 = 2.0, \quad s_{b_0} = 0.5$$
$$s_{b_1} = 0.25, \quad SST = 117.273, \quad SSE = 30.0$$

and $n = 24$. Use this information to answer the following questions:

a Test the hypotheses

$$H_0: \quad \beta_1 = 0$$
$$H_a: \quad \beta_1 \neq 0$$

using a 5% level of significance. State the decision rule, test statistic, and decision. Use a t test.

b Perform the same test as in (a) using an F test. Use a 10% level of significance.

c Compute the R^2 for the regression.

20 Suppose a regression analysis provides the following results:

$$b_0 = 4.0, \quad b_1 = 10.0, \quad s_{b_0} = 1.0,$$
$$s_{b_1} = 4.0, \quad SST = 67.36, \quad SSE = 50.0$$

and $n = 20$. Use this information to answer the following questions:

a Test the hypotheses

$$H_0: \quad \beta_0 = 0$$
$$H_a: \quad \beta_0 \neq 0$$

using a 5% level of significance. State the decision rule, test statistic, and decision.

b Test the hypotheses

$$H_0: \quad \beta_1 \leq 0$$
$$H_a: \quad \beta_1 > 0$$

using a 5% level of significance. State the decision rule, test statistic, and decision. What conclusion can be drawn from the test result?

c Compute the R^2 for the regression.

21 **Salary/Education** Data on beginning salary (Y) and years of education (X) for 93 employees of Harris Bank Chicago in 1977 are shown in Table 3.13. These data were taken from an article by Daniel W. Schafer, "Measurement-Error Diagnostics and the Sex Discrimination Problem," *Journal of Business and Economic Statistics*, 5: 529–537, 1987.

The MINITAB scatterplot and regression output for a regression of salary on education are shown in Figures 3.38 and 3.39, respectively. The SAS regression output is shown in Figure 3.40. Use the output to answer the following questions:

a Is there a linear relationship between salary and education? State the hypotheses to be tested, decision rule, test statistic, and decision. Use a 10% level of significance.

b What percentage of the variation in salary has been explained by the regression?

c For an individual with 12 years of education, find a point prediction of beginning salary.

d For all individuals with 12 years of education, find a point estimate of the conditional mean beginning salary.

e What other factors, in addition to education, might be useful in helping to estimate beginning salary?

These data are available on the data disk for further analysis. In MINITAB, they are read using

```
READ 'SALED3' C1, C2
```

where C1 will contain salary and C2 will contain education.

In SAS, the data can be read from the file SALED3.DAT using

```
INPUT SALARY EDUC;
```

T A B L E 3.13
Salary and Education Data

SALARY	EDUC	SALARY	EDUC
3900	12	5520	12
4020	10	5520	12
4290	12	5580	12
4380	8	5640	12
4380	8	5700	12
4380	12	5700	12
4380	12	5700	15
4380	12	5700	15
4440	15	5700	15
4500	8	6000	12
4500	12	6000	15
4620	12	6120	12
4800	8	6300	12
4800	12	6300	15
4800	12	4620	12
4800	12	5040	15
4800	12	5100	12
4800	12	5100	12
4800	12	5220	12
4800	12	5400	12
4800	12	5400	12
4800	16	5400	12
4980	8	5400	15
5100	8	5400	15
5100	12	5700	15
5100	12	6000	8
5100	15	6000	12
5100	15	6000	12
5100	16	6000	12
5160	12	6000	12
5220	8	6000	12
5220	12	6000	12
5280	8	6000	15
5280	8	6000	15
5280	12	6000	15
5400	8	6000	15
5400	8	6000	15
5400	12	6000	16
5400	12	6300	15
5400	12	6600	15
5400	12	6600	15
5400	12	6600	15
5400	12	6840	15
5400	15	6900	12
5400	15	6900	15
5400	15	8100	16
5400	15		

F I G U R E 3.38

MINITAB Scatterplot for Salary/Education Exercise

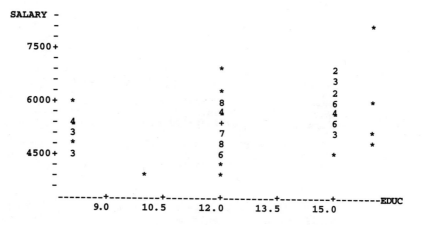

```
SALARY -
       -
       -
 7500+                                                    *
       -
       -                    *              2
       -                               3
 6000+  *                   *              2          *
       -                   8              6
       -   4               4              4
       -   3               +              6
       -   *               7              3          *
 4500+  3                  8                          *
       -                   6              *
       -                   *
       -         *         *
       --------+---------+---------+---------+---------+--------EDUC
              9.0      10.5      12.0      13.5      15.0
```

F I G U R E 3.39

MINITAB Regression Output for Salary/Education Exercise

```
The regression equation is
salary = 3819 + 128 educ

Predictor       Coef      Stdev    t-ratio        p
Constant      3818.6      377.4      10.12    0.000
educ          128.09      29.70       4.31    0.000

s = 650.1      R-sq = 17.0%     R-sq(adj) = 16.1%

Analysis of Variance

SOURCE          DF          SS          MS        F        p
Regression       1     7862535     7862535    18.60    0.000
Error           91    38460756      422646
Total           92    46323292

Unusual Observations
Obs.      educ      salary      Fit  Stdev.Fit   Residual   St.Resid
  1       12.0      3900.0   5355.6       69.1    -1455.6     -2.25R
  9       15.0      4440.0   5739.8      100.2    -1299.8     -2.02R
 91       12.0      6900.0   5355.6       69.1     1544.4      2.39R
 93       16.0      8100.0   5867.9      123.8     2232.1      3.50R

R denotes an obs. with a large st. resid.
```

22 **Income/Consumption** The following data are annual disposable income and total annual consumption for 12 families selected at random from a large metropolitan area. Regard annual disposable income as the explanatory variable and total annual consumption as the dependent variable. From the regression of y on x, answer the questions.

F I G U R E **3.40**
SAS Regression Output for Salary/Education Exercise

```
Dependent Variable: SALARY

                         Analysis of Variance

                       Sum of          Mean
Source          DF     Squares        Square      F Value      Prob>F

Model            1 7862534.2916 7862534.2916       18.603       0.0001
Error           91 38460756.031 422645.67067
C Total         92 46323290.323

          Root MSE        650.11204    R-square        0.1697
          Dep Mean       5420.32258    Adj R-sq        0.1606
          C.V.             11.99397

                        Parameter Estimates

                   Parameter     Standard     T for H0:
Variable   DF      Estimate        Error      Parameter=0    Prob > |T|

INTERCEP    1    3818.559794   377.43765814      10.117        0.0001
EDUC        1     128.085932    29.69671216       4.313        0.0001
```

Annual Disposable Income ($)	Total Annual Consumption ($)
16,000	14,000
30,000	24,545
43,000	36,776
70,000	63,254
56,000	40,176
50,000	49,548
16,000	16,000
26,000	22,386
14,000	16,032
12,000	12,000
24,000	20,768
30,000	34,780

a What is the estimated regression equation relating y to x?

b What percentage of the variation in y has been explained by the regression?

c Construct a 90% confidence interval estimate of β_1.

d Use a t test to test the hypotheses H_0: $\beta_1 = 0$ versus H_a: $\beta_1 \neq 0$ at the .05 level of significance. State the decision rule, test statistic, and decision. What conclusion can be drawn from the result of the test?

e Use an F test to test the hypotheses H_0: $\beta_1 = 0$ versus H_a: $\beta_1 \neq 0$ at the .05 level of significance. State the decision rule, test statistic, and decision.

f Can the F test be used to test H_0: $\beta_1 \leq 0$ versus H_a: $\beta_1 > 0$?

T A B L E **3.14**
Data for APEX Exercise

COST	MACHINE	COST	MACHINE
1102	218	1287	259
1008	199	1451	286
1227	249	1828	389
1395	277	1903	404
1710	363	1997	430
1881	399	1363	271
1924	411	1421	286
1246	248	1543	317
1255	259	1774	376
1314	266	1929	415
1557	334	1317	260
1887	401	1302	255
1204	238	1388	281
1211	246		

These data were created by Professor Roger L. Wright,
RLW Analytics, Inc., and are used (with modification)
with his permission.

g　Test the hypotheses $H_0: \beta_1 = 1$ versus $H_a: \beta_1 \neq 1$ at the .05 level of significance. State the decision rule, test statistic, and decision. What conclusion can be drawn from the result of the test?

These data are available on the data disk. In MINITAB, they can be read using

```
READ 'INCONS3' C1, C2
```

where C1 will contain annual disposable income and C2 will contain total annual consumption.

In SAS, the data can be read from the file INCONS3.DAT using

```
INPUT INCOME CONS;
```

23　**Apex Corporation**　The Apex Corporation produces corrugated paper. It has collected monthly data on the following two variables:

y, total manufacturing cost per month (in thousands of dollars)

x, total machine hours used per month

The data are shown in Table 3.14. These time-series data refer to the period January 1992 through March 1994. Perform any analyses necessary to answer the following questions:

a　What is the estimated regression equation relating y to x?

b　What percentage of the variation in y has been explained by the regression?

c   Are y and x linearly related? Conduct a hypothesis test to answer this question and use a 5% level of significance. State the hypotheses to be tested, the decision rule, the test statistic, and your decision. What conclusion can be drawn from the result of the test?

d   Use the equation developed to estimate the average manufacturing cost in a month with 350 machine hours. Find a point estimate and a 95% confidence interval estimate. How reliable do you believe this forecast might be?

e   Use the equation developed to estimate the average manufacturing cost in a month with 550 machine hours. Find a point estimate and a 95% confidence interval estimate. How reliable do you believe this forecast might be?

These data are available on the data disk. In MINITAB, they can be read using

```
READ 'APEX3' C1, C2
```

where C1 contains manufacturing cost and C2 contains machine hours.

In SAS, the data can be read from the file APEX3.DAT using

```
INPUT COST MACHINE;
```

24   **Wheat Exports**   The relationship between exchange rates and agricultural exports is of interest to agricultural economists. One such export of interest is wheat. Table 3.15 lists data on the following variables:

y, U.S. wheat export shipments

x, the real index of weighted-average exchange rates for the U.S. dollar

These time-series data were observed monthly from January 1974 through March 1985. Perform any analyses necessary to answer the following questions:

a   What is the estimated regression equation relating y to x?

b   Are y and x linearly related? Conduct a hypothesis test to answer this question and use a 5% level of significance. State the hypotheses to be tested, the decision rule, the test statistic, and your decision. What conclusion can be drawn from the result of the test?

c   What percentage of the variation in the dependent variable has been explained by the regression?

d   Construct a 95% confidence interval estimate for β_1.

These data are available on the data disk. In MINITAB, they can be read using

```
READ 'WHEAT3' C1,C2
```

where C1 will contain y and C2 will contain x.

In SAS, the data can be read from the file WHEAT3.DAT using

```
INPUT SHIPMENT EXCRATE;
```

T A B L E 3.15
Data for Wheat Export Exercise

SHIPMENT	EXCRATE	SHIPMENT	EXCRATE	SHIPMENT	EXCRATE
2264	104.142	1881	106.701	3760	109.238
1983	101.705	1567	104.882	3958	111.529
1787	97.857	2378	102.368	5284	107.243
1519	97.813	1764	100.715	4273	106.059
1500	96.250	2576	100.118	3470	104.473
1556	97.757	2870	98.637	3749	105.432
2256	98.164	2811	98.386	3379	107.414
2503	99.703	3268	100.022	3775	110.954
2346	100.450	2965	97.929	4329	113.599
2495	99.725	2888	95.475	4033	115.587
2676	101.497	3590	92.913	3170	112.341
2247	96.896	3255	92.346	4270	117.854
2951	95.162	3144	88.609	3209	119.634
1957	93.528	2514	91.297	3383	120.571
1774	92.920	2450	90.805	3565	122.312
2099	94.951	1916	90.001	2681	124.902
1778	94.723	1826	90.129	2575	126.268
2111	94.600	2056	90.069	2407	121.503
2721	98.184	2096	91.132	3896	120.526
3033	101.109	2131	91.706	3990	122.656
3428	102.870	2847	90.650	3569	123.793
3368	102.639	3627	88.004	3060	125.055
3228	102.567	3206	87.986	2619	125.394
2516	103.561	3528	87.483	3087	128.639
2506	104.059	4056	88.498	3176	130.112
1974	104.547	2963	88.730	2388	133.188
2105	106.535	3127	86.734	3246	133.413
2099	108.225	2250	86.010	3125	131.639
1845	108.547	2436	86.687	2800	134.792
1818	108.955	2578	90.213	3508	137.699
2330	108.707	2676	91.175	3221	140.244
3081	108.143	2411	86.894	3024	137.112
3004	107.990	2618	84.960	3231	133.865
2736	108.605	3364	84.693	2644	136.153
1478	108.894	3849	86.025	3070	140.147
1561	108.600	3737	85.473	2867	140.467
1346	108.949	3183	86.470	3627	145.506
1572	108.992	3054	89.057	3979	145.425
1433	108.737	3594	90.491	6605	151.073
1911	108.593	3537	91.082	3736	153.787
1810	108.539	3386	95.509	2648	151.330
2098	108.313	3504	95.911	3591	155.922
2277	106.419	3474	98.784	1897	160.254
2543	107.189	2124	103.492	2327	166.005
3011	108.054	3389	106.459	1576	165.932

The data were obtained from the journal article "Forecasting Wheat Exports: Do Exchange Rates Really Matter?" by D. A. Bessler and R. A. Babubla, which appeared in the *Journal of Business and Economic Statistics*, 5 (1987): 397–406.

T A B L E **3.16**

Number of Wins and Average Starting Salary for NFL Teams (1992)

Team Name	Wins	Average Starting Salary (in $1000)	Team Name	Wins	Average Starting Salary (in $1000)
Buffalo	11	829.217	Atlanta	6	699.279
Cincinnati	5	597.200	Chicago	5	620.326
Cleveland	7	652.750	Dallas	13	642.083
Denver	8	683.100	Detroit	5	593.460
Houston	10	803.333	Green Bay	9	657.609
Indianapolis	9	965.417	LA Rams	6	691.667
Kansas City	10	530.795	Minnesota	11	614.563
LA Raiders	7	650.345	New Orleans	12	783.500
Miami	11	983.200	NY Giants	6	658.333
New England	2	562.479	Philadelphia	11	757.424
NY Jets	4	468.717	Phoenix	4	561.773
Pittsburgh	11	406.211	San Francisco	14	839.240
San Diego	11	462.354	Tampa Bay	5	458.594
Seattle	2	539.940	Washington	9	744.674

From *Fort Worth Star Telegram*, 26 December 1992 and 2 January 1993. Reprinted courtesy of the *Fort Worth Star Telegram*.

25   **NFL Salaries**   The owners of NFL (National Football League) teams are concerned with rising salaries (as are owners of all professional sports teams). Table 3.16 provides the average starting salaries of the players on the 28 teams of the NFL for the 1992 season. Also provided is the number of wins for each team. Do you think that teams with higher average salaries tend to be more successful? Justify your answer.

The data are on the data disk and can be read in MINITAB using

```
READ 'NFL3' C1,C2
```

where C1 is WINS and C2 is average SALARY.

In SAS, the data can be read from the file NFL3.DAT using

```
INPUT WINS SALARY;
```

26   **Work Orders**   During the construction phase of a nuclear plant, the number of corrective work orders open should gradually decline until reaching a steady state that would be present during the operational phase. The Nuclear Regulatory Commission has licensing requirements that the number of work orders open at licensing and for operational plants be less than 1000. This number is set to provide a goal indicating operational readiness. Table 3.17 shows the number of work orders for a consecutive 120-working-day period during the construction phase of a nuclear plant. (These data have been disguised to protect confidentiality.)

As a consultant to the plant, you have been asked to estimate how many days it will take to reach the operational level of 1000 work orders. In determining the number of days, state any assumptions you make and any caveats that might be in order.

These data are on the data disk and can be read in MINITAB using

```
READ 'WKORDER3' C1
```

where C1 is the number of daily work orders.

T A B L E **3.17**

Data for Work-Orders Exercise

Day	Work Orders	Day	Work Orders	Day	Work Orders
1	3332	41	3118	81	2545
2	3348	42	3106	82	2553
3	3348	43	3075	83	2534
4	3387	44	3047	84	2541
5	3391	45	3018	85	2545
6	3421	46	3014	86	2527
7	3400	47	3019	87	2470
8	3408	48	2982	88	2442
9	3420	49	2977	89	2424
10	3431	50	2985	90	2398
11	3425	51	3000	91	2396
12	3416	52	2980	92	2333
13	3407	53	2984	93	2301
14	3395	54	3001	94	2267
15	3377	55	3000	95	2253
16	3363	56	3021	96	2266
17	3335	57	3004	97	2270
18	3315	58	2955	98	2236
19	3307	59	2893	99	2231
20	3292	60	2843	100	2219
21	3304	61	2827	101	2205
22	3275	62	2827	102	2211
23	3242	63	2828	103	2217
24	3217	64	2823	104	2204
25	3179	65	2827	105	2197
26	3220	66	2828	106	2210
27	3205	67	2801	107	2202
28	3206	68	2806	108	2181
29	3198	69	2761	109	2197
30	3197	70	2763	110	2230
31	3209	71	2764	111	2218
32	3192	72	2734	112	2210
33	3184	73	2700	113	2198
34	3178	74	2660	114	2177
35	3201	75	2618	115	2162
36	3209	76	2608	116	2136
37	3183	77	2603	117	2091
38	3176	78	2603	118	2111
39	3132	79	2576	119	2123
40	3104	80	2566	120	2149

In SAS, the data can be read from the file WKORDER3.DAT using

```
INPUT WKORDER;
```

Multiple Regression Analysis

4.1
Using Multiple Regression to Describe a Linear Relationship

In Chapter 3, the method of least squares was used to develop the equation of a line that best described the relationship between a dependent variable y and an explanatory variable x. In business and economic applications, however, there may be more than one explanatory variable that would be useful in explaining variation in the dependent variable y or obtaining better predictions of y. An equation of the form

$$\hat{y} = b_0 + b_1 x_1 + b_2 x_2,$$

where x_1 and x_2 are the explanatory variables, and b_1 and b_2 are estimates of the population regression coefficients may be desired. The relationship is still "linear"; each term on the right-hand side of the equation is additive and the regression coefficients do not enter the equation in a nonlinear manner (such as $b_1^2 x_1$). The graph of the relationship is no longer a line, however, because there are three variables involved.

Graphing the equation thus requires the use of three dimensions rather than two, and the equation would graph as a plane passing through the three-dimensional space. Figure 4.1 shows how this graph might appear. The x_1- and y-axes are drawn as before; the x_2-axis can be thought of as moving toward you to imitate the three-dimensional space. Because of the difficulty of drawing graphs on paper in more than two dimensions, the usefulness of graphical methods such as scatterplots is somewhat limited.

Still, when two or more explanatory variables are involved, two-dimensional scatterplots between the dependent variable and each explanatory variable can provide an initial indication of the relationships present. The relationship involving more than one explanatory variable may differ, however, from that involving each explanatory variable individually. The least squares method can still be used to develop regression equations involving more than one explanatory variable. These equations are referred

F I G U R E **4.1**

Graph Showing Regression "Plane"

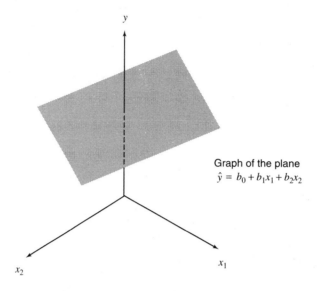

Graph of the plane
$$\hat{y} = b_0 + b_1 x_1 + b_2 x_2$$

to as *multiple regression equations.* As discussed, the equations no longer graph as lines, but the terms "linear regression" and even regression "line" (when perhaps regression "surface" would be more appropriate) still are used.

As the number of explanatory variables increases, the formulas for computing the estimates of the regression coefficients become increasingly complex. The availability of computerized regression routines precludes the need for hand computation of the estimates. The equations for the two or more explanatory variables case will not be presented in this text. There is a convenient method for writing the equations for the least squares estimates for any number of explanatory variables. This requires using matrices and matrix algebra, however. Because this text attempts to avoid as much mathematical detail as possible and concentrate on the use of computer regression output, the matrix presentation has been avoided; however, Appendix D does contain a brief introduction to the topic. A more advanced treatment of multiple regression that utilizes the matrix presentation is found, for example, in *Classical and Modern Regression with Applications* by Raymond H. Myers and in *Regression Analysis: Concepts and Applications* by Franklin A. Graybill and Hariharan K. Iyer.[1]

The concepts involved in producing least squares coefficient estimates for a multiple regression equation are very similar to those for simple regression. An equation

---

[1] See References for complete publication information.

that "best" describes the relationship between a dependent variable y and K explanatory variables $x_1, x_2, \ldots, x_K$ can be written

$$\hat{y} = b_0 + b_1 x_1 + b_2 x_2 + b_3 x_3 + \cdots + b_K x_K,$$

where $b_0, b_1, b_2, \ldots, b_K$ are the least squares coefficients. The case $K = 1$ is simple regression. The criterion for "best" is the same as it was for a simple regression; the difference between the true values of y and the values predicted by the multiple regression equation, $\hat{y}$, should be as small as possible. As before, this is accomplished by choosing $b_0, b_1, b_2, \ldots, b_K$ so that the sum of squares of the differences between the y and $\hat{y}$ values $\sum_{i=1}^{n}(y_i - \hat{y}_i)^2$, is a minimum. The optimizing values $b_0, b_1, b_2, \ldots, b_K$ are the least squares coefficients printed out by regression routines such as those available in MINITAB and SAS.

E X A M P L E 4.1 **Meddicorp Sales**

Meddicorp Company sells medical supplies to hospitals, clinics, and doctors' offices. The company currently markets in three regions of the Unites States: the South, the West, and the Midwest. These regions are each divided into many smaller sales territories.

Meddicorp's management is concerned with the effectiveness of a new bonus program. This program is overseen by regional sales managers and provides bonuses to salespeople based on performance. Management wants to know whether the bonuses paid in 1994 were related to sales. (Obviously, if there is a relationship here, the managers would expect it to be a direct one.) In determining whether this relationship exists, management also wants to take into account the effects of advertising. The variables to be used in the study include:

y, Meddicorp's sales (in thousands of dollars) in each territory for 1994 (SALES)

x_1, the amount Meddicorp spent on advertising in each territory (in hundreds of dollars) in 1994 (ADV)

x_2, the total amount of bonuses paid in each territory (in hundreds of dollars) in 1994 (BONUS)

These data for a random sample of 25 of Meddicorp's sales territories are shown in Table 4.1.

Figure 4.2 shows the MINITAB regression obtained relating SALES (y) to ADV (x_1) and BONUS (x_2). Figure 4.3 shows the regression output using SAS.

After rounding, the multiple regression equation describing the relationship between sales and the two explanatory variables may be written

$$\hat{y} = -516.4 + 2.47x_1 + 1.86x_2$$

or SALES $= -516.4 + 2.47$ADV $+ 1.86$BONUS.

This equation can be interpreted as providing an estimate of mean sales for a given level of advertising and bonus payment. Moreover, if advertising is held fixed, the equation shows that mean sales tends to rise by \$1860 (1.86 thousands of dollars) for each unit increase in BONUS. Also, if bonus payment is held fixed, it shows that mean sales tends to rise by \$2470 (2.47 thousands of dollars) for each unit increase in ADV. (Note that a "unit" increase in either BONUS or ADV represents a \$100 increase.) Clearly, such information provides a useful summary of the data. ∎

T A B L E **4.1**

Data for Meddicorp Example

Territory	SALES (in $1000)	ADV (in $100)	BONUS (in $100)	Territory	SALES (in $1000)	ADV (in $100)	BONUS (in $100)
1	963.50	374.27	230.98	14	1045.25	440.86	249.68
2	893.00	408.50	236.28	15	1102.25	487.79	232.99
3	1057.25	414.31	271.57	16	1225.25	537.67	272.20
4	1183.25	448.42	291.20	17	1508.00	612.21	266.64
5	1419.50	517.88	282.17	18	1564.25	601.46	277.44
6	1547.75	637.60	321.16	19	1634.75	585.10	312.25
7	1580.00	635.72	294.32	20	1159.25	524.56	292.87
8	1071.50	446.86	305.69	21	1202.75	535.17	268.27
9	1078.25	489.59	238.41	22	1294.25	486.03	309.85
10	1122.50	500.56	271.38	23	1467.50	540.17	291.03
11	1304.75	484.18	332.64	24	1583.75	583.85	289.29
12	1552.25	618.07	261.80	25	1124.75	499.15	272.55
13	1040.00	453.39	235.63				

F I G U R E **4.2**

MINITAB Output for Regression of SALES on ADV and BONUS for Meddicorp Example

```
The regression equation is
sales = - 516 + 2.47 adv + 1.86 bonus

Predictor        Coef        Stdev      t-ratio         p
Constant        -516.4       189.9       -2.72       0.013
adv             2.4732      0.2753        8.98       0.000
bonus           1.8562      0.7157        2.59       0.017

s = 90.75        R-sq = 85.5%       R-sq(adj) = 84.2%

Analysis of Variance

SOURCE        DF            SS           MS         F         p
Regression     2        1067797       533899     64.83     0.000
Error         22         181176         8235
Total         24        1248974

SOURCE        DF        SEQ SS
adv            1        1012408
bonus          1          55389
```

SAS Output for Regression of SALES on ADV and BONUS for Meddicorp Example

```
Dependent Variable: SALES

                    Analysis of Variance

                    Sum of          Mean
Source      DF      Squares         Square      F Value     Prob>F

Model        2   1067797.3206   533898.66029    64.831      0.0001
Error       22    181176.41942    8235.29179
C Total     24   1248973.74

        Root MSE        90.74851     R-square     0.8549
        Dep Mean      1269.02000     Adj R-sq     0.8418
        C.V.             7.15107

                    Parameter Estimates

                    Parameter    Standard    T for H0:
Variable    DF      Estimate     Error       Parameter=0   Prob > |T|

INTERCEP     1    -516.444282   89.87569701    -2.720       0.0125
ADV          1       2.473177    0.27531110     8.983       0.0001
BONUS        1       1.856179    0.71572507     2.593       0.0166
```

4.2
Inferences from a Multiple Regression Analysis

4.2.1 Assumptions Concerning the Population Regression Line

In general, a population regression equation involving K explanatory variables can be written as

$$\mu_{y|x_1,\ldots,x_K} = \beta_0 + \beta_1 x_1 + \beta_2 x_2 + \cdots + \beta_K x_K$$

This equation says that the conditional mean of y given $x_1, x_2, \ldots, x_K$ is a point on the regression surface described by the terms on the right-hand side of the equation.

An alternative way of writing the relationship is

$$y_i = \beta_0 + \beta_1 x_{1i} + \beta_2 x_{2i} + \cdots + \beta_K x_{Ki} + e_i,$$

where i denotes the ith observation and e_i is a random error or disturbance. Thus, y_i is related to the explanatory variables $x_{1i}, \ldots, x_{Ki}$ although the relationship is not an exact one. The random error e_i shows that, given the same values of $x_{1i}, \ldots, x_{Ki}$, each point y_i will not be exactly on the regression surface. Rather, the individual y_i values will be distributed around the regression surface in the manner discussed for a simple regression line in Chapter 3.

The following assumptions about the e_i are made:

1   The e_i are random variables and are normally distributed. Because the y_i are sums of a deterministic term involving only explanatory variables plus a random component e_i, this also makes the y_i normally distributed.

$$y_i = \underbrace{\beta_0 + \beta_1 x_{1i} + \beta_2 x_{2i} + \cdots + \beta_K x_{Ki}}_{\text{deterministic term}} + \underbrace{e_i}_{\substack{\text{normal random} \\ \text{error}}}$$

Another way to express this assumption would be to say that the y_i are normally distributed around the regression line conditional on the values of $x_{1i}, x_{2i}, \ldots, x_{Ki}$.

2   The e_i have an expected value (or mean) of zero:

$$E(e_i) = 0$$

3   The variance of each e_i is equal to σ_e^2. The variance around the regression line is assumed to be constant. The variance does not change for different values of explanatory variables.

4   The e_i are independent. This is an assumption that is very important when data are gathered over time. When the data are cross-sectional (that is, gathered at the same point in time for different individual units), this is typically not an assumption of concern.

These assumptions allow inferences to be made about the population multiple regression line from a sample multiple regression line. The first inferences to be considered are those made about the individual population regression coefficients, $\beta_0, \beta_1, \ldots, \beta_K$.

The effects of violations of the assumptions will be considered in Chapter 5. In this chapter, each assumption is assumed to hold so that an ideal situation exists for the use of least squares inference procedures.

4.2.2   Inferences about the Population Regression Coefficients

This section considers estimates of the population regression coefficients and tests of hypotheses about the population coefficients. Much of the information required to construct estimates and perform tests of hypotheses can be found in standard multiple regression output. For example, Figure 4.4 shows, in general, what information will be provided by the multiple regression output for MINITAB and SAS.

The least squares estimates $b_0, b_1, \ldots, b_K$ will be unbiased estimators of the corresponding population regression coefficients. Confidence interval estimates can be formed. A $(1 - \alpha)100\%$ confidence interval estimate of the population regression coefficient, β_k, is

$$b_k \pm t_{\alpha/2} s_{b_k}$$

F I G U R E **4.4**

Illustration of MINITAB and SAS Multiple Regression Outputs

(a) MINITAB

Predictor	Coef	Stdev	t-ratio	p
Constant	b_0	s_{b_0}	b_0/s_{b_0}	p value
x_1 variable name 1	b_1	s_{b_1}	b_1/s_{b_1}	p value
x_2 variable name 2	b_2	s_{b_2}	b_2/s_{b_2}	p value
.				
.				
.				
x_K variable name K	b_K	s_{b_K}	b_K/s_{b_K}	p value

(b) SAS

VARIABLE	DF	PARAMETER ESTIMATE	STANDARD ERROR	T FOR H0: PARAMETER = 0	PROB > |T|
INTERCEPT	1	b_0	s_{b_0}	b_0/s_{b_0}	p value
x_1 VARIABLE NAME 1	1	b_1	s_{b_1}	b_1/s_{b_1}	p value
x_2 VARIABLE NAME 2	1	b_2	s_{b_2}	b_1/s_{b_2}	p value
.					
.					
.					
x_K VARIABLE NAME K	1	b_K	s_{b_K}	b_K/s_{b_K}	p value

Here, k refers to the kth regression coefficient, $k = 0, 1, \ldots, K$. The value $t_{\alpha/2}$ is a number chosen from the t table to ensure the appropriate level of confidence, and s_{b_k} is the standard deviation of the sampling distribution of b_k. The number of degrees of freedom used in determining the t value is $n - (K + 1)$, where $K + 1$ is the number of regression coefficients to be estimated (K coefficients corresponding to the K explanatory variables and one intercept or constant). Note that $n - (K + 1)$ can also be written as $n - K - 1$.

Hypothesis tests about the individual β_k also can be performed. The general form of two-tailed hypotheses about the individual β_k is

$$H_0: \quad \beta_k = \beta_k^*$$
$$H_a: \quad \beta_k \neq \beta_k^*,$$

where β_k^* is any number chosen as the hypothesized value of the kth regression coefficient.

The decision rule for this test is:

$$\text{Reject } H_0 \quad \text{if} \quad t > t_{\alpha/2} \quad \text{or} \quad t < -t_{\alpha/2}$$
$$\text{Accept } H_0 \quad \text{if} \quad -t_{\alpha/2} \leq t \leq t_{\alpha/2}$$

where the test statistic is

$$t = \frac{b_k - \beta_k^*}{s_{b_k}}$$

and α is the probability of a Type I error.

When the null hypothesis is true, t should be small in absolute value because the estimate, b_k, will be close to the hypothesized value, β_k^*, making the numerator, $b_k - \beta_k^*$, close to zero. When the null hypothesis is false, the difference between b_k and β_k^* will be large in absolute value, leading to a large absolute value of the test statistic and resulting in the decision to reject H_0.

The most common hypothesis test encountered in multiple regression analysis is

$$H_0: \quad \beta_k = 0$$
$$H_a: \quad \beta_k \neq 0$$

as in simple regression. This test is typically most important when β_k refers to the coefficient of the explanatory variable x_k rather than the constant.

If the null hypothesis $H_0: \beta_k = 0$ is accepted, then it can be concluded that, once the effects of all other variables in the multiple regression are included, x_k is not linearly related to y. In other words, adding x_k to the regression equation is of no help in explaining any additional variation in y left unexplained by the other explanatory variables.

On the other hand, if the null hypothesis is rejected, then there is evidence that y and x_k are linearly related and that x_k does help to explain some of the variation in y not accounted for by the other explanatory variables.

From Figure 4.4, it can be seen that the test statistic used for testing

$$H_0: \quad \beta_k = 0$$

is printed out on the regression output. The test statistic is

$$t = \frac{b_k}{s_{b_k}}$$

and is found on the t-ratio column for MINITAB and the T for H0: Parameter=0 column for SAS. Also, note that the p values for testing whether each population regression coefficient is equal to zero are found in the prob > |T| column in SAS and in the p column in MINITAB.

E X A M P L E   **4.2**   **Meddicorp (continued)**

Refer again to the MINITAB output in Figure 4.2 or the SAS output in Figure 4.3.

1. Use the regression output to test the following hypotheses:

$$H_0: \quad \beta_1 = 0$$
$$H_a: \quad \beta_1 \neq 0,$$

where β_1 is the coefficient of ADV. Use a 5% level of significance. What conclusion can be drawn from the result of the test?

Answer
(a) Decision rule:

Reject H_0 if $t > 2.074$ or $t < -2.074$

Accept H_0 if $-2.074 \leq t \leq 2.074$

Note: The t value with 22 degrees of freedom is 2.074 when a two-tailed test with a 5% level of significance is required.

Test statistic: 8.98
Decision: Reject H_0.
Conclusion: ADV is related to SALES (even when the effect of BONUS is taken into account).

(b) Decision rule (using the p value from the output):

Reject H_0 if p value $< .05$

Accept H_0 if p value $\geq .05$

Test statistic: p value $= 0.000$
Decision: Reject H_0.

2. Use the regression output to test the following hypotheses:

$$H_0: \quad \beta_2 = 0$$
$$H_a: \quad \beta_2 \neq 0,$$

where β_2 is the coefficient of BONUS. Use a 5% level of significance. What conclusion can be drawn from the result of the test?

Answer
(a) Decision rule:

Reject H_0 if $t > 2.074$ or $t < -2.074$

Accept H_0 if $-2.074 \leq t \leq 2.074$

Test statistic: 2.59
Decision: Reject H_0.
Conclusion: BONUS is related to SALES (even when the effect of ADV is taken into account).

(b) Decision rule (using the p value from the output):

Reject H_0 if p value $< .05$

Accept H_0 if p value $\geq .05$

Test statistic: p value $= 0.017$

Decision: Reject H_0.

3. Use the regression output to test the following hypotheses:

$$H_0: \quad \beta_2 \le 0$$
$$H_a: \quad \beta_2 > 0,$$

where β_2 is the coefficient of BONUS. Use a 5% level of significance. What conclusion can be drawn from the result of the test?

Answer

(a) Decision rule:

Reject H_0	if	$t > 1.717$
Accept H_0	if	$t \le 1.717$

Note: The t value with 22 degrees of freedom is 1.717 when a one-tailed test with a 5% level of significance is required.

Test statistic: 8.98

Decision: Reject H_0.

Conclusion: BONUS is *directly* related to SALES (even when the effect of ADV is taken into account).

4. What would be the 95% confidence interval estimate of β_1, the coefficient of ADV?

Answer

$[2.4732 - (2.074)(.2753), \quad 2.4732 + (2.074)(.2753)]$ or $(1.9022, 3.0442)$ ∎

4.3
Assessing the Fit of the Regression Line

4.3.1 The ANOVA Table, the Coefficient of Determination, and the Multiple Correlation Coefficient

As with simple regression, the variation in the dependent variable y in a multiple regression can be written as follows:

$$SST = SSE + SSR$$

The total variation in y is given by the total sum of squares:

$$SST = \sum_{i=1}^{n} (y_i - \bar{y})^2$$

F I G U R E 4.5

Analysis of Variance Tables from MINITAB and SAS Multiple Regressions

(a) MINITAB

Source	DF	SS	MS	F	p
Regression	K	SSR	MSR = SSR/(K)	F = MSR/MSE	p value
Error	$n - K - 1$	SSE	MSE = SSE/$(n - K - 1)$		
Total	$n - 1$	SST			

(b) SAS

Source	DF	Sum of Squares	Mean Square	F Value	Prob>F
Model	K	SSR	MSR = SSR/(K)	F = MSR/MSE	p value
Error	$n - K - 1$	SSE	MSE = SSE/$(n - K - 1)$		
C Total	$n - 1$	SST			

The error sum of squares represents the variation in y left "unexplained" by the regression:

$$SSE = \sum_{i=1}^{n}(y_i - \hat{y}_i)^2$$

The regression sum of squares represents the variation in y "explained" by the regression:

$$SSR = \sum_{i=1}^{n}(\hat{y}_i - \bar{y})^2$$

In SSE and SSR, the $\hat{y}_i$ values are the predicted or fitted values from the multiple regression equation. These three sums of squares can be interpreted as in a simple regression context.

The values of each of the three sums of squares are listed in the analysis of variance (ANOVA) table as shown in Figure 4.5. Also listed in the ANOVA table are the number of degrees of freedom associated with each of the sums of squares. For SSR, the number of degrees of freedom is equal to the number of explanatory variables, K. For SSE, the number of degrees of freedom is $n - (K + 1)$ or, equivalently, $n - K - 1$. As in the simple regression ANOVA table, the mean squares also are shown. These are computed by dividing the sums of squares by the appropriate number of degrees of freedom.

SST, SSR, and SSE can be used to evaluate how well the regression equation is explaining the variation in y. One measure of the goodness of fit of the regression is the coefficient of determination, R^2. The R^2 value, as for a simple regression, is computed by dividing SSR by SST:

$$R^2 = \frac{SSR}{SST}$$

Thus, R^2 represents the proportion of the variation in y explained by the regression. As before, R^2 will range between 0 and 1. The closer to 1 the value of R^2, the better the fit of the regression equation to the data. If R^2 is multiplied by 100, it represents the percentage of the variation in y explained by the regression.

Although R^2 has a nice interpretation, there is a drawback to its use in multiple regression. As more explanatory variables are added to the regression model, the value of R^2 will never decrease, even if the additional variables are explaining an insignificant proportion of the variation in y. The addition of these unnecessary explanatory variables is not desirable. An alternative measure of the goodness of fit useful in multiple regression is R^2 adjusted for degrees of freedom (or, simply, adjusted R^2). Recall that another way of writing R^2 is

$$R^2 = 1 - \frac{SSE}{SST}$$

SSE/SST can be interpreted as the unexplained proportion of the total variation in y. Because the addition of explanatory variables to the model causes SSE to decrease, R^2 will get increasingly closer to 1. This will happen even if the added explanatory variables have no significant relationship to y.

The adjusted R^2 does not suffer from this limitation. The adjusted R^2 will be denoted as R^2_{ADJ}. It is computed

$$R^2_{ADJ} = 1 - \frac{SSE/(n - K - 1)}{SST/(n - 1)}$$

Note that the sums of squares have been divided by their degrees of freedom before they are used in computing R^2_{ADJ}. Now, suppose an explanatory variable is added to the regression model that produces only a very small decrease in SSE. The divisor, $n - K - 1$, also will decrease because the number of explanatory variables, K, has been incremented by 1. It is possible that $SSE/(n - K - 1)$ may increase if the decrease in SSE from the addition of an explanatory variable is very small, because there is also a decrease in the size of the divisor. Thus, the R^2_{ADJ} may decrease when the added explanatory variable adds little to the ability of the model to explain the variation in y. (It is also possible that negative R^2_{ADJ} values may occur. This is not a mistake, but a result of a model that fits the data very poorly. In MINITAB, when negative R^2_{ADJ} values occur, they are simply printed as 0.0%; in SAS, the actual value is printed.)

R^2_{ADJ} no longer represents the proportion of variation in y explained by the regression, but it can be useful when comparing two regressions with different numbers of explanatory variables (say, a two-variable model with a three- or more variable model). A decrease in R^2_{ADJ} from the addition of one or more explanatory variables would signal that the added variable(s) was of little importance in the regression equation. R^2_{ADJ} is purely a descriptive measure, however. A more structured approach to compare two regression models will be presented in Section 4.4.

MINITAB and SAS both print out the R^2 value for the regression and the value of R^2_{ADJ}. For regression routines that do not print out R^2_{ADJ}, it can be computed easily using the equation

$$R^2_{ADJ} = 1 - \frac{SSE/(n - K - 1)}{SST/(n - 1)}$$

or by using the relationship

$$R^2_{ADJ} = 1 + \frac{(n - 1)}{(n - K - 1)}(R^2 - 1)$$

SAS computes a measure called the *multiple correlation coefficient*, R, which is the positive square root of R^2:

$$R = +\sqrt{R^2}$$

The multiple correlation coefficient is equal to the simple correlation between the predicted y values, $\hat{y}$, and the true y values. Thus, it represents a measure of how closely associated the true values of y are with the points on the regression line. The R^2, however, may be a preferable measure of goodness of fit because of its interpretation as percentage of variance explained.

4.3.2 The F Statistic

Another measure of how well the multiple regression equation fits the data is the F statistic:

$$F = \frac{MSR}{MSE}$$

MSR is the mean square due to the regression, or the regression sum of squares divided by its degrees of freedom:

$$MSR = \frac{SSR}{K}$$

Note that the degrees of freedom associated with SSR is K, the number of explanatory variables in the model. MSE is the mean square due to error, or the error sum of squares divided by its degrees of freedom:

$$MSE = \frac{SSE}{n - K - 1}.$$

The degrees of freedom associated with the error sum of squares is equal to the sample size, n, minus the number of regression coefficients to be estimated, $K + 1$.

The F statistic is used to test the hypotheses

$$H_0: \quad \beta_1 = \beta_2 = \cdots = \beta_K = 0$$
$$H_a: \quad \text{At least one coefficient is not equal to zero.}$$

The decision rule for the test is:

$$\text{Reject } H_0 \quad \text{if} \quad F > F(\alpha; K, n - K - 1)$$
$$\text{Accept } H_0 \quad \text{if} \quad F \leq F(\alpha; K, n - K - 1)$$

where $F(\alpha; K, n - K - 1)$ is a value chosen from the F table for the appropriate level of significance, α. The critical value depends on the number of degrees of freedom associated with the numerator of the F statistic, K, and the number of degrees of freedom associated with the denominator, $n - K - 1$.

Acceptance of the null hypothesis implies that the explanatory variables in the regression equation are of little or no use in explaining the variation in the dependent variable, y. Rejection of the null hypothesis implies that *at least one* of the explanatory variables helps to explain the variation in y. Rejection does not mean that all the population regression coefficients are different from zero (although this *may* be the case). Rejection does mean that the regression equation is useful, however.

If the hypothesis that all the population regression coefficients are zero is rejected, the t test discussed previously can be used to determine which of the individual variables are significant contributors to the model's ability to explain the variation in y. If the null hypothesis is accepted, there is no need to perform the individual t tests. The F test can be thought of as a global test designed to assess the overall fit of the regression.

The information necessary to perform F tests is typically included in the computer regression output in the ANOVA table. The SAS and MINITAB outputs provide the computed value of the F statistic and p value associated with the statistic (as shown in Figure 4.5).

E X A M P L E   4.3   **Meddicorp (continued)**

Refer to the MINITAB output in Figure 4.2 or the SAS output in Figure 4.3.

1. What percentage of the variation in sales has been explained by the regression?

Answer: 85.5% (R-sq on MINITAB or R-SQUARE on SAS output.)

2. What is the adjusted R^2?

Answer: 84.2% (R-sq(adj) on MINITAB or ADJ R-SQ on SAS output.)

3. Conduct the F test for overall fit of the regression. Use a 5% level of significance.

$$H_0: \quad \beta_1 = \beta_2 = 0$$
$$H_a: \quad \text{At least one the coefficients is not equal to zero}$$

Answer
(a) Decision rule:

$$\text{Reject } H_0 \quad \text{if} \quad F > F(.05; 2, 22) = 3.44$$
$$\text{Accept } H_0 \quad \text{if} \quad F \leq F(.05; 2, 22) = 3.44$$

Test statistic: $F = 64.83$
Decision: Reject H_0.
(b) Decision rule:

$$\text{Reject } H_0 \quad \text{if} \quad p \text{ value} < .05$$

$$\text{Accept } H_0 \quad \text{if} \quad p \text{ value} \geq .05$$

Test statistic: p value $= 0.000$
Decision: Reject H_0.
4. What conclusion can be drawn from the result of the F test for overall fit?

Answer: At least one of the coefficients (β_1, β_2) is not equal to zero. In other words, at least one of the variables (x_1, x_2) is important in explaining the variation in y. ∎

Exercises

1   **Cost Control**   Ms. Karen Ainsworth is an employee of a well-known accounting firm's management services division. She is currently on a consulting assignment to the Apex Corporation, a firm that produces corrugated paper for use in making boxes and other packing materials. Apex called in consulting help to improve its cost control program, and Ms. Ainsworth is analyzing manufacturing costs to understand more fully the important influences on these costs. She has assembled monthly data on a group of variables, and she is using regression analysis to help her assess how these variables are related to total manufacturing costs. The variables Ms. Ainsworth has selected to study are

y, total manufacturing cost per month in thousands of dollars (COST)
x_1, total production of paper per month in tons (PAPER)
x_2, total machine hours used per month (MACHINE)
x_3, total variable overhead costs per month in thousands of dollars (OVERHEAD)
x_4, total direct labor hours used each month (LABOR)

The data shown in Table 4.2 refer to the period January 1992 through March 1994. Use the MINITAB regression output in Figure 4.6 or the SAS output in Figure 4.7 to answer the following questions:

a   If Ms. Ainsworth wants to use a cost function developed by means of regression analysis, what is the equation that will be empirically determined using all four explanatory variables?

b   Conduct the F test for overall fit of the regression. State the hypotheses to be tested, the decision rule, the test statistic, and the decision. Use a 5% level of significance. What conclusion can be drawn from the result of the test?

c   In the cost-accounting literature, the sample regression coefficient corresponding to x_k is regarded as an estimate of the true marginal cost of output associated with the variable x_k. Find a point estimate of the true marginal cost associated with total machine hours per month. Also, find a 95% confidence interval estimate of the true marginal cost associated with total machine hours.

TABLE 4.2

Data for Cost Control Exercise

COST	PAPER	MACHINE	OVERHEAD	LABOR
1102	550	218	112	325
1008	502	199	99	301
1227	616	249	126	376
1395	701	277	143	419
1710	838	363	191	682
1881	919	399	210	751
1924	939	411	216	813
1246	622	248	124	371
1255	626	259	127	383
1314	659	266	135	402
1557	740	334	181	546
1887	901	401	216	655
1204	610	238	117	351
1211	598	246	124	370
1287	646	259	127	387
1451	732	286	155	433
1828	891	389	208	878
1903	932	404	216	660
1997	964	430	233	694
1363	680	271	129	405
1421	723	286	146	426
1543	784	317	158	478
1774	841	376	199	601
1929	922	415	228	679
1317	647	260	126	378
1302	656	255	117	380
1388	704	281	142	429

SOURCE: These data were created by Professor Roger L. Wright, RLW Analytics, Inc. and have been modified with his permission.

d   Test the hypothesis that the true marginal cost of output associated with total production of paper is 1.0. Use a 5% level of significance and a two-tailed test procedure. State the hypotheses to be tested, the decision rule, the test statistic, and the decision. What conclusion can be drawn from the result of the test?

e   What percentage of the variation in y has been explained by the regression?

f   What is the adjusted R^2 for this regression?

g   Based on the regression equation, what actions might be taken to control costs?

These data are available on the data disk for further analysis. In MINITAB, they can be read using

FIGURE 4.6

MINITAB Regression Output for Cost Control Exercise

```
The regression equation is
cost = 51.7 + 0.948 paper + 2.47 machine + 0.048 overhead
     - 0.0506 labor

Predictor        Coef       Stdev      t-ratio        p
Constant        51.72       21.70        2.38      0.026
paper          0.9479      0.1200        7.90      0.000
machine        2.4710      0.4656        5.31      0.000
overhead       0.0483      0.5250        0.09      0.927
labor        -0.05058     0.04030       -1.26      0.223

s = 11.08      R-sq = 99.9%     R-sq(adj) = 99.9%

Analysis of Variance

SOURCE         DF          SS          MS          F          p
Regression      4     2271423      567856    4629.17      0.000
Error          22        2699         123
Total          26     2274122

SOURCE         DF      SEQ SS
paper           1     2255666
machine         1       15561
overhead        1           3
labor           1         193

Unusual Observations
Obs.     paper        cost        Fit   Stdev.Fit   Residual   St.Resid
 17        891     1828.00    1823.22        8.68       4.78      0.69 X
 25        647     1317.00    1294.48        3.58      22.52      2.15R

R denotes an obs. with a large st. resid.
X denotes an obs. whose X value gives it large influence.
```

```
READ 'COST4' C1-C5
```

where C1 is COST, C2 is PAPER, C3 is MACHINE, C4 is OVERHEAD, and C5 is LABOR.

In SAS, the data can be read from the file COST4.DAT using

```
INPUT COST PAPER MACHINE OVERHEAD LABOR;
```

2 **Salaries** The data in Table 4.3 show the values of the following variables for 93 employees of Harris Bank Chicago in 1977:

y, beginning salary in dollars (SALARY)

x_1, years of schooling at the time of hire (EDUC)

x_2, number of months of previous work experience (EXPER)

x_3, number of months after January 1, 1969, that the individual was hired (TIME)

F I G U R E **4.7**

SAS Regression Output for Cost Control Exercise

Dependent Variable: COST

Analysis of Variance

Source	DF	Sum of Squares	Mean Square	F Value	Prob>F
Model	4	2271423.3537	567855.83844	4629.168	0.0001
Error	22	2698.72033	122.66911		
C Total	26	2274122.0741			

Root MSE	11.07561	R-square	0.9988
Dep Mean	1497.18519	Adj R-sq	0.9986
C.V.	0.73976		

Parameter Estimates

Variable	DF	Parameter Estimate	Standard Error	T for H0: Parameter=0	Prob > |T|
INTERCEP	1	51.723142	21.70396993	2.383	0.0262
PAPER	1	0.947942	0.12002341	7.898	0.0001
MACHINE	1	2.471040	0.46556012	5.308	0.0001
OVERHEAD	1	0.048339	0.52500975	0.092	0.9275
LABOR	1	-0.050578	0.04029511	-1.255	0.2226

T A B L E **4.3**

Data for the Salaries Exercise

SALARY	EDUC	EXPER	TIME	SALARY	EDUC	EXPER	TIME
3900	12	0.0	1	4800	12	144.0	24
4020	10	44.0	7	4800	12	163.0	12
4290	12	5.0	30	4800	12	228.0	26
4380	8	6.2	7	4800	12	381.0	1
4380	8	7.5	6	4800	16	214.0	15
4380	12	0.0	7	4980	8	318.0	25
4380	12	0.0	10	5100	8	96.0	33
4380	12	4.5	6	5100	12	36.0	15
4440	15	75.0	2	5100	12	59.0	14
4500	8	52.0	3	5100	15	115.0	1
4500	12	8.0	19	5100	15	165.0	4
4620	12	52.0	3	5100	16	123.0	12
4800	8	70.0	20	5160	12	18.0	12
4800	12	6.0	23	5220	8	102.0	29
4800	12	11.0	12	5220	12	127.0	29
4800	12	11.0	17	5280	8	90.0	11
4800	12	63.0	22	5280	8	190.0	1

T A B L E 4.3 (Cont.)

Data for the Salaries Exercise

SALARY	EDUC	EXPER	TIME	SALARY	EDUC	EXPER	TIME
5280	12	107.0	11	5100	12	315.0	2
5400	8	173.0	34	5220	12	29.0	14
5400	8	228.0	33	5400	12	7.0	21
5400	12	26.0	11	5400	12	38.0	11
5400	12	36.0	33	5400	12	113.0	3
5400	12	38.0	22	5400	15	17.5	8
5400	12	82.0	29	5400	15	359.0	11
5400	12	169.0	27	5700	15	36.0	5
5400	12	244.0	1	6000	8	320.0	21
5400	15	24.0	13	6000	12	24.0	2
5400	15	49.0	27	6000	12	32.0	17
5400	15	51.0	21	6000	12	49.0	8
5400	15	122.0	33	6000	12	56.0	33
5520	12	97.0	17	6000	12	252.0	11
5520	12	196.0	32	6000	12	272.0	19
5580	12	132.5	30	6000	15	25.0	13
5640	12	55.0	9	6000	15	35.5	32
5700	12	90.0	23	6000	15	56.0	12
5700	12	116.5	25	6000	15	64.0	33
5700	15	51.0	17	6000	15	108.0	16
5700	15	61.0	11	6000	16	45.5	3
5700	15	241.0	34	6300	15	72.0	17
6000	12	121.0	30	6600	15	64.0	16
6000	15	78.5	13	6600	15	84.0	33
6120	12	208.5	21	6600	15	215.5	16
6300	12	86.5	33	6840	15	41.5	7
6300	15	231.0	15	6900	12	175.0	10
4620	12	11.5	22	6900	15	132.0	24
5040	15	14.0	3	8100	16	54.5	33
5100	12	180.0	15				

SOURCE: These data were obtained from D. W. Schafer. Measurement-error diagnostics and the sex discrimination problem. *Journal of Business and Economic Statistics*, 5 (1987): 529–537.

The MINITAB regression output for the regression of SALARY on the three explanatory variables is shown in Figure 4.8. The SAS output is in Figure 4.9. Use the outputs to answer the following questions:

a What is the estimated regression equation relating salary to education, experience, and time?

F I G U R E **4.8**

MINITAB Regression Output for Salaries Exercise

```
The regression equation is
salary = 3180 + 140 educ + 1.48 exper + 20.6 time

Predictor        Coef       Stdev     t-ratio        p
Constant       3179.7       383.5        8.29    0.000
educ           139.62       27.72        5.04    0.000
exper          1.4807      0.6970        2.12    0.036
time           20.633       6.155        3.35    0.001

s = 602.8      R-sq = 30.2%     R-sq(adj) = 27.8%

Analysis of Variance

SOURCE        DF          SS          MS        F        p
Regression     3    13984437     4661479    12.83    0.000
Error         89    32338854      363358
Total         92    46323292

SOURCE        DF      SEQ SS
educ           1     7862535
exper          1     2038491
time           1     4083411

Unusual Observations

Obs.     educ     salary       Fit   Stdev.Fit    Residual    St.Resid
   3     12.0     4290.0    5481.6       126.9     -1191.6       -2.02R
  21     12.0     4800.0    5439.9       232.0      -639.9       -1.15 X
  22     16.0     4800.0    6040.0       145.2     -1240.0       -2.12R
  90     15.0     6840.0    5479.9       112.4      1360.1        2.30R
  91     12.0     6900.0    5320.6        93.2      1579.4        2.65R
  93     16.0     8100.0    6175.2       158.9      1924.8        3.31R

R denotes an obs. with a large st. resid.
X denotes an obs. whose X value gives it large influence.
```

b Conduct the F test for overall fit of the regression. Use a 5% level of significance. State the hypotheses to be tested, the decision rule, the test statistic, and the decision. What conclusion can be drawn from the result of the test?

c Is education linearly related to beginning salary (after taking into account the effect of experience and time)? Perform the hypothesis test necessary to answer this question. State the hypotheses to be tested, the decision rule, the test statistic, and the decision. Use a 5% level of significance.

d What percentage of the variation in salary has been explained by the regression?

These data are available on the data disk for further analysis. In MINITAB, they can be read using

```
READ 'HARRIS4' C1-C4
```

where C1 is SALARY, C2 is EDUC, C3 is EXPER, and C4 is TIME.

In SAS, the data can be read from the file HARRIS4.DAT using

```
INPUT SALARY EDUC EXPER TIME;
```

FIGURE 4.9

SAS Regression Output for Salaries Exercise

Dependent Variable: SALARY

Analysis of Variance

Source	DF	Sum of Squares	Mean Square	F Value	Prob>F
Model	3	13984436.814	4661478.9381	12.829	0.0001
Error	89	32338853.508	363357.90459		
C Total	92	46323290.323			

Root MSE	602.79176	R-square	0.3019
Dep Mean	5420.32258	Adj R-sq	0.2784
C.V.	11.12096		

Parameter Estimates

Variable	DF	Parameter Estimate	Standard Error	T for H0: Parameter=0	Prob > |T|
INTERCEP	1	3179.743949	383.48451825	8.292	0.0001
EDUCAT	1	139.618208	27.71635324	5.037	0.0001
EXPER	1	1.480699	0.69699668	2.124	0.0364
TIME	1	20.633372	6.15497008	3.352	0.0012

4.4
Comparing Two Regression Models

4.4.1 Full and Reduced Model Comparisons Using Separate Regressions

Thus far, two types of hypothesis tests for multiple regression models have been considered:

1 a test of the overall fit of the regression

$$H_0: \quad \beta_1 = \beta_2 = \cdots = \beta_K = 0$$
$$H_a: \quad \text{At least one coefficient is not equal to zero}$$

2 a test of the significance of each individual regression coefficient

$$H_0: \quad \beta_k = 0$$
$$H_a: \quad \beta_k \neq 0$$

In multiple regression models it also may be useful to test whether subtests of coefficients are equal to zero. In this section, the use of *partial F* tests to test whether any subset of coefficients in a multiple regression is equal to zero is considered.

To set up this hypotheses test, consider the following regression model:

$$y = \beta_0 + \beta_1 x_1 + \cdots + \beta_L x_L + \beta_{L+1} x_{L+1} + \cdots + \beta_K x_K + e$$

Testing whether the variables $x_{L+1}, \ldots, x_K$ are useful in explaining any variation in y after taking account of the variation already explained by $x_1, \ldots, x_L$ can be viewed as a comparison of two regression models to determine whether it is worthwhile to include the additional variables. The two models for comparison will be called the *full* and *reduced* models.

Full Model

$$y = \beta_0 + \beta_1 x_1 + \cdots + \beta_L x_L + \beta_{L+1} x_{L+1} + \cdots + \beta_K x_K + e$$

This is called the full model because all K explanatory variables of interest are included.

Reduced Model

$$y = \beta_0 + \beta_1 x_1 + \cdots + \beta_L x_L + e$$

This is called the reduced model because the variables $x_{L+1}, \ldots, x_K$ have been removed.

The question to be answered is, "Is the full model significantly better than the reduced model at explaining the variation in y?" This question can be formalized by setting up the following null and alternative hypotheses:

H_0: $\beta_{L+1} = \cdots = \beta_K = 0$

H_a: At least one of the coefficients $\beta_{L+1}, \ldots, \beta_K$ is not equal to zero

If the null hypothesis is accepted, accept the reduced model; if the null hypothesis is rejected, at least one of $x_{L+1}, \ldots, x_K$ is contributing to the explanation of the variation in y, and the full model is chosen as superior to the reduced.

To test the hypotheses—that is, to compare the full and reduced models—an F statistic is used. The F statistic can be written:

$$F = \frac{(SSE_R - SSE_F)/(K - L)}{SSE_F/(n - K - 1)},$$

where the subscript F stands for full model, and the subscript R stands for reduced model.

Now consider what is being computed in the F statistic. If the full and reduced models are estimated, the regression output would include the error sum of squares for each of these regressions. In the F statistic, SSE_F refers to the error sum of squares from the full model output using all K explanatory variables. SSE_R refers to the error sum of squares from the reduced model output using only L explanatory variables. Recall that the error sum of squares represents the variation in y unexplained by the regression. Also, the reduced model error sum of squares can never be less than the full model error sum of squares, so the difference

$$SSE_R - SSE_F$$

will always be greater than or equal to zero. This difference represents the additional amount of variation in y explained by adding $x_{L+1}, \ldots, x_K$ to the regression model. This measure of improvement is then divided by the number of additional variables to be added to the model, $K - L$. The numerator thus represents the additional variation in y explained per additional variable used. Note that the numerator degrees of freedom, $K - L$, is equal to the number of coefficients included in the null hypothesis, or, equivalently, to the difference in the number of explanatory variables in the full and reduced models.

The mean square error for the full regression model is used in the denominator:

$$MSE_F = \frac{SSE_F}{n - K - 1}$$

If the measure of improvement is large relative to the mean square error for the full model, then the F statistic will be large. If the improvement measure is small relative to MSE_F, then the value of the F statistic will be small. The decision rule for the test is:

Reject H_0 if $F > F(\alpha; K - L, n - K - 1)$

Accept H_0 if $F \leq F(\alpha; K - L, n - K - 1)$

Here α is the probability of a Type I error, and $F(\alpha; K - L, n - K - 1)$ is a value chosen from the F table for level of significance α, $K - L$ numerator degrees of freedom and $n - K - 1$ denominator degrees of freedom. This test will be referred to as a *partial F* test and can be performed with any statistical package by running both the full and reduced model regressions.

E X A M P L E   4.4   Meddicorp (continued)

The management of Meddicorp feels that, in addition to advertising and bonus, two other explanatory variables may be important in explaining the variation in sales. These variables are

MKTSHR, or market share percentage currently held by Meddicorp in each territory

COMPET, or the largest competitor's sales in thousands of dollars in each territory

These two additional variables are shown in Table 4.4 for each territory.

The MINITAB regression of SALES on ADV, BONUS, MKTSHR, and COMPET is shown in Figure 4.10. The SAS regression is shown in Figure 4.11.

The hypothesized population regression model is

$$y_i = \beta_0 + \beta_1 x_{1i} + \beta_2 x_{2i} + \beta_3 x_{3i} + \beta_4 x_{4i} + e_i$$

T A B L E 4.4

Additional Data for Meddicorp Example

Territory	MKTSHR	COMPET	Territory	MKTSHR	COMPET
1	33	202.22	14	28	333.66
2	29	252.77	15	28	232.55
3	34	293.22	16	30	273.00
4	24	202.22	17	29	323.55
5	32	303.33	18	32	404.44
6	29	353.88	19	36	283.11
7	28	374.11	20	34	222.44
8	31	404.44	21	31	283.11
9	20	394.33	22	32	242.66
10	30	303.33	23	28	333.66
11	25	333.66	24	27	313.44
12	34	353.88	25	26	374.11
13	42	262.88			

F I G U R E 4.10

MINITAB Regression Output for the Regression of SALES on ADV, BONUS, MKTSHR, and COMPET

```
The regression equation is
sales = - 594 + 2.51 adv + 1.91 bonus + 2.65 mktshr - 0.121 compet

Predictor        Coef        Stdev      t-ratio          p
Constant       -593.5        259.2        -2.29      0.033
adv            2.5131       0.3143         8.00      0.000
bonus          1.9059       0.7424         2.57      0.018
mktshr          2.651        4.636         0.57      0.574
compet        -0.1207       0.3718        -0.32      0.749

s = 93.77      R-sq = 85.9%      R-sq(adj) = 83.1%

Analysis of Variance

SOURCE        DF            SS           MS          F          p
Regression     4       1073119       268280      30.51      0.000
Error         20        175855         8793
Total         24       1248974

SOURCE        DF        SEQ SS
adv            1       1012408
bonus          1         55389
mktshr         1          4394
compet         1           927

Unusual Observations
Obs.      adv       sales          Fit   Stdev.Fit     Residual    St.Resid
  20      525      1159.2       1346.2        39.4       -187.0       -2.20R

R denotes an obs. with a large st. resid.
```

F I G U R E  4.11

SAS Regression Output for the Regression of SALES on ADV, BONUS, MKTSHR, and COMPET

Dependent Variable: SALES

Analysis of Variance

Source	DF	Sum of Squares	Mean Square	F Value	Prob>F
Model	4	1073118.542	268279.63549	30.511	0.0001
Error	20	175855.19803	8792.75990		
C Total	24	1248973.74			

Root MSE	93.76972	R-square	0.8592	
Dep Mean	1269.02000	Adj R-sq	0.8310	
C.V.	7.38914			

Parameter Estimates

Variable	DF	Parameter Estimate	Standard Error	T for H0: Parameter=0	Prob > |T|
INTERCEP	1	-593.537452	259.19585077	-2.290	0.0330
ADV	1	2.513138	0.31427550	7.997	0.0001
BONUS	1	1.905948	0.74238560	2.567	0.0184
MKTSHR	1	2.651007	4.63565540	0.572	0.5738
COMPET	1	-0.120731	0.37181490	-0.325	0.7488

Consider the test of the hypotheses

$$H_0: \quad \beta_3 = \beta_4 = 0$$

$$H_a: \quad \text{At least one of the coefficients } \beta_3 \text{ and } \beta_4 \text{ is not equal to zero}$$

The full model output is shown in Figures 4.10 and 4.11 and the reduced model output in Figures 4.2 and Figure 4.3. The F statistic can be computed as

$$F = \frac{(SSE_R - SSE_F)/(K - L)}{SSE_F/(n - K - 1)}$$

$$= \frac{(181{,}176 - 175{,}855)/2}{175{,}855/20} = 0.303$$

(Note that $K = 4$ and $L = 2$, so $K - L = 2$.) If a 5% level of significance is used, the decision rule is:

Reject H_0	if	$F > 3.49$
Accept H_0	if	$F \leq 3.49$

where 3.49 is the 5% F critical value with 2 numerator and 20 denominator degrees of freedom.

The decision is to accept H_0 and conclude that both coefficients β_3 and β_4 are equal to zero. Thus, the variables x_3 and x_4 are not useful in explaining any of the remaining variation in y. ∎

4.4.2 Full and Reduced Model Comparisons, Using Conditional Sums of Squares[2]

Another way to view partial F tests is through the use of conditional or sequential sums of squares. For a regression model with two explanatory variables,

$$\hat{y} = b_0 + b_1 x_1 + b_2 x_2,$$

the standard ANOVA table would appear as in Figure 4.12(a). In Figure 4.12(b) an alternative ANOVA table is presented. In this figure, the regression sum of squares has been decomposed into two parts. The first, $SSR(x_1)$, is the sum of squares explained by x_1 if it were the only explanatory variable. The second, $SSR(x_2|x_1)$, is called a *conditional* or *sequential sum of squares*. It represents the sum of squares explained by x_2 in addition to that explained by x_1. That is, given that x_1 has explained a certain amount of variation in y, $SSR(x_2|x_1)$ shows how much of the remaining variation that x_2 will explain. Note that

$$SSR = SSR(x_1) + SSR(x_2|x_1)$$

Here SSR is the variation explained by both x_1 and x_2.

To test the hypotheses

$$H_0: \quad \beta_2 = 0$$
$$H_a: \quad \beta_2 \neq 0,$$

an F statistic can be constructed using the conditional sum of squares.

$$F = \frac{SSR(x_2|x_1)/1}{SSE/(n-3)}$$

The numerator of F is the conditional sum of squares for x_2, given that x_1 is in the model, divided by its degrees of freedom. The conditional sum of squares has 1 degree of freedom because it represents the sum of squares explained by only one variable. The denominator is the error sum of squares for the full model, the model with both x_1 and x_2, divided by its degrees of freedom. If x_2 explains little of the additional unexplained variation in y, then $SSR(x_2|x_1)$ will be small, as will the F statistic. The more variation explained by x_2, the bigger the F statistic will be. The decision rule for the test is:

$$\text{Reject } H_0 \quad \text{if} \quad F > F(\alpha; 1, n-3)$$
$$\text{Accept } H_0 \quad \text{if} \quad F \leq F(\alpha; 1, n-3)$$

where $F(\alpha; 1, n-3)$ is chosen from an F table for level of significance α, 1 numerator degree of freedom, and $n-3$ denominator degrees of freedom.

Of course, this hypothesis could be tested with a two-tailed t test as described in Section 4.2 because it involves only one coefficient. It can be shown that an F

---

[2]Optional section.

F I G U R E **4.12**

ANOVA Tables for Two Explanatory Variable Regression

(a) Standard ANOVA Table

Source of Variation	DF	SS
Regression	2	SSR
Error	$n - 3$	SSE
Total	$n - 1$	SST

(b) ANOVA with Conditional Sums of Squares Explained by Each Explanatory Variable

Source of Variation	DF	SS
Regression		
x_1	1	$SSR(x_1)$
$x_2 \mid x_1$	1	$SSR(x_2 \mid x_1)$
Error	$n - 3$	SSE
Total	$n - 1$	SST

statistic with 1 numerator degree of freedom is equal to the square of a t statistic, and that the F critical value will equal the square of a t critical value for appropriately chosen levels of significance and degrees of freedom, denoted df:

$$F(\alpha; 1, df) = t^2_{\alpha/2, df}$$

Therefore, the decision made will be the same regardless of which test is used. Because t statistics routinely appear on regression output, the t test is typically used when testing hypotheses about individual coefficients. The t test has additional advantages over the F test. The t test can be used to perform one-tailed hypothesis tests, while the F is restricted to the two-tailed test. It is also easier to test whether a coefficient is equal to some value other than zero by using a t test than it is using an F test.

The F test gains its advantage when testing whether a subset of coefficients are all equal to zero—for example, to test

$$H_0: \quad \beta_{L+1} = \cdots = \beta_K = 0$$

$$H_a: \quad \text{At least one } \beta_{L+1}, \ldots, \beta_K \text{ is not equal to zero}$$

for the general model presented earlier. In this case, the t test cannot be used. Even performing individual t tests on each coefficient may not provide as much information as performing the F test on the coefficients as a group.

F I G U R E **4.13**

Conditional Components of SSR as Provided by MINITAB Regression Output

SOURCE	DF	SEQ SS
x_1	1	$SSR(x_1)$
x_2	1	$SSR(x_2|x_1)$
.	.	.
.	.	.
.	.	.
x_L	1	$SSR(x_L|x_1,...,x_{L-1})$
x_{L+1}	1	$SSR(x_{L+1}|x_1,...,x_L)$
.	.	.
.	.	.
.	.	.
x_K	1	$SSR(x_K|x_1,...,x_{K-1})$

To test whether $\beta_{L+1}, \dots, \beta_K$ are all zero, the following F statistic is used:

$$F = \frac{SSR(x_{L+1}, \dots, x_K | x_1, x_2, \dots, x_L)/(K - L)}{SSE/(n - K - 1)}$$

$SSR(x_{L+1}, \dots, x_K | x_1, x_2, \dots, x_L)$ is the additional variation in y explained by $x_{L+1}, \dots, x_K$ given that $x_1, x_2, \dots, x_L$ are already in the model. The number of degrees of freedom associated with this conditional sum of squares is $K - L$, the number of coefficients to be included in the test. SSE is the error sum of squares from the model with all the variables included, and is divided by its degrees of freedom, $n - K - 1$. The conditional sum of squares can be computed as

$$SSR(x_{L+1}, \dots, x_K | x_1, x_2, \dots, x_L) =$$
$$SSR(x_{L+1}|x_1, x_2, \dots, x_L) + SSR(x_{L+2}|x_1, x_2, \dots, x_{L+1})$$
$$+ \cdots + SSR(x_K|x_1, x_2, \dots, x_{K-1})$$

The regression output from certain statistical packages will contain the necessary information to compute the conditional sums of squares. For example, in MINITAB, an additional sum of squares breakdown would be provided as in Figure 4.13. The table provides the conditional sums of squares for each of the variables, individually, given that the previous variables are in the model. By adding these sums of squares for appropriate individual variables, the conditional sum of squares for x_{L+1} through x_K is obtained. In the MINITAB output the conditional sums of squares are denoted SEQ SS for sequential sums of squares. This term is used to indicate that the sums of squares explained by each of the x variables when entered sequentially are represented.

The order in which the variables enter the regression is very important when using the conditional sums of squares to construct a partial F statistic. In MINITAB, for example, the explanatory variables whose coefficients are included in the null hypothesis must be the last ones listed in the REGR command. This ensures that the conditional sums of squares will be computed appropriately for the hypothesis to be tested.

A more extensive look at the use of these conditional sums of squares will be provided in the following example.

E X A M P L E **4.5** **Meddicorp (continued)**

Consider the problem posed in Example 4.4. In addition to BONUS and ADV, Meddicorp wants to consider the possibility that MKTSHR and COMPET are important in explaining the variation in sales. The MINITAB regression of SALES on ADV, BONUS, MKTSHR, and COMPET is shown in Figure 4.10.

The hypothesized population regression model is again

$$y_i = \beta_0 + \beta_1 x_{1i} + \beta_2 x_{2i} + \beta_3 x_{3i} + \beta_4 x_{4i} + e_i$$

Consider the test of the hypotheses

$$H_0: \quad \beta_3 = \beta_4 = 0$$

$H_a:$ At least one of the coefficients β_3 and β_4 is not equal to zero

The MINITAB regression output gives the conditional sums of squares explained by each variable. The regression sum of squares for the full regression is $SSR = 1,073,119$. The conditional sums of squares are as follows:

$$SSR(x_1) = 1,012,408$$
$$SSR(x_2|x_1) = 55,389$$
$$SSR(x_3|x_1, x_2) = 4394$$
$$SSR(x_4|x_1, x_2, x_3) = 927$$

The decision rule for the test is:

Reject H_0 if $F > 3.49$

Accept H_0 if $F \leq 3.49$

where 3.49 is the F critical value using a 5% level of significance with 2 and 20 degrees of freedom.

The test statistic, F, is

$$F = \frac{SSR(x_3, x_4|x_1, x_2)/2}{SSE/20}$$
$$= \frac{[SSR(x_4|x_1, x_2, x_3) + SSR(x_3|x_1, x_2)]/2}{SSE/20}$$
$$= \frac{(927 + 4394)/2}{175,855/20} = 0.303$$

F I G U R E 4.14

SAS Regression Output Showing the Partial F Test for the MKTSHR and COMPET Variables

```
Dependent Variable: SALES

                    Analysis of Variance

                    Sum of        Mean
Source      DF      Squares       Square      F Value    Prob>F

Model        4   1073118.542  268279.63549    30.511     0.0001
Error       20    175855.19803   8792.75990
C Total     24   1248973.74

        Root MSE       93.76972    R-square     0.8592
        Dep Mean     1269.02000    Adj R-sq     0.8310
        C.V.            7.38914

                    Parameter Estimates

                Parameter       Standard     T for H0:
Variable DF     Estimate         Error     Parameter=0   Prob > |T|

INTERCEP  1    -593.537452    259.19585077    -2.290       0.0330
ADV       1       2.513138      0.31427550     7.997       0.0001
BONUS     1       1.905948      0.74238560     2.567       0.0184
MKTSHR    1       2.651007      4.63565540     0.572       0.5738
COMPET    1      -0.120731      0.37181490    -0.325       0.7488


Dependent Variable: SALES
Test:   Numerator:    2660.6107   DF:   2   F value:   0.3026
        Denominator:   8792.76    DF:  20   Prob>F:    0.7422
```

The null hypothesis is accepted. The variables x_3 and x_4 do not significantly improve the model's ability to explain sales.

In SAS, tests of hypotheses concerning subsets of coefficients can be requested and SAS will compute the F statistic and its associated p value. The output is shown in Figure 4.14. The test statistic value is .303, as was previously computed, and the p value is 0.7422. Using the p-value decision rule the null hypothesis would be accepted at reasonable levels of significance. ▪

Exercises

3   Cost Control (continued)   Consider the cost data from Exercise 1 and the regression output in either Figure 4.6 or Figure 4.7. Consider this output to be for the full model

$$y_i = \beta_0 + \beta_1 x_{1i} + \beta_2 x_{2i} + \beta_3 x_{3i} + \beta_4 x_{4i} + e_i,$$

F I G U R E **4.15**

MINITAB Regression Output for Cost-Control Exercise 3

```
The regression equation is
cost = 59.4 + 0.949 paper + 2.39 machine

Predictor        Coef       Stdev     t-ratio        p
Constant        59.43       19.64        3.03    0.006
paper          0.9489      0.1101        8.62    0.000
machine        2.3864      0.2101       11.36    0.000

s = 10.98      R-sq = 99.9%      R-sq(adj) = 99.9%

Analysis of Variance

SOURCE        DF          SS          MS         F         p
Regression     2     2271227     1135613   9413.48    0.000
Error         24        2895         121
Total         26     2274122

SOURCE        DF      SEQ SS
paper          1     2255666
machine        1       15561

Unusual Observations
Obs.    paper       cost      Fit  Stdev.Fit   Residual   St.Resid
 25       647    1317.00  1293.83       2.59      23.17      2.17R

R denotes an obs. with a large st. resid.
```

where $y, x_1, x_2, x_3,$ and x_4 were defined in the first exercise.
Now consider the reduced model

$$y_i = \beta_0 + \beta_1 x_{1i} + \beta_2 x_{2i} + e_i$$

Conduct the test to compare these two models. State the hypotheses to be tested, the decision rule, the test statistic, and the decision. What conclusion can be drawn from the result of the test? The MINITAB and SAS regression outputs for the reduced model can be found in Figures 4.15 and 4.16, respectively. Use a 5% level of significance.

4 **Cost Control (continued)**   Now consider the SAS output in Figure 4.17. From the test result at the bottom of the output, find the F statistic for comparison of the full and reduced models. Compare this to the F statistic computed in Exercise 3.

Use the p-value decision rule with $\alpha = 0.05$ and conduct the test of full versus reduced models. State the hypotheses to be tested, the decision rule, the test statistic, and your decision. Which model should be chosen?

5 **Salaries (continued)**   Consider the salary data from Exercise 2 and the regression output in either Figure 4.8 or Figure 4.9. Consider this output to be for the full model

$$y_i = \beta_0 + \beta_1 x_{1i} + \beta_2 x_{2i} + \beta_3 x_{3i} + e_i,$$

where $y, x_1, x_2,$ and x_3 were defined in Exercise 2.
Now consider the reduced model

$$y_i = \beta_0 + \beta_1 x_{1i} + e_i$$

F I G U R E **4.16**

SAS Regression Output for Cost-Control Exercise 3

Dependent Variable: COST

Analysis of Variance

Source	DF	Sum of Squares	Mean Square	F Value	Prob>F
Model	2	2271226.7874	1135613.3937	9413.479	0.0001
Error	24	2895.28666	120.63694		
C Total	26	2274122.0741			

Root MSE	10.98349	R-square	0.9987	
Dep Mean	1497.18519	Adj R-sq	0.9986	
C.V.	0.73361			

Parameter Estimates

Variable	DF	Parameter Estimate	Standard Error	T for H0: Parameter=0	Prob > |T|
INTERCEP	1	59.431816	19.63883728	3.026	0.0058
PAPER	1	0.948883	0.11006005	8.622	0.0001
MACHINE	1	2.386442	0.21012138	11.357	0.0001

F I G U R E **4.17**

SAS Regression Output for Cost-Control Exercise 4

Dependent Variable: COST

Analysis of Variance

Source	DF	Sum of Squares	Mean Square	F Value	Prob>F
Model	4	2271423.3537	567855.83844	4629.168	0.0001
Error	22	2698.72033	122.66911		
C Total	26	2274122.0741			

Root MSE	11.07561	R-square	0.9988	
Dep Mean	1497.18519	Adj R-sq	0.9986	
C.V.	0.73976			

Parameter Estimates

Variable	DF	Parameter Estimate	Standard Error	T for H0: Parameter=0	Prob > |T|
INTERCEP	1	51.723142	21.70396993	2.383	0.0262
PAPER	1	0.947942	0.12002341	7.898	0.0001
MACHINE	1	2.471040	0.46556012	5.308	0.0001
OVERHEAD	1	0.048339	0.52500975	0.092	0.9275
LABOR	1	-0.050578	0.04029511	-1.255	0.2226

Test:	Numerator:	98.2832	DF:	2	F value:	0.8012
	Denominator:	122.6691	DF:	22	Prob>F:	0.4615

F I G U R E 4.18

MINITAB Regression Output for Salaries Exercise 5

```
The regression equation is
salary = 3819 + 128 educ

Predictor        Coef       Stdev    t-ratio        p
Constant       3818.6       377.4      10.12    0.000
educ           128.09       29.70       4.31    0.000

s = 650.1       R-sq = 17.0%    R-sq(adj) = 16.1%

Analysis of Variance

SOURCE         DF          SS          MS        F        p
Regression      1     7862535     7862535    18.60    0.000
Error          91    38460756      422646
Total          92    46323292

Unusual Observations
Obs.      educ      salary      Fit   Stdev.Fit   Residual   St.Resid
  1       12.0      3900.0     5355.6      69.1     -1455.6     -2.25R
  9       15.0      4440.0     5739.8     100.2     -1299.8     -2.02R
 91       12.0      6900.0     5355.6      69.1      1544.4      2.39R
 93       16.0      8100.0     5867.9     123.8      2232.1      3.50R

R denotes an obs. with a large st. resid.
```

Conduct the test to compare these two models. State the hypotheses to be tested, the decision rule, the test statistic, and the decision. What conclusion can be drawn from the result of the test? The MINITAB and SAS regression output for the reduced model can be found in Figures 4.18 and 4.19, respectively. Use a 5% level of significance.

6 **Salaries (continued)** Consider the SAS output in Figure 4.20. From the test results at the bottom of the output, find the F statistic for comparison of the full and reduced models. Compare this to the F statistic computed in Exercise 5.

Use the p-value decision rule with $\alpha = 0.05$ and conduct the test of full versus reduced models. State the hypotheses to be tested, the decision rule, the test statistic, and your decision. Which model should be chosen?

4.5
Prediction with a Multiple Regression Equation

As with simple regression, one of the possible goals of fitting a multiple regression equation is using it to predict values of the dependent variable. The two cases considered here are the same as in simple regression.

F I G U R E **4.19**
SAS Regression Output for Salaries Exercise 5

Dependent Variable: SALARY

Analysis of Variance

Source	DF	Sum of Squares	Mean Square	F Value	Prob>F
Model	1	7862534.2916	7862534.2916	18.603	0.0001
Error	91	38460756.031	422645.67067		
C Total	92	46323290.323			

Root MSE	650.11204	R-square	0.1697	
Dep Mean	5420.32258	Adj R-sq	0.1606	
C.V.	11.99397			

Parameter Estimates

Variable	DF	Parameter Estimate	Standard Error	T for H0: Parameter=0	Prob > |T|
INTERCEP	1	3818.559794	377.43765814	10.117	0.0001
EDUCAT	1	128.085932	29.69671216	4.313	0.0001

F I G U R E **4.20**
SAS Regression Output for Salaries Exercise 6

Dependent Variable: SALARY

Analysis of Variance

Source	DF	Sum of Squares	Mean Square	F Value	Prob>F
Model	3	13984436.814	4661478.9381	12.829	0.0001
Error	89	32338853.508	363357.90459		
C Total	92	46323290.323			

Root MSE	602.79176	R-square	0.3019	
Dep Mean	5420.32258	Adj R-sq	0.2784	
C.V.	11.12096			

Parameter Estimates

Variable	DF	Parameter Estimate	Standard Error	T for H0: Parameter=0	Prob > |T|
INTERCEP	1	3179.743949	383.48451825	8.292	0.0001
EDUCAT	1	139.618208	27.71635324	5.037	0.0001
EXPER	1	1.480699	0.69699668	2.124	0.0364
TIME	1	20.633372	6.15497008	3.352	0.0012

Test:	Numerator:3060951.2613	DF:	2	F value:	8.4241
	Denominator: 363357.9	DF:	89	Prob>F:	0.0004

4.5.1 Estimating the Conditional Mean of y Given $x_1, x_2, \ldots, x_K$

In this case, the goal is to estimate the point on the regression surface for specific values of the explanatory variables. For example, in the territorial sales problem (Example 4.1), consider the population regression equation

$$\mu_{y|x_1,x_2} = \beta_0 + \beta_1 x_1 + \beta_2 x_2,$$

where x_1 is ADV and x_2 is BONUS. The estimated regression equation from Figure 4.2 or 4.3 is

$$\hat{y} = -516.4 + 2.47x_1 + 1.86x_2$$

A point estimate of the conditional mean of y given x_1 and x_2 can be written as

$$\hat{y}_m = b_0 + b_1 x_1 + b_2 x_2$$

In the Meddicorp problem, the point estimate of the conditional mean of y given $x_1 = 500$ and $x_2 = 250$ is

$$\hat{y}_m = -516.4 + 2.47(500) + 1.86(250) = 1183.6$$

This is an estimate of average sales for *all* territories with advertising 500 and bonus 250. Confidence interval estimates also can be constructed. The formula for the standard deviation of $\hat{y}_m$, s_m, is omitted here because of its complexity.

Figure 4.21 shows the MINITAB output for this example. Here $\hat{y}_m$ = Fit, s_m = Stdev.Fit, and 95% C.I. shows the limits of the 95% confidence interval. (The difference in $\hat{y}_m$ computed by MINITAB and by hand is due to rounding. The MINITAB forecast, 1184.2, would be more accurate and, therefore, preferred.)

4.5.2 Predicting an Individual Value of y Given $x_1, x_2, \ldots, x_K$

Write the population regression for a single individual as

$$y_i = \beta_0 + \beta_1 x_{1i} + \beta_2 x_{2i} + e_i,$$

where e_i is the random disturbance. Denote the predicted value of y for an individual as $\hat{y}_p$. To predict the value of a dependent variable for a single individual, the point on the regression surface is used:

$$\hat{y}_p = b_0 + b_1 x_1 + b_2 x_2$$

As in simple regression, the point estimate of

$$\mu_{y|x_1,\ldots,x_K}$$

F I G U R E 4.21

Prediction in the Meddicorp Example Using MINITAB

```
The regression equation is
sales = - 516 + 2.47 adv + 1.86 bonus

Predictor        Coef        Stdev      t-ratio        p
Constant       -516.4        189.9        -2.72    0.013
adv            2.4732       0.2753         8.98    0.000
bonus          1.8562       0.7157         2.59    0.017

s = 90.75       R-sq = 85.5%       R-sq(adj) = 84.2%

Analysis of Variance

SOURCE        DF          SS          MS        F        p
Regression     2     1067797      533899    64.83    0.000
Error         22      181176        8235
Total         24     1248974

SOURCE        DF      SEQ SS
adv            1     1012408
bonus          1       55389


      Fit   Stdev.Fit       95% C.I.              95% P.I.
   1184.2        25.2   ( 1131.8,  1236.6)  (  988.8,  1379.6)
```

and the point prediction for an individual are the same. But the standard error of the prediction, s_p, is larger than the standard error of the forecast, s_m. Thus, the prediction interval will be wider than the confidence interval, reflecting the greater uncertainty in predicting for individuals than in estimating a conditional mean.

MINITAB produces a 95% prediction interval as shown in Figure 4.21. Note that the forecast standard error, s_m, also is printed. If the prediction standard error is desired, it can be computed using the relationship

$$s_p^2 = s_m^2 + s_e^2,$$

where s_e^2 is the *MSE* of the regression.

4.6
Lagged Variables as Explanatory Variables in Time-Series Regression

When using time-series data, it is possible to relate values of the dependent variable in the current time period to explanatory variable values in the current time period. For example, sales for a firm in the current month can be related to advertising expenditures in the current month. It may be, however, that sales in the current month are not affected as much by advertising expenditures in the current month as

T A B L E **4.5**

Creation of Lagged Values of the Explanatory Variables

i	x_i	x_{i-1}	x_{i-2}
1	4	*	*
2	7	4	*
3	8	7	4
4	10	8	7
5	11	10	8
6	9	11	10
7	15	9	11
8	16	15	9

* Indicates a missing value

by advertising expenditures from the previous month or from two months ago. This fact can be incorporated into a time-series regression. To illustrate, let y_i represent sales in time period i, x_i represent advertising expenditures in time period i, x_{i-1} represent advertising expenditures in time period $i - 1$, and so on. Then a possible model for sales could be written

$$y_i = \beta_0 + \beta_1 x_i + \beta_2 x_{i-1} + \beta_3 x_{i-2} + e_i$$

Here sales are modeled as a function of advertising expenditures in the current month and the two previous months.

The variables x_{i-1} and x_{i-2} are called *lagged variables.* Any lags felt to be appropriate may be used. Here the one- and two-period lags are used. Some caution must be exercised, however, because including several such lagged variables may result in multicollinearity problems (discussed in Chapter 5).

When lagged variables are used, a certain number of data points in the initial time periods will be lost. This is illustrated in Table 4.5. Note that no value can be computed for x_{i-1} in time period 1. No prior time period exists from which to take this value. For the same reason, no value for the first or second time period can be computed from x_{i-2}. These time periods will have to be omitted from the analysis, reducing the effective sample size from eight to six in the example.

Lagged values of the dependent variable also can be used as explanatory variables. Consider again the sales example. Now, however, assume that no information on advertising is available. Sales in the current month will be modeled simply as a function of sales in the previous month:

$$y_i = \beta_0 + \beta_1 y_{i-1} + e_i$$

The data are illustrated in Table 4.6. Of course, further lags can be used if desired. One observation will be lost for each lag.

T A B L E 4.6

Creation of Lagged Values of the Dependent Variables

i	y_i	y_{i-1}
1	22	*
2	24	22
3	27	24
4	35	27
5	38	35
6	42	38
7	47	42
8	50	47

* Indicates a missing value

Note that the model with the lagged value of the dependent variable as an explanatory variable may be viewed as an extrapolative time-series model. We are using only past information from the series itself to help describe the behavior of the series and, possibly, to forecast future values.

It should be noted, however, that regressions that include lagged dependent variable values are still sometimes interpreted as causal relationships. For example, the one-period lagged value of sales might be included along with the current and lagged values of advertising:

$$y_i = \beta_0 + \beta_1 y_{i-1} + \beta_2 x_i + \beta_3 x_{i-1} + e_i$$

If it is believed that last month's sales might help to generate new sales in the current month or to maintain sales, then this model could be justified as causal.

In the economics literature, a model with lagged values of the dependent variable (and possible lagged values of other explanatory variables) might be called an *adaptive expectations model* or a *partial adjustment model* (see, for example, G. G. Judge et al., *The Theory and Practice of Econometrics*, pp. 379–380). For alternatives to regression analysis useful in analyzing time-series data, see J. D. Cryer, *Time Series Analysis*; N. R. Farnum and L. W. Stanton, *Quantitative Forecasting Methods*; or B. L. Bowerman and R. T. O'Connel, *Time Series Forecasting: An Applied Approach*.[3]

E X A M P L E 4.6 **Unemployment Rate**

Table 4.7 lists the monthly unemployment rates from January 1975 through December 1993. (These data were obtained from *Business Statistics* and *Survey of Current Business*, both

---

[3] See References for complete publication information.

T A B L E **4.7**
Data for Unemployment Rate Example

Month	Rate	Month	Rate	Month	Rate	Month	Rate
1/75	8.1	6/78	5.9	11/81	8.3	4/85	7.3
2/75	8.1	7/78	6.2	12/81	8.5	5/85	7.2
3/75	8.6	8/78	5.9	1/82	8.6	6/85	7.3
4/75	8.8	9/78	6.0	2/82	8.9	7/85	7.3
5/75	9.0	10/78	5.8	3/82	9.0	8/85	7.1
6/75	8.8	11/78	5.9	4/82	9.3	9/85	7.1
7/75	8.6	12/78	6.0	5/82	9.4	10/85	7.1
8/75	8.4	1/79	5.9	6/82	9.6	11/85	7.0
9/75	8.4	2/79	5.9	7/82	9.8	12/85	7.0
10/75	8.4	3/79	5.8	8/82	9.8	1/86	6.8
11/75	8.3	4/79	5.8	9/82	10.1	2/86	7.2
12/75	8.2	5/79	5.6	10/82	10.4	3/86	7.2
1/76	7.9	6/79	5.7	11/82	10.8	4/86	7.1
2/76	7.7	7/79	5.7	12/82	10.8	5/86	7.2
3/76	7.6	8/79	6.0	1/83	10.4	6/86	7.1
4/76	7.7	9/79	5.9	2/83	10.4	7/86	7.0
5/76	7.4	10/79	6.0	3/83	10.3	8/86	6.8
6/76	7.6	11/79	5.9	4/83	10.2	9/86	7.0
7/76	7.8	12/79	6.0	5/83	10.1	10/86	6.9
8/76	7.8	1/80	6.3	6/83	10.1	11/86	6.9
9/76	7.6	2/80	6.3	7/83	9.4	12/86	6.7
10/76	7.7	3/80	6.3	8/83	9.4	1/87	6.6
11/76	7.8	4/80	6.9	9/83	9.2	2/87	6.6
12/76	7.8	5/80	7.5	10/83	8.8	3/87	6.6
1/77	7.5	6/80	7.6	11/83	8.5	4/87	6.3
2/77	7.6	7/80	7.8	12/83	8.3	5/87	6.3
3/77	7.4	8/80	7.7	1/84	8.1	6/87	6.2
4/77	7.2	9/80	7.5	2/84	7.8	7/87	6.1
5/77	7.0	10/80	7.5	3/84	7.8	8/87	6.0
6/77	7.2	11/80	7.5	4/84	7.7	9/87	5.9
7/77	6.9	12/80	7.2	5/84	7.4	10/87	6.0
8/77	7.0	1/81	7.5	6/84	7.2	11/87	5.8
9/77	6.8	2/81	7.4	7/84	7.4	12/87	5.7
10/77	6.8	3/81	7.4	8/84	7.5	1/88	5.7
11/77	6.8	4/81	7.2	9/84	7.3	2/88	5.7
12/77	6.4	5/81	7.5	10/84	7.3	3/88	5.7
1/78	6.4	6/81	7.5	11/84	7.2	4/88	5.3
2/78	6.3	7/81	7.2	12/84	7.3	5/88	5.6
3/78	6.3	8/81	7.4	1/85	7.4	6/88	5.4
4/78	6.1	9/81	7.6	2/85	7.3	7/88	5.4
5/78	6.0	10/81	7.9	3/85	7.2	8/88	5.6

T A B L E 4.7 (*Cont.*)

Data for Unemployment Rate Example

Month	Rate	Month	Rate	Month	Rate	Month	Rate
9/88	5.5	1/90	5.5	5/91	7.1	9/92	7.5
10/88	5.5	2/90	5.4	6/91	7.2	10/92	7.4
11/88	5.5	3/90	5.4	7/91	7.1	11/92	7.3
12/88	5.3	4/90	5.6	8/91	7.1	12/92	7.3
1/89	5.5	5/90	5.5	9/91	7.0	1/93	7.1
2/89	5.2	6/90	5.3	10/91	7.1	2/93	7.0
3/89	5.1	7/90	5.5	11/91	7.2	3/93	7.0
4/89	5.3	8/90	5.8	12/91	7.4	4/93	7.0
5/89	5.2	9/90	5.9	1/92	7.1	5/93	6.9
6/89	5.3	10/90	6.0	2/92	7.3	6/93	6.9
7/89	5.4	11/90	6.3	3/92	7.3	7/93	6.8
8/89	5.4	12/90	6.3	4/92	7.3	8/93	6.7
9/89	5.5	1/91	6.5	5/92	7.4	9/93	6.7
10/89	5.4	2/91	6.8	6/92	7.7	10/93	6.7
11/89	5.5	3/91	7.1	7/92	7.6	11/93	6.5
12/89	5.4	4/91	6.9	8/92	7.6	12/93	6.4

F I G U R E 4.22

MINITAB Time-Series Plot of the Unemployment Rate

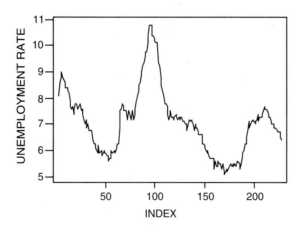

publications of the U.S. Department of Commerce, Bureau of Economic Analysis.) The data in Table 4.7 have been seasonally adjusted.

In Figure 4.22, the MINITAB time-series plot of the unemployment rate is shown. The horizontal axis in this plot is an index that numbers each month from 1 to 228.

F I G U R E 4.23

MINITAB Regression Output for Regression of Unemployment on One-Period Lagged Unemployment

```
The regression equation is
unemp = 0.0800 + 0.988 unempl1

227 cases used 1 cases contain missing values

Predictor       Coef       Stdev      t-ratio      p
Constant      0.08004     0.07295       1.10     0.274
unempl1       0.98768     0.01012      97.63     0.000

s = 0.1888     R-sq = 97.7%     R-sq(adj) = 97.7%

Analysis of Variance

SOURCE        DF        SS         MS         F         p
Regression     1      339.91     339.91    9531.01    0.000
Error        225        8.02       0.04
Total        226      347.94

Unusual Observations
Obs.   unempl1     unemp       Fit   Stdev.Fit   Residual   St.Resid
  3       8.1      8.6000    8.0802    0.0161      0.5198      2.76R
 36       6.8      6.4000    6.7963    0.0129     -0.3963     -2.10R
 64       6.3      6.9000    6.3024    0.0149      0.5976      3.17R
 65       6.9      7.5000    6.8950    0.0127      0.6050      3.21R
 83       7.9      8.3000    7.8827    0.0149      0.4173      2.22R
 94      10.1     10.4000   10.0556    0.0328      0.3444      1.85 X
 95      10.4     10.8000   10.3519    0.0356      0.4481      2.42RX
 96      10.8     10.8000   10.7470    0.0394      0.0530      0.29 X
 97      10.8     10.4000   10.7470    0.0394     -0.3470     -1.88 X
 98      10.4     10.4000   10.3519    0.0356      0.0481      0.26 X
 99      10.4     10.3000   10.3519    0.0356     -0.0519     -0.28 X
100      10.3     10.2000   10.2531    0.0347     -0.0531     -0.29 X
101      10.2     10.1000   10.1544    0.0337     -0.0544     -0.29 X
102      10.1     10.1000   10.0556    0.0328      0.0444      0.24 X
103      10.1      9.4000   10.0556    0.0328     -0.6556     -3.53RX
134       6.8      7.2000    6.7963    0.0129      0.4037      2.14R
160       5.7      5.3000    5.7098    0.0189     -0.4098     -2.18R

R denotes an obs. with a large st. resid.
X denotes an obs. whose X value gives it large influence.
```

In Figure 4.23, the MINITAB regression of the unemployment rate on the one-period lagged unemployment rate is shown. The regression for SAS is shown in Figure 4.24.

The one-period lagged variable is denoted UNEMPL1. Note that the first entry in the column for this variable will be missing (see Figure 4.23, line 3), as discussed in the creation of Table 4.6. In any subsequent analyses involving UNEMPL1 there will be one less observation than the total time-series length because missing cases will not be used.

The regression of the monthly unemployment rate on the previous month's rate obviously produces a good fit. The t value for UNEMPL1 is 97.63 (with p value $= 0.000$), resulting in rejection of the hypothesis H_0: $\beta_1 = 0$. Also, 97.7% of the variation in unemployment rate has been explained by the regression.

F I G U R E   **4.24**

SAS Regression Output for Regression of Unemployment on One-Period Lagged Unemployment

```
Dependent Variable: UNEMP

                          Analysis of Variance

                            Sum of          Mean
Source            DF        Squares         Square      F Value      Prob>F

Model              1       339.91281      339.91281    9531.013      0.0001
Error            225         8.02437        0.03566
C Total          226       347.93718


        Root MSE       0.18885      R-square      0.9769
        Dep Mean       7.09648      Adj R-sq      0.9768
        C.V.           2.66116

                          Parameter Estimates

                    Parameter      Standard      T for H0:
Variable    DF       Estimate         Error     Parameter=0    Prob > |T|

INTERCEP     1       0.080040      0.07295472       1.097         0.2738
UNEMPL1      1       0.987679      0.01011687      97.627         0.0001
```

Now consider adding a two-period lagged variable, UNEMPL2, to the equation. The MINITAB regression of unemployment on UNEMPL1 and UNEMPL2 is shown in Figure 4.25, with the SAS regression in Figure 4.26. The regression model can now be written

$$y_i = \beta_0 + \beta_1 y_{i-1} + \beta_2 y_{i-2} + e_i$$

To test whether the two-period lag is of any importance in the model the following hypotheses should be tested:

$$H_0: \quad \beta_2 = 0$$
$$H_a: \quad \beta_2 \neq 0$$

The test statistic value is -1.71 (or p value $= 0.088$). At a 5% level of significance the decision rule for the test is:

$$\text{Reject } H_0 \quad \text{if} \quad t > 1.96 \text{ or } t < -1.96$$
$$\text{Accept } H_0 \quad \text{if} \quad -1.96 \leq t \leq 1.96$$

The z value of 1.96 is used because a large number of degrees of freedom are available (223). The null hypothesis is accepted, suggesting that the two-period lagged variable is not useful in explaining any of the additional variation in unemployment rates. (Note that the hypothesis would be rejected at the 10% level of significance, however, since the critical value would be $z = 1.645$).

A three-period lagged variable was created and included in the regressions shown in Figures 4.27 and 4.28. The three-period lagged variable is significant at the 5% level. You can conduct

F I G U R E 4.25

MINITAB Regression Output for Regression of Unemployment on One- and Two-Period Lagged Unemployment

```
The regression equation is
unemp = 0.0898 + 1.10 unempl1 - 0.114 unempl2

226 cases used 2 cases contain missing values

Predictor       Coef      Stdev    t-ratio       p
Constant      0.08981    0.07307      1.23    0.220
unempl1       1.10024    0.06657     16.53    0.000
unempl2      -0.11384    0.06651     -1.71    0.088

s = 0.1885     R-sq = 97.7%     R-sq(adj) = 97.7%

Analysis of Variance

SOURCE          DF         SS        MS         F        p
Regression       2     339.01    169.50   4772.66    0.000
Error          223       7.92      0.04
Total          225     346.93

SOURCE          DF     SEQ SS
unempl1          1     338.90
unempl2          1       0.10

Unusual Observations
Obs.   unempl1      unemp       Fit   Stdev.Fit   Residual    St.Resid
  3        8.1     8.6000    8.0797      0.0161     0.5203        2.77R
  4        8.6     8.8000    8.6298      0.0381     0.1702        0.92 X
 36        6.8     6.4000    6.7974      0.0129    -0.3974       -2.11R
 64        6.3     6.9000    6.3042      0.0150     0.5958        3.17R
 65        6.9     7.5000    6.9643      0.0425     0.5357        2.92RX
 66        7.5     7.6000    7.5561      0.0422     0.0439        0.24 X
 83        7.9     8.3000    7.9166      0.0248     0.3834        2.05R
 95       10.4    10.8000   10.3826      0.0400     0.4174        2.27RX
 96       10.8    10.8000   10.7885      0.0464     0.0115        0.06 X
 97       10.8    10.4000   10.7430      0.0395    -0.3430       -1.86 X
 98       10.4    10.4000   10.3029      0.0456     0.0971        0.53 X
103       10.1     9.4000   10.0525      0.0329    -0.6525       -3.52R
104        9.4     9.4000    9.2823      0.0545     0.1177        0.65 X
134        6.8     7.2000    6.7746      0.0180     0.4254        2.27R
160        5.7     5.3000    5.7123      0.0190    -0.4123       -2.20R

R denotes an obs. with a large st. resid.
X denotes an obs. whose X value gives it large influence.
```

the hypothesis test to verify this using either the *t* value or the associated *p* value. Note that although the three-period lagged variable is significant, the resulting increase in R^2 is relatively small (from 97.7% to 97.9% or only .2%).

Obviously, this process of lagging the dependent variable can be continued for additional lags if desired. However, the use of continued lagged values as explanatory variables is questionable in this problem. The increases in R^2 due to the addition of variables is very small after the first lag. A regression using the one- and three-period lagged variables might be the best

F I G U R E 4.26

SAS Regression Output for Regression of Unemployment on One- and Two-Period Lagged Unemployment

Dependent Variable: UNEMP

Analysis of Variance

Source	DF	Sum of Squares	Mean Square	F Value	Prob>F
Model	2	339.00574	169.50287	4772.662	0.0001
Error	223	7.91993	0.03552		
C Total	225	346.92566			

Root MSE	0.18846	R-square	0.9772	
Dep Mean	7.09204	Adj R-sq	0.9770	
C.V.	2.65728			

Parameter Estimates

Variable	DF	Parameter Estimate	Standard Error	T for H0: Parameter=0	Prob > |T|
INTERCEP	1	0.089814	0.07307398	1.229	0.2203
UNEMPL1	1	1.100243	0.06656941	16.528	0.0001
UNEMPL2	1	-0.113840	0.06650913	-1.712	0.0884

model choice among the alternatives examined (or, for the sake of simplicity, perhaps using only the one-period lagged variable).

If additional lags are examined, problems can arise. For example, the lagged variables are highly correlated among themselves producing problems (discussed in Chapter 5, see Section 5.9, Multicollinearity). Also, for each additional lag used, one data point is lost. Since there were originally 228 monthly observations on unemployment this loss is not a substantial part of the data set. However, in smaller data sets the loss could be significant. ■

Exercises

7 Silver Prices Table 4.8 shows the monthly price of silver per ounce in dollars from January 1983 to December 1992. (These figures were obtained from *Business Statistics* and *Survey of Current Business*.) Figure 4.29 provides the MINITAB time-series plot of these prices. The following model is used to forecast silver prices:

$$\text{SILVER}_i = \beta_0 + \beta_1 \text{SILVER}_{i-1} + e_i,$$

where SILVER_i is the price of silver at time i and SILVER_{i-1} is the price at time $i - 1$. The MINITAB regression output is shown in Figure 4.30 and the SAS output is in

F I G U R E 4.27

MINITAB Regression Output for Regression of Unemployment on One- and Three-Period Lagged Unemployment

```
The regression equation is
unemp = 0.116 + 1.13 unempl1 - 0.148 unempl3

225 cases used 3 cases contain missing values

Predictor        Coef      Stdev    t-ratio       p
Constant      0.11555    0.07091       1.63   0.105
unempl1       1.13108    0.04349      26.00   0.000
unempl3      -0.14846    0.04340      -3.42   0.001

s = 0.1821    R-sq = 97.9%    R-sq(adj) = 97.8%

Analysis of Variance

SOURCE         DF          SS         MS          F        p
Regression      2      337.28     168.64    5084.18    0.000
Error         222        7.36       0.03
Total         224      344.64

SOURCE         DF      SEQ SS
unempl1         1      336.89
unempl3         1        0.39

Unusual Observations
Obs.   unempl1      unemp       Fit   Stdev.Fit   Residual   St.Resid
  36       6.8     6.4000    6.7973      0.0125    -0.3973     -2.19R
  64       6.3     6.9000    6.3060      0.0145     0.5940      3.27R
  65       6.9     7.5000    6.9847      0.0295     0.5153      2.87R
  66       7.5     7.6000    7.6633      0.0538    -0.0633     -0.36 X
  95      10.4    10.8000   10.4238      0.0416     0.3762      2.12RX
  96      10.8    10.8000   10.8317      0.0469    -0.0317     -0.18 X
  97      10.8    10.4000   10.7872      0.0408    -0.3872     -2.18RX
  98      10.4    10.4000   10.2754      0.0400     0.1246      0.70 X
  99      10.4    10.3000   10.2754      0.0400     0.0246      0.14 X
 103      10.1     9.4000   10.0251      0.0325    -0.6251     -3.49R
 104       9.4     9.4000    9.2482      0.0411     0.1518      0.86 X
 105       9.4     9.2000    9.2482      0.0411    -0.0482     -0.27 X
 134       6.8     7.2000    6.7676      0.0147     0.4324      2.38R
 160       5.7     5.3000    5.7165      0.0184    -0.4165     -2.30R

R denotes an obs. with a large st. resid.
X denotes an obs. whose X value gives it large influence.
```

Figure 4.31. Note that SILVERL1 in the output represents the variable of silver prices lagged one time period. Use the outputs to answer the following questions:

a What is the estimated regression equation?

b Is there a relationship between current and previous period silver prices? State the hypotheses to be tested, the decision rule, the test statistic, and your decision. Use a 5% level of significance.

c What percent of the variation in silver prices has been explained by the regression?

d Use the estimated equation to produce a forecast of the price of silver in January 1993. Find out what the actual price of silver was and compare it to the forecast. How

F I G U R E **4.28**

SAS Regression Output for Regression of Unemployment on One- and Three-Period Lagged Unemployment

Dependent Variable: UNEMP

Analysis of Variance

Source	DF	Sum of Squares	Mean Square	F Value	Prob>F
Model	2	337.27800	168.63900	5084.179	0.0001
Error	222	7.36360	0.03317		
C Total	224	344.64160			

Root MSE	0.18212	R-square	0.9786	
Dep Mean	7.08533	Adj R-sq	0.9784	
C.V.	2.57044			

Parameter Estimates

Variable	DF	Parameter Estimate	Standard Error	T for H0: Parameter=0	Prob > |T|
INTERCEP	1	0.115551	0.07091229	1.629	0.1046
UNEMPL1	1	1.131077	0.04349488	26.005	0.0001
UNEMPL3	1	-0.148462	0.04340294	-3.421	0.0007

T A B L E **4.8**

Data for Silver Price Example

Month	Price	Month	Price	Month	Price	Month	Price
1/83	12.396	9/84	7.263	5/86	5.115	1/88	6.732
2/83	13.964	10/84	7.317	6/86	5.153	2/88	6.325
3/83	10.619	11/84	7.488	7/86	5.049	3/88	6.413
4/83	11.694	12/84	6.694	8/86	5.218	4/88	6.478
5/83	12.976	1/85	6.098	9/86	5.683	5/88	6.543
6/83	11.749	2/85	6.069	10/86	5.667	6/88	7.037
7/83	12.088	3/85	6.014	11/86	5.596	7/88	7.146
8/83	12.096	4/85	6.458	12/86	5.364	8/88	6.708
9/83	11.915	5/85	6.280	1/87	5.529	9/88	6.365
10/83	9.841	6/85	6.172	2/87	5.488	10/88	6.285
11/83	8.837	7/85	6.104	3/87	5.682	11/88	6.275
12/83	9.121	8/85	6.247	4/87	7.428	12/88	6.108
1/84	8.182	9/85	6.054	5/87	8.439	1/89	5.972
2/84	9.126	10/85	6.188	6/87	7.411	2/89	5.891
3/84	9.651	11/85	6.134	7/87	7.678	3/89	5.930
4/84	9.220	12/85	5.888	8/87	7.847	4/89	5.791
5/84	8.972	1/86	6.053	9/87	7.590	5/89	5.447
6/84	8.744	2/86	5.874	10/87	7.562	6/89	5.280
7/84	7.416	3/86	5.639	11/87	6.662	7/89	5.236
8/84	7.613	4/86	5.229	12/87	6.790	8/89	5.179

T A B L E **4.8** *(Cont.)*

Data for Silver Price Example

Month	Price	Month	Price	Month	Price	Month	Price
9/89	5.133	7/90	4.859	5/91	4.040	3/92	4.100
10/89	5.133	8/90	4.982	6/91	4.390	4/92	4.030
11/89	5.465	9/90	4.790	7/91	4.300	5/92	4.070
12/89	5.533	10/90	4.366	8/91	3.940	6/92	4.060
1/90	5.243	11/90	4.169	9/91	4.030	7/92	3.950
2/90	5.278	12/90	4.068	10/91	4.100	8/92	3.800
3/90	5.058	1/91	4.028	11/91	4.060	9/92	3.760
4/90	5.046	2/91	3.723	12/91	3.910	10/92	3.740
5/90	5.074	3/91	3.960	1/92	4.120	11/92	3.760
6/90	4.906	4/91	3.970	2/92	4.140	12/92	3.720

F I G U R E **4.29**

MINITAB Time-Series Plot of Silver Prices

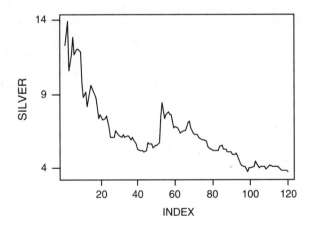

well did the equation do? Repeat this process for the remainder of 1993. Discuss any difficulties you encounter in forecasting for more than one month ahead.

These data are available on the data disk for any further analysis desired. In MINITAB, they can be read using

```
READ 'SILVER4' C1
```

In SAS, the data can be read from the file SILVER4.DAT using

```
INPUT SILVER;
```

F I G U R E **4.30**

MINITAB Regression Output for Silver Prices Exercise 7

```
The regression equation is
silver = 0.297 + 0.941 silver11

119 cases used 1 cases contain missing values

Predictor        Coef        Stdev      t-ratio        p
Constant       0.2973       0.1528         1.95    0.054
silver11       0.94146      0.02281       41.27    0.000

s = 0.5503      R-sq = 93.6%      R-sq(adj) = 93.5%

Analysis of Variance

SOURCE          DF           SS           MS         F         p
Regression       1        515.81       515.81   1703.34    0.000
Error          117         35.43         0.30
Total          118        551.24

Unusual Observations
Obs. silver11      silver        Fit   Stdev.Fit    Residual    St.Resid
   2     12.4     13.9640    11.9677      0.1474      1.9963      3.77RX
   3     14.0     10.6190    13.4439      0.1814     -2.8249     -5.44RX
   4     10.6     11.6940    10.2947      0.1102      1.3993      2.60R
   5     11.7     12.9760    11.3068      0.1325      1.6692      3.13RX
   6     13.0     11.7490    12.5138      0.1599     -0.7648     -1.45 X
   7     11.7     12.0880    11.3586      0.1336      0.7294      1.37 X
   8     12.1     12.0960    11.6777      0.1408      0.4183      0.79 X
   9     12.1     11.9150    11.6853      0.1410      0.2297      0.43 X
  10     11.9      9.8410    11.5149      0.1371     -1.6739     -3.14RX
  14      8.2      9.1260     8.0004      0.0659      1.1256      2.06R
  19      8.7      7.4160     8.5295      0.0748     -1.1135     -2.04R
  52      5.7      7.4280     5.6467      0.0525      1.7813      3.25R
  53      7.4      8.4390     7.2905      0.0564      1.1485      2.10R
```

R denotes an obs. with a large st. resid.
X denotes an obs. whose X value gives it large influence.

4.7
Using the Computer

4.7.1 MINITAB

Multiple Regression

```
REGR C1 K C_, . . . , C_       (STAT: REGRESSION: REGRESSION)
```

The dependent (y) variable data values are listed in the first column shown (C1 in this example) and the independent variables are listed in the K subsequent columns (which have not been numbered here). The K in the command tells MINITAB that K independent variables are to be used.

F I G U R E 4.31

SAS Regression Output for Silver Prices Exercise 7

```
Dependent Variable: SILVER

                        Analysis of Variance

                        Sum of          Mean
    Source      DF      Squares         Square      F Value     Prob>F

    Model        1      515.81106      515.81106    1703.335    0.0001
    Error      117       35.43043        0.30282
    C Total    118      551.24149


         Root MSE        0.55029     R-square        0.9357
         Dep Mean        6.25196     Adj R-sq        0.9352
         C.V.            8.80196

                        Parameter Estimates

                     Parameter      Standard     T for H0:
    Variable   DF     Estimate         Error    Parameter=0    Prob > |T|

    INTERCEP    1     0.297328     0.15284412        1.945       0.0541
    SILVERL1    1     0.941463     0.02281148       41.271       0.0001
```

With new versions of MINITAB, choice of dependent and independent variables are requested by menu, in which case the number of independent variables need not be specified.

Forecasting with the Multiple Regression Equation

```
REGR C1 1 C2 C3;
PRED E1 E2.
```

The PREDICT (PRED) subcommand is used to generate confidence intervals for the estimate of a conditional mean and prediction intervals for predictions of individual values. The example here is for a regression with two explanatory variables. The values E1 and E2 in the PREDICT subcommand are used for the two explanatory variables (in the order given in the REGR command). E1 and E2 can be either single numbers or columns of numbers if forecasts for several different values of the *x* variables are desired.

New versions of MINITAB work in a similar manner, with choices made through menus.

Creating a Lagged Variable (STAT: TIME SERIES)

In MINITAB, to create a new variable that contains the one-period lagged values of the variable in C1, use the following command:

```
LAG 1 C1 C2
```

A two-period lagged variable is created by replacing the 1 in the command with 2. Further lags can be created in a similar manner.

4.7.2 SAS

Multiple Regression

The following command sequence will produce the regression results in Figure 4.3:

```
PROC REG;
  MODEL SALES=ADV BONUS;
```

The dependent variable (SALES) is listed first; the independent variables (ADV and BONUS) follow the equal sign.

Partial *F* Tests in Multiple Regression

The TEST command in SAS will produce the partial F statistic for testing whether several coefficients are equal to zero. The following command sequence illustrates the use of the TEST command:

```
PROC REG;
  MODEL SALES=ADV BONUS MKTSHR COMPET;
  TEST MKTSHR COMPET;
```

This sequence will produce the output in Figure 4.14. The coefficients of MKTSHR and COMPET are those in the null hypothesis.

When the SAS TEST command is used, the explanatory variables in the MODEL command do not have to be listed in any particular order. For example, the following command sequence will produce the same test result as the previous sequence:

```
PROC REG;
  MODEL SALES=ADV MKTSHR BONUS COMPET;
  TEST MKTSHR COMPET;
```

Forecasting with the Multiple Regression Equation

Forecasts in SAS for multiple regression are generated using an "appended" data set just as with simple regression. To the values of the independent variables in the original data set, add the values for which predictions are desired. Then to the values of dependent variables add '.' (SAS for missing data), since we do not know those values. Now rerun the regression as follows:

```
PROC REG;
  MODEL SALES=ADV BONUS/P CLM CLI;
```

The option P requests forecasts (or predicted values), CLM requests upper and lower confidence interval limits for the estimate of the conditional mean, and CLI requests upper and lower prediction interval limits for an individual prediction.

Creating a Lagged Variable

In the data input phase in SAS use the LAG_ command to create lagged variables. For example, to create a one-period lagged variable for the unemployment variable in Example 4.6, use

```
UNEMPL1=LAG1(UNEMP);
```

For a two-period lagged variable use

```
UNEMPL2=LAG2(UNEMP);
```

Additional Exercises

8   **Wheat Exports**   The relationship between exchange rates and agricultural exports is of interest to agricultural economists. One such export of interest is wheat. Table 4.9 lists data on the following variables:

y, U.S. wheat export shipments (SHIPMENT)
x_1, the real index of weighted-average exchange rates of the U.S. dollar (EXCRATE)
x_2, the per-bushel real price of no. 1 red winter wheat (PRICE)

The dependent variable is U.S. wheat export shipments. The explanatory variables are exchange rate and price. The MINITAB and SAS regression outputs are shown in Figures 4.32 and 4.33, respectively. Use the outputs to answer the questions.

a   What is the estimated regression equation relating SHIPMENT to EXCRATE and PRICE?

b   Test the overall fit of the regression. State the hypotheses to be tested, the decision rule, the test statistic, and your decision. Use a 5% level of significance. What conclusion can be drawn from the result of the test?

c   After taking account of the effect of PRICE, are SHIPMENT and EXCRATE related? Conduct a hypothesis test to answer this question and use a 5% level of significance. State the hypotheses to be tested, the decision rule, the test statistic, and your decision. What conclusion can be drawn from the result of the test?

d   What percentage of the variation in the dependent variable has been explained by the regression?

T A B L E   4.9

Data for Wheat Export Exercise

SHIPMENT	EXCRATE	PRICE	SHIPMENT	EXCRATE	PRICE
2264	104.142	0.675969	1810	108.539	0.230318
1983	101.705	0.684394	2098	108.313	0.223497
1787	97.857	0.593693	2277	106.419	0.232193
1519	97.813	0.479903	2543	107.189	0.228678
1500	96.250	0.421644	3011	108.054	0.237409
1556	97.757	0.463543	1881	106.701	0.246300
2256	98.164	0.499162	1567	104.882	0.264202
2503	99.703	0.488550	2378	102.368	0.270112
2346	100.450	0.491222	1764	100.715	0.266093
2495	99.725	0.548979	2576	100.118	0.269372
2676	101.497	0.530823	2870	98.637	0.285304
2247	96.896	0.522932	2811	98.386	0.297034
2951	95.162	0.459886	3268	100.022	0.279991
1957	93.528	0.426019	2965	97.929	0.282057
1774	92.920	0.407098	2888	95.475	0.282499
2099	94.951	0.394918	3590	92.913	0.282695
1778	94.723	0.361930	3255	92.346	0.287967
2111	94.600	0.346000	3144	88.609	0.298474
2721	98.184	0.390863	2514	91.297	0.299235
3033	101.109	0.437014	2450	90.805	0.292863
3428	102.870	0.441748	1916	90.001	0.294996
3368	102.639	0.424429	1826	90.129	0.295454
3228	102.567	0.387923	2056	90.069	0.292349
2516	103.561	0.374701	2096	91.132	0.288898
2506	104.059	0.376692	2131	91.706	0.291523
1974	104.547	0.399818	2847	90.650	0.338378
2105	106.535	0.397904	3627	88.004	0.348430
2099	108.225	0.378107	3206	87.986	0.333526
1845	108.547	0.366381	3528	87.483	0.340297
1818	108.955	0.374828	4056	88.498	0.344550
2330	108.707	0.362312	2963	88.730	0.341522
3081	108.143	0.323255	3127	86.734	0.342148
3004	107.990	0.304265	2250	86.010	0.329736
2736	108.605	0.279868	2436	86.687	0.319842
1478	108.894	0.268899	2578	90.213	0.298573
1561	108.600	0.265363	2676	91.175	0.281348
1346	108.949	0.272095	2411	86.894	0.286996
1572	108.992	0.273863	2618	84.960	0.278684
1433	108.737	0.262259	3364	84.693	0.297887
1911	108.593	0.248590	3849	86.025	0.299195

T A B L E **4.9** *(Cont.)*

Data for Wheat Export Exercise

SHIPMENT	EXCRATE	PRICE	SHIPMENT	EXCRATE	PRICE
3737	85.473	0.312402	3896	120.526	0.246865
3183	86.470	0.323602	3990	122.656	0.246697
3054	89.057	0.332600	3569	123.793	0.247752
3594	90.491	0.307294	3060	125.055	0.247244
3537	91.082	0.312945	2619	125.394	0.235778
3386	95.509	0.301696	3087	128.639	0.223716
3504	95.911	0.288256	3176	130.112	0.217042
3474	98.784	0.294955	2388	133.188	0.221998
2124	103.492	0.279304	3246	133.413	0.227979
3389	106.459	0.272203	3125	131.639	0.221738
3760	109.238	0.267277	2800	134.792	0.220599
3958	111.529	0.268925	3508	137.699	0.221591
5284	107.243	0.267571	3221	140.244	0.220712
4273	106.059	0.264126	3024	137.112	0.216040
3470	104.473	0.278931	3231	133.865	0.221864
3749	105.432	0.278236	2644	136.153	0.225505
3379	107.414	0.268141	3070	140.147	0.220339
3775	110.954	0.263977	2867	140.467	0.215567
4329	113.599	0.261508	3627	145.506	0.212044
4033	115.587	0.246816	3979	145.425	0.216859
3170	112.341	0.256175	6605	151.073	0.219725
4270	117.854	0.235281	3736	153.787	0.215539
3209	119.634	0.227856	2648	151.330	0.214202
3383	120.571	0.227389	3591	155.922	0.209881
3565	122.312	0.228175	1897	160.254	0.208585
2681	124.902	0.218801	2327	166.005	0.206186
2575	126.268	0.231150	1576	165.932	0.202214
2407	121.503	0.239250			

SOURCE: The data were observed monthly from January 1974 through March 1985 and obtained from D. A. Bessler and R. A. Babubla. Forecasting wheat exports: Do exchange rates really matter? *Journal of Business and Economic Statistics*, 5 (1987): 397–406.

e Construct a 95% confidence interval estimate for the population regression coefficient of PRICE.

f What is the value of R^2 adjusted for degrees of freedom? What, if any, is the advantage of this number over the coefficient of determination?

These data are available on the data disk for further analysis. In MINITAB, they can be read using

FIGURE 4.32

MINITAB Regression Output for Wheat Export Exercise

```
The regression equation is
shipment = 3362 + 1.87 excrate - 2414 price

Predictor          Coef        Stdev      t-ratio        p
Constant         3361.9        633.2         5.31    0.000
excrate           1.869        4.223         0.44    0.659
price           -2413.8        846.5        -2.85    0.005

s = 798.3       R-sq = 8.8%        R-sq(adj) = 7.4%

Analysis of Variance

SOURCE          DF           SS           MS        F        p
Regression       2      8117338      4058669     6.37    0.002
Error          132     84112920       637219
Total          134     92230256

SOURCE          DF       SEQ SS
excrate          1      2935648
price            1      5181689

Unusual Observations
Obs.   excrate    shipment       Fit    Stdev.Fit    Residual    St.Resid
  1        104      2264.0    1924.9        310.7       339.1       0.46 X
  2        102      1983.0    1900.0        313.2        83.0       0.11 X
  3         98      1787.0    2111.8        233.5      -324.8      -0.43 X
 93        107      5284.0    2916.5         77.9      2367.5       2.98R
129        151      6605.0    3113.9        171.4      3491.1       4.48R
134        166      2327.0    3174.5        224.7      -847.5      -1.11 X
135        166      1576.0    3184.0        223.9     -1608.0      -2.10RX

R denotes an obs. with a large st. resid.
X denotes an obs. whose X value gives it large influence.
```

FIGURE 4.33

SAS Regression Output for Wheat Export Exercise

```
Dependent Variable: SHIPMENT

                      Analysis of Variance

                        Sum of         Mean
Source       DF        Squares        Square     F Value    Prob>F

Model         2   8117335.4604  4058667.7302       6.369    0.0023
Error       132  84112924.688   637219.12642
C Total     134  92230260.148

        Root MSE        798.26006     R-square      0.0880
        Dep Mean       2821.29630     Adj R-sq      0.0742
        C.V.             28.29409

                      Parameter Estimates

                   Parameter       Standard       T for H0:
Variable    DF      Estimate          Error    Parameter=0   Prob > |T|

INTERCEP     1   3361.933416   633.19549783         5.309       0.0001
EXCRATE      1      1.869142     4.22305754         0.443       0.6588
PRICE        1  -2413.838385   846.47982425        -2.852       0.0051
```

```
READ 'WHEAT4' C1-C3
```

where C1 is SHIPMENT, C2 is EXCRATE, and C3 is PRICE.
In SAS, the data also can be read from the file WHEAT4.DAT using

```
INPUT SHIPMENT EXCRATE PRICE;
```

9   **Dividends**   A random sample of 50 firms were chosen from the June 1994 *Standard and Poor's Security Owner's Stock Guide*.[4] The indicated dividend yield (DIVYIELD), the earnings per share (EPS), and the stock price (PRICE) were recorded for these 50 firms.

Using DIVYIELD as the dependent variable and EPS and PRICE as the independent variables, a regression was run. The list of firms and the accompanying data are shown in Table 4.10. The MINITAB and SAS regression outputs are shown in Figures 4.34 and 4.35, respectively. Use the outputs to answer the questions.

T A B L E **4.10**

Dividend Yield, Price, and EPS Data for Dividends Exercise

Firm Name	DIVYIELD	EPS	PRICE
Bristol-Myers Squibb	5.3	3.83	55
Intel	0.4	5.36	62
Fansteel Inc.	5.5	0.10	7
Waterhouse Investor Svc.	1.1	1.95	15
Schering-Plough	3.1	4.41	65
Weyerhaeuser	2.9	2.33	42
PNC Bank	4.2	3.22	31
Marion Merrell Dow	5.7	1.35	18
Park Electrochemical	1.2	2.02	26
United Mobile Homes	4.8	0.29	8
Burlington Resources	1.3	1.98	42
Consolidated Papers	3.3	1.41	39
AMRESCO Inc.	2.9	2.01	7
Consolidated Natural Gas	5.1	2.08	38
Louisiana-Pacific	1.5	2.29	34
Wheelabrator Technologies	0.5	0.89	18
Baker Hughes	2.3	0.57	20
McGraw-Hill	3.5	0.22	66
Clorox	3.5	3.84	51
Nalco Chemical	2.9	2.02	33
Pioneer Hi-Bred Int'l	1.6	1.82	34
TJX	2.3	1.58	24
Loral	1.6	2.72	36
DPL	5.9	1.45	20

[4] *Standard and Poor's Security Owner's Stock Guide.* © 1994 Standard and Poor's, a division of McGraw-Hill Inc.

T A B L E **4.10** (*Cont.*)

Dividend Yield, Price, and EPS data for Dividends Exercise

Firm Name	DIVYIELD	EPS	PRICE
Johnson Controls	2.9	3.43	49
Tandy	1.6	1.26	37
Cyprus Amax Minerals	2.8	1.86	29
Betz Laboratories	3.1	2.04	45
Owens & Minor	1.2	0.98	23
Wendy's International	1.4	0.79	17
General Signal	2.9	1.57	31
Kansas City Southern Inds.	0.7	2.28	45
New Plan Realty Trust	6.0	0.96	22
Ohio Casualty	5.4	2.12	27
Maybelline Inc.	1.0	1.30	29
Tidewater	1.9	0.67	21
Brooklyn Union Gas	5.7	1.75	24
Stone & Webster	1.8	0.91	33
Wilmington Trust	4.2	2.29	26
Idaho Power	8.0	2.03	23
BIC	2.8	1.92	21
PacifiCorp	6.1	1.60	18
Millipore	1.1	1.87	53
Masco Corp.	2.5	1.51	28
Central Maine Power	8.0	1.31	11
Lance Inc.	5.3	0.95	18
Sealright Co.	3.3	0.95	14
Health Equity Prop.	10.1	0.78	10
Jones Medical Indus.	0.9	0.71	11
Diamond Shamrock	2.1	1.25	25

a   What is the sample regression equation relating DIVYIELD to EPS and PRICE?

b   What percentage of the variation of DIVYIELD has been explained by the regression?

c   Test the overall fit of the regression. Use $\alpha = .10$. State the hypotheses to be tested, the decision rule, the test statistic, and your decision.

d   What conclusion can be drawn from the test result?

These data are available on the data disk for further analysis. In MINITAB, they can be read using

```
READ 'DIV4' C1-C3
```

where C1 is DIVYIELD, C2 is EPS, and C3 is PRICE.

F I G U R E **4.34**

MINITAB Regression Output for Dividends Exercise 9

```
The regression equation is
divyield = 4.49 + 0.231 eps - 0.0540 price

Predictor        Coef       Stdev     t-ratio        p
Constant       4.4935      0.6807        6.60    0.000
eps            0.2308      0.3726        0.62    0.539
price         -0.05400    0.02619       -2.06    0.045

s = 2.101      R-sq = 9.8%      R-sq(adj) = 6.0%

Analysis of Variance

SOURCE         DF          SS          MS         F        p
Regression      2      22.644      11.322      2.57    0.088
Error          47     207.376       4.412
Total          49     230.019

SOURCE         DF      SEQ SS
eps             1       3.886
price           1      18.758

Unusual Observations
Obs.      eps    divyield      Fit   Stdev.Fit   Residual   St.Resid
   2     5.36       0.400     2.382      1.060     -1.982     -1.09 X
  18     0.22       3.500     0.980      1.431      2.520      1.64 X
  40     2.03       8.000     3.720      0.385      4.280      2.07R
  48     0.78      10.100     4.133      0.493      5.967      2.92R

R denotes an obs. with a large st. resid.
X denotes an obs. whose X value gives it large influence.
```

F I G U R E **4.35**

SAS Regression Output for Dividends Exercise 9

```
Dependent Variable: DIVYIELD

                        Analysis of Variance

                            Sum of        Mean
Source         DF         Squares       Square      F Value     Prob>F

Model           2        22.64355     11.32177       2.566      0.0876
Error          47       207.37565      4.41225
C Total        49       230.01920

         Root MSE       2.10054     R-square       0.0984
         Dep Mean       3.30400     Adj R-sq       0.0601
         C.V.          63.57552

                        Parameter Estimates

                  Parameter      Standard     T for H0:
Variable   DF      Estimate         Error   Parameter=0    Prob > |T|

INTERCEP    1      4.493485    0.68074825        6.601        0.0001
EPS         1      0.230803    0.37261796        0.619        0.5386
PRICE       1     -0.054002    0.02619073       -2.062        0.0448
```

In SAS the data can be read from the file DIV4.DAT using

```
INPUT DIVYIELD EPS PRICE;
```

10   **Pricing Communications Nodes**   Refer to Chapter 3, Examples 3.3 and 3.6, on communications nodes. The cost of adding a new communications node at a location not currently included on the network was of concern for a major Fort Worth manufacturing company. To try to predict the price of new communications nodes, data were obtained on a sample of existing nodes. The installation cost and the number of ports available for access in each existing node were readily available. Data on two additional characteristics of communications nodes that might impact cost, the bandwidth on each node, and the port operating speeds, were also obtained. These data are shown in Table 4.11.

The network administrator wants to develop a method of estimating the price of new nodes in a quick and fairly accurate manner. You have been asked to help in this project. Using the data available, develop an equation to help in the pricing of new communications nodes. Justify your choice of equation.

The data are available on the data disk. In MINITAB, they can be read using

```
READ 'COMNODE4' C1-C4
```

where C1 is cost (COST), C2 is the number of ports (NUMPORTS), C3 is the bandwidth (BANDWIDT), and C4 is port speed (PORTSPED).

In SAS, the data can be read from the file COMNODE4.DAT using

```
INPUT COST NUMPORTS BANDWIDT PORTSPED;
```

11   **College Spending**   In the *U.S. News and World Report 1994 College Guide*, a variety of information on major universities is provided. The data include the following variables:

average SAT score (SAT)
freshmen in the top 10% of their high school class, percentage (TOP10)
acceptance rate, percentage (ACCRATE)
faculty with PhD, percentage (PHD)
student faculty ratio (#:1) (RATIO)
educational spending per full-time equivalent (FTE) student, in dollars (SPEND)
graduation rate, percentage (GRADRATE)
alumni giving rate, percentage (ALUMNI)

The data are shown in Table 4.12. Note that only schools with complete data on all variables are included in this data set.[5]

One of the universities, HSU, is studying their educational spending per FTE. The board of directors' concern is whether the spending per student for HSU is in line with that of other universities. In these days of increasing competition for students, the board does not want HSU to be perceived as one that spends too little for the benefit of the students. However, with the ever-increasing need to keep costs low, neither do they want to spend indiscriminately.

Your task is to build a regression model with educational spending per full-time equivalent (SPEND) as the dependent variable. By determining variables related to

---

[5]Copyright, 1994, *U.S. News & World Report.*

T A B L E 4.11
Data for Pricing Communications Nodes Exercise*

Cost	Number of Ports	Bandwidth	Port Speeds
52,388	68	58	653
51,761	52	179	499
50,221	44	123	422
36,095	32	38	307
27,500	16	29	154
57,088	56	141	538
54,475	56	141	538
33,969	28	48	269
31,309	24	29	230
23,444	24	10	230
24,269	12	56	115
53,479	52	131	499
33,543	20	38	192
33,056	24	29	230

* Note: These data have been modified as requested by the company to provide confidentiality.

SPEND, the board then hopes to be able to assess whether HSU is in line regarding spending on FTE students. The board has determined that HSU has the following values for the variables in the data set:

SAT = 1100
TOP10 = 50
ACCRATE = 50
PHD = 95
RATIO = 10
SPEND = 16,000
GRADRATE = 70
ALUMNI = 30

The data for HSU has not been included in the data set used for estimating the model. Once the model has been developed, use it to assess spending on FTE students for HSU. What is your recommendation to the board?

These data are available on the data disk. In MINITAB, they can be read using

```
READ 'COLLEGE4' C1-C8
```

where C1 is SAT, C2 is TOP10, C3 is ACCRATE, C4 is PHD, C5 is RATIO, C6 is SPEND, C7 is GRADRATE, and C8 is ALUMNI.

In SAS, the data can be read from the file COLLEGE4.DAT using

```
INPUT SAT TOP10 ACCRATE PHD RATIO SPEND GRADRATE ALUMNI;
```

T A B L E **4.12**

Data for College-Spending Exercise

College	SAT	TOP10	ACCRATE	PHD	RATIO	SPEND	GRADRATE	ALUMNI
Harvard University	1,385	90	16	98	12	36,291	97	27
Princeton University	1,355	90	16	97	8	27,792	95	44
Yale University	1,345	95	22	95	11	39,110	95	42
MIT	1,375	94	33	100	10	32,825	90	34
California Tech	1,415	98	28	100	6	60,623	82	33
Stanford University	1,345	91	22	99	14	35,854	92	18
Duke University	1,315	88	27	97	13	26,498	93	47
Dartmouth College	1,320	85	26	99	9	29,556	95	54
University of Chicago	1,300	71	44	100	6	36,937	85	35
Cornell University	1,275	84	32	98	13	20,923	88	26
Columbia University	1,300	78	30	98	11	31,029	90	17
Brown University	1,300	87	24	100	13	19,570	94	36
Northwestern University	1,240	85	42	100	11	25,385	88	23
Rice University	1,364	86	19	100	9	21,266	88	41
Johns Hopkins University	1,315	72	43	95	9	55,101	88	30
University of Pennsylvania	1,290	83	40	98	11	22,337	89	39
Georgetown University	1,230	68	29	90	13	19,486	90	24
Washington University	1,220	65	65	99	10	45,946	80	28
University of Calif., Berkeley	1,235	95	43	98	19	13,901	77	9
Vanderbilt University	1,195	64	56	98	11	23,051	79	26
University of Virginia	1,220	74	35	92	13	12,934	91	30
UCLA	1,160	93	42	99	19	19,738	72	12
University of Michigan	1,185	64	69	98	16	14,882	83	20
Carnegie Mellon University	1,240	58	59	92	9	22,903	72	30
Emory University	1,205	71	58	96	13	26,151	83	23
University of Notre Dame	1,265	78	49	95	13	13,193	93	46
Boston College	1,200	69	46	95	17	10,202	87	28
Boston University	1,150	41	70	81	17	15,997	68	17
Brandeis University	1,215	36	72	90	9	16,905	79	21
Case Western Reserve Univ.	1,220	68	79	97	12	19,416	64	32
College of William and Mary	1,215	68	41	92	14	9,248	87	24
Georgia Institute of Tech.	1,240	76	51	92	18	10,209	67	27
Lehigh University	1,145	40	64	99	13	14,330	87	46
New York University	1,145	70	61	98	12	20,849	68	11
Rensselaer Polytechnic Inst.	1,200	56	81	98	16	13,479	69	22
Rutgers State Univ., New Bruns.	1,115	38	54	95	20	9,785	74	17
SUNY at Binghamton	1,155	75	42	100	18	8,050	75	16
Tufts University	1,280	73	44	100	13	18,451	90	33
Tulane University	1,155	47	73	98	14	14,251	68	23
Univ. of California, Davis	1,085	90	64	100	22	15,226	73	11

T A B L E **4.12** (*Cont.*)
Data for College-Spending Exercise

College	SAT	TOP10	ACCRATE	PHD	RATIO	SPEND	GRADRATE	ALUMNI
Univ. of California, Irvine	1,018	85	72	96	19	16,252	60	17
Univ. of California, Riverside	1,005	80	76	98	13	12,608	58	13
Univ. of California, San Diego	1,142	95	59	97	28	17,243	61	14
Univ. of California, Santa Bar.	1,050	90	80	100	23	9,992	65	7
Univ. of Illinois, Urbana	1,151	55	72	92	17	8,228	78	14
Univ. of North Carolina	1,125	76	35	94	15	15,045	79	21
University of Rochester	1,170	57	61	99	13	21,850	76	26
Univ. of Southern California	1,100	44	68	94	14	16,803	65	12
Univ. of Texas at Austin	1,130	48	65	99	20	6,994	62	11
University of Washington	1,045	40	56	96	14	15,215	60	12
Univ. of Wisconsin at Madison	1,080	35	73	95	15	10,485	67	18
American University	1,133	35	81	91	14	11,400	67	11
Catholic University of America	1,040	27	86	95	9	12,128	74	15
Clark University	1,075	27	67	100	11	11,397	77	36
Clarkson University	1,140	38	84	95	15	10,871	75	31
Clemson University	1,035	36	67	84	18	7,752	70	26
Colorado School of Mines	1,165	60	85	89	14	12,101	55	25
Florida State University	1,085	50	72	89	22	6,804	54	10
Fordham University	1,070	32	68	97	16	10,923	77	15
George Washington University	1,120	33	79	92	11	13,497	68	16
Illinois Institute of Tech.	1,130	41	84	88	12	13,528	54	32
Indiana Univ., Bloomington	1,003	24	84	93	22	8,690	65	13
Iowa State University	995	27	88	89	20	7,837	64	21
Marquette University	1,010	34	86	94	17	9,082	74	25
Miami University, Ohio	1,110	41	77	88	19	7,780	78	23
Michigan State University	985	26	81	95	19	9,201	67	10
New School for Social Research	1,175	19	62	73	7	12,484	65	22
No. Carolina St. Univ., Raleigh	1,055	38	62	98	16	8,869	60	11
Ohio State University	1,005	26	79	95	17	11,609	54	16
Penn. State Univ., Univ. Park	1,095	42	47	88	18	8,656	60	19
Pepperdine University	1,050	85	50	98	11	15,045	62	8
Polytechnic University, NY	1,070	55	74	80	10	14,505	61	11
Purdue Univ., West Lafayette	1,015	34	83	93	19	8,335	69	15
Rutgers State Univ., Newark	950	23	47	95	18	11,533	55	16
SUNY, Albany	1,150	17	63	99	19	8,801	70	15
SUNY, Buffalo	1,100	32	55	97	17	11,113	51	14
SUNY, Stony Brook	960	27	53	95	16	13,489	56	8
Southern Methodist University	1,055	39	63	87	13	12,430	69	19
Stevens Institute of Tech.	1,150	51	79	83	13	12,693	76	23
Syracuse University	1,095	28	72	83	12	14,403	63	17

T A B L E **4.12** (*Cont.*)
Data for College-Spending Exercise

College	SAT	TOP10	ACCRATE	PHD	RATIO	SPEND	GRADRATE	ALUMNI
Texas A&M Univ., College St.	1,065	49	71	91	29	8,375	67	32
Texas Christian University	1,005	33	79	91	16	9,011	62	22
University of Arizona	985	30	86	94	23	9,732	47	13
Univ. of Calif., Santa Cruz	1,070	94	78	100	19	10,947	52	11
University of Cincinnati	985	26	83	95	17	12,651	42	13
Univ. of Colorado, Boulder	1,075	28	76	96	23	8,120	61	12
Univ. of Connecticut, Storrs	1,025	23	70	94	17	11,036	68	15
University of Delaware	1,065	25	70	83	19	10,210	70	15
University of Florida	1,145	50	66	95	18	10,120	61	18
University of Georgia	1,080	40	64	95	15	7,174	60	19
Univ. of Maryland, College Park	1,080	24	73	92	17	8,466	59	13
University of Miami, Florida	1,075	38	70	100	14	16,889	56	17
Univ. of Minnesota, Twin Cities	1,070	26	58	87	14	14,509	42	11
University of Missouri, Columbia	1,045	32	77	86	18	9,066	55	18
University of Missouri, Rolla	1,160	48	98	93	15	9,286	49	25
Univ. of Pittsburgh, Main Campus	995	21	76	92	15	13,393	64	15
University of Tennessee, Knoxville	995	27	73	87	18	8,059	52	12
University of Tulsa	1,085	42	92	96	11	11,173	46	15
University of Vermont	1,040	17	82	88	14	12,138	78	19
Virginia Tech	1,085	32	65	88	14	8,704	71	22
Arizona State University	965	23	82	94	21	7,835	46	8
Auburn University, Main Campus	1,077	24	89	91	19	6,488	65	22
Baylor University	1,045	40	88	73	18	7,384	69	10
Bowling Green State University	950	13	75	93	21	6,694	60	15
Colorado State University	1,011	23	68	87	21	7,875	57	12
Drake University	1,025	34	90	91	16	8,812	59	20
Drexel University	1,010	24	83	96	15	8,910	58	23
Duquesne University	1,005	34	84	93	14	7,749	69	20
Florida Institute of Technology	1,060	28	50	94	13	8,165	55	4
Hofstra University	1,055	25	70	91	14	9,442	57	6
Loyola University, Chicago	1,000	25	85	92	12	11,740	61	19
St. Louis University	1,020	24	88	78	7	17,142	63	19
Temple University	969	17	64	87	15	11,226	44	14
Texas Tech University	945	25	70	91	25	4,954	41	20
University of Denver	1,015	29	67	88	14	10,955	63	21
Univ. of Houston, Main Campus	975	22	60	79	21	6,602	27	11
University of Idaho	970	23	95	95	14	9,053	44	18
Univ. of Maryland, Baltimore Co.	1,065	31	58	86	20	7,322	50	11
Univ. of Massachusetts, Amherst	985	13	88	97	17	8,537	64	15
University of New Hampshire	1,040	26	74	85	15	7,149	69	16

T A B L E **4.12** (*Cont.*)

Data for College-Spending Exercise

College	SAT	TOP10	ACCRATE	PHD	RATIO	SPEND	GRADRATE	ALUMNI
University of North Dakota	950	22	85	82	21	9,718	47	12
University of Oregon	1,020	25	81	85	19	7,629	50	13
University of Rhode Island	950	10	78	83	16	7,958	57	28
University of San Francisco	980	23	74	86	15	9,522	56	9
Univ. of So. Carolina, Columbia	940	24	82	87	19	7,861	61	19
University of South Florida	1,035	27	77	86	21	10,347	45	5
Utah State University	925	26	91	94	17	7,117	58	10
Virginia Commonwealth University	925	15	70	87	14	11,080	42	12
Washington State University	900	31	91	90	17	10,529	53	32
Ball State University	783	16	79	60	18	7,356	50	19
Biola University	983	20	82	66	16	9,492	35	14
Cleveland State University	815	5	99	97	19	7,269	33	11
Georgia State University	890	9	65	90	20	7,280	27	11
Indiana State Univ., Terre Haute	820	10	84	72	15	7,299	39	15
Kent State University	875	10	81	86	21	6,597	44	7
La Sierra University	895	13	80	75	15	12,103	42	22
Mississippi College	928	30	65	78	16	5,788	49	18
Northeastern University	975	13	74	83	14	7,813	45	17
Northern Arizona University	925	23	86	86	22	6,045	39	6
Old Dominion University	985	12	82	87	17	6,228	44	19
University of Maine, Orono	980	20	85	82	16	7,256	51	21
Univ. of Missouri, St. Louis	980	16	58	78	15	5,920	26	12
Univ. of No. Carol., Greensboro	955	18	78	80	15	7,190	49	18
University of North Texas	977	16	68	89	22	5,107	33	6
University of Northern Colorado	905	12	70	77	20	6,044	38	9
University of Texas, Arlington	930	18	83	72	23	4,309	28	3
West Virginia University	910	23	81	86	19	8,121	55	13

12 **NFL** The following data were obtained from the *Fort Worth Star Telegram*[6] and refers to the 1992 NFL season:

wins (WINS)
net yards rushing (RUSH)
net yards passing (PASS)
passes attempted (PATT)
passes completed (PCOMP)
passes intercepted (PINT)

[6]From *Fort Worth Star Telegram*, 26 December 1992 and 2 January 1993. Reprinted courtesy of the *Fort Worth Star Telegram*.

yards penalties (PENALTY)

fumbles lost (FUMBLE)

net rushing yards allowed (RUSHOPP)

net passing yards allowed (PASSOPP)

passes attempted by opponents (PATTOPP)

passes completed by opponents (PCOMPOPP)

passes intercepted by opponents (PIOPP)

The dependent variable is the number of wins (WINS) for the season. The other variables are to be considered possible explanatory variables. The data for the 28 NFL teams are shown in Table 4.13.

Your NFL team is interested in what makes a winning season. You have gathered the data in Table 4.13 on various offensive and defensive statistics. Your job is to try to determine which combination of the variables will provide the best explanation of what makes a winning team. Once you have determined your choice of the best equation, use your results to answer the following questions:

a   What is the estimated regression equation relating WINS to your set of explanatory variables?

b   Test the overall fit of the regression. Use a 5% level of significance. State the hypotheses to be tested, decision rule, test statistic, and decision.

c   What percent of the variation in WINS is explained by the regression?

d   Why did you omit certain variables? Why did you decide to keep others in the regression? Justify your choice of variables.

These data are available on the data disk. In MINITAB, they can be read using

```
READ 'NFL4' C1-C13
```

where C1 is WINS, C2 is RUSH, C3 is PASS, C4 is PATT, C5 is PCOMP, C6 is PINT, C7 is PENALTY, C8 is FUMBLE, C9 is RUSHOPP, C10 is PASSOPP, C11 is PATTOPP, C12 is PCOMPOPP, and C13 is PIOPP.

In SAS, the data can be read from the file NFL4.DAT using

```
INPUT WINS RUSH PASS PATT PCOMP PINT PENALTY FUMBLE RUSHOPP
   PASSOPP PATTOPP PCOMPOPP PIOPP;
```

13   **Prime Rate**   Table 4.14 shows the monthly prime rate during the time period from January 1983 through December 1992. (These data were obtained from *Business Statistics 1963–91* and *Survey of Current Business.*) Develop an extrapolative model to forecast prime rate for each month in 1993. Be sure to examine a time-series plot of the data.

Find the actual rates for each month in 1993 and compare them to your forecasts. How well did your model do?

These data are available on the data disk. In MINITAB, they can be read using

```
READ 'PRIME4' C1
```

In SAS, the data can be read from the file PRIME4.DAT using

```
INPUT PRIMERT;
```

T A B L E 4.13
Data for NFL Exercise

Name	WINS	RUSH	PASS	PATT	PCOMP	PINT	PENALTY	FUMBLE	RUSHOPP	PASSOPP	PATTOPP	PCOMPOPP	PIOPP
Buffalo	11	2436	3457	509	293	21	775	17	1395	3209	520	305	23
Cincinnati	5	1976	1943	435	227	17	755	10	2007	3326	489	288	16
Cleveland	7	1607	2885	398	238	16	765	12	1605	3152	486	291	13
Denver	8	1500	2930	473	258	29	768	14	1963	3120	462	268	15
Houston	10	1626	4029	573	373	23	824	12	1634	2577	445	248	20
Indianapolis	9	1102	3266	546	305	26	958	11	2174	2900	470	260	20
Kansas City	10	1532	2792	413	230	12	675	9	1787	2537	458	253	24
LA Raiders	7	1794	2590	471	233	23	832	15	1683	2833	450	243	12
Miami	11	1525	3975	563	332	17	656	17	1600	2983	512	294	18
New England	2	1550	2034	444	244	19	1051	26	1951	3097	459	258	14
NY Jets	4	1752	2679	495	251	24	873	15	1919	2961	465	257	21
Pittsburgh	11	2156	2750	431	249	14	941	18	1841	2817	478	252	22
San Diego	11	1875	3346	496	282	21	813	12	1395	2832	491	271	25
Seattle	2	1596	1778	476	230	23	918	18	1922	2661	428	251	20
Atlanta	6	1270	3633	548	336	15	656	14	2294	3255	439	277	11
Chicago	5	1871	3070	479	266	24	776	10	1948	3004	442	261	14
Dallas	13	2121	3485	491	314	15	650	9	1244	2687	484	263	17
Detroit	5	1644	2796	406	231	21	903	15	1841	3217	487	296	21
Green Bay	9	1555	3230	527	340	15	749	21	1821	3277	483	277	15
LA Rams	6	1659	3218	495	289	20	592	17	2230	3293	507	305	18
New Orleans	12	1628	3178	426	251	16	567	13	1605	2470	511	387	18
NY Giants	6	2077	2345	433	232	10	647	13	2012	3031	440	270	14
Philadelphia	11	2388	2592	429	255	13	807	15	1481	2931	517	263	24
Phoenix	4	1491	3086	517	298	24	722	18	1635	3491	452	276	16
San Francisco	14	2315	3880	480	319	9	636	13	1418	3369	551	320	17
Tampa Bay	5	1706	3065	511	299	20	754	9	1675	3510	508	293	20
Washington	9	1727	3163	485	272	17	741	7	1696	2742	466	258	23
Minnesota	11	2030	2869	458	258	15	809	17	1733	2782	508	320	20

T A B L E **4.14**

Data for Prime Rate Exercise

Month	Rate	Month	Rate	Month	Rate
1/83	11.16	5/86	8.50	9/89	10.50
2/83	10.98	6/86	8.50	10/89	10.50
3/83	10.50	7/86	8.16	11/89	10.50
4/83	10.50	8/86	7.90	12/89	10.50
5/83	10.50	9/86	7.50	1/90	10.11
6/83	10.50	10/86	7.50	2/90	10.00
7/83	10.50	11/86	7.50	3/90	10.00
8/83	10.89	12/86	7.50	4/90	10.00
9/83	11.00	1/87	7.50	5/90	10.00
10/83	11.00	2/87	7.50	6/90	10.00
11/83	11.00	3/87	7.50	7/90	10.00
12/83	11.00	4/87	7.75	8/90	10.00
1/84	11.00	5/87	8.14	9/90	10.00
2/84	11.00	6/87	8.25	10/90	10.00
3/84	11.21	7/87	8.25	11/90	10.00
4/84	11.93	8/87	8.25	12/90	10.00
5/84	12.39	9/87	8.70	1/91	9.52
6/84	12.60	10/87	9.07	2/91	9.05
7/84	13.00	11/87	8.78	3/91	9.00
8/84	13.00	12/87	8.75	4/91	9.00
9/84	12.97	1/88	8.75	5/91	8.50
10/84	12.58	2/88	8.51	6/91	8.50
11/84	11.77	3/88	8.50	7/91	8.50
12/84	11.06	4/88	8.50	8/91	8.50
1/85	10.61	5/88	8.84	9/91	8.20
2/85	10.50	6/88	9.00	10/91	8.00
3/85	10.50	7/88	9.29	11/91	7.58
4/85	10.50	8/88	9.84	12/91	7.21
5/85	10.31	9/88	10.00	1/92	6.50
6/85	9.78	10/88	10.00	2/92	6.50
7/85	9.50	11/88	10.05	3/92	6.50
8/85	9.50	12/88	10.50	4/92	6.50
9/85	9.50	1/89	10.50	5/92	6.50
10/85	9.50	2/89	10.93	6/92	6.50
11/85	9.50	3/89	11.50	7/92	6.02
12/85	9.50	4/89	11.50	8/92	6.00
1/86	9.50	5/89	11.50	9/92	6.00
2/86	9.50	6/89	11.07	10/92	6.00
3/86	9.10	7/89	10.98	11/92	6.00
4/86	8.83	8/89	10.50	12/92	6.00

14 **Suicide** In the February 1989 issue of *Journal of Marriage and the Family*, Steven Stack investigated the relationship between the number of suicides per 100,000 population in Norway (SUICIDE) and a number of explanatory variables. The explanatory variables used were

x_1, unemployment rate in Norway (UNEMP)
x_2, divorce rate in Norway, used as an indicator of marital stress (DIVORCE)
x_3, religious book production, used as a measure of national religiosity levels (RELIG)

These data are shown in Table 4.15 for the years 1951 to 1980. Use the explanatory variables UNEMP, DIVORCE, and RELIG to develop a model of SUICIDE in Norway. What factors appear to be related to SUICIDE in Norway? Can we conclude that these factors cause suicides to occur? Why or why not?

These data are available on the data disk. In MINITAB, they can be read using

```
READ 'SUICIDE4' C1-C4
```

where C1 is SUICIDE, C2 is UNEMP, C3 is DIVORCE, and C4 is RELIG.
In SAS, the data can be read from the file SUICIDE4.DAT using

```
INPUT SUICIDE UNEMP DIVORCE RELIG;
```

15 **Absenteeism** The ABX Company is interested in conducting a study of the factors that affect absenteeism among its production employees. After reviewing the literature on absenteeism and interviewing several production supervisors and a number of employees, the researcher in charge of the project defined the variables shown in Table 4.16. Then a sample of 77 employees were randomly selected and the data shown in Table 4.17 collected. The dependent variable is absenteeism. The other seven variables are considered possible explanatory variables.

Use the procedures discussed in Chapters 3 and 4 to identify factors that may be related to absenteeism. Write down your final model and justify your choice of variables in the model. Check to see whether your choice of variables and the coefficient estimates make intuitive sense. How much variation in absenteeism has been explained? What does this tell you? Does your model give you some sense of which employees might be absent most often? If so, which ones? What might be done to reduce absenteeism?

These data are available on the data disk. In MINITAB, they can be read using

```
READ 'ABSENT4' C1-C8
```

where C1 is ABSENT, C2 is JOBCLAS, C3 is COMPLX, C4 is PAY, C5 is SATIS, C6 is SENIOR, C7 is AGE, and C8 is DEPEND.
In SAS, the data can be read from the file ABSENT4.DAT using

```
INPUT ABSENT JOBCLAS COMPLX PAY SATIS SENIOR AGE DEPEND;
```

T A B L E **4.15**

Data for Suicide Exercise

Year	SUICIDE	UNEMP	DIVORCE	RELIG
1951	6.5	3.6	7.3	5.3
1952	6.9	2.4	7.2	8.8
1953	7.7	3.3	7.2	6.4
1954	7.4	2.2	7.2	5.5
1955	7.4	2.5	7.1	5.2
1956	7.3	3.1	7.6	4.8
1957	7.4	3.2	7.7	4.0
1958	7.3	2.9	8.0	4.7
1959	7.8	2.7	8.7	5.6
1960	6.4	2.5	9.1	4.9
1961	6.6	2.0	9.2	4.2
1962	7.9	2.1	9.2	4.2
1963	8.0	2.5	9.2	3.5
1964	7.3	2.0	9.2	4.7
1965	7.7	1.8	9.6	4.6
1966	7.1	1.8	8.8	4.0
1967	7.0	1.2	9.0	5.0
1968	8.1	1.4	9.4	5.2
1969	8.2	1.4	9.6	5.5
1970	8.4	1.5	10.4	4.2
1971	8.1	1.6	11.2	4.5
1972	9.0	1.7	12.3	4.2
1973	8.6	1.5	14.3	5.6
1974	10.4	1.5	15.8	3.7
1975	9.9	2.3	17.6	3.1
1976	10.8	1.8	18.7	4.4
1977	11.4	1.5	20.4	4.7
1978	11.7	1.7	21.0	6.1
1979	12.1	2.0	22.1	4.5
1980	12.4	1.7	23.1	4.9

T A B L E **4.16**

Absenteeism Study Variables

	Variable	Description
1.	Absenteeism (ABSENT)	The number of distinct occasions that the worker was absent during 1994. Each occasion consists of one or more consecutive days of absence.
2.	Job Classification (JOBCLAS)	An integer identifying the 29 different jobs included in the study: 1 = Foundry molder 2 = Automatic screw machine operator 3 = Aluminum extrusion inspector 4 = Warehouse order picker 5 = Heavy hydraulic press operator etc.
3.	Job Complexity (COMPLX)	An index ranging from 0 to 100, measured according to procedures developed by Turner and Lawrence (1965).
4.	Base Pay (PAY)	Base hourly pay rate in dollars.
5.	Supervisor Satisfaction (SATIS)	Determined by employee response to the question: "How satisfied are you with your supervisor?" 1 = Very dissatisfied 2 = Somewhat dissatisfied 3 = Neither satisfied nor dissatisfied 4 = Fairly well satisfied 5 = Very satisfied
6.	Seniority (SENIOR)	Number of complete years with the company on December 31, 1994.
7.	Age (AGE)	Employee's age on December 31, 1994.
8.	Number of Dependents (DEPEND)	Determined by employee response to the question: "How many individuals other than yourself depend on you for most of their financial support?"

T A B L E **4.17**

Data for Absenteeism Exercise

Absenteeism	Job Classification	Job Complexity	Base Pay	Supervisor Satisfaction	Seniority	Age	Number of Dependents
0	14	45	5.86	4	3	28	2
1	22	76	7.74	4	10	42	1
0	21	56	5.08	1	9	40	5
2	22	76	7.74	3	7	34	2
0	9	70	7.92	3	14	39	2
1	7	69	6.31	3	9	44	0
1	21	56	5.78	4	3	40	1
1	21	56	4.70	4	1	35	0
2	19	43	6.99	1	9	32	0
1	22	76	5.63	3	1	41	1
3	11	30	5.02	2	1	27	1
2	15	50	6.88	4	9	40	0
1	17	10	4.80	4	1	30	1
3	7	69	6.48	2	4	35	0
2	12	67	7.61	3	3	33	1
0	7	69	6.44	1	4	32	1
4	9	70	7.34	2	8	37	1
7	1	13	6.17	2	1	26	2
3	25	16	7.87	3	3	36	2
2	8	52	7.39	1	5	28	2
2	8	52	6.87	1	16	40	1
4	24	3	6.04	2	2	26	0
2	18	6	5.38	3	4	38	2
0	12	67	8.42	3	6	33	1
3	17	10	4.66	3	1	26	0
3	6	89	9.51	3	18	48	0
3	23	21	4.83	2	2	34	1
0	28	34	6.27	3	4	26	1
2	4	12	8.47	4	6	40	2
3	9	70	6.71	2	2	34	2
1	7	69	6.39	3	11	49	2
4	1	13	5.77	2	1	35	1
2	11	30	6.28	4	13	51	5
1	19	43	5.19	2	1	25	1
3	5	8	6.40	2	2	29	0
2	3	69	7.03	2	2	34	2
4	11	30	4.84	4	1	36	2
4	16	23	4.81	2	1	31	2
4	25	16	6.57	4	1	28	2
3	26	11	5.60	3	1	32	2

T A B L E 4.17 *(Cont.)*

Data for Absenteeism Exercise

Absenteeism	Job Classification	Job Complexity	Base Pay	Supervisor Satisfaction	Seniority	Age	Number of Dependents
2	25	16	5.89	3	1	30	2
6	15	50	6.24	1	2	30	2
3	15	50	5.61	3	2	28	0
1	3	69	8.79	3	4	31	4
2	17	10	5.53	3	2	34	1
1	19	43	6.86	3	26	54	1
1	4	12	5.93	4	1	28	0
3	22	76	7.20	2	5	28	2
2	21	56	5.22	3	2	35	2
0	18	6	5.88	3	8	43	4
0	5	8	6.73	5	3	29	4
1	14	45	5.37	4	2	32	3
3	19	43	5.84	3	5	31	3
6	16	23	4.64	3	1	26	1
3	27	1	7.18	5	7	46	1
2	10	82	7.58	3	1	23	1
2	27	1	5.94	3	1	20	0
4	27	1	5.84	5	1	35	3
3	9	70	7.80	3	4	32	2
0	22	76	7.00	3	6	34	0
0	10	82	9.47	3	7	38	0
1	15	50	6.21	3	9	33	2
1	9	70	8.56	3	8	45	1
1	2	81	6.60	3	5	27	1
2	9	70	7.61	3	9	33	4
3	27	1	7.35	4	2	30	3
2	5	8	5.51	5	1	32	2
2	16	23	5.27	4	2	24	3
2	23	21	5.67	4	12	47	4
2	20	82	8.54	3	7	33	5
1	12	67	8.82	4	28	54	3
0	2	81	7.00	3	18	45	2
1	19	43	7.50	3	6	40	0
4	18	6	5.58	3	3	21	1
3	1	13	7.44	2	8	29	4
2	8	52	7.24	1	7	31	1
3	8	52	5.26	3	1	27	1

SOURCE: These data were created by Professor Roger L. Wright, RLW Analytics, Inc., and are modified here with his permission.

5

Assessing the Assumptions
of the Regression Model

5.1
Introduction

In Chapter 4, the multiple linear regression model was presented as

$$y_i = \beta_0 + \beta_1 x_{1i} + \beta_2 x_{2i} + \cdots + \beta_K x_{Ki} + e_i \tag{5.1}$$

Certain assumptions were made concerning the disturbances, e_i, of this model. The e_i's represent the differences between the true values of the dependent variable and the corresponding points on the population regression line. Because the true disturbances cannot be observed, they are modeled as realizations of a random variable, about which certain assumptions are made. Under a set of ideal assumptions, the method of least squares provides the best possible estimates of the population regression coefficients. Certain of the assumptions also are necessary for inference procedures (confidence interval estimates and hypothesis tests) to perform as expected. In this chapter, we consider the problems with estimation and inference that may arise if any of these assumptions are violated. Methods of assessing the validity of the assumptions also are discussed. Graphical procedures such as scatterplots and residual plots may be used to examine certain of the assumptions, and statistical tests are available for a more formal examination. Finally, we discuss appropriate techniques to correct for violated assumptions.

5.2
Assumptions of the Multiple Linear Regression Model

The "ideal" conditions for estimation and inference in the multiple regression model are as follows:

a The relationship is linear.

b The disturbances in Equation (5.1), e_i, have constant variance σ_e^2.

c The disturbances are independent.

d The disturbances are normally distributed.

An additional condition is added to this list that applies only to the explanatory variables in the equation:

e The explanatory variables are not highly interrelated.

The effects of violations of each of these assumptions on the least squares estimates of the regression coefficients will be examined in subsequent sections. Methods of assessing the validity of the assumptions will be discussed and possible corrections for violations will be offered. Because many of the methods of assessing assumption validity depend on the use of the residuals (the sample counterpart of the disturbances), the next section is devoted to a brief discussion of the computation and properties of the residuals.

5.3
The Regression Residuals

The regression equation estimated from the sample data may be written

$$\hat{y}_i = b_0 + b_1 x_{1i} + b_2 x_{2i} + \cdots + b_K x_{Ki} \qquad (5.2)$$

By substituting in the values for each explanatory variable in the sample, the predicted or fitted y value for each data point in the sample is obtained. The fitted y values are denoted $\hat{y}_i$. The y values for each point in the sample also are available and will be referred to as y_i. The differences between the true and fitted y values for the points in the sample are called the *sample residuals*, or simply *residuals*. The residuals will be denoted $\hat{e}_i$:

$$\hat{e}_i = y_i - \hat{y}_i$$

They represent the distance that each dependent variable value is from the estimated regression line or the portion of the variation in y that cannot be "explained" with the data available. Because these "sample disturbances" approximate the population disturbances, they can be used to examine assumptions concerning the population disturbances.

After estimating a sample regression equation it is highly recommended that some sort of analysis be conducted to assess the model assumptions. No regression analysis can be considered complete without such further examination. The residuals can be used to conduct such analyses through graphical techniques called *residual plots*. Often, violations of assumptions can be detected through the use of residual plots in combination with scatterplots, without the use of statistical tests. The use of graphical techniques, however, is not an exact science. It might, in fact, be considered an "art."

It takes some experience at examining plots to become adept at determining which, if any, assumptions may be violated. Several examples will be presented later to illustrate this art and to aid in mastering residual analysis.

First, consider some properties of the residuals.

Property 1: The average of the residuals will be equal to zero. This property holds regardless of whether the assumptions are true or not and is a direct result of the way the least-squares method works. Least squares "forces" the mean of the residuals to be zero when it chooses the estimates of the regression coefficients.

Property 2: If assumptions (a) through (c) of Section 5.2 are true, then the residuals should be randomly distributed about their mean (zero). There should be no systematic pattern in a residual plot.

Property 3: If assumptions (a) through (c) are true and the disturbances also are normally distributed (assumption (d)), then the residuals should look like random numbers chosen from a normal distribution.

The residuals can be thought of as representing the variation in y that cannot be explained using the proposed regression model. Thus, if an assumption is violated, an indication of this violation will appear as some type of pattern in the residuals. Identification of such patterns is a first step in correcting for the violation.

In a residual analysis it is suggested that the following plots be used:

1   Plot the residuals versus each explanatory variable.

2   Plot the residuals versus the predicted or fitted values.

3   If the data are measured over time, plot the residuals versus some variable representing the time sequence.

As will be seen in subsequent sections, each of these three types of plots plays a part in identifying violations of the basic assumptions.

If no assumptions are violated, then the residuals should be randomly distributed around their mean of zero and should look like numbers drawn randomly from a normal distribution. Figure 5.1 shows how a residual plot might appear when assumptions (a) through (d) are all true. There is no pattern visible in the scatter of residuals. For comparison, Figure 5.2 shows a residual plot with an obvious pattern to the residuals. Compare this to the random scatter of the residuals in Figure 5.1. A residual plot such as Figure 5.2 would indicate that some assumption had been violated. (There are other patterns that could suggest violations, as will be seen throughout this chapter.)

In certain regression software packages (SAS and MINITAB, for example), residual plots are easily requested after a regression analysis has been performed. These plots may be constructed using the actual residuals, $\hat{e}_i$, or the standardized residuals. The standardized residuals are simply the residuals divided by their standard deviation. There is very little difference in the way residual plots with actual residuals or those with standardized residuals are used. To illustrate the difference in the two types of plots, compare Figure 5.1, a plot of actual residuals, to Figure 5.3, a plot of the same residuals after standardization. The residuals plotted in Figure 5.2 also

F I G U R E **5.1**

MINITAB Residual Plot Assuming No Violation of Assumptions (a) Through (d) of Section 5.2

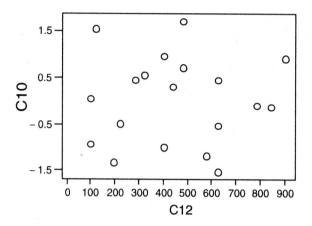

F I G U R E **5.2**

MINITAB Residual Plot Indicating That at Least One of Assumptions (a) Through (d) of Section 5.2 Has Been Violated

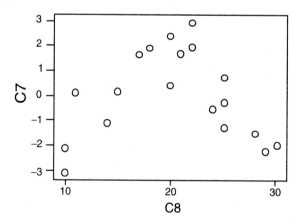

have been standardized and plotted in Figure 5.4. The patterns in the actual and standardized plots are much the same. One advantage of using the standardized plots will become more evident when the assumption of normality is discussed in Section 5.6. In this text, the residual plots shown will be standardized plots unless otherwise indicated.

F I G U R E 5.3

MINITAB Plot of the Residuals from Figure 5.1 after Standardizing

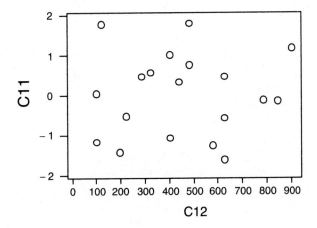

F I G U R E 5.4

MINITAB Plot of the Residuals from Figure 5.2 after Standardizing

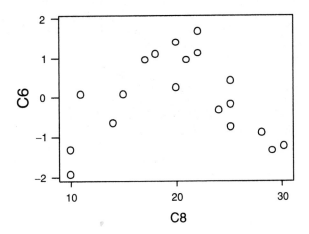

5.4
Assessing the Assumption That the Relationship Is Linear

5.4.1 Using Plots to Assess the Linearity Assumption

The first assumption given in Section 5.2 was that the relationship between the dependent variable, y, and the explanatory variables was linear. After performing a regression, this assumption can be checked visually through residual plots. The scatterplots of y versus each of the explanatory variables also may give an indication of whether the linearity assumption is an appropriate one. Small deviations from linearity that are not evident in the scatterplots, however, may show up clearly in the residual plots. The following example illustrates a violation of the linearity assumption.

E X A M P L E 5.1 Telemarketing

A company that sells transportation services uses a telemarketing division to help sell its services. The division manager is interested in the time spent on the phone by the telemarketers in the division. Data on the number of months of employment and the number of calls placed per day (an average for 20 working days) is recorded for 20 employees. These data are shown in Table 5.1.

The average number of calls for all 20 employees is 28.95. The division manager, however, suspects that there may be a relationship between time on the job and number of calls. As time on the job increases, the employee becomes more familiar with the calling system and the correct procedures to use on the phone and also will begin to acquire increasing numbers of regular clients. Thus, the longer the time on the job, the greater should be the number of calls per day. To investigate this possible relationship further, the scatterplot of y (CALLS) versus x (MONTHS) is produced in Figure 5.5. The MINITAB regression output relating CALLS to MONTHS is shown in Figure 5.6 and the SAS output in Figure 5.7.

Plots of the standardized residuals versus the fitted values are shown in Figures 5.8 and 5.10 for MINITAB and SAS, respectively. Figures 5.9 and 5.11 show plots of the standardized residuals versus the explanatory variable values. The standardized residuals have been labeled SRES1 in the MINITAB plots. In the SAS plots, they are referred to as "studentized residuals." The fitted values are labeled FITS1 in the MINITAB plot. In the SAS plot, they are referred to as predicted values.

A systematic pattern can be observed in both of the residual plots. The standardized residuals plot in a curvilinear pattern, suggesting a curvilinear component may be omitted from the equation expressing the relationship between CALLS and MONTHS. The plots of the standardized residuals versus the fitted values and MONTHS show identical patterns in this case. The plot versus the fitted values may differ from the plot versus one of the explanatory variables, especially in a multiple regression. The fitted values combine the effects of all the explanatory variables used in the regression. In a multiple regression, the plot of the standardized residuals versus the fitted values will provide an overall picture, while the plots of the standardized residuals versus each explanatory variable may help in identifying any violation specifically related to an individual explanatory variable.

TABLE 5.1

Data for Telemarketing Example

Months of Employment	Calls Placed per Day
10	18
10	19
11	22
14	23
15	25
17	28
18	29
20	29
20	31
21	31
22	33
22	32
24	31
25	32
25	32
25	33
25	31
28	33
29	33
30	34

FIGURE 5.5

MINITAB Scatterplot for Telemarketing Example

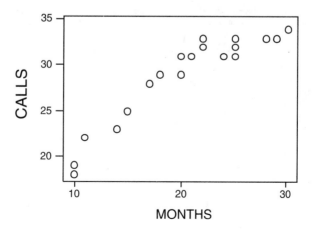

F I G U R E 5.6

MINITAB Regression Output for Telemarketing Example

```
The regression equation is
calls = 13.7 + 0.744 months

Predictor        Coef        Stdev     t-ratio         p
Constant       13.671        1.427        9.58     0.000
months        0.74351      0.06666       11.15     0.000

s = 1.787        R-sq = 87.4%     R-sq(adj) = 86.7%

Analysis of Variance

SOURCE         DF          SS           MS         F         p
Regression      1       397.45       397.45    124.41     0.000
Error          18        57.50         3.19
Total          19       454.95
```

F I G U R E 5.7

SAS Regression Output for Telemarketing Example

```
Dependent Variable: CALLS

                      Analysis of Variance

                      Sum of        Mean
Source         DF     Squares       Square      F Value      Prob>F

Model           1   397.44586    397.44586     124.409      0.0001
Error          18    57.50414      3.19467
C Total        19   454.95000

          Root MSE       1.78737     R-square      0.8736
          Dep Mean      28.95000     Adj R-sq      0.8666
          C.V.           6.17397

                      Parameter Estimates

                  Parameter     Standard     T for H0:
Variable    DF    Estimate        Error    Parameter=0    Prob > |T|

INTERCEP     1   13.670770    1.42697114        9.580        0.0001
MONTHS       1    0.743515    0.06665979       11.154        0.0001
```

The systematic pattern observed in the residual plots suggests a violation of the linearity assumption. Looking back at the scatterplot of CALLS (y) versus MONTHS (x) will help to verify that the relationship may not be linear. As the number of months on the job increases, the number of calls also increases. But the rate of increase begins to slow over time, thus resulting in a pattern that may be better modeled by a curve than a straight line.

In Figure 5.12, the plot of y versus x has been reproduced with a curve approximating the relationship between the two variables drawn in.

Note that the residual plots were used to determine whether the linearity assumption had been violated, although this violation might have been suspected from looking at only the

F I G U R E **5.8**

MINITAB Residual Plot of Standardized Residuals versus Fitted Values for Telemarketing Example

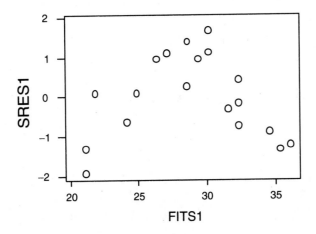

F I G U R E **5.9**

MINITAB Residual Plot of Standardized Residuals versus Explanatory Variable MONTHS for Telemarketing Example

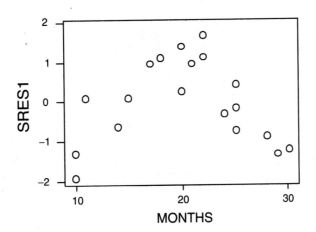

scatterplot of CALLS versus MONTHS. In many cases the violation of an assumption will not be obvious from a scatterplot. The residual plot, however, is intended to magnify the consequences of any possible violation. Thus, the residual plot should be depended upon to identify the violation. ∎

F I G U R E **5.10**

SAS Residual Plot of Standardized Residuals versus Fitted Values for Telemarketing Example

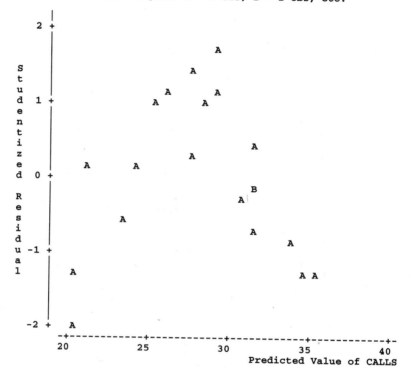

```
Plot of STRES*FITS.   Legend: A = 1 obs, B = 2 obs, etc.
```

5.4.2 Tests for Lack of Fit [1]

MINITAB provides two tests to determine whether a curvilinear model might fit the data better than a linear model. These tests are referred to as *tests for lack of fit*. The first test is called the *pure error lack-of-fit test*. To perform this test, the error sum of squares is decomposed into two parts: the pure error component and the lack-of-fit component. These two components are used to construct an F statistic to test the hypotheses

H_0:   The relationship is linear
H_a: The relationship is not linear

If H_0 is accepted, the linear regression model is appropriate. If H_0 is rejected, the linear model does not fit the data well, and some other function may provide a better

---

[1]This section refers specifically to MINITAB output, but the tests could be performed with other software.

F I G U R E **5.11**

SAS Residual Plot of Standardized Residuals versus Explanatory Variable MONTHS for Telemarketing Example

Plot of STRES*MONTHS. Legend: A = 1 obs, B = 2 obs, etc.

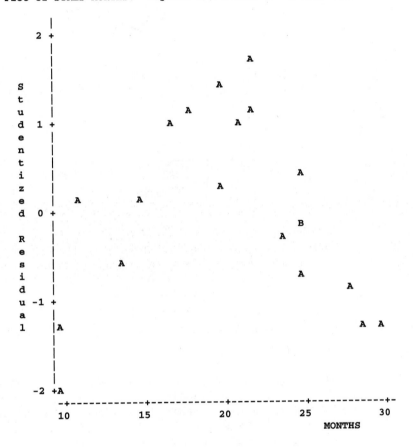

fit, although the test does not specify what that function is. Determination of the appropriate function to fit to the data will be examined in the next section.

To conduct the F test, the decision rule is:

$$\text{Reject } H_0 \quad \text{if} \quad F > F(\alpha; c - K - 1, n - c)$$
$$\text{Accept } H_0 \quad \text{if} \quad F \leq F(\alpha; c - K - 1, n - c)$$

where K is the number of explanatory variables and n is the sample size. The value c requires some additional explanation.

The pure error lack-of-fit test requires that there be repeated observations (replications) for at least one level of the variables. In the telemarketing data in Table 5.1,

F I G U R E   **5.12**

MINITAB Scatterplot for Telemarketing Example with Curve Drawn to Represent the Relationship Between CALLS and MONTHS

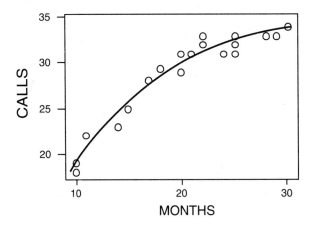

there are replicates for $x = 10, 20, 22,$ and 25. The value, c, is the number of distinct levels of x. In the telemarketing example, there are 14 levels of (or distinct values of) the explanatory variable. The decision rule to perform this test on the telemarketing data is:

$$\text{Reject } H_0 \quad \text{if} \quad F > F(\alpha; 12, 6)$$
$$\text{Accept } H_0 \quad \text{if} \quad F \leq F(\alpha; 12, 6)$$

(because, $c = 14$, $K = 1$, and $n = 20$). The results are shown in Figure 5.13. From the output, the F statistic value is 5.25. If a 5% level of significance is used, the critical value for the test is $F(.05; 12, 6) = 4.00$, and the decision is to reject H_0 and conclude that a curvilinear model may fit the data better than the linear model. Also, the p value (.0264) can be used in the usual manner to perform this test.

Note that this test cannot be performed unless there are replicates for at least one level of x. MINITAB does provide another test for lack of fit that does not require replicates. The test is new, however, and some caution should be exercised in its use. The *experimental lack-of-fit test* actually involves a series of tests, results of several of which may be printed out on the output. For example, in Figure 5.14, results of tests examining curvilinearity in the variable MONTHS, lack of fit at the outer x values, and overall lack of fit are reported. These results are reported in terms of the p values, so the p-value decision rule can be applied:

$$\text{Reject } H_0 \quad \text{if} \quad p \text{ value} < \alpha$$
$$\text{Accept } H_0 \quad \text{if} \quad p \text{ value} \geq \alpha$$

For $\alpha = 0.05$, the test result indicates possible curvature in the variable MONTHS and an overall lack of fit.

F I G U R E 5.13

MINITAB Output Showing Use of Pure Error Lack-of-Fit Test for Telemarketing Example

```
The regression equation is
calls = 13.7 + 0.744 months

Predictor      Coef       Stdev     t-ratio       p
Constant     13.671       1.427        9.58   0.000
months      0.74351     0.06666       11.15   0.000

s = 1.787     R-sq = 87.4%    R-sq(adj) = 86.7%

Analysis of Variance

SOURCE        DF          SS          MS        F       p
Regression     1      397.45      397.45   124.41   0.000
Error         18       57.50        3.19
Total         19      454.95


Pure error test - F = 5.25   P = 0.0264   DF(pure error) = 6
10 rows with no replicates
```

F I G U R E 5.14

MINITAB Output Showing Experimental Lack-of-Fit Test for Telemarketing Example

```
The regression equation is
calls = 13.7 + 0.744 months

Predictor      Coef       Stdev     t-ratio       p
Constant     13.671       1.427        9.58   0.000
months      0.74351     0.06666       11.15   0.000

s = 1.787     R-sq = 87.4%    R-sq(adj) = 86.7%

Analysis of Variance

SOURCE        DF          SS          MS        F       p
Regression     1      397.45      397.45   124.41   0.000
Error         18       57.50        3.19
Total         19      454.95


Lack of fit test
Possible curvature in variable months (P = 0.000)
Possible lack of fit at outer X values      (P = 0.097)
Overall lack of fit test is significant at P = 0.000
```

5.4.3 Corrections for Violations of the Linearity Assumption

When the linearity assumption is violated, it is not always clear how to correct for it. The violation of this assumption implies that y and x are related in some curvilinear fashion, but there are many equations that describe curvilinear relationships. The idea behind the use of any equation of this sort is to transform the variables in such a way that a linear relationship is achieved. If x and y are related in a curvilinear fashion, then perhaps x^2 and y would have a linear relationship.

The violation of the linearity assumption was originally noted in the residual plots. If we have corrected for the violation, we should not see the same patterns in the residual plots from the corrected model. The residuals from a properly corrected model should be randomly scattered.

In this text, the following four commonly used corrections will be considered:

1   polynomial regression
2   reciprocal transformation of the x variable
3   log transformation of the x variable
4   log transformation of both the x and y variables

After trying one of these transformations, check the new residual plots to see if the violation was effectively corrected. If not, try one of the other corrections.

Polynomial Regression

A common correction when the linearity assumption is violated is to add powers of the explanatory variable that is viewed as the curvilinear component of the model. This type of model is called a *polynomial regression*. The order of the model is the highest power used for the explanatory variable. For example, a second-order polynomial regression in one variable would be written as

$$y = \beta_0 + \beta_1 x + \beta_2 x^2 + e$$

Higher-order polynomial models may be developed by adding higher powers of x. A Kth-order polynomial regression model in one variable, x, would be written as

$$y = \beta_0 + \beta_1 x + \beta_2 x^2 + \cdots + \beta_K x^K + e$$

In practice, the second-order model is often sufficient to describe curvilinear relationships encountered.

E X A M P L E   **5.2** **Telemarketing (continued)**

To model the curvilinear relationship in the telemarketing data a second-order polynomial regression will be tried. The model can be written

$$CALLS = \beta_0 + \beta_1 MONTHS + \beta_2 XSQR + e,$$

where XSQR is a variable created by squaring each value of the MONTHS variable.

Figures 5.15 and 5.19 show, respectively, the MINITAB and SAS regression estimates of the second-order model. The estimated regression is

$$\hat{y} = -0.14 + 2.31 MONTHS - 0.0401 XSQR$$

F I G U R E **5.15**

MINITAB Regression Output for Telemarketing Example with Second-Order Term Added

```
The regression equation is
calls = - 0.14 + 2.31 months - 0.0401 xsqr

Predictor        Coef       Stdev     t-ratio        p
Constant       -0.140       2.323       -0.06     0.952
months         2.3102      0.2501        9.24     0.000
xsqr        -0.040118    0.006333       -6.33     0.000

s = 1.003      R-sq = 96.2%     R-sq(adj) = 95.8%

Analysis of Variance

SOURCE         DF          SS          MS         F         p
Regression      2       437.84      218.92    217.50     0.000
Error          17        17.11        1.01
Total          19       454.95

SOURCE         DF      SEQ SS
months          1      397.45
xsqr            1       40.39
```

Two checks should be made at this point to determine whether the second-order model is preferred to the original linear model: (1) test to see whether the coefficient of the second-order term is significantly different from zero, and (2) check to see whether the new residual plots indicate an improved model.

To determine whether the x^2 variable has significantly improved the fit of the regression, the following hypotheses can be tested:

$$H_0: \quad \beta_2 = 0$$
$$H_a: \quad \beta_2 \neq 0,$$

where β_2 is the coefficient of x^2. The t test discussed in Chapter 4 for multiple regression can be used to conduct the test. For $\alpha = 0.05$, the decision rule is:

Reject H_0 if $t > 2.11$ or $t < -2.11$
Accept H_0 if $-2.11 \leq t \leq 2.11$

The test statistic value is (see Figure 5.15)

$$t = -6.33$$

The null hypothesis is rejected. The x^2 term adds significantly to the ability of the regression to explain the variation in y. Thus, the term should remain in the equation. Note that the p value could also have been used to conduct this test (p value = 0.000 < .05, so reject H_0).

Once a decision is made to keep the second-order term in the model, the lower-order term is typically kept in the model regardless of the t test result on its coefficient. There are good statistical reasons for keeping lower-order terms in a polynomial regression when the higher-order terms are judged important.[2]

---

[2] See "A Property of Well-Formulated Polynomial Regression Models," J. L. Peixoto, *The American Statistician* 44 (1990): 26–30.

F I G U R E **5.16**

MINITAB Residual Plot of Standardized Residuals versus Fitted Values for Second-Order Model

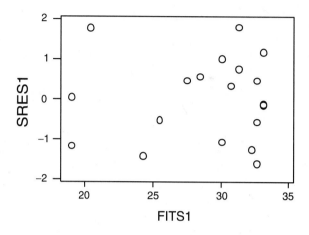

FITS1

F I G U R E **5.17**

MINITAB Residual Plot of Standardized Residuals versus Explanatory Variable MONTHS for Second-Order Model

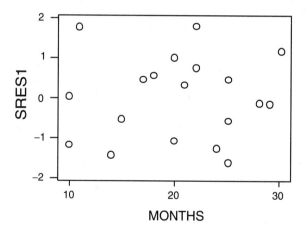

MONTHS

The test result on the second-order term by itself is not sufficient evidence to judge this model to be adequate. The goal in adding the second-order term was to correct for the curvilinear patterns noted in the original residual plots. To see if this has been accomplished, the residual plots from the new equation must be examined. The residual plots of the standardized residuals versus the fitted values (FITS1), the MONTHS variable, and the XSQR variable, are shown in Figures 5.16, 5.17, and 5.18, respectively. The equivalent SAS plots are shown in Figures 5.20, 5.21, and 5.22.

F I G U R E 5.18

MINITAB Residual Plot of Standardized Residuals versus Explanatory Variable XSQR for Second-Order Model

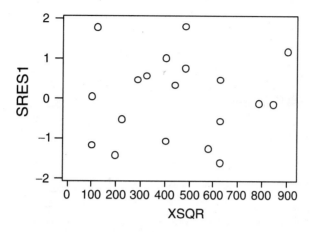

F I G U R E 5.19

SAS Output for Telemarketing Example with Second-Order Term Added

Dependent Variable: CALLS

Analysis of Variance

Source	DF	Sum of Squares	Mean Square	F Value	Prob>F
Model	2	437.83927	218.91964	217.503	0.0001
Error	17	17.11073	1.00651		
C Total	19	454.95000			

Root MSE	1.00325	R-square	0.9624	
Dep Mean	28.95000	Adj R-sq	0.9580	
C.V.	3.46546			

Parameter Estimates

Variable	DF	Parameter Estimate	Standard Error	T for H0: Parameter=0	Prob > |T|
INTERCEP	1	-0.140471	2.32263036	-0.060	0.9525
MONTHS	1	2.310202	0.25012170	9.236	0.0001
XSQR	1	-0.040118	0.00633281	-6.335	0.0001

Looking at these residual plots, no distinct patterns can be seen. Contrast this with the obvious patterns of Figures 5.8 and 5.9 or 5.10 and 5.11. The addition of the x^2 variable appears to have corrected for the curvilinearity. The second-order model is an improvement over the first-order model, and the regression assumptions appear to be satisfied.

F I G U R E 5.20

SAS Residual Plot of Standardized Residuals versus Fitted Values for Second-Order Model

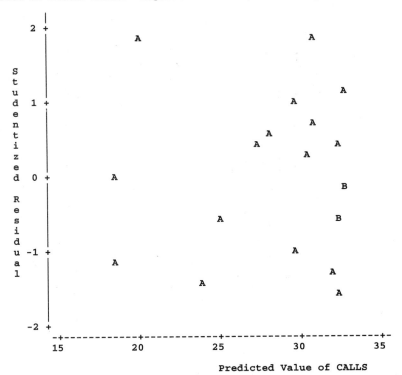

Higher-order terms could be added to the model, but there appears to be little justification in doing so from looking at the second-order model regression output and residual plots.

Other indicators that the regression has been improved by adding the x^2 term include the reduction in the standard error of the regression from 1.787 to 1.003, and the increase in adjusted R^2 from 86.7% to 95.8%. ∎

One caution should be observed in using higher-order polynomial regression models. Correlations between powers of a variable can cause computational problems for least squares. These correlations result in a problem called *multicollinearity*, which will be discussed in more detail later in this chapter. To reduce the possibility of computational difficulties, the use of explanatory variables that have been centered often is recommended. For example, instead of using the explanatory variables, x, x^2, x^3, and x^4, use instead

$$x - \bar{x}, (x - \bar{x})^2, (x - \bar{x})^3, \quad \text{and} \quad (x - \bar{x})^4,$$

F I G U R E 5.21

SAS Residual Plot of Standardized Residuals versus Explanatory Variable MONTHS for Second-Order Model

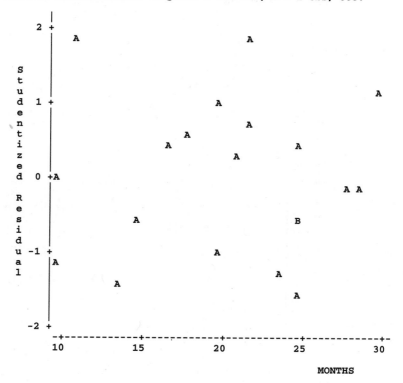

where $\bar{x}$ is the sample mean of the variable values. Using the centered variables helps to avoid multicollinearity problems to some extent.

Reciprocal Transformation of the x Variable

Other transformations may produce a linear relationship. A fairly common example is the reciprocal transformation:

$$y = \beta_0 + \beta_1 \left(\frac{1}{x} \right) + e$$

In this equation, x and y are inversely related, but the inverse relationship is not a linear one. (Note that this transformation is not defined when $x = 0$.)

F I G U R E   **5.22**

SAS Residual Plot of Standardized Residuals versus Explanatory Variable XSQR for Second-Order Model

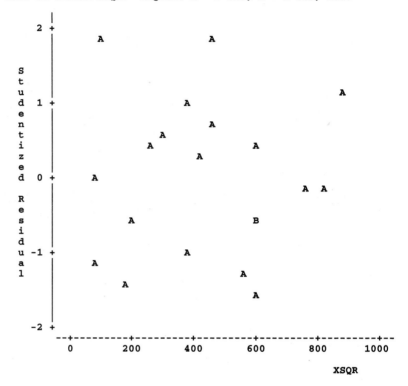

```
Plot of STRES1*XSQR.   Legend: A = 1 obs, B = 2 obs, etc.
```

E X A M P L E   **5.3**   **MPG versus WEIGHT**

A scatterplot of a possible curvilinear inverse relationship is shown in Figure 5.23. The variables are CITYMPG (y), the number of miles per gallon obtained by a car in city driving, and WEIGHT (x), the weight of the car in pounds. (This information was available for 144 cars listed in Road and Track's *The Complete '94 Car Buyer's Guide.* The complete data set is listed in Table 7.3.)

As WEIGHT increases, the mileage decreases, as would be expected. The MINITAB regression output for the regression of CITYMPG on WEIGHT is shown in Figure 5.24 and the SAS output is in Figure 5.27. The MINITAB residual plots are shown in Figures 5.25 and 5.26, with the SAS residual plots in Figures 5.28 and 5.29. Note that the residuals tend to be positive for lower and higher weights (see Figures 5.26 and 5.29) and negative for middle weights (at least, in general). This again suggests a curvilinear pattern. Looking back at the

F I G U R E **5.23**

MINITAB Scatterplot of CITYMPG versus WEIGHT

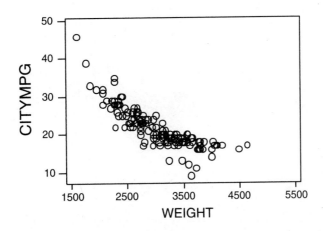

F I G U R E **5.24**

MINITAB Regression Output for Regression of CITYMPG on WEIGHT

```
The regression equation is
citympg = 45.1 - 0.00772 weight

Predictor        Coef       Stdev     t-ratio        p
Constant       45.078       1.278       35.27    0.000
weight      -0.0077206   0.0004133      -18.68    0.000

s = 2.943      R-sq = 71.1%     R-sq(adj) = 70.9%

Analysis of Variance

SOURCE          DF          SS          MS          F         p
Regression       1       3022.7      3022.7     348.91    0.000
Error          142       1230.2         8.7
Total          143       4252.9

Unusual Observations
Obs.    weight   citympg       Fit   Stdev.Fit    Residual    St.Resid
  22      4477    16.000    10.513       0.645       5.487      1.91 X
  45      3235    13.000    20.102       0.259      -7.102     -2.42R
  53      1621    46.000    32.563       0.634      13.437      4.67RX
  56      2275    34.000    27.514       0.399       6.486      2.22R
  57      2265    35.000    27.591       0.402       7.409      2.54R
  69      3640     9.000    16.975       0.350      -7.975     -2.73R
  82      2790    17.000    23.538       0.265      -6.538     -2.23R
  88      4630    17.000     9.332       0.703       7.668      2.68RX
 130      1780    39.000    31.336       0.574       7.664      2.65R

R denotes an obs. with a large st. resid.
X denotes an obs. whose X value gives it large influence.
```

FIGURE **5.25**

MINITAB Residual Plot of Standardized Residuals versus Fitted Values

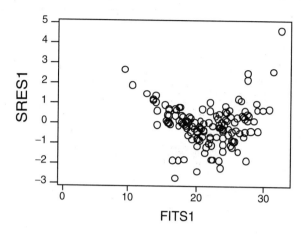

FIGURE **5.26**

MINITAB Residual Plot of Standardized Residuals versus Explanatory Variable WEIGHT

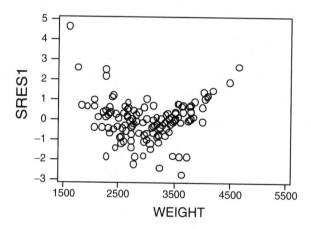

scatterplot in Figure 5.23, it is obvious that mileage decreases as weight increases. Combining information from the residual plots and scatterplot suggests the curvilinear inverse relationship

$$CITYMPG = \beta_0 + \beta_1 \left(\frac{1}{WEIGHT} \right) + e$$

Figure 5.30 shows the scatterplot of CITYMPG versus the transformed explanatory variable 1/WEIGHT (named WTINV). This scatterplot appears linear. The regression output for the

F I G U R E 5.27

SAS Regression Output for Regression of CITYMPG on WEIGHT

```
Dependent Variable: CITYMPG

                    Analysis of Variance

                    Sum of        Mean
Source      DF      Squares       Square      F Value     Prob>F

Model        1    3022.73254    3022.73254    348.908     0.0001
Error      142    1230.20496       8.66342
C Total    143    4252.93750

        Root MSE        2.94337    R-square      0.7107
        Dep Mean       21.64583    Adj R-sq      0.7087
        C.V.           13.59785

                    Parameter Estimates

                 Parameter    Standard    T for H0:
Variable    DF    Estimate      Error    Parameter=0    Prob > |T|

INTERCEP     1    45.078317   1.27823220    35.266         0.0001
WEIGHT       1    -0.007721   0.00041333   -18.679         0.0001
```

regression of CITYMPG on WTINV is shown in Figure 5.31 for MINITAB and Figure 5.34 for SAS.

The R^2 value has increased from 71.1% to 81.3%. The standard error of the regression has decreased from 2.943 to 2.367. Both of these facts also support the use of the curvilinear model. The residual plots from the curvilinear model are shown in Figures 5.32 and 5.33 for MINITAB, and 5.35 and 5.36 for SAS. The patterns observed in the residual plots from the linear model (Figures 5.25 and 5.26, or 5.28 and 5.29) are no longer apparent in these plots. ■

Log Transformation of the *x* Variable

Another useful curvilinear equation is

$$y = \beta_0 + \beta_1 \ln(x) + e,$$

where $\ln(x)$ is the natural logarithm of x. It is assumed here that the x values are positive (because $\ln(x)$ is not defined for $x \leq 0$).

Log Transformation of Both the *x* and *y* Variables

It is also possible to transform the y variable in attempting to achieve a linear relationship. The natural logarithm of y often is used as the dependent variable, with the natural logarithm of x as the explanatory variable:

$$\ln(y) = \beta_0 + \beta_1 \ln(x) + e$$

F I G U R E **5.28**

SAS Residual Plot of Standardized Residuals versus Fitted Values

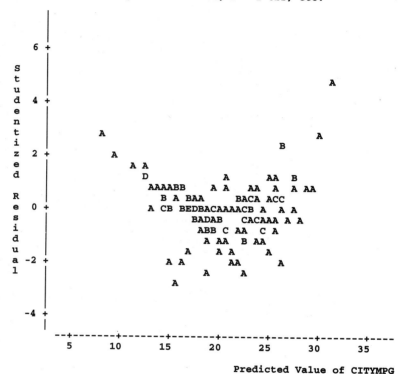

    Some caution must be exercised if this model is chosen. First, all *x* and *y* values must be positive for the natural log transformation to be defined. Second, because ln(*y*) is used as the dependent variable, it becomes more difficult to compare this regression to any model using *y* as the dependent variable. The R^2 values of the two regressions cannot be compared, for example, because two different units of measurement are used for the dependent variable. Thus, increases in R^2 when the natural logarithm transformation is applied to *y* do not necessarily suggest an improved model. (Note that transformations of the explanatory variables do not create this type of problem. It is only when the *y* variable is transformed that comparison becomes more difficult.)

    It is important to keep in mind that the type of transformation to correct for curvilinearity will not always be obvious. If *y* and *x* are related in a curvilinear manner, the goal is to transform the variables in some manner to achieve a linear relationship. Different transformations may be tried (including transformations not discussed in this section) and the one that appears to do the best job chosen.

F I G U R E **5.29**

SAS Residual Plot of Standardized Residuals versus Explanatory Variable WEIGHT

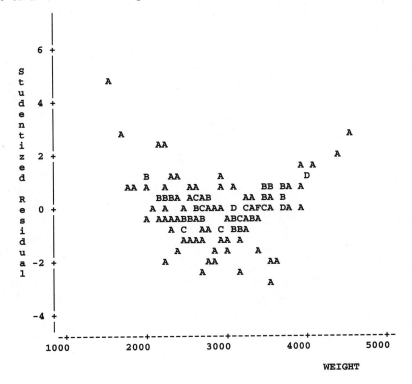

```
Plot of STRES*WEIGHT.  Legend: A = 1 obs, B = 2 obs, etc.
```

In deciding what type of transformation to use, look at the scatterplot showing the relationship between y and x. This will help to identify the form of the relationship between the two variables. The residual plot will indicate when the linearity assumption has been violated but not the appropriate transformation to correct for the violation.

When deciding between two or more possible transformations, ease of interpretation can also be used to help in the decision. Other things being equal (or nearly so), it is best to keep the regression model as simple as possible or to use the transformation that is easiest to explain in practical terms.

Fitting Curvilinear Trends

In Chapter 3, the linear trend model was presented:

$$y_i = \beta_0 + \beta_1 t + e_i,$$

F I G U R E   **5.30**

MINITAB Scatterplot of CITYMPG versus WTINV = 1/WEIGHT

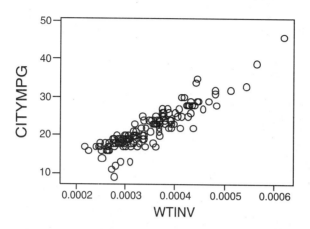

where t is simply a variable indicating time sequence, $t = 1, 2, \ldots, n$. Just as curvilinear patterns can be observed with regard to x variables as discussed in this section, so can curvilinear trends occur. It is possible to model certain curvilinear trends using regression. This is done in a very similar manner to the corrections for violations of the linearity assumption just discussed. A few basic curvilinear trend models are presented here.

A quadratic trend equation can be written

$$y_i = \beta_0 + \beta_1 t + \beta_2 t^2 + e_i$$

Examples of the linear and quadratic trends are shown in Figure 5.37(a) and 5.37(b), respectively.

The equation for a curve called an *S-curve* is given by

$$y_i = \exp\left(\beta_0 + \beta_1\left(\frac{1}{t}\right)\right),$$

where exp denotes the exponential operator. The value $e = 2.7$ (approximately) is raised to the power $\beta_0 + \beta_1(1/t)$. The *S-curve* is shown in Figure 5.37(c). This type of trend might be used to model demand for certain products over their lifetime. Demand is slow initially until the product becomes better known. Then demand picks up until a saturation point is reached. At that time, demand levels off.

The *S-curve* equation cannot be estimated directly using least squares. By taking natural logarithms of both sides of the equation, however, a new equation will be

F I G U R E 5.31

MINITAB Regression Output for Regression of CITYMPG on WTINV = 1/WEIGHT

```
The regression equation is
citympg = - 1.66 + 67931 wtinv

Predictor      Coef      Stdev    t-ratio        p
Constant     -1.6639     0.9587      -1.74    0.085
wtinv         67931        2734      24.84    0.000

s = 2.367      R-sq = 81.3%     R-sq(adj) = 81.2%

Analysis of Variance

SOURCE         DF        SS         MS         F        p
Regression      1     3457.5     3457.5    617.25    0.000
Error         142      795.4        5.6
Total         143     4252.9

Unusual Observations
Obs.     wtinv    citympg      Fit   Stdev.Fit   Residual   St.Resid
  40   0.000288    13.000   17.879      0.249     -4.879      -2.07R
  45   0.000309    13.000   19.335      0.218     -6.335      -2.69R
  46   0.000269    11.000   16.622      0.282     -5.622      -2.39R
  53   0.000617    46.000   40.243      0.774      5.757       2.57RX
  56   0.000440    34.000   28.196      0.329      5.804       2.48R
  57   0.000442    35.000   28.328      0.334      6.672       2.85R
  69   0.000275     9.000   16.999      0.272     -7.999      -3.40R
  79   0.000436    22.000   27.962      0.322     -5.962      -2.54R
  82   0.000358    17.000   22.684      0.202     -5.684      -2.41R
 119   0.000279    12.000   17.258      0.265     -5.258      -2.24R
 127   0.000542    33.000   35.155      0.578     -2.155      -0.94 X
 130   0.000562    39.000   36.500      0.630      2.500       1.10 X
 137   0.000513    32.000   33.173      0.504     -1.173      -0.51 X

R denotes an obs. with a large st. resid.
X denotes an obs. whose X value gives it large influence.
```

obtained that can be estimated. Because $\ln(\exp(x)) = x$ for any x, taking natural logarithms of both sides of the equation produces

$$\ln(y_i) = \beta_0 + \beta_1 \left(\frac{1}{t} \right)$$

Regressing $\ln(y_i)$ on $1/t$ will produce estimates of β_0 and β_1. When forecasting with this model, care should be taken. For example, write $y_i' = \ln(y_i)$ and $t' = 1/t$, and write the estimated regression equation as

$$\hat{y}_i' = b_0 + b_1 t'$$

F I G U R E **5.32**

MINITAB Residual Plot of Standardized Residuals versus Fitted Values for Transformed Model

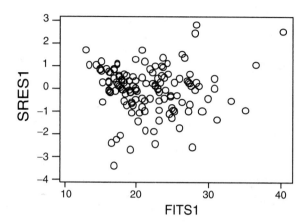

F I G U R E **5.33**

MINITAB Residual Plot of Standardized Residuals versus Explanatory Variable WTINV = 1/WEIGHT

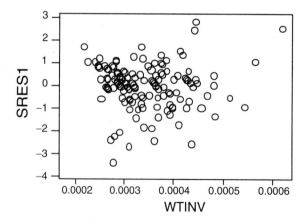

F I G U R E 5.34

SAS Regression Output for Regression of CITYMPG on WTINV = 1/WEIGHT

Dependent Variable: CITYMPG

Analysis of Variance

Source	DF	Sum of Squares	Mean Square	F Value	Prob>F
Model	1	3457.52190	3457.52190	617.247	0.0001
Error	142	795.41560	5.60152		
C Total	143	4252.93750			

Root MSE	2.36675	R-square	0.8130	
Dep Mean	21.64583	Adj R-sq	0.8117	
C.V.	10.93399			

Parameter Estimates

Variable	DF	Parameter Estimate	Standard Error	T for H0: Parameter=0	Prob > |T|
INTERCEP	1	-1.663875	0.95873178	-1.735	0.0848
WTINV	1	67931	2734.2531192	24.844	0.0001

The estimated equation provides the forecast for time period T

$$\hat{y}'_T = b_0 + b_1 \left(\frac{1}{T} \right)$$

Note that this is a forecast of y'_T or the natural logarithm of y_T. To obtain a forecast of the original dependent variable, y_T, the conversion back to the original units from logarithmic units must be made:

$$\exp(\hat{y}'_T) = \hat{y}_T$$

Exponential trends also are used in time-series applications. The equation for an exponential trend is

$$y_i = \exp(\beta_0 + \beta_1 t)$$

Again, to estimate β_0 and β_1, the equation is transformed using natural logarithms. Writing $y'_i = \ln(y_i)$, the transformed equation is

$$y'_i = \beta_0 + \beta_1 t$$

Regressing $\ln(y_i) = y'_i$ on t will produce estimates of β_0 and β_1. As with the S-curve, exercise caution when using this equation for forecasting. The natural logarithm of y_i

FIGURE 5.35

SAS Residual Plot of Standardized Residuals versus Fitted Values for Transformed Model

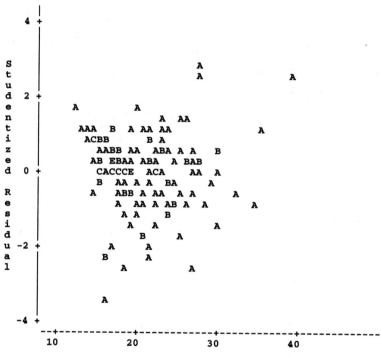

```
Plot of STRES1*FITS1.   Legend: A = 1 obs, B = 2 obs, etc.

         |
      4 +
S        |
t        |
u        |                              A
d     2 +                              A            A
e        |
n        |      A          A
t        |                        A  AA
i        |       AAA  B   A AA  AA              A
z        |       ACBB       B A
e        |        AABB AA   ABA A A    B
d        |        AB EBAA ABA   A BAB
      0 +         CACCCE  ACA      AA  A
R        |        B  AA A A  BA       A
e        |      A    ABB A AA  A A       A
s        |           A  AA A AB A  A        A
i        |           A A     B
d        |            A   A        A
u    -2 +         A      A
a        |        B      A
l        |           A          A
         |
         |        A
     -4 +
         --+-------------+-------------+-------------+-------------
           10           20            30            40

                                    Predicted Value of CITYMPG
```

F I G U R E 5.36

SAS Residual Plot of Standardized Residuals versus Explanatory Variable WTINV = 1/WEIGHT

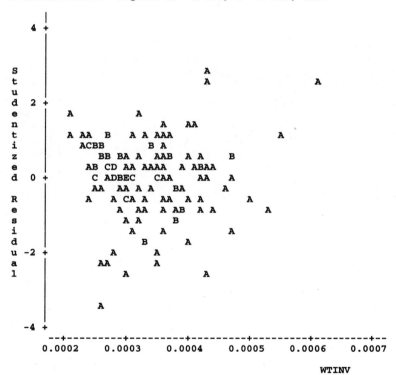

Plot of STRES1*WTINV.   Legend: A = 1 obs, B = 2 obs, etc.

F I G U R E 5.37

Examples of Types of Trends

(a) Linear trend

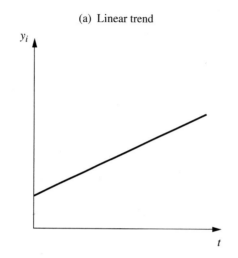

(c) S-curve

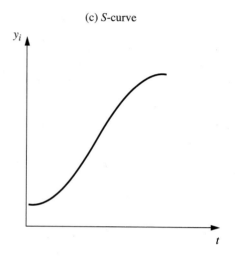

(b) Quadratic trend

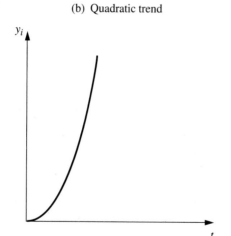

(b) Exponential trend ($\beta_0 = 0.0$)

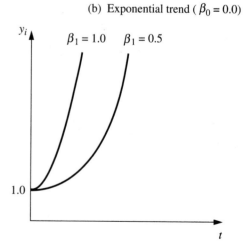

FIGURE 5.38
MINITAB Scatterplot of y versus x for Parabola Exercise

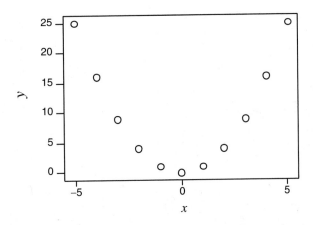

must be transformed back to its original units to obtain the desired forecast. Examples of exponential trends are shown in Figure 5.37(d).

Exercises

1 **Parabola** Consider the following data:

y	16	4	1	9	1	25	16	4	0	9	25
x	−4	−2	1	3	−1	−5	4	2	0	−3	5

Regard x as the explanatory variable and y as the dependent variable. Figure 5.38 shows the scatterplot of y versus x. Figure 5.39 shows the MINITAB regression output.

a Examine the scatterplot of y versus x. Is there a relationship between y and x?

b What is the estimated linear regression equation relating y to x?

c Test the hypothesis $H_0 : \beta_1 = 0$ against the alternative $H_a: \beta_1 \neq 0$ at the 1% level of significance. What conclusion can be drawn from the result of the test?

d Despite the outcome of the test in (c), does there appear to be a "strong" or "weak" association between x and y? Express this association in the form of an equation.

2 **Research and Development** A company is interested in the relationship between profit on a number of projects and two explanatory variables. These variables are the expenditure on research and development for the project (RD) and a measure of risk assigned at the outset of the project (RISK). Table 5.2 shows the data on the three variables PROFIT, RISK, and RD. PROFIT is measured in thousands of dollars and

F I G U R E **5.39**

MINITAB Regression Output for Regression of y on x for Parabola Exercise

```
The regression equation is
y = 10.0 + 0.000 x

Predictor        Coef        Stdev      t-ratio         p
Constant       10.000        2.944         3.40     0.008
x              0.0000        0.9309        0.00     1.000

s = 9.764      R-sq = 0.0%     R-sq(adj) = 0.0%

Analysis of Variance

SOURCE          DF          SS          MS         F         p
Regression       1        0.00        0.00      0.00     1.000
Error            9      858.00       95.33
Total           10      858.00
```

T A B L E **5.2**

Data for Research and Development Exercise

RD	RISK	PROFIT	RD	RISK	PROFIT
132.580	8.5	396	74.816	7.5	102
81.928	7.5	130	108.752	6.0	214
145.992	10.0	508	92.372	8.5	200
90.020	8.0	172	92.260	7.0	158
114.408	7.0	256	60.732	6.5	32
53.704	7.5	32	78.120	7.5	116
76.244	7.0	102	90.000	5.5	120
71.680	8.0	102	105.532	9.0	270
151.592	9.5	536	111.832	8.0	270

RD is measured in hundreds of dollars. The scatterplots of PROFIT versus RISK and PROFIT versus RD are shown in Figures 5.40 and 5.41, respectively. The MINITAB and SAS regressions are in Figures 5.42 and 5.43, respectively. The MINITAB residual plots of the standardized residuals versus the fitted values, RISK, and RD are shown in Figures 5.44, 5.45, and 5.46, respectively. The corresponding SAS plots are in Figures 5.47, 5.48, and 5.49.

F I G U R E **5.40**

MINITAB Scatterplot of PROFIT versus RISK for Research and Development Exercise

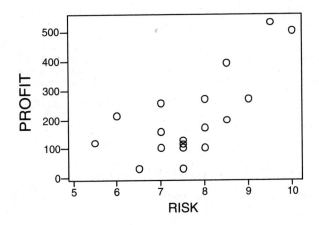

F I G U R E **5.41**

MINITAB Scatterplot of PROFIT versus RD for Research and Development Exercise

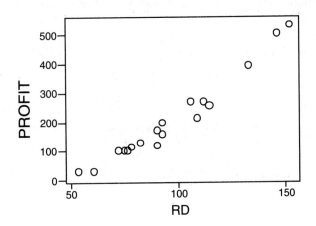

F I G U R E 5.42

MINITAB Regression Output for Regression of PROFIT on RISK and RD for Research and Development Exercise

```
The regression equation is
profit = - 453 + 4.51 rd + 29.3 risk

Predictor       Coef        Stdev      t-ratio          p
Constant     -453.18        23.51       -19.28      0.000
rd             4.5100       0.1538       29.33      0.000
risk          29.309        3.669         7.99      0.000

s = 14.34      R-sq = 99.2%     R-sq(adj) = 99.0%

Analysis of Variance

SOURCE          DF           SS           MS          F          p
Regression       2       361639       180820     879.08      0.000
Error           15         3085          206
Total           17       364724

SOURCE          DF       SEQ SS
rd               1       348510
risk             1        13129

Unusual Observations
Obs.      rd     profit      Fit   Stdev.Fit   Residual     St.Resid
   9     152     536.00   508.94        7.98      27.06         2.27R

R denotes an obs. with a large st. resid.
```

F I G U R E 5.43

SAS Regression Output for Regression of PROFIT on RISK and RD for Research and Development Exercise

```
Dependent Variable: PROFIT

                     Analysis of Variance

                      Sum of          Mean
Source       DF      Squares         Square      F Value      Prob>F

Model         2  361639.05686  180819.52843      879.077      0.0001
Error        15    3085.38758    205.69251
C Total      17  364724.44444

           Root MSE       14.34198      R-square        0.9915
           Dep Mean      206.44444      Adj R-sq        0.9904
           C.V.            6.94714

                     Parameter Estimates

                   Parameter      Standard     T for H0:
Variable    DF     Estimate         Error    Parameter=0   Prob > |T|

INTERCEP     1  -453.176321   23.50614355      -19.279       0.0001
RD           1     4.510005    0.15375017       29.333       0.0001
RISK         1    29.309040    3.66858555        7.989       0.0001
```

F I G U R E **5.44**

MINITAB Residual Plot of Standardized Residuals versus Fitted Values for Research and Development Exercise

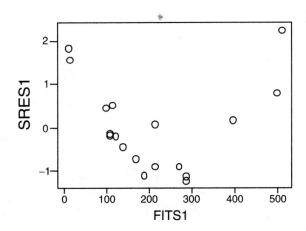

F I G U R E **5.45**

MINITAB Residual Plot of Standardized Residuals versus RISK for Research and Development Exercise

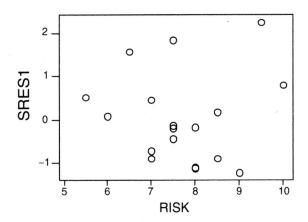

F I G U R E   5.46

MINITAB Residual Plot of Standardized Residuals versus RD for Research and Development Exercise

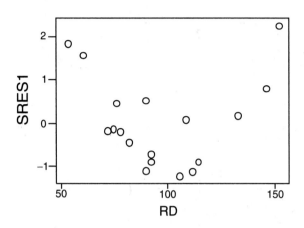

F I G U R E   5.47

SAS Residual Plot of Standardized Residuals versus Fitted Values for Research and Development Exercise

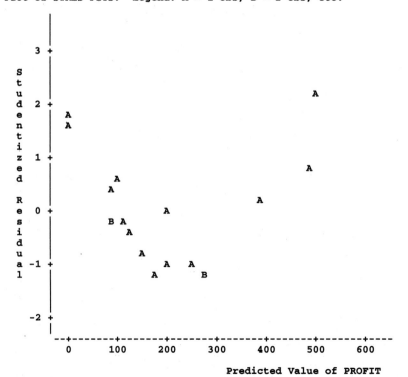

F I G U R E **5.48**

SAS Residual Plot of Standardized Residuals versus RISK for Research and Development Exercise

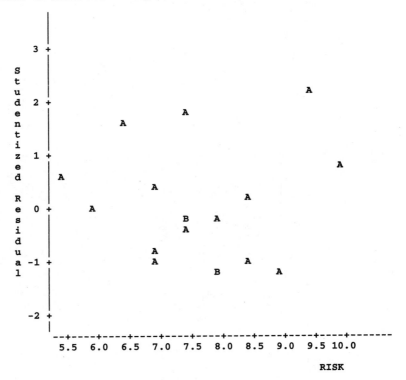

Plot of STRES*RISK.   Legend: A = 1 obs, B = 2 obs, etc.

Using any of the given outputs, does the linearity assumption appear to be violated? Justify your answer. If you answered yes, state how the violation might be corrected. Then try your correction using a computer regression routine. Does your model appear to be an improvement over the original model? Justify your answer.

These data are available on the data disk. In MINITAB, they can be read using

```
READ 'RD5' C1-C3
```

where C1 is RD, C2 is RISK, and C3 is PROFIT.

In SAS, the data can be read from the file RD5.DAT using

```
INPUT RD RISK PROFIT;
```

3 **Personal Consumption** Table 5.3 shows quarterly data on personal consumption (in billions of dollars) for the years 1975 through 1990. Seasonal effects have been removed.

F I G U R E **5.49**

SAS Residual Plot of Standardized Residuals versus RD for Research and Development Exercise

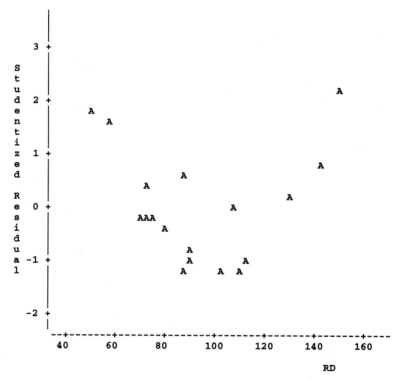

T A B L E **5.3**

Data for Personal Consumption Exercise

Date	Personal Consumption	Date	Personal Consumption	Date	Personal Consumption
1975.1	244.725	1977.2	313.375	1979.3	401.775
1975.2	252.075	1977.3	321.175	1979.4	413.125
1975.3	260.525	1977.4	330.600	1980.1	425.375
1975.4	267.575	1978.1	337.925	1980.2	426.225
1976.1	276.200	1978.2	352.525	1980.3	440.575
1976.2	281.125	1978.3	360.675	1980.4	455.900
1976.3	288.475	1978.4	370.075	1981.1	469.000
1976.4	297.275	1979.1	380.100	1981.2	477.225
1977.1	306.375	1979.2	388.700	1981.3	488.025

T A B L E **5.3** *(Cont.)*
Data for Personal Consumption Exercise

Date	Personal Consumption	Date	Personal Consumption	Date	Personal Consumption
1981.4	492.000	1985.1	647.300	1988.1	799.775
1982.1	501.350	1985.2	659.100	1988.2	815.125
1982.2	507.350	1985.3	676.050	1988.3	831.650
1982.3	518.275	1985.4	684.950	1988.4	849.550
1982.4	532.175	1986.1	696.200	1989.1	859.125
1983.1	540.725	1986.2	703.075	1989.2	872.650
1983.2	557.975	1986.3	720.500	1989.3	887.925
1983.3	572.175	1986.4	730.775	1989.4	898.200
1983.4	586.700	1987.1	740.700	1990.1	916.825
1984.1	598.100	1987.2	757.525	1990.2	926.500
1984.2	611.125	1987.3	772.850	1990.3	946.300
1984.3	619.450	1987.4	781.150	1990.4	953.000
1984.4	640.600				

These data were taken from *Business Statistics 1963–91*.

Figure 5.50 shows the MINITAB time-series plot of the data. A regression of personal consumption on a linear trend variable is shown in Figure 5.51 for MINITAB and in Figure 5.52 for SAS. Plots of the standardized residuals versus the fitted values are shown, respectively, for MINITAB in Figure 5.53 and for SAS in Figure 5.55. The MINITAB time-series plot of the standardized residuals is shown in Figure 5.54. Use the outputs to help answer the following questions:

a What is the estimated regression equation?

b What percentage of the variation in personal consumption has been explained by the regression?

c From the residual plots, do any of the assumptions of the linear regression model appear to be violated? If so, what correction would you suggest? Write out the corrected regression equation clearly.

These data are available on the data disk for further analysis. In MINITAB, they can be read using

```
READ 'PERCON5' C1
```

In SAS, the data can be read from the file PERSCON5.DAT using

```
INPUT PERCONS;
```

F I G U R E **5.50**

MINITAB Time-Series Plot of Personal Consumption Data

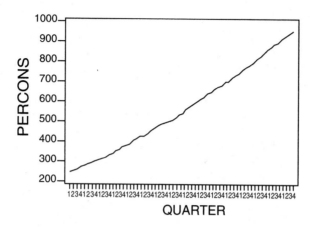

F I G U R E **5.51**

MINITAB Regression Output for Regression of Personal Consumption on Linear Trend Variable

```
The regression equation is
percons = 193 + 11.4 trend

Predictor        Coef       Stdev      t-ratio       p
Constant      192.935       4.632        41.65    0.000
trend         11.3864       0.1239       91.90    0.000

s = 18.31       R-sq = 99.3%      R-sq(adj) = 99.3%

Analysis of Variance

SOURCE        DF          SS          MS         F        p
Regression     1      2831550     2831550   8445.27   0.000
Error         62        20788         335
Total         63      2852337

Unusual Observations
Obs.    trend    percons     Fit   Stdev.Fit   Residual   St.Resid
  1      1.0     244.73   204.32      4.52       40.40       2.28R
  2      2.0     252.07   215.71      4.42       36.37       2.05R
 63     63.0     946.30   910.28      4.42       36.02       2.03R

R denotes an obs. with a large st. resid.
```

F I G U R E 5.52

SAS Regression Output for Regression of Personal Consumption on Linear Trend

```
Dependent Variable: PERCONS

                      Analysis of Variance

                        Sum of           Mean
Source        DF       Squares          Square      F Value      Prob>F

Model          1  2831549.4451  2831549.4451      8445.269      0.0001
Error         62    20787.50325    335.28231
C Total       63  2852336.9483

          Root MSE      18.31072      R-square      0.9927
          Dep Mean     562.99258      Adj R-sq      0.9926
          C.V.           3.25239

                      Parameter Estimates

                   Parameter      Standard      T for H0:
Variable    DF      Estimate         Error    Parameter=0    Prob > |T|

INTERCEP     1    192.935156    4.63185453        41.654        0.0001
TREND        1     11.386382    0.12390220        91.898        0.0001
```

F I G U R E 5.53

MINITAB Residual Plot of Standardized Residuals versus Fitted Values for Personal Consumption Exercise

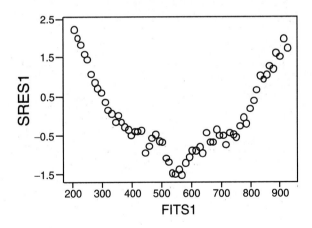

F I G U R E **5.54**

MINITAB Time-Series Plot of Standardized Residuals for Personal Consumption Exercise

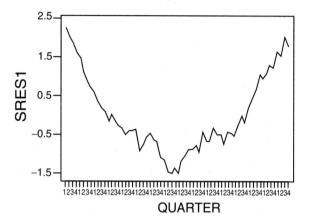

F I G U R E **5.55**

SAS Residual Plot of Standardized Residuals versus Fitted Values for Personal Consumption Exercise

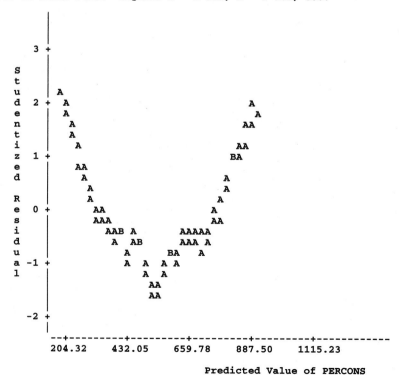

5.5
Assessing the Assumption That the Variance Around the Regression Line Is Constant

5.5.1 Using Plots to Assess the Assumption of Constant Variance

Assumption (b) of Section 5.2 states that the disturbances in the population regression equation e_i have constant variance σ_e^2. In a residual plot of $\hat{e}_i$ versus an explanatory variable x, the residuals should appear scattered randomly about the zero line with no differences in the amount of variation in the residuals regardless of the value of x. If there appears to be a difference in variation (for example, if the residuals are more spread out for large values of x than for small values), then the assumption of constant variance may be violated. In a residual plot, nonconstant variance often is identified by a "cone-shaped" pattern as shown in Figure 5.56. Again, the violation is indicated by a systematic pattern in the residuals. In many texts, the term *heteroscedasticity* is used in place of "nonconstant variance." Example 5.4 illustrates the use of plots to assess the constant variance assumption.

E X A M P L E **5.4** **Automobile Price**

The scatterplot of price (PRICE) versus horsepower (HP) for 152 cars listed in Road and Track's *Complete '94 Car Buyer's Guide* is shown in Figure 5.57. The MINITAB regression output relating price (y) to horsepower (HP) is shown in Figure 5.58 and the SAS output is in Figure 5.61. The MINITAB plots of the standardized residuals versus the fitted values and the standardized residuals versus HP are shown in Figures 5.59 and 5.60, respectively (with the equivalent SAS plots in Figures 5.62 and 5.63). In each of these plots the cone-shaped pattern of residuals is observed. Note that the variability of the residuals increases as the horsepower of the car increases. This suggests that there is more variability in the price of more powerful cars than in the price of less powerful cars. This pattern also can be seen in the scatterplot of PRICE versus HP. Such violations of assumptions, however, are typically magnified in the residual plots, as in this case. ∎

When the disturbance variance is not constant, using the least-squares method has two major drawbacks:

1   The estimates of the regression coefficients are no longer minimum variance estimates.

2   The estimates of the standard errors of the coefficients are biased.

The first drawback suggests that estimates of the coefficients with smaller sampling variability may exist. Because of the second drawback, hypothesis tests about the population regression parameters may provide misleading results.

F I G U R E **5.56**

Cone-shaped Pattern in Residual Plot Suggesting Nonconstant Variance

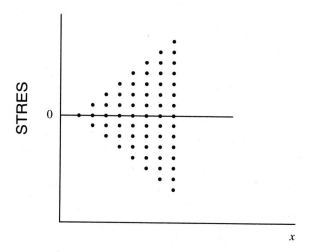

F I G U R E **5.57**

MINITAB Scatterplot of Automobile Price versus Horsepower

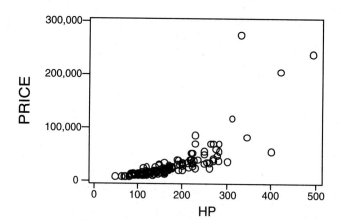

F I G U R E 5.58

MINITAB Regression Output for Automobile Price Example

```
The regression equation is
price = - 32776 + 369 hp

152 cases used 2 cases contain missing values

Predictor       Coef      Stdev     t-ratio       p
Constant      -32776       4544       -7.21   0.000
hp            369.47       25.18      14.67   0.000

s = 22564      R-sq = 58.9%    R-sq(adj) = 58.7%

Analysis of Variance

SOURCE        DF          SS           MS          F         p
Regression     1 1.09581E+11 1.09581E+11     215.22   0.000
Error        150 76372066304    509147104
Total        151 1.85953E+11

Unusual Observations
Obs.       hp      price      Fit  Stdev.Fit   Residual   St.Resid
  7       330     275000    89150       4537     185850      8.41RX
 44       400      55000   115013       6191     -60013     -2.77RX
 50       421     206000   122772       6699      83228      3.86RX
 76       492     240000   149004       8433      90996      4.35RX
127       345      82260    94692       4885     -12432     -0.56 X

R denotes an obs. with a large st. resid.
X denotes an obs. whose X value gives it large influence.
```

F I G U R E 5.59

MINITAB Residual Plot of Standardized Residuals versus Fitted Values for Automobile Price Example

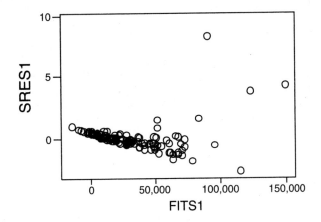

FIGURE **5.60**

MINITAB Residual Plot of Standardized Residuals versus HP for Automobile Price Example

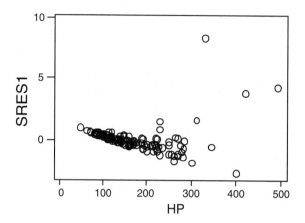

FIGURE **5.61**

SAS Regression Output for Automobile Price Example

```
Dependent Variable: PRICE

                    Analysis of Variance

                     Sum of         Mean
Source      DF      Squares        Square      F Value      Prob>F

Model        1 109580875373 109580875373      215.224      0.0001
Error      150   76372063740   509147091.6
C Total    151  185952939113

           Root MSE     22564.28797    R-square      0.5893
           Dep Mean     28240.16447    Adj R-sq      0.5866
           C.V.            79.90140

                    Parameter Estimates

               Parameter       Standard      T for H0:
Variable   DF   Estimate          Error    Parameter=0    Prob > |T|

INTERCEP    1     -32776    4543.9990426      -7.213        0.0001
HP          1 369.472752    25.18469328       14.671        0.0001
```

5.5.2 Test for Nonconstant Variance

Several tests are available for nonconstant variance, although a recent study by Griffiths and Surekha (1986) demonstrated that a test from J. Szroeter tends to be better at detecting nonconstant variance. The hypotheses to be tested are

F I G U R E 5.62

SAS Residual Plot of Standardized Residuals versus Fitted Values for Automobile Price
Example

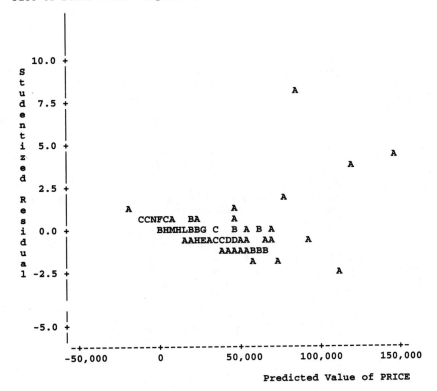

```
Plot of STRES*FITS.   Legend: A = 1 obs, B = 2 obs, etc.
```

H_0: Variance is constant
H_a: Variance is not constant

Szroeter's test statistic is

$$Q = \left(\frac{6n}{n^2 - 1}\right)^{1/2}\left(h - \frac{n+1}{2}\right),$$

where n is the sample size,

$$h = \frac{\sum\limits_{i=1}^{n} i\hat{e}_i^2}{\sum\limits_{i=1}^{n} \hat{e}_i^2},$$

and $\hat{e}_i$ is the residual from the ith observation in the regression equation. The decision
rule for the test is:

F I G U R E **5.63**

SAS Residual Plot of Standardized Residuals versus HP for Automobile Price Example

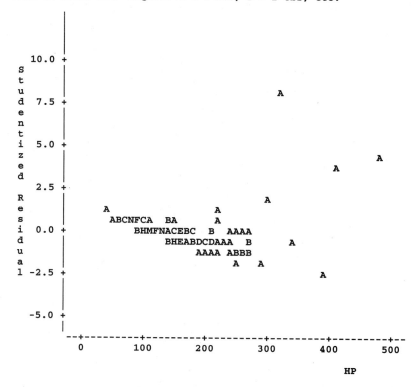

Plot of STRES*HP.   Legend: A = 1 obs, B = 2 obs, etc.

$$\text{Reject } H_0 \quad \text{if} \quad Q > Z_\alpha$$
$$\text{Accept } H_0 \quad \text{if} \quad Q \le Z_\alpha$$

where α is the level of significance for the test, and Z_α is chosen from the standard normal table with upper-tail area α.

Szroeter's test assumes that all the observations can be arranged in order of increasing variance. Typically, it is assumed that the variance will increase as the value of one of the explanatory variables increases. Thus, the data need to be arranged according to the values of this explanatory variable. As a simple example, suppose the values of x and y in a simple regression are as follows:

x	3	2	7	9	4
y	6	4	16	15	8

Arranging the values of x in ascending order and maintaining the associated values of y would result in the following arrangement of the data:

x	2	3	4	7	9
y	4	6	8	16	15

After reordering the data in this way, a regression is run and the residuals, $\hat{e}_i$, are saved and used to compute h. The value for h then is substituted into the equation to compute the test statistic Q.

5.5.3 Corrections for Nonconstant Variance

There are several possible corrections for nonconstant variance. All require a transformation of the dependent variable. This often makes comparison of the new regression equation with the old equation difficult. Some commonly used corrections for nonconstant variances are as follows:

1 In place of the dependent variable y, use the natural logarithm of y, $\ln(y)$. The natural logarithms of the y values will be less variable than the original y values and may stabilize the variance. For example, consider the numbers in Table 5.4. Note the difference in variation between the original y values and their natural logarithms.

As mentioned earlier in this chapter, the natural logarithm transformation is only defined for positive numbers.

The natural logarithm transformation is the appropriate transformation to be used when the error standard deviation is proportional to the mean of the dependent variable.

2 In place of the dependent variable y, use the square root of y, $\sqrt{y}$. The square roots of the y values will be less variable than the original y values and may stabilize the variance. Note that the square root transformation is not defined for negative numbers.

The square root transformation is appropriate when the dependent variable is a count variable that follows a Poisson distribution.

3 If the disturbance variance is thought to be proportional to some function of one of the x variables, the values of that variable can be used to stabilize the variance. For example, if

$$\sigma_{e_i}^2 = \sigma^2 x_i^2$$

is thought to express the relationship between the variance at each observation i and the associated value of the x variable, then dividing each variable in the regression by x will stabilize the variance. If the original equation is

$$y_i = \beta_0 + \beta_1 x_i + e_i$$

T A B L E 5.4

Example of Using the Natural Logarithm Transformation to Reduce Variability

y	1	2	5	10	50
$\ln(y)$	0	0.69	1.61	2.30	3.91

then, after dividing through by x_i, the transformed model will be

$$\frac{y_i}{x_i} = \beta_0 \left(\frac{1}{x_i}\right) + \beta_1 + e_i',$$

where $e_i' = e_i / x_i$ is a new disturbance with constant variance. Note that the roles played by β_0 and β_1 have been reversed in the transformed equation. Furthermore, the transformation is not defined when x_i is zero.

E X A M P L E   **5.5** **Automobile Price (continued)**

The MINITAB regression output for the regression of the natural log of price (LOGPRICE) on horsepower (HP) is shown in Figure 5.64 and the residual plots are in Figures 5.65 and 5.66. In the residual plots, the cone-shaped pattern has been greatly reduced. Using the log transformation stabilized the variance, so it is now relatively constant for all values of x. Caution should be exercised in interpreting and using the regression output, however. The output in Figure 5.64 shows results concerning the relationship of the log of price to x. All information from the output must be interpreted in light of this fact. Thus, 83.6% of the variation in the log of price has been explained. This value is not directly comparable to the R^2 from the regression of y on x in Figure 5.58 (58.9%). No conclusions can be drawn concerning which regression does "better" based on the R^2 because two different measures of the dependent variable are used.

Also, keep in mind that, if the equation from Figure 5.64 is used for forecasting, natural logs of the y values will be forecasted, not the y values themselves. For example, "What will be the price of cars, on average, for all cars with 200 HP?" Using the estimated regression equation

$$\text{LOGPRICE} = 8.5 + 0.00869(200) = 10.238$$

The forecast value for LOGPRICE is 10.238. The resulting forecast for y must be computed as

$$\text{PRICE} = e^{10.238} = \$27,945.18$$

When deciding whether the transformation has improved our results, comparing the R^2 is not always dependable as noted. The residual plots can be used to help in this decision. If the pattern suggesting a violation in the original residual plots is no longer present in the plots from a transformed model, then the transformed model would be chosen as preferable. If there is little or no improvement in the residual plots, then another transformation should be tried and the resulting residual plots examined to see whether they indicate an improved model. Choosing the correct transformation to produce an adequate model is thus an iterative process that may take several tries. And when all else fails, consult your neighborhood statistician!   ■

Exercises

4 **Coal-Mining Fatalities** The data in Table 5.5 show the annual number of fatalities from gas and dust explosions in coal mines for the years 1915 to 1978 (FATALS) and the number of labor hours of production work (HOURS).

MINITAB Regression Output for Regression of the Natural Logarithm of Price on HP

```
The regression equation is
logprice = 8.50 + 0.00869 hp

152 cases used 2 cases contain missing values

Predictor        Coef       Stdev     t-ratio        p
Constant      8.49913     0.05671      149.86    0.000
hp          0.0086940   0.0003143       27.66    0.000

s = 0.2816     R-sq = 83.6%     R-sq(adj) = 83.5%

Analysis of Variance

SOURCE         DF          SS          MS         F        p
Regression      1      60.675      60.675    765.01    0.000
Error         150      11.897       0.079
Total         151      72.572

Unusual Observations
Obs.        hp    logprice        Fit   Stdev.Fit   Residual   St.Resid
   6       120     10.1266      9.5424      0.0269     0.5842      2.08R
   7       330     12.5245     11.3681      0.0566     1.1564      4.19RX
  21       260     10.0858     10.7596      0.0376    -0.6738     -2.41R
  32       300     10.4964     11.1073      0.0482    -0.6109     -2.20R
  44       400     10.9151     11.9767      0.0773    -1.0616     -3.92RX
  50       421     12.2356     12.1593      0.0836     0.0763      0.28 X
  76       492     12.3884     12.7766      0.1052    -0.3882     -1.49 X
  95       228     11.1648     10.4814      0.0302     0.6834      2.44R
  96       228     11.3528     10.4814      0.0302     0.8714      3.11R
 127       345     11.3176     11.4986      0.0610    -0.1809     -0.66 X

R denotes an obs. with a large st. resid.
X denotes an obs. whose X value gives it large influence.
```

MINITAB Residual Plot of Standardized Residuals versus Explanatory Variable HP for Transformed Model

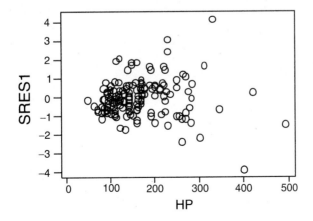

FIGURE 5.66

MINITAB Residual Plot of Standardized Residuals versus Fitted Values for Transformed Model

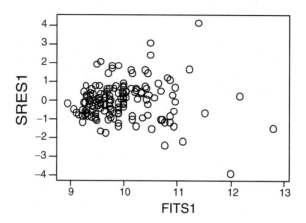

TABLE 5.5

Data for Coal-Mining Fatalities Exercise

	FATALS	HOURS		FATALS	HOURS
1915	270	97,933,888	1936	41	79,474,032
1916	183	109,076,112	1937	116	80,094,992
1917	319	121,058,944	1938	84	59,940,640
1918	103	123,566,736	1939	43	62,918,720
1919	149	99,216,192	1940	292	73,732,624
1920	124	116,558,640	1941	89	81,381,232
1921	62	84,526,048	1942	148	92,164,880
1922	298	82,702,064	1943	166	86,265,424
1923	330	107,454,592	1944	32	83,806,144
1924	486	90,955,584	1945	72	75,690,256
1925	302	98,775,488	1946	27	63,350,416
1926	373	109,827,152	1947	154	72,860,336
1927	187	97,814,144	1948	44	71,673,360
1928	347	91,544,880	1949	3	51,300,992
1929	168	95,045,776	1950	3	57,035,424
1930	234	79,800,752	1951	153	57,219,200
1931	68	62,047,040	1952	11	46,988,608
1932	162	50,502,128	1953	9	41,339,072
1933	27	58,928,608	1954	17	36,797,120
1934	40	68,520,560	1955	2	41,559,840
1935	26	69,799,616	1956	5	42,825,680

T A B L E **5.5** (*Cont.*)

Data for Coal-Mining Fatalities Exercise

	FATALS	HOURS		FATALS	HOURS
1957	63	40,705,344	1968	88	22,337,968
1958	41	30,538,256	1969	0	22,236,256
1959	10	28,100,560	1970	41	24,688,032
1960	3	26,713,472	1971	2	22,955,296
1961	26	23,902,688	1972	5	24,919,936
1962	52	23,536,464	1973	2	25,660,160
1963	31	23,667,760	1974	0	24,480,272
1964	3	23,617,792	1975	0	30,713,872
1965	19	24,470,896	1976	23	32,400,048
1966	10	23,137,008	1977	4	30,601,984
1967	12	23,205,312	1978	0	24,920,528

These data were obtained from K. D. Lawrence and L. C. March. "Robust Ridge Estimation Methods for Predicting U.S. Coal Mining Fatalities." *Communications in Statistics* 13 (1984): 139–149.

The scatterplot of fatalities versus labor hours is shown in Figure 5.67. The MINITAB regression output is shown in Figure 5.68. The residual plots of the standardized residuals versus the fitted values and the explanatory variable are shown in Figures 5.69 and 5.70, respectively.

Is there evidence that the constant variance assumption has been violated? Justify your answer. If yes, suggest a correction for the violation of the constant variance assumption for this example. Try the correction using a regression routine. Does the correction appear to have eliminated the problem of nonconstant variance? State why or why not.

These data are available on the data disk. In MINITAB, they can be read using

```
READ 'COAL5' C1-C2
```

where C1 is FATALS and C2 is HOURS.

In SAS, the data can be read from the file COAL5.DAT using

```
INPUT FATALS HOURS;
```

5 **Aerospace Exports** Table 5.6 shows annual exports of aerospace aircraft for the years 1963 through 1993 (in millions of dollars). The MINITAB time-series plot of the data is shown in Figure 5.71. The MINITAB and SAS regression outputs for the regression of exports on one-period lagged exports are shown in Figures 5.72 and 5.73, respectively. The MINITAB time-series plot of the standardized residuals is shown in Figure 5.74 and the plot of the standardized residuals versus the fitted values is shown in Figure 5.75.

F I G U R E 5.67
MINITAB Scatterplot for Coal-Mining Fatalities Exercise

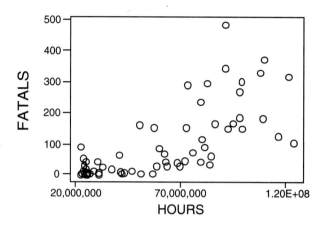

F I G U R E 5.68
MINITAB Regression of FATALS on HOURS for Coal-Mining Fatalities Exercise

```
The regression equation is
fatals = - 63.4 +0.000003 hours

Predictor       Coef        Stdev      t-ratio        p
Constant      -63.40        22.33        -2.84    0.006
hours     0.00000266  0.00000033         8.06    0.000

s = 81.29       R-sq = 51.2%     R-sq(adj) = 50.4%

Analysis of Variance

SOURCE         DF          SS          MS        F        p
Regression      1      429505      429505    65.00    0.000
Error          62      409679        6608
Total          63      839184

Unusual Observations
Obs.    hours    fatals      Fit  Stdev.Fit   Residual   St.Resid
   4 123566736   103.0    265.8       23.3     -162.8     -2.09R
  10  90955584   486.0    178.9       14.4      307.1      3.84R
  14  91544880   347.0    180.5       14.5      166.5      2.08R

R denotes an obs. with a large st. resid.
```

F I G U R E 5.69

MINITAB Residual Plot of Standardized Residuals versus Fitted Values for Coal-Mining Fatalities Exercise

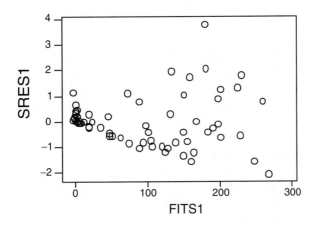

F I G U R E 5.70

MINITAB Residual Plot of Standardized Residuals versus Explanatory Variable HOURS for Coal-Mining Fatalities Exercise

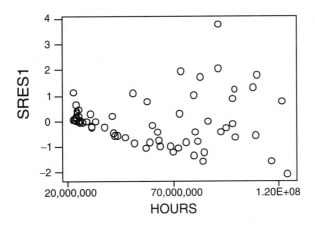

T A B L E **5.6**

Aerospace Exports (in millions of dollars)

Date	Aerospace Exports	Date	Aerospace Exports
1963	244	1979	6,149
1964	287	1980	8,250
1965	473	1981	8,551
1966	554	1982	4,775
1967	786	1983	5,569
1968	1,403	1984	3,989
1969	1,239	1985	6,252
1970	1,527	1986	7,207
1971	1,907	1987	7,380
1972	1,609	1988	9,971
1973	2,311	1989	13,711
1974	3,360	1990	18,444
1975	3,228	1991	22,629
1976	3,207	1992	23,580
1977	2,605	1993	20,164
1978	3,589		

The data were obtained from *Business Statistics 1963–91*
and *Survey of Current Business.*

F I G U R E **5.71**

MINITAB Time-Series Plot of Aerospace Exports

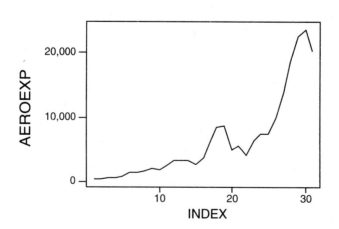

F I G U R E **5.72**

MINITAB Regression Output for Regression of Aerospace Exports on One-Period Lagged Exports

```
The regression equation is
aeroexp = 503 + 1.03 lagexp

30 cases used 1 cases contain missing values

Predictor        Coef       Stdev      t-ratio          p
Constant        503.4       468.3         1.08      0.292
lagexp        1.02756     0.05518        18.62      0.000

s = 1865        R-sq = 92.5%      R-sq(adj) = 92.3%

Analysis of Variance

SOURCE         DF          SS          MS          F          p
Regression      1  1205728640  1205728640     346.74      0.000
Error          28    97364160     3477291
Total          29  1303092736

Unusual Observations
Obs.    lagexp   aeroexp       Fit   Stdev.Fit   Residual   St.Resid
 20       8551      4775      9290         372      -4515      -2.47R
 28      13711     18444     14592         552       3852       2.16R
 30      22629     23580     23756         988       -176      -0.11 X
 31      23580     20164     24733        1037      -4569      -2.95RX

R denotes an obs. with a large st. resid.
X denotes an obs. whose X value gives it large influence.
```

F I G U R E **5.73**

SAS Regression Output for Regression of Aerospace Exports on One-Period Lagged Exports

```
Dependent Variable: AEROEXP

                    Analysis of Variance

                       Sum of         Mean
Source      DF        Squares        Square      F Value     Prob>F

Model        1  1205728653.5  1205728653.5      346.744     0.0001
Error       28  97364161.318   3477291.4756
C Total     29  1303092814.8

           Root MSE      1864.74971     R-square       0.9253
           Dep Mean      6490.20000     Adj R-sq       0.9226
           C.V.            28.73178

                    Parameter Estimates

                  Parameter      Standard      T for H0:
Variable    DF     Estimate         Error    Parameter=0    Prob > |T|

INTERCEP     1   503.402139   468.26961068          1.075        0.2915
LAGEXP       1     1.027565     0.05518296         18.621        0.0001
```

F I G U R E 5.74

MINITAB Time-Series Plot of Standardized Residuals for Aerospace Exports Exercise

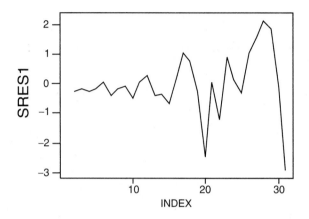

F I G U R E 5.75

MINITAB Residual Plot of Standardized Residuals versus Fitted Values for Aerospace Exports Exercise

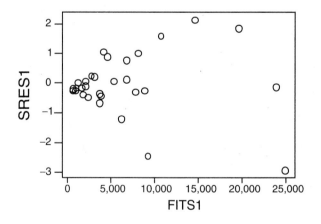

Do any of the assumptions of the linear regression model appear to be violated? Justify your answer. If yes, suggest a correction for the violation. Try the correction and see if it works.

These data are available on the data disk and can be read in MINITAB using

```
READ 'AERO5' C1
```

In SAS, the data can be read from the file AERO5.DAT using

```
INPUT AEROEXP;
```

5.6
Assessing the Assumption That the Disturbances Are Normally Distributed

5.6.1 Using Plots to Assess the Assumption of Normality

Residual plots of the standardized residuals versus the fitted values can be used to assess graphically whether the sample residuals have come from a normally distributed population. For normally distributed data, about 68% of the standardized residuals should be between -1 and $+1$; about 95% should be between -2 and $+2$; and about 99% should be between -3 and $+3$.

Normal probability plots also can be a useful graphical technique in assessing normality.

E X A M P L E 5.6 **Communications Nodes**

Figure 5.76 shows the MINITAB regression of cost (COST) on the number of ports (NUMPORTS) and the bandwidth (BANDWIDT) for the communications nodes data discussed in several examples in Chapters 3 and 4. The SAS regression is shown in Figure 5.77. The plots of the standardized residuals versus the fitted values are shown in Figure 5.78 for MINITAB and Figure 5.79 for SAS. A printout of the residuals is shown in Figure 5.80.

F I G U R E **5.76**

MINITAB Regression Output for Regression of COST on NUMPORTS and BANDWIDT

```
The regression equation is
cost = 17086 + 469 numports + 81.1 bandwidt

Predictor         Coef       Stdev     t-ratio         p
Constant         17086        1865        9.16     0.000
numports        469.03       66.98        7.00     0.000
bandwidt         81.07       21.65        3.74     0.003

s = 2983        R-sq = 95.0%     R-sq(adj) = 94.1%

Analysis of Variance

SOURCE          DF          SS          MS          F          p
Regression       2  1876012672   938006336     105.45     0.000
Error           11    97849856     8895441
Total           13  1973862528

SOURCE          DF      SEQ SS
numports         1  1751268352
bandwidt         1   124744288

Unusual Observations
Obs. numports      cost        Fit   Stdev.Fit    Residual    St.Resid
  1      68.0     52388      53682        2532       -1294       -0.82 X
 10      24.0     23444      29153        1273       -5709       -2.12R

R denotes an obs. with a large st. resid.
X denotes an obs. whose X value gives it large influence.
```

F I G U R E **5.77**

SAS Regression Output for Regression of COST on NUMPORTS and BANDWIDT

```
Dependent Variable: COST

                    Analysis of Variance

                      Sum of         Mean
Source      DF        Squares        Square      F Value      Prob>F

Model        2  1876012661.8  938006330.89      105.448      0.0001
Error       11    97849859.724  8895441.7931
C Total     13  1973862521.5

        Root MSE      2982.52272     R-square       0.9504
        Dep Mean     40185.50000     Adj R-sq       0.9414
        C.V.             7.42189

                    Parameter Estimates

                Parameter      Standard      T for H0:
Variable    DF    Estimate         Error    Parameter=0    Prob > |T|

INTERCEP     1       17086  1865.4068660          9.159        0.0001
NUMPORTS     1  469.032482    66.98412592          7.002        0.0001
BANDWIDT     1   81.074269    21.64992865          3.745        0.0032
```

F I G U R E 5.78

MINITAB Residual Plot of Standardized Residuals versus Fitted Values

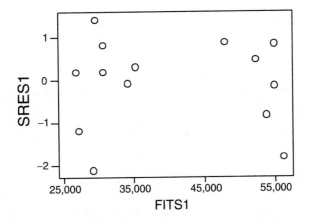

F I G U R E 5.79

SAS Residual Plot of Standardized Residuals versus Fitted Values

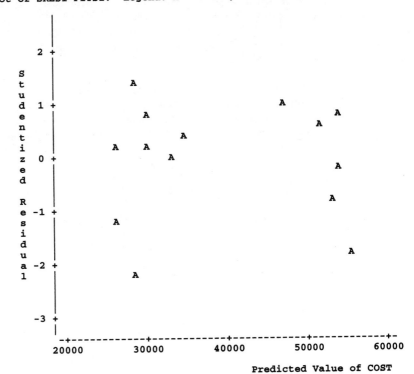

F I G U R E **5.80**

Printout of Standardized Residuals for the Communications Nodes Regression

```
-0.82145 -1.80142  0.91086   0.32777   0.20567   0.85903  -0.11480
-0.04969  0.22068 -2.11672  -1.17904   0.50409   1.44088   0.84722
```

As can be seen from the plots and the printout, 13 out of the 14 residuals (93%) are between ±2. So there are about the number of residuals we would expect to see if they came from a normal distribution. From these plots we would conclude that the normality assumption seems reasonable.

Note that MINITAB also flags any observations with standardized residuals that are greater than or equal to 2 in absolute value. These values are shown with an R next to the value of the standardized residual in the table of Unusual Observations. Often, it is the observations with large standardized residuals with which we are concerned. This is why MINITAB takes the time to flag these observations. This does not mean that there is anything wrong with these data values or that they should be deleted. It simply means that these observations may be different from the others in our data set for some reason and may deserve special attention. When examining the normality assumption, concern should be placed on relatively large standardized residuals. Thus, an excessive number of residuals outside the ±2 limit or ±3 limit might cause concern about this assumption. But remember to expect some values outside these limits, especially in large data sets.

Figure 5.81 shows the normal probability plot for the standardized residuals produced by MINITAB. In this plot, the observed standardized residuals (horizontal axis) are plotted against the "normal scores." The normal scores can be thought of as the values that would be expected if a sample of the same size as the one used (14 in this case) were selected from a normal distribution. The vertical scale shows the cumulative probabilities at or below the normal scores rather than the normal scores themselves. The normal scores and the probabilities are computed by MINITAB.

When the plot of the normal scores and the data is approximately a straight line, the normality assumption appears reasonable. The normal scores are numbers we would expect to see from a sample from a normal distribution, so for the two to plot on a straight line, the two sets of data would have to be similar. So we reason that the data must also have come from a normal distribution. If the data did not come from a normal distribution, the plot will show curvature. (Note that whether the normal probability plot is linear or not has nothing to do with whether the relationship between y and x is linear. We are not assessing whether the relationship among the original data is linear, but whether the disturbances come from a normal distribution.)

In this example, the plot of the normal scores versus the data is nearly linear (MINITAB has drawn in the line). This suggests that the standardized residuals could have come from a normal distribution. Thus, the normality assumption is supported. ∎

5.6.2 Test for Normality

The plot of the standardized residuals in the normal probability plot should be approximately linear if the disturbances are normal. The "straightness" of the line in the

F I G U R E   5.81

MINITAB Normal Probability Plot and Test for Normality

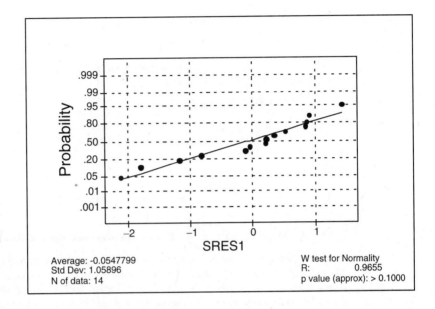

plot can be measured by computing a statistic that will be referred to as the "normal probability plot test statistic, R" (we use R to represent the test statistic since this is what MINITAB uses; note, however, that this has nothing to do with the R that MINITAB uses to flag large standardized residuals).

The hypotheses to be tested can be stated as

$$H_0: \quad \text{Disturbances are normal}$$
$$H_a: \quad \text{Disturbances are nonnormal}$$

The decision rule is:

$$\text{Reject } H_0 \quad \text{if} \quad R < c_\alpha$$
$$\text{Accept } H_0 \quad \text{if} \quad R \geq c_\alpha$$

Here, c_α represents a critical value chosen from Table 6 in Appendix B for level of significance α. If a p value for the test statistic is provided (as in MINITAB) this can also be used to conduct the test.

Note that the test for normality is referred to as the "W test" in the MINITAB output. The test used here is essentially equivalent to a test called the "Shapiro–Wilk W test" (see Shapiro and Wilk (1965)) and takes its name from this test.

E X A M P L E 5 . 7 **Communications Nodes (continued)**

The test statistic for the test for normality is given in Figure 5.81 as $R = 0.96$. Using a 5% level of significance, the decision rule for the normality test is:

$$\text{Reject } H_0 \quad \text{if} \quad R < 0.9383$$
$$\text{Accept } H_0 \quad \text{if} \quad R \geq 0.9383$$

Since $n = 14$ in the example, we used .9383 for $n = 15$. Our decision is to accept the null hypothesis. The disturbances are normally distributed.

Or, using the p value:

$$\text{Reject } H_0 \quad \text{if} \quad p \text{ value} < .05$$
$$\text{Accept } H_0 \quad \text{if} \quad p \text{ value} \geq .05$$

Since the p value is greater than .10, accept H_0. ▪

E X A M P L E 5 . 8 **Saving and Loan (S&L) Rates of Return**

In "Return, Risk, and Cost of Equity for Stock S&L Firms: Theory and Empirical Results," *Journal of the American Real Estate and Urban Economics Association*, 1985, Lee and Lynge discuss methods of estimating the cost of equity capital for S&L associations. One aspect of their analysis includes an examination of the relationship between the rate of return of S&L stocks (y) and two measures of the risk of the stocks: the beta coefficient (x_1), which is a measure of nondiversifiable risk, and the standard deviation of the security return (x_2), which measures total risk. The data for their sample of 35 S&Ls is shown in Table 5.7. Scatterplots of y versus x_1 and y versus x_2 are shown in Figures 5.82 and 5.83, respectively. The MINITAB regression output is in Figure 5.84 and the SAS output is in Figure 5.85. Figures 5.86 through 5.88 show the residual plots of the standardized residuals versus the fitted values, x_1, and x_2, respectively. These plots highlight the presence of one standardized residual that lies well above the $+3$ limit. The normal probability plot and results of the normal probability plot test for normality (W) are shown in Figure 5.89.

To perform the test for normal disturbances at the 5% level of significance, the decision rule is:

$$\text{Reject } H_0 \quad \text{if} \quad R < .9715$$
$$\text{Accept } H_0 \quad \text{if} \quad R \geq .9715$$

(The cirical value for $n = 40$ was used because $n = 35$ was not in the table.) The test statistic computed by MINITAB is $R = .8275$, so the null hypothesis is rejected. The disturbances do not appear to be normally distributed. ▪

T A B L E 5.7

Data for the S&L Rate of Return Example

Name of Institution	Time Period	RETURN	BETA	SIGMA
H. F. Ahmanson	1/78–12/82	2.29	1.2862	14.2896
Alamo Savings Bank	9/78–12/82	0.34	0.6254	10.9786
American Federal S&L	12/80–12/82	2.57	1.1706	9.7917
American S&L	1/78–12/82	2.91	1.6328	17.7219
Bell National Ind.	1/78–12/82	3.50	1.2492	18.4450
Beverly Hills S&L	11/78–12/82	0.47	1.1363	12.4691
Broadview Financial Ind.	1/78–12/82	−0.28	1.3585	12.3396
Buckeye Financial Ind.	10/80–12/82	0.40	1.5415	14.7000
Citizens Savings Financial	6/80–12/82	2.42	2.1457	18.9970
City Federal Bank	6/80–12/82	5.48	2.2701	18.0840
Danney S&L	1/78–12/82	1.67	1.4527	14.2785
Far West Financial	1/78–12/82	1.01	1.4532	13.8673
Financial Corp. of America	1/78–12/82	6.06	1.8826	18.1800
Financial Corp. of Santa Barbara	1/78–12/82	0.48	1.4493	14.7792
Financial Federation	1/78–12/82	0.96	1.5590	14.9088
First Charter Financial	1/78–12/82	1.24	1.2247	12.3504
First City Federal Ind.	5/81–12/82	6.39	2.2567	22.0455
First Financial S&L	1/81–12/82	2.39	1.7003	12.8343
First Lincoln Financial Bank	1/78–12/82	0.30	2.2226	1.8750
First Western Financial Bank	1/78–12/82	2.09	1.6535	16.5737
Freedom S&L Bank	5/80–12/82	2.46	1.3616	14.2680
Gibraltar Financial	1/78–12/82	2.10	1.9851	17.8500
Golden West Financial Corp.	1/78–12/82	2.76	1.4311	14.1036
Great Western Financial	1/78–12/82	2.06	1.3448	12.4630
Guarantee Financial Ind.	1/78–12/82	1.42	1.4560	13.9728
Homestead Financial Bank	1/78–12/82	4.12	1.5543	17.2628
Imperial Corp. of America	1/78–12/82	1.82	1.7280	15.2880
Land of Lincoln Ind.	12/79–12/82	1.59	1.3389	10.3032
Mercury Saving	1/78–12/82	13.05	1.2973	13.3110
Naples Federal	2/80–12/82	3.04	1.0945	10.5792
Palmetto Federal S&L	11/79–12/82	3.72	1.2051	12.9456
Prudential Federal S&L	1/78–12/82	0.75	1.0756	11.5200
Texas Federal Bank	7/81–12/82	1.00	1.9157	16.6000
Transohio Financial	1/78–12/82	−0.35	1.4456	11.7705
Western Financial Corp.	1/78–12/82	2.26	1.9128	16.8370

F I G U R E **5.82**

MINITAB Scatterplot of RETURN versus BETA for the S&L Rate of Return Example

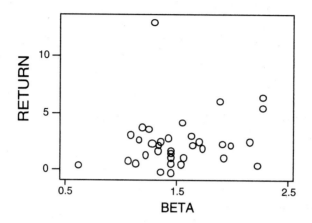

F I G U R E **5.83**

MINITAB Scatterplot of RETURN versus SIGMA for the S&L Rate of Return Example

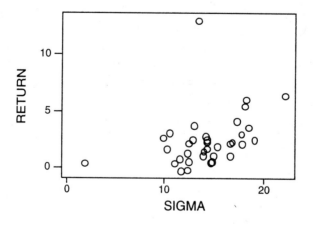

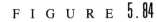

F I G U R E **5.84**

MINITAB Regression Output for the S&L Rate of Return Example

```
The regression equation is
return = - 1.33 + 0.30 beta + 0.231 sigma

Predictor       Coef       Stdev     t-ratio        p
Constant      -1.330       2.012       -0.66    0.513
beta           0.300       1.198        0.25    0.804
sigma         0.2307      0.1255        1.84    0.075

s = 2.377     R-sq = 12.5%    R-sq(adj) = 7.0%

Analysis of Variance

SOURCE         DF          SS          MS         F        p
Regression      2      25.808      12.904      2.28    0.118
Error          32     180.815       5.650
Total          34     206.624

SOURCE         DF      SEQ SS
beta            1       6.708
sigma           1      19.100

Unusual Observations
Obs.     beta     return     Fit  Stdev.Fit  Residual  St.Resid
  19     2.22      0.300  -0.231      2.078     0.531     0.46 X
  29     1.30     13.050   2.130      0.474    10.920     4.69R

R denotes an obs. with a large st. resid.
X denotes an obs. whose X value gives it large influence.
```

F I G U R E **5.85**

SAS Regression Output for the S&L Rate of Return Example

```
Dependent Variable: RETURN

                   Analysis of Variance

                 Sum of        Mean
Source     DF    Squares       Square     F Value    Prob>F

Model       2   25.80815     12.90407      2.284    0.1183
Error      32  180.81549      5.65048
C Total    34  206.62364

        Root MSE      2.37707    R-square     0.1249
        Dep Mean      2.41400    Adj R-sq     0.0702
        C.V.         98.47037

                   Parameter Estimates

                Parameter     Standard    T for H0:
Variable   DF    Estimate        Error  Parameter=0   Prob > |T|

INTERCEP    1   -1.329738   2.01191665       -0.661       0.5134
BETA        1    0.299787   1.19775847        0.250       0.8040
SIGMA       1    0.230686   0.12547133        1.839       0.0753
```

F I G U R E **5.86**

MINITAB Residual Plot of the Standardized Residuals versus the Fitted Values for the S&L
Rate of Return Example

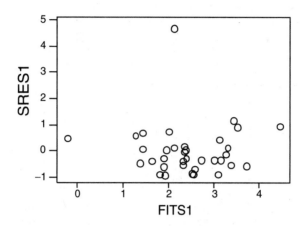

F I G U R E **5.87**

MINITAB Residual Plot of the Standardized Residuals versus the Explanatory Variable BETA
for the S&L Rate of Return Example

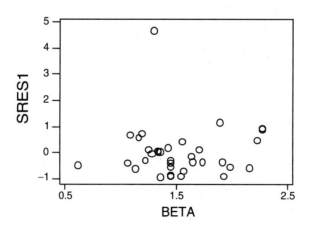

FIGURE 5.88

MINITAB Residual Plot of the Standardized Residuals versus the Explanatory Variable SIGMA for the S&L Rate of Return Example

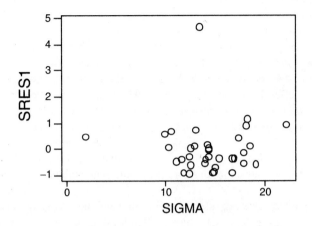

FIGURE 5.89

MINITAB Normal Probability Plot and *W* Test for Normality for the S&L Rate of Return Example

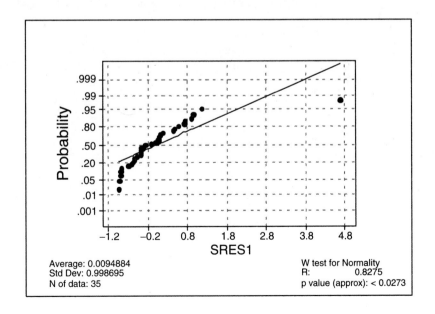

5.6.3   Corrections for Nonnormality

The assumption of normally distributed disturbances is not necessary to use least squares estimation to produce an estimated regression equation. However, for making inferences with small samples, it is necessary. In large samples the assumption is not as important because the sampling distribution of the estimators of the regression coefficients still will be approximately normal. Recall that when estimating a population mean, μ, the cutoff point for a large sample is $n = 30$. When $n \geq 30$, the Central Limit Theorem guarantees that the sampling distribution of the sample mean will be approximately normal. A similar theorem operates in the regression context for the sampling distribution of the regression coefficients, b_k. The cutoff for a large sample may differ, however, because several coefficients may be estimated in a multiple regression context. It is uncertain exactly how many observations ensure normality of the sampling distributions in the multiple regression context. If the assumption of normal disturbances does not hold, additional observations will be necessary for each additional explanatory variable. Thirty observations for a simple regression with 10 to 20 additional observations for *each* additional explanatory variable is commonly suggested.

When the normality assumption is violated and the sample size is too small to ensure normality of the sampling distributions, there are a variety of possible corrections. Some of these corrections involve transformations of the dependent variable that are beyond the scope of this text. These transformations are called *Box–Cox transformations* and include the natural logarithm transformation as a special case. (For more on the use of Box–Cox transformations, the interested reader is referred to Neter, Wasserman, and Kutner's *Applied Linear Statistical Models* (pages 394–400).)

When considering the normality assumption, be sure to correct for other violations before worrying about normality. A violation of the linearity or the constant variance assumption can introduce outliers (discussed in Section 5.7) into a data set that would make the normality assumption appear to be violated also. Choosing the correct model by correcting for nonlinearity or nonconstant variance may eliminate the outliers, however. So check for violations of the linearity and constant variance assumptions before being too concerned with the normality assumption.

In some cases, the primary reason for the nonnormality of the disturbances may be the presence of one or a few data points that are much different from the remaining observations in the data set. Even in large samples it is important to be able to recognize such unusual observations because their presence may drastically alter results. In such instances, the sampling distributions of the estimated regression coefficients should not be assumed normal, even if the sample size is large. These cases, and some possible corrections, will be discussed in the next section.

5.7
Influential Observations

5.7.1 Introduction to Influential Observations

The method of least squares estimation chooses the regression coefficient estimates so the error sum of squares, *SSE*, is a minimum. In doing this, the distances from the true y values, y_i, to the points on the regression line or surface, $\hat{y}_i$, are minimized. Least squares thus tries to avoid any large distances from y_i to $\hat{y}_i$. As shown in Figure 5.90, this can have an effect on the placement of the regression line. In Figure 5.90(a), the points are all clustered near the regression line. In Figure 5.90(b), one of the points has been moved so that its y value is much different from the y values of the remaining sample points. The effect of moving this one point on the placement of the estimated regression also is shown. Note that the regression line has been pulled toward the point that was moved to the extreme position. This is a result of the requirement of the least squares method to minimize the error sum of squares. Squaring the residuals gives proportionately more weight to extreme points in the error sum of squares. The least squares regression line often will be drawn toward such extreme points.

When a sample data point has a y value that is much different from the y values of the other points in the sample, it is called an *outlier*. Outliers can be either good or bad. They can provide information concerning the behavior of the process studied that would be unavailable otherwise. In this sense, the presence of the outlier could be viewed as of positive value. On the other hand, the presence of an outlier can at times produce confusing results and mask important information that could otherwise be obtained from the regression. In either case, it is important to recognize an outlier when it is present. Outlier detection techniques will be discussed in this section.

Now consider Figure 5.91. In both Figure 5.91(a) and 5.91(b), the same five initial points are used as in Figure 5.90. One additional point is added to each figure but is placed in a different position. The positioning of this point has a large effect on the estimated regression line. In Figure 5.91(a), the slope of the line appears to have changed little from its value with only the five original points (see Figure 5.90(a)). In Figure 5.91(b), the placement of the additional point has drastically changed the slope of the line.

In fact, the slope of the line appears to be determined almost entirely by this one point. This sixth observation is said to have high leverage and is referred to as a *leverage point*. The term "leverage point" means that the point is placed in such a way that it has the *potential* to affect the regression line.

In both Figure 5.91(a) and 5.91(b), the added point is a leverage point. This is because of its extreme placement on the x-axis. The x value for this point is much different from the x values for the other sample points. The point, however, does not exert much influence in Figure 5.91(a) because it is in line with all the other points in terms of its y value relative to its x value. It would be important to recognize any

F I G U R E   **5. 90 (a)**

MINITAB Scatterplot with Regression Line for Data Shown Below

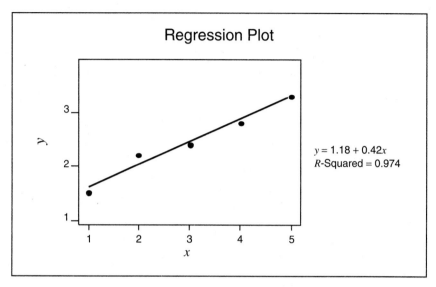

Data

x	y
1	1.5
2	2.2
3	2.4
4	2.8
5	3.3

leverage points because of their possible effect on the regression line. As with outliers, leverage points may be good or bad depending on whether they add information about the process under study or mask information that otherwise would be obtained.

Finally, it is important to note that an observation can be both a leverage point and an outlier.

5 . 7 . 2   Identifying Outliers

The use of standardized residuals already has been discussed. Standardized residuals are computed by dividing the raw residual $\hat{e}_i = y_i - \hat{y}_i$, by the standard deviation of $\hat{e}_i$:

$$\hat{e}_{is} = \frac{\hat{e}_i}{\text{stdev}(\hat{e}_i)},$$

F I G U R E **5. 90 (b)**

MINITAB Scatterplot Showing Effect on Regression Line of Outlier

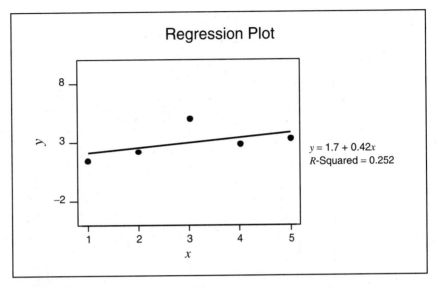

Data

x	y
1	1.5
2	2.2
3	5.0
4	2.8
5	3.3

where $\hat{e}_{is}$ indicates the standardized residual. The variance of the standardized residuals is 1 (note that in this section it is necessary to distinguish between the raw residual $\hat{e}_i$ and the standardized residual $\hat{e}_{is}$).

If the residuals come from a normal distribution, then a standardized residual larger than 2 would be expected only about 5% of the time. Thus, any observation with a standardized residual larger than 2 might be classified as an outlier. MINITAB, for example, will indicate any such observations in a table following the regression results.

Another measure sometimes used in place of the standardized residual is the standardized residual computed after deleting the ith observation. This measure is called the *studentized residual* or *studentized deleted residual*. (Note that SAS refers to the standardized residual, $\hat{e}_{is}$, as the studentized residual. The terminology in this area of study often is confusing because of interchanging of terms.) To compute the studentized deleted residual, the residual, $\hat{e}_i$, is again standardized, but the divisor is

FIGURE **5.91 (a)**

MINITAB Scatterplot Showing Effect of Leverage Point in Line with Other Data

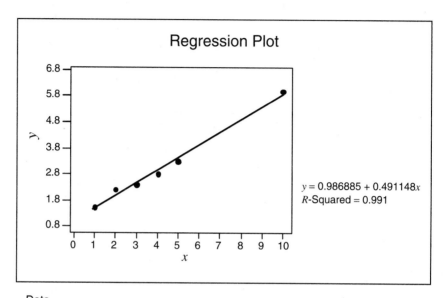

Data

x	y
1	1.5
2	2.2
3	2.4
4	2.8
5	3.3
10	6.0

different from that used to compute the standardized residual. The standard deviation of the ith residual is computed from the regression with the ith observation deleted. By doing this, the ith observation exerts no influence over the value of the standard deviation. If the ith observation's y value is unusual, this will be reflected in the residual but not in its divisor. Thus, unusual y values should stand out. Furthermore, because of the way they are computed, the studentized deleted residuals are known to follow a t distribution with $n - K - 2$ degrees of freedom. The studentized deleted residuals can be compared to a value chosen from the t table to determine whether they should be classified as outliers. (The standardized residuals do not follow a t distribution.) But this approach should not be used as a test of significance to determine whether the observation should be discarded. What to do about outliers once they are identified will be discussed later in this section.

F I G U R E **5.91 (b)**
MINITAB Scatterplot Showing Effect of Moving the Leverage Point to Alternate Position

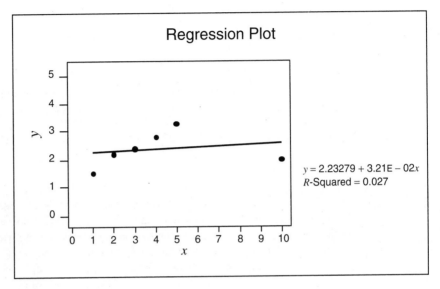

Data

x	y
1	1.5
2	2.2
3	2.4
4	2.8
5	3.3
10	2.0

5.7.3 Identifying Leverage Points

Leverage was previously defined as the potential of an observation to affect the regression line. As shown in Figure 5.91, a point can possess leverage without significantly altering the position of the regression line. On the other hand, given sufficient leverage, a single point can significantly affect the slope of the regression line.

The leverage of the ith point in a sample is denoted h_i and is computed by most regression software packages. Leverage is a measure of how extreme the point is in terms of the values of the explanatory variables. Observations with extreme x values will possess greater leverage than observations with x values that are similar to the other sample points. In Figure 5.90(a), the observation that was changed has smaller leverage than the observation that was changed in Figure 5.91(a). Note that the slope of the regression line is affected more by changes in the point with greater leverage.

MINITAB indicates certain observations with very high leverage. Any data value with leverage greater than $2(K + 1)/n$ will be indicated in a table following the regression results along with observations that have large standardized residuals.

5.7.4 Combining Measures to Detect Outliers and Leverage Points

The effect of an observation on the regression line is determined both by the y value of the point and the x value(s). As shown in Figures 5.90 and 5.91, an observation with an unusual y value will have a much greater effect on the regression line if it also has high leverage. Several statistics have been developed that consider both extremity in the y and x dimensions in an attempt to determine which points will be highly influential on the regression line. Two of these measures, the DFITS statistic and Cook's D statistic, will be discussed in this section.

Both of these measures combine information from the residuals and the leverage of each observation to try to pick out observations that may have a large influence on the regression line. As with the individual measures, unusual values of the DFITS statistic or Cook's D statistic are not indications that anything is wrong with the particular data value or that it should be discarded. It does indicate that the value with the unusual statistic is somehow different from the remaining values in the data set and should be given additional consideration before accepting the regression model.

The DFITS statistic can be written as

$$\text{DFITS}_i = \hat{e}_i \sqrt{\frac{n - K - 2}{SSE(1 - h_i) - \hat{e}_i^2}} \sqrt{\frac{h_i}{1 - h_i}},$$

where $\hat{e}_i$ is the residual for the ith observation, h_i is the leverage value for the ith observation, and SSE is the error sum of squares for the regression.

Cook's D statistic is computed as

$$c_i = \frac{\hat{e}_i^2}{MSE(K + 1)} \left(\frac{h_i}{(1 - h_i)^2} \right),$$

where $\hat{e}_i$ and h_i are as defined for the DFITS statistic and MSE is the mean square error for the regression.

As can be seen, both statistics use the residuals and the leverage of each individual point. Since they use the values in different ways, however, different information may be obtained from each of the statistics. Cook's D statistic is usually thought to represent the combined impact on all the regression coefficients of the ith observation. DFITS represents the combined impact on the fitted values of the ith observation.

There are two different schools of thought about how the DFITS statistic and the Cook's D statistic should be used:

1   The values should be compared to some absolute cutoff. For example, the Cook's value often is compared to an $F(\alpha; K + 1, n - K - 1)$ value. The

DFITS value is compared to $2\sqrt{(K+1)/n}$. Values bigger than either of the numbers should be further examined. But these are not to be viewed as statistical tests to reject or throw out observations.

2 Do not use absolute cutoffs. Simply pick out those observations with Cook's or DFITS values, if any, that appear to be appreciably different from most of the values.

The second approach will be used in this text. Much recent research has shown that comparison to absolute cutoffs is not as effective in identifying influential observations as examining observations with unusually large DFITS or Cook's D values.

When specific cutoffs are not used, a method is needed to compare the different values of each statistic to determine which observations may be unusual. A particularly effective way of doing this is simply to graph the DFITS (or Cook's D) values for each observation on the vertical axis and the number of the observation on the horizontal axis. This can also be accomplished by doing a time-series plot of the DFITS values, remembering that the index on the horizontal axis refers to the number of the observation and not necessarily to a time period. This method of presenting the DFITS and Cook's D statistics will be demonstrated in the next example.

5.7.5 What to Do with Unusual Observations

As noted earlier, the fact that an observation has been classified as unusual does not mean that it is useless or that it should be deleted from the analysis. It is merely a flag to indicate that the observation deserves further examination. This is true regardless of which measure of "unusualness" has been used (standardized residual, DFITS, Cook's D statistic, and so on).

There are many reasons why an observation may appear unusual. If there is a violation of the linearity or constant variance assumptions, this can cause certain observations to appear unusual until the violation has been corrected by choosing an appropriate transformation of the data.

If a data value has been typed in incorrectly, the value may be flagged as unusual. This is useful since incorrectly coded values should not be included in our data set. If this is the case, then the true data value should be located and used to replace the incorrect value. If the true value cannot be found, then this is one case when it is almost always better to omit the incorrect data value before running the analysis.

If the unusual value is not due to the violation of an assumption or incorrect coding but is a correct value that is simply unusual with respect to most of the values in the data set, then the choice of what to do with it is more difficult. There are certain cases when deleting the observation from the data set is appropriate. These cases occur when the unusual observation is somehow very different from the observations included in the analysis. For example, if a production process is being examined, unusual observations may occur at the beginning of the process due to start-up problems. When the process reaches a steady state of performance the data values generated may be quite different from those generated initially. The initial observations may be deleted if the process in its steady state is to be studied.

Consider another example. Suppose the data on price and size of houses is obtained in order to develop an equation to help set prices for the houses. If interest lies in pricing houses with 1500 to 2500 square feet of space, then it would be proper to exclude a house if it contains 4500 square feet. If the x values for the unusual observation fall outside the range of interest, it may be proper to discard the observation and run the regression without that value.

In any case, before deleting an observation from an analysis, the observation should be studied carefully to see whether deletion is an appropriate option. If the observation is somehow so different from the others in the data set that it is inappropriate to include it in the analysis or if the value has been coded incorrectly and the true value is unknown, then deletion is a viable option. However, this option should not be used indiscriminately.

E X A M P L E 5 . 9 **S&L Rate of Return (continued)**

Figure 5.92 shows the MINITAB plot of DFITS for the S&L rate of return data. Figure 5.93 shows the plot of the Cook's D statistic. Both of these plots were created by doing a time-series plot of the statistics. The index on the horizontal axis refers to the number of the observation from the sample. From each of these plots, the 29th observation stands out as unusual relative to the rest of the observations in the sample. In Table 5.7, the 29th observation is Mercury Saving. Note that the return for Mercury Saving is much higher than that for the other S&Ls. Mercury Saving then has a very unusual y value. In the table of Unusual Observations in Figure 5.84, Mercury Saving has been identified by MINITAB as an outlier (note the R next to this entry in the table). The standardized residual is 4.69, which is far greater than would be expected if the disturbances were normally distributed.

This observation should definitely be examined further. The question at this point is what to do with it. In the case of Mercury Saving, it is unclear whether the return of 13.05% is correct. In the article from which these data were taken, however, it appears that Mercury Saving has been deleted from the analysis. Because the true return is not known, Mercury Saving will be excluded from the data set and the analysis redone. It is important to emphasize that casual deletion of points from the data set is not recommended. If there is a good reason for not including a particular value, then it can be deleted. If the return for Mercury Saving is incorrect and the correct value is unknown, it would be better to delete this observation rather than use the incorrect information. Or, if Mercury Saving is believed somehow so different from the other S&Ls that it should not be included in the analysis, this would be a reason for deletion. For example, perhaps Mercury Saving had undertaken a particularly risky line of investments, different from those of the other S&Ls, which led to its very high return. Because the investment behavior of Mercury would be extremely different from the other S&Ls in this case, there might be grounds for excluding it from the analysis. It is assumed here that there is sufficient reason for omitting Mercury Saving since that appears to be what was done in the original article. In a real application it would be beneficial to further study Mercury to see what makes it so different from the other S&Ls.

In the following example, note the difference between the analyses with and without Mercury Saving. ■

F I G U R E 5.92
MINITAB Plot of DFITS for S&L Rate of Return Data

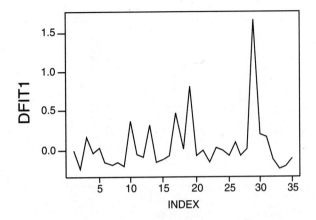

F I G U R E 5.93
MINITAB Plot of Cook's *D* Statistic for S&L Rate of Return Data

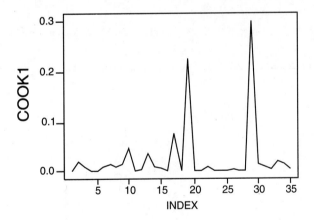

E X A M P L E 5.10 **S&L Rate of Return Without Mercury Saving**

Figures 5.94 and 5.95 show the scatterplots with Mercury Saving omitted. The MINITAB regression output is in Figure 5.96, the residual plots are in Figures 5.97 to 5.99, and the plots of the DFITS and Cook's *D* statistics are in Figures 5.100 and 5.101.

The regression results differ considerably from those with Mercury Saving included. Compare the Figure 5.96 regression (without Mercury) to the Figure 5.84 (or 5.85) regression (with Mercury). In the initial regression, neither variable is significant at the 5% level. In the regression without Mercury, SIGMA is now significant. Thus, the conclusions drawn from these

F I G U R E **5.94**
MINITAB Scatterplot of RETURN versus BETA with Mercury Saving Omitted

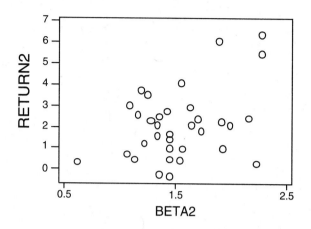

F I G U R E **5.95**
MINITAB Scatterplot of RETURN versus SIGMA with Mercury Saving Omitted

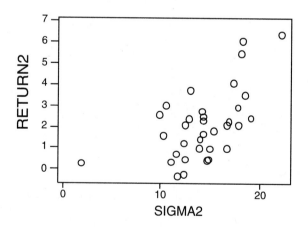

F I G U R E **5.96**

MINITAB Regression with Mercury Saving Omitted

```
The regression equation is
return2 = - 2.51 + 0.846 beta2 + 0.232 sigma2

Predictor      Coef       Stdev     t-ratio        p
Constant      -2.510      1.153       -2.18     0.037
beta2         0.8463      0.6843       1.24     0.225
sigma2        0.23220     0.07135      3.25     0.003

s = 1.352      R-sq = 37.2%      R-sq(adj) = 33.1%

Analysis of Variance

SOURCE        DF         SS          MS         F         p
Regression    2          33.537      16.768     9.18      0.001
Error         31         56.635      1.827
Total         33         90.172

SOURCE        DF         SEQ SS
beta2         1          14.185
sigma2        1          19.351

Unusual Observations
Obs.     beta2     return2       Fit   Stdev.Fit  Residual   St.Resid
 13      1.88       6.060       3.304     0.367     2.756      2.12R
 19      2.22       0.300      -0.194     1.181     0.494      0.75 X

R denotes an obs. with a large st. resid.
X denotes an obs. whose X value gives it large influence.
```

F I G U R E **5.97**

MINITAB Residual Plot of Standardized Residuals versus Fitted Values for S&L Rate of Return Example with Mercury Saving Omitted

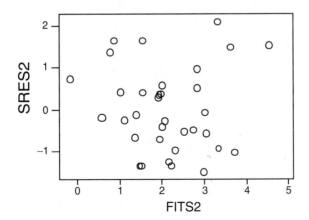

F I G U R E **5.98**

MINITAB Residual Plot of Standardized Residuals versus BETA for S&L Rate of Return Example with Mercury Saving Omitted

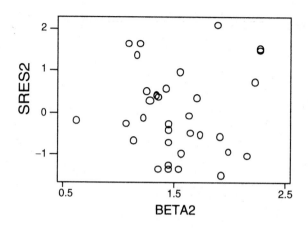

F I G U R E **5.99**

MINITAB Residual Plot of Standardized Residuals versus SIGMA for S&L Rate of Return Example with Mercury Saving Omitted

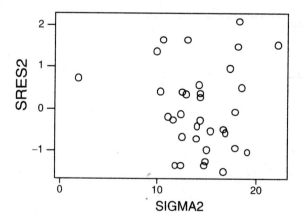

F I G U R E **5.100**

MINITAB Plot of DFITS (DFIT2) for S&L Rate of Return Example with Mercury Saving Omitted

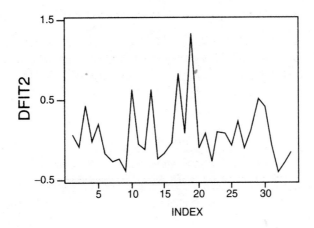

F I G U R E **5.101**

MINITAB Plot of Cook's *D* Statistic for S&L Rate of Return Example with Mercury Saving Omitted

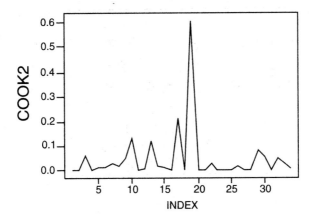

two regressions are completely different because of the presence (or absence) of one influential observation. This highlights the need to be careful when deleting influential observations. Knowing whether Mercury Saving belongs in our analysis is especially important since omitting it causes a reversal in our conclusion concerning the importance of the variable SIGMA. ▪

6   **Petroleum Imports**   The data for monthly petroleum imports from 1976 through 1991 appear in Table 5.8. Figure 5.102 shows the MINITAB regression output for the regression of monthly petroleum imports (in millions of barrels) on the one-period lagged imports. Figure 5.103 is a time-series plot of the standardized residuals from this regression. Figure 5.104 shows the plot of the standardized residuals versus the fitted values. Figures 5.105 and 5.106, respectively, show plots of the DFITS and Cook's D statistics.

T A B L E **5.8**

Monthly Petroleum Imports (in millions of barrels)

Date	Petroleum Imports	Date	Petroleum Imports	Date	Petroleum Imports	Date	Petroleum Imports
1/76	144.0	5/78	178.4	9/80	142.3	1/83	99.0
2/76	123.7	6/78	195.0	10/80	148.8	2/83	69.4
3/76	147.8	7/78	197.1	11/80	141.8	3/83	77.6
4/76	145.2	8/78	201.1	12/80	158.2	4/83	102.5
5/76	146.0	9/78	212.3	1/81	155.5	5/83	112.4
6/76	169.3	10/78	205.3	2/81	139.7	6/83	117.5
7/76	180.3	11/78	205.9	3/81	143.7	7/83	129.0
8/76	172.7	12/78	217.6	4/81	133.8	8/83	140.1
9/76	177.1	1/79	216.0	5/81	136.8	9/83	136.0
10/76	176.8	2/79	183.1	6/81	125.5	10/83	115.3
11/76	179.1	3/79	198.9	7/81	135.4	11/83	108.9
12/76	184.8	4/79	186.8	8/81	135.3	12/83	110.0
1/77	195.8	5/79	196.2	9/81	147.9	1/84	105.2
2/77	187.1	6/79	201.3	10/81	140.7	2/84	93.8
3/77	208.7	7/79	206.8	11/81	125.9	3/84	115.5
4/77	105.2	8/79	212.9	12/81	134.1	4/84	115.0
5/77	212.3	9/79	194.2	1/82	120.9	5/84	134.0
6/77	212.6	10/79	215.9	2/82	89.3	6/84	115.4
7/77	219.7	11/79	189.9	3/82	93.8	7/84	122.5
8/77	199.4	12/79	199.0	4/82	91.4	8/84	108.6
9/77	193.8	1/80	202.1	5/82	110.0	9/84	109.2
10/77	202.8	2/80	176.4	6/82	122.0	10/84	127.3
11/77	190.5	3/80	178.4	7/82	139.0	11/84	117.7
12/77	197.4	4/80	170.0	8/82	126.6	12/84	104.5
1/78	193.9	5/80	161.0	9/82	115.5	1/85	90.6
2/78	162.1	6/80	166.5	10/82	120.3	2/85	68.5
3/78	191.8	7/80	151.2	11/82	122.8	3/85	97.8
4/78	169.3	8/80	149.5	12/82	100.7	4/85	116.2

T A B L E **5.8** (*Cont.*)

Monthly Petroleum Imports (in millions of barrels)

Date	Petroleum Imports	Date	Petroleum Imports	Date	Petroleum Imports	Date	Petroleum Imports
5/85	134.2	1/87	144.3	9/88	167.2	5/90	215.2
6/85	107.9	2/87	118.7	10/88	183.8	6/90	210.2
7/85	112.9	3/87	129.7	11/88	167.2	7/90	226.3
8/85	111.5	4/87	134.2	12/88	172.3	8/90	213.1
9/85	104.6	5/87	144.3	1/89	187.1	9/90	183.5
10/85	110.4	6/87	157.9	2/89	163.1	10/90	172.8
11/85	130.4	7/87	173.9	3/89	170.1	11/90	171.0
12/85	123.6	8/87	182.3	4/89	188.0	12/90	155.7
1/86	117.4	9/87	162.9	5/89	190.6	1/91	180.1
2/86	89.7	10/87	172.2	6/89	191.5	2/91	163.6
3/86	101.0	11/87	160.6	7/89	205.1	3/91	169.2
4/86	123.2	12/87	156.2	8/89	216.2	4/91	177.8
5/86	144.7	1/88	157.6	9/89	195.2	5/91	215.2
6/86	149.5	2/88	145.0	10/89	204.4	6/91	199.2
7/86	155.3	3/88	161.8	11/89	197.0	7/91	201.4
8/86	159.9	4/88	169.4	12/89	178.4	8/91	220.2
9/86	161.0	5/88	180.8	1/90	208.4	9/91	190.3
10/86	146.6	6/88	174.1	2/90	178.0	10/91	189.3
11/86	148.3	7/88	172.8	3/90	204.0	11/91	182.9
12/86	146.1	8/88	169.6	4/90	186.8	12/91	182.8

The data were taken from *Business Statistics 1963–91*.

Are there any unusual observations that should be checked before accepting these regression results? If so, which observations? Can you determine what might be causing certain observations to appear unusual? Justify your answers.

These data are available on the data disk and can be read in MINITAB using

```
READ 'PETRO5' C1
```

In SAS, the data can be read from the file PETRO5.DAT using

```
INPUT PETRO;
```

F I G U R E **5.102**

MINITAB Regression Output for Regression of Petroleum Imports on the Lagged Value of Petroleum Imports

```
The regression equation is
petro = 18.6 + 0.884 petrolag

191 cases used 1 cases contain missing values

Predictor         Coef      Stdev    t-ratio        p
Constant        18.592      5.547       3.35    0.001
petrolag       0.88352    0.03419      25.84    0.000

s = 17.62      R-sq = 77.9%      R-sq(adj) = 77.8%

Analysis of Variance

SOURCE          DF          SS         MS         F        p
Regression       1      207238     207238    667.65    0.000
Error          189       58665        310
Total          190      265903

Unusual Observations
Obs. petrolag      petro       Fit  Stdev.Fit  Residual   St.Resid
  16       209     105.20    202.98       2.16    -97.78      -5.59R
  17       105     212.30    111.54       2.21    100.76       5.76R
  74       121      89.30    125.41       1.80    -36.11      -2.06R
  86        99      69.40    106.06       2.38    -36.66      -2.10R
  87        69      77.60     79.91       3.28     -2.31      -0.13 X
 111        69      97.80     79.11       3.31     18.69       1.08 X
 185       178     215.20    175.68       1.45     39.52       2.25R

R denotes an obs. with a large st. resid.
X denotes an obs. whose X value gives it large influence.
```

F I G U R E **5.103**

MINITAB Time-Series Plot of Standardized Residuals for Petroleum Imports Regression

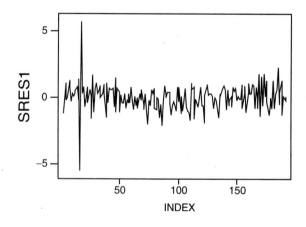

F I G U R E 5.104
MINITAB Plot of Standardized Residuals versus the Fitted Values for the Petroleum
Imports Regression

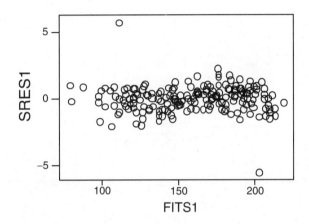

F I G U R E 5.105
MINITAB Plot of DFITS Statistic for Petroleum Imports Regression

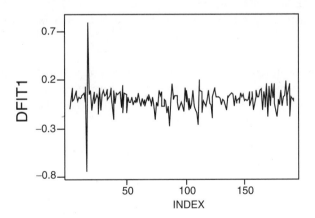

FIGURE **5.106**

MINITAB Plot of Cook's D Statistic for Petroleum Imports Regression

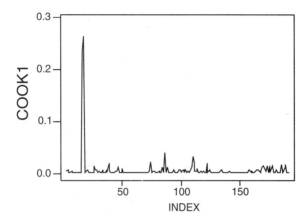

5.8
Assessing the Assumption That the Disturbances Are Independent

5.8.1 Autocorrelation

One assumption that is frequently violated when using time-series data is the independence of disturbances, e_i. Disturbances in adjacent time periods often are correlated because an event in one time period may influence an event in the next time period. The relationship between disturbances in adjacent time periods often is represented by

$$e_i = \rho e_{i-1} + u_i$$

In this equation, e_i is the disturbance in the ith time period, e_{i-1} is the disturbance in the previous time period, ρ is called the *serial correlation coefficient* or *autocorrelation coefficient*, and u_i represents a disturbance that meets the assumption of independence. The regression relationship will be written as

$$y_i = \beta_0 + \beta_1 x_i + e_i,$$

where $e_i = \rho e_{i-1} + u_i$.

When disturbances exhibit autocorrelation, least-squares estimates of the regression coefficients will be unbiased, but the estimated standard errors of the coefficients will be biased. As a result, confidence intervals and hypothesis tests will not perform as expected. The estimated regression coefficients also will have larger sampling variance than certain other estimators that correct for autocorrelation.

The autocorrelation coefficient, ρ, determines the strength of the relationship between disturbances in successive time periods. Like any other correlation coefficient, it varies between -1 and $+1$, with values close to ± 1 indicating very strong relationships and values close to zero indicating weak relationships. Ideally, a value of $\rho = 0$ is desired because this would mean that the disturbances were independent and the independence assumption had not been violated.

To determine whether autocorrelation is present, the Durbin–Watson test is used. This test will be discussed in the next section.

When autocorrelation is present in business and economic data, it is typically positive autocorrelation ($\rho > 0$). When the Durbin–Watson test for autocorrelation is applied, it will be conducted as a test for positive autocorrelation. The null hypothesis will be stated as H_0: $\rho = 0$ and the alternative as H_a: $\rho > 0$.

5.8.2 A Test for First-Order Autocorrelation

A well-known and widely used test for first-order autocorrelation is the Durbin–Watson test. The hypotheses to be tested may be written as follows:

$$H_0: \quad \rho = 0$$
$$H_a: \quad \rho > 0,$$

where ρ is the first-order autocorrelation coefficient. If the null hypothesis is accepted, the correlation, ρ, of adjacent disturbances is zero and no problem of first-order autocorrelation exists. If the null hypothesis is rejected, the disturbances are correlated and some correction for autocorrelation needs to be made.

The Durbin–Watson statistic is computed by first using least squares to estimate the regression equation and then by computing the residuals

$$\hat{e}_i = y_i - \hat{y}_i,$$

where y_i represents one of the sample y values, and $\hat{y}_i$ is the corresponding predicted y value. The residuals are used to compute the Durbin–Watson statistic, d:

$$d = \frac{\sum_{i=2}^{n} (\hat{e}_i - \hat{e}_{i-1})^2}{\sum_{i=1}^{n} \hat{e}_i^2}$$

When the disturbances are independent, d should be approximately equal to 2. When the disturbances are positively correlated, d will tend to be less than 2.

The decision rule for the test is:

$$\text{Reject } H_0 \quad \text{if} \quad d < d_L(\alpha; n, K)$$
$$\text{Accept } H_0 \quad \text{if} \quad d > d_U(\alpha; n, K)$$

Here, $d_L(\alpha; n, K)$ and $d_U(\alpha; n, K)$ are the critical values found in Table 7 of Appendix B. The critical values depend on the level of significance of the test, α; the sample size, n; and the number of explanatory variables in the equation, K. For the Durbin–Watson test, there is a range of values for the test statistic where the test is said to be inconclusive. The inconclusive range of values for d is

$$d_L \leq d \leq d_U$$

If the test statistic d falls in this region, there is some question as to how to proceed. Rejection of the null hypothesis suggests that a correction for autocorrelation is necessary. Acceptance means that no correction is necessary. But what should be done when d falls in the inconclusive region? There have been additional procedures developed to further examine those cases where d falls in the inconclusive region, but these have not been incorporated into many computer regression routines. Without easy access to the additional procedures, one possibility would be to treat values of d in the inconclusive region as if they suggested autocorrelation. If the regression results after correction for autocorrelation differ from those prior to the correction, then we conclude that the correction was necessary. If the results are similar, then the correction was unnecessary and the original uncorrected results can be used.

E X A M P L E **5.11** **Corporate Profits**

Table 5.9 shows data on corporate profits (in billions) and GNP (in billions). These are annual data covering the period from 1960 to 1991. The MINITAB regression output for the regression of corporate profits on GNP is shown in Figure 5.107. The Durbin–Watson statistic is shown in the output. The SAS regression output, including the D–W statistic and an estimate of ρ, is shown in Figure 5.108. The MINITAB time-series plot of the residuals is shown in Figure 5.109. To test for positive first-order autocorrelation, the following decision rule is used:

$$\text{Reject } H_0 \quad \text{if} \quad d < d_L(.05; 32, 1) = 1.37$$
$$\text{Accept } H_0 \quad \text{if} \quad d > d_U(.05; 32, 1) = 1.50$$
$$\text{Indeterminate} \quad \text{if} \quad 1.37 \leq d \leq 1.50$$

Because $d = 0.48$, the null hypothesis of no autocorrelation is rejected. First-order autocorrelation is a problem and should be corrected before inferences or forecasts are made. ∎

5.8.3 Correction for First-Order Autocorrelation

There are several possible causes of autocorrelation. One possibility is that an important variable has been omitted from the regression. If the time-ordered effects of such a missing variable are positively correlated, then the disturbances in the regression will tend to be positively correlated. The remedy to this problem is to locate the missing variable and include it in the regression equation, although this is easier said than done in many cases.

T A B L E **5.9**

Annual Data: Corporate Profits and GNP

Date	CORPROF	GNP	Date	CORPROF	GNP
1960	28.4	516.6	1976	109.5	1785.5
1961	28.2	535.4	1977	130.3	1994.6
1962	32.4	575.8	1978	154.4	2254.5
1963	34.9	607.7	1979	173.4	2520.8
1964	40.0	653.0	1980	156.1	2742.1
1965	47.9	708.1	1981	147.8	3063.8
1966	51.4	774.9	1982	113.2	3179.8
1967	49.2	819.8	1983	133.5	3434.4
1968	51.2	895.5	1984	146.4	3801.5
1969	49.4	965.6	1985	128.5	4053.6
1970	44.0	1017.1	1986	111.3	4277.7
1971	52.4	1104.9	1987	160.8	4544.5
1972	62.6	1215.7	1988	210.5	4908.2
1973	81.6	1362.3	1989	206.6	5248.2
1974	91.0	1474.3	1990	197.0	5524.5
1975	89.5	1599.1	1991	188.1	5685.8

The data were obtained from *Business Statistics 1963–91*.

F I G U R E **5.107**

MINITAB Regression of Corporate Profits on GNP Including Durbin–Watson Statistic

```
The regression equation is
corprof = 30.1 + 0.0317 gnp

Predictor      Coef       Stdev     t-ratio       p
Constant     30.051       7.604        3.95   0.000
gnp        0.031686    0.002682       11.81   0.000

s = 24.99      R-sq = 82.3%      R-sq(adj) = 81.7%

Analysis of Variance

SOURCE        DF          SS          MS         F        p
Regression     1       87178       87178    139.59    0.000
Error         30       18736         625
Total         31      105915

Unusual Observations
Obs.      gnp     corprof       Fit  Stdev.Fit  Residual   St.Resid
  19     2254      154.40    101.49       4.42     52.91       2.15R
  20     2521      173.40    109.93       4.45     63.47       2.58R
  27     4278      111.30    165.59       6.89    -54.29      -2.26R

R denotes an obs. with a large st. resid.

Durbin-Watson statistic = 0.48
```

F I G U R E   5.108

SAS Regression Output for Regression of Corporate Profits on GNP Including Durbin–Watson Statistic

```
Dependent Variable: CORPROF

                      Analysis of Variance

                        Sum of          Mean
Source      DF         Squares         Square     F Value     Prob>F

Model        1    87178.04825    87178.04825     139.586     0.0001
Error       30    18736.47644      624.54921
C Total     31   105914.52469

          Root MSE        24.99098     R-square       0.8231
          Dep Mean       103.17188     Adj R-sq       0.8172
          C.V.            24.22267

                      Parameter Estimates

                    Parameter      Standard     T for H0:
Variable    DF       Estimate         Error    Parameter=0    Prob > |T|

INTERCEP     1      30.051591    7.60397138         3.952        0.0004
GNP          1       0.031686    0.00268191        11.815        0.0001


Durbin-Watson D                        0.478
(For Number of Obs.)                      32
1st Order Autocorrelation              0.739
```

F I G U R E   5.109

MINITAB Time-Series Plot of Standardized Residuals for Corporate Profits/GNP Example

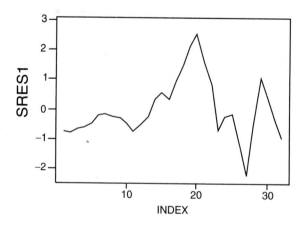

Another possible correction for first-order autocorrelation involves the transformation of the original time-series variables in the regression into new series that have independent disturbances. The original regression model for the time period i can be written

$$y_i = \beta_0 + \beta_1 x_i + e_i,$$

where the disturbances, e_i, have first-order autocorrelation

$$e_i = \rho e_{i-1} + u_i$$

To remove the autocorrelation from the original series, the following transformations are used. Create new dependent and explanatory variable values y_i^* and x_i^*, using

$$y_i^* = y_i - \rho y_{i-1}$$

and

$$x_i^* = x_i - \rho x_{i-1},$$

for time periods $i = 2, \ldots, n$.

In addition, transform the first time-period observation as

$$y_1^* = \sqrt{1 - \rho^2}\, y_1$$

and

$$x_1^* = \sqrt{1 - \rho^2}\, x_1$$

The new regression can be written as

$$y_i^* = \beta_0 + \beta_1 x_i^* + u_i$$

and the disturbances u_i will be independent. Now regress y_i^* on x_i^* to obtain estimates of β_0 and β_1.

In practice, there are various refinements to this process. In choosing a statistical package to perform these transformations and run the regressions, one of the most important things to keep in mind is that the transformation should include the first observation (y_1^*). Many statistical packages incorporated routines that simply dropped the first observation rather than transforming it as shown and including it in the new regression. Recent research shows that dropping this observation results in the loss of important information and adversely affects the results of the new regression. One common estimation procedure that drops the first observation is the Cochrane–Orcutt method, and it should be avoided. Procedures that incorporate the first observation include the Prais–Winsten method and full maximum likelihood. When using an automatic method from a statistical package to correct for autocorrelation, only those methods incorporating the initial observation should be used. Statistical packages such as SAS and SHAZAM have single commands that will transform the data appropriately, rerun the regression on the transformed data, and print the results so that correcting for autocorrelation in this case is a simple matter.

A third option is to add a lagged value of the dependent variable as an explanatory variable. This is a viable option if building an extrapolative model and if the number of observations is reasonably large (since one observation will be lost because of the lagged variable).

Alternative procedures for treating time-series data are discussed in Bowerman and O'Connell's *Time Series Forecasting* and Cryer's *Time Series Analysis*.

Forecasts are computed in a slightly different manner when disturbances are autocorrelated. The T-period-ahead forecast can be written in general as

$$\hat{y}_{n+T} = \hat{\beta}_0 + \hat{\beta}_1 x_{n+T} + \rho^T \hat{e}_n,$$

where $\hat{\beta}_0$ and $\hat{\beta}_1$ are used to represent the estimates of β_0 and β_1 from the transformed regression model (rather than the least-squares estimates b_0 and b_1), x_{n+T} is the value of the explanatory variable in the period to be forecast, ρ is the autocorrelation coefficient, and $\hat{e}_n$ is the residual from the last sample time period. Note that only the last residual in the sample contains any information about the future. Also note that the value of this information declines as forecasts are generated further into the future. The term ρ^T can be seen to decrease (because $-1 < \rho < 1$) as T increases.

5.8.4 *H* Test for Autocorrelation

When lagged values of the dependent variable are used as explanatory variables, the Durbin–Watson test is no longer appropriate. An alternative test typically recommended in this case is Durbin's h. The hypotheses to be tested are

$$H_0: \rho = 0$$
$$H_a: \rho \neq 0$$

The test statistic is

$$h = r \left(\frac{T}{1 - T\sigma_{b_1}^2} \right)^{1/2},$$

where r is the estimate of the first-order autocorrelation coefficient, T is the sample size, and $\sigma_{b_1}^2$ is the variance of the regression coefficient of the lagged dependent variable (y_{i-1}). If the null hypothesis is true, h will have a standard normal distribution. The decision rule to conduct the test is:

Reject H_0	if	$h > z_{\alpha/2}$ or $h < -z_{\alpha/2}$
Accept H_0	if	$-z_{\alpha/2} < h < z_{\alpha/2}$

Note that the test statistic h cannot be computed if $1 - T\sigma_{b_1}^2 < 0$ because this would result in the need to take the square root of a negative number. (Alternative test procedures are available in this case. The reader is referred to Judge et al. (1985), pp. 326–327, for example.) In practice, $\sigma_{b_1}^2$ in the formula for h would be replaced by its estimate $s_{b_1}^2$.

Finally, it should be noted that other procedures are available for analyzing time-series data. Certain of these procedures are designed especially for extrapolative models using lagged dependent variables, autocorrelated errors, or both. For more detail on such time-series forecasting methods, the reader is referred to Farnum and Stanton (1989) or Cryer (1986).

Exercises

7   **Personal Consumption Expenditures** Table 5.10 shows data on the M1 measure of money stock and personal consumption expenditures (both in billions of dollars). These are annual data covering the period from 1963 to 1991. The MINITAB scatterplot of personal consumption expenditures versus M1 is shown in Figure 5.110. The MINITAB regression output for the regression of personal consumption expenditures on M1 is shown in Figure 5.111. The Durbin–Watson statistic is shown in the output. The SAS regression output, including the D–W statistic and an estimate of ρ, is shown in Figure 5.112. The MINITAB time-series plot of the residuals is shown in Figure 5.113.

Test whether the disturbances are autocorrelated. Use a 5% level of significance. Be sure to state the hypotheses to be tested, the decision rule, the test statistic, and your decision.

T A B L E **5.10**

Annual Data: M1 and Personal Consumption Expenditures

Date	M1	CONSUMP	Date	M1	CONSUMP
1963	151.0	384.2	1978	346.5	1421.2
1964	156.8	412.5	1979	372.9	1583.7
1965	163.5	444.6	1980	396.0	1748.1
1966	171.0	481.6	1981	425.1	1926.2
1967	177.7	509.3	1982	453.2	2059.2
1968	190.2	559.1	1983	503.4	2257.5
1969	201.5	603.7	1984	538.9	2460.3
1970	209.2	646.5	1985	587.3	2667.4
1971	223.3	700.3	1986	666.8	2850.6
1972	239.2	767.8	1987	744.1	3052.2
1973	256.5	848.1	1988	775.8	3296.1
1974	269.3	927.7	1989	783.3	3517.9
1975	281.6	1024.9	1990	812.0	3742.6
1976	297.3	1143.1	1991	860.4	3889.1
1977	320.1	1271.5			

The data were obtained from *Business Statistics 1963–91*.

F I G U R E 5.110

MINITAB Scatterplot of Personal Consumption Expenditures versus M1

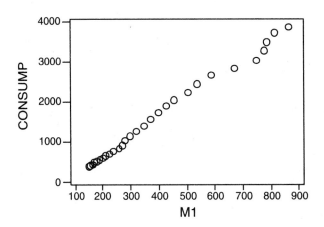

F I G U R E 5.111

MINITAB Regression Output for Regression of Personal Consumption Expenditures on M1
Including Durbin–Watson Statistic

```
The regression equation is
consump = - 336 + 4.92 m1

Predictor       Coef       Stdev     t-ratio        p
Constant     -336.18       39.14       -8.59    0.000
m1           4.92022      0.08552       57.53    0.000

s = 103.2       R-sq = 99.2%      R-sq(adj) = 99.2%

Analysis of Variance

SOURCE       DF          SS          MS          F        p
Regression    1    35248232    35248232    3310.25    0.000
Error        27      287502       10648
Total        28    35535732

Unusual Observations
Obs.        m1     consump      Fit   Stdev.Fit    Residual    St.Resid
  25       744      3052.2   3325.0        35.2      -272.8      -2.81R

R denotes an obs. with a large st. resid.

Durbin-Watson statistic = 0.51
```

F I G U R E 5.112

SAS Regression Output for Regression of Personal Consumption Expenditures on M1 Including Durbin–Watson Statistic

Dependent Variable: CONSUMP

Analysis of Variance

Source	DF	Sum of Squares	Mean Square	F Value	Prob>F
Model	1	35248230.043	35248230.043	3310.245	0.0001
Error	27	287502.05871	10648.22440		
C Total	28	35535732.101			

Root MSE	103.19023	R-square	0.9919	
Dep Mean	1627.48276	Adj R-sq	0.9916	
C.V.	6.34048			

Parameter Estimates

Variable	DF	Parameter Estimate	Standard Error	T for H0: Parameter=0	Prob > |T|
INTERCEP	1	-336.176407	39.14122852	-8.589	0.0001
M1	1	4.920218	0.08551737	57.535	0.0001

Durbin-Watson D	0.508
(For Number of Obs.)	29
1st Order Autocorrelation	0.745

F I G U R E 5.113

MINITAB Time-Series Plot of Standardized Residuals from Regression of Personal Consumption Expenditures on M1

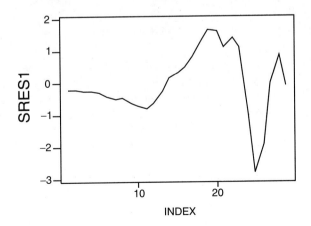

These data are available on the data disk for further analysis. In MINITAB, the data can be read using

```
READ 'M15' C1,C2
```

where C1 is M1 and C2 is personal consumption expenditures.

In SAS, the data can be read from the file M15.DAT using

```
INPUT M1 CONSUMP;
```

5.9
Multicollinearity

5.9.1 Consequences of Multicollinearity

For a regression of y on K explanatory variables $x_1, \ldots, x_K$, it is hoped that the explanatory variables will be highly correlated with the dependent variable. A relationship is sought that will explain a large portion of the variation in y. At the same time, however, it is not desirable for strong relationships to exist among the explanatory variables. When explanatory variables are correlated with one another, the problem of *multicollinearity* is said to exist. How serious the problem is depends on the degree of multicollinearity. Low correlations among the explanatory variables generally will not result in serious deterioration of the quality of the least-squares estimates. High correlations may result in highly unstable least-squares estimates of the regression coefficients.

The presence of a high degree of multicollinearity among the explanatory variables will result in the following problems:

1   The standard deviations of the regression coefficients will be disproportionately large. As a result, the t values computed to test whether the population regression coefficients are zero will be small. The null hypothesis that the coefficients are zero may be accepted even when the associated variable is important in explaining variation in y.

2   The regression coefficient estimates will be unstable. Because of the high standard errors, reliable estimates of the regression coefficients will be difficult to obtain. Signs of the coefficients may be the opposite of what is intuitively reasonable. Dropping one variable from the regression or adding a variable will cause large changes in the estimates of the coefficients of other variables.

5.9.2 Detecting Multicollinearity

Numerous ways have been suggested in the literature to help detect multicollinearity. These will be listed with some recommendations on their usefulness:

1 Compute the pairwise correlations between the explanatory variables. Because multicollinearity exists when explanatory variables are highly correlated, these correlations should help to identify any highly correlated pairs of variables. One rule of thumb suggested by some researchers is that multicollinearity may be a serious problem if any pairwise correlation is bigger than 0.5.

There are two limitations to this approach. First, the correlation cutoff of 0.5 is somewhat arbitrary and not always effective in identifying serious pairwise multicollinearity problems. Second, only relationships between two explanatory variables can be investigated. For example, if there are three explanatory variables in the model, x_1, x_2, and x_3, the pairwise correlations can be computed between x_1 and x_2, x_1 and x_3, and x_2 and x_3. But the relationships resulting in the multicollinearity may be more complex than simple pairwise correlations. The variable x_1 may not be highly correlated with x_2 or x_3 individually, but it may be highly correlated with some linear combination of the two variables. That is, x_1 may be highly correlated with $a_1 x_2 + a_2 x_3$.

Another suggested rule of thumb is that multicollinearity may be a serious problem if any of the pairwise correlations among the x variables is larger than the largest of the correlations between the y variable and the x variables. Although this rule does not suffer from an arbitrary cutoff point (such as 0.5) it does suffer from the same limitations concerning more complex relationships among the x variables.

2 An indication of multicollinearity is a large overall F statistic but small t statistics. As mentioned, multicollinearity results in large standard deviations of the regression coefficients and small t ratios. Thus, the test for whether the individual regression coefficients are equal to zero may result in a decision to accept the null hypothesis H_0: $\beta_k = 0$ even when the variables included in the regression are important in explaining the variation in y. The overall F statistic is typically not affected by the multicollinearity, however. If the variables are important, the F statistic should be large, indicating a good overall fit even if the t statistics appear to be saying that none of the variables are important.

This method of detecting multicollinearity will not always be effective because multicollinearity may result in some of the t values being small, but not all of them. The question of whether the variable is unimportant or whether it just appears so because of multicollinearity cannot be answered by looking at the output. Although this approach also may be helpful in pointing out that multicollinearity exists in some instances, it does not provide any information on which of the explanatory variables are highly correlated with others.

3 Compute variance inflation factors (VIFs). Let $x_1, \ldots, x_K$ be the K explanatory variables in a regression. Perform the regression of x_j on the remaining $K - 1$ explanatory variables and call the coefficient of determination from this regression R_j^2. The VIF for the variable x_j will be

$$\text{VIF}_j = \frac{1}{1 - R_j^2}$$

A variance inflation factor can be computed for each explanatory variable. It is a measure of the strength of the relationship between each explanatory variable and all other explanatory variables in the regression. Thus, pairwise correlations are taken into account as well as more complex relationships with two or more of the other variables. The value R_j^2 measures the strength of the relationship between x_j and the other $K - 1$ explanatory variables. If there is no relationship (an ideal case), then $R_j^2 = 0.0$ and $\text{VIF}_j = 1/(1 - 0) = 1$. As R_j^2 increases, VIF_j increases also. For example, if $R_j^2 = 0.9$, then $\text{VIF}_j = 1/(1 - 0.9) = 10$; if $R_j^2 = 0.99$, then $\text{VIF}_j = 1/(1 - 0.99) = 100$. Large values of VIF_j suggest that x_j may be highly related to other explanatory variables and, thus, multicollinearity may be a problem.

How large the VIFs have to be to suggest a serious problem with multicollinearity is not completely clear. Some suggested guidelines are as follows:

a   An individual VIF_j larger than 10 indicates that multicollinearity may be influencing the least squares estimates of the regression coefficients.

b   If the average of the VIF_j, $\overline{\text{VIF}} = \sum_{j=1}^{K} \text{VIF}_j / K$, is considerably larger than 1, then serious problems may exist. $\overline{\text{VIF}}$ indicates how many times larger the error sum of squares for the regression is due to multicollinearity than it would be if the variables were uncorrelated.

5.9.3   Corrections for Multicollinearity

One obvious solution to the multicollinearity problem is to remove those variables that are highly correlated with others and thus eliminate the problem. This solution has obvious drawbacks. No information will be obtained on the omitted variables. Also, the omission of one variable causes changes in the estimates of the regression coefficients of variables left in the equation.

In certain cases, adding more data can break the pattern of multicollinearity. This solution is not always possible, especially in many business and economics situations, and also will not always work even when it is possible.

When multicollinearity is present it will affect the regression coefficient estimates in the ways noted earlier, but it does not affect the ability to obtain a good fit of the regression (high R^2). Neither does it affect the quality of forecasts or predictions from the regression (as long as the pattern of multicollinearity continues for those observations where forecasts are desired). Thus, if the regression model is to be used strictly for forecasting, corrections may be unnecessary. Even when developing a model for forecasting, however, it often is desirable to test whether individual variables are contributing significantly to the explanatory power of the model. In this case, multicollinearity remains a problem.

Finally, several other statistical procedures have been proposed as possible remedial measures with multicollinearity. These include ridge regression and principle-components regression. These techniques are beyond the scope of this text. The interested reader is referred to pages 243–263 of *Classical and Modern Regression with Applications* by Raymond H. Myers.

5.10
Using the Computer

5.10.1 MINITAB

Storing Standardized Residuals and Fitted Values

REGR C1 K C_,..., C_, STORE C_,C_ (STAT: REGRESSION: REGRESSION)

The dependent (y) variable data values are listed in the first column shown (C1 in this example) and the independent variables are listed in the K subsequent columns (which have not been numbered here). The K in the command tells MINITAB that K independent variables are to be used. The standardized residuals are stored in the next column (the first column listed after STORE) and the fitted values or predicted values are stored next. Residual plots are created by using the PLOT command with the column for the standardized residuals listed first and the column for the fitted values or one of the x variables listed next.

With new versions of MINITAB, choices of dependent and independent variables are requested by menu, in which case the number of independent variables need not be specified. The standardized residuals and fitted values can also be requested from a menu of options.

Requesting Other Influence Statistics

Influence statistics other than standardized residuals and fitted values can be requested in MINITAB using subcommands. For example:

```
REGR C1 2 C3 C4;
 HI C5;
 TRESIDS C6;
 COOKD C7;
 DFITS C8.
```

stores the leverage values (h_i) in C5, the studentized deleted residuals in C6, the Cook's D statistics in C7, and the DFITS values in C8.

In newer versions of MINITAB, all of these measures can be requested from the Regression menu.

Requesting the Durbin–Watson Statistic

```
REGR C1 K C_,...,C_;
DW.
```

requests that the Durbin–Watson statistic be printed.

Variable Transformations

(CALC: MATHEMATICAL EXPRESSIONS)

In MINITAB, variable transformations are performed using the LET command. Here are some typical examples:

Create the square of the variable in C1 and put the result in C3:

```
LET C3=C1**2
```

Create the natural log of the variable in C1 and put the result in C4:

```
LET C4=LOGE(C1)
```

These transformed variables can then be used as variables in the REGR command, the PLOT command, and so on.

Testing for Normality

(GRAPH: NORMAL PLOT)

In older versions of MINITAB, a normal probability plot for data in C1 (for example) can be created as follows:

```
NSCORES C1 C2
PLOT C1 C2
```

NSCORES creates the "normal scores" or expected values of the order statistics chosen from a standard normal distribution. These are placed in C2 and matched from smallest to largest with the actual data in C1. The plot created is the normal probability plot. If the data came from a normal distribution, the plot should be approximately linear. If not, the plot will show some sort of curvature. To perform a test for normality, use the command

```
CORR C1 C2
```

The correlation of the data and the normal scores measures the "straightness" of the normal probability plot. These correlations (the test statistics) can be compared to critical values in Table 6 of Appendix B.

In new versions of MINITAB, a version of the probability plot can be requested by accessing the GRAPH menu, choosing NORMAL PLOT from this menu, and then picking the Ryan–Joiner test (rather than the Andersen–Darling test).

This will produce the normal probability plot, the correlation test statistic described, and an approximate p value associated with this test statistic.

Szroeter's Test for Nonconstant Variance

Although this test cannot be requested in MINITAB (or SAS) with a single command, it can be computed through a sequence of commands. This will be demonstrated for MINITAB.

Assume that the dependent (y) variable is in C1 and the (one) explanatory variable (x) is in C2. First, recall that the data must be ordered according to increasing values of x. The SORT command accomplishes this. The standardized residuals from the regression of y on x are then stored in C10.

```
SORT C2, CARRY C1, PUT IN C20,C21
REGR Y IN C21 ON 1 PRED IN C20, STORE IN C10
```

A patterned set command is used to put integers 1 through n (the sample size) in C25.

```
SET IN C25
1:n
END
```

Now compute the quantities needed to compute h in Szroeter's test statistic:

```
LET C16=C10*C10
LET C17=C16*C25
SUM C17 K2
SUM C16 K1
LET K3=K2/K1
```

The value of K3 printed will be h.

```
PRINT K3
```

Szroeter's Q statistic can then be computed using the formula

$$Q = \left(\frac{6n}{n^2 - 1} \right)^{1/2} \left(h - \frac{n+1}{2} \right)$$

5.10.2 SAS

Storing Standardized Residuals and Fitted Values

The following command sequence will produce the regression results in Figure 4.3, as well as the associated residual plots.

```
PROC REG;
  MODEL SALES=ADV BONUS;
  OUTPUT PREDICTED=FITS1 STUDENT=SRES1;
PROC PLOT;
  PLOT SRES1*FITS1 SRES1*ADV SRES1*BONUS;
```

In the model statement, the dependent variable (SALES) is listed first; the independent variables (ADV and BONUS) follow the equal sign. In the output statement the fitted (predicted) values are requested and labeled FITS1. The standardized residuals (student) are also requested and labeled SRES1. PROC PLOT is used to produce residual plots. As shown, residual plots of the standardized residuals versus the fitted values and each of the two explanatory variables will be generated.

Requesting Other Influence Statistics

Influence statistics other than standardized residuals and fitted values can be requested in SAS as follows:

```
PROC REG;
  MODEL Y=X/INFLUENCE;
  OUTPUT COOK=COOKD;
```

The INFLUENCE option requests that SAS print out the leverage values (h_i), the studentized deleted residuals, and the DFITS statistics (among others not discussed in this text). The OUTPUT command requests that Cook's D statistic be computed, stored, and labeled COOKD.

Requesting the Durbin–Watson Statistic

```
PROG REG;
MODEL CORPROF=GNP/DW;
```

requests that the Durbin–Watson statistic be printed. SAS also prints out an estimate of the first-order autocorrelation statistic.

Variable Transformations

In SAS, variable transformations are performed during the data input phase. Here are some typical examples:

Create the square of the variable MONTHS and call it XSQR:

```
XSQR=MONTHS**2;
```

Create the natural log of the variable MONTHS and call it LOGMONTH:

```
LOGMONTH=LOG(MONTH);
```

These transformed variables can then be used in PROC REG, PROC PLOT, and so on.

Testing for Normality

In SAS, a normal probability plot can be produced as follows:

```
PROC UNIVARIATE PLOT;
VAR SRES1;
```

A variety of descriptive statistics on the variable SRES1 will be printed along with a stem-and-leaf plot, a box plot, and a normal probability plot. When the sample size is 50 or less, the Shapiro–Wilk test statistic is computed. When $n > 50$, the Kolmogorov D statistic is used. In either case, a p value corresponding to the observed statistic is computed and printed. (Note that the Shapiro–Wilk test is essentially the same test as the Ryan–Joiner test produced in MINITAB.)

Prais–Winsten Transformation

The Prais–Winsten transformation to correct for first-order autocorrelation was discussed earlier in this chapter. Although SAS does not have a procedure to correct for autocorrelation, the associated statistical package SAS/ETS does. This procedure is outlined briefly here:

```
PROC AUTOREG;
  MODEL CORPROF=GNP/NLAG=1 ITER;
```

These commands request the Prais–Winsten transformation through the PROC AUTOREG command. The dependent variable here is CORPROF and the explanatory variable is GNP (more than one explanatory variable can be included if necessary). The NLAG=1 option tells the procedure that first-order autocorrelation is to be corrected (AUTOREG is a general procedure that can correct for higher-order autocorrelation not discussed in this text). The ITER option requests an iterative procedure, which has in general been shown superior in various studies.

Additional Exercises

8 Imports The Gross National Product (GNP) and imports for 25 countries are shown in Table 5.11. The scatterplot of IMPORTS versus GNP is shown in Figure 5.114. The MINITAB and SAS regressions are shown in Figures 5.115 and 5.116, respectively. Plots of the standardized residuals versus the fitted values and the explanatory variable

T A B L E   **5.11**

Data for Imports Exercise

Country	IMPORTS	GNP (or GDP)
1. Argentina	8.0	101.2
2. Australia	43.7	311.0
3. Bolivia	0.8	4.8
4. Brazil	23.0	338.0
5. Canada	124.0	521.0
6. Costa Rica	2.5	5.6
7. Denmark	32.3	91.0
8. Egypt	11.5	39.2
9. Finland	21.2	80.0
10. France	239.0	1000.0
11. Greece	21.5	77.0
12. Haiti	0.3	2.7
13. India	25.2	328.0
14. Israel	18.1	54.6
15. Jamaica	1.8	3.6
16. Japan	233.0	2300.0
17. Liberia	0.4	1.0
18. Malaysia	38.7	48.0
19. Mauritius	1.5	2.5
20. Netherlands	156.0	249.0
21. Nigeria	9.5	28.0
22. Panama	1.5	5.2
23. Saudi Arabia	21.5	104.0
24. United Kingdom	221.0	915.0
25. United States	553.0	5600.0

These data were obtained from the *World Almanac and Book of Facts 1994.*

are shown in Figures 5.117 and 5.118 for MINITAB and Figures 5.119 and 5.120 for SAS. Use the outputs to help answer the following questions:

a Using the scatterplot, regression outputs, and the residual plots, do any of the assumptions of the regression model appear to be violated? If so, which one (or ones)? Justify your answers.

b Using a computer statistical package, construct the scatterplot and rerun the regression with the United States omitted. Construct the residual plots for this new regression. Do the results appear any different from the original regression results? If so, how do they differ? Do you prefer the original results or the results with the United States omitted? On what do you base your choice? Do there still appear to be problems with this regression?

c Try to develop a curvilinear model using the original data (with the United States included) that provides improved results over the linear model. Be sure to examine

F I G U R E 5.114

MINITAB Scatterplot of IMPORTS versus GNP

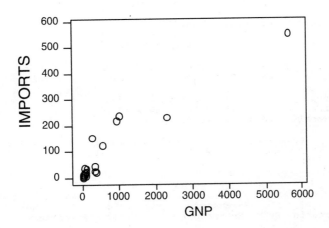

F I G U R E 5.115

MINITAB Regression Output for Regression of IMPORTS on GNP

```
The regression equation is
imports = 23.3 + 0.100 gnp

Predictor        Coef       Stdev     t-ratio         p
Constant       23.314       9.866        2.36     0.027
gnp          0.100418    0.007880       12.74     0.000

s = 45.42        R-sq = 87.6%      R-sq(adj) = 87.1%

Analysis of Variance

SOURCE         DF           SS          MS          F         p
Regression      1       335034      335034     162.38     0.000
Error          23        47456        2063
Total          24       382490

Unusual Observations
Obs.      gnp    imports      Fit   Stdev.Fit    Residual   St.Resid
  10     1000     239.00   123.73        9.94      115.27       2.60R
  20      249     156.00    48.32        9.28      107.68       2.42R
  24      915     221.00   115.20        9.69      105.80       2.38R
  25     5600     553.00   585.66       41.29      -32.66      -1.73 X

R denotes an obs. with a large st. resid.
X denotes an obs. whose X value gives it large influence.
```

F I G U R E 5.116

SAS Regression Output for Regression of IMPORTS on GNP

```
Dependent Variable: IMPORTS

                      Analysis of Variance

                      Sum of          Mean
Source      DF        Squares         Square       F Value      Prob>F

Model        1  335034.36035  335034.36035       162.377      0.0001
Error       23   47456.03965    2063.30607
C Total     24  382490.40000

          Root MSE       45.42363      R-square      0.8759
          Dep Mean       72.36000      Adj R-sq      0.8705
          C.V.           62.77450

                    Parameter Estimates

                 Parameter      Standard     T for H0:
Variable   DF     Estimate        Error    Parameter=0    Prob > |T|

INTERCEP    1    23.314057    9.86643403        2.363        0.0270
GNP         1     0.100418    0.00788044       12.743        0.0001
```

F I G U R E 5.117

MINITAB Residual Plot of Standardized Residuals versus Fitted Values for Imports Exercise

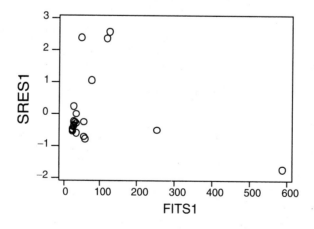

F I G U R E **5.118**

MINITAB Residual Plot of Standardized Residuals versus GNP for Imports Exercise

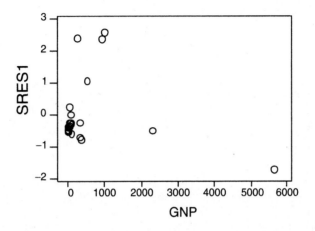

F I G U R E **5.119**

SAS Residual Plot of Standardized Residuals versus Fitted Values for Imports Exercise

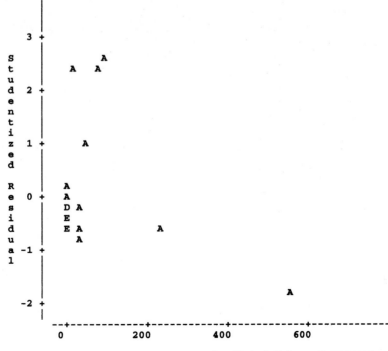

F I G U R E **5.120**

SAS Residual Plot of Standardized Residuals versus GNP for Imports Exercise

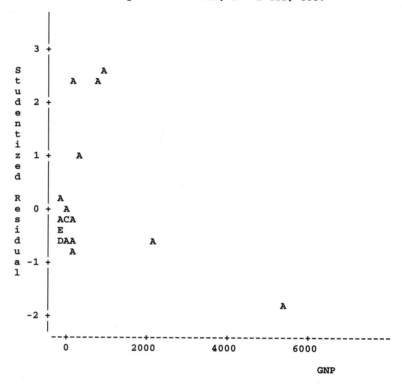

```
Plot of SRES1*GNP.  Legend: A = 1 obs, B = 2 obs, etc.
```

the residual plots from the curvilinear model to see whether any assumptions are violated for this model.

d   Finally, state what you believe is the best model for these data, and why.

These data are available on the data disk and can be read in MINITAB using

```
READ 'IMPORT5' C1,C2
```

where C1 is IMPORTS and C2 is GNP.

In SAS, the data can be read from the file IMPORT5.DAT using

```
INPUT IMPORTS GNP;
```

9   **Piston Corporation (Part A)**   Reginald Jackson was employed as a cost accountant by the Piston Corporation, a medium-sized auto parts company located in the outskirts of Detroit. Kelly Jones, the controller for Piston, decided that she needed an assistant. Jackson was selected to fill that position. As part of his training program, Jackson was sent to night school to study quantitative applications in cost accounting.

Because the Piston Corporation's products were replacement parts, its sales were, fortunately, not as volatile as the new car market's. Piston had experienced a rather stable growth in sales in recent years and had been required to increase its capacity regularly. It appeared to be time for another expansion, but with an uncertain stock market prevailing and uncertainty concerning interest rates, Jones was worried about obtaining funds at a reasonable cost. On the other hand, Piston's production manager had been complaining, more than usual, about various personnel, material handling, and scheduling bottlenecks that arose from the high level of output demanded of his present facilities.

The executive officers thus had been asked by Piston's directors to formulate a proposal for expansion and price adjustments. Jones asked Jackson what he could determine statistically about the effect of inflation and the level of production on unit costs.

By looking at old budgets, Jackson was able to obtain quarterly data on manufacturing costs per unit, production level (a percentage of the total capacity), and the index of direct material and direct labor costs for a five-year period (see Table 5.12). He immediately went to the computer terminal, on which he had been assigned time for his class, and ran a regression of unit cost on production volume (PROD) and the cost index (INDEX). He began to wonder about the validity of modeling unit costs as a linear function of production level and the cost index. He decided to examine residual plots to determine the validity of his model.

The scatterplots of the dependent variable (COST) versus each explanatory variable are shown in Figures 5.121 and 5.122. The MINITAB regression output is in Figure 5.123 and the SAS output is in Figure 5.124. The residual plots are shown in Figures 5.125 through 5.127 for MINITAB and Figures 5.128 through 5.130 for SAS. To help Jackson achieve a better fit, examine the residual plots. Does it appear that any assumptions of the linear regression model have been violated? If so, state which one (or ones) and justify your choice.

10   Piston Corporation (Part B)   After spending several days trying to improve his model, Jackson had several new solutions but was still unsure which one was best. That night after his quantitative accounting class, he asked his professor for advice. The professor suggested that Jackson first derive a theoretically plausible solution and then see whether the data satisfied this relationship.

Jackson knew that the basic relationship with which he was dealing was

$$\text{total cost} = \text{variable cost per unit} \times \text{volume} + \text{fixed cost}$$

He also theorized that variable cost per unit was composed of a constant multiple of the index of direct materials and labor (x_2), and that fixed cost was simply the current capacity of the company times some constant.

Jackson realized that the basic equation could be rewritten as

$$\text{total cost} = \beta_1 \times \text{capacity} + \beta_2 \times x_2 \times \text{volume}$$

Then it dawned on him that he actually wanted cost per unit. This equation could be divided by volume to get

$$\text{total cost/volume} = \beta_1 \times \text{capacity/volume} + \beta_2 x_2$$

T A B L E 5.12

Data for Piston Exercise

Quarter	Average Mfg. Cost per Unit (y) (COST)	Production Level As a Fraction of Rated Capacity (x_1) (PROD)	Direct Material and Labor Costs (x_2) (INDEX)
1	3.65	.85	80
2	4.22	.78	93
3	4.29	.82	107
4	5.43	.64	115
5	6.42	.50	130
6	5.71	.62	128
7	5.39	.70	116
8	3.99	.90	92
9	4.08	.94	94
10	4.38	1.00	110
11	4.28	1.04	115
12	4.42	.82	117
13	5.11	.75	128
14	4.88	.84	134
15	4.99	.86	135
16	4.57	.90	135
17	4.84	.94	139
18	5.16	.80	142
19	5.67	.72	147
20	6.26	.60	150

F I G U R E 5.121

MINITAB Scatterplot of COST versus PROD for Piston Exercise

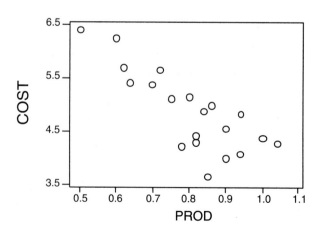

F I G U R E 5.122

MINITAB Scatterplot of COST versus INDEX for Piston Exercise

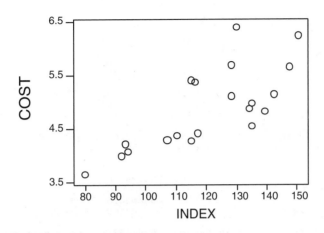

F I G U R E 5.123

MINITAB Regression Output for Piston Exercise

```
The regression equation is
cost = 5.18 - 3.45 prod + 0.0205 index

Predictor        Coef       Stdev     t-ratio         p
Constant       5.1829      0.5364        9.66     0.000
prod          -3.4482      0.3961       -8.70     0.000
index         0.020492    0.002796       7.33     0.000

s = 0.2280      R-sq = 91.9%     R-sq(adj) = 91.0%

Analysis of Variance

SOURCE          DF          SS          MS         F         p
Regression       2     10.0586      5.0293     96.78     0.000
Error           17      0.8834      0.0520
Total           19     10.9420

SOURCE          DF      SEQ SS
prod             1      7.2677
index            1      2.7909
```

Capacity/volume, however, is simply the reciprocal of production level, so the new equation becomes

$$y = \beta_1 \left(\frac{1}{x_1}\right) + \beta_2 x_2,$$

where y is total cost/volume (or cost per unit), x_1 is production level, and x_2 is cost index. Allowing for random error and allowing the equation to have a y intercept term produces:

$$y = \beta_0 + \beta_1(1/x_1) + \beta_2 x_2 + e$$

SAS Regression Output for Piston Exercise

```
Dependent Variable: COST

                    Analysis of Variance

                     Sum of         Mean
Source      DF       Squares        Square      F Value      Prob>F

Model        2       10.05862       5.02931      96.784       0.0001
Error       17        0.88340       0.05196
C Total     19       10.94202

        Root MSE      0.22796      R-square      0.9193
        Dep Mean      4.88700      Adj R-sq      0.9098
        C.V.          4.66456

                    Parameter Estimates

                   Parameter      Standard      T for H0:
Variable    DF     Estimate       Error         Parameter=0    Prob > |T|

INTERCEP     1      5.182864      0.53643393       9.662         0.0001
PROD         1     -3.448235      0.39614626      -8.704         0.0001
INDEX        1      0.020492      0.00279613       7.329         0.0001
```

MINITAB Residual Plot of Standardized Residuals versus Fitted Values for Piston Exercise

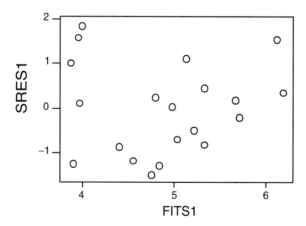

Try Jackson's new model by regressing y on $1/x_1$ and x_2 (note that this introduces a constant into the equation). As in Part A, check residual plots to see whether any assumptions are violated in this new model. How does this model compare with the original regression? In answering this question, use the R^2 values, the residual plots,

F I G U R E   5.126

MINITAB Residual Plot of Standardized Residuals versus PROD for Piston Exercise

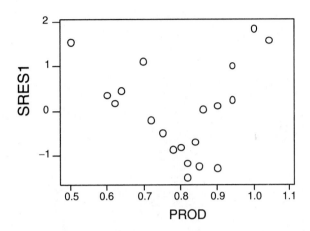

F I G U R E   5.127

MINITAB Residual Plot of Standardized Residuals versus INDEX for Piston Exercise

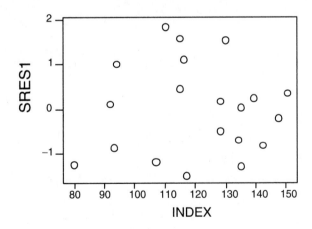

and any other information you feel might be useful in the comparisons. Which model do you prefer?

These data are available on the data disk. In MINITAB, they can be read using

```
READ 'PISTON5' C1-C3
```

where C1 is COST, C2 is PROD, and C3 is INDEX.

F I G U R E **5.128**

SAS Residual Plot of Standardized Residuals versus Fitted Values for Piston Exercise

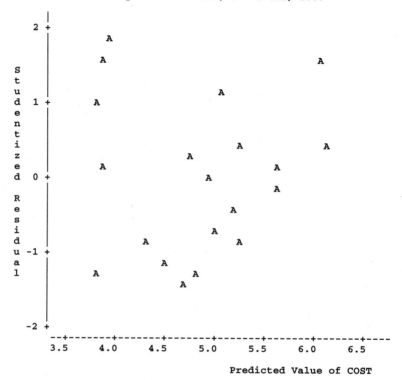

Plot of STRES*FITS. Legend: A = 1 obs, B = 2 obs, etc.

In SAS, the data can be read from the file PISTON5.DAT using

```
INPUT COST PROD INDEX;
```

11 **Piston Corporation (Part C)**   Use the model developed in Part B to answer the following questions:

a A three-point rise in the cost index will cause what change in unit costs (assuming production level remains constant)?

b What is the marginal unit cost of a rise in production volume from 0.94 to 0.95 of capacity (marginal cost implies all other variables remain constant)?

c If forecasts of a production level of 0.87 and a cost index of 120 are obtained, find a prediction of the manufacturing cost per unit (use a point prediction).

d Construct a 95% prediction interval for manufacturing cost per unit under the conditions described in (c).

12 **ABX Company**   Consider again the data used in Exercise 15 of Chapter 4. The dependent variable is absenteeism among employees at the ABX Company. In this exercise,

F I G U R E **5.129**

SAS Residual Plot of Standardized Residuals versus PROD for Piston Exercise

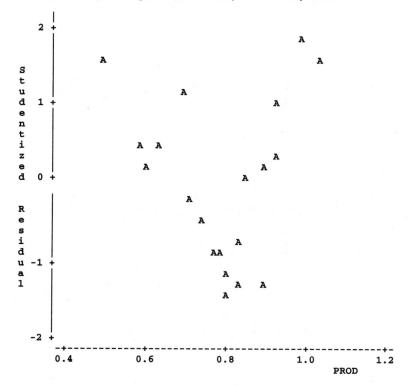

```
Plot of STRES*PROD.   Legend: A = 1 obs, B = 2 obs, etc.
```

the explanatory variable to be considered is seniority (SENIOR). The data were shown in Table 4.16. The scatterplot of absenteeism versus seniority is shown in Figure 5.131. The MINITAB and SAS regressions of absenteeism on seniority are shown in Figures 5.132 and 5.133, respectively. The MINITAB residual plots are shown in Figures 5.134 and 5.135 and the SAS residual plots are in Figures 5.136 and 5.137.

From the outputs, do any assumptions of the linear regression model appear to be violated? If so, which one (or ones)? If any violations are detected, suggest possible corrections. Rerun the regression with the suggested corrections and compare your results to the original results. Be sure to do residual plots for the model using the suggested correction. Which model do you prefer and why?

These data are available on the data disk. In MINITAB, they can be read using

```
READ 'ABSENT5' C1-C2
```

where C1 is ABSENT and C2 is SENIOR.

F I G U R E **5.130**

SAS Residual Plot of Standardized Residuals versus INDEX for Piston Exercise

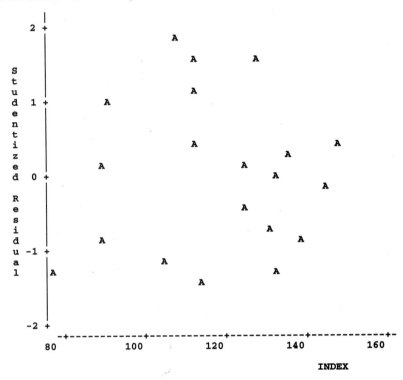

F I G U R E **5.131**

MINITAB Scatterplot of ABSENT versus SENIOR for ABX Company Exercise

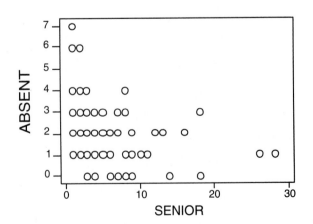

F I G U R E 5.132

MINITAB Regression Output for ABX Company Exercise

```
The regression equation is
absent = 2.58 - 0.0906 senior

Predictor        Coef       Stdev     t-ratio        p
Constant       2.5814      0.2255       11.45    0.000
senior       -0.09056     0.02935       -3.09    0.003

s = 1.403     R-sq = 11.3%    R-sq(adj) = 10.1%

Analysis of Variance

SOURCE         DF          SS          MS        F        p
Regression      1      18.738      18.738     9.52    0.003
Error          75     147.625       1.968
Total          76     166.364

Unusual Observations
Obs.    senior    absent      Fit   Stdev.Fit   Residual   St.Resid
  18       1.0     7.000     2.491      0.206      4.509      3.25R
  26      18.0     3.000     0.951      0.402      2.049      1.52 X
  42       2.0     6.000     2.400      0.189      3.600      2.59R
  46      26.0     1.000     0.227      0.625      0.773      0.62 X
  54       1.0     6.000     2.491      0.206      3.509      2.53R
  71      28.0     1.000     0.046      0.682      0.954      0.78 X
  72      18.0     0.000     0.951      0.402     -0.951     -0.71 X

R denotes an obs. with a large st. resid.
X denotes an obs. whose X value gives it large influence.
```

F I G U R E 5.133

SAS Regression Output for ABX Company Exercise

```
Dependent Variable: ABSENT

                    Analysis of Variance

                      Sum of        Mean
Source       DF      Squares      Square    F Value    Prob>F

Model         1    18.73828    18.73828      9.520    0.0028
Error        75   147.62536     1.96834
C Total      76   166.36364

          Root MSE      1.40297    R-square     0.1126
          Dep Mean      2.09091    Adj R-sq     0.1008
          C.V.         67.09879

                    Parameter Estimates

                 Parameter    Standard     T for H0:
Variable   DF     Estimate       Error   Parameter=0    Prob > |T|

INTERCEP    1     2.581360  0.22545566        11.450        0.0001
SENIOR      1    -0.090563  0.02935183        -3.085        0.0028
```

F I G U R E **5.134**

MINITAB Residual Plot of Standardized Residuals versus Fitted Values for ABX Exercise

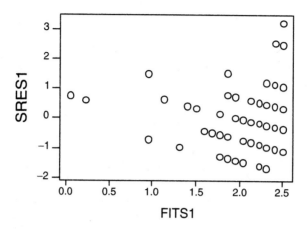

F I G U R E **5.135**

MINITAB Residual Plot of Standardized Residuals versus SENIOR for ABX Exercise

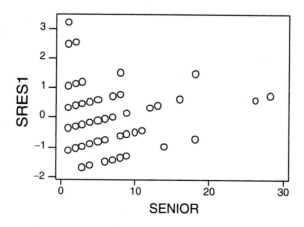

F I G U R E **5.136**

SAS Residual Plot of Standardized Residuals versus Fitted Values for ABX Company Exercise

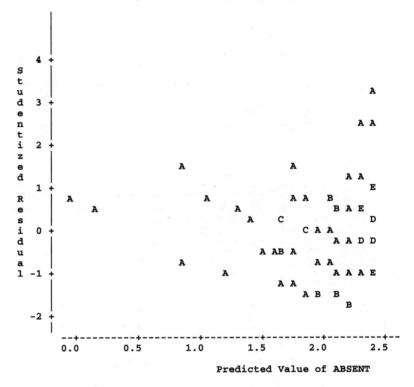

Plot of STRES*FITS. Legend: A = 1 obs, B = 2 obs, etc.

In SAS, the data can be read from the file ABSENT5.DAT using

```
INPUT ABSENT SENIOR;
```

13 **Coal-Mining Fatalities** The data in Table 5.13 show the annual number of fatalities from gas and dust explosions in coal mines for the years 1915 to 1978 and the number of cutting machines in use.

The scatterplot of fatalities (FATALS) versus the number of cutting machines in use (CUTTING) is shown in Figure 5.138. The MINITAB regression of FATALS on CUTTING is shown in Figure 5.139, and the residual plots are shown in Figures 5.140 and 5.141.

From the outputs, do any of the assumptions of the linear regression model appear to be violated? If so, which one (or ones)? If any assumptions appear to be violated, suggest a possible correction. Rerun the regression with the suggested correction and compare your results to the original results. Be sure to do residual plots for the model using the suggested correction. Which model do you prefer and why?

F I G U R E **5.137**

SAS Residual Plot of Standardized Residuals versus SENIOR for ABX Company Exercise

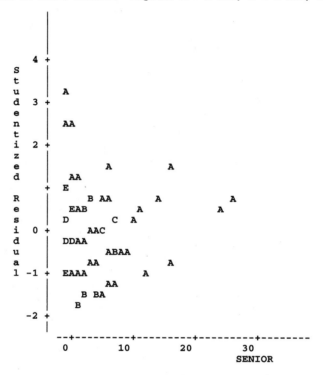

```
Plot of STRES*SENIOR.   Legend: A = 1 obs, B = 2 obs, etc.
```

These data are available on the data disk. In MINITAB, they can be read using

```
READ 'CUTTING5' C1-C2
```

where C1 is FATALS and C2 is CUTTING.

In SAS, the data can be read from the file CUTTING5.DAT using

```
INPUT FATALS CUTTING;
```

14   **Piston Corporation (Part D)**   Reexamine the data from the Piston exercise. Use the variables 1/PROD and INDEX as explanatory variables (these were the variables chosen in Exercise 5.10). Test to see whether the disturbances are positively autocorrelated. State the hypotheses to be tested, the decision rule, the test statistic, and your decision. On the basis of the test result, what action should be taken? Use a 0.05 level of significance.

15   **Cost Control**   Consider again the data from Exercise 1 in Chapter 4. Use the variables PAPER and MACHINE as explanatory variables. Test to see whether the disturbances are positively autocorrelated. State the hypotheses to be tested, the decision rule, the test

T A B L E 5.13

Data for Coal-Mining Fatalities Exercise

Year	FATALS	CUTTING	Year	FATALS	CUTTING
1915	270	15,692	1947	154	13,865
1916	183	16,198	1948	44	14,445
1917	319	17,235	1949	3	14,424
1918	103	18,463	1950	3	14,315
1919	149	18,959	1951	153	13,761
1920	124	19,103	1952	11	12,471
1921	62	19,618	1953	9	10,960
1922	298	20,436	1954	17	9,218
1923	330	21,229	1955	2	9,054
1924	486	18,660	1956	5	9,218
1925	302	17,551	1957	63	8,817
1926	373	17,466	1958	41	7,744
1927	187	17,388	1959	10	6,907
1928	347	15,261	1960	3	6,440
1929	168	14,731	1961	26	6,021
1930	234	14,237	1962	52	5,561
1931	68	13,216	1963	31	5,309
1932	162	12,017	1964	3	5,320
1933	27	11,845	1965	19	4,784
1934	40	11,905	1966	10	4,311
1935	26	11,881	1967	12	3,663
1936	41	11,974	1968	88	3,060
1937	116	11,892	1969	0	2,779
1938	84	11,810	1970	41	2,623
1939	43	12,076	1971	2	2,058
1940	292	12,342	1972	5	1,890
1941	89	12,608	1973	2	1,535
1942	148	13,049	1974	0	1,515
1943	166	11,656	1975	0	1,595
1944	32	13,305	1976	23	1,803
1945	72	13,390	1977	4	1,495
1946	27	13,625	1978	0	1,432

Data were obtained from K. D. Lawrence and L. C. March. "Robust Ridge Estimation Methods for Predicting U.S. Coal Mining Fatalities." *Communications in Statistics* 13 (1984): 139–149.

statistic, and your decision. On the basis of the test result, what action should be taken? Use a 0.05 level of significance.

These data are available on the data disk. In MINITAB, they can be read using

```
READ 'COST5' C1-C3
```

where C1 is COST (y), C2 is PAPER, and C3 is MACHINE.

F I G U R E **5.138**

MINITAB Scatterplot of FATALS versus CUTTING for Coal-Mining Fatalities Exercise

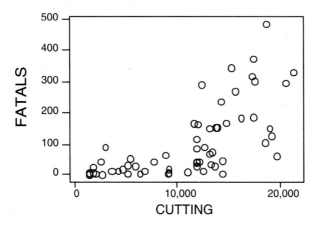

F I G U R E **5.139**

MINITAB Regression Output for Coal-Mining Fatalities Exercise

```
The regression equation is
fatals = - 47.7 + 0.0134 cutting

Predictor        Coef        Stdev      t-ratio         p
Constant        -47.71       23.17        -2.06     0.044
cutting       0.013432    0.001903         7.06     0.000

s = 86.62       R-sq = 44.6%      R-sq(adj) = 43.7%

Analysis of Variance

SOURCE          DF            SS           MS          F         p
Regression       1        373953       373953      49.84     0.000
Error           62        465230         7504
Total           63        839184

Unusual Observations
Obs.   cutting    fatals        Fit   Stdev.Fit   Residual   St.Resid
  10     18660     486.0      202.9        18.5      283.1      3.35R
  12     17466     373.0      186.9        16.7      186.1      2.19R
  14     15261     347.0      157.3        13.8      189.7      2.22R
  26     12342     292.0      118.1        11.2      173.9      2.03R

R denotes an obs. with a large st. resid.
```

In SAS, the data can be read from the file COST5.DAT using

```
INPUT COST PAPER MACHINE;
```

16   Computer Repair   A computer repair service is examining the time taken on service calls to repair computers. Data are obtained for 30 service calls. The data are shown in Table 5.14. Information obtained includes:

F I G U R E **5.140**
MINITAB Residual Plot of Standardized Residuals versus Fitted Values for Coal-Mining Fatalities Exercise

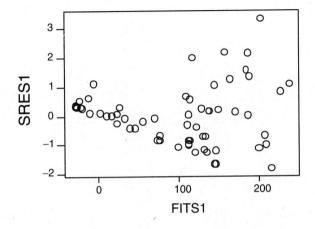

F I G U R E **5.141**
MINITAB Residual Plot of Standardized Residuals versus CUTTING for Coal-Mining Fatalities Exercise

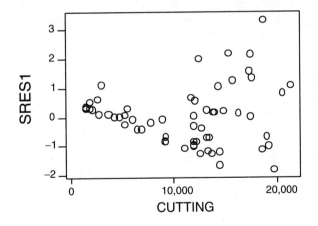

x_1, the number of machines to be repaired (NUMBER)
x_2, the years of experience of service person (EXPER)
y, the time taken (in minutes) to provide service (TIME)

Develop a model to predict average time on the service calls using EXPER and NUMBER as explanatory variables. Use scatterplots and residual plots to determine

T A B L E **5.14**

Data for Computer Repair Exercise

NUMBER	EXPER	TIME	NUMBER	EXPER	TIME
1	9	.66	16	11	383
1	11	74	17	10	383
3	11	88	20	9	515
4	8	99	19	9	474
6	9	134	20	9	495
6	9	120	22	9	628
7	10	178	22	9	636
8	9	139	23	10	660
9	8	187	24	10	731
11	10	227	25	11	752
11	10	225	26	8	800
12	7	270	27	10	863
13	9	265	28	9	918
14	9	301	29	9	976
15	10	343	30	10	1027

whether any of the assumptions of the linear regression model have been violated. If any of the assumptions have been violated, state which one (or ones) and suggest possible corrections. Try the new model to see whether it is an improvement over the original one. Be sure to examine residual plots from the corrected model (or models) that you try. Indicate your choice for the best model.

These data are available on the data disk. In MINITAB, they can be read using

```
READ 'COMPREP5' C1-C3
```

where C1 is NUMBER (x_1), C2 is EXPER (x_2), and C3 is TIME (y).

In SAS, the data can be read from the file COMPREP5.DAT using

```
INPUT NUMBER EXPER TIME;
```

17   **Estimating Residential Real Estate Values**   The Tarrant County Appraisal District must appraise properties for all of the county. The appraisal district uses data such as square footage of the individual houses as well as location, depreciation, and physical condition of an entire neighborhood to derive individual appraisal values on each house. This avoids labor-intensive reinspection each year.

Regression can be used to establish the weight assigned to various factors used in assessing values. For example, Table 5.15 shows the current value, size in square feet, a physical condition index, and a depreciation factor for a sample of 100 Tarrant County homes (in 1990). Using these data, develop an equation that might be useful to the appraisal district in evaluating homes.

The data are available on the data disk and can be read in MINITAB using

```
READ 'REALEST5' C1-C4
```

where C1 is VALUE, C2 is SIZE, C3 is PHYSICAL, and C4 is DEPREC.
    In SAS, the data can be read from the file REALEST5.DAT using

```
INPUT VALUE SIZE PHYSICAL DEPREC;
```

Discuss how the equation developed here could be used to value homes. What would be the value assigned to a 1400-square-foot house with physical condition index 0.70 and depreciation factor 0.02?

T A B L E **5.15**
Data for Real Estate Valuation Exercise

Value	Size	Physical Condition	Depreciation	Value	Size	Physical Condition	Depreciation
23,974	1442	0.40	0.00	43,403	1268	0.55	0.10
24,087	1426	0.40	0.00	38,112	1008	0.55	0.10
16,781	1632	0.50	0.00	27,710	1120	0.50	0.00
29,061	910	0.50	0.18	27,621	960	0.60	0.00
37,982	972	0.55	0.18	22,258	920	0.35	0.00
29,433	912	0.55	0.18	29,064	1259	0.50	0.00
33,624	1400	0.45	0.05	12,001	783	0.40	0.00
27,032	1087	0.45	0.18	37,650	1874	0.35	0.02
28,653	1139	0.45	0.18	27,930	1242	0.50	0.00
33,075	1386	0.55	0.05	16,066	772	0.40	0.00
17,474	756	0.50	0.05	20,411	908	0.45	0.00
33,852	1044	0.50	0.07	23,672	1155	0.45	0.00
29,046	1032	0.50	0.00	24,215	1004	0.50	0.00
20,715	720	0.55	0.00	22,020	958	0.45	0.00
19,461	734	0.50	0.00	52,863	1828	0.60	0.02
21,377	720	0.50	0.00	41,822	1146	0.60	0.02
52,881	1635	0.60	0.02	45,104	1368	0.60	0.02
43,889	1381	0.55	0.02	28,154	1392	0.65	0.24
45,134	1372	0.55	0.02	20,943	1058	0.65	0.24
47,655	1349	0.60	0.02	17,851	1375	0.55	0.26
53,088	1599	0.60	0.02	16,616	648	0.40	0.06
38,923	1171	0.50	0.02	38,752	1313	0.50	0.00
57,870	1966	0.55	0.02	44,377	1780	0.55	0.00
30,489	1504	0.45	0.00	43,566	1148	0.55	0.32
29,207	1296	0.35	0.00	38,950	1363	0.55	0.32
44,919	1356	0.55	0.12	44,633	1262	0.55	0.32
48,090	1553	0.55	0.10	12,372	840	0.35	0.00
40,521	1142	0.55	0.10	12,148	840	0.40	0.00

T A B L E **5.15** *(Cont.)*
Data for Real Estate Valuation Exercise

Value	Size	Physical Condition	Depreciation	Value	Size	Physical Condition	Depreciation
19,852	839	0.50	0.00	49,683	966	0.60	0.05
20,012	852	0.55	0.00	60,647	1469	0.65	0.05
20,314	852	0.55	0.00	49,024	1322	0.70	0.02
22,814	974	0.55	0.00	52,092	1509	0.65	0.02
24,696	1135	0.50	0.00	55,645	1724	0.65	0.04
23,443	1170	0.70	0.02	51,919	1559	0.65	0.02
35,904	960	0.50	0.00	55,174	2133	0.55	0.00
21,799	1052	0.50	0.00	48,760	1233	0.55	0.00
28,212	1296	0.55	0.00	45,906	1323	0.55	0.00
27,553	1282	0.55	0.00	52,013	1733	0.55	0.00
15,826	916	0.35	0.00	56,612	1357	0.60	0.00
18,660	864	0.50	0.00	69,197	1234	0.60	0.17
21,536	1404	0.40	0.00	84,416	1434	0.60	0.15
24,147	1676	0.40	0.00	60,962	1384	0.55	0.17
17,867	1131	0.40	0.00	47,359	995	0.55	0.05
21,583	1397	0.40	0.00	56,302	1372	0.65	0.14
15,482	888	0.40	0.00	88,285	1774	0.70	0.06
24,857	1448	0.45	0.00	91,862	1903	0.70	0.08
17,716	1022	0.45	0.00	242,690	3581	0.80	0.07
224,182	2251	0.75	0.04	296,251	4343	0.80	0.04
182,012	1126	0.55	0.04	107,132	1861	0.75	0.08
201,597	2617	0.90	0.03	77,797	1542	0.65	0.30

18   Criminal Justice Expenditures   Table 5.16 shows the following data for each of the 50 states:

total expenditures on a state's criminal justice system (in millions of dollars)
total number of police employed in the state
population of the state (in thousands)
total number of incarcerated prisoners in the state

State governments must try to project spending in many areas. Expenditures on the criminal justice system is one area of continually rising cost. Your job is to build a model that can be used to forecast spending on a state's criminal justice system. Any of the three possible explanatory variables can be used. Be sure to consider violations of any assumptions in building your model and correct for any violations. Once your model is complete, predict expenditures for a state that plans to hire 10,000 police personnel, has a population of 3 million and expects 600 prisoners. Find a point prediction and a 95% prediction interval.

The data are available on the data disk and can be read in MINITAB using

```
READ 'CRIMSPN5' C1-C4
```

where C1 is EXPEND, C2 is POLICE, C3 is POP, and C4 is PRISONER.
In SAS, the data can be read from the file CRIMSPN5.DAT using

```
INPUT EXPEND POLICE POP PRISONER;
```

T A B L E 5.16

Data for Exercise on Expenditures on Criminal Justice System

State	Expenditure	Police	Population	Prisoners
Alabama	561	10,312	2,780	12,357
Alaska	283	1,928	223	1,862
Arizona	962	10,315	2,718	11,578
Arkansas	233	4,875	955	5,519
California	8,940	75,043	27,808	73,780
Colorada	701	9,141	2,703	5,765
Connecticut	692	9,282	2,969	4,723
Delaware	158	1,841	444	2,207
Florida	2,810	39,853	11,496	34,681
Georgia	1,187	18,118	4,175	18,018
Hawaii	271	3,122	849	1,510
Idaho	133	2,305	203	1,581
Illinois	2,340	36,925	9,590	21,081
Indiana	688	12,072	3,809	11,271
Iowa	354	5,631	1,233	3,034
Kansas	404	6,506	1,344	5,817
Kentucky	496	7,234	1,719	7,119
Louisiana	748	13,349	3,033	16,242
Maine	169	2,914	452	1,214
Maryland	1,091	13,351	4,363	13,572
Massachusetts	1,449	18,475	5,388	6,455
Michigan	2,132	22,873	7,416	27,612
Minnesota	735	8,798	2,900	27,499
Mississippi	263	5,616	800	7,251
Missouri	829	14,037	3,408	12,176
Montana	104	1,799	195	1,272
Nebraska	216	3,696	767	2,066
Nevada	332	3,379	918	4,881
New Hampshire	170	2,978	591	1,019
New Jersey	2,118	29,049	7,736	16,936
New Mexico	290	4,520	746	2,723
New York	7,145	77,571	16,378	44,560
North Carolina	1,042	16,259	3,641	16,251

T A B L E **5.16**   *(Cont.)*

Data for Exercise on Expenditures on Criminal Justice System

State	Expenditure	Police	Population	Prisoners
North Dakota	71	1,280	253	414
Ohio	1,809	23,780	8,594	26,462
Oklahoma	442	7,593	1,894	10,448
Oregon	593	6,221	1,909	5,991
Pennsylvania	1,919	26,199	10,203	17,883
Rhode Island	194	2,838	936	1,179
South Carolina	553	8,641	2,127	12,902
South Dakota	83	1,569	208	1,020
Tennessee	756	12,205	3,286	7,732
Texas	2,939	43,745	13,807	40,437
Utah	282	3,793	1,321	1,944
Vermont	84	1,254	108	553
Virginia	1,195	15,500	4,401	13,928
Washington	887	10,398	3,886	5,816
West Virginia	168	3,352	677	1,455
Wisconsin	864	12,905	3,247	6,325
Wyoming	98	1,598	139	945

These data were obtained from the 1990 *Sourcebook of Criminal Justice Statistics.*

19   **Intersections**   One factor related to the number of accidents at an intersection is the peak-hour volume of traffic. Data on both the volume of traffic during the peak hour and the total number of accidents are available for 62 intersections in Fort Worth, Texas. These data are shown in Table 5.17. The city would like to be able to identify intersections that have an unusual number of accidents. Their definition of unusual involves first establishing some type of base level forecast of the number of accidents, taking account of the peak-hour volume of traffic, and then judging which intersections still have an unusual number of accidents. As a consultant to the city, your job is to determine which, if any, of these 62 intersections appear to have an unusually high number of accidents given the volume of traffic.

These data are available on the data disk and can be read in MINITAB using

```
READ 'TRAFFIC5' C1,C2
```

where C1 is the number of accidents and C2 is the peak-hour traffic volume.

In SAS, the data can be read from the file TRAFFIC5.DAT using

```
INPUT ACCIDENT VOLUME;
```

T A B L E **5.17**

Data for Intersections Exercise

Number	Accidents	Volume	Number	Accidents	Volume
1	2	2025	32	14	4168
2	7	4526	33	0	632
3	3	2028	34	10	1620
4	2	3723	35	2	1315
5	2	1337	36	10	2860
6	1	1985	37	2	1723
7	4	2673	38	0	1147
8	7	1958	39	0	1917
9	7	5811	40	3	2035
10	8	2870	41	6	3257
11	4	2239	42	10	2841
12	1	1909	43	8	2790
13	1	2372	44	6	1940
14	7	3485	45	8	1733
15	5	2768	46	4	1881
16	6	2068	47	11	1932
17	4	3453	48	3	1554
18	4	3731	49	7	2498
19	3	1972	50	5	1699
20	2	2357	51	5	2769
21	2	2049	52	10	3353
22	9	3014	53	4	2252
23	2	3190	54	6	3837
24	0	1122	55	1	1763
25	4	1341	56	5	2294
26	2	3473	57	10	3910
27	2	2297	58	2	2922
28	3	3944	59	6	1760
29	6	2173	60	5	1521
30	28	4250	61	11	3778
31	21	2109	62	3	2200

6

Using Indicator and Interaction Variables

6.1
Using and Interpreting Indicator Variables

Indicator variables or dummy variables are a special type of variable used in a variety of ways in regression analysis. Indicator variables take on only two values, either 0 or 1. They can be used to indicate whether a sample unit either does (1) or does not (0) belong in a certain category. For example, a dummy variable could be used to indicate whether an individual in the sample was employed by constructing the variable as

$D_{1i} = 1$ if individual i is employed

$\quad = 0$ if individual i is not employed

To indicate whether an individual is unemployed, the variable could be constructed as

$D_{2i} = 1$ if individual i is unemployed

$\quad = 0$ if individual i is employed

Obviously, any type of split into two groups can be easily represented by indicator variables.

If there are more than two groups into which individuals may be classified, this simply requires the use of additional indicator variables. Suppose firms in a sample are to be categorized according to the exchange on which they are listed: NYSE, AMEX, or OTC. This could be accomplished by constructing the following dummy variables:

$D_{1i} = 1$ if firm i is listed on the NYSE

$\quad = 0$ if firm i is not listed on the NYSE

$D_{2i} = 1$ if firm i is listed on the AMEX

$\quad = 0$ if firm i is not listed on the AMEX

$D_{3i} = 1$ if firm i is listed on the OTC

$\quad = 0$ if firm i is not listed on the OTC

Thus far, when sample individuals could belong to one of m different groups, m indicator variables were constructed, one for each group. When indicator variables are used in a regression analysis, however, only $m - 1$ of the indicator variables will be included in the regression. Only $m - 1$ indicator variables are needed to indicate m groups. The one group whose indicator is omitted will serve as what might be called a "base-level" group. Consider the following example to clarify this point.

E X A M P L E 6.1 Employment Discrimination

Regression analysis has been used increasingly in employment discrimination cases. The desire in such cases is typically to compare mean salaries of male and female employees in order to determine whether one group has significantly lower salaries than the other group. Evidence of lower average salaries would provide some support for a discrimination suit against the employer. It is recognized that a simple two-sample comparison of mean salaries would not be sufficient to conclude that one group has been discriminated against. Obviously, there are many factors that affect salary to which differences in average salary might be attributed other than discrimination. Regression is used to adjust for the effects of these other factors before the two groups are compared. An indicator variable is added to the regression to separate the employees into two groups: male and female.

Table 6.1 presents a portion of the data from the case of *United States Department of the Treasury vs. Harris Trust and Savings Bank* (1981). The data include the salary of 93 employees of the bank, their educational level, and an indicator variable in the third column, signifying whether the employee is male (1) or female (0). Figure 6.1 shows a MINITAB scatterplot of salary versus education for all 93 employees. Figure 6.2 shows the same plot but with the two groups indicated by different symbols (male $= +$ and female $= 0$). There is some indication from the plot in Figure 6.2 that male salaries are higher than female salaries, even when differing education levels have been taken into account. To obtain a better sense of the magnitude of these differences and to provide a test for whether the differences are significant or whether they are small enough that they could have occurred by chance, the regression of SALARY on the two explanatory variables EDUCAT and MALES is shown in Figure 6.3 for MINITAB and in Figure 6.4 for SAS.

The resulting equation is

$$\text{SALARY} = 4173 + 80.7\text{EDUCAT} + 692\text{MALES}$$

The next questions is, How do we interpret this equation? Consider a regression like the one in Example 6.1 with one quantitative explanatory variable (x_1) and one indicator variable (D):

$$y = \beta_0 + \beta_1 x_1 + \beta_2 D$$

The indicator variable D is coded as 1 if an item in the sample belongs to a certain group and as 0 if the item does not belong to the group. The equation can be separated into two parts as follows:

If the sample item is in the indicated group ($D = 1$):

$$y = \beta_0 + \beta_1 x_1 + \beta_2(1) = (\beta_0 + \beta_2) + \beta_1 x_1$$

T A B L E **6.1**

Data for Employment Discrimination Example

SALARY	EDUCAT	MALES	SALARY	EDUCAT	MALES
3900	12	0	5400	12	0
4020	10	0	5400	15	0
4290	12	0	5400	15	0
4380	8	0	5400	15	0
4380	8	0	5400	15	0
4380	12	0	5520	12	0
4380	12	0	5520	12	0
4380	12	0	5580	12	0
4440	15	0	5640	12	0
4500	8	0	5700	12	0
4500	12	0	5700	12	0
4620	12	0	5700	15	0
4800	8	0	5700	15	0
4800	12	0	5700	15	0
4800	12	0	6000	12	0
4800	12	0	6000	15	0
4800	12	0	6120	12	0
4800	12	0	6300	12	0
4800	12	0	6300	15	0
4800	12	0	4620	12	1
4800	12	0	5040	15	1
4800	16	0	5100	12	1
4980	8	0	5100	12	1
5100	8	0	5220	12	1
5100	12	0	5400	12	1
5100	12	0	5400	12	1
5100	15	0	5400	12	1
5100	15	0	5400	12	1
5100	16	0	5400	15	1
5160	12	0	5400	15	1
5220	8	0	5700	15	1
5220	12	0	6000	8	1
5280	8	0	6000	12	1
5280	8	0	6000	12	1
5280	12	0	6000	12	1
5400	8	0	6000	12	1
5400	8	0	6000	12	1
5400	12	0	6000	15	1
5400	12	0	6000	15	1
5400	12	0	6000	15	1
5400	12	0	6000	15	1
5400	12	0	6000	15	1

T A B L E **6**.1 *(Cont.)*

Data for Employment Discrimination Example

SALARY	EDUCAT	MALES	SALARY	EDUCAT	MALES
6000	16	1	6840	15	1
6300	15	1	6900	12	1
6600	15	1	6900	15	1
6600	15	1	8100	16	1
6600	15	1			

These data were published in "Measurement-Error Diagnostics and the Sex Discrimination Problem" by D. W. Schafer in *Journal of Business and Economic Statistics* 5 (1987): 529–537.

F I G U R E **6**.1

Scatterplot of Salary versus Education for Employment Discrimination Example

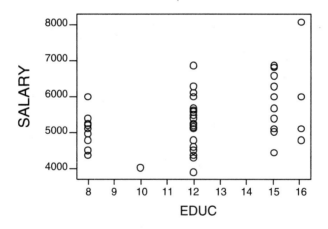

If the sample item is not in the indicated group ($D = 0$):

$$y = \beta_0 + \beta_1 x_1 + \beta_2(0) = \beta_0 + \beta_1 x_1$$

Using the indicator variable results in one equation for the indicated group and another for the other group. Note that the equation for the indicated group has been rewritten with two components making up the intercept term: the original intercept β_0 and the coefficient of the indicator variable β_2. Two lines have been fit with the same slope but different intercepts, even through only one regression has been run. Figure 6.5 shows an example of how we might draw

F I G U R E **6.2**

Scatterplot of Salary Versus Education with Males (+) and Females (o) Indicated

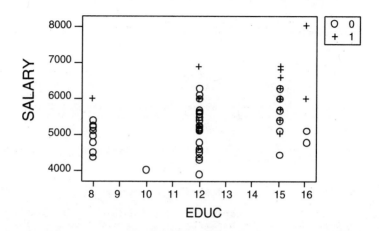

F I G U R E **6.3**

Regression Output for MINITAB Regression of SALARY on EDUCAT and MALES for the Employment Discrimination Example

```
The regression equation is
salary = 4173 + 80.7 educat + 692 males

Predictor       Coef      Stdev     t-ratio        p
Constant      4173.1      339.2       12.30    0.000
educat         80.70      27.67        2.92    0.004
males          691.8      132.2        5.23    0.000

s = 572.4      R-sq = 36.3%     R-sq(adj) = 34.9%

Analysis of Variance

SOURCE        DF          SS          MS         F        p
Regression     2    16831744     8415872     25.68    0.000
Error         90    29491546      327684
Total         92    46323288

SOURCE        DF      SEQ SS
educat         1     7862535
males          1     8969210

Unusual Observations
Obs.   educat    salary       Fit   Stdev.Fit   Residual   St.Resid
  1     12.0    3900.0    5141.5        73.3     -1241.5      -2.19R
 60     12.0    6300.0    5141.5        73.3      1158.5       2.04R
 62     12.0    4620.0    5833.3       109.7     -1213.3      -2.16R
 73      8.0    6000.0    5510.5       183.5       489.5       0.90 X
 93     16.0    8100.0    6156.1       122.1      1943.9       3.48R

R denotes an obs. with a large st. resid.
X denotes an obs. whose X value gives it large influence.
```

F I G U R E **6.4**

Regression Output for SAS Regression of SALARY on EDUCAT and MALES for the Employment Discrimination Example

```
Dependent Variable: SALARY

                    Analysis of Variance

                       Sum of          Mean
Source      DF         Squares        Square      F Value      Prob>F

Model        2  16831743.945  8415871.9726       25.683       0.0001
Error       90  29491546.377  327683.84864
C Total     92  46323290.323

          Root MSE      572.43676    R-square      0.3634
          Dep Mean     5420.32258    Adj R-sq      0.3492
          C.V.           10.56094

                    Parameter Estimates

                   Parameter      Standard     T for H0:
Variable    DF     Estimate         Error     Parameter=0    Prob > |T|

INTERCEP     1   4173.125108   339.18110059      12.304         0.0001
EDUCAT       1     80.697765    27.67290568       2.916         0.0045
MALES        1    691.808260   132.23188019       5.232         0.0001
```

F I G U R E **6.5**

Graph Showing Relative Placement of Regression Lines If β_2 Is Assumed to Be Positive

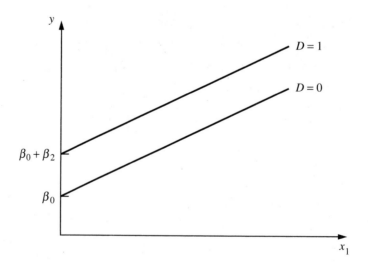

the two estimated lines. The difference in the intercepts is given by β_2 (which is assumed to be positive in the graph). This process allows us to answer the question of whether there is a difference in the average value of the y variable for the two groups after adjusting for the effect of the quantitative variable (or variables if there are more than one) and how much the average difference is. The adjusted difference in the averages is represented by the difference in the intercepts, that is, by the coefficient of the indicator variable. A t test on this coefficient will help to decide whether the difference is large enough to be considered statistically significant. ∎

E X A M P L E 6.2 Employment Discrimination (continued)

The equation in the employment discrimination example can be interpreted as follows: Salary increases by $80.70 for each year of education. Males earn, on average, $692 more per year than females (this was in 1977 so $692 was more than it sounds like now).

The next question is whether $692 is large enough to be considered statistically significant. Or could this difference have occurred purely by chance? To determine this, the coefficient of the indicator variable can be tested to see if it is equal to zero:

$$H_0: \quad \beta_2 = 0$$
$$H_a: \quad \beta_2 \neq 0$$

If the null hypothesis is accepted, we conclude that there is no significant difference in average salaries (after taking into account education). If the null hypothesis is rejected, we conclude that the difference observed is too large to have occurred by chance.

Decision rule:

Reject H_0 if p value $< .05$

Accept H_0 if p value $\geq .05$

Test statistic: p value $= 0.000$

Decision: Reject H_0.

Of course, the t ratio could also have been used to conduct the test.

Our conclusion is that there is evidence of employment discrimination. Males, on average, appear to be earning significantly more than females, even after we take into account education. Lawyers in such a case would point out that education is not the only factor that could cause a difference in salary. Factors like previous experience and time on the job might also have an effect. These factors, if measurable, could be included in the regression as well (and typically are in such applications).[1]

One question that arises is whether the way the two groups were coded matters. Would the results be the same if males were coded 0 and females were coded 1? Yes, they would. Figure 6.6 shows the MINITAB regression of SALARY on EDUCAT and a new variable called FEMALES. This variable is coded 0 for males and 1 for females. Note that the overall equation intercept and the coefficient of EDUCAT are exactly the same as they were for the regression

[1]For a more detailed examination of the use of regression in employment discrimination cases, see "Regression Analyses in Employment Discrimination Cases," by D. A. Conway and H. V. Roberts in *Statistics and the Law*, New York: John Wiley and Sons, 1986.

F I G U R E 6.6

Regression Output for MINITAB Regression of SALARY on EDUCAT and FEMALES for the Employment Discrimination Example

```
The regression equation is
salary = 4865 + 80.7 educat - 692 females

Predictor        Coef       Stdev     t-ratio        p
Constant       4864.9       387.9       12.54    0.000
educat          80.70       27.67        2.92    0.004
females        -691.8       132.2       -5.23    0.000

s = 572.4       R-sq = 36.3%     R-sq(adj) = 34.9%

Analysis of Variance

SOURCE          DF          SS          MS        F        p
Regression       2    16831744     8415872    25.68    0.000
Error           90    29491546      327684
Total           92    46323288

SOURCE          DF      SEQ SS
educat           1     7862535
females          1     8969210

Unusual Observations
Obs.    educat    salary      Fit  Stdev.Fit   Residual   St.Resid
  1      12.0    3900.0    5141.5       73.3    -1241.5     -2.19R
 60      12.0    6300.0    5141.5       73.3     1158.5      2.04R
 62      12.0    4620.0    5833.3      109.7    -1213.3     -2.16R
 73       8.0    6000.0    5510.5      183.5      489.5      0.90 X
 93      16.0    8100.0    6156.1      122.1     1943.9      3.48R

R denotes an obs. with a large st. resid.
X denotes an obs. whose X value gives it large influence.
```

in Figures 6.3 and 6.4. The coefficient of the indicator variable is the same except for the sign. In the original regression it was positive and now it is negative. However, the interpretation of the results will be exactly the same. When the variable MALES was used our interpretation was that males earned, on average, $692 per year *more* than females. Using the FEMALES variable, our interpretation is that females earned, on average, $692 per year *less* than males. Also, the *t* test will again tell us that the difference is statistically significant.

The coefficient of the indicator variable always represents the difference between the intercept of the indicated group and the nonindicated group. The nonindicated group, referred to as the *base-level group*, is used for comparisons. Thus, in the regression using the indicator variable MALES, $692 is the difference between males' salaries (the indicated group) and females' salaries (the base-level group).

Also, note that since there are two groups (males and females) only one indicator variable is needed in the regression to separate the sample elements. When the indicator labeled MALES was used, males were indicated with a 1 and females with a 0. No other variable is needed since we can see which group each person is in from the associated value of just the one variable. ∎

In the employment discrimination example, an indicator variable was used to indicate when sample observations fell into one of two groups. The groups represented qualitative variables, that is, variables that could not be quantified in a meaningful way. For example, there is no meaningful way to quantify the difference between males and females. An indicator variable was used to separate the two groups for separate analyses, but no numeric values were assigned to express the difference between being male or female. Indicator variables can be used in this manner to incorporate qualitative information into the regression equation. The next example illustrates the use of indicator variables to represent qualitative information when there are more than two categories.

E X A M P L E **6.3** **Meddicorp (continued)**

In the Meddicorp example in Chapter 4, the relationship between sales and several other variables was investigated. The data for the dependent variable SALES and two explanatory variables, ADV and BONUS, were shown in Table 4.1.

It also was noted in the example that Meddicorp sold in three different regions of the country. These regions were denoted South, West, and Midwest.

A variable has been added to the data set to indicate each of these three regions. The variable is called REGION and is coded as follows:

$$REGION = 1 \quad \text{if} \quad \text{South}$$
$$= 2 \quad \text{if} \quad \text{West}$$
$$= 3 \quad \text{if} \quad \text{Midwest}$$

The new variable and the original variables are shown in Table 6.2. The new variable is included in a regression along with the ADV and BONUS variables. The results are shown in Figures 6.7 and 6.8 for MINITAB and SAS, respectively.

The estimated regression equation is

$$\hat{y} = -84 + 1.55 ADV + 1.11 BONUS + 119 REGION$$

The coefficient of REGION indicates that as the value assigned to the region increases, so does the amount of sales. On average, there is a difference of 119 units between sales in the territories of the three regions. Each unit is \$1000. Sales in territories of Region 2 (West) would be \$119,000 more (on average) than sales in territories of Region 1 (South), and sales in territories of Region 3 (Midwest) would be \$119,000 more than sales in Region 2. Note that the difference in territorial sales between regions is forced to be \$119,000. Although this situation may not be realistic, it is required by the direct use of the variable REGION in the regression equation. A more flexible representation of the changes in average sales between regions is allowed by using indicator or dummy variables.

Indicator variables can be used to transform the REGION variable. An indicator variable SOUTH can be developed that indicates whether or not a territory is in the South. SOUTH is made to take on the value 1 whenever the REGION variable is 1, and SOUTH is given the value 0 if REGION is 2 or 3. An indicator variable WEST can be developed that indicates whether or not a territory is in the West. WEST is made to take on the value 1 whenever the REGION variable is 2 (that is, when the territory is in the West), and is given the value 0 if REGION is

T A B L E **6.2**

Meddicorp Data for Example 6.2 Showing Variable REGION and Three Resulting Indicator Variables, SOUTH, WEST, and MIDWEST

SALES	ADV	BONUS	REGION	SOUTH	WEST	MIDWEST
963.50	374.27	230.98	1	1	0	0
893.00	408.50	236.28	1	1	0	0
1057.25	414.31	271.57	1	1	0	0
1183.25	448.42	291.20	2	0	1	0
1419.50	517.88	282.17	3	0	0	1
1547.75	637.60	321.16	3	0	0	1
1580.00	635.72	294.32	3	0	0	1
1071.50	446.86	305.69	1	1	0	0
1078.25	489.59	238.41	1	1	0	0
1122.50	500.56	271.38	2	0	1	0
1304.75	484.18	332.64	3	0	0	1
1552.25	618.07	261.80	3	0	0	1
1040.00	453.39	235.63	1	1	0	0
1045.25	440.86	249.68	2	0	1	0
1102.25	487.79	232.99	2	0	1	0
1225.25	537.67	272.20	2	0	1	0
1508.00	612.21	266.64	3	0	0	1
1564.25	601.46	277.44	3	0	0	1
1634.75	585.10	312.35	3	0	0	1
1159.25	524.56	292.87	1	1	0	0
1202.75	535.17	268.27	2	0	1	0
1294.25	486.03	309.85	2	0	1	0
1467.50	540.17	291.03	3	0	0	1
1583.75	583.85	289.29	3	0	0	1
1124.75	499.15	272.55	2	0	1	0

1 or 3. Similarly, an indicator variable for the Midwest can be developed. The three indicator variables are as follows:

SOUTH = 1 if the territory is in the South

= 0 otherwise

WEST = 1 if the territory is in the West

= 0 otherwise

MIDWEST = 1 if the territory is in the Midwest

= 0 otherwise

These three indicator variables, SOUTH, WEST, and MIDWEST, indicate into which of the three mutually exclusive regions each territory falls. Table 6.2 shows the SALES, ADV, BONUS, and REGION variables and the resulting indicators. As stated previously, only two

F I G U R E **6.7**

MINITAB Regression of SALES on ADV, BONUS, and REGION

```
The regression equation is
sales = - 84 + 1.55 adv + 1.11 bonus + 119 region

Predictor        Coef       Stdev     t-ratio        p
Constant        -84.2       177.9       -0.47     0.641
adv            1.5460      0.3061        5.05     0.000
bonus          1.1062      0.5727        1.93     0.067
region         118.90       28.69        4.14     0.000

s = 68.89       R-sq = 92.0%     R-sq(adj) = 90.9%

Analysis of Variance

SOURCE          DF           SS            MS        F        p
Regression       3      1149317        383106    80.73    0.000
Error           21        99657          4746
Total           24      1248974

SOURCE          DF       SEQ SS
adv              1      1012408
bonus            1        55389
region           1        81519
```

F I G U R E **6.8**

SAS Regression of SALES on ADV, BONUS, and REGION

```
Dependent Variable: SALES

                      Analysis of Variance

                       Sum of         Mean
Source      DF        Squares        Square     F Value     Prob>F

Model        3  1149316.7391  383105.57969      80.729     0.0001
Error       21    99657.00093    4745.57147
C Total     24  1248973.74

          Root MSE        68.88811    R-square      0.9202
          Dep Mean      1269.02000    Adj R-sq      0.9088
          C.V.             5.42845

                    Parameter Estimates

                  Parameter       Standard     T for H0:
Variable   DF      Estimate          Error   Parameter=0    Prob > |T|

INTERCEP    1    -84.219166   177.90672375       -0.473        0.6408
ADV         1      1.546015     0.30613713        5.050        0.0001
BONUS       1      1.106244     0.57265172        1.932        0.0670
REGION      1    118.899157    28.68748638        4.145        0.0005
```

of the three indicators need to be used in the regression. The territories indicated by the third indicator will serve as a base-level group.

If MIDWEST is used as the base-level group, the MINITAB and SAS regressions shown in Figures 6.9 and 6.10 are obtained. The regression equation is

$$\hat{y} = 435 + 1.37\text{ADV} + 0.975\text{BONUS} - 258\text{SOUTH} - 210\text{WEST}$$

The interpretation of this equation is similar to that of the equation developed in the employment discrimination example. Here, however, the territories have been separated into three groups through the use of the indicator variables. The coefficient of each dummy variable represents the difference in the intercept between the indicated group and the base level (MIDWEST) group. This can be expressed through the use of three separate equations:

$$\text{SOUTH: } \hat{y} = 435 + 1.37\text{ADV} + 0.975\text{BONUS} - 258$$
$$= 177 + 1.37\text{ADV} + 0.975\text{BONUS}$$
$$\text{WEST: } \hat{y} = 435 + 1.37\text{ADV} + 0.975\text{BONUS} - 210$$
$$= 225 + 1.37\text{ADV} + 0.975\text{BONUS}$$
$$\text{MIDWEST: } \hat{y} = 435 + 1.37\text{ADV} + 0.975\text{BONUS}$$

The slopes of the equations are constrained to be the same, but the intercepts are allowed to differ. As a further interpretation, consider the values of $\hat{y}$ for a given level of ADV and BONUS—say ADV = 500 and BONUS = 250. These values are

$$\text{SOUTH: } \hat{y} = 177 + 1.37(500) + 0.975(250) = 1105.8$$
$$\text{WEST: } \hat{y} = 225 + 1.37(500) + 0.975(250) = 1153.8$$
$$\text{MIDWEST: } \hat{y} = 435 + 1.37(500) + 0.975(250) = 1363.8$$

The conditional mean sales for advertising equal to 500 and bonus payment equal to 250 are shown by these computations. The sales figures differ according to the coefficients of the indicator variables: \$1,105,800 for SOUTH, \$1,153,800 for WEST, and \$1,363,800 for MIDWEST.

To determine whether there is a significant difference in sales for territories in different regions, the following hypotheses should be tested:

$$H_0: \quad \beta_3 = \beta_4 = 0$$
$$H_a: \quad \text{At least one of } \beta_3 \text{ and } \beta_4 \text{ is not equal to zero}$$

The model hypothesized is

$$y = \beta_0 + \beta_1\text{ADV} + \beta_2\text{BONUS} + \beta_3\text{SOUTH} + \beta_4\text{WEST} + e,$$

so the null hypothesis states that the coefficients of the dummy variables are both zero. If this hypothesis is accepted, then no difference between the various regions exists, and the indicator variables can be dropped from the model. The simpler model

$$y = \beta_0 + \beta_1\text{ADV} + \beta_2\text{BONUS} + e$$

F I G U R E 6.9

MINITAB Regression of SALES on ADV, BONUS, and the Indicator Variables WEST and SOUTH

```
The regression equation is
sales = 435 + 1.37 adv + 0.975 bonus - 258 south - 210 west

Predictor        Coef        Stdev     t-ratio         p
Constant        435.1        206.2        2.11     0.048
adv            1.3678       0.2622        5.22     0.000
bonus          0.9752       0.4808        2.03     0.056
south         -257.89        48.41       -5.33     0.000
west          -209.75        37.42       -5.61     0.000

s = 57.63      R-sq = 94.7%     R-sq(adj) = 93.6%

Analysis of Variance

SOURCE          DF           SS           MS         F         p
Regression       4      1182560       295640     89.03     0.000
Error           20        66414         3321
Total           24      1248974

SOURCE          DF       SEQ SS
adv              1      1012408
bonus            1        55389
south            1        10435
west             1       104328


Unusual Observations
Obs.     adv     sales         Fit    Stdev.Fit    Residual    St.Resid
 11      484    1304.8      1421.7         37.0      -117.0       -2.65R
 22      486    1294.3      1192.3         27.7       102.0        2.02R

R denotes an obs. with a large st. resid.
```

will explain just as much variation in sales. This hypothesis can be tested using the partial F test discussed in Chapter 4. The full model contains the indicator variables; the reduced model does not. The test statistic is computed exactly as discussed in Chapter 4:

$$F = \frac{(SSE_R - SSE_F)/(K - L)}{MSE_F} = \frac{(181,176 - 66,414)/2}{3321} = 17.3,$$

using the reduced output in Figures 6.11 or 6.12 to get SSE_R, and the full model output in Figures 6.9 or 6.10 to get SSE_F.

The decision rule is:

$$\text{Reject } H_0 \quad \text{if} \quad F > 3.49$$
$$\text{Accept } H_0 \quad \text{if} \quad F \leq 3.49$$

where 3.49 is the 5% F critical value with 2 numerator and 20 denominator degrees of freedom.

The null hypothesis is rejected because $17.3 > 3.49$. Thus, at least one of the coefficients of the indicator variables is not zero. This means that there are differences in average sales levels between the three regions in which Meddicorp does business. ∎

F I G U R E **6.10**

SAS Regression of SALES on ADV, BONUS, and the Indicator Variables WEST and SOUTH

```
Dependent Variable: SALES

                        Analysis of Variance

                      Sum of          Mean
Source       DF       Squares         Square      F Value      Prob>F

Model         4  1182559.8959   295639.97397      89.030       0.0001
Error        20    66413.84412     3320.69221
C Total      24  1248973.74

            Root MSE        57.62545     R-square      0.9468
            Dep Mean      1269.02000     Adj R-sq      0.9362
            C.V.             4.54094

                        Parameter Estimates

                   Parameter       Standard      T for H0:
Variable    DF      Estimate          Error    Parameter=0    Prob > |T|

INTERCEP     1    435.098908   206.23415310         2.110        0.0477
ADV          1      1.367798     0.26220747         5.216        0.0001
BONUS        1      0.975153     0.48081612         2.028        0.0561
SOUTH        1   -257.891592    48.41294648        -5.327        0.0001
WEST         1   -209.745723    37.42033058        -5.605        0.0001
```

F I G U R E **6.11**

MINITAB Regression of SALES on ADV and BONUS

```
The regression equation is
sales = - 516 + 2.47 adv + 1.86 bonus

Predictor        Coef       Stdev     t-ratio        p
Constant       -516.4       189.9       -2.72    0.013
adv            2.4732      0.2753        8.98    0.000
bonus          1.8562      0.7157        2.59    0.017

s = 90.75      R-sq = 85.5%     R-sq(adj) = 84.2%

Analysis of Variance

SOURCE         DF          SS          MS        F         p
Regression      2     1067797      533899    64.83     0.000
Error          22      181176        8235
Total          24     1248974

SOURCE         DF      SEQ SS
adv             1     1012408
bonus           1       55389
```

F I G U R E **6.12**

SAS Regression of SALES on ADV and BONUS

```
Dependent Variable: SALES

                    Analysis of Variance

                    Sum of          Mean
Source      DF      Squares         Square       F Value      Prob>F

Model        2   1067797.3206   533898.66029      64.831      0.0001
Error       22    181176.41942    8235.29179
C Total     24   1248973.74

        Root MSE      90.74851      R-square      0.8549
        Dep Mean    1269.02000      Adj R-sq      0.8418
        C.V.           7.15107

                    Parameter Estimates

                  Parameter     Standard     T for H0:
Variable   DF     Estimate        Error    Parameter=0    Prob > |T|

INTERCEP    1   -516.444282   189.87569701     -2.720       0.0125
ADV         1      2.473177     0.27531110      8.983       0.0001
BONUS       1      1.856179     0.71572507      2.593       0.0166
```

When using indicator variables, the partial F statistic is used to test whether the variables are important as a group. The t test on individual coefficients should not be used to decide whether individual indicator variables should be retained or dropped from the equation. The indicator variables are designed to have a particular meaning as a group. They are either all retained in or all dropped from the equation as a group. Dropping individual indicators will change the meaning of the coefficients of the remaining indicators. In the Meddicorp example, each indicator coefficient represents the difference in sales between the indicated group and the base level group (MIDWEST). If one of the other indicators is dropped—say, WEST—the remaining coefficients then will represent the differences in sales between the indicated group and the new base level group, which now becomes the MIDWEST and WEST regions combined. The interpretation of the coefficients is totally different because of the change in the base-level group. To answer the question of whether there is a difference in the intercepts for the groups involved, the indicators must be retained and tested as a group (although there is not universal acceptance of this point of view).

Recall that in the discrimination example, a t test was used to determine whether the intercepts for the males and females differed. Because there were only two groups and therefore only one indicator, the partial F test and t test were equivalent. If more than two indicators are used, the partial F test will be required.

Figures 6.13 and 6.14 show the MINITAB and SAS regressions of SALES on ADV, BONUS, and the indicators WEST and MIDWEST. The base-level group is

F I G U R E **6.13**

MINITAB Regression of SALES on ADV, BONUS, and the Indicator Variables WEST and MIDWEST

```
The regression equation is
sales = 177 + 1.37 adv + 0.975 bonus + 48.1 west + 258 midwest

Predictor        Coef       Stdev     t-ratio        p
Constant        177.2       170.1        1.04     0.310
adv            1.3678      0.2622        5.22     0.000
bonus          0.9752      0.4808        2.03     0.056
west            48.15       32.80        1.47     0.158
midwest        257.89       48.41        5.33     0.000

s = 57.63      R-sq = 94.7%      R-sq(adj) = 93.6%

Analysis of Variance

SOURCE        DF          SS          MS          F        p
Regression     4     1182560      295640      89.03    0.000
Error         20       66414        3321
Total         24     1248974


SOURCE        DF      SEQ SS
adv            1     1012408
bonus          1       55389
west           1       20535
midwest        1       94228

Unusual Observations
Obs.     adv    sales       Fit  Stdev.Fit   Residual   St.Resid
 11      484   1304.8    1421.7       37.0     -117.0      -2.65R
 22      486   1294.3    1192.3       27.7      102.0       2.02R

R denotes an obs. with a large st. resid.
```

now the SOUTH region. The coefficients of the indicator variables measure the difference in sales between the base-level group and the indicated group. Although the regression coefficient estimates have different values from the previous regression (see Figures 6.9 and 6.10), the results are the same. For example, consider the value of $\hat{y}$ for ADV $= 500$ and BONUS $= 250$ for the SOUTH region:

$$\hat{y} = 177 + 1.37(500) + 0.975(250) = 1105.8$$

This is the same value determined from the regression using the WEST and SOUTH indicator variables. Comparisons for the other regions also show the same values regardless of which set of indicators is used. Any one of the three indicators can be omitted, and the omitted group will simply serve as the base-level group. The remaining indicator coefficients will equal the difference between the indicated group and the chosen base-level group.

F I G U R E 6.14

SAS Regression of SALES on ADV, BONUS, and the Indicator Variables WEST and MID-
WEST

```
Dependent Variable: SALES

                    Analysis of Variance

                    Sum of          Mean
Source      DF      Squares         Square       F Value      Prob>F

Model        4 1182559.8959  295639.97397         89.030      0.0001
Error       20   66413.84412    3320.69221
C Total     24 1248973.74

          Root MSE      57.62545    R-square      0.9468
          Dep Mean    1269.02000    Adj R-sq      0.9362
          C.V.           4.54094

                    Parameter Estimates

                Parameter     Standard     T for H0:
Variable   DF    Estimate        Error    Parameter=0    Prob > |T|

INTERCEP    1   177.207316  170.11586070        1.042       0.3100
ADV         1     1.367798    0.26220747        5.216       0.0001
BONUS       1     0.975153    0.48081612        2.028       0.0561
WEST        1    48.145868   32.80134113        1.468       0.1577
MIDWEST     1   257.891592   48.41294648        5.327       0.0001
```

Exercises

1   Discrimination   The data in Table 6.3 show the values of the following variables for
93 employees of Harris Bank Chicago in 1977:

   y = beginning salaries in dollars (SALARY)

   x_1 = years of schooling at the time of hire (EDUCAT)

   x_2 = number of months of previous work experience (EXPER)

   x_3 = number of months after January 1, 1969, that the individual was hired
        (MONTHS)

   x_4 = indicator variable coded 1 for males and 0 for females (MALES)

The MINITAB and SAS regression outputs for the regression of y on all four explanatory
variables are shown in Figures 6.15 and 6.16, respectively. In this example, we are still
concerned with whether there is evidence of discrimination, but we are now taking into
account two other possibly important variables besides education. Use the outputs to
help answer the following questions:

T A B L E **6.3**
Data for Discrimination Exercise

SALARY	EDUCAT	EXPER	MONTHS	MALES	SALARY	EDUCAT	EXPER	MONTHS	MALES
3900	12	0.0	1	0	5400	12	169.0	27	0
4020	10	44.0	7	0	5400	12	244.0	1	0
4290	12	5.0	30	0	5400	15	24.0	13	0
4380	8	6.2	7	0	5400	15	49.0	27	0
4380	8	7.5	6	0	5400	15	51.0	21	0
4380	12	0.0	7	0	5400	15	122.0	33	0
4380	12	0.0	10	0	5520	12	97.0	17	0
4380	12	4.5	6	0	5520	12	196.0	32	0
4440	15	75.0	2	0	5580	12	132.5	30	0
4500	8	52.0	3	0	5640	12	55.0	9	0
4500	12	8.0	19	0	5700	12	90.0	23	0
4620	12	52.0	3	0	5700	12	116.5	25	0
4800	8	70.0	20	0	5700	15	51.0	17	0
4800	12	6.0	23	0	5700	15	61.0	11	0
4800	12	11.0	12	0	5700	15	241.0	34	0
4800	12	11.0	17	0	6000	12	121.0	30	0
4800	12	63.0	22	0	6000	15	78.5	13	0
4800	12	144.0	24	0	6120	12	208.5	21	0
4800	12	163.0	12	0	6300	12	86.5	33	0
4800	12	228.0	26	0	6300	15	231.0	15	0
4800	12	381.0	1	0	4620	12	11.5	22	1
4800	16	214.0	15	0	5040	15	14.0	3	1
4980	8	318.0	25	0	5100	12	180.0	15	1
5100	8	96.0	33	0	5100	12	315.0	2	1
5100	12	36.0	15	0	5220	12	29.0	14	1
5100	12	59.0	14	0	5400	12	7.0	21	1
5100	15	115.0	1	0	5400	12	38.0	11	1
5100	15	165.0	4	0	5400	12	113.0	3	1
5100	16	123.0	12	0	5400	15	17.5	8	1
5160	12	18.0	12	0	5400	15	359.0	11	1
5220	8	102.0	29	0	5700	15	36.0	5	1
5220	12	127.0	29	0	6000	8	320.0	21	1
5280	8	90.0	11	0	6000	12	24.0	2	1
5280	8	190.0	1	0	6000	12	32.0	17	1
5280	12	107.0	11	0	6000	12	49.0	8	1
5400	8	173.0	34	0	6000	12	56.0	33	1
5400	8	228.0	33	0	6000	12	252.0	11	1
5400	12	26.0	11	0	6000	12	272.0	19	1
5400	12	36.0	33	0	6000	15	25.0	13	1
5400	12	38.0	22	0	6000	15	35.5	32	1
5400	12	82.0	29	0	6000	15	56.0	12	1

T A B L E **6.3** (*Cont.*)

Data for Discrimination Exercise

SALARY	EDUCAT	EXPER	MONTHS	MALES	SALARY	EDUCAT	EXPER	MONTHS	MALES
6000	15	64.0	33	1	6600	15	215.5	16	1
6000	15	108.0	16	1	6840	15	41.5	7	1
6000	16	45.5	3	1	6900	12	175.0	10	1
6300	15	72.0	17	1	6900	15	132.0	24	1
6600	15	64.0	16	1	8100	16	54.5	33	1
6600	15	84.0	33	1					

F I G U R E **6.15**

MINITAB Regression Output for Discrimination Exercise

```
The regression equation is
salary = 3526 + 90.0 educat + 1.27 exper + 23.4 months + 722 males

Predictor        Coef        Stdev      t-ratio          p
Constant       3526.4       327.7        10.76      0.000
educat          90.02       24.69         3.65      0.000
exper          1.2690      0.5877         2.16      0.034
months         23.406       5.201         4.50      0.000
males           722.5       117.8         6.13      0.000

s = 507.4       R-sq = 51.1%      R-sq(adj) = 48.9%

Analysis of Variance

SOURCE        DF            SS           MS        F          p
Regression     4      23665352      5916338    22.98      0.000
Error         88      22657938       257477
Total         92      46323288


SOURCE        DF        SEQ SS
educat         1       7862535
exper          1       2038491
months         1       4083411
males          1       9680915

Unusual Observations
Obs.    educat      salary        Fit   Stdev.Fit    Residual    St.Resid
   3      12.0      4290.0     5315.2       110.2     -1025.2       -2.07R
  62      12.0      4620.0     5858.7       119.4     -1238.7       -2.51R
  90      15.0      6840.0     5815.7       109.4      1024.3        2.07R
  91      12.0      6900.0     5785.3       109.1      1114.7        2.25R
  93      16.0      8100.0     6530.8       145.8      1569.2        3.23R

R denotes an obs. with a large st. resid.
```

F I G U R E **6.16**
SAS Regression Output for Discrimination Exercise

Dependent Variable: SALARY

Analysis of Variance

Source	DF	Sum of Squares	Mean Square	F Value	Prob>F
Model	4	23665351.393	5916337.8481	22.978	0.0001
Error	88	22657938.93	257476.57875		
C Total	92	46323290.323			

Root MSE	507.42150	R-square	0.5109	
Dep Mean	5420.32258	Adj R-sq	0.4886	
C.V.	9.36146			

Parameter Estimates

Variable	DF	Parameter Estimate	Standard Error	T for H0: Parameter=0	Prob > |T|
INTERCEP	1	3526.422111	327.72542145	10.760	0.0001
EDUCAT	1	90.020311	24.69356079	3.645	0.0005
EXPER	1	1.268990	0.58773685	2.159	0.0336
MONTHS	1	23.406236	5.20086281	4.500	0.0001
MALES	1	722.460671	117.82159054	6.132	0.0001

a Conduct the F test for the overall fit of the regression. State the hypotheses to be tested, the decision rule, the test statistic, and your decision. Use a 5% level of significance.

b What conclusion can be drawn from the test result in (a)?

c Is there a difference in salaries, on average, for male and female workers after accounting for the effect of the three other explanatory variables? Use a 5% level of significance to answer this question. State the hypotheses to be tested, the decision rule, the test statistic, and your decision.

d What conclusion can be drawn from the test result in (c)?

e What salary would you forecast, on average, for males with 12 years of education, 10 years of experience, and with MONTHS equal to 15? A point forecast will be sufficient. What salary would you forecast, on average, for females if all other factors are equal?

These data are available on the data disk for further analysis. In MINITAB, they can be read using

```
READ 'HARRIS6' C1-C5
```

where C1 is SALARY, C2 is EDUCAT, C3 is EXPER, C4 is MONTHS, and C5 is MALES.

In SAS, the data can be read from the file HARRIS6.DAT using

```
INPUT SALARY EDUCAT EXPER MONTHS MALES;
```

F I G U R E **6.17**
MINITAB Regression Output for Automobile Transmission Exercise

```
The regression equation is
citympg = - 4.99 + 75332 wtinv + 1.98 auto

Predictor        Coef       Stdev     t-ratio       p
Constant       -4.987       1.184       -4.21    0.000
wtinv           75332        3089       24.39    0.000
auto           1.9798      0.4556        4.35    0.000

s = 2.230      R-sq = 83.5%     R-sq(adj) = 83.3%

Analysis of Variance

SOURCE           DF          SS         MS         F         p
Regression        2      3551.5     1775.7    356.93     0.000
Error           141       701.5        5.0
Total           143      4252.9

SOURCE           DF      SEQ SS
wtinv             1      3457.5
auto              1        93.9

Unusual Observations
Obs.     wtinv   citympg       Fit   Stdev.Fit   Residual   St.Resid
  45   0.000309   13.000    18.299      0.315     -5.299      -2.40R
  53   0.000617   46.000    41.485      0.784      4.515       2.16RX
  55   0.000333   25.000    20.082      0.273      4.918       2.22R
  56   0.000440   34.000    28.126      0.311      5.874       2.66R
  57   0.000442   35.000    28.272      0.315      6.728       3.05R
  69   0.000275    9.000    15.709      0.392     -6.709      -3.06R
  79   0.000436   22.000    27.866      0.304     -5.866      -2.65R
  82   0.000358   17.000    22.014      0.245     -5.014      -2.26R
 127   0.000542   33.000    35.843      0.568     -2.843      -1.32 X
 130   0.000562   39.000    37.334      0.624      1.666       0.78 X

R denotes an obs. with a large st. resid.
X denotes an obs. whose X value gives it large influence.
```

2   Automobile Transmissions   Data for 144 cars were obtained from Road and Track's *The Complete '94 Car Buyer's Guide*. The full data set is listed in Table 7.3. Only complete cases (those with missing data are omitted from the analysis) of the following variables will be considered here:

y = mileage in city driving (CITYMPG)

x_1 = weight in pounds (WEIGHT)

x_2 = indicator variable coded as 1 for cars with automatic transmissions and 0 for cars with manual transmissions (AUTO)

MINITAB and SAS outputs for the regression of y on $1/x_1$ (WTINV) and x_2 are shown in Figures 6.17 and 6.18, respectively. The decision to use the variable WTINV rather than WEIGHT was based on examination of residual plots and scatterplots. Use the outputs to answer the following questions:

F I G U R E **6.18**
SAS Regression Output for Automobile Transmission Exercise

```
Dependent Variable: CITYMPG

                    Analysis of Variance

                  Sum of        Mean
Source      DF    Squares       Square     F Value     Prob>F

Model        2   3551.46527   1775.73264   356.933     0.0001
Error      141    701.47223      4.97498
C Total    143   4252.93750

        Root MSE       2.23047    R-square     0.8351
        Dep Mean      21.64583    Adj R-sq     0.8327
        C.V.          10.30437

                    Parameter Estimates

              Parameter    Standard    T for H0:
Variable  DF    Estimate       Error   Parameter=0    Prob > |T|

INTERCEP   1   -4.987049   1.18371822      -4.213        0.0001
WTINV      1      75332   3088.7712054      24.389        0.0001
AUTO       1    1.979801   0.45560040        4.345        0.0001
```

a Conduct the *F* test for the overall fit of the regression. State the hypotheses to be tested, the decision rule, the test statistic, and your decision. Use a 5% level of significance.

b What conclusion can be drawn from the test result in (a)?

c Is there a difference in mileage, on average, for cars with manual and automatic transmissions after the effect of weight is taken into account? State the hypotheses to be tested, the decision rule, the test statistic, and your decision. Use a 5% level of significance.

d What conclusion can be drawn from the test result in (c)?

e What mileage would you forecast, on average, for cars weighing 3500 pounds with automatic transmissions? A point forecast will be sufficient. What mileage would you forecast, on average, for cars weighing 3500 pounds with manual transmissions?

These data are available on the data disk for further analysis. In MINITAB, they can be read using

```
READ 'MPG6' C1-C3
```

where C1 is CITYMPG, C2 is WEIGHT, and C3 is AUTO.

In SAS, the data can be read from the file MPG6.DAT using

```
INPUT CITYMPG WEIGHT AUTO;
```

6.2

Interaction Variables

Another type of variable used in regression is called an *interaction variable*. It is formed as the product of two (or more) variables. To illustrate the effect of using an interaction variable, consider a regression equation with dependent variable y and independent variables x_1 and x_2. Construct the interaction variable $x_1 x_2$, which is the product of the two explanatory variables. Now consider two possible regression models, one with the interaction term and one without:

$$y = \beta_0 + \beta_1 x_1 + \beta_2 x_2 + e$$

and

$$y = \beta_0 + \beta_1 x_1 + \beta_2 x_2 + \beta_3 x_1 x_2 + e$$

Now determine the change in y given a one-unit change in x_1 with each of these models. For the model without the interaction term, a one-unit change in x_1 will produce a change in y of β_1 units. For the model with the interaction term, rewrite the equation as

$$y = \beta_0 + (\beta_1 + \beta_3 x_2)x_1 + \beta_2 x_2 + e$$

Then a one-unit change in x_1 will produce a change of $\beta_1 + \beta_3 x_2$ units in y. As shown, the change in y resulting from a one-unit change in x_1 also depends on the value of the variable x_2. If x_2 is small, smaller changes will result; if x_2 is large, larger changes will result. Thus, the effect of movements in x_1 cannot be judged independently of the value of x_2 (and the effect of movements in x_2 cannot be judged independently of movements in x_1).

An important application of interaction variables is in testing for differences in the slopes of two regression lines. This is done in a manner similar to the procedure to test for differences in the intercepts. Consider a regression with one quantitative explanatory variable (x_1) and one indicator variable (D):

$$y = \beta_0 + \beta_1 x_1 + \beta_2 D$$

The indicator variable D is coded as 1 if an item in the sample belongs to a certain group and as 0 if the item does not belong to the group. Now add the variable representing the interaction between x_1 and D, $x_1 D$:

$$y = \beta_0 + \beta_1 x_1 + \beta_2 D + \beta_3 x_1 D$$

This equation can be separated into two parts as follows:

If the sample item is in the indicated group ($D = 1$):

$$y = \beta_0 + \beta_1 x_1 + \beta_2(1) + \beta_3 x_1 = (\beta_0 + \beta_2) + (\beta_1 + \beta_3)x_1$$

If the sample item is not in the indicated group ($D = 0$):

$$y = \beta_0 + \beta_1 x_1 + \beta_2(0) + \beta_3 x_1(0) = \beta_0 + \beta_1 x_1$$

Using the indicator variable allows us to examine differences in the intercepts for the two groups. Using the interaction variable allows us to examine differences in the slopes. Note that the equation for the indicated group has been rewritten with two components making up the intercept term, the original intercept β_0 and the coefficient of the indicator variable β_2, and two components making up the slope term, the original slope β_1 and the coefficient of the interaction term, β_3. Two lines have been fit with different slopes and different intercepts, even though only one regression has been run. The difference in the intercepts is given by β_2, the difference in the slopes by β_3.

Not only can we determine whether there is a difference in the average value of the y variable for the two groups after adjusting for the effect of the quantitative variable, but we can also tell whether there is a difference in the slopes for the two groups. A t test for whether β_3 is equal to zero will help to determine whether the slopes differ. Also, a partial F test of the hypotheses

$$H_0: \quad \beta_2 = \beta_3 = 0$$

$$H_a: \quad \text{At least one of } \beta_2 \text{ and } \beta_3 \text{ are different from zero}$$

can be used to tell us whether there is any difference in the regression lines for the two groups (intercept or slope). The following example illustrates.

E X A M P L E   **6.4** **Employment Discrimination (again)**

In Examples 6.1 and 6.2, we concluded that there is evidence of employment discrimination at Harris Bank even after taking into account education. Now suppose the following question is to be considered: Does the difference in average salaries increase between the two groups as education increases? This is one question an interaction term will allow us to investigate. The equation can be written as

$$\text{SALARY} = \beta_0 + \beta_1 \text{EDUCAT} + \beta_2 \text{MALES} + \beta_3 \text{MSLOPE},$$

where MSLOPE represents the interaction between EDUCAT and MALES. Thus,

$$\text{MSLOPE} = \text{EDUCAT} * \text{MALES}$$

The MINITAB regression output for this equation is shown in Figure 6.19 and the SAS output in Figure 6.20.

We ask the question, Is there *any* difference between the two groups (males and females)? To answer this, the following hypotheses can be tested:

$$H_0: \quad \beta_2 = \beta_3 = 0$$

$$H_a: \quad \text{At least one of } \beta_2 \text{ and } \beta_3 \text{ is different from zero}$$

To test these hypotheses, a partial F test should be used. The reduced model will have only the variable EDUCAT. This regression is shown in Figure 6.21 for MINITAB and Figure 6.22 for SAS. The F statistic is

$$F = \frac{(38,460,756 - 29,054,426)/2}{326,454} = 14.41$$

FIGURE 6.19

MINITAB Regression Output for Discrimination Example with Interaction Variable to Represent Different Slopes

```
The regression equation is
salary = 4395 + 62.1 educat - 275 males + 73.6 mslope

Predictor        Coef      Stdev     t-ratio        p
Constant       4395.3      389.2       11.29    0.000
educat          62.13      31.94        1.95    0.055
males          -274.9      845.7       -0.32    0.746
mslope          73.59      63.59        1.16    0.250

s = 571.4       R-sq = 37.3%     R-sq(adj) = 35.2%

Analysis of Variance

SOURCE        DF          SS           MS         F        p
Regression     3    17268864      5756288     17.63    0.000
Error         89    29054426       326454
Total         92    46323288

SOURCE        DF      SEQ SS
educat         1     7862535
males          1     8969210
mslope         1      437121

Unusual Observations
Obs.     educat    salary      Fit   Stdev.Fit   Residual   St.Resid
  1       12.0    3900.0     5140.9      73.2     -1240.9     -2.19R
 60       12.0    6300.0     5140.9      73.2      1159.1      2.05R
 62       12.0    4620.0     5749.1     131.5     -1129.1     -2.03R
 63       15.0    5040.0     6156.2     129.3     -1116.2     -2.01R
 73        8.0    6000.0     5206.2     320.5       793.8      1.68 X
 91       12.0    6900.0     5749.1     131.5      1150.9      2.07R
 93       16.0    8100.0     6291.9     169.2      1808.1      3.31R

R denotes an obs. with a large st. resid.
X denotes an obs. whose X value gives it large influence.
```

Using a 5% level of significance, the decision rule is:

$$\text{Reject } H_0 \quad \text{if} \quad F > 3.15$$
$$\text{Accept } H_0 \quad \text{if} \quad F \leq 3.15$$

The critical value used is the $F(.05; 2,60)$ value since the value for $F(.05; 2,89)$ is not in the tables. The decision is to reject H_0. We should already have guessed that this would be the decision since the test in Example 6.2 showed that the coefficient of the indicator variable was not zero.

The coefficients can be tested individually to see whether one or both are different from zero. Note that this results in some conflicting results. The p values (or t ratios) on each of the individual coefficients for MALES and MSLOPE suggest that the coefficients are equal to zero. But the F test just told us that at least one of the coefficients is different from zero. The reason for these conflicting results is the high correlation between MALES and MSLOPE (0.986). This is an example of the multicollinearity problem discussed in Chapter 5. Since we already have concluded that the indicator variable is important in the regression and the

F I G U R E **6.20**

SAS Regression Output for Discrimination Example with Interaction Variable to Represent
Different Slopes

```
Dependent Variable: SALARY

                         Analysis of Variance

                         Sum of          Mean
    Source       DF      Squares         Square      F Value      Prob>F

    Model         3 17268864.766 5756288.2554      17.633       0.0001
    Error        89 29054425.556 326454.21974
    C Total      92 46323290.323

           Root MSE       571.36172     R-square       0.3728
           Dep Mean      5420.32258     Adj R-sq       0.3516
           C.V.            10.54110

                        Parameter Estimates

                     Parameter      Standard      T for H0:
    Variable  DF      Estimate         Error     Parameter=0   Prob > |T|

    INTERCEP   1   4395.322812   389.20996006      11.293       0.0001
    EDUCAT     1     62.130560    31.94336442       1.945       0.0549
    MALES      1   -274.859715   845.74886657      -0.325       0.7460
    MSLOPE     1     73.585794    63.59227682       1.157       0.2503
```

F I G U R E **6.21**

MINITAB Regression Output for Reduced Model in Discrimination Example with Interaction
Variable

```
The regression equation is
salary = 3819 + 128 educat

Predictor        Coef       Stdev      t-ratio         p
Constant       3818.6       377.4        10.12     0.000
educat         128.09       29.70         4.31     0.000

s = 650.1       R-sq = 17.0%      R-sq(adj) = 16.1%

Analysis of Variance

SOURCE          DF          SS          MS          F          p
Regression       1     7862535     7862535      18.60     0.000
Error           91    38460756      422646
Total           92    46323292

Unusual Observations
Obs.    educat     salary       Fit    Stdev.Fit    Residual    St.Resid
  1       12.0     3900.0     5355.6        69.1     -1455.6      -2.25R
  9       15.0     4440.0     5739.8       100.2     -1299.8      -2.02R
 91       12.0     6900.0     5355.6        69.1      1544.4       2.39R
 93       16.0     8100.0     5867.9       123.8      2232.1       3.50R

R denotes an obs. with a large st. resid.
```

F I G U R E **6.22**

SAS Regression Output for Reduced Model in Discrimination Example with Interaction Variable

```
Dependent Variable: SALARY

                    Analysis of Variance

                      Sum of          Mean
Source         DF    Squares         Square      F Value      Prob>F

Model           1 7862534.2916 7862534.2916      18.603      0.0001
Error          91 38460756.031 422645.67067
C Total        92 46323290.323

          Root MSE      650.11204   R-square       0.1697
          Dep Mean     5420.32258   Adj R-sq       0.1606
          C.V.           11.99397

                    Parameter Estimates

                   Parameter     Standard     T for H0:
Variable     DF     Estimate       Error     Parameter=0    Prob > |T|

INTERCEP      1   3818.559794  377.43765814      10.117       0.0001
EDUCAT        1    128.085932   29.69671216       4.313       0.0001
```

addition of the interaction variable does not add much (R^2 only increases by 1%), it might be best in this example to stick to the simpler model in Example 6.2. ∎

Example 6.4 illustrates one caution in using interaction variables. If the correlation is high between interaction variables and the original variables in the regression, multicollinearity problems can result. In a regression with several variables, the number of interaction variables that could be created is very large and the likelihood of multicollinearity problems is high. Therefore, it is wise not to use interaction variables indiscriminately. There should be some good reason to suspect that two variables might be related, or some specific question that can be answered by an interaction variable before this type of explanatory variable is used.

Exercises

3 **More on Possible Discrimination** Suppose that legal counsel representing Harris Bank suggests that an interaction exists between education and experience and that the introduction of this term into the regression may account for the difference in average salaries. The interaction term

$$\text{EDUCEXPR} = \text{EDUCAT} * \text{EXPER}$$

F I G U R E 6.23

MINITAB Regression Output for Discrimination Example Using Interaction Term Between Education and Experience

```
The regression equation is
salary = 3006 + 134 educat + 5.68 exper + 22.4 months + 688 males
         - 0.364 educexpr
```

Predictor	Coef	Stdev	t-ratio	p
Constant	3006.2	490.7	6.13	0.000
educat	134.47	39.81	3.38	0.001
exper	5.679	3.164	1.79	0.076
months	22.421	5.218	4.30	0.000
males	687.6	119.7	5.74	0.000
educexpr	-0.3643	0.2569	-1.42	0.160

```
s = 504.5      R-sq = 52.2%     R-sq(adj) = 49.4%
```

Analysis of Variance

SOURCE	DF	SS	MS	F	p
Regression	5	24177362	4835473	19.00	0.000
Error	87	22145928	254551		
Total	92	46323288			

SOURCE	DF	SEQ SS
educat	1	7862535
exper	1	2038491
months	1	4083411
males	1	9680915
educexpr	1	512011

Unusual Observations

Obs.	educat	salary	Fit	Stdev.Fit	Residual	St.Resid
3	12.0	4290.0	5299.0	110.2	-1009.0	-2.05R
23	8.0	4980.0	5521.6	261.7	-541.6	-1.26 X
62	12.0	4620.0	5815.7	122.5	-1195.7	-2.44R
71	15.0	5400.0	6034.4	268.7	-634.4	-1.49 X
73	8.0	6000.0	6125.1	268.3	-125.1	-0.29 X
91	12.0	6900.0	5760.4	109.9	1139.6	2.31R
93	16.0	8100.0	6577.0	148.6	1523.0	3.16R

```
R denotes an obs. with a large st. resid.
X denotes an obs. whose X value gives it large influence.
```

is created and introduced into the regression. The MINITAB regression output is in Figure 6.23 and the SAS output is in Figure 6.24. Use the outputs to help answer the following questions:

a What is the adjusted R^2 for this regression? Compare this value to the adjusted R^2 for the regression without the interaction variable (see Figure 6.15 or 6.16). Which model appears to be the best choice based on the adjusted R^2?

b Test to see whether the interaction term is important in this regression model. Use a 5% level of significance. State the hypotheses to be tested, the decision rule, the test statistic, and your decision.

F I G U R E **6.24**

SAS Regression Output for Discrimination Example Using Interaction Term Between Education and Experience

```
Dependent Variable: SALARY

                    Analysis of Variance

                       Sum of          Mean
    Source     DF     Squares         Square      F Value     Prob>F

    Model       5 24177362.322 4835472.4643      18.996      0.0001
    Error      87 22145928.001 254550.89656
    C Total    92 46323290.323

         Root MSE       504.53037    R-square       0.5219
         Dep Mean      5420.32258    Adj R-sq       0.4945
         C.V.             9.30812

                    Parameter Estimates

                     Parameter      Standard     T for H0:
    Variable   DF     Estimate         Error    Parameter=0    Prob > |T|

    INTERCEP    1   3006.167477  490.65980385       6.127      0.0001
    EDUCAT      1    134.470416   39.81376691       3.377      0.0011
    EXPER       1      5.679213    3.16406201       1.795      0.0761
    MONTHS      1     22.420506    5.21772841       4.297      0.0001
    MALES       1    687.629703  119.69686616       5.745      0.0001
    EDUCEXPR    1     -0.364326    0.25688446      -1.418      0.1597
```

   c Does the interaction variable seem to be important in explaining SALARY?

(See Exercise 1 for instructions on how to read the data into MINITAB or SAS.)

4   **Automobile Transmissions (continued)**   Consider again the data from Exercise 2:

y = mileage in city driving (CITYMPG)

x_1 = weight in pounds (WEIGHT)

x_2 = indicator variable coded as 1 for cars with automatic transmissions and 0 for cars with manual transmissions (AUTO)

Instead of x_1 (WEIGHT), the variable $1/x_1$ (WTINV) will be used as before. We define the interaction variable

$$WTSLOPE = WTINV * AUTO$$

When WTSLOPE is included in the regression, it allows the slopes of the regression lines for cars with manual and automatic transmissions to differ. The regression model can be written

$$y = \beta_0 + \beta_1 WTINV + \beta_2 AUTO + \beta_3 WTSLOPE + e$$

F I G U R E **6.25**

MINITAB Regression Output for MPG Interaction Variable Exercise

```
The regression equation is
citympg = - 6.23 + 78647 wtinv + 7.98 auto - 19493 wtslope
```

Predictor	Coef	Stdev	t-ratio	p
Constant	-6.231	1.273	-4.89	0.000
wtinv	78647	3334	23.59	0.000
auto	7.980	2.529	3.16	0.002
wtslope	-19493	8085	-2.41	0.017

s = 2.193   R-sq = 84.2%   R-sq(adj) = 83.8%

Analysis of Variance

SOURCE	DF	SS	MS	F	p
Regression	3	3579.4	1193.1	248.02	0.000
Error	140	673.5	4.8		
Total	143	4252.9			

SOURCE	DF	SEQ SS
wtinv	1	3457.5
auto	1	93.9
wtslope	1	28.0

Unusual Observations

Obs.	wtinv	citympg	Fit	Stdev.Fit	Residual	St.Resid
26	0.000248	18.000	13.255	0.486	4.745	2.22R
27	0.000398	26.000	25.269	0.817	0.731	0.36 X
28	0.000375	25.000	23.946	0.665	1.054	0.50 X
45	0.000309	13.000	18.080	0.323	-5.080	-2.34R
49	0.000372	26.000	23.739	0.642	2.261	1.08 X
53	0.000617	46.000	42.286	0.839	3.714	1.83 X
55	0.000333	25.000	19.941	0.275	5.059	2.32R
56	0.000440	34.000	28.339	0.318	5.661	2.61R
57	0.000442	35.000	28.491	0.322	6.509	3.00R
69	0.000275	9.000	15.375	0.410	-6.375	-2.96R
79	0.000436	22.000	28.067	0.310	-6.067	-2.79R
82	0.000358	17.000	21.958	0.242	-4.958	-2.27R
88	0.000216	17.000	14.525	0.644	2.475	1.18 X
130	0.000562	39.000	37.952	0.665	1.048	0.50 X

R denotes an obs. with a large st. resid.
X denotes an obs. whose X value gives it large influence.

The MINITAB and SAS regression outputs for this model are shown in Figures 6.25 and 6.26, respectively. Figures 6.27 and 6.28 contain the outputs for the following model:

$$y = \beta_0 + \beta_1 \text{WTINV} + e$$

Use the outputs to answer the following questions:

a   Is there *any* difference between the regression lines for cars with manual and automatic transmissions? State the hypotheses to be tested, the decision rule, the test statistic, and your decision. Use a 5% level of significance.

F I G U R E 6.26

SAS Regression Output for MPG Interaction Variable Exercise

Dependent Variable: CITYMPG

Analysis of Variance

Source	DF	Sum of Squares	Mean Square	F Value	Prob>F
Model	3	3579.43201	1193.14400	248.016	0.0001
Error	140	673.50549	4.81075		
C Total	143	4252.93750			

Root MSE	2.19334	R-square	0.8416	
Dep Mean	21.64583	Adj R-sq	0.8382	
C.V.	10.13286			

Parameter Estimates

Variable	DF	Parameter Estimate	Standard Error	T for H0: Parameter=0	Prob > |T|
INTERCEP	1	-6.231283	1.27327818	-4.894	0.0001
WTINV	1	78647	3334.0569610	23.589	0.0001
AUTO	1	7.980480	2.52878106	3.156	0.0020
WTSLOPE	1	-19493	8084.8715019	-2.411	0.0172

b Is there a difference, on average, in mileages for cars with manual and automatic transmissions? State the hypotheses to be tested, the decision rule, the test statistic, and your decision. Use a 5% level of significance.

c Is there a difference between the slopes of the regression lines representing the relationship between CITYMPG and WTINV for cars with manual and automatic transmissions? State the hypotheses to be tested, the decision rule, the test statistic, and your decision. Use a 5% level of significance.

d Write out the estimated equation as it would appear for cars with manual transmissions.

e Write out the estimated equation as it would appear for cars with automatic transmissions.

(See Exercise 2 for instructions on how to read the data into MINITAB or SAS.)

F I G U R E **6.27**

MINITAB Regression Output for Reduced Model for MPG Interaction Variable Exercise

```
The regression equation is
citympg = - 1.66 + 67931 wtinv

Predictor        Coef       Stdev      t-ratio        p
Constant       -1.6639     0.9587       -1.74      0.085
wtinv           67931        2734       24.84      0.000

s = 2.367       R-sq = 81.3%     R-sq(adj) = 81.2%

Analysis of Variance

SOURCE          DF         SS          MS         F          p
Regression       1       3457.5      3457.5    617.25     0.000
Error          142        795.4         5.6
Total          143       4252.9

Unusual Observations
Obs.     wtinv   citympg        Fit   Stdev.Fit    Residual   St.Resid
  40   0.000288   13.000     17.879      0.249      -4.879     -2.07R
  45   0.000309   13.000     19.335      0.218      -6.335     -2.69R
  46   0.000269   11.000     16.622      0.282      -5.622     -2.39R
  53   0.000617   46.000     40.243      0.774       5.757      2.57RX
  56   0.000440   34.000     28.196      0.329       5.804      2.48R
  57   0.000442   35.000     28.328      0.334       6.672      2.85R
  69   0.000275    9.000     16.999      0.272      -7.999     -3.40R
  79   0.000436   22.000     27.962      0.322      -5.962     -2.54R
  82   0.000358   17.000     22.684      0.202      -5.684     -2.41R
 119   0.000279   12.000     17.258      0.265      -5.258     -2.24R
 127   0.000542   33.000     35.155      0.578      -2.155     -0.94 X
 130   0.000562   39.000     36.500      0.630       2.500      1.10 X
 137   0.000513   32.000     33.173      0.504      -1.173     -0.51 X

R denotes an obs. with a large st. resid.
X denotes an obs. whose X value gives it large influence.
```

F I G U R E 6.28

SAS Regression Output for Reduced Model for MPG Interaction Variable Exercise

Dependent Variable: CITYMPG

Analysis of Variance

Source	DF	Sum of Squares	Mean Square	F Value	Prob>F
Model	1	3457.52190	3457.52190	617.247	0.0001
Error	142	795.41560	5.60152		
C Total	143	4252.93750			

Root MSE	2.36675	R-square	0.8130	
Dep Mean	21.64583	Adj R-sq	0.8117	
C.V.	10.93399			

Parameter Estimates

Variable	DF	Parameter Estimate	Standard Error	T for H0: Parameter=0	Prob > |T|
INTERCEP	1	-1.663875	0.95873178	-1.735	0.0848
WTINV	1	67931	2734.2531192	24.844	0.0001

6.3
Seasonal Effects in Time-Series Regression

Seasonal effects are fairly regular patterns of movement in a time series, repeating within a one-year period. For example, sales of swimsuits would be expected to be higher in spring and summer months and lower in fall and winter. Although the influence of the seasonal effects are not expected to be exactly the same every year, the same general pattern is expected to persist.

Seasonal patterns can be modeled in a regression equation by using indicator variables, which can be created to indicate the time period to which each observation belongs. For example, if quarterly data were being analyzed, the following indicator variables could be created:

$Q1 = 1$ if the observation is from the first quarter of any year

$\quad = 0$ otherwise

$Q2 = 1$ if the observation is from the second quarter of any year

$\quad = 0$ otherwise

$Q3 = 1$ if the observation is from the third quarter of any year

$\quad = 0$ otherwise

$Q4 = 1$ if the observation is from the fourth quarter of any year

$\quad = 0$ otherwise

Four indicator variables have been created to denote the quarter to which each observation belongs, but only three of the variables should be included in the regression equation. The excluded quarter will simply serve as a base-level quarter from which changes in the seasonal levels will be measured. The interpretation of the coefficients of the indicator variables is the same as for any set of indicator variables. To illustrate, consider the following estimated regression equation with only quarterly indicator variables:

$$\hat{y}_i = b_0 + b_1 Q1 + b_2 Q2 + b_3 Q3$$

Note that the fourth quarter will serve as the base-level quarter. Observations in the fourth quarter will be represented by the equation

$$\hat{y}_i = b_0$$

because $Q1 = Q2 = Q3 = 0$. This point has been located on the graph in Figure 6.29. Observations in the first quarter will be represented by

$$\hat{y}_i = b_0 + b_1$$

because $Q1 = 1$ and $Q2 = Q3 = 0$.

Similarly, observations in the second quarter will be represented by

$$\hat{y}_i = b_0 + b_2$$

and in the third quarter by

$$\hat{y}_i = b_0 + b_3$$

The coefficients b_1, b_2, and b_3 represent the differences between the fitted values for the indicated quarter (first, second, and third, respectively) and the base-level quarter. The graph in Figure 6.29 has been constructed with the assumption that b_1 and b_2 are positive and b_3 is negative. The lines shown for each quarter have a zero slope because no term has been included in the regression except the dummy variables. Differences in the overall level of the series in different quarters are shown by the quarterly indicators. The regression coefficients are estimating the differences in the mean levels of y in the indicated quarters. Obviously, additional variables could be used in the regression in addition to the seasonal indicator variables. This will be illustrated in the following example.

F I G U R E **6.29**

Graph Showing Placement of Seasonal Levels and Interpretation of Seasonal Indicator Coefficients

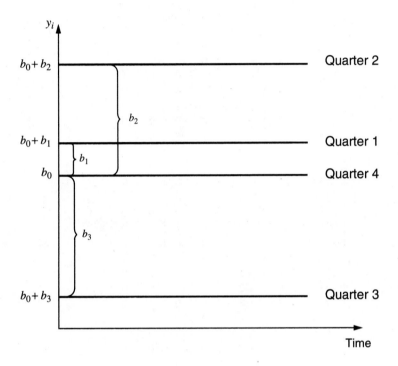

E X A M P L E **6.5** **ABX Company Sales**

Consider again the ABX Company of Example 3.11. The ABX Company sells winter sports merchandise including skis, ice skates, sleds, and so on. Quarterly sales in thousands of dollars for the ABX Company are shown in Table 6.4. The time period represented starts in the first quarter of 1985 and ends in the fourth quarter of 1994.

A MINITAB time-series plot of the sales figures in shown in Figure 6.30. In Chapter 3, it was decided that a strong linear trend in the sales figures appeared in this plot. The regression with the linear trend variable was estimated and the resulting output is shown again in Figure 6.31 for MINITAB and Figure 6.32 for SAS. The MINITAB residual plot of the standardized residuals versus the fitted values is shown in Figure 6.33. From this plot, no obvious violations of assumptions can be observed.

T A B L E **6.4**

Data for ABX Company Sales Example Showing Seasonal Indicator Variables

Sales	Trend	Quarter	Q1	Q2	Q3	Q4
221.0	1	1	1	0	0	0
203.5	2	2	0	1	0	0
190.0	3	3	0	0	1	0
225.5	4	4	0	0	0	1
223.0	5	1	1	0	0	0
190.0	6	2	0	1	0	0
206.0	7	3	0	0	1	0
226.5	8	4	0	0	0	1
236.0	9	1	1	0	0	0
214.0	10	2	0	1	0	0
210.5	11	3	0	0	1	0
237.0	12	4	0	0	0	1
245.5	13	1	1	0	0	0
201.0	14	2	0	1	0	0
230.0	15	3	0	0	1	0
254.5	16	4	0	0	0	1
257.0	17	1	1	0	0	0
238.0	18	2	0	1	0	0
228.0	19	3	0	0	1	0
255.0	20	4	0	0	0	1
260.5	21	1	1	0	0	0
244.0	22	2	0	1	0	0
256.0	23	3	0	0	1	0
276.5	24	4	0	0	0	1
291.0	25	1	1	0	0	0
255.5	26	2	0	1	0	0
244.0	27	3	0	0	1	0
291.0	28	4	0	0	0	1
296.0	29	1	1	0	0	0
260.0	30	2	0	1	0	0
271.5	31	3	0	0	1	0
299.5	32	4	0	0	0	1
297.0	33	1	1	0	0	0
271.0	34	2	0	1	0	0
270.0	35	3	0	0	1	0
300.0	36	4	0	0	0	1
306.5	37	1	1	0	0	0
283.5	38	2	0	1	0	0
283.5	39	3	0	0	1	0
307.5	40	4	0	0	0	1

F I G U R E 6.30

MINITAB Time-Series Plot of ABX Sales

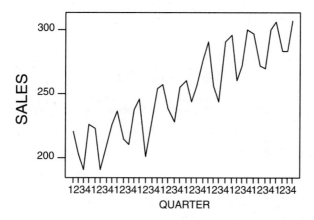

F I G U R E 6.31

MINITAB Regression Output for Regression of Sales on Linear Trend Variable for ABX Sales
Example

```
The regression equation is
sales = 199 + 2.56 trend

Predictor        Coef        Stdev      t-ratio          p
Constant       199.017       5.128        38.81      0.000
trend           2.5559       0.2180       11.73      0.000

s = 15.91        R-sq = 78.3%      R-sq(adj) = 77.8%

Analysis of Variance

SOURCE         DF           SS           MS          F          p
Regression      1         34818        34818     137.50      0.000
Error          38          9622          253
Total          39         44440

Unusual Observations
Obs.    trend     sales        Fit   Stdev.Fit    Residual    St.Resid
 14      14.0    201.00     234.80        2.89      -33.80       -2.16R

R denotes an obs. with a large st. resid.
```

A time-series plot of the standardized residuals is shown in Figure 6.34. Here a clear
pattern emerges. The residuals tend to be higher in the first and fourth quarters and lower
in the second and third quarters. This is not unexpected since the ABX Company sells winter sports merchandise. This pattern is the result of seasonal variation in the data that has not
been accounted for in the regression. Note that the pattern can also be seen in the time-series plot

F I G U R E **6.32**

SAS Regression Output for Regression of Sales on Linear Trend Variable for ABX Sales Example

Dependent Variable: SALES

Analysis of Variance

Source	DF	Sum of Squares	Mean Square	F Value	Prob>F
Model	1	34817.88322	34817.88322	137.505	0.0001
Error	38	9622.06053	253.21212		
C Total	39	44439.94375			

Root MSE	15.91264	R-square	0.7835
Dep Mean	251.41250	Adj R-sq	0.7778
C.V.	6.32930		

Parameter Estimates

Variable	DF	Parameter Estimate	Standard Error	T for H0: Parameter=0	Prob > |T|
INTERCEP	1	199.017308	5.12787526	38.811	0.0001
TREND	1	2.555863	0.21796092	11.726	0.0001

F I G U R E **6.33**

MINITAB Residual Plot of Standardized Residuals versus Fitted Values for ABX Sales Example

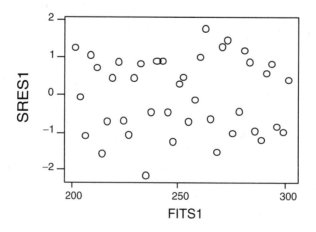

of the original data in Figure 6.30. Again, the residual plot emphasizes the pattern and points out some systematic variation in the data that we should try to model with our regression.

Figure 6.35 shows the MINITAB regression of sales on the linear trend variable and indicator variables designed to indicate the first, second, and third quarters. The SAS regression is in Figure 6.36. The original sales data, the trend variable, a variable representing the number of the quarter (1 through 4) labeled QUARTER, and four indicator variables labeled $Q1$, $Q2$, $Q3$, and $Q4$ are shown in Table 6.4. Remember that only three of the four indicator variables should be used in the regression. (Also, note that the variable QUARTER is not used in the regression. It is merely in the table to indicate the number of each quarter.)

The residual plot of the standardized residuals versus the fitted values for the regression with the quarterly indicators is shown in Figure 6.37. A time-series plot of the standardized residuals is shown in Figure 6.38. No further violations of any assumptions appear in either of these plots. ■

An important question to be asked in seasonal time-series models is, "Are there seasonal differences in the level of the dependent variable?" Another way of asking this question is, "Are the seasonal indicator variables necessary in the model?" The partial F test discussed in Chapter 4 can be used to answer the question.

Consider the following model with explanatory variable x and quarterly seasonal indicators $Q1$, $Q2$, and $Q3$:

$$y_i = \beta_0 + \beta_1 x_i + \beta_2 Q1 + \beta_3 Q2 + \beta_4 Q3 + e_i$$

This will be referred to as the *full model*. The hypotheses to be tested are

H_0: $\beta_2 = \beta_3 = \beta_4 = 0$
H_a: At least one of the coefficients β_2, β_3, and β_4 is not zero

If the null hypothesis is accepted, the seasonal indicator variables add nothing to the model and can be removed. In other words, there are no seasonal differences. In this case, the following *reduced model* would be adopted:

$$y_i = \beta_0 + \beta_1 x_i + e_i$$

If the null hypothesis is rejected, then there are seasonal differences and the quarterly indicators should remain in the model.

To conduct the test, the partial F test statistic is computed as

$$F = \frac{(SSE_R - SSE_F)/(K - L)}{MSE_F},$$

where SSE_R is the error sum of squares from the reduced model, SSE_F is the error sum of squares from the full model, and MSE_F is the mean square error from the full model. Because the hypothesis test determines whether three coefficients are equal to zero, a divisor of 3 is used in the numerator in place of $K - L$ ($K = 4$, $L = 1$). The decision rule for the test is:

Reject H_0 if $F > F(\alpha; K - L, n - K - 1)$
Accept H_0 if $F \leq F(\alpha; K - L, n - K - 1)$

F I G U R E **6.34**

MINITAB Time-Series Plot of Standardized Residuals for ABX Sales Example

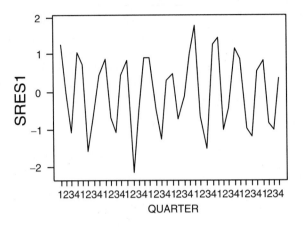

F I G U R E **6.35**

MINITAB Regression Output for Regression of Sales on Linear Trend Variable and Quarterly Indicator Variables for ABX Sales Example

```
The regression equation is
sales = 211 + 2.57 trend + 3.75 q1 - 26.1 q2 - 25.8 q3

Predictor        Coef       Stdev     t-ratio         p
Constant      210.846       3.148       66.98     0.000
trend         2.56610     0.09895       25.93     0.000
q1              3.748       3.229        1.16     0.254
q2            -26.118       3.222       -8.11     0.000
q3            -25.784       3.217       -8.01     0.000

s = 7.190      R-sq = 95.9%      R-sq(adj) = 95.5%

Analysis of Variance

SOURCE         DF          SS          MS          F         p
Regression      4       42630       10658     206.14     0.000
Error          35        1810          52
Total          39       44440

SOURCE         DF      SEQ SS
trend           1       34818
q1              1        3335
q2              1        1156
q3              1        3321

Unusual Observations
Obs.     trend      sales         Fit   Stdev.Fit    Residual    St.Resid
   2       2.0     203.50      189.86        2.89       13.64       2.07R
  14      14.0     201.00      220.65        2.35      -19.65      -2.89R

R denotes an obs. with a large st. resid.
```

F I G U R E **6.36**

SAS Regression Output for Regression of Sales on Linear Trend Variable and Quarterly Indicator Variables for ABX Sales Example

Dependent Variable: SALES

Analysis of Variance

Source	DF	Sum of Squares	Mean Square	F Value	Prob>F
Model	4	42630.43712	10657.60928	206.143	0.0001
Error	35	1809.50663	51.70019		
C Total	39	44439.94375			

Root MSE	7.19028	R-square	0.9593	
Dep Mean	251.41250	Adj R-sq	0.9546	
C.V.	2.85996			

Parameter Estimates

Variable	DF	Parameter Estimate	Standard Error	T for H0: Parameter=0	Prob > |T|
INTERCEP	1	210.845833	3.14788865	66.980	0.0001
TREND	1	2.566098	0.09895303	25.932	0.0001
Q1	1	3.748295	3.22926667	1.161	0.2536
Q2	1	-26.117803	3.22167731	-8.107	0.0001
Q3	1	-25.783902	3.21711510	-8.015	0.0001

F I G U R E **6.37**

MINITAB Residual Plot of Standardized Residual versus Fitted Values for ABX Sales Example with Quarterly Indicator Variables

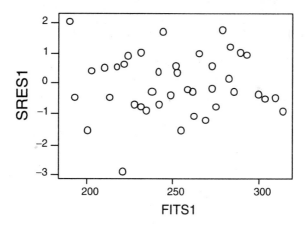

F I G U R E   **6.38**

MINITAB Time-Series Plot of Standardized Residuals for ABX Sales Example with Quarterly Indicator Variables

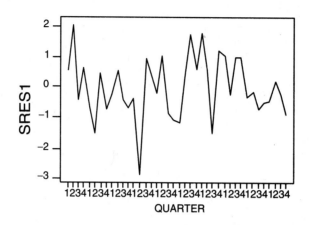

E X A M P L E   **6.6**   **ABX Company Sales (continued)**

In Example 6.5, the following model was examined for ABX Company Sales:

$$\text{SALES} = \beta_0 + \beta_1 \text{TREND} + \beta_2 Q1 + \beta_3 Q2 + \beta_4 Q3 + e$$

To determine whether there are seasonal components affecting sales, the following hypotheses should be tested:

$$H_0: \quad \beta_2 = \beta_3 = \beta_4 = 0$$

$$H_a: \quad \text{At least one of } \beta_2, \beta_3, \text{ and } \beta_4 \text{ is not zero}$$

To test this hypothesis, the partial F test is used. The test statistic is

$$F = \frac{(SSE_R - SSE_F)/3}{MSE_F} = \frac{(9622 - 1810)/3}{52} = 50.1$$

Note that the reduced model output is in Figure 6.31 or 6.32, and the full model output is in Figure 6.35 or 6.36. Using a 5% level of significance, the decision rule for the test is:

Reject H_0 if $F > F(.05; 3, 35) = 2.92$ (approximately)

Accept H_0 if $F \le 2.92$

The null hypothesis should be rejected. Thus, the conclusion is that seasonal components do affect sales and should be taken into account as was done in Example 6.5.

When computing forecasts with seasonal models, the coefficients of the seasonal indicators are used to adjust the appropriate time periods. The quarterly forecasts for 1995 are as follows, using the seasonal model with trend:

Time Period	Point Forecast
1995 $Q1$	$211 + 2.57(41) + 3.75 = 320.12$
1995 $Q2$	$211 + 2.57(42) - 26.1 = 292.84$
1995 $Q3$	$211 + 2.57(43) - 25.8 = 295.71$
1995 $Q4$	$211 + 2.57(44) = 324.08$ ∎

Throughout this section the use of quarterly indicator variables has been discussed. If monthly data are used instead of quarterly the applications are similar. Instead of four quarterly indicators, twelve monthly indicators would be created. Eleven of the twelve monthly indicators would be used in the regression with the estimated coefficients interpreted in a manner similar to those of the quarterly coefficients. Tests for seasonal variation would involve the complete set of eleven indicator variable coefficients. Since the use of monthly indicators is so similar to quarterly indicators, the demonstration of their use is reserved for the exercises.

Exercises

5   **Milk Production**   Data representing monthly milk production in pounds per cow for the period January 1962 through December 1975 are shown in Table 6.5. An extrapolative model to forecast milk production for each month in 1976 was developed. The MINITAB regression output for the model is presented in Figure 6.39 with the SAS output in Figure 6.40. The model used can be written as follows:

$$MILKPROD = \beta_0 + \beta_1 TREND + \beta_2 LAGMILK + \beta_3 JAN + \beta_4 FEB + \beta_5 MAR$$
$$+ \beta_6 APRIL + \beta_7 MAY + \beta_8 JUNE + \beta_9 JULY + \beta_{10} AUG$$
$$+ \beta_{11} SEPT + \beta_{12} OCT + \beta_{13} NOV + e$$

The variable TREND is a linear trend variable, LAGMILK is MILKPROD lagged one period, and JAN through NOV are eleven monthly seasonal indicators. Note that December has been used as the base-level month.

Figures 6.41 and 6.42 show the MINITAB and SAS regressions, respectively, for the model without the seasonal indicators.

Use the computer outputs to help answer the following questions. For any hypothesis tests, use a 5% level of significance. Be sure to state the hypotheses to be tested, the decision rule, the test statistic, and your decision.

a   Is there seasonal variation in milk production?

b   Are the TREND and LAGMILK variables important to the equation explaining milk production?

c   Using the better of the two equations (with or without seasonal indicators) as determined by you, develop a forecast of milk production for each month in 1976.

T A B L E **6.5**

Data for Milk Production Exercise

Mo/Yr	Lb/Cow/Mo	Mo/Yr	Lb/Cow/Mo	Mo/Yr	Lb/Cow/Mo
1/62	589	1/65	658	1/68	717
2/62	561	2/65	622	2/68	696
3/62	640	3/65	709	3/68	775
4/62	656	4/65	722	4/68	796
5/62	727	5/65	782	5/68	858
6/62	697	6/65	756	6/68	826
7/62	640	7/65	702	7/68	783
8/62	599	8/65	653	8/68	740
9/62	568	9/65	615	9/68	701
10/62	577	10/65	621	10/68	706
11/62	553	11/65	602	11/68	677
12/62	582	12/65	635	12/68	711
1/63	600	1/66	677	1/69	734
2/63	566	2/66	635	2/69	690
3/63	653	3/66	736	3/69	785
4/63	673	4/66	755	4/69	805
5/63	742	5/66	811	5/69	871
6/63	716	6/66	798	6/69	845
7/63	660	7/66	735	7/69	801
8/63	617	8/66	697	8/69	764
9/63	583	9/66	661	9/69	725
10/63	587	10/66	667	10/69	723
11/63	565	11/66	645	11/69	690
12/63	598	12/66	688	12/69	734
1/64	628	1/67	713	1/70	750
2/64	618	2/67	667	2/70	707
3/64	688	3/67	762	3/70	807
4/64	705	4/67	784	4/70	824
5/64	770	5/67	837	5/70	886
6/64	736	6/67	817	6/70	859
7/64	678	7/67	767	7/70	819
8/64	639	8/67	722	8/70	783
9/64	604	9/67	681	9/70	740
10/64	611	10/67	687	10/70	747
11/64	594	11/67	660	11/70	711
12/64	634	12/67	698	12/70	751

T A B L E **6.5** *(Cont.)*
Data for Milk Production Exercise

Mo/Yr	Lb/Cow/Mo	Mo/Yr	Lb/Cow/Mo
1/71	804	7/73	881
2/71	756	8/73	837
3/71	860	9/73	784
4/71	878	10/73	791
5/71	942	11/73	760
6/71	913	12/73	802
7/71	869	1/74	828
8/71	834	2/74	778
9/71	790	3/74	889
10/71	800	4/74	902
11/71	763	5/74	969
12/71	800	6/74	947
1/72	826	7/74	908
2/72	799	8/74	867
3/72	890	9/74	815
4/72	900	10/74	812
5/72	961	11/74	773
6/72	935	12/74	813
7/72	894	1/75	834
8/72	855	2/75	782
9/72	809	3/75	892
10/72	810	4/75	903
11/72	766	5/75	966
12/72	805	6/75	937
1/73	821	7/75	896
2/73	773	8/75	858
3/73	883	9/75	817
4/73	898	10/75	827
5/73	957	11/75	797
6/73	924	12/75	843

F I G U R E 6.39

MINITAB Regression Output for Regression of MILKPROD on TREND, LAGMILK, and
Seasonal Indicators for Milk Production Exercise

```
The regression equation is
milkprod = 98.3 + 0.192 trend + 0.887 lagmilk - 8.11 jan - 69.3 feb
           + 58.3 march - 8.92 april + 38.9 may - 43.6 june
     - 68.2 july - 66.3 aug - 71.4 sept - 30.1 oct - 64.2 nov

167 cases used 1 cases contain missing values
```

Predictor	Coef	Stdev	t-ratio	p
Constant	98.28	19.99	4.92	0.000
trend	0.19207	0.06635	2.89	0.004
lagmilk	0.88699	0.03769	23.53	0.000
jan	-8.109	3.240	-2.50	0.013
feb	-69.265	3.688	-18.78	0.000
march	58.273	2.980	19.56	0.000
april	-8.915	5.185	-1.72	0.088
may	38.908	5.660	6.87	0.000
june	-43.554	7.732	-5.63	0.000
july	-68.185	6.750	-10.10	0.000
aug	-66.310	5.111	-12.97	0.000
sept	-71.372	3.892	-18.34	0.000
oct	-30.110	3.040	-9.91	0.000
nov	-64.213	3.087	-20.80	0.000

```
s = 7.559       R-sq = 99.5%     R-sq(adj) = 99.4%
```

Analysis of Variance

SOURCE	DF	SS	MS	F	p
Regression	13	1708077	131391	2299.66	0.000
Error	153	8742	57		
Total	166	1716819			

SOURCE	DF	SEQ SS
trend	1	1104988
lagmilk	1	316779
jan	1	2364
feb	1	29173
march	1	91446
april	1	11427
may	1	105492
june	1	13193
july	1	2926
aug	1	880
sept	1	4405
oct	1	281
nov	1	24723

Unusual Observations

Obs.	trend	milkprod	Fit	Stdev.Fit	Residual	St.Resid
3	3	640.000	654.730	2.246	-14.730	-2.04R
26	26	618.000	591.038	2.135	26.962	3.72R
27	27	688.000	709.898	2.283	-21.898	-3.04R
74	74	696.000	679.200	2.022	16.800	2.31R
109	109	804.000	777.236	2.118	26.764	3.69R
135	135	883.000	868.126	2.156	14.874	2.05R
158	158	782.000	799.112	2.469	-17.112	-2.40R

R denotes an obs. with a large st. resid.

F I G U R E **6.40**

SAS Regression Output for Regression of MILKPROD on TREND, LAGMILK, and Seasonal Indicators for Milk Production Exercise

Dependent Variable: MILKPROD

Analysis of Variance

Source	DF	Sum of Squares	Mean Square	F Value	Prob>F
Model	13	1708077.4267	131390.57129	2299.665	0.0001
Error	153	8741.60321	57.13466		
C Total	166	1716819.0299			

Root MSE	7.55875	R-square	0.9949	
Dep Mean	755.70060	Adj R-sq	0.9945	
C.V.	1.00023			

Parameter Estimates

Variable	DF	Parameter Estimate	Standard Error	T for H0: Parameter=0	Prob > |T|
INTERCEP	1	98.276875	19.99022285	4.916	0.0001
TREND	1	0.192068	0.06635307	2.895	0.0044
LAGMILK	1	0.886994	0.03769342	23.532	0.0001
JAN	1	-8.109176	3.24017218	-2.503	0.0134
FEB	1	-69.264852	3.68838286	-18.779	0.0001
MAR	1	58.273080	2.97991997	19.555	0.0001
APRIL	1	-8.915098	5.18530590	-1.719	0.0876
MAY	1	38.908357	5.66023660	6.874	0.0001
JUNE	1	-43.553785	7.73182794	-5.633	0.0001
JULY	1	-68.185218	6.74954320	-10.102	0.0001
AUG	1	-66.309630	5.11091948	-12.974	0.0001
SEPT	1	-71.372214	3.89220232	-18.337	0.0001
OCT	1	-30.109942	3.03968783	-9.906	0.0001
NOV	1	-64.212766	3.08691704	-20.802	0.0001

These data are available on the data disk for further analysis. In MINITAB, they can be read using

```
READ 'MILK6' C1
```

where C1 is milk production.

In SAS, the data can be read from the file MILK6.DAT using

```
INPUT MILKPROD;
```

F I G U R E **6.41**

MINITAB Regression Output for Regression of MILKPROD on TREND and LAGMILK for
Milk Production Exercise

```
The regression equation is
milkprod = 173 + 0.459 trend + 0.721 lagmilk

167 cases used 1 cases contain missing values

Predictor        Coef       Stdev     t-ratio        p
Constant        173.01       33.77        5.12    0.000
trend           0.4589      0.1149        3.99    0.000
lagmilk        0.72089     0.05433       13.27    0.000

s = 42.42       R-sq = 82.8%     R-sq(adj) = 82.6%

Analysis of Variance

SOURCE          DF          SS          MS        F        p
Regression       2     1421767      710884   395.13    0.000
Error          164      295052        1799
Total          166     1716819

SOURCE          DF      SEQ SS
trend            1     1104988
lagmilk          1      316779

Unusual Observations
Obs.   trend  milkprod       Fit  Stdev.Fit   Residual   St.Resid
111     111    860.00    768.94       4.39      91.06      2.16R
113     113    942.00    857.81       5.61      84.19      2.00R
123     123    890.00    805.45       4.32      84.55      2.00R
135     135    883.00    792.21       5.95      90.79      2.16R
147     147    889.00    801.32       6.95      87.68      2.10R

R denotes an obs. with a large st. resid.
```

F I G U R E 6.42

SAS Regression Output for Regression of MILKPROD on TREND and LAGMILK for Milk Production Exercise

Dependent Variable: MILKPROD

Analysis of Variance

Source	DF	Sum of Squares	Mean Square	F Value	Prob>F
Model	2	1421767.315	710883.65748	395.134	0.0001
Error	164	295051.71498	1799.09582		
C Total	166	1716819.0299			

Root MSE	42.41575	R-square	0.8281	
Dep Mean	755.70060	Adj R-sq	0.8260	
C.V.	5.61277			

Parameter Estimates

Variable	DF	Parameter Estimate	Standard Error	T for H0: Parameter=0	Prob > |T|
INTERCEP	1	173.013874	33.76541787	5.124	0.0001
TREND	1	0.458869	0.11491939	3.993	0.0001
LAGMILK	1	0.720893	0.05432749	13.269	0.0001

6.4
Using the Computer

6.4.1 MINITAB

Creating and Using Indicator Variables

(CALC: MAKE INDICATOR VARIABLES)

Indicator variables have values of either 0 or 1. Obviously, one way to create an indicator variable (or variables) is simply to type it into a data set. The INDICATOR command in MINITAB can be useful in creating indicator variables more quickly in some cases.

Consider the data in Table 6.2 for the Meddicorp example. The variable REGION was typed into the original data set. This variable numbers the three regions as 1, 2, or 3. It can be used to create the indicator variables for the three regions after they are defined as follows:

SOUTH = 1 whenever REGION is 1 and 0 otherwise

WEST = 1 whenever REGION is 2 and 0 otherwise

MIDWEST = 1 whenever REGION is 3 and 0 otherwise

The following INDICATOR command creates these three variables:

```
INDICATOR C6 PUT IN C7,C8,C9
```

where C6 is the variable REGION and C7, C8, and C9 will contain the three indicator variables defined as SOUTH, WEST, and MIDWEST, respectively. After creating the three indicator variables, any two of them can be used on the REGR command.

Creating and Using Interaction Variables

Interaction variables are created by multiplying one variable by another. In MINITAB, multiplication is performed using the LET command.

For example, the following command creates the interaction variable used in Exercise 3. In this exercise, C2 is EDUCAT, C3 is EXPER, and the interaction variable is created in C8 and named EDUCEXPR.

```
LET C8=C2*C3
NAME C3 'EDUCEXPR'
```

The interaction variable, EDUCEXPR, can then be used in the REGR, PLOT, or other commands just like other variables.

In the Windows version of MINITAB, these operations can be performed by using the CALC menu, MATHEMATICAL EXPRESSIONS subheading.

Creating and Using Seasonal Indicators for Time-Series Regression

Seasonal indicators are simply indicator variables so their creation is much like that of indicator variables, discussed previously. There are some shortcuts that can be helpful in efficiently creating certain seasonal indicators, however.

For quarterly data, the following command sequence can be useful:

```
SET IN C20
K(1:4)
END
INDICATOR C20, PUT IN C21-C24
```

The SET command creates a variable in C20 that contains the numbers 1 through 12 repeated K times. If K is set to be the number of years in the data set, then C20 will number each observation with the number of the month in which it occurred. The INDICATOR command is then used to create four indicators, one for each quarter. C21 will be equal to 1 whenever C20 is equal to 1 (first quarter) and equal to 0 otherwise. C22 will be equal to 1 whenever C20 is equal to 2 (second quarter) and equal to 0 otherwise, and so on. This creates the four quarterly indicators. Three of these four are then included in the regression.

For monthly data, the following command sequence can be useful:

```
SET IN C20
K(1:12)
END
INDICATOR C20, PUT IN C21-C32
```

The SET command creates a variable in C20 that contains the numbers 1 through 12 repeated K times. If K is set to be the number of years in the data set, then C20 will number each observation with the number of the month in which it occurred. The INDICATOR command is then used to create twelve indicators, one for each month. C21 will be equal to 1 whenever C20 is equal to 1 (first month) and equal to 0 otherwise. C22 will be equal to 1 whenever C20 is equal to 2 (second month) and equal to 0 otherwise, and so on. This creates the twelve monthly indicators. Eleven of these twelve are then included in the regression.

In the Windows version of MINITAB, create any patterned data using CALC: SET PATTERNED DATA. Then create the seasonal dummies using CALC: MAKE INDICATOR VARIABLES.

6.4.2 SAS

Creating and Using Indicator Variables

Indicator variables have values of either 0 or 1. Obviously, one way to create an indicator variable (or variables) is simply to type it into a data set. There are certain shortcuts in SAS that may be helpful in creating indicator variables more efficiently in some cases.

Consider the data in Table 6.2 for the Meddicorp example. The variable REGION was typed into the original data set. This variable numbers the three regions as 1, 2, or 3. It can be used to create the indicator variables for the three regions after they are defined as follows:

SOUTH = 1 whenever REGION is 1 and 0 otherwise

WEST = 1 whenever REGION is 2 and 0 otherwise

MIDWEST = 1 whenever REGION is 3 and 0 otherwise

The three indicators can be created during the INPUT phase in SAS as follows:

```
INPUT SALES ADV BONUS REGION;
    IF REGION=1 THEN SOUTH=1;
    ELSE SOUTH=0;
    IF REGION=2 THEN WEST=1;
    ELSE WEST=0;
    IF REGION=3 THEN MIDWEST=1;
    ELSE MIDWEST=0.
```

After creating the three indicator variables, any two of them can be used in PROC REG. For example,

```
PROC REG;
  MODEL SALES=ADV BONUS SOUTH WEST;
```

will generate the output in Figure 6.10.

Creating and Using Interaction Variables

Interaction variables are created by multiplying one variable by another. In SAS, such variable transformations are performed during the data input phase.

For example, the following commands create the interaction variable used in Exercise 3:

```
INPUT SALARY EDUCAT EXPER MONTHS MALES;
EDUCEXPR=EDUCAT*EXPER;
```

The interaction variable, EDUCEXPR, can then be used in PROC REG, PROC PLOT, and so on, just like other variables.

Creating and Using Seasonal Indicators for Time-Series Regression

Seasonal indicators are simply indicator variables so their creation is much like that of indicator variables, discussed previously. The only difference would be that, instead of the variable representing REGION in the example given there, a variable numbering the quarters or the months in the seasonal cycle would be needed.

For quarterly data, a variable numbering the quarters 1, 2, 3, or 4 would be used with the following command sequence in the input phase. Call the variable that numbers the quarters QUARTER and proceed as follows:

```
IF QUARTER=1 THEN Q1=1;
ELSE Q1=0;
IF QUARTER=2 THEN Q2=1;
ELSE Q2=0;
IF QUARTER=3 THEN Q3=1;
ELSE Q3=0;
IF QUARTER=4 THEN Q4=1;
ELSE Q4=0;
```

Q1, Q2, Q3, and Q4 are the four quarterly indicator variables. Three of these four can then be used in PROC REG.

For monthly data, a variable that numbers each of the months as 1, 2, ..., 12 would be needed. The same type of sequence used for quarterly indicators could then be used to create twelve monthly indicators.

Additional Exercises

6   **Absenteeism**   In Exercise 15 in Chapter 4, data on 77 employees of the ABX Company were introduced. The dependent variable was absenteeism. The possible explanatory variables were defined in Table 4.16 and shown in Table 4.17.

In this exercise use the following explanatory variables:

COMPLX = job complexity

SENINV = 1/SENIOR = the reciprocal of the seniority variable

Indicator variables created from the variable SATIS. These variables are as follows:

$FS1$ = 1 if SATIS = 1 (very dissatisfied)
   = 0 otherwise

$FS2$ = 1 if SATIS = 2 (somewhat dissatisfied)
   = 0 otherwise

$FS3$ = 1 if SATIS = 3 (neither satisfied nor dissatisfied)
   = 0 otherwise

$FS4$ = 1 if SATIS = 4 (somewhat satisfied)
   = 0 otherwise

$FS5$ = 1 if SATIS = 5 (very satisfied)
   = 0 otherwise

Five dummy variables are created to represent all five supervisor satisfaction categories. Recall that only four need to be used in the regression. Run the regression with the explanatory variables shown here. Answer the following questions:

a   Is there a difference in average absenteeism for employees in different supervisor satisfaction groups? Perform a hypothesis test to answer this question. State the hypotheses to be tested, the decision rule, the test statistic, and your decision. Use a 5% level of significance.

b   Using the model chosen in (a) (and keeping the variables COMPLX and SENINV in the model), what would be your estimate of average absenteeism rate for all employees with COMPLX = 60 and SENIOR = 30 who were very dissatisfied with their supervisor? What if they were very satisfied with their supervisor but COMPLX and SENIOR were the same values?

c   How do you account for the differences in the estimates in (b)?

d How could this equation be used to help identify employees who might be prone to absenteeism?

These data are available on the data disk and can be read in MINITAB using

READ 'ABSENT6' C1-C4

where C1 is ABSENT, C2 is COMPLX, C3 is SENIOR, and C4 is SATIS.
In SAS, the data can be read from the file ABSENT6.DAT using

INPUT ABSENT COMPLX SENIOR SATIS;

7 **Work-Order Closing** Management at the TCU Physical Plant Department is interested in reducing the average time to completion of routine work orders. The time to completion is defined as the difference between the date of receipt of a work order and the date closing information is entered. The number of labor hours charged to each work order and the cost of materials are two variables believed to be related to the time to closing of the work order. Management wants to know if there is any difference in the time to completion of work orders, on average, for different types of buildings. Buildings are classified into four types on the TCU campus: residence halls, athletic, academic, and administrative. In answering the question, take into account the possible effect of labor hours charged and materials cost. The data for a random sample of 72 work orders (chosen from a population of 11,720) are shown in Table 6.6. The variables are labeled as follows:

$y = $ DAYS $ = $ number of days to complete each work order

$x_1 = $ HOURS $ = $ number of hours of labor charged to each work order

$x_2 = $ MATERIAL $ = $ cost of materials charged to each work order

$x_3 = $ BUILDING $ = $ 1 for residence halls

2 for athletic buildings

3 for academic buildings

4 for administrative buildings

These data are available on the data disk and can be read in MINITAB using

READ 'WORKORD6' C1-C4

where C1 is DAYS, C2 is HOURS, C3 is MATERIAL, and C4 is BUILDING.
In SAS, the data can be read from the file WORKORD6.DAT using

INPUT DAYS HOURS MATERIAL BUILDING;

8 **Beer Production** Table 6.7 shows monthly U.S. beer production in millions of barrels for January 1982 through December 1991.[2] Develop an extrapolative model for these data and use it to examine whether there is seasonal variation in beer production and whether beer production seems to be increasing, decreasing, or staying fairly constant over this time period. Use the model you select as best for beer production to forecast average monthly production for each month in 1992. Find the 1992 data and compare your forecasts to the actual data. How did your model do?

[2]Data were obtained from *Business Statistics 1963–91* and *Survey of Current Business*.

T A B L E **6.6**

Data for Work-Order Closing Exercise

DAYS	HOURS	MATERIAL	BUILDING	DAYS	HOURS	MATERIAL	BUILDING
7	0.50	0	1	3	0.50	0	1
9	6.50	117	3	5	1.00	28	3
3	1.00	6	1	25	0.50	1350	2
4	0.50	0	1	1	0.50	4	1
1	1.00	4	1	30	0.50	3	1
1	1.50	27	1	1	0.75	13	1
1	0.50	0	3	5	0.50	0	3
1	0.25	0	3	7	0.25	0	3
13	0.50	87	4	10	0.50	0	3
19	30.00	131	3	1	1.00	139	4
3	0.25	0	3	2	0.25	0	1
6	7.00	18	4	1	2.00	14	3
0	0.50	0	1	50	11.00	33	3
1	0.25	0	1	4	0.50	4	4
2	0.50	0	4	3	0.50	0	1
2	1.00	6	1	5	1.00	0	3
1	3.50	6	1	6	0.25	0	1
1	0.50	0	1	1	0.45	4	1
1	0.50	0	3	21	0.50	0	1
1	0.25	0	1	5	0.50	0	1
1	0.25	10	4	8	2.00	0	3
29	2.75	4	1	12	1.00	0	1
7	1.00	242	4	3	0.50	0	1
5	0.25	2	4	2	0.25	44	1
3	2.50	93	1	1	0.25	2	4
13	0.50	1	1	4	0.50	8	3
1	0.50	8	1	3	0.75	6	1
4	0.25	0	2	1	0.50	0	2
3	0.50	0	1	1	0.50	0	4
12	0.25	2	1	1	0.50	0	1
14	2.00	4	1	1	0.50	4	1
4	4.00	0	1	3	1.00	10	3
4	1.00	2	1	1	0.50	0	1
29	2.00	25	1	2	1.00	13	3
1	0.50	0	1	17	1.50	0	3
3	0.50	0	1	3	0.50	1	3

T A B L E **6.7**

Data for Beer Production Exercise

Mo/Yr	Barrels (million)	Mo/Yr	Barrels (million)
1/82	15.19	1/85	15.50
2/82	15.00	2/85	14.46
3/82	17.65	3/85	16.76
4/82	17.62	4/85	17.97
5/82	18.22	5/85	18.86
6/82	18.19	6/85	18.23
7/82	17.17	7/85	18.59
8/82	19.50	8/85	17.71
9/82	15.64	9/85	14.54
10/82	15.07	10/85	14.36
11/82	13.65	11/85	13.12
12/82	13.31	12/85	13.13
1/83	14.77	1/86	15.71
2/83	14.56	2/86	15.21
3/83	16.78	3/86	16.50
4/83	15.54	4/86	17.99
5/83	18.17	5/86	18.67
6/83	18.47	6/86	18.65
7/83	18.50	7/86	18.33
8/83	18.27	8/86	17.06
9/83	15.71	9/86	15.26
10/83	15.30	10/86	15.62
11/83	13.62	11/86	13.53
12/83	12.46	12/86	13.97
1/84	14.15	1/87	15.60
2/84	14.75	2/87	15.63
3/84	17.72	3/87	17.66
4/84	16.81	4/87	17.42
5/84	18.59	5/87	17.44
6/84	18.47	6/87	18.59
7/84	18.64	7/87	18.09
8/84	17.59	8/87	16.81
9/84	14.58	9/87	15.82
10/84	15.14	10/87	15.50
11/84	13.06	11/87	13.18
12/84	12.89	12/87	13.69

These data are available on the data disk. In MINITAB, they can be read using

```
READ 'BEER6' C1
```

where C1 is BEERPROD.

T A B L E **6.7** *(Cont.)*
Data for Beer Production Exercise

Mo/Yr	Barrels (million)	Mo/Yr	Barrels (million)
1/88	15.80	1/90	16.46
2/88	15.85	2/90	15.74
3/88	17.12	3/90	17.97
4/88	17.73	4/90	17.48
5/88	18.31	5/90	18.10
6/88	18.58	6/90	18.58
7/88	18.17	7/90	18.25
8/88	17.72	8/90	18.96
9/88	15.78	9/90	16.08
10/88	15.61	10/90	16.62
11/88	14.02	11/90	15.44
12/88	13.32	12/90	13.97
1/89	15.88	1/91	16.27
2/89	15.29	2/91	15.17
3/89	17.57	3/91	16.08
4/89	17.30	4/91	17.23
5/89	18.41	5/91	18.90
6/89	18.82	6/91	19.16
7/89	18.28	7/91	19.88
8/89	18.88	8/91	18.63
9/89	15.28	9/91	16.11
10/89	15.82	10/91	16.65
11/89	14.78	11/91	14.47
12/89	13.45	12/91	13.64

In SAS, the data can be read from the file BEER6.DAT using

```
INPUT BEERPROD;
```

9 **Monthly Temperatures** Table 6.8 shows the average monthly temperatures from January 1978 to December 1993 for the Dallas–Fort Worth, Texas, area.[3] Develop an extrapolative model for these data and use the model to forecast average monthly temperatures for each month in 1994.

These data are available on the data disk. In MINITAB, they can be read using

```
READ 'TEMPDFW6' C1
```

where C1 is TEMP.

In SAS, the data can be read from the file TEMPDFW6.DAT using

```
INPUT TEMP;
```

[3]Data were obtained from *Local Climatological Data, Annual Summary with Comparative Data, Dallas–Ft. Worth TX*, published by the National Oceanic and Atmospheric Administration.

T A B L E **6.8**

Average Monthly Temperatures for Dallas–Ft. Worth

Mo/Yr	Temp (°F)	Mo/Yr	Temp (°F)	Mo/Yr	Temp (°F)	Mo/Yr	Temp (°F)
1/78	33.8	1/81	44.6	1/84	39.3	1/87	44.5
2/78	36.7	2/81	48.9	2/84	50.9	2/87	50.8
3/78	54.1	3/81	55.7	3/84	56.3	3/87	53.9
4/78	67.1	4/81	69.2	4/84	63.7	4/87	65.0
5/78	73.1	5/81	70.5	5/84	73.7	5/87	75.1
6/78	82.3	6/81	80.3	6/84	82.5	6/87	79.6
7/78	88.4	7/81	85.9	7/84	85.5	7/87	83.4
8/78	84.6	8/81	83.4	8/84	85.8	8/87	86.5
9/78	80.2	9/81	76.2	9/84	76.1	9/87	77.1
10/78	68.9	10/81	66.1	10/84	67.0	10/87	66.5
11/78	57.7	11/81	57.5	11/84	54.6	11/87	55.7
12/78	46.1	12/81	47.3	12/84	52.6	12/87	47.3
1/79	35.4	1/82	44.6	1/85	37.8	1/88	42.2
2/79	42.2	2/82	44.5	2/85	45.0	2/88	47.1
3/79	56.7	3/82	59.8	3/85	60.8	3/88	56.0
4/79	64.4	4/82	62.5	4/85	67.2	4/88	64.5
5/79	69.7	5/82	72.5	5/85	74.0	5/88	72.8
6/79	81.0	6/82	79.2	6/85	80.2	6/88	80.4
7/79	84.5	7/82	84.6	7/85	84.4	7/88	85.3
8/79	82.5	8/82	86.7	8/85	87.6	8/88	87.9
9/79	77.0	9/82	78.1	9/85	77.7	9/88	79.2
10/79	70.8	10/82	67.0	10/85	67.6	10/88	65.7
11/79	52.9	11/82	55.6	11/85	56.3	11/88	58.1
12/79	49.4	12/82	49.2	12/85	42.3	12/88	49.1
1/80	45.5	1/83	43.4	1/86	48.8	1/89	50.0
2/80	46.6	2/83	48.5	2/86	51.2	2/89	42.2
3/80	54.2	3/83	54.5	3/86	60.2	3/89	56.7
4/80	63.1	4/83	60.6	4/86	67.2	4/89	66.4
5/80	75.0	5/83	69.5	5/86	71.5	5/89	74.3
6/80	87.0	6/83	77.3	6/86	80.8	6/89	77.9
7/80	92.0	7/83	83.6	7/86	86.4	7/89	82.8
8/80	88.5	8/83	84.9	8/86	83.4	8/89	82.3
9/80	80.3	9/83	77.1	9/86	80.2	9/89	74.7
10/80	65.4	10/83	67.8	10/86	65.7	10/89	69.0
11/80	54.9	11/83	57.3	11/86	52.4	11/89	58.2
12/80	49.4	12/83	34.8	12/86	46.1	12/89	39.0

T A B L E **6.8** (*Cont.*)

Average Monthly Temperatures for Dallas–Ft. Worth

Mo/Yr	Temp (°F)	Mo/Yr	Temp (°F)
1/90	51.8	1/92	46.9
2/90	53.9	2/92	54.4
3/90	57.7	3/92	59.1
4/90	64.0	4/92	66.0
5/90	73.4	5/92	71.1
6/90	84.0	6/92	79.4
7/90	82.5	7/92	84.3
8/90	84.6	8/92	80.2
9/90	80.0	9/92	77.7
10/90	66.4	10/92	69.5
11/90	59.8	11/92	52.7
12/90	44.0	12/92	49.9
1/91	42.8	1/93	45.1
2/91	53.7	2/93	49.0
3/91	59.8	3/93	56.1
4/91	67.4	4/93	63.3
5/91	75.4	5/93	71.9
6/91	81.0	6/93	81.7
7/91	85.0	7/93	87.3
8/91	82.5	8/93	87.5
9/91	75.2	9/93	78.2
10/91	68.1	10/93	63.8
11/91	51.7	11/93	51.6
12/91	50.3	12/93	49.5

10 **BigTex Services** BigTex Services is undergoing scrutiny for a possible wage discrimination suit. As consulting statistician hired by the corporate lawyer you are to examine data on BigTex employees to further investigate the charges. The data are shown in Table 6.9 and are as follows:

monthly salary for each employee (SALARY)

years with the company (YEARS)

position with the company (POSITION) coded as

1 = manual labor

2 = secretary

3 = lab technician

4 = chemist

5 = management

T A B L E **6.9**

Data for BigTex Services Exercise

SALARY	YEARS	POSITION	EDUCAT	GENDER
1720	6.0	3	2	0
2400	4.9	1	1	1
1600	4.2	2	2	0
2900	3.7	4	3	0
1200	1.6	3	1	0
1000	0.3	3	1	0
2900	1.0	4	3	1
2400	1.8	4	3	1
1900	6.8	3	1	0
2200	1.2	4	3	1
1000	0.3	3	1	0
900	0.2	3	1	0
1250	0.6	3	1	0
950	0.5	3	1	0
2000	0.7	4	3	1
2000	1.9	4	3	1
1900	1.6	1	1	1
1000	1.4	3	1	0
1000	1.4	3	1	0
2800	3.4	4	3	0
2900	3.5	4	3	1
1550	3.1	3	1	0
1550	3.0	2	1	0
2200	2.5	4	3	1
1650	2.2	1	1	1
2200	2.0	4	3	1
900	0.5	3	1	0
1000	0.5	3	2	0
1220	2.0	3	1	0
2100	0.5	4	3	1
900	0.5	3	1	0
900	0.2	3	1	0
2000	0.5	4	3	1
2330	0.6	4	3	1
2400	0.3	4	3	1
900	1.0	1	1	1
1069	0.5	3	1	0
1400	0.5	1	1	1
1650	1.0	1	1	1
1200	0.3	1	1	1

T A B L E **6.9** (*Cont.*)

Data for BigTex Services Exercise

SALARY	YEARS	POSITION	EDUCAT	GENDER
3500	13.5	5	4	1
1750	11.0	5	3	0
4000	6.4	5	3	1
1800	7.2	2	1	0
4000	6.1	5	3	1
4600	5.8	5	4	1
1350	5.1	4	3	1

amount of education completed (EDUCAT) coded as

1 = high school degree

2 = some college

3 = college degree

4 = graduate degree

gender (GENDER) coded as

0 = female

1 = male

What would you conclude from the data? Should BigTex Services be worried about possible wage discrimination charges? Why or why not?

These data are available on the data disk. In MINITAB, they can be read using

```
READ 'BIGTEX6' C1-C5
```

where C1 is SALARY, C2 is YEARS, C3 is POSITION, C4 is EDUCAT, and C5 is GENDER.

In SAS, the data can be read from the file BIGTEX6.DAT using

```
INPUT SALARY YEARS POSITION EDUCAT GENDER;
```

7

Variable Selection

7.1
Introduction to Variable Selection

One of the primary tasks discussed in this text has been choosing which variables to include in the regression equation. Several hypothesis tests have been suggested to aid this task. The F test for overall fit of the regression, the partial F test, and the t test are all designed to help decide whether certain variables should be included in the regression.

Several additional procedures, usually called *variable selection techniques*, also can be used to help choose which variables are important. These procedures will be discussed in this chapter.

The importance of choosing the correct variables is highlighted by examining what happens when either (1) important variables are omitted from the regression equation or (2) unimportant variables are included in the equation.

If an important variable is omitted from the regression, the effect of this variable will not be taken into account. The estimates of the other regression coefficients will be biased (either systematically too high or too low). Forecasts generated by the regression also will be biased.

If an unimportant variable is included in the regression equation, the standard errors of the coefficients and forecasts will be inflated. Thus, forecasts and coefficient estimates will be more variable than they would be with a proper choice of variables. The larger standard errors also may make results from inferences less dependable.

Whether identifying important variables to be included or unimportant variables to be deleted, variable choice is an important aspect of regression analysis. As a result, considerable work has been done in developing methods to help choose the "best" group of variables to include in the regression equation. A word of caution is in order before these techniques are introduced, however. None of these methods is guaranteed to automatically pick the "best" of all regression models. Otherwise, this text could have started with these procedures and stopped after one chapter.

Any regression analysis requires considerable input from the researcher who is performing the analysis. This person must define the problem to be solved, determine what variables might be useful in the regression equation, obtain data on these variables, and set up the data to be analyzed in a data file. During the analysis itself, the researcher must check the regression assumptions to ensure that none have been violated. The automatic methods will not do that. For example, if $\ln(y)$ rather than y is the appropriate dependent variable for analysis, the variable selection procedures will not be able to determine this. The functional form of the relationship must be determined separately from the use of these procedures. In fact, any correction for a violation of one of the assumptions of regression must be determined by the researcher. These methods also cannot suggest explanatory variables to add to the regression unless they have been initially determined by the researcher and included in the data set. Finally, none of these automatic procedures has the ability to use the researcher's knowledge of the business or economic situation being analyzed. This knowledge should be used to help in establishing what form the regression model will take, what variables should be included, and so on.

The variable selection techniques discussed here are tools to aid the researcher in sifting through several explanatory variables to determine which one(s) should be included in the regression equation. With the knowledge that the techniques cannot be reliably applied without the judgement of the person researching the problem, the following variable selection procedures will be discussed in this chapter:

1   all possible regressions (along with several criteria to choose which is the best regression)

2   backward elimination

3   forward selection

4   stepwise regression

5   maximum R^2 improvement

7.2
All Possible Regressions

One of the possible variable selection techniques suggested to aid in choosing the best regression model is called "all possible regressions." As the name suggests, the procedure is designed to run all possible regressions between the dependent variable and all possible subsets of explanatory variables. For example, if the three possible explanatory variables identified for consideration in the problem are denoted x_1, x_2, and x_3, then a total of eight possible regressions may be best. The possible regressions include the following subsets of the three explanatory variables:

1   no variables

2   x_1

3   x_2

4 x_3

5 x_1 and x_2

6 x_1 and x_3

7 x_2 and x_3

8 all three variables

The all-possible regressions procedure will evaluate each regression and print out summary statistics to aid in choosing which of the eight possibilities is best. The choice of the criterion to use and the final choice of a model then is up to the researcher.

Two commonly used criteria to help in choosing between the alternative regressions are:

1 R^2 (adjusted or unadjusted, as the researcher prefers)

2 C_p

The coefficient of determination, R^2, has been discussed extensively in previous chapters, but the statistic C_p has not. C_p measures the total mean square error of the fitted values of the regression. The total mean square error involves two components, one resulting from random error and one resulting from bias. When there is no bias in the estimated regression model, the expected value of C_p will be equal to p, which, in the notation of this text, is equal to $K + 1$, the number of coefficients to be estimated. When evaluating which regression is best, it is recommended that regressions with small C_p values and those with values near $K + 1$ be considered. If the value of C_p is large, then the mean square error of the fitted values is large, indicating either a poor fit or substantial bias in the fit or both. If the value of C_p is much greater than $K + 1$, then there is a large bias component in the regression, usually indicating omission of an important variable.

The formula for computing C_p is

$$C_p = \frac{SSE_p}{MSE_F} - (n - 2p),$$

where SSE_p is the error sum of squares for the regression with p coefficients to be estimated, and MSE_F is the mean square error for the model with all possible explanatory variables included.

Although the C_p measure is highly recommended as a useful criterion in choosing between alternative regressions, keep in mind that the bias is measured with respect to the total group of variables provided by the researcher. This criteria cannot determine when the researcher has forgotten about some variable not included in the total group. In other words, the input of the researcher is still important. The all-possible regressions procedure will be illustrated in the following example.

E X A M P L E *7.1* **Meddicorp Revisited**

Consider again Example 4.1, the study of sales in the Meddicorp Company. The complete data set for this example is shown in Table 7.1, with descriptions of each variable as follows:

T A B L E **7.1**

Data for Meddicorp Example

Territory	SALES	ADV	BONUS	MKTSHR	COMPET	REGION
1	963.50	374.27	230.98	33.	202.22	1
2	893.00	408.50	236.28	29.	252.77	1
3	1057.25	414.31	271.57	34.	293.22	1
4	1183.25	448.42	291.20	24.	202.22	2
5	1419.50	517.88	282.17	32.	303.33	3
6	1547.75	637.60	321.16	29.	353.88	3
7	1580.00	635.72	294.32	28.	374.11	3
8	1071.50	446.86	305.69	31.	404.44	1
9	1078.25	489.59	238.41	20.	394.33	1
10	1122.50	500.56	271.38	30.	303.33	2
11	1304.75	484.18	332.64	25.	333.66	3
12	1552.25	618.07	261.80	34.	353.88	3
13	1040.00	453.39	235.63	42.	262.88	1
14	1045.25	440.86	249.68	28.	333.66	2
15	1102.25	487.79	232.99	28.	232.55	2
16	1225.25	537.67	272.20	30.	273.00	2
17	1508.00	612.21	266.64	29.	323.55	3
18	1564.25	601.46	277.44	32.	404.44	3
19	1634.75	585.10	312.35	36.	283.11	3
20	1159.25	524.56	292.87	34.	222.44	1
21	1202.75	535.17	268.27	31.	283.11	2
22	1294.25	486.03	309.85	32.	242.66	2
23	1467.50	540.17	291.03	28.	333.66	3
24	1583.75	583.85	289.29	27.	313.44	3
25	1124.75	499.15	272.55	26.	374.11	2

y, Meddicorp's sales (in thousands of dollars) in each territory for 1994 (SALES)

x_1, the amount (in hundreds of dollars) that Meddicorp spent on advertising in each territory in 1994 (ADV)

x_2, the total amount of bonuses paid (in hundreds of dollars) in each territory in 1994 (BONUS)

x_3, the market share currently held by Meddicorp in each territory (MKTSHR)

x_4, the largest competitor's sales (in thousands of dollars) in each territory (COMPET)

x_5, a variable coded to indicate the region in which each territory is located: 1 = SOUTH, 2 = WEST, and 3 = MIDWEST (REGION)

The REGION variable was transformed to a set of three possible indicator variables—SOUTH, WEST, and MIDWEST—in Chapter 6. The interpretation of the coefficients of these variables was preferred to the single REGION variable. Recall from Chapter 6, however, that indicator variables should be treated as a group rather than individually. The all-possible regressions technique would combine each indicator variable with each other possible combination

F I G U R E 7.1

SAS All-Possible Regression Summary Output

N = 25   Regression Models for Dependent Variable: SALES

Number in Model	R-square	C(p)	Variables in Model
1	0.81059186	5.90461	ADV
1	0.32284527	75.18692	BONUS
1	0.14217889	100.84980	COMPET
1	0.00053415	120.96983	MKTSHR
2	0.85493977	1.60518	ADV BONUS
2	0.81230552	7.66119	ADV MKTSHR
2	0.81174811	7.74037	ADV COMPET
2	0.38729555	68.03203	BONUS COMPET
2	0.32796886	76.45913	BONUS MKTSHR
2	0.16100040	100.17629	MKTSHR COMPET
3	0.85845798	3.10544	ADV BONUS MKTSHR
3	0.85689789	3.32704	ADV BONUS COMPET
3	0.81279843	9.59118	ADV MKTSHR COMPET
3	0.40902300	66.94574	BONUS MKTSHR COMPET
4	0.85920024	5.00000	ADV BONUS MKTSHR COMPET

of variables. To keep the indicator variables grouped together, they will not be included as possible explanatory variables in the all-possible regressions procedure. Instead, they will be examined later as a group (this also greatly reduces the amount of computation necessary and simplifies this example).

The SAS all-possible regressions output is shown in Figure 7.1. The regressions in the output have been divided into sets: first, all possible simple regressions are run; second, all regressions with two explanatory variables are shown; and so on. Figure 7.2 provides a useful plot to help determine which of the $2^4 = 16$ possible regressions is best according to the C_p criterion. (Note: Only 15 regressions are actually summarized. The missing one is the "regression" with no variables included, which would be chosen as best only if none of the possible explanatory variables were linearly related to the dependent variable.) In Figure 7.2, the C_p value has been plotted on the vertical axis and the value p (or $K + 1$) on the horizontal axis. Recall that small values of C_p and values close to p are of interest in choosing good sets of explanatory variables. The smallest C_p value in the plot is for a two-variable regression. Referring to Figure 7.1, this is the regression with ADV and BONUS as explanatory variables; it has a C_p value of approximately 1.6. The R^2 for the regression is 85.5%.

As competing models, for example, there are two three-variable models denoted by the "B" for $p = 4$. The summary models for these measures are repeated here:

Variables	C_p	R^2
1. ADV BONUS COMPET	3.3	85.7
2. ADV BONUS MKTSHR	3.1	85.8

F I G U R E 7.2

C_p Plot

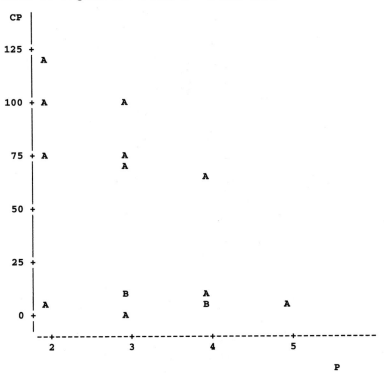

Plot of CP*P. Legend: A = 1 obs, B = 2 obs, etc.

Note that only modest increases in R^2 are achieved in these models. Although SAS does not print out the adjusted R^2, it is easily calculated. The adjusted R^2's for the four models examined so far are

Variables	R^2_{ADJ}
1. ADV BONUS	84.2
2. ADV BONUS COMPET	83.7
3. ADV BONUS MKTSHR	83.8

R^2_{ADJ} was computed using the formula from Chapter 4:

$$R^2_{\text{ADJ}} = 1 + \left(\frac{n-1}{n-K-1} \right) (R^2 - 1)$$

As can be seen, the adjusted R^2 is highest for the two-variable model, again supporting this model as best. Other models with small C_p values could be examined, but there appears to be little bias in the two-variable model with ADV and BONUS (the small deviation from the $C_p = p$ line probably results from random variation), and it has the smallest C_p value. Therefore, the all-possible regressions procedure suggests using this model.

Note that the number of computations involved in the all-possible regressions technique is very large. Although SAS has no built-in limit on the number of variables that can be included, it is recommended that no more than 14 explanatory variables be used in a single analysis. This is a primary limitation of the all-possible regressions procedure. ∎

7.3
Other Variable Selection Techniques

As noted in the previous section, the all-possible regressions technique becomes computationally unwieldy when the number of possible explanatory variables is large. SAS, for example, suggests at most 14 explanatory variables be included in the list. The techniques examined in this section attempt to cut down on the computational expense while still choosing variables that are important in explaining variation in the dependent variable.

Four procedures will be discussed in this section:

1   backward elimination
2   forward selection
3   stepwise regression
4   maximum R^2 improvement

Again, it should be stressed that none of these procedures is guaranteed to produce the best possible regression equation. The judgement of the researcher as well as careful examination of scatterplots, residual plots, and regression diagnostics is vital in choosing an appropriate model. The stepwise techniques are merely tools to help the researcher sort through a large number of possible explanatory variables. They will help in identifying some important variables but by themselves are not sufficient to produce a good regression model.

7.3.1 Backward Elimination

The backward elimination procedure begins with a regression on all possible explanatory variables. After this regression is run, the explanatory variables will be examined to determine which one has the smallest partial F statistical value. Calling this variable x_k, the following hypothesis test will be performed:

$$
\begin{aligned}
H_0&: \quad \beta_k = 0 \\
H_a&: \quad \beta_k \neq 0
\end{aligned}
$$

The decision rule is:

$$\text{Reject } H_0 \quad \text{if} \quad F > F_c$$
$$\text{Accept } H_0 \quad \text{if} \quad F \leq F_c$$

where F_c represents some critical value chosen as a cutoff for the test. If H_0 is rejected, the coefficient is judged to be nonzero and the variable is considered important in the relationship. Because the partial F statistics for all other coefficients are known to exceed the partial F statistic for β_k, the null hypothesis will be rejected for these coefficients also. The backward elimination procedure will terminate at this point and produce summary statistics of the chosen regression.

On the other hand, if the null hypothesis is accepted, then the variable is deleted from the equation and a new regression is run with one less explanatory variable. The procedure is repeated until the null hypothesis is rejected, at which point the procedure terminates.

In this way, the backward elimination procedure sorts through the list of possible explanatory variables, eliminating those that are of little importance in explaining the variation in y and keeping those that are important. Importance is judged by the size of the partial F statistic for testing H_0: $\beta_k = 0$ relative to some critical value.

Two additional aspects of this procedure to note are

1 Although the test was described as a partial F test, it can just as easily be thought of as a t test. Rather than the partial F statistic, the t statistic would be used and the decision rule would be:

$$\text{Reject } H_0 \quad \text{if} \quad t > t_c \quad \text{or} \quad t < -t_c$$
$$\text{Accept } H_0 \quad \text{if} \quad -t_c \leq t \leq t_c$$

where t_c is the chosen critical value. The t test and the partial F test for a *single* coefficient are equivalent, as was discussed in Chapter 4, as long as the same levels of significance are used for both tests.

2 Another way the test could be performed would be by using p values. Whether the t or F statistic is computed, the p value could be calculated and compared to the decision rule:

$$\text{Reject } H_0 \quad \text{if} \quad p \text{ value } < \alpha$$
$$\text{Accept } H_0 \quad \text{if} \quad p \text{ value } \geq \alpha$$

where α is the chosen level of significance. When using p values the critical value is α, while with the t or F tests it is a value chosen from the t or F tables. The p value form of the test would be a better choice, if available, because the level of significance used to determine whether a variable stays or goes would be the same regardless of the sample size or the number of variables in the equation. When a single t or F critical value is chosen, level of significance will vary depending on the sample size and number of variables.

Example 7.2 will demonstrate the backward elimination procedure as well as the other procedures. First, however, the remaining techniques will be discussed.

7.3.2 Forward Selection

Forward selection starts by examining the list of possible explanatory variables and computing a simple regression for each one. The partial F statistic (or t statistic or the p value) is computed for the slope coefficient in each of these regressions and the variable with the largest F statistic is noted. The hypothesis test

$$H_0: \quad \beta_k = 0$$
$$H_a: \quad \beta_k \neq 0$$

is conducted just as was done in the backward elimination procedure. If the null hypothesis is accepted, then the conclusion is that x_k is of no importance to the regression, and none of the other variables are important because they must have smaller partial F statistics. The forward selection procedure terminates at this point.

If the null hypothesis is rejected, then x_k is judged important and is retained in the regression. Next, each remaining variable is examined to determine which one will have the largest partial F statistic if added to the regression that already contains x_k. The hypothesis test is performed for this variable and the decision is made to either keep the variable in the regression or to discard it. When no more variables are judged to have nonzero coefficients, the procedure terminates and summary statistics are printed.

7.3.3 Stepwise Regression

The stepwise regression procedure combines elements of both backward elimination and forward selection. It begins like forward selection by examining the list of all possible explanatory variables in simple regressions and choosing the one with the largest partial F statistic. The hypothesis test for significance is performed and, if the variable is judged to be important, this variable is added to the model. Each of the remaining variables then is examined. The variable with the largest partial F statistic is chosen, and the hypothesis test for significance is performed on the coefficient of this variable to determine whether it should be added to the model. If the variable is judged important, it is added as in the forward selection procedure.

At this point, however, the stepwise procedure begins to act like the backward elimination procedure. After adding a new variable to the model, the stepwise procedure will retest the coefficients of the previously added variables, deleting these variables if the test judges them to be unnecessary and retaining them otherwise. Because the addition of one variable can result in a change in the partial F statistic associated with another variable, it is possible for the stepwise procedure to allow a variable to enter the equation at one step, delete the variable at a later step, and even to allow the variable to reenter at an even later step.

Once none of the remaining out-of-equation variables test as significant and all of the variables in the equation are judged to be necessary, the stepwise regression procedure terminates.

7.3.4 Maximum R^2 Improvement

Unlike the procedures discussed previously, the maximum R^2 improvement technique does not attempt to identify a single best model. Rather, the procedure tries to find a best model with one variable, two variables, and so on up to the total number of explanatory variables.

The maximum R^2 improvement technique begins by examining all simple regressions and choosing the one with the largest R^2. Then, from the remaining list of variables, the one producing the greatest increase in R^2 is chosen. After this two-variable model is estimated, each of the variables in the model is compared to each of the variables not in the model to determine whether removing one variable and replacing it by another will increase the R^2. This process is called *pair switching*. After comparing all possible switches, the model producing the largest R^2 is chosen. Another variable is added to the model, and the comparing-and-switching process is repeated to find the best three-variable model. This process continues through the list of possible explanatory variables.

7.4
Which Variable Selection Procedure Is Best?

In an attempt to identify the best set of variables for a regression model, several techniques have been examined. This leaves the user to decide which technique is best for his or her purposes. As noted, none of the techniques examined is guaranteed to find the best possible regression model. The judgment of the researcher as well as careful examination of scatterplots, residual plots, and regression diagnostics is vital in choosing an appropriate model. With this caveat in mind, several trade-offs must be considered when choosing the variable selection technique to be used.

The all-possible regressions technique is considered the best because it examines every possible model given a certain list of variables. From the summary statistics such as R^2 and C_p, the researcher can decide which model is best. Note that even with the all-possible regressions technique, a single best model might not be identifiable. There may be several competing models that have nearly identical summary statistics, leaving the researcher with the task of using judgment in choosing between these similar best models. This should not be looked upon as a drawback, however, but as a benefit. With a variety of models from which to choose, the researcher has more freedom to pick the one, say, with the most easily obtainable data, or the simplest interpretation.

The maximum R^2 improvement technique is considered better than forward selection, backward elimination, and stepwise regression and almost as good as the all-possible regressions technique. It is not guaranteed to find the model of each size with the maximum R^2, but it should be successful in identifying models with nearly the highest R^2.

The remaining three procedures are not as highly favored as variable-selection procedures, but they do have one advantage over the all-possible regressions and maximum R^2 improvement procedures: computational cost. The all-possible regressions and maximum R^2 improvement procedures can be very expensive in terms of the computer time needed to produce a solution. If the variable list is a very large one, the researcher may be forced to avoid these procedures in favor of the computationally less expensive forward selection, backward elimination, and stepwise procedures. As will be shown in Example 7.2, the forward selection, backward elimination, and stepwise regression procedures can be useful in identifying important variables, but research also has shown that these procedures can choose unimportant variables for inclusion in the regressions by chance and may miss important variables. Thus, some caution must be exercised in their use. Among the three procedures, the stepwise and backward elimination procedures are very similar. The forward selection procedure is generally considered the least reliable of the techniques.

E X A M P L E *7.2* **Meddicorp Once Again**

Figure 7.3 shows the MINITAB backward elimination output when applied to the Meddicorp data. Again, the indicator variables have not been included in this (or any subsequent) analysis since these variables will be treated as a group rather than individually. The forward selection output is shown in Figure 7.4 and the stepwise output is in Figure 7.5.

The MINITAB outputs summarize the results of each step of these variable selection procedures in a column. For example, in the backward elimination output shown in Figure 7.3, the variables included in the model are shown in the left-hand column. In the column numbered Step 1, a summary of the regression equation at the first step is given. The estimated equation is

$$SALES = -593.5 + 2.51ADV + 191BONUS$$
$$+2.70MKTSHR - 0.12COMPET$$

Below the estimated coefficients in the columns are the t ratios for testing H_0: $\beta_k = 0$. At the bottom of the column are the standard error of the regression and the R^2 (unadjusted). The variable with the smallest partial F statistic (or t ratio) is chosen: COMPET. The hypothesis test

$$H_0: \quad \beta_k = 0$$
$$H_a: \quad \beta_k \neq 0$$

is performed and the null hypothesis is accepted. COMPET is removed from the regression and a new equation is estimated. This regression is summarized in the Step 2 column. This process continues until the null hypothesis H_0: $\beta_k = 0$ is rejected for all remaining variables. The last column (Step 3 in this example) shows the result of the final regression.

The SAS outputs for backward elimination, forward selection, stepwise and the maximum R^2 improvement procedure are shown in Figures 7.6, 7.7, 7.8, and 7.9, respectively.

At each step of the SAS stepwise procedures, a summary table is printed. A general description of the summary table is shown in Figure 7.10. The variable entered (or removed)

F I G U R E 7.3

MINITAB Output for Backward Elimination

```
Stepwise Regression

  F-to-Enter: 100000.00    F-to-Remove:      4.00

  Response is  sales   on  4 predictors, with N =    25

        Step        1        2        3
    Constant    -593.5   -620.6   -516.4

    adv           2.51     2.47     2.47
    T-Ratio       8.00     8.87     8.98

    bonus         1.91     1.90     1.86
    T-Ratio       2.57     2.62     2.59

    mktshr        2.7      3.1
    T-Ratio       0.57     0.72

    compet       -0.12
    T-Ratio      -0.32

    S            93.8     91.8     90.7
    R-Sq        85.92    85.85    85.49
```

F I G U R E 7.4

MINITAB Output for Forward Selection

```
Stepwise Regression

  F-to-Enter:      4.00    F-to-Remove:      0.00

  Response is  sales   on  4 predictors, with N =    25

        Step        1        2
    Constant    -157.3   -516.4

    adv           2.77     2.47
    T-Ratio       9.92     8.98

    bonus                  1.86
    T-Ratio                2.59

    S             101     90.7
    R-Sq        81.06    85.49
```

is noted on the first line, and the R^2 and C_p values for the resulting regression are printed. This is followed by the ANOVA table for the regression and then a table with information about each coefficient in the regression. The Type-II Sum of Squares column is something not included in previous SAS outputs discussed in this text. The Type-II Sum of Squares is a conditional sum

F I G U R E 7.5

MINITAB Output for Stepwise Regression

```
Stepwise Regression

 F-to-Enter:      4.00    F-to-Remove:      4.00

 Response is  sales   on  4 predictors, with N =    25

      Step        1        2
  Constant    -157.3   -516.4

  adv           2.77     2.47
  T-Ratio       9.92     8.98

  bonus                  1.86
  T-Ratio                2.59

  S              101     90.7
  R-Sq         81.06    85.49
```

F I G U R E 7.6

SAS Output for Backward Elimination

```
Backward Elimination Procedure for Dependent Variable SALES

Step 0  All Variables Entered  R-square = 0.85920024  C(p) = 5.00000000

              DF    Sum of Squares      Mean Square        F    Prob>F

Regression     4   1073118.5419660   268279.63549150    30.51    0.0001
Error         20    175855.19803401    8792.75990170
Total         24   1248973.7400000

              Parameter        Standard        Type II
Variable      Estimate            Error    Sum of Squares     F    Prob>F

INTERCEP   -593.53745160    259.19585077    46106.84227386    5.24   0.0330
ADV           2.51313803      0.31427550   562259.55825002   63.95   0.0001
BONUS         1.90594801      0.74238560    57954.64361276    6.59   0.0184
MKTSHR        2.65100700      4.63565540     2875.57485025    0.33   0.5738
COMPET       -0.12073131      0.37181490      927.06772802    0.11   0.7488

 Bounds on condition number:      1.479887,     20.83795
-------------------------------------------------------------------------

Step 1 Variable COMPET Removed  R-square = 0.85845798 C(p) = 3.10543535

              DF    Sum of Squares      Mean Square        F    Prob>F

Regression     3   1072191.4742380   357397.15807932    42.46    0.0001
Error         21    176782.26576203    8418.20313153
Total         24   1248973.7400000
```

F I G U R E **7.6**   *(Cont.)*
SAS Output for Backward Elimination

Variable	Parameter Estimate	Standard Error	Type II Sum of Squares	F	Prob>F
INTERCEP	-620.63774039	240.10769251	56244.96036250	6.68	0.0173
ADV	2.46979329	0.27839114	662566.97761023	78.71	0.0001
BONUS	1.90029797	0.72620177	57643.21538026	6.85	0.0161
MKTSHR	3.11646156	4.31354025	4394.15365784	0.52	0.4780

Bounds on condition number: 1.221189,   10.32487

Step 2 Variable MKTSHR Removed R-square = 0.85493977 C(p) = 1.60518216

	DF	Sum of Squares	Mean Square	F	Prob>F
Regression	2	1067797.3205801	533898.66029007	64.83	0.0001
Error	22	181176.41941987	8235.29179181		
Total	24	1248973.7400000			

Variable	Parameter Estimate	Standard Error	Type II Sum of Squares	F	Prob>F
INTERCEP	-516.44428206	189.87569701	60923.82699593	7.40	0.0125
ADV	2.47317740	0.27531110	664572.05087384	80.70	0.0001
BONUS	1.85617938	0.71572507	55389.37007911	6.73	0.0166

Bounds on condition number: 1.212554,   4.850218

All variables left in the model are significant at the 0.1000 level.

Summary of Backward Elimination Procedure for Dependent Variable SALES

Step	Variable Removed	Number In	Partial R**2	Model R**2	C(p)	F	Prob>F
1	COMPET	3	0.0007	0.8585	3.1054	0.1054	0.7488
2	MKTSHR	2	0.0035	0.8549	1.6052	0.5220	0.4780

of squares, as discussed in Chapter 4. In this case, it is the conditional sum of squares due to the regression ("explained") for the variable x_k given in the corresponding row of the table. The sum of squares is computed conditional on the other variables included in the regression. Thus, for the first variable, x_1, the Type-II Sum of Squares could be written $SSR(x_1|x_2, \ldots, x_K)$. When this sum of squares is divided by the *MSE* for the equation, the partial F statistic for testing $H_0: \beta_k = 0$ is obtained. (Note that the square root of this partial F statistic with an appropriate sign attached would provide the t statistic for testing the same hypothesis.)

Figure 7.11 shows the summary table printed by SAS at the end of the backward elimination, forward selection, and stepwise procedures. The variable entered or removed at each step is shown, as are the number of variables in the model at that step and a number called the Partial R^2, which represents the added (or removed) variable's contribution to the Model R^2 (shown in the next column). The C_p for the model at each step and the partial F statistics for the individual variables entered or removed also are printed.

FIGURE 7.7

```
Forward Selection Procedure for Dependent Variable SALES

Step 1  Variable ADV Entered  R-square = 0.81059186   C(p) = 5.90461154

                DF      Sum of Squares      Mean Square        F    Prob>F

Regression      1     1012407.9505010    1012407.9505010    98.43  0.0001
Error          23      236565.78949898    10285.46910865
Total          24     1248973.7400000

                Parameter      Standard         Type II
Variable        Estimate         Error       Sum of Squares      F    Prob>F

INTERCEP     -157.33011359   145.19119861     12077.22717564    1.17  0.2898
ADV             2.77211593     0.27941239   1012407.9505010    98.43  0.0001

 Bounds on condition number:              1,             1
-----------------------------------------------------------------------

Step 2  Variable BONUS Entered  R-square = 0.85493977 C(p) = 1.60518216

                DF      Sum of Squares      Mean Square        F    Prob>F

Regression      2     1067797.3205801    533898.66029007    64.83  0.0001
Error          22      181176.41941987     8235.29179181
Total          24     1248973.7400000

                Parameter      Standard         Type II
Variable        Estimate         Error       Sum of Squares      F    Prob>F

INTERCEP     -516.44428206   189.87569701     60923.82699593    7.40  0.0125
ADV             2.47317740     0.27531110    664572.05087384   80.70  0.0001
BONUS           1.85617938     0.71572507     55389.37007911    6.73  0.0166

 Bounds on condition number:     1.212554,     4.850218
-----------------------------------------------------------------------

Step 3 Variable MKTSHR Entered  R-square = 0.85845798 C(p) = 3.10543535

                DF      Sum of Squares      Mean Square        F    Prob>F

Regression      3     1072191.4742380    357397.15807932    42.46  0.0001
Error          21      176782.26576203     8418.20313153
Total          24     1248973.7400000

                Parameter      Standard         Type II
Variable        Estimate         Error       Sum of Squares      F    Prob>F

INTERCEP     -620.63774039    40.10769251     56244.96036250    6.68  0.0173
ADV             2.46979329     0.27839114    662566.97761023   78.71  0.0001
BONUS           1.90029797     0.72620177     57643.21538026    6.85  0.0161
MKTSHR          3.11646156     4.31354025      4394.15365784    0.52  0.4780

 Bounds on condition number:     1.221189,     10.32487
-----------------------------------------------------------------------

No other variable met the 0.5000 significance level for entry into the model.

Summary of Forward Selection Procedure for Dependent Variable SALES

       Variable  Number   Partial     Model
Step   Entered     In      R**2        R**2      C(p)        F     Prob>F

  1    ADV          1      0.8106     0.8106    5.9046    98.4309   0.0001
  2    BONUS        2      0.0443     0.8549    1.6052     6.7259   0.0166
  3    MKTSHR       3      0.0035     0.8585    3.1054     0.5220   0.4780
```

F I G U R E 7.8

SAS Output for Stepwise Regression

```
Stepwise Procedure for Dependent Variable SALES

Step 1  Variable ADV Entered   R-square = 0.81059186  C(p) =  5.90461154

                DF      Sum of Squares      Mean Square        F    Prob>F

Regression       1    1012407.9505010    1012407.9505010    98.43   0.0001
Error           23     236565.78949898     10285.46910865
Total           24    1248973.7400000

                Parameter       Standard         Type II
Variable         Estimate         Error     Sum of Squares      F    Prob>F

INTERCEP    -157.33011359   145.19119861     12077.22717564    1.17   0.2898
ADV            2.77211593     0.27941239   1012407.9505010    98.43   0.0001

Bounds on condition number:                1,           1
------------------------------------------------------------------

Step 2 Variable BONUS Entered  R-square = 0.85493977  C(p) =  1.60518216

                DF      Sum of Squares      Mean Square        F    Prob>F

Regression       2    1067797.3205801    533898.66029007    64.83   0.0001
Error           22     181176.41941987      8235.29179181
Total           24    1248973.7400000

                Parameter       Standard         Type II
Variable         Estimate         Error     Sum of Squares      F    Prob>F

INTERCEP    -516.44428206   189.87569701     60923.82699593    7.40   0.0125
ADV            2.47317740     0.27531110    664572.05087384   80.70   0.0001
BONUS          1.85617938     0.71572507     55389.37007911    6.73   0.0166

Bounds on condition number:      1.212554,      4.850218
------------------------------------------------------------------

All variables left in the model are significant at the 0.1500 level.
No other variable met the 0.1500 significance level for entry into the model.

Summary of Stepwise Procedure for Dependent Variable SALES

         Variable        Number   Partial    Model
Step  Entered Removed      In      R**2       R**2     C(p)       F    Prob>F

  1   ADV                  1      0.8106     0.8106   5.9046   98.4309  0.0001
  2   BONUS                2      0.0443     0.8549   1.6052    6.7259  0.0166
```

The SAS output for the maximum R^2 improvement method is shown in Figure 7.9. It is essentially the same as the output for the stepwise techniques. Note, however, that throughout the output, SAS indicates which output refers to the best model with a certain number of explanatory variables. For example,

THE ABOVE MODEL IS THE BEST 1-VARIABLE MODEL FOUND.

F I G U R E 7.9
SAS Output for Maximum R^2 Improvement

```
Maximum R-square Improvement for Dependent Variable SALES

Step 1  Variable ADV Entered    R-square = 0.81059186  C(p) =  5.90461154

                   DF       Sum of Squares      Mean Square       F    Prob>F

Regression          1      1012407.9505010   1012407.9505010   98.43   0.0001
Error              23       236565.78949898    10285.46910865
Total              24      1248973.7400000

                 Parameter      Standard        Type II
Variable         Estimate          Error    Sum of Squares      F    Prob>F

INTERCEP      -157.33011359   145.19119861     12077.22717564   1.17   0.2898
ADV              2.77211593     0.27941239   1012407.9505010   98.43   0.0001

  Bounds on condition number:            1,            1
-----------------------------------------------------------------------
  The above model is the best  1-variable model found.

Step 2  Variable BONUS Entered  R-square = 0.85493977 C(p) =  1.60518216

                   DF       Sum of Squares      Mean Square       F    Prob>F

Regression          2      1067797.3205801    533898.66029007   64.83   0.0001
Error              22       181176.41941987     8235.29179181
Total              24      1248973.7400000

                 Parameter      Standard        Type II
Variable         Estimate          Error    Sum of Squares      F    Prob>F

INTERCEP      -516.44428206   189.87569701     60923.82699593   7.40   0.0125
ADV              2.47317740     0.27531110    664572.05087384   80.70   0.0001
BONUS            1.85617938     0.71572507     55389.37007911   6.73   0.0166

  Bounds on condition number:      1.212554,      4.850218
-----------------------------------------------------------------------
  The above model is the best  2-variable model found.

Step 3  Variable MKTSHR Entered R-square = 0.85845798 C(p) =  3.10543535

                   DF       Sum of Squares      Mean Square       F    Prob>F

Regression          3      1072191.4742380    357397.15807932   42.46   0.0001
Error              21       176782.26576203     8418.20313153
Total              24      1248973.7400000

                 Parameter      Standard        Type II
Variable         Estimate          Error    Sum of Squares      F    Prob>F

INTERCEP      -620.63774039   240.10769251     56244.96036250   6.68   0.0173
ADV              2.46979329     0.27839114    662566.97761023   78.71   0.0001
BONUS            1.90029797     0.72620177     57643.21538026   6.85   0.0161
MKTSHR           3.11646156     4.31354025      4394.15365784   0.52   0.4780

  Bounds on condition number:      1.221189,     10.32487
-----------------------------------------------------------------------
  The above model is the best  3-variable model found.
```

F I G U R E **7.9** *(Cont.)*
SAS Output for Maximum R^2 Improvement

Step 4 Variable COMPET Entered R-square = 0.85920024 C(p) = 5.00000000

	DF	Sum of Squares	Mean Square	F	Prob>F
Regression	4	1073118.5419660	268279.63549150	30.51	0.0001
Error	20	175855.19803401	8792.75990170		
Total	24	1248973.7400000			

Variable	Parameter Estimate	Standard Error	Type II Sum of Squares	F	Prob>F
INTERCEP	-593.53745160	259.19585077	46106.84227386	5.24	0.0330
ADV	2.51313803	0.31427550	562259.55825002	63.95	0.0001
BONUS	1.90594801	0.74238560	57954.64361276	6.59	0.0184
MKTSHR	2.65100700	4.63565540	2875.57485025	0.33	0.5738
COMPET	-0.12073131	0.37181490	927.06772802	0.11	0.7488

Bounds on condition number: 1.479887,   20.83795

The above model is the best 4-variable model found.

No further improvement in R-square is possible.

Recall that this procedure finds what it considers the best model for each number of explanatory variables from 1 to K, where $K =$ the entire set of possible explanatory variables. (Also, recall that the maximum R^2 improvement technique is not guaranteed to find the model with the largest R^2.)

There may be differences between the models chosen by MINITAB and SAS, even when the same technique is used. When there are differences for the same technique, they result from the critical values chosen for the test. For the three procedures available in MINITAB (backward elimination, forward selection, and stepwise) a value of 4 is used as the critical value for all partial F tests. This is the default critical value—that is, the value chosen by MINITAB if no other value is provided. The researcher, however, can enter his or her own choice for a critical value. The subcommands to do this are discussed in Section 7.5: Using the Computer.

The justification for the partial F test cutoff value of 4 is that it will result in a test with a 5% level of significance (approximately) if a large number of observations are available. When using stepwise procedures, it is often recommended that a smaller cutoff value be used, say $F_c = 2$ or $F_c = 1$. After examining the variables chosen by the procedure(s) at this critical value, the researcher is left to make the final choice about which variables should remain in the model.

In SAS, the entry and removal of variables is controlled by the p values of the F statistics through the SLENTRY and SLSTAY options. SLENTRY is the p value for entry of a new

F I G U R E 7.10

Summary Output for Backward Elimination, Forward Selection, Stepwise Regression, and Maximum R^2 Improvement Techniques

Step K Variable _____ Entered   R-square =   C(p) =
                      (Removed)

	DF	Sum of Squares	Mean Square	F	Prob>F
Regression	1	SSR	MSR	$\dfrac{MSR}{MSE}$	p-value
Error	n – K – 1	SSE	MSE		
Total	n – 1	SST			

Variable	Parameter Estimate	Standard Error	Type II Sum of Squares	F	Prob>F
INTERCEPT	b_0	s_{b_0}			
VAR1	b_1	s_{b_1}			
VAR2					
.	.	.			
.	.	.	(See text.)		
.	.	.			
VARK	b_K	s_{b_K}			

Bounds on condition number: (not discussed)

F I G U R E 7.11

SAS Summary Table for Backward Elimination, Forward Selection, and Stepwise Regression

Step	Variable Entered (Removed)	Number In	Partial R**2	Model R**2	C(p)	F	Prob>F

(See text for explanation of each column)

variable into the equation. SLSTAY is the *p* value for removal of a variable. The default *p* values used are SLENTRY = 0.5 for forward selection, SLSTAY = 0.1 for backward elimination, and SLENTRY and SLSTAY = 0.15 for the stepwise procedure. The SAS default *p* values can also be changed to suit the researcher's needs (see Section 7.5).

Note that the default values used by SAS are more conservative than the MINITAB cutoff (the MINITAB cutout would correspond to a cutoff *p* value of about 0.05, but it would vary

F I G U R E 7.12

MINITAB Output for Model Including Indicator Variables

```
The regression equation is
sales = 435 + 1.37 adv + 0.975 bonus - 258 south - 210 west

Predictor        Coef      Stdev     t-ratio         p
Constant        435.1      206.2        2.11     0.048
adv            1.3678     0.2622        5.22     0.000
bonus          0.9752     0.4808        2.03     0.056
south         -257.89      48.41       -5.33     0.000
west          -209.75      37.42       -5.61     0.000

s = 57.63        R-sq = 94.7%      R-sq(adj) = 93.6%

Analysis of Variance

SOURCE         DF          SS          MS        F         p
Regression      4     1182560      295640    89.03     0.000
Error          20       66414        3321
Total          24     1248974

SOURCE         DF      SEQ SS
adv             1     1012408
bonus           1       55389
south           1       10435
west            1      104328

Unusual Observations
Obs.      adv      sales      Fit   Stdev.Fit   Residual   St.Resid
  11      484     1304.8   1421.7        37.0     -117.0     -2.65R
  22      486     1294.3   1192.3        27.7      102.0      2.02R

R denotes an obs. with a large st. resid.
```

depending on the sample size because only the F value rather than the actual p value is specified). For the forward selection procedure, a much more conservative cutoff is used and the variable MKTSHR also is chosen for the final model. From the all-possible regressions result, MKTSHR appears to be unnecessary in the model.

Combining all information gathered from the all-possible regressions procedure and the various stepwise procedures, the best model appears to be

$$\text{SALES} = -516.4 + 2.47\text{ADV} + 1.86\text{BONUS}$$

Before concluding, recall that the indicator variables for the region have not been included in any of this analysis. They could be added to the regression at this point to see whether they improve the model. The MINITAB regression output with the indicators included is shown in Figure 7.12. The partial F test to test the hypotheses

$$H_0: \quad \beta_3 = \beta_4 = 0$$

$$H_a: \quad \text{At least one of } \beta_3 \text{ and } \beta_4 \text{ is not equal to zero}$$

can be used to determine whether the indicator variables improve the model. The null hypothesis will be rejected, and the conclusion will be to retain the indicator variables as well. ∎

7.5
Using the Computer

7.5.1 MINITAB

All Possible Regressions (STAT: REGRESSION: BEST SUBSETS)

```
BREG C1 C2,C3,C4,C5
```

MINITAB has a procedure that is similar to the all-possible regressions approach discussed in this chapter. The command used is BREG. The first column shown is the dependent variable (C1 is this example) and the remaining columns (C2 through C5) are possible explanatory variables. MINITAB calls this procedure "Best Subsets Regression." The command produces output containing the two simple regressions with the highest R^2's, the two two-variable multiple regressions with the highest R^2's, the two three-variable multiple regressions with the highest R^2's, and so on. The last regression listed will be the regression with all the explanatory variables listed on the BREG command.

An example of the output from the command shown applied to the Meddicorp example is in Figure 7.13. MINITAB prints out the R^2, R^2_{ADJ}, C_p, and s (the standard deviation around the regression). The column on the left-hand side of the output shows the number of variables in the regression summarized in that row and the columns on the right-hand side show the variables in the regression.

If more than the two highest R^2 regressions are desired this can be requested with a subcommand as follows:

```
BREG C1,C2,C3,C4,C5;
BEST K.
```

This command sequence requests MINITAB to print out the K highest R^2 regressions with each subset of variables. K can range from 1 to 5.

Note that this command is *not* the same as all possible regressions since not all regressions will be shown even if the BEST 5 subcommand is used (unless there are three or fewer possible explanatory variables).

Stepwise Regression (STAT: REGRESSION: STEPWISE)

```
STEPWISE Y IN C1 PREDICTION IN C_, ..., C_
```

The dependent (y) variable is the first column shown (C1 in this example) and the independent variables are listed in the subsequent columns (which

F I G U R E **7.13**

Example of MINITAB BREG Output for Meddicorp

```
Best Subsets Regression

Response is sales
```

Vars	R-sq	Adj. R-sq	C-p	s	m a d u v	b k o n s r	c o t s h r	m p e t
1	81.1	80.2	5.9	101.42	X			
1	32.3	29.3	75.2	191.76		X		
2	85.5	84.2	1.6	90.749	X	X		
2	81.2	79.5	7.7	103.23	X		X	
3	85.8	83.8	3.1	91.751	X	X	X	
3	85.7	83.6	3.3	92.255	X	X		X
4	85.9	83.1	5.0	93.770	X	X	X	X

have not been numbered here). With new versions of MINITAB, choice of dependent and independent variables can be made by menu.

This form of the command performs stepwise regression as described in this chapter. Default critical values of 4.0 are used for both the partial F test to include and the partial F test to delete variables. The critical values can be altered using subcommands. For example, to change the critical values to 1.0, the following command sequence could be used:

```
STEPWISE Y IN C1 PREDICTORS IN C_,...,C_;
FENTER=1.0;
FREMOVE=1.0.
```

Backward Elimination (STAT: REGRESSION: STEPWISE: OPTIONS)

```
STEPWISE Y IN C1 PREDICTORS IN C_,...,C_;
FENTER=100000;
ENTER C_,...,C_.
```

The FENTER=100000 subcommand tells MINITAB that the F value to enter the regression must be greater than 100,000 (or some other big number; the actual number here does not matter as long as a very big number is used). For practical purposes, this means that no variable removed from the regression will reenter. The ENTER C_,...,C_ subcommand gives MINITAB the list of variables to start with. Backward elimination then starts with this list of variables, sequentially removes the ones that have partial F values below the critical value to remove (4.0 by default), starting with the one with the smallest partial F value. No variable that has been removed is allowed to reenter.

Forward Selection (STAT: REGRESSION: STEPWISE: OPTIONS)

```
STEPWISE Y IN C1 PREDICTORS IN C_,...,C_;
FREMOVE=0.
```

The FREMOVE=0 subcommand tells MINITAB that the partial F value for a variable to be removed from the regression must be less than zero, which is impossible. F values are always nonnegative. So the effect of this subcommand is to make sure that any variable that enters the regression is never removed. Forward selection starts by sequentially entering variables with partial F values above the critical value to enter (4.0 by default), starting with the variable with the largest partial F value. Once a variable has entered the regression it is never removed.

7.5.2 SAS

In SAS, the PROC REG command can be used to request all possible regressions, backward elimination, forward selection, stepwise and maximum R^2 improvement. The choice of variable selection procedure is made using the SELECTION option in the MODEL statement. Each of the choices is demonstrated here.

All Possible Regressions

```
PROC REG CP;
    MODEL SALES=ADV BONUS MKTSHR COMPET/SELECTION=RSQUARE;
```

This command sequence produces the output in Figure 7.1. The CP option requests that the C_p value associated with each regression be printed. In addition the R^2 value (unadjusted) is printed. The MODEL statement works just like it does for PROC REG. The dependent variable is listed to the left of the equal sign and the possible explanatory variables are listed to the right. The SELECTION=RSQUARE option requests all possible regressions.

Maximum R-Square Improvement

```
PROC REG;
    MODEL SALES=ADV BONUS MKTSHR COMPET/SELECTION=MAXR;
```

Stepwise Regression

```
PROC REG;
    MODEL SALES=ADV BONUS MKTSHR COMPET/SELECTION=STEPWISE;
```

Control of the variables to enter or leave the regression is through the p values for the partial F test (rather than the F critical values as in MINITAB). SLENTRY represents the maximum p value the coefficient of a variable can have and still have the variable enter the model. SLSTAY represents the maximum p value the coefficient of a variable can have for the variable to remain in the model. For stepwise regression these values are set at SLENTRY=0.15 and SLSTAY=0.15. These default values can be changed. For example, to change SLENTRY and SLSTAY each to 0.2 the following sequence could be used:

```
PROC REG;
    MODEL SALES=ADV BONUS MKTSHR COMPET/SELECTION=STEPWISE/
            SLENTRY=0.2 SLSTAY=0.2;
```

Backward Elimination

```
PROC REG;
    MODEL SALES=ADV BONUS MKTSHR COMPET/SELECTION=BACKWARD;
```

Backward elimination uses SLSTAY=0.1 in SAS. Of course, SLENTRY is set so that once a variable leaves the regression it will not reenter.

Forward Selection

```
PROC REG;
    MODEL SALES=ADV BONUS MKTSHR COMPET/SELECTION=FORWARD;
```

Backward selection uses SLENTRY=0.5 in SAS. Of course, SLSTAY is set so that once a variable enters the regression it will not leave.

Exercises

1   **Cost Control**   Exercise 1 in Chapter 4 discussed data available for a firm that produces corrugated paper for use in making boxes and other packing materials. The variables that were discussed were

y, total manufacturing cost per month in thousands of dollars (COST)

x_1, total production of paper per month in tons (PAPER)

x_2, total machine hours used per month (MACHINE)

x_3, total variable overhead costs per month in thousands of dollars (OVERHEAD)

x_4, total direct labor hours used each month (LABOR)

The data, shown in Table 4.2, are monthly and refer to the period from January 1992 to March 1994.

F I G U R E 7.14

MINITAB Backward Elimination Output for Cost Control Exercise

```
Stepwise Regression

  F-to-Enter: 100000.00    F-to-Remove:      4.00

  Response is   cost   on  4 predictors, with N =   27

       Step        1        2        3
   Constant    51.72    51.17    59.43

   paper        0.95     0.94     0.95
   T-Ratio      7.90     8.69     8.62

   machine      2.47     2.51     2.39
   T-Ratio      5.31    11.01    11.36

   overhead     0.05
   T-Ratio      0.09

   labor      -0.051   -0.051
   T-Ratio     -1.26    -1.29

   S           11.1     10.8     11.0
   R-Sq       99.88    99.88    99.87
```

The following outputs are as shown:

Figure 7.14, the MINITAB backward elimination output
Figure 7.15, the SAS backward elimination output
Figure 7.16, the SAS all-possible regressions output

A. Use the MINITAB or SAS backward elimination output to answer the following questions:

a What is the regression equation chosen by the backward elimination procedure?

b What is the R^2 for the chosen equation?

c What is the adjusted R^2 for the chosen equation?

d What is the standard error of the chosen equation?

e What variables were omitted? Do you feel these variables are unrelated to $y =$ COST? Why or why not? Do you feel the omitted variables are necessary in the regression equation? Why or why not?

B. Use the SAS all-possible regressions output to answer the following questions:

a Plot the C_p values versus p for each regression evaluated.

b Using the plot in (a), which set of variables would you choose as best? Explain why.

c For the regression with your chosen set of explanatory variables, find R^2, R^2_{ADJ}, s_e, and C_p.

These data are available on the data disk for further analysis. In MINITAB, they can be read using

READ 'COST7' C1-C5

F I G U R E 7.15

SAS Backward Elimination Output for Cost Control Exercise

```
Backward Elimination Procedure for Dependent Variable COST

Step 0   All Variables Entered   R-square = 0.99881329   C(p) = 5.00000000

                  DF      Sum of Squares      Mean Square        F      Prob>F

Regression    4     2271423.3537458    567855.83843646    4629.17    0.0001
Error        22        2698.72032824       122.66910583
Total        26     2274122.0740741

                 Parameter        Standard           Type II
Variable         Estimate           Error      Sum of Squares       F     Prob>F

INTERCEP     51.72314206     21.70396993       696.66924724      5.68    0.0262
PAPER         0.94794209      0.12002341      7651.85726210     62.38    0.0001
MACHINE       2.47103960      0.46556012      3455.75591927     28.17    0.0001
OVERHEAD      0.04833872      0.52500975         1.03989798      0.01    0.9275
LABOR        -0.05057756      0.04029511       193.26191106      1.58    0.2226

Bounds on condition number:     228.9054,      1591.037
-----------------------------------------------------------------------

Step 1 Variable OVERHEAD Removed R-square = 0.99881283 C(p) = 3.00847726

                  DF      Sum of Squares      Mean Square        F      Prob>F

Regression    3     2271422.3138479    757140.77128262    6450.29    0.0001
Error        23        2699.76022622       117.38087940
Total        26     2274122.0740741

                 Parameter        Standard           Type II
Variable         Estimate           Error      Sum of Squares       F     Prob>F

INTERCEP     51.17024497     20.40217916       738.37883116      6.29    0.0196
PAPER         0.94375121      0.10863738      8858.37030823     75.47    0.0001
MACHINE       2.50816148      0.22771386     14240.63724580    121.32    0.0001
LABOR        -0.05078975      0.03935247       195.52642983      1.67    0.2097

Bounds on condition number:      57.22967,       342.0691
-----------------------------------------------------------------------

Step 2   Variable LABOR Removed   R-square = 0.99872686   C(p) = 2.60241103

                  DF      Sum of Squares      Mean Square        F      Prob>F

Regression    2     2271226.7874180   1135613.3937090    9413.48    0.0001
Error        24        2895.28665605       120.63694400
Total        26     2274122.0740741

                 Parameter        Standard           Type II
Variable         Estimate           Error      Sum of Squares       F     Prob>F

INTERCEP     59.43181579     19.63883728      1104.80792820      9.16    0.0058
PAPER         0.94888292      0.11006005      8966.97972707     74.33    0.0001
MACHINE       2.38644225      0.21012138     15561.15059686    128.99    0.0001

Bounds on condition number:      47.41326,       189.653
-----------------------------------------------------------------------
```

F I G U R E **7.15** *(Cont.)*
SAS Backward Elimination Output for Cost Control Exercise

All variables left in the model are significant at the 0.1000 level.

Summary of Backward Elimination Procedure for Dependent Variable COST

Step	Variable Removed	Number In	Partial R**2	Model R**2	C(p)	F	Prob>F
1	OVERHEAD	3	0.0000	0.9988	3.0085	0.0085	0.9275
2	LABOR	2	0.0001	0.9987	2.6024	1.6657	0.2097

F I G U R E **7.16**
SAS All-Possible Regressions Output for Cost Control Exercise

N = 27   Regression Models for Dependent Variable: COST

Number in Model	R-square	C(p)	Variables in Model
1	0.99478380	73.70134	MACHINE
1	0.99188415	127.45709	PAPER
1	0.97885891	368.92766	OVERHEAD
1	0.88073363	2188	LABOR
2	0.99872686	2.60241	PAPER MACHINE
2	0.99729305	29.18317	PAPER OVERHEAD
2	0.99529336	66.25488	MACHINE OVERHEAD
2	0.99491754	73.22202	MACHINE LABOR
2	0.99255080	117.09832	PAPER LABOR
2	0.97975894	354.24241	OVERHEAD LABOR
3	0.99881283	3.00848	PAPER MACHINE LABOR
3	0.99872831	4.57547	PAPER MACHINE OVERHEAD
3	0.99729369	31.17136	PAPER OVERHEAD LABOR
3	0.99544854	65.37803	MACHINE OVERHEAD LABOR
4	0.99881329	5.00000	PAPER MACHINE OVERHEAD LABOR

where C1 is COST, C2 is PAPER, C3 is MACHINE, C4 is OVERHEAD, and C5 is LABOR.

In SAS, the data can be read from the file COST7.DAT using

```
INPUT COST PAPER MACHINE OVERHEAD LABOR;
```

2   **Sales Force Performance**   Data on the following variables were obtained for a random sample of 25 sales territories for a company (many of the data have been transformed to preserve confidentiality).

y, sales in units for the territory (SALES)

x_1, length of time that territory salespersons have been with the company (TIME)

x_2, industry sales in units for the territory (POTENT)

x_3, dollar expenditures on advertising (ADV)

x_4, weighted average of past market share for four previous years (SHARE)

x_5, change in market share over the four years before the time period analyzed (SHARECHG)

x_6, total number of accounts assigned to salesperson (ACCTS)

x_7, average workload per account using a weighted index based on annual purchases of accounts and concentration of accounts (WORKLOAD)

x_8, aggregate rating on a 1–7 scale for eight dimensions of performance by applicable field sales manager (RATING)

The data are shown in Table 7.2.

The goal of the study is to identify factors that influence territory sales (y). The equation to be developed then will be used to assess whether salespersons in respective territories are performing up to standard.

Develop an appropriate model to explain sales territory performance. Use any of the techniques discussed to select appropriate variables. Be sure to examine scatterplots and residual plots for violations of assumptions and to correct for any such violations.

a For the model you select, report the estimated regression equation. Be sure to define the variables used.

b For the model you select, report any corrections for violations of assumptions

c For the model you select, report the R^2, R^2_{ADJ}, standard error, and C_p value for the selected regression

d Discuss how this equation could be used to set a performance standard for sales territories. How would average performance be determined? below-average performance? What limitations would this approach have for setting performance standards?

These data are available on the data disk. In MINITAB, they can be read using

```
READ 'TERRITR7' C1-C9
```

where C1 is SALES, C2 is TIME, C3 is POTENT, C4 is ADV, C5 is SHARE, C6 is SHARECHG, C7 is ACCTS, C8 is WORKLOAD, and C9 is RATING.

In SAS, the data can be read from the file TERRITR7.DAT using

```
INPUT SALES TIME POTENT ADV SHARE SHARECHG ACCTS WORKLOAD
    RATING;
```

3 **1994 Cars** Data on 154 cars were obtained from Road and Track's *The Complete '94 Car Buyer's Guide*. The data shown in Table 7.3 (on pages 444–448) are as follows:

name of car

price, in dollars (PRICE)

weight, in pounds (WEIGHT)

mileage in city driving (CITYMPG)

mileage in highway driving (HWYMPG)

displacement, in cubic centimeters (DISP)

T A B L E 7.2
Data for Sales Force Performance Exercise

SALES	TIME	POTENT	ADV	SHARE	SHARECHG	ACCTS	WORKLOAD	RATING
3669.88	43.10	74065.1	4582.9	2.51	0.34	74.86	15.05	4.9
3473.95	108.13	58117.3	5539.8	5.51	0.15	107.32	19.97	5.1
2295.10	13.82	21118.5	2950.4	10.91	−0.72	96.75	17.34	2.9
4675.56	186.18	68521.3	2243.1	8.27	0.17	195.12	13.40	3.4
6125.96	161.79	57805.1	7747.1	9.15	0.50	180.44	17.64	4.6
2134.94	8.94	37806.9	402.4	5.51	0.15	104.88	16.22	4.5
5031.66	365.04	50935.3	3140.6	8.54	0.55	256.10	18.80	4.6
3367.45	220.32	35602.1	2086.2	7.07	−0.49	126.83	19.86	2.3
6519.45	127.64	46176.8	8846.2	12.54	1.24	203.25	17.42	4.9
4876.37	105.69	42053.2	5673.1	8.85	0.31	119.51	21.41	2.8
2468.27	57.72	36829.7	2761.8	5.38	0.37	116.26	16.32	3.1
2533.31	23.58	33612.7	1991.8	5.43	−0.65	142.28	14.51	4.2
2408.11	13.82	21412.8	1971.5	8.48	0.64	89.43	19.35	4.3
2337.38	13.82	20416.9	1737.4	7.80	1.01	84.55	20.02	4.2
4586.95	86.99	36272.0	10694.2	10.34	0.11	119.51	15.26	5.5
2729.24	165.85	23093.3	8618.6	5.15	0.04	80.49	15.87	3.6
3289.40	116.26	26878.6	7747.9	6.64	0.68	136.58	7.81	3.4
2800.78	42.28	39572.0	4566.0	5.45	0.66	78.86	16.00	4.2
3264.20	52.84	51866.1	6022.7	6.31	−0.10	136.58	17.44	3.6
3453.62	165.04	58749.8	3721.1	6.35	−0.03	138.21	17.98	3.1
1741.45	10.57	23990.8	861.0	7.37	−1.63	75.61	20.99	1.6
2035.75	13.82	25694.9	3571.5	8.39	−0.43	102.44	21.66	3.4
1578.00	8.13	23736.3	2845.5	5.15	0.04	76.42	21.46	2.7
4167.44	58.54	34314.3	5060.1	12.88	0.22	136.58	24.78	2.8
2799.97	21.14	22809.5	3552.0	9.14	−0.74	88.62	24.96	3.9

These data were analyzed in "An Analytical Approach for Evaluating Sales Territory Performance," D. W. Cravens, R. B. Woodruff, and J. C. Stamper, *Journal of Marketing*, 36, 1972, pp. 31–37. They also have been analyzed in *A First Course in Linear Regression* by M. S. Younger.

compression ratio (#:1) (COMP)
horsepower, @6300 RPM (HP)
torque, @5200 RPM (TORQUE)
type of transmission: 1 = automatic, 0 = manual (AUTO)
number of cylinders (CYLIN)
country of origin (COUNTRY)

    1 = Japan
    2 = USA
    3 = South Korea
    4 = Italy

    5 = United Kingdom
    6 = Germany
    7 = USA/Canada
    8 = USA/Mexico
    9 = Japan/USA
    10 = Japan/Canada
    11 = Australia
    12 = Sweden
    13 = Germany/Mexico
    14 = Sweden/Belgium

In the table, an asterisk (*) is used to represent missing data.

    Using the available data, try to determine what factors involved in the construction of a car affect either mileage in city driving or mileage in highway driving. (Choose either CITYMPG or HWYMPG as your dependent variable. If you choose CITYMPG, don't use HWYMPG as a possible explanatory variable and vice versa.) Use any of the techniques discussed to select appropriate variables. Be sure to examine scatterplots and residual plots for violations of assumptions and to correct for any such violations. (Note: You have to decide what to do about the missing data.)

a   For the model you select, report the estimated regression. Be sure to define the variables used.

b   For the model you select, report any corrections for violations of assumptions. Explain why the correction was needed and justify the correction you used.

c   Justify your choice of variables from both a statistical and a practical standpoint.

d   State any limitations of the model

These data are available on the data disk. In MINITAB, they can be read using

```
READ 'CARS7' C1-C12
```

where C1 is an identification number corresponding to the number in the table, C2 is PRICE, C3 is WEIGHT, C4 is CITYMPG, C5 is HWYMPG, C6 is DISP, C7 is COMP, C8 is HP, C9 is TORQUE, C10 is AUTO, C11 is CYLIN, and C12 is COUNTRY.

    In SAS, the data can be read from the file CARS7.DAT using

```
INPUT NUMBER PRICE WEIGHT CITYMPG HWYMPG DISP COMP HP TORQUE AUTO CYLIN
    COUNTRY;
```

4   **1993 American League Pitchers**   Data on 43 American League pitchers were obtained for the 1993 season. The pitchers included in the data set must have pitched in at least 40 innings to be listed here. Also, these pitchers were used only as starting pitchers (pitchers with even one appearance in relief were not included). The data shown in Table 7.4 are as follows:

name of pitcher
team: coded as
    1 = Baltimore
    2 = Boston
    3 = Cleveland

4 = Detroit

5 = California

6 = Chicago

7 = Kansas City

8 = Milwaukee

9 = Minnesota

10 = Seattle

11 = New York

12 = Oakland

13 = Texas

14 = Toronto

number of wins (W)

number of losses (L)

earned run average (ERA)

games in which an appearance was made (G)

innings pitched (IP)

hits allowed (H)

runs allowed (R) (earned + unearned runs)

home runs allowed (HR)

base on balls (BB)

strikeouts (SO)

As a consultant to the Texas Rangers' coaching staff, you have been hired to determine what makes a starting pitcher successful. During the Rangers' 1994 season, they have become painfully aware of the need for good starting pitchers. At midseason they are in first place in their division but are five games under .500 and have the second-worst pitching staff in the American League (based on ERA). You have data available for American League starting pitchers in the 1993 season. Your goal is to try to determine what factors might be important in the success of a starting pitcher during a particular season. First, you must define success (the dependent variable). Then decide which of the variables available might make sense in evaluating a pitcher's success.

a For the model you select, report the estimated regression equation. Be sure to define the variables used.

b For the model you select, report any corrections for violations of assumptions. Explain why the correction was needed and justify the correction you used.

c Justify your choice of variables from both a statistical and a practical standpoint.

These data are available on the data disk. In MINITAB, they can be read using

```
READ 'ALPITCH7' C1-C12
```

where C1 is an identification number corresponding to the number in the table, C2 is TEAM, C3 is W, C4 is L, C5 is ERA, C6 is G, C7 is IP, C8 is H, C9 is R, C10 is HR, C11 is BB, and C12 is SO.

In SAS, the data can be read from the file ALPITCH7.DAT using

```
INPUT NUMBER TEAM W L ERA G IP H R HR BB SO;
```

Model	PRICE	WEIGHT	CITYMPG	HWYMPG	DISP	COMP	HP	TORQUE	AUTO	CYLIN	COUNTRY
1. Acura Integra	14,670	2,685	25	31	1,834	9.2	142	127	0	4	1
2. Acura Legend	33,800	3,515	18	26	3,206	8.6	200	210	0	6	1
3. Acura NSX	70,000	3,010	19	24	2,977	10.2	270	210	0	6	1
4. Acura Vigor	26,350	3,150	20	26	2,451	9.0	176	170	0	5	1
5. Alfa Romeo 164	34,890	3,413	17	24	2,959	10.0	210	198	0	6	4
6. Alfa Romeo Spider	25,000	2,550	22	30	1,962	9.0	120	117	0	4	4
7. Aston Martin Virage	275,000	3,850	*	*	5,340	9.5	330	350	0	8	5
8. Audi 90	27,000	3,185	20	26	2,771	10.3	172	184	0	6	6
9. Audi 100	23,200	3,329	19	26	2,771	10.3	172	184	0	6	6
10. Audi V8	59,000	3,991	14	20	4,172	10.6	276	295	1	8	6
11. Bentley	147,100	5,340	*	*	6,750	8.0	*	*	1	8	5
12. BMW 3-Series	24,675	3,020	22	30	1,796	10.0	138	129	0	4	4
13. BMW 5-Series	38,425	3,600	17	25	2,494	10.0	189	184	0	6	4
14. BMW 7-Series	55,950	3,795	16	22	3,892	10.0	282	295	1	8	4
15. BMW 8-Series	70,000	4,125	*	*	3,982	10.0	282	295	1	8	4
16. Buick Century	15,495	2,976	24	34	2,189	9.0	120	130	1	4	2
17. Buick Le Sabre	20,860	3,449	19	29	3,792	8.5	170	225	1	6	2
18. Buick Park Avenue	26,999	3,637	19	28	3,792	8.5	170	225	1	6	2
19. Buick Regal	17,999	3,240	19	29	3,135	9.5	160	185	1	6	2
20. Buick Riviera	28,000	3,800	16	25	3,792	8.5	170	225	1	6	2
21. Buick Roadmaster Wagon	23,999	4,191	17	25	5,733	10.5	260	330	1	8	2
22. Buick Skylark	13,599	2,791	23	31	2,260	9.5	115	140	1	4	2
23. Cadillac De Ville	32,990	3,757	16	25	4,893	9.5	200	275	1	8	2
24. Cadillac Eldorado	37,290	3,774	16	25	4,572	10.3	270	300	1	8	2
25. Cadillac Fleetwood	33,990	4,477	16	25	5,710	9.7	260	335	1	8	2
26. Cadillac Seville & STS	40,990	3,830	16	25	4,572	10.3	270	300	1	8	2
27. Chevrolet Beretta	12,415	2,795	25	34	2,189	9.0	120	130	0	4	2
28. Chevrolet Camaro	13,399	3,247	19	28	3,352	9.0	160	200	1	6	7
29. Chevrolet Caprice	18,995	4,036	18	26	4,293	9.8	200	245	0	8	2
30. Chevrolet Cavalier	8,845	2,515	26	37	2,189	9.0	120	140	1	4	2
31. Chevrolet Corsica	13,145	2,665	25	31	2,189	9.0	120	130	1	4	2

444

Model	PRICE	WEIGHT	CITYMPG	HWYMPG	DISP	COMP	HP	TORQUE	AUTO	CYLIN	COUNTRY
32. Chevrolet Corvette	36,185	3,335	17	25	5,733	10.5	300	340	0	8	2
33. Chevrolet Lumina	15,305	3,333	19	29	3,137	8.9	140	185	1	6	7
34. Chrysler Concorde	19,457	3,379	20	28	3,293	8.9	161	181	1	6	7
35. Chrysler Le Baron Conv.	16,999	3,122	21	28	2,972	8.9	142	171	1	6	2
36. Chrysler Le Baron Sedan	15,121	2,971	20	27	2,972	8.9	142	171	1	6	8
37. Chrysler NY & LHS	24,294	3,457	18	26	3,518	10.5	214	221	1	6	7
38. Dodge (Plymouth) Colt	9,120	2,085	32	40	1,468	9.2	92	93	0	4	1
39. Dodge Intrepid	17,251	3,271	20	28	3,301	8.9	161	181	1	6	7
40. Dodge(Plymouth) Neon	9,500	2,320	*	*	2,005	*	132	129	0	4	8
41. Dodge Shadow (P Sundance)	8,806	2,608	27	32	2,205	9.5	93	122	0	4	8
42. Dodge Spirit (P Acclaim)	12,470	2,824	23	28	2,502	8.9	100	135	1	4	8
43. Dodge Stealth	20,935	3,064	18	24	2,972	8.9	164	185	0	6	1
44. Dodge Viper RT/10	55,000	3,476	13	21	7,990	9.1	400	480	0	10	2
45. Eagle Summit	9,120	2,085	32	40	1,468	9.2	92	93	0	4	1
46. Eagle Summit Wagon	12,979	2,725	23	29	2,834	9.5	113	116	0	4	1
47. Eagle Talon (P Laser)	11,542	2,550	23	32	1,755	9.0	92	105	0	4	9
48. Eagle Vision	19,308	3,344	20	28	3,301	8.9	161	181	1	6	7
49. Ferrari 348	118,000	3,235	13	19	3,405	10.4	312	229	0	8	4
50. Ferrari 512 TR	206,000	3,715	11	16	4,943	10.0	421	360	0	12	4
51. Ford Aspire	7,500	2,053	*	*	1,324	9.7	63	73	0	4	3
52. Ford Contour (M Mystique)	12,000	*	*	*	1,989	10.0	136	133	0	4	2
53. Ford Crown Victoria	19,300	3,786	17	23	4,601	9.0	190	260	1	8	7
54. Ford Escort	9,035	2,325	26	31	1,856	9.0	88	108	0	4	8
55. Ford Mustang	13,365	3,055	*	*	3,802	9.0	145	215	0	6	2
56. Ford Probe	13,685	2,690	26	33	1,991	9.0	118	127	1	4	9
57. Ford Taurus	16,140	3,104	20	29	2,931	9.3	140	165	1	6	2
58. Ford Tempo	10,735	2,569	24	33	2,307	9.0	96	126	0	4	2
59. Ford Thunderbird	16,830	3,570	20	27	3,805	9.0	140	215	0	6	2
60. Geo Metro	7,195	1,621	46	50	993	9.5	49	58	0	3	10
61. Geo Prizm	10,730	2,347	28	33	1,587	9.5	105	100	0	4	9
62. Honda Accord	14,330	3,005	25	31	2,156	8.8	130	139	0	4	9

Data for 1994 Cars Exercise

Model	PRICE	WEIGHT	CITYMPG	HWYMPG	DISP	COMP	HP	TORQUE	AUTO	CYLIN	COUNTRY
63. Honda Civic	9,400	2,275	34	40	1,493	9.2	102	98	0	4	9
64. Honda Civic del Sol	14,100	2,265	35	41	1,493	9.2	102	98	0	4	1
65. Honda Prelude	18,100	2,765	23	29	2,156	8.8	135	142	0	4	1
66. Hyundai Elantra	9,749	2,450	22	29	1,596	9.2	113	102	0	4	3
67. Hyundai Excel	7,190	2,150	29	33	1,468	9.4	81	92	0	4	3
68. Hyundai Scoupe	9,499	2,200	27	35	1,495	10.0	92	97	0	4	3
69. Hyundai Sonata	12,799	2,725	20	27	1,997	9.0	128	121	0	4	3
70. Infiniti G20	20,045	2,880	24	32	1,998	9.5	140	132	0	4	1
71. Infiniti J30	34,400	3,530	18	23	2,960	10.5	210	193	1	6	1
72. Infiniti Q45	47,500	4,040	17	22	4,494	10.2	278	292	1	8	1
73. Jaguar XJS	51,950	3,805	17	23	3,980	9.5	219	273	1	6	5
74. Jaguar XJ6	51,750	4,075	17	24	3,980	9.5	223	278	1	6	5
75. KIA Sephia	8,500	2,340	28	33	1,597	9.0	88	98	0	4	3
76. Lamborghini Diablo	240,000	3,640	9	14	5,707	10.0	492	428	0	12	4
77. Lexus ES300	30,600	3,362	18	24	2,995	10.5	188	200	1	6	1
78. Lexus GS300	39,900	3,652	18	23	2,997	10.0	220	210	1	6	1
79. Lexus LS400	49,900	3,858	18	23	3,969	10.0	250	260	1	8	1
80. Lexus SC300 & SC400	38,000	3,495	18	23	2,997	10.2	225	210	1	6	1
81. Lincoln Continental	33,750	3,576	18	26	3,802	9.0	160	225	1	6	2
82. Lincoln Mark VII	38,050	3,768	18	25	4,601	9.8	280	285	1	8	2
83. Lincoln Town Car	34,750	4,040	17	23	4,601	9.0	210	270	1	8	2
84. Lotus Esprit S4	69,000	2,955	17	27	2,174	8.0	264	261	0	4	5
85. Mazda MX-3	13,500	2,332	29	37	1,597	9.0	105	100	0	4	1
86. Mazda MX-5 Miata	16,450	2,293	22	27	1,839	9.0	128	110	0	4	1
87. Mazda MX-6	17,195	2,600	26	34	1,991	9.0	118	127	0	4	9
88. Mazda Protege	11,295	2,425	30	37	1,839	8.9	103	111	0	4	1
89. Maxda RX-7	34,000	2,790	17	25	1,308	9.0	255	217	0	*	1
90. Mazda 323	7,995	2,240	29	37	1,597	9.3	82	92	0	4	1
91. Mazda 626	14,255	2,670	26	34	1,991	9.0	118	127	0	4	9
92. Mazda 929	30,500	3,650	19	24	2,954	9.2	195	200	1	6	1
93. Mercedes-Benz C-Class	29,900	3,175	21	28	2,198	10.0	147	155	1	4	6

T A B L E 7.3 (*Cont.*)
Data for 1994 Cars Exercise

Model	PRICE	WEIGHT	CITYMPG	HWYMPG	DISP	COMP	HP	TORQUE	AUTO	CYLIN	COUNTRY
94. Mercedes-Benz E-Class	40,000	3,525	19	25	3,199	10.0	217	229	1	6	6
95. Mercedes-Benz S-Class	70,600	4,630	17	24	3,199	10.0	228	232	1	6	6
96. Mercedes-Benz SL-Class	85,200	4,090	17	24	3,199	10.0	228	232	1	6	6
97. Mercury Capri	13,190	2,423	25	31	1,598	9.4	100	95	0	4	11
98. Mercury Cougar XR7	16,260	3,564	20	27	3,805	9.0	140	205	1	6	2
99. Mercury Grand Marquis	20,330	3,787	18	24	4,601	9.0	190	260	1	8	7
100. Mercury Sable	17,740	3,126	20	29	2,931	9.3	140	165	1	6	2
101. Mercury Topaz	11,270	2,531	23	33	2,307	9.0	96	126	0	4	2
102. Mercury Tracer	10,250	2,393	30	37	1,839	9.0	88	108	0	4	8
103. Mitsubishi Diamante	25,525	3,430	18	25	2,972	10.0	175	185	1	6	1
104. Mitsubishi Eclipse	11,979	2,525	23	32	1,755	9.0	92	105	0	4	9
105. Mitsubishi Expo and LRV	13,019	2,735	21	28	1,834	9.5	113	116	0	4	1
106. Mitsubishi Galant	13,600	2,755	23	30	2,350	9.5	141	148	0	4	9
107. Mitsubishi Mirage	8,989	2,083	31	39	1,468	9.2	92	93	0	4	1
108. Mitsubishi 3000 GT	27,175	3,220	18	24	2,972	10.0	222	201	0	6	1
109. Morgan	40,000	2,015	*	*	3,974	9.4	188	232	0	8	5
110. Nissan Altima	13,739	2,765	24	30	2,389	9.5	150	154	0	4	9
111. Nissan Maxima	22,199	3,130	19	26	2,960	9.1	160	182	0	6	1
112. Nissan Sentra	10,049	2,265	29	37	1,597	9.5	110	108	0	4	9
113. Nissan 240SX Convertible	23,969	2,870	21	26	2,389	9.5	155	160	1	4	1
114. Nissan 300ZX	32,000	3,185	18	24	2,960	10.5	222	198	0	6	1
115. Oldsmobile Achieva	13,510	2,717	24	31	2,260	9.5	115	140	0	4	2
116. Oldsmobile Aurora	32,500	4,000	16	25	3,995	10.3	250	260	0	8	2
117. Oldsmobile Cutlass Ciera	13,470	2,833	24	32	2,189	9.0	120	130	1	4	2
118. Oldsmobile Cutlass Sup.	16,470	3,405	19	28	3,137	9.5	160	185	0	6	2
119. Oldsmobile 88 Royale	19,420	3,439	19	28	3,791	9.0	170	225	1	6	2
120. Oldsmobile 98	24,370	3,512	19	27	3,791	9.0	170	225	1	6	2
121. Pontiac Bonneville	20,424	3,446	19	28	3,791	9.0	170	225	1	6	2
122. Pontiac Firebird	13,995	3,232	19	28	3,352	9.0	160	200	0	6	7
123. Pontiac Grand Am	12,514	2,736	22	32	2,260	9.5	115	140	1	4	2
124. Pontiac Grand Prix	16,174	3,275	19	28	3,137	9.5	160	185	1	6	2

447

T A B L E 7.3 (Cont.)
Data for 1994 Cars Exercise

Model	PRICE	WEIGHT	CITYMPG	HWYMPG	DISP	COMP	HP	TORQUE	AUTO	CYLIN	COUNTRY
125. Pontiac Sunbird	9,764	2,484	25	35	1,998	9.2	110	124	0	4	2
126. Porsche 911	54,800	2,950	17	25	3,600	11.3	247	228	0	6	6
127. Porsche 928 GTS	82,260	3,590	12	19	5,395	10.4	345	369	0	8	6
128. Porsche 968	39,950	3,090	17	26	2,990	11.0	236	225	0	4	6
129. Rolls Royce	189,900	5,340	*	*	6,750	9.5	*	*	1	8	5
130. Saab 900	22,000	2,999	20	28	2,290	10.5	150	155	0	4	12
131. Saab 9000	28,725	2,966	19	27	2,290	10.5	147	151	0	4	12
132. Saturn Sports Coupe	11,695	2,279	28	37	1,901	9.3	85	107	0	4	2
133. Saturn Sedan	9,995	2,314	28	37	1,901	9.3	85	107	0	4	2
134. Saturn Wagon	11,695	2,362	28	37	1,901	9.3	85	107	0	4	2
135. Subaru Impreza	10,500	2,350	25	31	1,820	9.6	110	110	0	4	1
136. Subaru Justy	7,500	1,845	33	37	1,189	9.1	73	71	0	3	1
137. Subaru Legacy	14,200	2,800	23	31	2,212	9.5	130	137	0	4	9
138. Subaru Loyale Wagon	13,553	2,635	24	29	1,781	9.5	90	101	0	4	1
139. Subaru SVX	23,500	*	17	25	3,318	10.0	230	228	1	6	1
140. Suzuki Swift	7,549	1,780	39	43	1,298	9.5	70	74	0	4	1
141. Toyota Camry	16,148	2,945	22	30	2,163	9.5	130	145	1	4	9
142. Toyota Celica	16,168	2,675	27	34	1,762	9.5	110	115	0	4	1
143. Toyota Corolla	11,198	2,460	27	34	1,587	9.5	105	100	0	4	9
144. Toyota MR2	19,000	2,590	22	29	2,164	9.5	135	145	0	4	1
145. Toyota Paseo	11,498	2,070	28	34	1,497	9.4	100	91	0	4	1
146. Toyota Supra	33,900	3,215	18	23	2,997	8.5	220	210	0	6	1
147. Toyota Tercel	8,698	1,950	32	36	1,457	9.3	82	89	0	4	1
148. Volkswagen Corrado	24,000	2,815	18	25	2,792	10.0	178	177	0	6	6
149. Volkswagen Golf	12,500	2,575	24	32	1,984	10.1	115	122	0	4	13
150. Volkswagen Jetta	13,700	2,645	23	30	1,984	10.1	115	122	0	4	13
151. Volkswagen Passat	22,700	3,220	17	24	2,792	10.0	172	177	0	6	6
152. Volvo 850	24,300	3,140	23	29	2,435	10.5	168	162	0	5	14
153. Volvo 940	22,900	3,175	20	28	2,316	9.8	114	136	1	4	12
154. Volvo 960	28,950	3,460	18	26	2,922	10.7	201	197	1	6	12

T A B L E 7.4

Data for 1993 American League Pitchers Exercise

Name	Team	W	L	ERA	G	IP	H	R	HR	BB	SO
1. McDonald	1	13	14	3.39	34	220.1	185	92	17	86	171
2. Moyer	1	12	9	3.43	25	152.0	154	63	11	38	90
3. Mussina	1	14	6	4.46	25	167.2	163	84	20	44	117
4. Sele	2	7	2	2.74	18	111.2	100	42	5	48	93
5. Viola	2	11	8	3.14	29	183.2	180	76	12	72	91
6. Darwin	2	15	11	3.26	34	229.1	196	93	31	49	130
7. Clemens	2	11	14	4.46	29	191.2	175	99	17	67	160
8. Bielecki	3	4	5	5.90	13	68.2	90	47	8	23	38
9. Lopez	3	3	1	5.98	9	49.2	49	34	7	32	25
10. Nagy	3	2	6	6.29	9	48.2	66	38	6	13	30
11. Moore	4	13	9	5.22	36	213.2	227	135	35	89	89
12. Gullickson	4	13	9	5.37	28	159.1	186	106	28	44	70
13. Finley	5	16	14	3.15	35	251.1	243	108	22	82	187
14. Langston	5	16	11	3.20	35	256.1	220	100	22	85	196
15. Leftwich	5	4	6	3.79	12	80.2	81	35	5	27	31
16. Magrane	5	3	2	3.94	8	48.0	48	27	4	21	24
17. Sanderson	5	7	11	4.46	21	135.1	153	77	15	27	66
18. Hathaway	5	4	3	5.02	11	57.1	71	35	6	26	11
19. Alvarez	6	15	8	2.95	31	207.2	168	78	14	122	155
20. Fernandez	6	18	9	3.13	34	247.1	221	95	27	67	169
21. McDowell	6	22	10	3.37	34	256.2	261	104	20	69	158
22. Bere	6	12	5	3.47	24	142.2	109	60	12	81	129
23. Appier	7	18	8	2.56	34	238.2	183	74	8	81	186
24. Cone	7	11	14	3.33	34	254.0	205	102	20	114	191
25. Haney	7	9	9	6.02	23	124.0	141	87	13	53	65
26. Eldred	8	16	16	4.01	36	258.0	232	120	32	91	180
27. Boddicker	8	3	5	5.67	10	54.0	77	35	6	15	24
28. Deshaies	9	11	13	4.41	27	167.1	159	85	24	51	80
29. Erickson	9	8	19	5.19	34	218.2	266	138	17	71	116
30. Fleming	10	12	5	4.36	26	167.1	189	84	15	67	75
31. Key	11	18	6	3.00	34	236.2	219	84	26	43	173
32. Abbott	11	11	14	4.37	32	214.0	221	115	22	73	95
33. Perez	11	6	14	5.19	25	163.0	173	103	22	64	148
34. Witt	11	3	2	5.27	9	41.0	39	26	7	22	30
35. Karsay	12	3	3	4.04	8	49.0	49	23	4	16	33
36. Van Poppel	12	6	6	5.04	16	84.0	76	50	10	62	47
37. Pavlik	13	12	6	3.41	26	166.1	157	67	18	80	131
38. Brown	13	15	12	3.59	34	233.0	228	105	14	74	142
39. Leibrandt	13	9	10	4.55	26	150.1	169	84	15	45	89
40. Ryan	13	5	5	4.88	13	66.1	54	47	5	40	46
41. Guzman	14	14	3	3.99	33	221.0	211	107	17	110	194
42. Stewart	14	12	8	4.44	26	162.0	146	86	23	72	96
43. Morris	14	7	12	6.19	27	152.2	189	116	18	65	103

Data were obtained from the Fort Worth *Star-Telegram* 3 October 1993 issue.

Introduction to Analysis of Variance

8.1
One-Way Analysis of Variance

Analysis of variance (ANOVA) was a term used with regression to describe the decomposition of the total sum of squares into two parts: the regression ("explained") sum of squares and the error ("unexplained") sum of squares. ANOVA also is used to describe a statistical technique used to test whether there is a difference between means of several populations. The procedure used is very similar to regression analysis. In fact, for one-way analysis of variance, the procedure is the same as if a regression were performed using only indicator variables as explanatory variables. The actual analyses are usually performed using ANOVA routines rather than regression routines because the analysis of variance routines are more efficient computationally for this specific type of problem.

To describe the ANOVA procedure, consider a problem with K populations. One way that the ANOVA model can be written is

$$y_{ij} = \mu_i + e_{ij},$$

where

y_{ij} is the jth observation from population i

μ_i is the population mean for population i

e_{ij} is a random disturbance for the jth observation from population i

Because there are K populations, i will range from 1 to K. Assuming that there are n_i observations from each population, j will range from 1 to n_i. The use of the subscript on n_i implies that the number of sample observations from each population can differ. The total number of observations combining all samples will be denoted

$$n = \sum_{i=1}^{K} n_i$$

The following assumptions are made concerning the disturbances, e_{ij}'s:

1　The e_{ij}'s have mean zero.

2　The e_{ij}'s have constant variance, σ^2.

3　The e_{ij}'s are normally distributed.

ANOVA has its own special terminology. As in regression, y_{ij} is called the *dependent variable*. The explanatory variables are called *factors*. A level of the factor is a particular value of the explanatory variable. The μ_i are called *factor-level means*. The ANOVA model allows for a different mean for each factor level. Factor levels also are referred to as *treatments* in one-way ANOVA.

An alternative way of writing the ANOVA model is

$$y_{ij} = \mu + \gamma_i + e_{ij},$$

where μ is a constant component common to all observations and γ_i is the effect of the ith treatment (or factor level). Here the treatment means are

$$\mu_1 = \mu + \gamma_1$$
$$\mu_2 = \mu + \gamma_2$$

.

.

.

$$\mu_K = \mu + \gamma_K$$

The question to be answered is, "Are the means of all K populations equal?" The hypotheses to be tested to answer this question can be stated as

$$H_0: \quad \mu_1 = \mu_2 = \cdots = \mu_K$$
$$H_a: \quad \text{Not all means are equal}$$

or as

$$H_0: \quad \gamma_1 = \gamma_2 = \cdots = \gamma_K$$
$$H_a: \quad \text{Not all treatment effects are equal}$$

depending on the form of the model used. The test procedure is the same regardless of the way the model is written.

The test statistic used to conduct the test is

$$F = \frac{MSTR}{MSE},$$

where *MSTR* is the mean square due to treatments and *MSE* is the mean square error. This statistic is similar to the F statistic used to test the overall fit of a regression. The ANOVA F statistic has an F distribution with $K - 1$ numerator and $n - K$

denominator degrees of freedom. K is the number of populations and n is the total sample size. The decision rule for the test is:

$$\text{Reject } H_0 \quad \text{if} \quad F > F(\alpha; \quad K-1, n-K)$$

$$\text{Accept } H_0 \quad \text{if} \quad F \leq F(\alpha; \quad K-1, n-K)$$

The reasoning behind the term *analysis of variance* can be seen by further examination of the test statistic. The F statistic is the ratio of two mean squares and each mean square is an estimate of the common population variance. One of the assumptions necessary for using ANOVA is that the variances of all populations are equal. This common variance is called σ^2.

MSE provides an unbiased estimate of the variance σ^2. Furthermore, if the μ_i's were all equal, *MSTR* also would provide an unbiased estimate of σ^2. But when some of the μ_i's are not equal, *MSTR* will be biased. Thus, if H_0 is false, *MSTR* will tend to be bigger than *MSE*, and the null hypothesis will likely be rejected. If H_0 is true, *MSTR* and *MSE* will provide similar estimates and the F statistic will be close to 1, leading to acceptance of the null hypothesis.

The formulas for *MSTR* and *MSE* are as follows:

$$MSTR = \frac{SSTR}{K-1}$$

The treatment sum of squares, *SSTR*, is

$$SSTR = \sum_{i=1}^{K} n_i (\bar{y}_{i.} - \bar{y}_{..})^2$$

and has $K-1$ degrees of freedom;

$$MSE = \frac{SSE}{n-K}$$

The error sum of squares, *SSE*, is

$$SSE = \sum_{i=1}^{K} \sum_{j=1}^{n_i} (y_{ij} - \bar{y}_{i.})^2$$

The notation in these formulas is as follows:

y_{ij} is the jth sample observation from population i,

$\bar{y}_{i.}$ is the mean of all the sample observations for the ith population:

$$\bar{y}_{i.} = \frac{\sum_{j=1}^{n_i} y_{ij}}{n_i}$$

$\bar{y}_{..}$ is the overall mean of all n observations:

$$\bar{y}_{..} = \frac{\sum\limits_{i=1}^{K}\sum\limits_{j=1}^{n_i} y_{ij}}{n}$$

As mentioned, the one-factor ANOVA model is equivalent to a regression model in which all the explanatory variables are indicator variables. The equivalent regression model can be written in two ways, just as the ANOVA model can written in two ways. For example, the following regression equation is equivalent to the first form of the ANOVA model:

$$y_{ij} = \mu_1 x_{ij1} + \mu_2 x_{ij2} + \cdots + \mu_K x_{ijK} + e_{ij}$$

In this equation, the x_{ijk}'s are defined as

$x_{ij1} = 1$ if the observation corresponds to factor-level one,

   $= 0$ otherwise,

$x_{ij2} = 1$ if the observation corresponds to factor-level two,

   $= 0$ otherwise,

and so on.

Note that no constant term is included in the regression equation. The constant is unnecessary (and would result in perfect multicollinearity if included). There is an alternate form of the regression model equivalent to the second ANOVA model, but it will not be discussed here because regression is typically not used for ANOVA-type problems.

E X A M P L E   **8.1**   **Automobile Injuries**

U.S. News and World Report, 28 September 1987, lists injury claims for 1984–1986 cars. The claims are listed for cars in the following categories:

small two-door

midsized two-door

large two-door

small four-door

midsized four-door

large four-door

small station wagons and vans

midsized station wagons and vans

large station wagons and vans

The variable CARCLAS is used to indicate into which category each car falls. This list is coded from 1 to 9 in the order shown. Table 8.1 shows the name of each car, the CARCLAS variable, and a variable INJURY that indicates the number of injury claims for each car.

T A B L E 8.1
Data for Automobile Injuries Example

Car Name	CARCLAS	INJURY
Saab 900	1	70
Honda Prelude	1	97
Mazda 626	1	103
Toyota Celica	1	109
Subaru Hatchback	1	115
Volkswagen Scirocco	1	115
Mitsubishi Starion	1	119
Dodge Daytona	1	120
Plymouth Colt	1	124
Ford Escort	1	125
Mercury Lynx	1	137
Mitsubishi Cordia	1	137
Dodge Colt	1	139
Renault Alliance	1	139
Nissan Sentra	1	139
Plymouth Turismo	1	140
Nissan Pulsar	1	151
Chevrolet Sprint	1	152
Chevrolet Spectrum	1	153
Mitsubishi Mirage	1	158
Oldsmobile Cutlass Ciera	2	80
Pontiac 6000	2	85
Chrysler Le Baron	2	91
Honda Accord	2	93
Chevrolet Monte Carlo	2	95
Buick Regal	2	97
Ford Thunderbird	2	102
Mercury Cougar	2	111
Plymouth Reliant	2	117
Pontiac Grand Am	2	117
Ford Tempo	2	123
Buick Skyhawk	2	123
Chevrolet Cavalier	2	131
Mercury Grand Marquis	3	55
Ford Crown Victoria	3	70
Oldsmobile Ninety-Eight	3	73
Chevrolet Caprice	3	75
Saab 900	4	66
Mazda 626	4	96
Volkswagen Jetta	4	102
Nissan Stanza	4	103
Honda Civic	4	112
Toyota Corolla	4	115

T A B L E **8**.1 *(Cont.)*

Data for Automobile Injuries Example

Car Name	CARCLAS	INJURY
Chevrolet Nova	4	115
Plymouth Horizon	4	116
Toyota Tercel	4	121
Ford Escort	4	121
Renault Alliance	4	131
Subaru DL/GL Sedan	4	132
Mazda 323	4	137
Dodge Colt	4	140
Nissan Sentra	4	142
Mitsubishi Tredia	4	149
Hyundai Excel	4	161
Chevrolet Spectrum	4	177
Ford Taurus	5	73
Volvo 240	5	78
Toyota Camry	5	80
Pontiac Bonneville	5	81
Plymouth Caravelle	5	84
Pontiac 6000	5	84
Mercury Marquis	5	86
Honda Accord	5	87
Chrysler Le Baron GTS	5	87
Ford LTD	5	90
Dodge Lancer	5	90
Chevrolet Celebrity	5	91
Nissan Maxima	5	91
Dodge 600	5	94
Audi 4000	5	95
Buick Skyhawk	5	102
Mitsubishi Galant	5	106
Plymouth Reliant	5	107
Mercury Topaz	5	107
Ford Tempo	5	110
Oldsmobile Firenza	5	113
Chevrolet Cavalier	5	118
Pontiac Sunbird	5	121
Dodge Diplomat	6	61
Mercury Grand Marquis	6	63
Plymouth Gran Fury	6	66
Buick Electra	6	68
Pontiac Parisienne	6	70
Oldsmobile Ninety-Eight	6	70
Toyota Van	7	75
Volkswagen Vanagon	7	78
Subaru DL/GL 4-Wh. Dr.	7	84

T A B L E **8.1** *(Cont.)*

Data for Automobile Injuries Example

Car Name	CARCLAS	INJURY
Toyota Tercel 4-Wh. Dr.	7	90
Nissan Stanza	7	93
Subaru DL/GL	7	98
Honda Civic	7	100
Volvo 240	8	58
Mercury Marquis	8	60
Buick Century	8	73
Chrysler Le Baron	8	74
Oldsmobile Cutlass Ciera	8	75
Nissan Maxima	8	81
Ford Celebrity	8	82
Pontiac Sunbird	8	89
Plymouth Reliant	8	91
Dodge Colt Vista	8	93
Plymouth Colt Vista	8	97
Chevrolet Cavalier	8	98
Buick Skyhawk	8	103
Pontiac Parisienne	9	52
Mercury Grand Marquis	9	53
Oldsmobile Custom Cruiser	9	54
Chevrolet Caprice	9	60
Plymouth Voyager	9	63
Dodge Caravan	9	65
Ford Aerostar	9	65
Chevrolet Astro Van	9	68

Figure 8.1 shows the MINITAB ANOVA output for this problem. Figure 8.2(a) shows the ANOVA table for MINITAB in general form. The sums of squares due to the treatment variable, error, and the total sum of squares are printed along with their degrees of freedom. *MSTR*, *MSE*, the F statistic, and a p value associated with the observed F statistic are computed.

The description of a general ANOVA table for SAS is given in Figure 8.2(b). Figure 8.3 shows the SAS ANOVA output for the example. The same information shown in the MINITAB ANOVA table is represented in the SAS ANOVA table.

The decision rule for the test using a 5% level of significance is:

$$\text{Reject } H_0 \quad \text{if} \quad F > 2.10$$
$$\text{Accept } H_0 \quad \text{if} \quad F \leq 2.10$$

The critical value is chosen from the $\alpha = 0.05$ level F table with 8 numerator and 103 (approximately) denominator degrees of freedom. The test statistic value, 22.80, exceeds the critical value, so the null hypothesis is rejected. There is a difference in the factor-level means—that is, the average level of injuries differs depending on the type of car. ∎

F I G U R E **8.1**

MINITAB ANOVA Output for Automobile Injuries Example

```
One-Way Analysis of Variance

Analysis of Variance on injuries
Source      DF        SS        MS        F        p
carclas      8     54762      6845    22.80    0.000
Error      103     30917       300
Total      111     85679
                                    Individual 95% CIs For Mean
                                    Based on Pooled StDev
Level        N      Mean     StDev  -+---------+---------+---------+-----
  1         20    127.10     21.89                              (--*--)
  2         13    105.00     16.29                      (---*---)
  3          4     68.25      9.07     (------*------)
  4         18    124.22     25.58                              (---*--)
  5         23     94.57     13.38                   (--*--)
  6          6     66.33      3.72     (-----*----)
  7          7     88.29      9.64              (----*-----)
  8         13     82.62     14.21            (---*---)
  9          8     60.00      6.23     (----*----)
                                    -+---------+---------+---------+-----
Pooled StDev =    17.33            50        75       100       125
```

Analysis of variance often is used in an experimental design situation. The term *experiment* refers to the data collection process. The term *design* refers to the plan for conducting the experiment. In many situations the researcher can assign objects upon which measurements are to be made (called *experimental units*) to the factor levels or treatments. This was not done in the previous example. Once a car was chosen for the example—say, a Ford Thunderbird—the researcher had no control over which factor level this case was assigned. A Ford Thunderbird is a midsized two-door, so it automatically is assigned to factor-level two.

E X A M P L E **8.2** **Computer Sales**

Consider another situation where experimental design can be used. The effect of different selling approaches on sales of computers is to be studied. Three different selling approaches are to be compared. The object is to determine whether avarage sales will differ among the three approaches. Fifteen salespeople are chosen to participate in the study. Five salespeople each are randomly assigned to use one of the three approaches for the next month. At the end of the month, sales figures will be computed for each salesperson. These data will be analyzed to determine whether the sales approaches produce the same or different average sales.

In this situation, the salespeople were randomly assigned to the factor levels or treatments. This random assignment is possible when an experiment is designed to help answer a particular question. The type of experimental design used in this case is called a *completely randomized design*. Analysis of variance can be used in this situation to analyze the data just as in the car injury example.

F I G U R E **8.2**

Structure of the MINITAB and SAS ANOVA Tables

(a) MINITAB

Analysis of Variance on (dependent variable name)

Source	DF	SS	MS	F	p
Treatment var	$K-1$	$SSTR = \sum_i n_i(\bar{y}_{i\cdot} - \bar{y}_{\cdot\cdot})^2$	$MSTR = SSTR/(K-1)$	$\dfrac{MSTR}{MSE}$	p value
Error	$n-K$	$SSE = \sum_i n_j(y_{ij} - \bar{y}_{i\cdot})^2$	$MSE = SSE/(n-K)$		
Total	$n-1$	$SST = \sum_i \sum_j (y_{ij} - \bar{y}_{\cdot\cdot})^2$			

(b) SAS

Analysis of Variance Procedure

Dependent Variable: (DEPENDENT VARIABLE NAME)

Source	DF	Sum of Squares	Mean Square	F Value	Pr > F
Model	$K-1$	$SSTR = \sum_i n_i(\bar{y}_{i\cdot} - \bar{y}_{\cdot\cdot})^2$	$MSTR = SSTR/(K-1)$	$\dfrac{MSTR}{MSE}$	p-value
Error	$n-K$	$SSE = \sum_i n_j(\bar{y}_{ij} - \bar{y}_{i\cdot})^2$	$MSE = SSE/(n-K)$		
Corrected Total	$n-1$	$SST = \sum_i \sum_j (\bar{y}_{ij} - \bar{y}_{\cdot\cdot})^2$			

R-square	C.V.	Root MSE	Y Var. Mean
$\dfrac{SSModel}{SST}$	$\dfrac{Root\ MSE}{Y\ Var.\ Mean}$ x 100	$\sqrt{MSE}$	$\bar{Y}$

Source	DF	Anova SS	Mean Square	F Value	Pr > F
Factor Name	$K-1$	SSTR	MSTR	MSTR/MSE	p-value

Suppose the following sales figures (in $1000) resulted from the experiment just described:

Selling Approaches

Salesperson	A	B	C
1	15	19	28
2	17	17	25
3	21	17	22
4	13	25	31
5	12	30	34

The hypotheses to be tested are

$$H_0: \quad \mu_A = \mu_B = \mu_C$$

$$H_a: \quad \text{All three means are not equal}$$

F I G U R E   **8.3**

SAS ANOVA Output for Automobile Injuries Example

Analysis of Variance Procedure
Class Level Information

Class   Levels   Values

CARTYPE   9   1 2 3 4 5 6 7 8 9

Number of observations in data set = 112

Analysis of Variance Procedure

Dependent Variable: INJURY

Source	DF	Sum of Squares	Mean Square	F Value	Pr > F
Model	8	54762.26752999	6845.28344125	22.80	0.0001
Error	103	30917.15211286	300.16652537		
Corrected Total	111	85679.41964286			

R-Square	C.V.	Root MSE	INJURY Mean
0.639153	17.38585	17.32531458	99.65178571

Source	DF	Anova SS	Mean Square	F Value	Pr > F
CARTYPE	8	54762.26752999	6845.28344125	22.80	0.0001

where μ_i is the population average sales for selling approach i. The MINITAB output for this analysis is shown in Figure 8.4 and the SAS output is in Figure 8.5. To test the hypotheses, either the F statistic or its associated p value could be used. If the F statistic is used, the decision rule is (with a 5% level of significance):

$$\text{Reject } H_0 \quad \text{if} \quad F > 3.89$$
$$\text{Accept } H_0 \quad \text{if} \quad F \le 3.89$$

where the critical value is chosen with 2 numerator and 12 denominator degrees of freedom. The test statistic is $F = 8.47$, so the decision is to reject the null hypothesis.

Rejection of the null hypothesis leads to the conclusion that the population average sales differ depending on what selling approach is used.   ∎

Note that rejection of the null hypothesis simply says that the population means are not all equal. It does not say they are all different or tell which ones are different from the others. In a case such as this, the researcher would probably want to know which population averages are different, or whether two particular ones differ. A

F I G U R E **8.4**

MINITAB ANOVA Output for Computer Sales Example

```
One-Way Analysis of Variance

Analysis of Variance on sales
Source      DF       SS        MS         F         p
approach     2      384.5     192.3      8.47     0.005
Error       12      272.4      22.7
Total       14      656.9
                                    Individual 95% CIs For Mean
                                    Based on Pooled StDev
  Level      N      Mean      StDev   --+---------+---------+---------+----
    1        5     15.600     3.578   (-------*-------)
    2        5     21.600     5.727            (-------*-------)
    3        5     28.000     4.743                      (-------*------)
                                    --+---------+---------+---------+----
Pooled StDev =     4.764            12.0      18.0      24.0      30.0
```

F I G U R E **8.5**

SAS ANOVA Output for Computer Sales Example

```
              Analysis of Variance Procedure
                 Class Level Information

           Class      Levels      Values

           APPROACH       3        1 2 3


        Number of observations in data set = 15


              Analysis of Variance Procedure

Dependent Variable: SALES

Source          DF    Sum of Squares    Mean Square    F Value    Pr > F

Model            2     384.53333333    192.26666667      8.47     0.0051
Error           12     272.40000000     22.70000000
Corrected Total 14     656.93333333


        R-Square          C.V.         Root MSE       SALES Mean

        0.585346        21.92232      4.76445170      21.73333333


Source      DF      Anova SS      Mean Square     F Value     Pr > F

APPROACH     2    384.53333333   192.26666667       8.47      0.0051
```

$(1 - \alpha)100\%$ confidence interval estimate of the difference between two means, μ_i and μ_j, can be constructed as follows:

$$(\bar{y}_i - \bar{y}_j) \pm t_{\alpha/2}s\sqrt{\left(\frac{1}{n_i}\right) + \left(\frac{1}{n_j}\right)},$$

where $t_{\alpha/2}$ is the value chosen to put $\alpha/2$ probability in the upper tail of the t distribution using $n - K$ degrees of freedom, s is the square root of *MSE*, and $\bar{y}_i$ and $\bar{y}_j$ are the sample means for samples i and j (or factors i and j).

E X A M P L E **8.3** **Computer Sales (continued)**

In the computer sales example, the following is the 95% confidence interval estimate of the difference between selling approaches A and C:

$$(15.6 - 28.0) \pm (2.179)(4.76)\sqrt{\left(\frac{1}{5}\right) + \left(\frac{1}{5}\right)}$$

or

$$(-18.96, -5.84)$$

Because the 95% confidence interval estimate of the difference between these two population means does not contain zero, this suggests that the population means for methods A and C are not equal. ∎

This type of comparison works when only two means are to be compared. If this type of interval estimate is used for a series of comparisons, the level of significance will no longer be appropriate. Three procedures can be used when such multiple comparisons are desired: the Tukey method, the Scheffé method, and the Bonferroni method. Only the Bonferroni method will be discussed here. The Bonferroni approach assumes that the user can specify in advance which means are to be compared.[1] The Bonferroni intervals used to compare pairs of means are constructed as

$$(\bar{y}_i - \bar{y}_j) \pm Bs\sqrt{\left(\frac{1}{n_i}\right) + \left(\frac{1}{n_j}\right)},$$

where B is a t value chosen to put $\alpha/2g$ probability in the upper tail of the t distribution using $n - K$ degrees of freedom. Here g is the number of comparisons to be made.

E X A M P L E **8.4** **Computer Sales (continued)**

Suppose all possible pairs of means are to be compared in the computer sales example with a 95% confidence level. Intervals are to be constructed to estimate $\mu_A - \mu_B, \mu_B - \mu_C$, and

---

[1]See page 584 of Neter, Wasserman, and Kutner (1985), *Applied Linear Statistical Models*, for a discussion of when the Tukey and Scheffé methods may be preferred to the Bonferroni.

$\mu_A - \mu_C$. Because there are three comparisons to be made ($g = 3$), the Bonferroni confidence coefficient, B, would be the t value that puts $.05/(2)(3) = .008$ probability in the upper tail of the t distribution. In this example, the .005 column will be used to ensure at least a 95% confidence level. The interval estimates are

$$\mu_A - \mu_B : (15.6 - 21.6) \pm (3.055)(4.76)\sqrt{\left(\frac{1}{5}\right) + \left(\frac{1}{5}\right)}$$

$$\text{or} \quad (-15.20, \quad 3.20)$$

$$\mu_B - \mu_C : (21.6 - 28.0) \pm (3.055)(4.76)\sqrt{\left(\frac{1}{5}\right) + \left(\frac{1}{5}\right)}$$

$$\text{or} \quad (-15.6, \quad 2.80)$$

$$\mu_A - \mu_C : (15.6 - 28.0) \pm (3.055)(4.76)\sqrt{\left(\frac{1}{5}\right) + \left(\frac{1}{5}\right)}$$

$$\text{or} \quad (-21.60, \quad -3.20)$$

The three estimates are said to have a *familywise* confidence level of 95%. This means that the estimates can be viewed simultaneously rather than one at a time and that the 95% confidence level will apply. ∎

The one-way ANOVA model presented in this text is referred to as a *fixed-effects model*. Another type of model is referred to as a *random-effects model*. The difference between the two models concerns whether inference is about the specific means, μ_i, in the problem or whether the μ_i's are a random sample from some population of many μ_i's.

For example, suppose the problem involves the study of whether the average number of defective items differs between three production lines. If the three production lines are the only lines or at least the only ones of interest, then the problem falls into the fixed-effects category. The three means of interest are μ_1, μ_2, and μ_3. It is these three means that are to be compared and to which inferences will refer.

On the other hand, suppose that there are many production lines and that the three chosen are a random sample of the total of all production lines. Also, suppose that it is not a comparison of the means of these three production lines that is to be performed. Instead, the question is whether any of the lines in the population of production lines differs, on average, from the others in the population. Here, the example falls into the random-effects category. The three means to be examined are a sample from some larger population of means and the inferences to be made concern the entire population.

It can be shown that the F test described in this section can be used in the random-effects model to test whether the means of the population differ. The performance of the test is exactly the same although the question asked is different.

Throughout this chapter all the examples used will be for fixed-effects models. Also note that, although in one-way ANOVA the same F test is used for both fixed- and random-effects models, this will not always be the case for more complicated designs. For further information on both fixed- and random-effects ANOVA models, see Neter, Wasserman, and Kutner (1985).

Exercises

1   **Automobile Collisions**   The *U.S. News and World Report*, 28 September 1987, issue lists numbers of collision claims (COLLISON) reported for 1984–1986 cars. The claims are listed in the same categories as described for Example 8.1 and are shown in Table 8.2. Using the classification variable (CARCLAS) described in that example, an ANOVA was run on the number of collisions. Figures 8.6 and 8.7 provide the MINITAB and SAS ANOVA outputs, respectively. Use the outputs to determine whether there is a difference in the average number of collisions for different types of cars. Use a 5% level of significance. State the hypotheses to be tested, the decision rule, the test statistic, and your decision.

These data are available on the data disk for further analysis. In MINITAB, they can be read using

```
READ 'CRASH8' C1-C2
```

where C1 is CARCLAS and C2 is COLLISON.

In SAS, the data can be read from the file CRASH8.DAT using

```
INPUT CARCLAS COLLISON;
```

T A B L E **8.2**

Data for Automobile Collision Exercise

Car Name	CARCLAS	COLLISON
Saab 900	1	155
Honda Prelude	1	119
Mazda 626	1	137
Toyota Celica	1	137
Subaru Hatchback	1	103
Volkswagen Scirocco	1	232
Mitsubishi Starion	1	254
Dodge Daytona	1	160
Plymouth Colt	1	122
Ford Escort	1	98
Mercury Lynx	1	98
Mitsubishi Cordia	1	186
Dodge Colt	1	111
Renault Alliance	1	118
Nissan Sentra	1	118
Plymouth Turismo	1	135
Nissan Pulsar	1	142
Chevrolet Sprint	1	106
Chevrolet Spectrum	1	103
Mitsubishi Mirage	1	147
Oldsmobile Cutlass Ciera	2	80
Pontiac 6000	2	70

T A B L E **8.2** (*Cont.*)
Data for Automobile Collision Exercise

Car Name	CARCLAS	COLLISON
Chrysler Le Baron	2	98
Honda Accord	2	103
Chevrolet Monte Carlo	2	108
Buick Regal	2	91
Ford Thunderbird	2	114
Mercury Cougar	2	119
Plymouth Reliant	2	88
Pontiac Grand Am	2	104
Ford Tempo	2	93
Buick Skyhawk	2	110
Chevrolet Cavalier	2	121
Mercury Grand Marquis	3	52
Ford Crown Victoria	3	68
Oldsmobile Ninety-Eight	3	72
Chevrolet Caprice	3	67
Saab 900	4	122
Mazda 626	4	108
Volkswagen Jetta	4	110
Nissan Stanza	4	109
Honda Civic	4	100
Toyota Corolla	4	88
Chevrolet Nova	4	91
Plymouth Horizon	4	87
Toyota Tercel	4	81
Ford Escort	4	82
Renault Alliance	4	102
Subaru DL/GL Sedan	4	113
Mazda 323	4	112
Dodge Colt	4	124
Nissan Sentra	4	111
Mitsubishi Tredia	4	145
Hyundai Excel	4	123
Chevrolet Spectrum	4	103
Ford Taurus	5	75
Volvo 240	5	95
Toyota Camry	5	70
Pontiac Bonneville	5	67
Plymouth Caravelle	5	78
Pontiac 6000	5	83
Mercury Marquis	5	76
Honda Accord	5	92
Chrysler Le Baron GTS	5	93
Ford LTD	5	75
Dodge Lancer	5	97
Chevrolet Celebrity	5	73

T A B L E **8.2** (*Cont.*)

Data for Automobile Collision Exercise

Car Name	CARCLAS	COLLISON
Nissan Maxima	5	121
Dodge 600	5	79
Audi 4000	5	158
Buick Skyhawk	5	87
Mitsubishi Galant	5	130
Plymouth Reliant	5	83
Mercury Topaz	5	85
Ford Tempo	5	84
Oldsmobile Firenza	5	83
Chevrolet Cavalier	5	91
Pontiac Sunbird	5	101
Dodge Diplomat	6	65
Mercury Grand Marquis	6	55
Plymouth Gran Fury	6	65
Buick Electra	6	79
Pontiac Parisienne	6	59
Oldsmobile Ninety-Eight	6	76
Toyota Van	7	77
Volkswagen Vanagon	7	76
Subaru DL/GL 4-Wh. Dr.	7	94
Toyota Tercel 4-Wh. Dr.	7	70
Nissan Stanza	7	79
Subaru DL/GL	7	87
Honda Civic	7	76
Volvo 240	8	84
Mercury Marquis	8	74
Buick Century	8	80
Chrysler Le Baron	8	90
Oldsmobile Cutlass Ciera	8	66
Nissan Maxima	8	113
Ford Celebrity	8	64
Pontiac Sunbird	8	80
Plymouth Reliant	8	69
Dodge Colt Vista	8	91
Plymouth Colt Vista	8	89
Chevrolet Cavalier	8	75
Buick Skyhawk	8	65
Pontiac Parisienne	9	59
Mercury Grand Marquis	9	82
Oldsmobile Custom Cruiser	9	59
Chevrolet Caprice	9	63
Plymouth Voyager	9	58
Dodge Caravan	9	57
Ford Aerostar	9	63
Chevrolet Astro Van	9	49

F I G U R E **8.6**

MINITAB ANOVA Output for Automobile Collision Exercise

```
One-Way Analysis of Variance

Analysis of Variance on collison
Source      DF        SS        MS        F        p
carclas      8     63790      7974    14.82    0.000
Error      103     55427       538
Total      111    119218
                                      Individual 95% CIs For Mean
                                      Based on Pooled StDev
Level      N      Mean     StDev   -------+---------+---------+---------
    1     20    139.05     42.47                               (--*---)
    2     13     99.92     15.18                   (---*----)
    3      4     64.75      8.77    (-------*------)
    4     18    106.17     16.63                       (--*---)
    5     23     90.26     21.04                 (--*--)
    6      6     66.50      9.38      (-----*-----)
    7      7     79.86      8.03           (-----*----)
    8     13     80.00     13.74            (----*---)
    9      8     61.25      9.45     (----*-----)
                                    -------+---------+---------+---------
Pooled StDev =    23.20              60        90       120
```

F I G U R E **8.7**

SAS ANOVA Output for Automobile Collision Exercise

```
                   Analysis of Variance Procedure
                     Class Level Information

          Class      Levels    Values

          CARTYPE       9       1 2 3 4 5 6 7 8 9


          Number of observations in data set = 112


                   Analysis of Variance Procedure

Dependent Variable: COLLISON

Source              DF    Sum of Squares    Mean Square    F Value    Pr > F

Model                8    63790.26356904    7973.78294613    14.82    0.0001
Error              103    55427.41500239     538.13024274
Corrected Total    111   119217.67857143


          R-Square         C.V.       Root MSE      COLLISON Mean

          0.535074      24.02566    23.19763442      96.55357143


Source        DF       Anova SS      Mean Square    F Value     Pr > F

CARTYPE        8    63790.26356904    7973.78294613    14.82     0.0001
```

8.2

Analysis of Variance Using a Randomized Block Design

In some situations designs other than the completely randomized design discussed in the previous section can be beneficial. Another type of experimental design is called a *randomized block design*. Only randomized block designs with one value per treatment–block combination will be considered in this text. (Randomized block designs with more than one value per treatment–block combination can be used, but there are adjustments that are needed—e.g., different equations for various degrees of freedom.) Consider again the problem in Example 8.2 involving the study of the three different selling approaches. In the completely randomized design, 15 salespeople were used. Five people each were randomly assigned to each selling approach (treatment). The one-way ANOVA technique then was used to determine whether the average sales for each group were significantly different. Two types of variation affect the sample averages computed in this case: (1) the variation that results from the differences in selling approaches, and (2) the variation from the individuals involved in the study. Certain individuals simply may be better salespeople than others regardless of the sales approach used.

The goal of the study is to determine whether the difference in the sample means that results from differences in selling approaches is significant. The second type of variation is a hindrance to this goal because the additional variation may make it difficult to determine what is actually causing the differences in the means. Is it the selling approaches themselves or the individuals assigned to the three groups? To eliminate this second source of variation, a randomized block design can be used. The idea of the randomized block design is to compare the means of treatments within fairly homogeneous blocks of experimental units.

In the example given, instead of choosing 15 people and randomly assigning them to use a particular selling approach, it might be better to choose 5 people and let each person use all three of the selling approaches. The treatments in this study are still the three selling approaches. The blocks are the salespeople themselves. The experimental units within a block are instances when the different treatments can be "applied" to the salespeople. Table 8.3 illustrates this situation. The treatments (selling approaches) are denoted T_1, T_2, and T_3. The three treatments have been applied to each block (salesperson) in a randomized order. Thus, during the first month, salespersons 1 and 5 will use approach 1, salespersons 3 and 4 will use approach 3, and salesperson 2 will use approach 2. The order of the treatments within each block is determined by using a random number table.

When the blocks are the subjects to be used in the experiment, the design often is referred to as a *repeated measures design*. One advantage of this type of randomized block design is that all sources of variability between subjects is removed. Another advantage is that fewer subjects are needed. In this example, 5 subjects were needed rather than the 15 when the completely randomized design was used.

One serious potential disadvantage of the repeated measures design is the effect of time order in the application of the treatments. In this example, sales may vary

TABLE 8.3
The Assignment of Treatments to Experimental Units for Computer Sales

Blocks	Treatment Order		
1	T_1	T_3	T_2
2	T_2	T_1	T_3
3	T_3	T_1	T_2
4	T_3	T_2	T_1
5	T_1	T_2	T_3

somewhat by month—that is, those treatments applied in month 1 may produce higher sales than in month 2 simply because of some type of monthly seasonal variation. An attempt has been made to minimize this variation by randomizing the treatment order independently for each subject.

Another example of a randomized block design that is not a repeated measures design follows. A company wishes to evaluate the effect of package design on one of its products, a certain brand of cereal. The four package designs (treatments) are to be tested in different stores throughout a large city. There are 20 stores available for the study. Cereal sales are known to vary depending on the size of the stores, so size will be used as a blocking variable. The 20 stores are divided into 5 groups of 4 stores each by size. Table 8.4 illustrates the design. The treatments are randomized within each block. The randomization is performed independently between blocks.

The model for a randomized block design can be written

$$y_{ij} = \mu + \gamma_i + B_j + e_{ij},$$

where

μ is an overall mean

γ_i is the ith treatment effect

B_j is the jth block effect

e_{ij} is the random disturbance for treatment i and block j

TABLE 8.4
The Assignment of Treatments to Experimental Units for Cereal Package Design Example

Blocks	Treatment Order			
1	T_2	T_1	T_3	T_4
2	T_1	T_2	T_4	T_3
3	T_4	T_3	T_1	T_2
4	T_3	T_1	T_2	T_4
5	T_1	T_4	T_3	T_2

There are K treatments and b blocks, so $i = 1, \ldots, K$ and $j = 1, \ldots, b$.

An example of the type of ANOVA table used to analyze this model is shown in Figure 8.8. Three sources of variation are identified: blocks, treatments, and error. The sums of squares, the mean squares, and the degrees of freedom associated with each of these sources are shown. Note that the degrees of freedom from the three sources will sum to the total degrees of freedom: $(b-1)+(K-1)+(b-1)(K-1) = bK - 1$. This also will be true for the sums of squares: $SSBL + SSTR + SSE = SST$.

The goal of the analysis is to determine whether the treatment effects differ:

$$H_0: \quad \gamma_1 = \gamma_2 = \cdots = \gamma_K$$
$$H_a: \quad \text{All treatment effects are not equal}$$

The decision rule to perform the test is:

$$\text{Reject } H_0 \quad \text{if} \quad F > F(\alpha; \quad K - 1, (b - 1)(K - 1))$$
$$\text{Accept } H_0 \quad \text{if} \quad F \leq F(\alpha; \quad K - 1, (b - 1)(K - 1))$$

The test statistic is

$$F = \frac{MSTR}{MSE}$$

If the null hypothesis is rejected, then the conclusion is that the treatment effects differ.

A test also can be conducted to determine whether the block effects differ:

$$H_0: \quad B_1 = B_2 = \cdots = B_b$$
$$H_a: \quad \text{All blocks effects are not equal}$$

The decision rule to perform the test is:

$$\text{Reject } H_0 \quad \text{if} \quad F > F(\alpha; \quad b - 1, (b - 1)(K - 1))$$
$$\text{Accept } H_0 \quad \text{if} \quad F \leq F(\alpha; \quad b - 1, (b - 1)(K - 1))$$

The test statistic is

$$F = \frac{MSBL}{MSE},$$

where $MSBL$ is the mean square due to blocks.

If the null hypothesis is rejected, then the conclusion is that the block effects differ. In this case, the use of blocking has helped and should be continued.

If the null hypothesis is accepted, then the conclusion is that the block effects are equal. The use of blocks appears to be unnecessary, and information may actually be lost by the use of blocking. In many cases, however, the use of blocking will be continued regardless of the outcome of this test if it is felt that blocking truly will produce more homogenous groups and therefore reduce variation. As a result, the test for block effects often will not be used.

A $(1 - \alpha)100\%$ confidence interval estimate for the difference between two treatment means is given by

$$(\bar{y}_i - \bar{y}_{i'}) \pm t_{\alpha/2} s \sqrt{\frac{2}{b}},$$

F I G U R E **8.8**

ANOVA Table for Randomized Block Design

Source	DF	SS	MS
Blocks	$b-1$	SSBL	MSBL
Treatments	$K-1$	SSTR	MSTR
Error	$(b-1)(K-1)$	SSE	MSE
Total	$bK-1$	SST	

where $\bar{y}_i$ and $\bar{y}_{i'}$ are sample means for treatments i and i', $t_{\alpha/2}$ is chosen with $(b-1)(K-1)$ degrees of freedom, s is the square root of *MSE*, and b is the number of blocks.

If more than one pair of treatment means is to be compared, a familywise $(1-\alpha)100\%$ level of confidence can be achieved by using the Bonferroni confidence coefficient described in the previous section.

E X A M P L E **8.5** **Cereal Package Design**

Consider the problem discussed in this section involving the design of cereal packages. Four package designs (treatments) are to be tested in 20 stores. The 20 stores are divided into 5 groups (blocks) of 4 stores each by size. The treatments are randomized within each block, independently between blocks. The data obtained are shown in Table 8.5. Table 8.6 shows the data in an alternate form. This is the way the data would be entered for analysis in either MINITAB or SAS.

The MINITAB output for this example is shown in Figure 8.9 and the SAS output is in Figure 8.10. In the output, the blocks are denoted SIZE and the treatments are denoted DESIGN. The MINITAB and SAS ANOVA tables contain the information in the general ANOVA table of Figure 8.8. The general structure of the MINITAB and SAS ANOVA tables is shown in Figure 8.11.

T A B L E **8.5**

Data for Cereal Package Design Example

Blocks	Sales (in $1000) Treatments			
	1	**2**	**3**	**4**
1	40	23	17	33
2	32	45	40	25
3	43	31	38	47
4	44	41	56	45
5	43	60	47	64

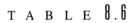

T A B L E **8.6**
Data for Cereal Package Design Example Listed As It Would
Be Entered for MINITAB or SAS Analysis

SALES	SIZE	DESIGN
40	1	1
23	1	2
17	1	3
33	1	4
32	2	1
45	2	2
40	2	3
25	2	4
43	3	1
31	3	2
38	3	3
47	3	4
44	4	1
41	4	2
56	4	3
45	4	4
43	5	1
60	5	2
47	5	3
64	5	4

To determine whether there is a difference in sales because of package design, the following hypotheses should be tested:

$$H_0: \quad \gamma_1 = \gamma_2 = \gamma_3 = \gamma_4$$

$$H_a: \quad \text{All treatment effects are not equal}$$

The decision rule for the test is:

Reject H_0 if $F > F(.05; \quad 3, 12) = 3.49$

Accept H_0 if $F \le F(.05; \quad 3, 12) = 3.49$

The test statistic is

$$F = \frac{MSTR}{MSE} = \frac{10.3}{91.1} = 0.11$$

The null hypothesis cannot be rejected. There is no evidence of a difference in sales because of package design.

A 95% confidence interval estimate for the difference between the treatment means for the first and second designs is

$$(40.4 - 40) \pm 2.179(9.54)\sqrt{\frac{2}{5}}$$

or

$$(-12.75, \quad 13.55) \quad \blacksquare$$

F I G U R E **8.9**

MINITAB ANOVA Output for Cereal Package Design Example

```
Two-way Analysis of Variance

Analysis of Variance for sales
Source       DF        SS        MS
size          4      1521.7     380.4
design        3        31.0      10.3
Error        12      1093.5      91.1
Total        19      2646.2
```

F I G U R E **8.10**

SAS ANOVA Output for Cereal Package Design Example

```
              Analysis of Variance Procedure
                 Class Level Information

         Class     Levels    Values

         SIZE         5      1 2 3 4 5

         DESIGN       4      1 2 3 4


      Number of observations in data set = 20


              Analysis of Variance Procedure

Dependent Variable: SALES

Source            DF   Sum of Squares    Mean Square   F Value   Pr > F
Model              7    1552.70000000   221.81428571     2.43    0.0842
Error             12    1093.50000000    91.12500000
Corrected Total   19    2646.20000000



       R-Square          C.V.        Root MSE      SALES Mean

       0.586766       23.45440      9.54594155     40.70000000


Source       DF       Anova SS       Mean Square   F Value   Pr > F

SIZE          4    1521.70000000    380.42500000     4.17    0.0240
DESIGN        3      31.00000000     10.33333333     0.11    0.9506
```

F I G U R E 8.11

Structure of the MINITAB and SAS ANOVA Tables for a Randomized Block Design

(a) MINITAB

Analysis of Variance for (dependent variable name)

Source	DF	SS	MS
Blocks	$b-1$	SSBL	MSBL
Treatments	$K-1$	SSTR	MSTR
Error	$(b-1)(K-1)$	SSE	MSE
Total	$bK-1$	SST	

(b) SAS

Analysis of Variance Procedure

Dependent Variable: DEPENDENT VARIABLE NAME

Source	DF	Sum of Squares	Mean Square	F Value	Pr > F
Model	$b+K-2$	SSModel = SSBL + SSTR	MSModel = SSModel/$b+K-2$	$\dfrac{\text{MSModel}}{\text{MSE}}$	p-value
Error	$(b-1)(K-1)$	SSE	MSE = SSE/$(b-1)(K-1)$		
Corrected Total	$bK-1$	SST			

R-square	C.V.	Root MSE	Y Var. Mean
$\dfrac{\text{SSModel}}{\text{SST}}$	$\dfrac{\text{Root MSE}}{\text{Y Var. Mean}} \times 100$	$\sqrt{\text{MSE}}$	$\bar{Y}$

Source	DF	Anova SS	Mean Square	F Value	Pr > F
BLOCK NAME	$b-1$	SSBL	SSBL/$(b-1)$	MSBL/MSE	p-value
TREATMENT NAME	$K-1$	SSTR	SSTR/$(K-1)$	MSTR/MSE	p-value

Exercises

2   **Advertising**   A study was undertaken by a company that markets iced tea to determine the effectiveness of three types of advertising: (1) price discounts, (2) manufacturer's coupons, and (3) rebates. Three cities of nearly equal size are selected for the experiment. Each of the advertising strategies is to be used for a period of two months in each city and the sales of the company's iced tea recorded for the two-month period. It is known, however, that iced tea sales are highly seasonal. Thus, the months selected for a particular advertising strategy could highly influence the level of sales. A randomized block design is used to eliminate the seasonal effects.

For each time period (block) the advertising strategies (treatments) are randomly assigned to the three cities. The results are shown in Table 8.7. The variable ADV is coded as 1 = price discounts, 2 = manufacturer's coupons, and 3 = rebates. The variable BLOCK is coded as 1 = first two-month period, 2 = second two-month period, and 3 = third two-month period.

Treating the experiment as a randomized block design, the MINITAB and SAS outputs in Figures 8.12 and 8.13 respectively, were obtained. Use the outputs to determine whether the effects of the advertising strategies differ. Use a 5% level of significance. State any hypotheses to be tested, the decision rule, the test statistic, and your decision to accept or reject the null hypothesis.

These data are available on the data disk for further analysis. In MINITAB, they can be read using

```
READ 'ADVERT8' C1-C3
```

where C1 is SALES (in $1000), C2 is ADV, and C3 is BLOCK.

In SAS, the data can be read from the file ADVERT8.DAT using

```
INPUT SALES ADV BLOCK;
```

T A B L E **8.7**
Data for Advertising Exercise

SALES (in $1000)	ADV	BLOCK
30	1	1
21	1	2
14	1	3
33	2	1
25	2	2
19	2	3
41	3	1
32	3	2
24	3	3

F I G U R E **8.12**

MINITAB ANOVA Output for Advertising Exercise

```
Two-way Analysis of Variance

Analysis of Variance for sales
Source     DF       SS       MS
adv         2    174.222   87.111
block       2    369.556  184.778
Error       4      2.444    0.611
Total       8    546.222
```

F I G U R E **8.13**

SAS ANOVA Output for Advertising Exercise

```
           Analysis of Variance Procedure
              Class Level Information

      Class      Levels     Values

      ADV            3      1 2 3

      BLOCK          3      1 2 3


   Number of observations in data set = 9


         Analysis of Variance Procedure

Dependent Variable: SALES

Source           DF   Sum of Squares   Mean Square        F    Pr > F

Model             4   543.77777778   135.94444444    222.45   0.0001
Error             4     2.44444444     0.61111111
Corrected Total   8   546.22222222


     R-Square        C.V.        Root MSE       SALES Mean

     0.995525      2.943776      0.78173596      26.55555556



Source     DF      Anova SS       Mean Square    F Value  Pr > F

   ADV      2   174.22222222      87.11111111    142.55   0.0002
 BLOCK      2   369.55555556     184.77777778    302.36   0.0001
```

8.3
Two-Way Analysis of Variance

Two-way ANOVA refers to a situation in which there are two factors or explanatory variables. For example, suppose a company wants to investigate the effect of selling price and type of advertising on sales of its top-of-the-line printer. The two possible prices investigated are $600 and $700. There are three types of advertising: television, radio, and newspaper.

In general, denote the two factors in the study as A and B and the number of levels of each factor as n_1 and n_2, respectively. Each combination of a factor level of A and a factor level of B is called a *treatment*. The total number of possible treatments in a two-factor study is $n_1 n_2$. In the example given, there are $2 \times 3 = 6$ possible treatments:

1   $600 price and television advertising
2   $600 price and radio advertising
3   $600 price and newspaper advertising
4   $700 price and television advertising
5   $700 price and radio advertising
6   $700 price and newspaper advertising

This type of design is called a *factorial design*. When all treatment combinations (or factor-level combinations) are used, the experiment is termed a *complete factorial experiment*. This will be the design considered in this section.

Equal sample sizes are assumed for each treatment. (Unequal sample sizes will not be considered in this text.) The number of observations for each treatment will be denoted r. The total number of observations used is $n = n_1 n_2 r$. The number of observations for each treatment must be at least two ($r \geq 2$).

The two-way ANOVA model is written

$$y_{ijk} = \mu + \alpha_i + \beta_j + (\alpha\beta)_{ij} + e_{ijk},$$

where

y_{ijk} is the kth observation for factor-level i of factor A and factor-level j of factor B

μ is a common component for all treatments

α_i is the effect of factor A at level i

β_j is the effect of factor B at level j

$(\alpha\beta)_{ij}$ is called the interaction effect for factors A and B

e_{ijk} is a random disturbance

Here, $i = 1, 2, \ldots, n_1$; $j = 1, 2, \ldots, n_2$; and $k = 1, 2, \ldots, r$ with $r \geq 2$.

In the two-way ANOVA setting, hypotheses can be tested to determine whether the effects from either factor A or factor B are equal or different. The factor effects due to A and B are called *main effects*. Hypotheses also can be tested to determine whether the interaction effects are equal. Interaction implies that the difference in mean levels of factor A depends on the levels of factor B. The model has no interaction effects if the difference is independent of the levels of B.

The first test that should be conducted is the test for interaction effects. The tests for main effects will be relevant only if no interaction exists. If interaction exists, then the tests for factor-level means will be inappropriate. In this case individual treatment means must be examined, as will be demonstrated in the example.

An example of the type of ANOVA table used in two-way analysis of variance problems is shown in Figure 8.14. Total variation in the dependent variable is attributed to four sources: the two factors A and B, the interaction between the two factors, and random error. The degrees of freedom, sums of squares, and mean square for each source are shown. The tests that can be performed using the ANOVA table are outlined next.

Test for Interaction Effects

H_0:   No interaction between factors A and B exists (all $(\alpha\beta)_{ij} = 0$)

H_a: Factors A and B interact (at least one $(\alpha\beta)_{ij}$ is not equal to zero)

The decision rule for the test is:

Reject H_0 if $F > F(\alpha;\quad (n_1 - 1)(n_2 - 1), n_1 n_2 (r - 1))$

Accept H_0 if $F \leq F(\alpha;\quad (n_1 - 1)(n_2 - 1), n_1 n_2 (r - 1))$

The test statistic is

$$F = \frac{MSINT}{MSE},$$

where *MSINT* is the mean square due to interaction. If the null hypothesis is accepted, then we conclude that there is no interaction between factors A and B. To determine whether the factor-level means are equal, the following tests can be performed.

Test for Factor *A* Effects

$$H_0: \quad \alpha_1 = \alpha_2 = \ldots = \alpha_{n_1}$$

$$H_a: \quad \text{The } \alpha_i \text{ are not all equal}$$

The decision rule for the test is:

Reject H_0 if $F > F(\alpha;\quad n_1 - 1, n_1 n_2 (r - 1))$

Accept H_0 if $F \leq F(\alpha;\quad n_1 - 1, n_1 n_2 (r - 1))$

The test statistic is

$$F = \frac{MSA}{MSE}$$

F I G U R E **8.14**

Sample ANOVA Table for Two-Way Design

Source	DF	SS	MS
Factor A	$n_1 - 1$	SSA	$MSA = SSA/(n_1 - 1)$
Factor B	$n_2 - 1$	SSB	$MSB = SSB/(n_2 - 1)$
Interaction	$(n_1 - 1)(n_2 - 1)$	SSINT	$MSINT = SSINT/[(n_1 - 1)(n_2 - 1)]$
Error	$n_1 n_2 (r - 1)$	SSE	$MSE = SSE/[n_1 n_2 (r - 1)]$
Total	$n_1 n_2 r - 1$	SST	

Test for Factor *B* Effects

$$H_0: \quad \beta_1 = \beta_2 = \ldots = \beta_{n_2}$$
$$H_a: \quad \text{The } \beta_j \text{ are not all equal}$$

The decision rule for the test is:

$$\text{Reject } H_0 \quad \text{if} \quad F > F(\alpha; \quad n_2 - 1, n_1 n_2 (r - 1))$$
$$\text{Accept } H_0 \quad \text{if} \quad F \leq F(\alpha; \quad n_2 - 1, n_1 n_2 (r - 1))$$

The test statistic is

$$F = \frac{MSB}{MSE}$$

To construct a $(1 - \alpha)100\%$ confidence interval estimate of the difference between two treatment means, we use the following formula:

$$\bar{y}_i - \bar{y}_{i'} \pm t_{\alpha/2} s \sqrt{\frac{2}{r}},$$

where s is the square root of MSE, $t_{\alpha/2}$ is chosen with $n_1 n_2 (r - 1)$ degrees of freedom, and $\bar{y}_i$ and $\bar{y}_{i'}$ are sample means using the r observations of the appropriate treatments (factor-level combinations).

If more than one pair of treatment means is to be compared, a familywise $(1 - \alpha)100\%$ level of confidence can be achieved by using the Bonferroni confidence coefficient described in the one-way ANOVA section.

E X A M P L E **8.6** **Printer Sales**

Consider again the company investigating sales of this top-of-the-line printer. An experiment was conducted to determine the effects of type of advertising and selling price on sales. The two levels of selling price considered were $600 and $700. The three types of advertising were television, radio, and newspaper.

Table 8.8 shows the data obtained from the experiment. The first column of the table (SALES) shows total sales for a period of one month (in $1000). The second column (PRICE) indicates the level of price (1 = $600 and 2 = $700), and the third column (ADV) indicates the type of advertising used (1 = television, 2 = radio, and 3 = newspaper).

T A B L E   **8.8**

Data for Printer Example

SALES (in $1000)	PRICE	ADV
18.0	1	1
16.8	1	1
12.0	1	2
13.2	1	2
7.8	1	3
9.9	1	3
14.0	2	1
14.7	2	1
10.8	2	2
9.6	2	2
9.8	2	3
8.4	2	3

The MINITAB output is shown in Figure 8.15 and the SAS output is in Figure 8.16. The MINITAB and SAS ANOVA tables contain the information in the general ANOVA table of Figure 8.14. The general structure of the MINITAB and SAS ANOVA table is shown in Figure 8.17.

First, we test to see whether interaction effects are present. The decision rule is:

$$\text{Reject } H_0 \quad \text{if} \quad F > F(.05; \quad 2, 6) = 5.14$$

$$\text{Accept } H_0 \quad \text{if} \quad F \leq 5.14.$$

The test statistic is

$$F = \frac{4.016}{0.684} = 5.87$$

The decision is to reject H_0.

We conclude that there are interaction effects. The F tests for main effects discussed in this section cannot be used to determine whether price effects differ or whether advertising effects differ because the two factors interact. In this case it may be helpful to examine the individual treatment means. These are obtained simply by averaging the r observations associated with each treatment (or factor-level combination).

The treatment means are computed by averaging the observations for each treatment. For example, for the treatment when price was $600 and television advertising was used the treatment mean would be $(18.0 + 16.8)/2 = 17.4$. These means can be computed by hand but some computer routines allow simple procedures that will compute the means. Figure 8.18 shows the output from MINITAB that results from using the TABLE command (see Section 8.5: Using the Computer). Each of the treatment means is shown in this table.

Figure 8.19 shows a plot of the treatment means. It appears from the plot that the highest level of sales is associated with television advertising and a $600 price. Sales are higher for the $600 price when either television or radio advertising is used. When newspaper advertising is used, however, the $700 price is associated with slightly higher sales. This crossover of the lines illustrates the interaction effects. If there were no interaction, the effects of factors A and B might appear as illustrated in Figure 8.20. The two lines are parallel, which indicates complete absence of interaction. Figure 8.21 illustrates another possible situation. Here the

F I G U R E 8.15

MINITAB ANOVA Output for Printer Sales Example

```
Two-way Analysis of Variance

Analysis of Variance for sales
Source          DF        SS        MS
price            1     7.521     7.521
adv              2   103.752    51.876
Interaction      2     8.032     4.016
Error            6     4.105     0.684
Total           11   123.409
```

F I G U R E 8.16

SAS ANOVA Output for Printer Sales Example

```
               Analysis of Variance Procedure
                  Class Level Information

        Class    Levels    Values

        PRICE        2     1 2

        ADV          3     1 2 3


      Number of observations in data set = 12


            Analysis of Variance Procedure

Dependent Variable: SALES

Source              DF   Sum of Squares   Mean Square   F Value   Pr > F

Model                5   119.30416667    23.86083333     34.88   0.0002
Error                6     4.10500000     0.68416667
Corrected Total     11   123.40916667
```

R-Square	C.V.	Root MSE	SALES Mean
0.966737	6.888081	0.82714368	12.00833333

Source	DF	Anova SS	Mean Square	F Value	Pr > F
PRICE	1	7.52083333	7.52083333	10.99	0.0161
ADV	2	103.75166667	51.87583333	75.82	0.0001
PRICE*ADV	2	8.03166667	4.01583333	5.87	0.0387

FIGURE 8.17

Structure of the MINITAB and SAS ANOVA Tables for a Two-Way Design

(a) MINITAB

Analysis of Variance for (dependent variable name)

Source	DF	SS	MS
Factor A	$n_1 - 1$	SSA	MSA
Factor B	$n_2 - 1$	SSB	MSB
Interaction	$(n_1 - 1)(n_2 - 1)$	SSINT	MSINT
Error	$n_1 n_2 (r - 1)$	SSE	MSE
Total	$n_1 n_2 r - 1$	SST	

(b) SAS

Analysis of Variance Procedure

Dependent Variable: DEPENDENT VARIABLE NAME

Source	DF	Sum of Squares	Mean Square	F Value	Pr > F
Model	$n_1 n_2 - 1$	SSModel = SSA + SSB + SSINT	MSModel = SSModel/$n_1 n_2 - 1$	$\dfrac{\text{MSModel}}{\text{MSE}}$	p-value
Error	$n_1 n_2 (r - 1)$	SSE	MSE = SSE/[$n_1 n_2 (r - 1)$]		
Corrected Total	$n_1 n_2 r - 1$	SST			

R-square	C.V.	Root MSE	Y Var. Mean
$\dfrac{\text{SSModel}}{\text{SST}}$	$\dfrac{\text{Root MSE}}{\text{Y Var. Mean}} \times 100$	$\sqrt{\text{MSE}}$	$\bar{Y}$

Source	DF	Anova SS	Mean Square	F Value	Pr > F
FACTOR A	$n_1 - 1$	SSA	SSA/$(n_1 - 1)$	MSA/MSE	p-value
FACTOR B	$n_2 - 1$	SSB	SSB/$(n_2 - 1)$	MSB/MSE	p-value
INTERACTION	$(n_1 - 1)(n_2 - 1)$	SSINT	SSINT/[$(n_1 - 1)(n_2 - 1)$]	MSINT/MSE	p-value

F I G U R E **8.18**

MINITAB Output for Printer Sales Example Showing Use of TABLE Command to Determine Treatment Means

Tabulated Statistics

```
ROWS: price      COLUMNS: adv

           1        2        3       ALL

 1     17.400   12.600   8.400   12.800
 2     14.350   10.200   9.100   11.217
ALL    15.875   11.400   8.750   12.008

CELL CONTENTS --
          sales:MEAN
```

F I G U R E **8.19**

Plot of Treatment Means for Printer Sales Example

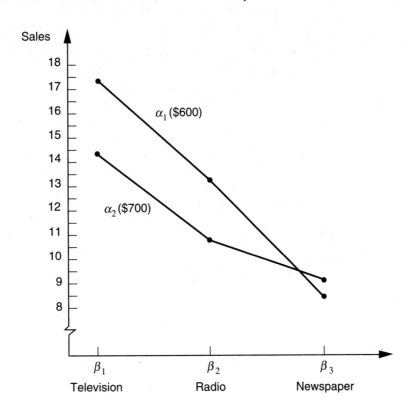

F I G U R E **8.20**
Example of Treatment Mean Plot Showing No Interaction Effects

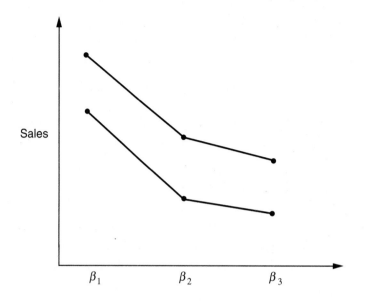

F I G U R E **8.21**
Example of Treatment Mean Plot Showing Weak Interaction Effects

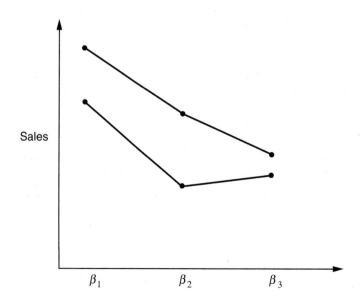

two lines are not parallel, but they do not cross. In this case, the interaction does not appear to be serious and the model could be treated as one without interaction. Thus, the F tests for main factor effects would be appropriate.

If there were no differences in the effects because of factor A, the two lines drawn would nearly coincide (see Figure 8.22, for example). If there were no differences in the effects from factor B, the two lines drawn would be nearly horizontal (see Figure 8.23, for example).

A 95% confidence interval estimate for the difference between the treatment means for $700 price and television advertising and $700 price and radio advertising is given by

$$(14.35 - 10.2) \pm 2.447(.887)\sqrt{\frac{2}{2}}$$

or $(2.13, 6.17)$. ■

F I G U R E **8.22**

Example of Treatment Mean Plot of No Interaction Effects and No Factor A Main Effects

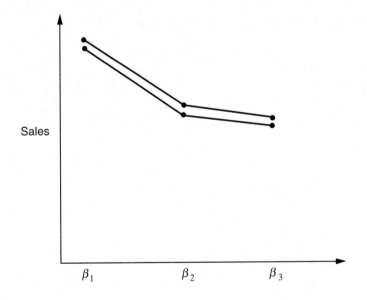

F I G U R E   **8.23**

Example of Treatment Mean Plot of No Interaction Effects and No Factor *B* Main Effects

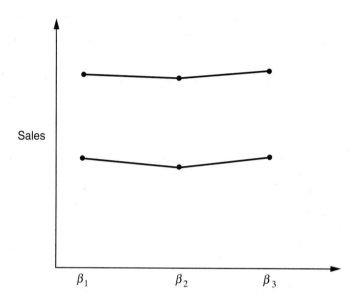

Exercises

3   **Satisfaction**   A company designs applications software for a large number of firms. A study is conducted to assess the level of satisfaction of these firms with the software supplied. The effects of two factors on the level of satisfaction are to be investigated:

1   the industry of the firm that receives the software, and

2   the contact person from whom the software was purchased.

   Four industries are served and there are three contact people. For each combination of industries and contacts, two firms are randomly selected and surveyed. A satisfaction score is obtained from the questionnaire administered. The results are shown in Table 8.9. MINITAB and SAS outputs for this two-factor study are shown in Figures 8.24 and 8.25, respectively. Use the outputs to determine whether the factor effects are different. Use a 5% level of significance. State any hypotheses to be tested, the decision rule, the test statistic, and your decision to accept or reject the null hypothesis.

   These data are available on the data disk for further analysis. In MINITAB, they can be read using

```
READ 'SATIS8' C1-C3
```

where C1 is SATIS, C2 is INDUSTRY, and C3 is CONTACT.
In SAS, the data can be read from the file SATIS8.DAT using

```
INPUT SATIS INDUSTRY CONTACT;
```

T A B L E 8.9

Data for Satisfaction Exercise

SATIS	INDUSTRY	CONTACT
74	1	1
72	1	1
73	1	2
71	1	2
75	1	3
69	1	3
73	2	1
71	2	1
75	2	2
70	2	2
71	2	3
72	2	3
81	3	1
84	3	1
83	3	2
82	3	2
85	3	3
82	3	3
84	4	1
81	4	1
85	4	2
83	4	2
82	4	3
85	4	3

F I G U R E 8.24

MINITAB ANOVA Output for Satisfaction Exercise

```
Two-way Analysis of Variance

Analysis of Variance for satis
Source        DF        SS        MS
industry       3     716.12    238.71
contact        2       0.25      0.13
Interaction    6       5.75      0.96
Error         12      57.50      4.79
Total         23     779.63
```

F I G U R E **8.25**

SAS ANOVA Output for Satisfaction Exercise

```
                 Analysis of Variance Procedure
                    Class Level Information

         Class     Levels    Values

         INDUSTRY     4      1 2 3 4

         CONTACT      3      1 2 3

      Number of observations in data set = 24


               Analysis of Variance Procedure

Dependent Variable: SATIS

  Source             DF  Sum of Squares  Mean Square  F Value  Pr > F

  Model              11   722.12500000  65.64772727    13.70  0.0001
  Error              12    57.50000000   4.79166667
  Corrected Total    23   779.62500000

           R-Square          C.V.      Root MSE      SATIS Mean
           0.926247       2.819952   2.18898759    77.62500000


  Source             DF    Anova SS     Mean Square   F Value  Pr > F

  INDUSTRY            3   716.12500000  238.70833333    49.82  0.0001
  CONTACT            2     0.25000000    0.12500000     0.03  0.9743
  INDUSTRY*CONTACT   6     5.75000000    0.95833333     0.20  0.9703
```

8.4
Analysis of Covariance

Analysis of covariance (ANCOVA) is a procedure sometimes used with models containing some quantitative and some qualitative independent variables. In ANCOVA, however, the main interest is in the qualitative variables. In this respect, ANCOVA might be viewed as a modification of ANOVA procedures rather than as a special case of regression analysis (it is, in fact, both). The term ANCOVA is used when the quantitative independent variables are added to the ANOVA model to reduce the variance of the error terms and thus provide more precise measurement of the treatment effects. These quantitative variables should be constructed in such a way that they are not influenced by the treatments.

Although programs such as SAS do provide specific routines for performing ANCOVA, these will not be discussed in this text. ANCOVA also can be performed using regression routines with appropriately constructed indicator variables.

8.5
Using the Computer

8.5.1 MINITAB

One-Way Analysis of Variance

There are two commands in MINITAB for one-way analysis of variance. The choice depends on how the data are arranged. If all data are in a single column and another column is used to specify the factor levels (or groups) the command is

```
ONEWAY ON DATA IN C2, LEVELS IN C1      (STAT: ANOVA: ONEWAY)
```

where the dependent variable is assumed to be in C2 and the variable specifying the factor levels is in C1.

If the data for each factor level are placed in separate columns (unstacked) then the command is

```
AOVONEWAY ON DATA IN C1-C9      (STAT: ANOVA: ONEWAY (UNSTACKED))
```

Either of these commands would generate the output in Figure 8.1 for data set up appropriately.

Analysis of Variance Using a Randomized Block Design
(STAT: ANOVA: TWOWAY: FIT ADDITIVE MODEL)

```
TWOWAY ON DATA IN C1, BLOCKS IN C2, LEVELS IN C3; ADDITIVE.
```

In Example 8.5, C1 is the variable SALES, C2 is SIZE (the blocking variable), and C3 is DESIGN (the treatment variable). The output is shown in Figure 8.9. The TWOWAY command indicates that there are two variables other than the dependent variable to be considered. The ADDITIVE subcommand is used for the randomized block design (this subcommand can be used in other instances too, but it should be used when using a randomized block design).

Two-Way Analysis of Variance (STAT: ANOVA: TWOWAY)

```
TWOWAY ON DATA IN C1, LEVELS IN C2, C3
```

In Example 8.6, C1 is SALES, C2 is PRICE, and C3 is ADV. The output is shown in Figure 8.15. The TWOWAY command (without the ADDITIVE subcommand) automatically assumes that an interaction term should be included in the model (as it should be for two-way analysis of variance).

The treatment means are easily obtained in MINITAB using the following command:

```
TABLE C2,C3;
MEANS C1.
```

This command requests a table with the levels of C2 to be used as rows and the levels of C3 as columns. In the table itself, the means of the values of C1 for all possible combinations of C2 and C3 are to be displayed. Output from Example 8.6, using the TABLE command is shown in Figure 8.18.

In the Windows version of MINITAB, the table can be generated using STAT: TABLES: CROSS TABULATION. CLASSIFICATION VARIABLES would be C2 and C3 in this example. Under SUMMARIES, ASSOCIATED VARIABLES would be C1 and MEANS should be requested.

8.5.2 SAS

One-Way Analysis of Variance

```
PROC ANOVA;
 CLASS CARTYPE;
 MODEL INJURY=CARTYPE;
```

Class indicates which variable is the classification variable—that is, which variable denotes the factor levels for each observation in the data set. Output for this example is shown in Figure 8.3.

Analysis of Variance Using a Randomized Block Design

```
PROC ANOVA;
 CLASS SIZE DESIGN;
 MODEL SALES=SIZE DESIGN;
```

The PROC ANOVA statement is the same as the statement used for a one-way analysis of variance. The CLASS statement now specifies both the blocking and treatment variables. The MODEL statement lists the dependent variable on the left-hand side of the equality and the blocking and treatment variables on the right-hand side. Output for this example is shown in Figure 8.10.

Two-Way Analysis of Variance

```
PROC ANOVA;
 CLASS PRICE ADV;
 MODEL SALES=PRICE ADV PRICE*ADV;
```

The SAS command sequence for two-way analysis of variance requires that the interaction term be explicitly included in the MODEL statement as shown: PRICE*ADV. Otherwise, the interaction term will be omitted (as in the randomized block design). Output for this example is shown in Figure 8.16.

Additional Exercises

4 **ANOVA Tables**

   a Assume that one-way analysis of variance is to be performed. Complete the ANOVA table for this analysis:

SOURCE	DF	SS	MS	F
Treatment	3			
ERROR		20		
TOTAL	23	170		

   b Assume that a randomized block experiment is to be performed. Complete the ANOVA table for this analysis:

SOURCE	DF	SS	MS	F
Blocks	4			
Treatment		80	40	
ERROR	39		2	
TOTAL	45	198		

5 **Assembly Line** Three assembly lines are used to produce a certain component for a computer. To examine the production rate of the assembly lines, a random sample of six hourly periods is chosen for each assembly line and the number of components produced during these periods for each line is recorded. The data are shown in Table 8.10.

   Is there a difference in the average production rates for the three assembly lines? Use a 5% level of significance in answering this question. State any hypotheses to be tested, the decision rule, the test statistic, and your decision to accept or reject the null hypothesis.

   These data are available on the data disk. In MINITAB, they can be read using

```
READ 'ASSEMBL8' C1,C2
```

where C1 is NUMBER, the number of components produced, and C2 is coded 1, 2, or 3 to indicate the assembly line (LINE).

   In SAS, the data can be read from the file ASSEMBL8.DAT using

```
INPUT NUMBER LINE;
```

T A B L E **8.10**

Data for Assembly Line Exercise

NUMBER	LINE	NUMBER	LINE
37	1	58	2
35	1	52	2
34	1	53	2
37	1	31	3
36	1	36	3
38	1	37	3
50	2	37	3
57	2	39	3
56	2	34	3

6   **Salaries**   A large state university is interested in comparing salaries of its graduates (BA or BS) in the following areas: business, education, engineering, and liberal arts. Five graduates in each major are randomly selected and their starting salaries recorded. The data are shown in Table 8.11.

The university wants to know whether there is a difference in the population average salaries for the four majors. Use a 5% level of significance in making the decision. State any hypotheses to be tested, the decision rule, the test statistic, and your decision to accept or reject the null hypothesis.

Find a 95% interval estimate for the difference between the business and engineering mean salaries.

Use the Bonferroni method to compare all possible pairs of means with a familywise confidence level of 90%. Use the familywise comparisons to answer the following questions: Is there a significant difference in the population mean salaries for (1) business and education majors, (2) business and engineering majors, and (3) education and liberal arts majors? If so, which major has a higher mean salary in each comparison?

These data are available on the data disk. In MINITAB, they can be read using

```
READ 'SALMAJ8' C1,C2
```

where C1 is SALARIES and C2 (MAJOR) is coded to indicate the major (1 = business, 2 = education, 3 = engineering, and 4 = liberal arts).

T A B L E **8.11**

Salaries (in $1000) for Majors Used in Salaries Exercise

	Major		
Business	**Education**	**Engineering**	**Liberal Arts**
14.5	12.2	24.7	10.6
22.4	13.4	25.6	14.7
24.1	12.8	26.7	15.2
21.7	11.7	24.9	12.1
17.9	12.5	28.7	16.4

In SAS, the data can be read from the file SALMAJ8.DAT using

```
INPUT SALARIES MAJOR;
```

7   **Test Scores**   A large financial-planning firm wants to compare the results of three training programs for its staff. Nine employees are grouped into three blocks for the comparison. The blocks are based on number of years since college graduation, with block 1 being most recent graduates and block 3 the most distant graduates. After the training programs are completed the employees are tested and the test scores recorded. These data are shown in Table 8.12 and are denoted SCORE for the test score, PRO-GRAM for the training program used (1, 2, or 3), and BLOCK for the block in which each employee was placed (1, 2, or 3).

   Determine whether there is a difference in average test scores because of the training programs. Use a 5% level of significance. State any hypotheses to be tested, the decision rule, the test statistic, and your decision to accept or reject the null hypothesis.

   Construct a 95% confidence interval estimate of the difference between the means for program 1 and program 2.

   These data are available on the data disk. In MINITAB, they can be read using

```
READ 'TESTSCR8'
```

where C1 is SCORE, C2 is PROGRAM, and C3 is BLOCK.
   In SAS, the data can be read from the file TESTSCR8.DAT using

```
INPUT SCORE PROGRAM BLOCK;
```

8   **Employee Productivity**   A study of productivity is to be conducted with employees who enter data at computer terminals. The amount of data entered is to be the dependent variable. Two factors that may influence the dependent variable are to be examined. One factor is the type of computer terminal used (three types are available in the company). The second factor is the time of day (morning or afternoon). Four employees are randomly assigned to each type of terminal. Two employees' production levels are recorded for a period of one hour in the morning. The other two are recorded in the afternoon. The production level is the number of forms completely entered at the terminal by each employee. The data are shown in Table 8.13. In the table, NUMBER is the number of

T A B L E   **8.12**
Data for Test Scores Exercise

SCORE	PROGRAM	BLOCK
82	1	1
95	2	1
81	3	1
83	1	2
96	2	2
82	3	2
82	1	3
97	2	3
78	3	3

T A B L E   **8.13**

Data for Employee Productivity Exercise

NUMBER	TERMINAL	TIME
14	1	1
15	1	1
10	1	2
8	1	2
17	2	1
19	2	1
12	2	2
13	2	2
20	3	1
18	3	1
14	3	2
12	3	2

forms processed by each employee, TERMINAL is the terminal type (1, 2, or 3), and TIME is coded as 1 for morning and 2 for afternoon.

Do the factors TERMINAL and TIME appear to influence production rate (NUMBER)? If so, how would you describe the influence in words? Use a 5% level of significance for any hypothesis tests used. State any hypotheses to be tested, the decision rule, the test statistic, and your decision to accept or reject the null hypothesis.

These data are available on the data disk. In MINITAB, they can be read using

```
READ 'PRODRAT8' C1-C3
```

where C1 is NUMBER, C2 is TERMINAL, and C3 is TIME.

In SAS, the data can be read from the file PRODRAT8.DAT using

```
INPUT NUMBER TERMINAL TIME;
```

9   **Bill's Sales**   Bill's is a popular restaurant/bar in southwest Fort Worth, Texas. Table 8.14 shows daily sales data for Bill's for the period from October 14 through December 8 (these data have been disguised for confidentiality). Also shown is the day of the week, coded as 1 = Monday, 2 = Tuesday, 3 = Wednesday, 4 = Thursday, 5 = Friday, 6 = Saturday, and 7 = Sunday. Determine whether there is a difference in Bill's average sales on different days of the week. If there is a difference, on which day (or days) do sales appear to be highest? What would this suggest to the owner of Bill's about staffing?

These data are available on the data disk. In MINITAB, they can be read using

```
READ 'BILLS8' C1,C2
```

where C1 is SALES and C2 is the coded variable for day of the week.

In SAS, the data can be read from the file BILLS8.DAT using

```
INPUT SALES DAY;
```

T A B L E **8.14**

Data for Bill's Sales Exercise

SALES	DAY	SALES	DAY	SALES	DAY
2,573.5	1	6,397.3	6	3,259.3	4
3,509.1	2	2,865.1	7	5,816.0	5
2,979.0	3	2,068.9	1	6,697.3	6
4,037.1	4	2,141.0	2	2,465.2	7
9,521.4	5	2,782.6	3	2,195.1	1
7,015.5	6	3,590.8	4	2,451.0	2
3,516.8	7	6,396.7	5	4,045.6	3
2,309.9	1	10,154.9	6	1,569.0	4
3,673.0	2	2,595.1	7	5,574.1	5
3,329.2	3	1,845.2	1	5,194.8	6
4,818.0	4	2,412.3	2	2,494.2	7
7,078.0	5	2,700.7	3	1,970.6	1
5,570.6	6	3,371.1	4	2,511.6	2
3,722.8	7	6,826.7	5	2,481.3	3
1,749.7	1	6,611.4	6	2,318.2	4
3,245.0	2	2,768.2	7	4,460.8	5
2,454.0	3	2,145.0	1	5,330.4	6
2,779.8	4	2,021.9	2	2,424.0	7
6,048.2	5	2,341.7	3		

Qualitative Dependent Variables: An Introduction to Discriminant Analysis and Logistic Regression

9.1
Introduction

A bank is interested in determining whether certain large borrowers are creditworthy. Should loans be made to these potential customers or not? The bank has a variety of quantitative information about each potential borrower and would like some way of trying to classify them into groups of qualifying and nonqualifying candidates.

An investment company is trying to determine the likelihood that certain firms will end up in bankruptcy. The investment company has a variety of quantitative information on the firms it is considering and would like to be able to classify them into two groups, those that will go bankrupt and those that will not.

The director of personnel for a large corporation would like to know which of a group of new trainees will be successful in a certain position at the company. The director has some demographic information on these people and the results of certain tests that will be given prior to hiring.

The marketing department of a retail firm is interested in predicting whether people will buy a new product within the next year. The marketing department will have the results from surveys given to the people and a quantitative score representing propensity to buy as a summary measure from these surveys. The department wants to use this score to divide the people into groups of potential buyers and nonbuyers in order to be able to better target future advertising.

Each of these examples represents a case in which certain observations (people, firms, and so on) are to be divided into two groups: firms that do and do not qualify for credit; firms that will and won't go bankrupt; people that will and won't be successful in new positions; people who will and won't purchase a new product. The goal is to try to pick which of the two groups each observation will fall into based on available information. This type of problem can be placed in a regression setting. Write the regression model as

$$y = \beta_0 + \beta_1 x_1 + \cdots + \beta_K x_K + e,$$

where

$y = 1$ if the observation falls into the group of interest

$y = 0$ if the observation does not fall into the group of interest

Recall that in Chapter 6 methods were discussed for dealing with explanatory variables representing qualitative information. Examples used were employed/unemployed, male/female, and so on. The way this information was incorporated into the regression was to use indicator variables. These variables took on values of either 0 or 1 to indicate whether an item was or was not in a certain group (male = 1, female = 0, for example). In this chapter, we adopt a similar approach for situations where the dependent variable of interest is qualitative in nature. Situations will be examined where the task is to try and determine whether items will or will not fall into a certain group. The dependent variable used to represent this situation will be a variable that has either the value 1 if the item is in the group or the value 0 if the item is not in the group.

Standard linear regression analysis is not designed for directly analyzing this situation. In the regression applications examined so far in this text the dependent variable was a variable that could be effectively modeled as a continuous variable. The assumptions of the regression model are designed for such a situation. When a 0/1 dependent variable is used there are several problems that occur. To discuss the first problem it is important to note that the conditional mean of y given x has a different interpretation when the dependent variable is a 0/1 variable than it did in the previous case when the dependent variable was modeled as continuous. It can be shown that $\mu_{y|x}$ is equal to the probability that the observation belongs to the indicated group:

$$\mu_{y|x} = p,$$

where $p = P(Y = 1)$. Probabilities must be between 0 and 1, of course, but when the regression is estimated there is nothing to guarantee that the predictions from the estimated regression equation will be between 0 and 1. The actual predictions can vary considerably with values above 1 or even negative values occurring.

Second, certain assumptions of the regression model will be violated. For example, the disturbances will not be normally distributed and the variance around the regression line will not be constant.

As a result of the problems that occur with applying standard regression techniques to situations with 0/1 dependent variables, several alternative methods of analysis have been proposed. Two of these methods will be discussed in this chapter: discriminant analysis and logistic regression. Both of these techniques have characteristics that are similar to the regression models that have been presented thus far in this text. Even though linear regression, discriminant analysis, and logistic regression differ, the similarities will help the reader to understand the use of these procedures.

9.2
Discriminant Analysis

E X A M P L E 9.1 Employee Classification

The personnel director for a firm that manufactures computers has classified the performance of each of the employees in a certain position as either satisfactory or unsatisfactory. The director has two tests that she would like to use to help determine which employees will perform in a satisfactory manner and which will not before they are assigned to the position. With this knowledge she will be better able to suggest jobs within the firm at which each employee will have a greater chance of success. To help determine whether the tests will be useful, she administers the tests to the current employees and records their scores. The resulting data are shown in Table 9.1. The first column notes whether the employee is currently classified as satisfactory (1) or unsatisfactory (0). The next two columns show the test score results on each of the two tests given. Her task is now to determine how to use the test scores to predict the correct classification of each employee.

Figure 9.1 shows a scatterplot of each employee's scores on the two tests. The employees classified as successful are denoted with + and those classified as unsuccessful as O. From the plot, it does appear that knowledge of the test score may provide information useful in classifying the employees. There is no exact cutoff to separate the two groups precisely, but there is enough separation of the members to indicate that the information provided on the tests may be useful. ■

Discriminant analysis can be used to help solve the type of problem posed in Example 9.1. Discriminant analysis can be described as follows: Let y represent the dependent variable, defined as

$y = 1$ if the observation falls into the group of interest

$y = 0$ if the observation does not fall into the group of interest

Let $x_1, \ldots, x_K$ be explanatory variables that will be used to help predict into which of the two groups each of the observations in the sample should be classified. The explanatory variables are assumed to be approximately normally distributed. Although discriminant analysis can be used when the explanatory variables are not normally distributed, it is not guaranteed to be optimal in such cases and may not provide good results. This is one of the more serious limitations of this technique since it limits the kinds of variables that can be used as explanatory variables in the equation. Discriminant analysis also assumes that the variation of the explanatory variables is the same for each group.

T A B L E **9.1**

Data and Discriminant Analysis Results for Employee Classification Examples

Group	TEST1	TEST2	Prediction	Regression d Score
1	96	85	1	0.99694
1	96	88	1	1.04291
1	91	81	1	0.64276
1	95	78	1	0.83111
1	92	85	1	0.76262
1	93	87	1	0.85185
1	98	84	1	1.09878
1	92	82	1	0.71666
1	97	89	1	1.11681
1	95	96	1	1.10691
1	99	93	1	1.29526
1	89	90	1	0.66350
1	94	90	1	0.95639
1	92	94	1	0.90052
1	94	84	1	0.86446
1	90	92	1	0.75272
1	91	70	0*	0.47421
1	90	81	1	0.58418
1	86	81	0*	0.34986
1	90	76	0*	0.50757
1	91	79	1	0.61211
1	88	83	0*	0.49766
1	87	82	0*	0.42376
0	93	74	1*	0.65266
0	90	84	1*	0.63014
0	91	81	1*	0.64276
0	91	78	1*	0.59679
0	88	78	0	0.42105
0	86	86	0	0.42647
0	79	81	0	−0.06020
0	83	84	0	0.22009
0	79	77	0	−0.12149
0	88	75	0	0.37508
0	81	85	0	0.11825
0	85	83	0	0.32192
0	82	72	0	−0.02236
0	82	81	0	0.11554
0	81	77	0	−0.00433
0	86	76	0	0.27325
0	81	84	0	0.10293
0	85	78	0	0.24531
0	83	77	0	0.11283
0	81	71	0	−0.09626

F I G U R E **9.1**

Scatterplot of TEST1 versus TEST2 for Satisfactory (+) and Unsatisfactory (○) Employees

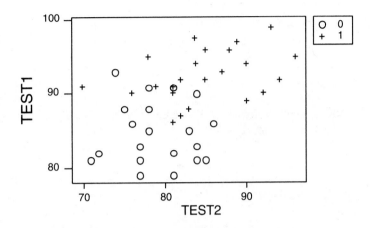

Write the equation representing the relationship between y and the explanatory variables as

$$y = \beta_0 + \beta_1 x_1 + \cdots + \beta_K x_K + e$$

Apply linear regression to the data and estimate the previous equation. The estimated equation will be written

$$d = b_0 + b_1 x_1 + \cdots + b_K x_K,$$

where d is called the *discriminant score*. The discriminant score is just the predicted value from the estimated regression equation. These discriminant scores are used to classify each of the observations in the sample. A cutoff value is chosen, call it c, and the following classification rule is used:

If $d \leq c$, assign the observation to group 0

If $d > c$, assign the observation to group 1

How is the cutoff value in the classification rule chosen? Our real goal in such a situation is not to be able to classify the items in the sample correctly. We know what group these items are in; the goal is to be able to classify future observations correctly. In the employee classification example, this would mean being able to correctly classify future employees as satisfactory or unsatisfactory in a particular position on the basis of their test scores. So, ideally, the estimates $b_0, b_1, \ldots, b_K$ should be chosen so that the number of misclassified future observations is minimized.

In the problem considered here this can be done as follows: Estimate the equation for the discriminant score with least-squares regression, using the 0/1 dependent variable. Record the predicted or fitted values from this estimated equation. These are the discriminant scores, d. Choose a value, c, as a cutoff in such a way that the probability of misclassification for future observations is minimized. This is done by choosing d halfway between the average discriminant scores for the two groups if the sample sizes are equal. If we write

$\bar{d}_1$ = average discriminant score for the 1 group, and

$\bar{d}_0$ = average discriminant score for the 0 group,

then

$$c = \frac{\bar{d}_0 + \bar{d}_1}{2}$$

If the sample sizes are not equal, then a weighted average of the two average discriminant scores can be used:

$$c = \frac{n_0 \bar{d}_0 + n_1 \bar{d}_1}{n_0 + n_1},$$

where n_0 is the sample size for the group labeled 0 and n_1 is the sample size for the group labeled 1.

E X A M P L E   **9.2**   **Employee Classification (continued)**

Continuing with Example 9.1, the discriminant scores for the employees in the sample in Table 9.1 have been computed and are shown in the fifth column of the table. Column 4 shows the result of a classification rule applied to the discriminant scores. The employees who were incorrectly classified have been denoted with an "*". Note that five employees who were in group 1 have been classified as being in group 0 and four employees who were in group 0 have been classified as being in group 1. These errors are termed misclassifications. The percentage of correct classifications in this example is 79.1%.

The average discriminant score computed from the linear regression for the satisfactory (1) group can be found from the data in column 5. This average is 0.7848. The average for the unsatisfactory (0) group is 0.2475. The weighted average of these two values is given by

$$\frac{20(0.2475) + 23(0.7848)}{20 + 23} = 0.5349$$

This number can be used to classify each of the observations in Table 9.1 and to check the classifications in column 4. Whenever the d score in column 5 is less than or equal to 0.5349 the observation should be classified as belonging to group 0. When the d score in column 5 is greater than 0.5349 the observation should be classified as belonging to group 1. This is how the classifications in the table were determined.

The MINITAB regression used to determine the d scores is shown in Figure 9.2. For future employees to be classified, this regression can be used to determine the d scores. ■

Even though linear regression was used to perform the discriminant analysis, this is not typically the method of choice. There are specific computer routines available for discriminant analysis. Figure 9.3 shows the MINITAB output for the employee classification problem when a procedure designed specifically for discriminant analysis is used. Figure 9.4 shows the SAS output. The results of the classification will

FIGURE 9.2

MINITAB Regression Output to Perform Discriminant Analysis for Employee Classification Example

```
The regression equation is
group = - 5.93 + 0.0586 test1 + 0.0153 test2

Predictor       Coef       Stdev     t-ratio        p
Constant      -5.9291      0.9633      -6.15      0.000
test1         0.05858     0.01119       5.23      0.000
test2         0.015322    0.009954      1.54      0.132

s = 0.3518      R-sq = 53.7%      R-sq(adj) = 51.4%

Analysis of Variance

SOURCE          DF          SS          MS         F         p
Regression       2       5.7472      2.8736     23.22     0.000
Error           40       4.9505      0.1238
Total           42      10.6977

SOURCE          DF      SEQ SS
test1            1       5.4540
test2            1       0.2932
```

be identical to those from the regression approach but the method used is somewhat different and the output differs considerably.

The primary reason that specific discriminant analysis routines are used rather than the regression approach is that discriminant analysis can be extended to more than two groups. When more than two groups are included in the analysis, the regression approach is not as straightforward. The case for more than two groups can be handled easily by specific discriminant analysis routines, however. Each group is given a different number. The numbers assigned do not have to include 0 and 1. (In fact, in the two-group case, the numbers used to identify the two groups can be any integers, not necessarily 0 and 1. The values 0 and 1 were used here for convenience in extending the discussion to the topic of logistic regression.)

Discriminant analysis routines proceed by computing the means of each of the different groups for each explanatory variable. Then a measure of the distance from each observation to each set of means is computed. The observation is classified into the group whose set of means is closest. Example 9.3 illustrates a discriminant analysis routine applied to the employee classification data.

EXAMPLE 9.3 Employee Classification (continued)

Figure 9.3 shows the MINITAB discriminant analysis output applied to the employee classification data. In this example the group counts are noted, 20 in the group denoted 0 and 23 in the group denoted 1. A Summary of Classification table is provided next. For example, for those employees who were actually unsatisfactory (0), 16 were classified as unsatisfactory and 4 were classified as satisfactory out of the total of 20. The 16 correct classifications for

F I G U R E **9.3**

MINITAB Discriminant Analysis Output for Employee Classification Example

```
Linear Discriminant Analysis for group

Group         0        1
Count        20       23

Summary of Classification

Put into     ....True Group....
Group         0        1
0            16        5
1             4       18
Total N      20       23
N Correct    16       18
Proport.   0.800    0.783

N =    43    N Correct =    34    Prop. Correct = 0.791

Squared Distance Between Groups
              0        1
0       0.00000  4.44946
1       4.44946  0.00000

Linear Discriminant Function for Group
              0        1
Constant  -298.27  -351.65
test1        5.20     5.68
test2        1.97     2.10

Summary of Misclassified Observations

Observation     True      Pred    Group Sqrd Distnc Probability
                Group     Group
       17 **      1         0        0        6.657     0.586
                                     1        7.352     0.414
       19 **      1         0        0       0.1911     0.799
                                     1       2.9454     0.201
       20 **      1         0        0        2.561     0.518
                                     1        2.703     0.482
       22 **      1         0        0        1.034     0.538
                                     1        1.340     0.462
       23 **      1         0        0       0.5264     0.682
                                     1       2.0567     0.318
       24 **      0         1        0        6.438     0.244
                                     1        4.177     0.756
       25 **      0         1        0       2.2891     0.280
                                     1       0.4008     0.720
       26 **      0         1        0       2.6389     0.259
                                     1       0.5416     0.741
       27 **      0         1        0        2.900     0.339
                                     1        1.564     0.661
```

this group yield a proportion correct of 0.800 (80.0%). The same information is given for each group. Overall there were 43 employees, 34 were correctly categorized and the overall proportion correct was 0.791 (79.1%).

The Squared Distance Between Groups table will not be discussed in this text.

The next item in the output is the Linear Discriminant Function for Group. When a discriminant analysis procedure is used, a separate equation is computed for each group. Note

F I G U R E 9.4
SAS Discriminant Analysis Output for Employee Classification Example

```
                    Discriminant Analysis

       43 Observations      42 DF Total
        2 Variables         41 DF Within Classes
        2 Classes            1 DF Between Classes


               Class Level Information
                                                   Prior
   GROUP    Frequency       Weight    Proportion  Probability

     0          20        20.0000      0.465116    0.500000
     1          23        23.0000      0.534884    0.500000



Discriminant Analysis    Pooled Covariance Matrix Information

           Covariance     Natural Log of the Determinant
           Matrix Rank    of the Covariance Matrix

               2                   6.05464747

Discriminant Analysis    Pairwise Generalized Squared Distances Between Groups
```

$$D^2(i|j) = (\bar{X}_i - \bar{X}_j)' \; COV^{-1} \; (\bar{X}_i - \bar{X}_j)$$

```
          Generalized Squared Distance to GROUP

      From GROUP               0              1

            0                  0         4.44946
            1             4.44946             0

Discriminant Analysis      Linear Discriminant Function
```

$$\text{Constant} = -.5 \; \bar{X}_j' \; COV^{-1} \; \bar{X}_j \qquad \text{Coefficient Vector} = COV^{-1} \; \bar{X}_j$$

```
                            GROUP

                         0              1

       CONSTANT     -298.26618     -351.64588
       TEST1           5.19936        5.68452
       TEST2           1.97076        2.09766
```

F I G U R E **9.4**   *(Cont.)*

SAS Discriminant Analysis Output for Employee Classification Example

Discriminant Analysis   Classification Summary for Calibration Data: WORK.DATA1

Resubstitution Summary using Linear Discriminant Function

Generalized Squared Distance Function: Posterior Probability of Membership in each GROUP:

$$D_j^2(X) = (X-\bar{X}_j)' \; COV^{-1} (X-\bar{X}_j) \qquad Pr(j|X) = exp(-.5 \; D_j^2(X)) \; / \; \underset{k}{SUM} \; exp(-.5 \; D_k^2(X))$$

Number of Observations and Percent Classified into GROUP:

From GROUP	0	1	Total
0	16 80.00	4 20.00	20 100.00
1	5 21.74	18 78.26	23 100.00
Total Percent	21 48.84	22 51.16	43 100.00
Priors	0.5000	0.5000	

Error Count Estimates for GROUP:

	0	1	Total
Rate	0.2000	0.2174	0.2087
Priors	0.5000	0.5000	

that these equations are not the same as the discriminant function computed using the regression approach. The two equations can be combined in a certain way to produce the overall discriminant function, however. The way this combination is achieved will not be discussed here, but the use of the equations for the separate groups will be demonstrated.

In this example the equations are

$$\text{Group } 0: -298.27 + 5.20\text{test1} + 1.97\text{test2}$$
$$\text{Group } 1: -351.65 + 5.68\text{test1} + 2.10\text{test2}$$

These equations are applied to each employee. The employee is then classified into the group for which his or her score is the highest. These equations can also be used to classify any future applicants. Administer the tests, record the test scores, and compute the values for each equation. The applicant is then assigned to the group for which the value from the equations is the highest. Although this method differs from the way the linear regression approach classified the employees, the results are the same as can be seen from the Summary of Misclassified Observations. This will always be true in the two-group case. For three or more groups, however, discriminant analysis procedures should be used.

In the Summary of Misclassified Observations, the number of each employee misclassified is shown along with the true group and the predicted group. The squared distance column shows the distance computed from the means of each group. Each employee has been classified into the group with the smaller distance. In the last column a probability has been computed that can be thought of as the predicted probability that the employee will belong to a particular group. The employee has been classified into the group that has the highest probability.

Figure 9.4 shows the SAS discriminant analysis output. Under the Discriminant Analysis heading note that there are 43 observations, two variables (one dependent and one independent), with two classes for the dependent variable. Under Class Level Information the number and proportion of observations for each value of the dependent variable are given. The prior probability will not be used in this text. For our purposes the prior probability will be assumed equal for each value of the dependent variable.

The Linear Discriminant Function section of Figure 9.4 shows the equations for each group used to classify the observations. In this example, the equations are

$$\text{Group 0:} -298.26618 + 5.19936\text{test1} + 1.97076\text{test2}$$
$$\text{Group 1:} -351.64588 + 5.68452\text{test1} + 2.09766\text{test2}$$

Near the end of the output is a table labeled Number of Observations and Percent Classified into GROUP. This table notes that of the 20 observations actually in group 0, 4 were classified into group 1 and 16 into group 0. Of the 23 observations actually in group 1, 5 were classified into group 0 and 18 into group 1. These numbers are converted into percentages and the total counts and percentages are listed at the end of the table. Below this is a table called Error Count Estimates for GROUP which summarizes the proportion of errors of classification for each group and overall. ■

In linear regression an equation was developed using a certain set of observations. It is typically not these observations for which predictions are desired, however. The quality of predictions is important for observations not included in the original sample. This situation is the same in discriminant analysis. What really matters in using discriminant analysis is how well the discriminant equations will classify future observations. The percentage of correctly classified observations given in the discriminant analysis output can be used as a guide for this, but this percentage will likely overstate the quality of future classifications. The same thing was true of the R^2 for a linear regression. The R^2 represents a measure of fit of the sample data, but may not reflect how well the equation will do in classifying future data.

There are other methods to assess the quality of future classifications when using discriminant analysis. One method is to split the original sample into two parts called an *estimation sample* and a *validation sample*. Use the estimation sample to determine the discriminant equations. Then use the discriminant equations to classify the items in the validation sample. The percentage of correct classifications in the validation sample should provide a better indication of how discriminant analysis will perform on future observations. After this has been done, the two samples can then be combined to compute the discriminant function for future use.[1]

---

[1] For more detail on discriminant analysis, including a discussion of discriminant analysis with more than two groups, see "Introducing Discriminant Analysis to the Business Statistics Curriculum" by C. T. Ragsdale and A. Stam in *Decision Sciences* 23(1992): 724–745 or Chapter 23 of *Applied Regression Analysis and Other Multivariable Methods* by D. Kleinbaum, L. L. Kupper, and K. Muller, Boston: Duxbury Press, 1988.

9.3
Logistic Regression

Discriminant analysis depends heavily on the assumption that the independent variable in the regression equation is normally distributed. When the equation has more than one independent variable the assumption is that the x variables have a multivariate normal distribution, a strong assumption that will not be discussed in detail here. Suffice it to say that this normality assumption excludes many possible variables from inclusion as explanatory variables in the discriminant function equation. *Logistic regression* is another procedure for modeling a 0/1 dependent variable that does not depend on the assumption that the independent variables are normally distributed. As a result many other types of variables, including indicator variables, are in the possible set of explanatory variables.

The logistic regression approach does have its own set of assumptions, however. To briefly describe logistic regression, the notion presented earlier that the conditional mean of y given x has a different interpretation when the dependent variable is a 0/1 variable must be reconsidered. When the dependent variable is either 0 or 1, it can be shown that the conditional mean of y given x, $\mu_{y|x}$, is equal to the probability that the observation belongs to the indicated group:

$$\mu_{y|x} = p = P(Y = 1)$$

Probabilities must be between 0 and 1 so, to model the conditional mean of y, a function that is restricted to lie between 0 and 1 must be used. The function considered in logistic regression is called the *logistic function* (what a coincidence!) and can be written as follows:

$$\mu_{y|x} = \frac{1}{1 + e^{-\left(\beta_0 + \sum_{j=1}^{k} \beta_j x_j\right)}}$$

This function works well for modeling probabilities since it is restricted to be between 0 and 1. The function forms an S-shaped curve like the one in Figure 9.5.[2]

---

[2] Some logistic regression programs estimate an equivalent nonlinear function, which can be written

$$\mu_{y|x} = \frac{e^{\left(\beta_0 + \sum_{j=1}^{k} \beta_j x_j\right)}}{1 + e^{\left(\beta_0 + \sum_{j=1}^{k} \beta_j x_j\right)}}$$

The numerical values of the coefficients will be exactly the same if this function is estimated, but the signs will be opposite.

FIGURE **9.5**
The *S*-shaped Curve of the Logistic Function

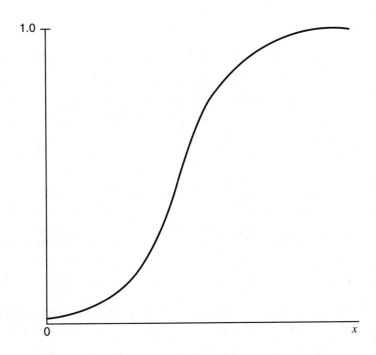

The logistic function is a nonlinear function of the regression coefficients and must be solved by a nonlinear regression routine. This makes the description of the solution process more complicated than that for linear least squares. However, logistic regression routines are available in certain statistical software packages and usually use a procedure called *maximum likelihood estimation* to estimate the regression coefficients in the logistic regression function.

Typically, logistic regression procedures will also print out information on how to test to see if variables are important in the nonlinear logistic regression function. In logistic regression, the sampling distribution of the test statistic used to test whether coefficients are equal to zero no longer has a *t* distribution as it did in linear regression. The distribution of the test statistic is called a chi-square distribution. To test the hypotheses

$$H_0: \quad \beta_k = 0$$
$$H_a: \quad \beta_k \neq 0$$

the decision rule is:

$$\text{Reject } H_0 \quad \text{if} \quad \chi^2 > \chi^2(\alpha, 1)$$
$$\text{Accept } H_0 \quad \text{if} \quad \chi^2 \leq \chi^2(\alpha, 1)$$

where $\chi^2(\alpha, 1)$ is a chi-square critical value chosen from the chi-square table in Appendix B. One degree of freedom is used in selecting the proper critical value for the α level of significance. The test statistic is printed out on most logistic regression outputs. The following example illustrates.

E X A M P L E   **9.4**   **Logistic Regression and Employee Classification**

Consider again the employee classification problem discussed in Example 9.1. Consider trying to estimate the probability that each employee belongs to the satisfactory group (the group coded 1). A possible nonlinear model to estimate this probability using only the result from TEST1 can be written

$$\mu_{y|x} = \frac{1}{1 + e^{-(\beta_0 + \beta_1 x_1)}},$$

where x_1 is the TEST1 result.

The SAS logistic regression output used to estimate this equation is shown in Figure 9.6. The Response Profile table shows the number of observations in each group (satisfactory = 1, unsatisfactory = 0). The table labeled Analysis of Maximum Likelihood Estimates contains the estimates of the regression coefficients and information used to test whether the population coefficients are equal to zero. The estimates of the regression coefficients are $b_0 = 43.3684$ and $b_1 = -0.4897$. The estimated logistic function can now be written

$$\mu_{y|x} = \frac{1}{1 + e^{-(43.3684 - 0.4897x_1)}}$$

To test whether the variable x_1 = TEST1 is useful in estimating the probability that the observations fall into group 1, the test statistic in the WALD CHI-SQUARE column or the p value in the PR > CHI-SQUARE column can be used. The chi-square statistic is used as follows:

Hypotheses:

$$H_0: \quad \beta_k = 0$$
$$H_a: \quad \beta_k \neq 0$$

Decision rule:

Reject H_0 if $\chi^2 > \chi^2(.05, 1) = 3.841$

Accept H_0 if $\chi^2 \leq 3.841$

Test statistic: $\chi^2 = 11.4070$

Decision: Reject H_0

Conclusion: TEST1 is useful in this model.

The p value can also be used to conduct the test in the usual manner:

Decision rule:

Reject H_0 if p value $< .05$

Accept H_0 if p value $\geq .05$

Test statistic: p-value $= 0.0007$

The same decision and conclusion will be reached whether the chi-square statistic or its p value is used.

F I G U R E **9.6**

SAS Logistic Regression Output for Employee Classification Example Using Only TEST1 As an Independent Variable

```
                    The LOGISTIC Procedure

Data Set: WORK.DATA1
Response Variable: GROUP
Response Levels: 2
Number of Observations: 43
Link Function: Logit

                        Response Profile

                  Ordered
                   Value    GROUP     Count

                      1       0        20
                      2       1        23


            Criteria for Assessing Model Fit

                                 Intercept
                     Intercept      and
     Criterion         Only      Covariates   Chi-Square for Covariates

     AIC               61.401      35.169        .
     SC                63.162      38.692        .
     -2 LOG L          59.401      31.169      28.232 with 1 DF (p=0.0001)
     Score               .           .         21.923 with 1 DF (p=0.0001)


              Analysis of Maximum Likelihood Estimates

               Parameter  Standard     Wald        Pr >     Standardized    Odds
     Variable DF Estimate    Error   Chi-Square  Chi-Square    Estimate     Ratio

     INTERCPT  1  43.3684   12.9243   11.2599      0.0008        .         999.000
     TEST1     1  -0.4897    0.1450   11.4070      0.0007    -1.466559       0.613


     Association of Predicted Probabilities and Observed Responses

              Concordant = 89.3%     Somers' D = 0.817
              Discordant =  7.6%     Gamma     = 0.843
              Tied       =  3.0%     Tau-a     = 0.416
              (460 pairs)            c         = 0.909
```

Information in the first row of the table can be used to test hypotheses about β_0, although interest is generally centered on the coefficients of the explanatory variables as in linear regression.

The tables labeled Criteria for Assessing Model Fit and Association of Predicted Probabilities and Observed Responses will not be discussed in this text.

Figure 9.7 shows the SAS logistic regression output when the TEST2 variable is added to the logistic regression function. The *p* value for TEST2 shows that this variable is not

F I G U R E

SAS Logistic Regression Output for Employee Classification Example Using TEST1 and TEST2 as Independent Variables

The LOGISTIC Procedure

Data Set: WORK.DATA1
Response Variable: GROUP
Response Levels: 2
Number of Observations: 43
Link Function: Logit

Response Profile

Ordered Value	GROUP	Count
1	0	20
2	1	23

Criteria for Assessing Model Fit

Criterion	Intercept Only	Intercept and Covariates	Chi-Square for Covariates
AIC	61.401	33.918	.
SC	63.162	39.202	.
-2 LOG L	59.401	27.918	31.483 with 2 DF (p=0.0001)
Score	.	.	23.101 with 2 DF (p=0.0001)

Analysis of Maximum Likelihood Estimates

Variable	DF	Parameter Estimate	Standard Error	Wald Chi-Square	Pr > Chi-Square	Standardized Estimate	Odds Ratio
INTERCPT	1	56.1704	17.4516	10.3597	0.0013	.	999.000
TEST1	1	-0.4833	0.1578	9.3834	0.0022	-1.447371	0.617
TEST2	1	-0.1652	0.1021	2.6201	0.1055	-0.556418	0.848

Association of Predicted Probabilities and Observed Responses

Concordant = 93.0%		Somers' D = 0.863
Discordant = 6.7%		Gamma = 0.865
Tied = 0.2%		Tau-a = 0.440
(460 pairs)		c = 0.932

significant at the 10% level. This suggests that the estimates of the probabilities of belonging to group 1 will be just as good using only the variable TEST1. TEST2 can be viewed as only marginally significant at best. ∎

When using logistic regression, the goal of the analysis may be to classify the observations into a particular group (as in discriminant analysis). In this case, some rule must be designed to help decide into which group each observation should be classified. Predicted values of the probability of group membership in the indicated group can be computed from the logistic regression. A rule using these predicted probabilities can then be designed. The form of such a rule would be to classify observations into the

$y = 0$ group if the predicted value is below the cutoff

$y = 1$ group otherwise

A cutoff value of 0.5 is reasonable when the 0 and 1 outcomes are equally likely and the costs of misclassification into each group are about equal. In other cases, a different cutoff may be considered superior.[3]

9.4
Using the Computer

9.4.1 MINITAB

Discriminant Analysis (STAT: MULTIVARIATE: DISCRIMINANT ANALYSIS)

```
DISCRIMINANT GROUPS IN C1, PREDICTORS IN C_, . . . , C_
```

performs a discriminant analysis. The dependent variable, which designates the two (or more) groups into which the observations are classified, is assumed to be in C1 in this example. The explanatory or predictor variables are listed in the remaining columns.

The subcommand

```
FITS C_
```

stores the fitted values. The fitted value for an observation is the group into which it would be classified by the discriminant analysis.

The subcommand

```
PREDICT e1, . . . . , eK
```

finds the predicted group membership for observations with predictor values listed in $e_1, \ldots, e_K$, which can be either single numbers or columns of predictor variable values.

---

[3]For a more complete presentation of logistic regression, see Chapters 16, 17, and 18 of *Modeling Experimental and Observational Data*, by C. E. Lunneborg, Belmont, CA: Duxbury Press, 1994 or Chapter 16 of *Applied Linear Regression Models*, by J. Neter, W. Wasserman, and M. Kutner, Homewood, IL: Irwin, 1989.

Logistic Regression

MINITAB currently has no command for logistic regression.

9.4.2 SAS

Discriminant Analysis

```
PROC DISCRIM;
 CLASS VAR1;
 VAR VAR2;
```

performs a discriminant analysis. The dependent variable, which designates the two (or more) groups into which the observations are classified, is denoted here as VAR1 and is listed on the CLASS statement. The explanatory or predictor variables are listed on the VAR statement. In this example only one predictor variable, VAR2, is used.

Logistic Regression

```
PROC LOGISTIC;
 MODEL VAR1=VAR2;
```

performs a logistic regression. VAR1 is assumed to be the dependent variable. This variable is a 0/1 variable (as discussed in this chapter). The explanatory variables are listed on the right-hand side of the equality in the MODEL statement. In this example, the only variable listed is VAR2. The MODEL statement setup is similar to PROC REG.

Exercises

1   **Harris Salaries**   In Exercise 1 in Chapter 6, data from Harris Bank was examined to test for possible discrimination. In that exercise the dependent variable was salary and one of the explanatory variables was an indicator variable to separate the employees into male and female groups. The coefficient of the indicator variable served as a measure of whether males earned more (or less), on average, than females.

Another way of examining this problem might be to use the male/female indicator variable as the dependent variable and see if the group membership can be predicted from knowledge of the salary. This can be done using either discriminant analysis or logistic regression. Try discriminant analysis and/or logistic regression and see how well these methods do in predicting whether employees are male or female based only on the knowledge of their salary. Does your result support the claim that Harris Bank discriminated by underpaying female employees?[4]

The data are the same as in Table 6.3, but only two variables will be used: SALARY and MALES. MALES has been coded as 1 for a male employee and 0 for a female employee.

These data can be read in MINITAB using

```
READ 'HARRIS9' C1,C2
```

where C1 is SALARY and C2 is MALES.

In SAS, the data can be read from the file HARRIS9.DAT using

```
INPUT SALARY MALES;
```

2 **Automatic versus Standard Transmissions** The mileage in city driving (CITYMPG) and the type of transmission of the car (AUTO) are available on the data disk and can be read in MINITAB using

```
READ 'TRANS9' C1,C2
```

where C1 is CITYMPG and C2 is AUTO. AUTO has been coded as 1 for cars with automatic transmissions and 0 for cars with manual transmissions.

In SAS, the data can be read from the file TRANS9.DAT using

```
INPUT CITYMPG AUTO;
```

These data are to be used to see whether the type of transmission can be predicted by knowing the mileage of the car in city driving. This can be investigated using either discriminant analysis or logistic regression. From the result does it appear that there may be differences in city mileage due to the type of transmission?

---

[4]Note: Using discriminant analysis or logistic regression in this manner would probably not be the preferred method of examining this question in a legal proceeding. The regression approach discussed in Chapter 6 would be preferred but this makes an interesting exercise.

Appendices

A

Summation Notation

A sample of n items chosen from a population can be denoted as $X_1, X_2, \ldots, X_n$. To represent the sum of these n items, the notation

$$\sum_{i=1}^{n} X_i$$

will be used. This is simply shorthand notation for writing

$$X_1 + X_2 + \cdots + X_n$$

As an example, suppose a sample of four items is drawn and the four sample values are 2, 3, 4, and 11.

The sum of these four items can be represented by

$$\sum_{i=1}^{4} X_i = 2 + 3 + 4 + 11 = 20$$

Some other useful examples are

1. $\displaystyle\sum_{i=1}^{4} X_i^2 = 4 + 9 + 16 + 121 = 150$

2. $\displaystyle\sum_{i=1}^{4} (X_i - 5) = (2 - 5) + (3 - 5) + (4 - 5) + (11 - 5) = 0$

3. $\displaystyle\sum_{i=1}^{4} (X_i - 5)^2 = (2 - 5)^2 + (3 - 5)^2 + (4 - 5)^2 + (11 - 5)^2 = 50$

4. $\displaystyle\sum_{i=1}^{4} 4X_i = 8 + 12 + 16 + 44 = 80 = 4\sum_{i=1}^{4} X_i$

Exercises

Use the following information to complete each exercise. A sample of six items is chosen with the following result values:

5, 8, 10, 11, 12, 20

a $\displaystyle\sum_{i=1}^{6} X_i =$

b $\displaystyle\sum_{i=1}^{6} X_i^2 =$

c $\displaystyle\sum_{i=1}^{6} (X_i - 11) =$

d $\displaystyle\sum_{i=1}^{6} (X_i - 11)^2 =$

e $\displaystyle\sum_{i=1}^{6} 2X_i =$

B

Statistical Tables

T A B L E **B.1**

Standard Normal Distribution

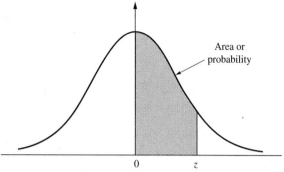

Area or probability

0   z

Entries in the table give the area under the curve between the mean and z standard deviations above the mean. For example, for $z = 1.25$ the area under the curve between the mean and z is .3944.

z	.00	.01	.02	.03	.04	.05	.06	.07	.08	.09
.0	.0000	.0040	.0080	.0120	.0160	.0199	.0239	.0279	.0319	.0359
.1	.0398	.0438	.0478	.0517	.0557	.0596	.0636	.0675	.0714	.0753
.2	.0793	.0832	.0871	.0910	.0948	.0987	.1026	.1064	.1103	.1141
.3	.1179	.1217	.1255	.1293	.1331	.1368	.1406	.1443	.1480	.1517
.4	.1554	.1591	.1628	.1664	.1700	.1736	.1772	.1808	.1844	.1879
.5	.1915	.1950	.1985	.2019	.2054	.2088	.2123	.2157	.2190	.2224
.6	.2257	.2291	.2324	.2357	.2389	.2422	.2454	.2486	.2518	.2549
.7	.2580	.2612	.2642	.2673	.2704	.2734	.2764	.2794	.2823	.2852
.8	.2881	.2910	.2939	.2967	.2995	.3023	.3051	.3078	.3106	.3133
.9	.3159	.3186	.3212	.3238	.3264	.3289	.3315	.3340	.3365	.3389
1.0	.3413	.3438	.3461	.3485	.3508	.3531	.3554	.3577	.3599	.3621
1.1	.3643	.3665	.3686	.3708	.3729	.3749	.3770	.3790	.3810	.3830
1.2	.3849	.3869	.3888	.3907	.3925	.3944	.3962	.3980	.3997	.4015
1.3	.4032	.4049	.4066	.4082	.4099	.4115	.4131	.4147	.4162	.4177
1.4	.4192	.4207	.4222	.4236	.4251	.4265	.4279	.4292	.4306	.4319
1.5	.4332	.4345	.4357	.4370	.4382	.4394	.4406	.4418	.4429	.4441
1.6	.4452	.4463	.4474	.4484	.4495	.4505	.4515	.4525	.4535	.4545
1.7	.4554	.4564	.4573	.4582	.4591	.4599	.4608	.4616	.4625	.4633
1.8	.4641	.4649	.4656	.4664	.4671	.4678	.4686	.4693	.4699	.4706
1.9	.4713	.4719	.4726	.4732	.4738	.4744	.4750	.4756	.4761	.4767
2.0	.4772	.4778	.4783	.4788	.4793	.4798	.4803	.4808	.4812	.4817
2.1	.4821	.4826	.4830	.4834	.4838	.4842	.4846	.4850	.4854	.4857
2.2	.4861	.4864	.4868	.4871	.4875	.4878	.4881	.4884	.4887	.4890
2.3	.4893	.4896	.4898	.4901	.4904	.4906	.4909	.4911	.4913	.4916
2.4	.4918	.4920	.4922	.4925	.4927	.4929	.4931	.4932	.4934	.4936
2.5	.4938	.4940	.4941	.4943	.4945	.4946	.4948	.4949	.4951	.4952
2.6	.4953	.4955	.4956	.4957	.4959	.4960	.4961	.4962	.4963	.4964
2.7	.4965	.4966	.4967	.4968	.4969	.4970	.4971	.4972	.4973	.4974
2.8	.4974	.4975	.4976	.4977	.4977	.4978	.4979	.4979	.4980	4981
2.9	.4981	.4982	.4982	.4983	.4984	.4984	.4985	.4985	.4986	.4986
3.0	.4986	.4987	.4987	.4988	.4988	.4989	.4989	.4989	.4990	.4990

Abridged from Table I of A. Hald, *Statistical Tables and Formulas* (New York: John Wiley and Sons, 1952). Reproduced by permission of the publisher.

T A B L E **B.2**

t Distribution

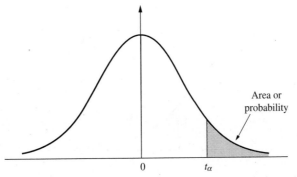

Area or probability

0   t_α

Entries in the table give t_α values, where α is the area or probability in the upper tail of the *t* distribution. For example, with 10 degrees of freedom and a .05 area in the upper tail, $t_{.05} = 1.812$.

Degrees of Freedom	.10	.05	Area in Upper Tail .025	.01	.005
1	3.078	6.314	12.706	31.821	63.657
2	1.886	2.920	4.303	6.965	9.925
3	1.638	2.353	3.182	4.541	5.841
4	1.533	2.132	2.776	3.747	4.604
5	1.476	2.015	2.571	3.365	4.032
6	1.440	1.943	2.447	3.143	3.707
7	1.415	1.895	2.365	2.998	3.499
8	1.397	1.860	2.306	2.896	3.355
9	1.383	1.833	2.262	2.821	3.250
10	1.372	1.812	2.228	2.764	3.169
11	1.363	1.796	2.201	2.718	3.106
12	1.356	1.782	2.179	2.681	3.055
13	1.350	1.771	2.160	2.650	3.012
14	1.345	1.761	2.145	2.624	2.977
15	1.341	1.753	2.131	2.602	2.947
16	1.337	1.746	2.120	2.583	2.921
17	1.333	1.740	2.110	2.567	2.898
18	1.330	1.734	2.101	2.552	2.878
19	1.328	1.729	2.093	2.539	2.861
20	1.325	1.725	2.086	2.528	2.845
21	1.323	1.721	2.080	2.518	2.831
22	1.321	1.717	2.074	2.508	2.819
23	1.319	1.714	2.069	2.500	2.807
24	1.318	1.711	2.064	2.492	2.797
25	1.316	1.708	2.060	2.485	2.787
26	1.315	1.706	2.056	2.479	2.779
27	1.314	1.703	2.052	2.473	2.771
28	1.313	1.701	2.048	2.467	2.763
29	1.311	1.699	2.045	2.462	2.756
30	1.310	1.697	2.042	2.457	2.750
40	1.303	1.684	2.021	2.423	2.704
60	1.296	1.671	2.000	2.390	2.660
120	1.289	1.658	1.980	2.358	2.617
∞	1.282	1.645	1.960	2.326	2.576

T A B L E **B**.3
Critical Values for the F Statistic ($\alpha = .10$)

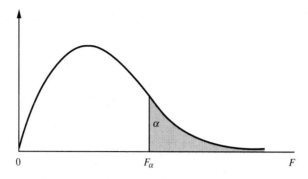

v_2 \ v_1	\multicolumn{9}{c}{**Numerator Degrees of Freedom**}
	1	**2**	**3**	**4**	**5**	**6**	**7**	**8**	**9**
1	39.86	49.50	53.59	55.83	57.24	58.20	58.91	59.44	59.86
2	8.53	9.00	9.16	9.24	9.29	9.33	9.35	9.37	9.38
3	5.54	5.46	5.39	5.34	5.31	5.28	5.27	5.25	5.24
4	4.54	4.32	4.19	4.11	4.05	4.01	3.98	3.95	3.94
5	4.06	3.78	3.62	3.52	3.45	3.40	3.37	3.34	3.32
6	3.78	3.46	3.29	3.18	3.11	3.05	3.01	2.98	2.96
7	3.59	3.26	3.07	2.96	2.88	2.83	2.78	2.75	2.72
8	3.46	3.11	2.92	2.81	2.73	2.67	2.62	2.59	2.56
9	3.36	3.01	2.81	2.69	2.61	2.55	2.51	2.47	2.44
10	3.39	2.92	2.73	2.61	2.52	2.46	2.41	2.38	2.35
11	3.23	2.86	2.66	2.54	2.45	2.39	2.34	2.30	2.27
12	3.18	2.81	2.61	2.48	2.39	2.33	2.28	2.24	2.21
13	3.14	2.76	2.56	2.43	2.35	2.28	2.23	2.20	2.16
14	3.10	2.73	2.52	2.39	2.31	2.24	2.19	2.15	2.12
15	3.07	2.70	2.49	2.36	2.27	2.21	2.16	2.12	2.09
16	3.05	2.67	2.46	2.33	2.24	2.18	2.13	2.09	2.06
17	3.03	2.64	2.44	2.31	2.22	2.15	2.10	2.06	2.03
18	3.01	2.62	2.42	2.29	2.20	2.13	2.08	2.04	2.00
19	2.99	2.61	2.40	2.27	2.18	2.11	2.06	2.02	1.98
20	2.97	2.59	2.38	2.25	2.16	2.09	2.04	2.00	1.96
21	2.96	2.57	2.36	2.23	2.14	2.08	2.02	1.98	1.95
22	2.95	2.56	2.35	2.22	2.13	2.06	2.01	1.97	1.93
23	2.94	2.55	2.34	2.21	2.11	2.05	1.99	1.95	1.92
24	2.93	2.54	2.33	2.19	2.10	2.04	1.98	1.94	1.91
25	2.92	2.53	2.32	2.18	2.09	2.02	1.97	1.93	1.89
26	2.91	2.52	2.31	2.17	2.08	2.01	1.96	1.92	1.88
27	2.90	2.51	2.30	2.17	2.07	2.00	1.95	1.91	1.87
28	2.89	2.50	2.29	2.16	2.06	2.00	1.94	1.90	1.87
29	2.89	2.50	2.28	2.15	2.06	1.99	1.93	1.89	1.86
30	2.88	2.49	2.28	2.14	2.05	1.98	1.93	1.88	1.85
40	2.84	2.44	2.23	2.09	2.00	1.93	1.87	1.83	1.79
60	2.79	2.39	2.18	2.04	1.95	1.87	1.82	1.77	1.74
120	2.75	2.35	2.13	1.99	1.90	1.82	1.77	1.72	1.68
∞	2.71	2.30	2.08	1.94	1.85	1.77	1.72	1.67	1.63

Denominator Degrees of Freedom

Source: From M. Merrington and C. M. Thompson, "Tables of Percentage Points of the Inverted Beta (F)-Distribution," *Biometrika* 33 (1943): 73–88. Reproduced by permission of the *Biometrika* Trustees.

T A B L E **B.3** (*Cont.*)
Critical Values for the F Statistic ($\alpha = .10$)

v_2 \ v_1	Numerator Degrees of Freedom									
	10	12	15	20	24	30	40	60	120	∞
1	60.19	60.71	61.22	61.74	62.00	62.26	62.53	62.79	63.06	63.33
2	9.39	9.41	9.42	9.44	9.45	9.46	9.47	9.47	9.48	9.49
3	5.23	5.22	5.20	5.18	5.18	5.17	5.16	5.15	5.14	5.13
4	3.92	3.90	3.87	3.84	3.83	3.82	3.80	3.79	3.78	3.76
5	3.30	3.27	3.24	3.21	3.19	3.17	3.16	3.14	3.12	3.10
6	2.94	2.90	2.87	2.84	2.82	2.80	2.78	2.76	2.74	2.72
7	2.70	2.67	2.63	2.59	2.58	2.56	2.54	2.51	2.49	2.47
8	2.54	2.50	2.46	2.42	2.40	2.38	2.36	2.34	2.32	2.29
9	2.42	2.38	2.34	2.30	2.28	2.25	2.23	2.21	2.18	2.16
10	2.32	2.28	2.24	2.20	2.18	2.16	2.13	2.11	2.08	2.06
11	2.25	2.21	2.17	2.12	2.10	2.08	2.05	2.03	2.00	1.97
12	2.19	2.15	2.10	2.06	2.04	2.01	1.99	1.96	1.93	1.90
13	2.14	2.10	2.05	2.01	1.98	1.96	1.93	1.90	1.88	1.85
14	2.10	2.05	2.01	1.96	1.94	1.91	1.89	1.86	1.83	1.80
15	2.06	2.02	1.97	1.92	1.90	1.87	1.85	1.82	1.79	1.76
16	2.03	1.99	1.94	1.89	1.87	1.84	1.81	1.78	1.75	1.72
17	2.00	1.96	1.91	1.86	1.84	1.81	1.78	1.75	1.72	1.69
18	1.98	1.93	1.89	1.84	1.81	1.78	1.75	1.72	1.69	1.66
19	1.96	1.91	1.86	1.81	1.79	1.76	1.73	1.70	1.67	1.63
20	1.94	1.89	1.84	1.79	1.77	1.74	1.71	1.68	1.64	1.61
21	1.92	1.87	1.83	1.78	1.75	1.72	1.69	1.66	1.62	1.59
22	1.90	1.86	1.81	1.76	1.73	1.70	1.67	1.64	1.60	1.57
23	1.89	1.84	1.80	1.74	1.72	1.69	1.66	1.62	1.59	1.55
24	1.88	1.83	1.78	1.73	1.70	1.67	1.64	1.61	1.57	1.53
25	1.87	1.82	1.77	1.72	1.69	1.66	1.63	1.59	1.56	1.52
26	1.86	1.81	1.76	1.71	1.68	1.65	1.61	1.58	1.54	1.50
27	1.85	1.80	1.75	1.70	1.67	1.64	1.60	1.57	1.53	1.49
28	1.84	1.79	1.74	1.69	1.66	1.63	1.59	1.56	1.52	1.48
29	1.83	1.78	1.73	1.68	1.65	1.62	1.58	1.55	1.51	1.47
30	1.82	1.77	1.72	1.67	1.64	1.61	1.57	1.54	1.50	1.46
40	1.76	1.71	1.66	1.61	1.57	1.54	1.51	1.47	1.42	1.38
60	1.71	1.66	1.60	1.54	1.51	1.48	1.44	1.40	1.35	1.29
120	1.65	1.60	1.55	1.48	1.45	1.41	1.37	1.32	1.26	1.19
∞	1.60	1.55	1.49	1.42	1.38	1.34	1.30	1.24	1.17	1.00

Denominator Degrees of Freedom

T A B L E **B.4**

Critical Values for the *F* Statistic ($\alpha = .05$)

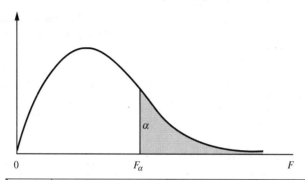

v_1	Numerator Degrees of Freedom								
v_2	1	2	3	4	5	6	7	8	9
1	161.40	199.50	215.70	224.60	230.20	234.00	236.80	238.90	240.50
2	18.51	19.00	19.16	19.25	19.30	19.33	19.35	19.37	19.38
3	10.13	9.55	9.28	9.12	9.01	8.94	8.89	8.85	8.81
4	7.71	6.94	6.59	6.39	6.26	6.16	6.09	6.04	6.00
5	6.61	5.79	5.41	5.19	5.05	4.95	4.88	4.82	4.77
6	5.99	5.14	4.76	4.53	4.39	4.28	4.21	4.15	4.10
7	5.59	4.74	4.35	4.12	3.97	3.87	3.79	3.73	3.68
8	5.32	4.46	4.07	3.84	3.69	3.58	3.50	3.44	3.39
9	5.12	4.26	3.86	3.63	3.48	3.37	3.29	3.23	3.18
10	4.96	4.10	3.71	3.48	3.33	3.22	3.14	3.07	3.02
11	4.84	3.98	3.59	3.36	3.20	3.09	3.01	2.95	2.90
12	4.75	3.89	3.49	3.26	3.11	3.00	2.91	2.85	2.80
13	4.67	3.81	3.41	3.18	3.03	2.92	2.83	2.77	2.71
14	4.60	3.74	3.34	3.11	2.96	2.85	2.76	2.70	2.65
15	4.54	3.68	3.29	3.06	2.90	2.79	2.71	2.64	2.59
16	4.49	3.63	3.24	3.01	2.85	2.74	2.66	2.59	2.54
17	4.45	3.59	3.20	2.96	2.81	2.70	2.61	2.55	2.49
18	4.41	3.55	3.16	2.93	2.77	2.66	2.58	2.51	2.46
19	4.38	3.52	3.13	2.90	2.74	2.63	2.54	2.48	2.42
20	4.35	3.49	3.10	2.87	2.71	2.60	2.51	2.45	2.39
21	4.32	3.47	3.07	2.84	2.68	2.57	2.49	2.42	2.37
22	4.30	3.44	3.05	2.82	2.66	2.55	2.46	2.40	2.34
23	4.28	3.42	3.03	2.80	2.64	2.53	2.44	2.37	2.32
24	4.26	3.40	3.01	2.78	2.62	2.51	2.42	2.36	2.30
25	4.24	3.39	2.99	2.76	2.60	2.49	2.40	2.34	2.28
26	4.23	3.37	2.98	2.74	2.59	2.47	2.39	2.32	2.27
27	4.21	3.35	2.96	2.73	2.57	2.46	2.37	2.31	2.25
28	4.20	3.34	2.95	2.71	2.56	2.45	2.36	2.29	2.24
29	4.18	3.33	2.93	2.70	2.55	2.43	2.35	2.28	2.22
30	4.17	3.32	2.92	2.69	2.53	2.42	2.33	2.27	2.21
40	4.08	3.23	2.84	2.61	2.45	2.34	2.25	2.18	2.12
60	4.00	3.15	2.76	2.53	2.37	2.25	2.17	2.10	2.04
120	3.92	3.07	2.68	2.45	2.29	2.17	2.09	2.02	1.96
∞	3.84	3.00	2.60	2.37	2.21	2.10	2.01	1.94	1.88

Denominator Degrees of Freedom

T A B L E **B.4** (*Cont.*)
Critical Values for the F Statistic ($\alpha = .05$)

v_2 \ v_1	Numerator Degrees of Freedom									
	10	**12**	**15**	**20**	**24**	**30**	**40**	**60**	**120**	**∞**
1	241.90	243.90	245.90	248.00	249.10	250.10	251.10	252.20	253.30	254.30
2	19.40	19.41	19.43	19.45	19.45	19.46	19.47	19.48	19.49	19.50
3	8.79	8.74	8.70	8.66	8.64	8.62	8.59	8.57	8.55	8.53
4	5.96	5.91	5.86	5.80	5.77	5.75	5.72	5.69	5.66	5.63
5	4.74	4.68	4.62	4.56	4.53	4.50	4.46	4.43	4.40	4.36
6	4.06	4.00	3.94	3.87	3.84	3.81	3.77	3.74	3.70	3.67
7	3.64	3.57	3.51	3.44	3.41	3.38	3.34	3.30	3.27	3.23
8	3.35	3.28	3.22	3.15	3.12	3.08	3.04	3.01	2.97	2.93
9	3.14	3.07	3.01	2.94	2.90	2.86	2.83	2.79	2.75	2.71
10	2.98	2.91	2.85	2.77	2.74	2.70	2.66	2.62	2.58	2.54
11	2.85	2.79	2.72	2.65	2.61	2.57	2.53	2.49	2.45	2.40
12	2.75	2.69	2.62	2.54	2.51	2.47	2.43	2.38	2.34	2.30
13	2.67	2.60	2.53	2.46	2.42	2.38	2.34	2.30	2.25	2.21
14	2.60	2.53	2.46	2.39	2.35	2.31	2.27	2.22	2.18	2.13
15	2.54	2.48	2.40	2.33	2.29	2.25	2.20	2.16	2.11	2.07
16	2.49	2.42	2.35	2.28	2.24	2.19	2.15	2.11	2.06	2.01
17	2.45	2.38	2.31	2.23	2.19	2.15	2.10	2.06	2.01	1.96
18	2.41	2.34	2.27	2.19	2.15	2.11	2.06	2.02	1.97	1.92
19	2.38	2.31	2.23	2.16	2.11	2.07	2.03	1.98	1.93	1.88
20	2.35	2.28	2.20	2.12	2.08	2.04	1.99	1.95	1.90	1.84
21	2.32	2.25	2.18	2.10	2.05	2.01	1.96	1.92	1.87	1.81
22	2.30	2.23	2.15	2.07	2.03	1.98	1.94	1.89	1.84	1.78
23	2.27	2.20	2.13	2.05	2.01	1.96	1.91	1.86	1.81	1.76
24	2.25	2.18	2.11	2.03	1.98	1.94	1.89	1.84	1.79	1.73
25	2.24	2.16	2.09	2.01	1.96	1.92	1.87	1.82	1.77	1.71
26	2.22	2.15	2.07	1.99	1.95	1.90	1.85	1.80	1.75	1.69
27	2.20	2.13	2.06	1.97	1.93	1.88	1.84	1.79	1.73	1.67
28	2.19	2.12	2.04	1.96	1.91	1.87	1.82	1.77	1.71	1.65
29	2.18	2.10	2.03	1.94	1.90	1.85	1.81	1.75	1.70	1.64
30	2.16	2.09	2.01	1.93	1.89	1.84	1.79	1.74	1.68	1.62
40	2.08	2.00	1.92	1.84	1.79	1.74	1.69	1.64	1.58	1.51
60	1.99	1.92	1.84	1.75	1.70	1.65	1.59	1.53	1.47	1.39
120	1.91	1.83	1.75	1.66	1.61	1.55	1.50	1.43	1.35	1.25
∞	1.83	1.75	1.67	1.57	1.52	1.46	1.39	1.32	1.22	1.00

Denominator Degrees of Freedom

T A B L E   **B.5**

Critical Values for the *F* Statistic ($\alpha = .01$)

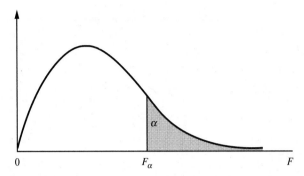

v_1				**Numerator Degrees of Freedom**					
v_2	**1**	**2**	**3**	**4**	**5**	**6**	**7**	**8**	**9**
1	4,052.00	4,999.50	5,403.00	5,625.00	5,764.00	5,859.00	5,928.00	5,982.00	6,022.00
2	98.50	99.00	99.17	99.25	99.30	99.33	99.36	99.37	99.39
3	34.12	30.82	29.46	28.71	28.24	27.91	27.67	27.49	27.35
4	21.20	18.00	16.69	15.98	15.52	15.21	14.98	14.80	14.66
5	16.26	13.27	12.06	11.39	10.97	10.67	10.46	10.29	10.16
6	13.75	10.92	9.78	9.15	8.75	8.47	8.26	8.10	7.98
7	12.25	9.55	8.45	7.85	7.46	7.19	6.99	6.84	6.72
8	11.26	8.65	7.59	7.01	6.63	6.37	6.18	6.03	5.91
9	10.56	8.02	6.99	6.42	6.06	5.80	5.61	5.47	5.35
10	10.04	7.56	6.55	5.99	5.64	5.39	5.20	5.06	4.94
11	9.65	7.21	6.22	5.67	5.32	5.07	4.89	4.74	4.63
12	9.33	6.93	5.95	5.41	5.06	4.82	4.64	4.50	4.39
13	9.07	6.70	5.74	5.21	4.86	4.62	4.44	4.30	4.19
14	8.86	6.51	5.56	5.04	4.69	4.46	4.28	4.14	4.03
15	8.68	6.36	5.42	4.89	4.56	4.32	4.14	4.00	3.89
16	8.53	6.23	5.29	4.77	4.44	4.20	4.03	3.89	3.78
17	8.40	6.11	5.18	4.67	4.34	4.10	3.93	3.79	3.68
18	8.29	6.01	5.09	4.58	4.25	4.01	3.84	3.71	3.60
19	8.18	5.93	5.01	4.50	4.17	3.94	3.77	3.63	3.52
20	8.10	5.85	4.94	4.43	4.10	3.87	3.70	3.56	3.46
21	8.02	5.78	4.87	4.37	4.04	3.81	3.64	3.51	3.40
22	7.95	5.72	4.82	4.31	3.99	3.76	3.59	3.45	3.35
23	7.88	5.66	4.76	4.26	3.94	3.71	3.54	3.41	3.30
24	7.82	5.61	4.72	4.22	3.90	3.67	3.50	3.36	3.26
25	7.77	5.57	4.68	4.18	3.85	3.63	3.46	3.32	3.22
26	7.72	5.53	4.64	4.14	3.82	3.59	3.42	3.29	3.18
27	7.68	5.49	4.60	4.11	3.78	3.56	3.39	3.26	3.15
28	7.64	5.45	4.57	4.07	3.75	3.53	3.36	3.23	3.12
29	7.60	5.42	4.54	4.04	3.73	3.50	3.33	3.20	3.09
30	7.56	5.39	4.51	4.02	3.70	3.47	3.30	3.17	3.07
40	7.31	5.18	4.31	3.83	3.51	3.29	3.12	2.99	2.89
60	7.08	4.98	4.13	3.65	3.34	3.12	2.95	2.82	2.72
120	6.85	4.79	3.95	3.48	3.17	2.96	2.79	2.66	2.56
∞	6.63	4.61	3.78	3.32	3.02	2.80	2.64	2.51	2.41

Denominator Degrees of Freedom (vertical label at left of table)

Source: From M. Merrington and C. M. Thompson, "Tables of Percentage Points of the Inverted Beta (*F*)-Distribution," *Biometrika* 33 (1943): 73–88. Reproduced by permission of the *Biometrika* Trustees.

T A B L E **B.5** (*Cont.*)
Critical Values for the *F* Statistic ($\alpha = .01$)

v_1 v_2	Numerator Degrees of Freedom									
	10	**12**	**15**	**20**	**24**	**30**	**40**	**60**	**120**	**∞**
1	6,056.00	6,106.00	6,157.00	6,209.00	6,235.00	6,261.00	6,287.00	6,313.00	6,339.00	6,366.00
2	99.40	99.42	99.43	99.45	99.46	99.47	99.47	99.48	99.49	99.50
3	27.23	27.05	26.87	26.69	26.60	26.50	26.41	26.32	26.22	26.13
4	14.55	14.37	14.20	14.02	13.93	13.84	13.75	13.65	13.56	13.46
5	10.05	9.89	9.72	9.55	9.47	9.38	9.29	9.20	9.11	9.02
6	7.87	7.72	7.56	7.40	7.31	7.23	7.14	7.06	6.97	6.88
7	6.62	6.47	6.31	6.16	6.07	5.99	5.91	5.82	5.74	5.65
8	5.81	5.67	5.52	5.36	5.28	5.20	5.12	5.03	4.95	4.86
9	5.26	5.11	4.96	4.81	4.73	4.65	4.57	4.48	4.40	4.31
10	4.85	4.71	4.56	4.41	4.33	4.25	4.17	4.08	4.00	3.91
11	4.54	4.40	4.25	4.10	4.02	3.94	3.86	3.78	3.69	3.60
12	4.30	4.16	4.01	3.86	3.78	3.70	3.62	3.54	3.45	3.36
13	4.10	3.96	3.82	3.66	3.59	3.51	3.43	3.34	3.25	3.17
14	3.94	3.80	3.66	3.51	3.43	3.35	3.27	3.18	3.09	3.00
15	3.80	3.67	3.52	3.37	3.29	3.21	3.13	3.05	2.96	2.87
16	3.69	3.55	3.41	3.26	3.18	3.10	3.02	2.93	2.84	2.75
17	3.59	3.46	3.31	3.16	3.08	3.00	2.92	2.83	2.75	2.65
18	3.51	3.37	3.23	3.08	3.00	2.92	2.84	2.75	2.66	2.57
19	3.43	3.30	3.15	3.00	2.92	2.84	2.76	2.67	2.58	2.49
20	3.37	3.23	3.09	2.94	2.86	2.78	2.69	2.61	2.52	2.42
21	3.31	3.17	3.03	2.88	2.80	2.72	2.64	2.55	2.46	2.36
22	3.26	3.12	2.98	2.83	2.75	2.67	2.58	2.50	2.40	2.31
23	3.21	3.07	2.93	2.78	2.70	2.62	2.54	2.45	2.35	2.26
24	3.17	3.03	2.89	2.74	2.66	2.58	2.49	2.40	2.31	2.21
25	3.13	2.99	2.85	2.70	2.62	2.54	2.45	2.36	2.27	2.17
26	3.09	2.96	2.81	2.66	2.58	2.50	2.42	2.33	2.23	2.13
27	3.06	2.93	2.78	2.63	2.55	2.47	2.38	2.29	2.20	2.10
28	3.03	2.90	2.75	2.60	2.52	2.44	2.35	2.26	2.17	2.06
29	3.00	2.87	2.73	2.57	2.49	2.41	2.33	2.23	2.14	2.03
30	2.98	2.84	2.70	2.55	2.47	2.39	2.30	2.21	2.11	2.01
40	2.80	2.66	2.52	2.37	2.29	2.20	2.11	2.02	1.92	1.80
60	2.63	2.50	2.35	2.20	2.12	2.03	1.94	1.84	1.73	1.60
120	2.47	2.34	2.19	2.03	1.95	1.86	1.76	1.66	1.53	1.38
∞	2.32	2.18	2.04	1.88	1.79	1.70	1.59	1.47	1.32	1.00

Denominator Degrees of Freedom

T A B L E .6

Critical Values for the Probability Plot Correlation Coefficient Test for Normality

	α		
n	**0.01**	**0.05**	**0.10**
4	.8951	.8734	.8318
5	.9033	.8804	.8320
10	.9347	.9180	.8804
15	.9506	.9383	.9110
20	.9600	.9503	.9290
25	.9662	.9582	.9408
30	.9707	.9639	.9490
40	.9767	.9715	.9597
50	.9807	.9764	.9664
60	.9835	.9799	.9710
75	.9865	.9835	.9757

SOURCE: *MINITAB Statistical Software Reference Manual—Release 6.1,* 1988, p. 63. Reproduced by permission of MINITAB, Inc.

T A B L E **B.7**
Critical Values for the Durbin–Watson Statistic ($\alpha = .05$)

n	K=1 d_L	K=1 d_U	K=2 d_L	K=2 d_U	K=3 d_L	K=3 d_U	K=4 d_L	K=4 d_U	K=5 d_L	K=5 d_U
15	1.08	1.36	0.95	1.54	0.82	1.75	0.69	1.97	0.56	2.21
16	1.10	1.37	0.98	1.54	0.86	1.73	0.74	1.93	0.62	2.15
17	1.13	1.38	1.02	1.54	0.90	1.71	0.78	1.90	0.67	2.10
18	1.16	1.39	1.05	1.53	0.93	1.69	0.82	1.87	0.71	2.06
19	1.18	1.40	1.08	1.53	0.97	1.68	0.86	1.85	0.75	2.02
20	1.20	1.41	1.10	1.54	1.00	1.68	0.90	1.83	0.79	1.99
21	1.22	1.42	1.13	1.54	1.03	1.67	0.93	1.81	0.83	1.96
22	1.24	1.43	1.15	1.54	1.05	1.66	0.96	1.80	0.86	1.94
23	1.26	1.44	1.17	1.54	1.08	1.66	0.99	1.79	0.90	1.92
24	1.27	1.45	1.19	1.55	1.10	1.66	1.01	1.78	0.93	1.90
25	1.29	1.45	1.21	1.55	1.12	1.66	1.04	1.77	0.95	1.89
26	1.30	1.46	1.22	1.55	1.14	1.65	1.06	1.76	0.98	1.88
27	1.32	1.47	1.24	1.56	1.16	1.65	1.08	1.76	1.01	1.86
28	1.33	1.48	1.26	1.56	1.18	1.65	1.10	1.75	1.03	1.85
29	1.34	1.48	1.27	1.56	1.20	1.65	1.12	1.74	1.05	1.84
30	1.35	1.49	1.28	1.57	1.21	1.65	1.14	1.74	1.07	1.83
31	1.36	1.50	1.30	1.57	1.23	1.65	1.16	1.74	1.09	1.83
32	1.37	1.50	1.31	1.57	1.24	1.65	1.18	1.73	1.11	1.82
33	1.38	1.51	1.32	1.58	1.26	1.65	1.19	1.73	1.13	1.81
34	1.39	1.51	1.33	1.58	1.27	1.65	1.21	1.73	1.15	1.81
35	1.40	1.52	1.34	1.58	1.28	1.65	1.22	1.73	1.16	1.80
36	1.41	1.52	1.35	1.59	1.29	1.65	1.24	1.73	1.18	1.80
37	1.42	1.53	1.36	1.59	1.31	1.66	1.25	1.72	1.19	1.80
38	1.43	1.54	1.37	1.59	1.32	1.66	1.26	1.72	1.21	1.79
39	1.43	1.54	1.38	1.60	1.33	1.66	1.27	1.72	1.22	1.79
40	1.44	1.54	1.39	1.60	1.34	1.66	1.29	1.72	1.23	1.79
45	1.48	1.57	1.43	1.62	1.38	1.67	1.34	1.72	1.29	1.78
50	1.50	1.59	1.46	1.63	1.42	1.67	1.38	1.72	1.34	1.77
55	1.53	1.60	1.49	1.64	1.45	1.68	1.41	1.72	1.38	1.77
60	1.55	1.62	1.51	1.65	1.48	1.69	1.44	1.73	1.41	1.77
65	1.57	1.63	1.54	1.66	1.50	1.70	1.47	1.73	1.44	1.77
70	1.58	1.64	1.55	1.67	1.52	1.70	1.49	1.74	1.46	1.77
75	1.60	1.65	1.57	1.68	1.54	1.71	1.51	1.74	1.49	1.77
80	1.61	1.66	1.59	1.69	1.56	1.72	1.53	1.74	1.51	1.77
85	1.62	1.67	1.60	1.70	1.57	1.72	1.55	1.75	1.52	1.77
90	1.63	1.68	1.61	1.70	1.59	1.73	1.57	1.75	1.54	1.78
95	1.64	1.69	1.62	1.71	1.60	1.73	1.58	1.75	1.56	1.78
100	1.65	1.69	1.63	1.72	1.61	1.74	1.59	1.76	1.57	1.78

Source: From J. Durbin and G. S. Watson, "Testing for Serial Correlation in Least Squares Regression, II." *Biometrika* 38 (1951): 159–178. Reproduced by permission of the *Biometrika* trustees.

T A B L E **B.8**

Critical Values for the Chi-Square Statistic

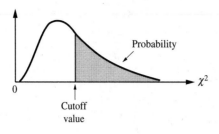

Cutoff
value

Note: Entries on this page are cutoff values to place a specified probability amount in the right tail. For example, to have probability $= .10$ in the right tail when $df = 4$, the table value is $\chi^2 = 7.779$.

Degrees of Freedom, *df*	Probability in Right Tail				
	.10	.05	.025	.01	.005
1	2.706	3.841	5.024	6.635	7.879
2	4.605	5.991	7.378	9.210	10.597
3	6.251	7.815	9.348	11.345	12.838
4	7.779	9.488	11.143	13.277	14.860
5	9.236	11.070	12.833	15.086	16.750
6	10.645	12.592	14.449	16.812	18.548
7	12.017	14.067	16.013	18.475	20.278
8	13.362	15.507	17.535	20.090	21.955
9	14.684	16.919	19.023	21.666	23.589
10	15.987	18.307	20.483	23.209	25.188
11	17.275	19.675	21.920	24.725	26.757
12	18.549	21.026	23.337	26.217	28.300
13	19.812	22.362	24.736	27.688	29.819
14	21.064	23.685	26.119	29.141	31.319
15	22.307	24.996	27.488	30.578	32.801
16	23.542	26.296	28.845	32.000	34.267
17	24.769	27.587	30.191	33.409	35.718
18	25.989	28.869	31.526	34.805	37.156
19	27.204	30.144	32.852	36.191	38.582
20	28.412	31.410	34.170	37.566	39.997
21	29.615	32.671	35.479	38.932	41.401
22	30.813	33.924	36.781	40.289	42.796
23	32.007	35.172	38.076	41.638	44.181
24	33.196	36.415	39.364	42.980	45.558
25	34.382	37.652	40.647	44.314	46.928
26	35.563	38.885	41.923	45.642	48.290
27	36.741	40.113	43.194	46.963	49.645
28	37.916	41.337	44.461	48.278	50.993
29	39.087	42.557	45.722	49.588	52.336
30	40.256	43.773	46.979	50.892	53.672
50	63.167	67.505	71.420	76.154	79.490
60	74.397	79.082	83.298	88.379	91.952
80	96.578	101.879	106.629	112.329	116.321
100	118.498	124.342	129.561	135.807	140.169

SOURCE: Computed by R. E. Shiffler and A. J. Adams.

C

A Summary of MINITAB
and SAS Commands

C.1
Introduction

This appendix will present a brief summary of MINITAB and SAS. As noted earlier, in this text Windows version 9.2 of MINITAB was used on an IBM-compatible personal computer. The mainframe version 6.07 of SAS was used. Depending on the version of MINITAB or SAS used, the commands and output may differ slightly from what is presented in this text (but should be fairly similar). In the MINITAB Windows version most of the procedures can be requested by menu. However, the commands that would be appropriate in most earlier versions will be given for those that prefer commands or have command-driven versions of MINITAB. Version 8.2 of MINITAB was used to determine the commands presented here.

The first step in any data analysis is to input the data to be analyzed. A very brief overview of the data input process for MINITAB and SAS will be presented. However, there may be some significant steps omitted depending on the version of the statistical package used and the mainframe system used if the package is being run on a mainframe. You should check with your instructor or computer center personnel to determine if additional or alternative steps are necessary to input the data.

C.2
MINITAB

A. Data Input

There are several different ways to enter data to be analyzed into MINITAB. These include:

1 Read data using the READ command from a disk file that has already been set up.
2 Read the data directly in at the terminal using the READ command.
3 Read the data directly in at the terminal using the SET command.
4 Use the IMPORT ASCII DATA menu option (if available).
5 Enter data with spreadsheet-type data entry (if available).

Storage of data during a MINITAB session is accomplished through the use of "columns." For example, Table 4.2 of the text provided a list of numbers representing COST, PAPER production, MACHINE hours used, OVERHEAD cost, and LABOR hours used for 27 months. These data were stored in a disk file called COST4.DAT on the data disk provided with the text.

To analyze these data in MINITAB, the COST data can be read into a storage space called C1 (for column 1), PAPER into a storage space called C2 (for column 2), MACHINE into C3, OVERHEAD into C4, and LABOR into C5. Columns are not of any fixed length nor do they have to be of equal length. (Note: There are two other storage modes in MINITAB: constants, which represent single numbers and are denoted K1, K2, . . . and matrices, which represent arrays of numbers and are denoted M1, M2, ... These storage modes will not be discussed.)

E X A M P L E C.1

Read data from the file COST4.DAT into five columns. The name of the file must be set off by single quotes:

```
MTB > READ 'A:COST4' INTO C1,C2,C3,C4,C5
```

(Note that MINITAB responses are indicated by the absence of underlining, and what is to be typed in at the terminal is indicated by the underline. Including the underline is unnecessary, of course, at the time the commands are actually typed in.) MINITAB assumes that the data file has the .DAT suffix so it is not necessary to include it in the READ command (although it will not be a problem if you do include it).

The READ command as used here assumes the data are in the disk file in columns with *each column separated by at least one space*. Also, note that the disk file is being read from disk drive A on a PC. If you are using a mainframe version of MINITAB the drive specification may be unnecessary.

At the terminal, you should see something similar to the following output when you enter the READ command:

Version 8.2

```
MTB > READ 'A:COST4' C1-C5
    27 ROWS READ

ROW    C1    C2    C3    C4    C5
  1   1102   550   218   112   325
  2   1008   502   199    99   301
  3   1227   616   249   126   376
  4   1395   701   277   143   419
   .     .     .
```

Windows Version

```
MTB > READ 'A:COST4' C1-C5
ENTERING DATA FROM FILE A:COST4.DAT
    27 ROWS READ
```

As an alternative to the READ command, to enter data from a file the more recent versions of MINITAB have a menu category called FILE that makes data entry very easy. Under the menu items in FILE is IMPORT ASCII DATA. This command serves the same function as the READ command and will prompt the user for the data file name, the columns into which data are to be stored, and so on.

Once the data have been read into columns in MINITAB, analyses can be performed to examine the data. Note that the original data in COST4.DAT are not altered in any way; the columns in MINITAB are merely copies of what exists in the file.

Once you are in a MINITAB session you can also enter data directly into columns at the terminal. To do this you can use either the READ or SET commands. For example, suppose you want to enter information on the height and weight of five people as follows:

Height (in inches)	Weight (in pounds)
60	140
66	195
70	185
71	190
73	210

Using the READ command, the terminal session would look like:

```
MTB > READ INTO C1,C2
60 140
66 195
70 185
71 190
73 210

END
    5 ROWS READ
```

Note that the number of data entries per row must be equal to the number of columns to be read in.

Using the SET command:

```
MTB > SET IN C1
60 66 70 71 73
END
MTB > SET IN C2
140 195 185 190 210
END
```

When using the READ command, the data are entered by row with one entry for each variable or column. With the SET command, the data are entered by typing in an entire column, one column at a time.

Finally, the more recent versions of MINITAB have spreadsheet data entry similar to spreadsheet software, such as LOTUS, when data are to be entered from the terminal while in MINITAB. In the MINITAB Windows version the spreadsheet or data screen will be available automatically when you access MINITAB. In earlier versions of MINITAB you may have to request the data screen. For example, in version 8.2 pressing ALT-D will request the data screen. Menus are used to control characteristics of the data screen.   ∎

The remainder of this appendix discusses MINITAB commands that may be useful. Also, MINITAB *subcommands* will be discussed. A subcommand simply adds to or modifies the directions given in a command. To indicate that a subcommand is to be used, end the command with a semicolon, type in the subcommand on the next line, and end the final subcommand line with a period.

Also, any of the MINITAB commands and subcommands given can be abbreviated by using just the first four letters.

B. Naming Columns

Columns in MINITAB can be named using the NAME command:

```
MTB > NAME C1 'HEIGHT' C2 'WEIGHT'
```

assigns the names HEIGHT and WEIGHT to C1 and C2, respectively. Additional columns can be named on the same line, if necessary. Column names can be at most eight characters long.

C. Statistics Commands

The following commands perform certain statistical analyses. Most of these are used in the text at some point. All of these commands are available as items on menus in more recent versions of MINITAB. The menu headings and subheadings used to access the commands will be noted in parentheses next to the commands. These headings and subheadings are from the Windows version of MINITAB but should be similar to those on other recent versions.

```
AOVONEWAY C,C,...,C    (STAT: ANOVA: ONEWAY(UNSTACKED))
```

requests a one-way analysis of variance on the data in the specified columns (see also ONEWAY command).

```
CORR C,C,...,C    (STAT: BASIC STATISTICS: CORRELATION)
```

produces a matrix of all pairwise correlations between the data in the listed columns.

`COUNT C`   (`CALC: MATHEMATICAL EXPRESSIONS: COUNT`)

counts the number of observations in the specified column.

`DESCRIBE C`   (`STAT: BASIC STATISTICS: DESCRIPTIVE STATISTICS`)

computes a number of descriptive statistics for the data in the specified column. The statistics requested by the DESCRIBE command are the count of the number of observations in the column, the mean, median, the 5% trimmed mean, the standard deviation, the standard error of the mean, the minimum and maximum, and the first and third quartiles.

`HISTOGRAM C`   (`GRAPH: HISTOGRAM`)

produces a histogram of the data in the specified column.

`INDICATOR FOR C, PUT RESULTS IN C,C,...,C` (`CALC: MAKE INDICATOR VARIABLES`)

creates a set of indicator variables equal to the number of distinct integer values in the first specified column. The remaining columns are where the indicator variables are stored.

`MAXIMUM C`   (`CALC: MATHEMATICAL EXPRESSIONS: MAX`)

finds the largest value in the specified column.

`MEAN C`   (`CALC: MATHEMATICAL EXPRESSIONS: MEAN`)

computes the sample mean (also AVERAGE C).

`MEDIAN C`   (`CALC: MATHEMATICAL EXPRESSIONS: MEDIAN`)

computes the median.

`MINIMUM C`   (`CALC: MATHEMATICAL EXPRESSIONS: MIN`)

finds the smallest value in the specified column.

`ONEWAY DATA IN C, SUBSCRIPTS IN C`   (`STAT: ANOVA: ONEWAY`)

requests a two-way analysis of variance on the data listed in the first column. The second column listed is used to indicate factor levels.

`PLOT C VS C`   (`GRAPH: PLOT`)

produces a scatterplot with the first column plotted on the vertical axis and the second on the horizontal axis.

`REGRESS Y IN C ON K PREDICTORS IN C...C, STORE IN C,C`

produces a regression analysis. The dependent variable Y is assumed to be in the first column listed. There are K predictor or explanatory variables and these are in the next K columns listed. The last two columns (listed after "STORE IN") will be used to store the standardized residuals and fitted values, respectively. These last two columns are optional. The regression results will still be produced whether the additional storage columns are specified or not. There are a variety of subcommands that can be used with the REGRESS command. Some of these include:

COOKD C, which stores the Cook's D statistic values in the specified column.

DFITS C, which stores the DFITS statistic values in the specified column.

DW, which produces the Durbin–Watson statistic value.

HI C, which stores the leverage values in the specified column.

PREDICT e1 e2...eK, which produces confidence and prediction intervals for a forecast of y given $x_1 = e1, x_2 = e2, \ldots, x_K = eK$.

PURE, which requests the pure error lack-of-fit test.

TRESIDS C, which stores the studentized deleted residuals in the specified column.

VIF, which causes the variance inflation factors to be printed.

XLOF, which requests the experimental lack-of-fit test.

(STAT: REGRESSION: REGRESSION) is the menu sequence that produces the regression output. You will be prompted for dependent and explanatory variables. There are boxes to check to request COOKD, DFITS, HI, STANDARDIZED RESIDUALS, FITS, and TRESIDS (among other things). Under the OPTIONS box you will be prompted for DW, PRED, PURE, VIF, and XLOF.

STANDARD DEVIATION C   (CALC: MATHEMATICAL EXPRESSIONS: STDEV)

> computes the standard deviation.

STEPWISE Y IN C, PREDICTORS IN C,C,...,C

> requests a stepwise regression of the dependent variable in the first column listed using the remaining columns as explanatory variables.

> (STAT: REGRESSION: STEPWISE)

> is the menu sequence that produces the regression output. You will be prompted for dependent and explanatory variables.

TINTERVAL WITH K FOR C
     (STAT: BASIC STATISTICS: 1-SAMPLE T: CONFIDENCE INTERVAL)

> requests a $K\%$ confidence interval using the data in the specified column.

TTEST OF MU=K ON C
     (STAT: BASIC STATISTICS: 1-SAMPLE T: TEST MENU)

> requests a t test of H_0: $\mu = K$ using the data in the specified column. The subcommand ALT=L can be used to indicate whether a two-tailed (ALT=0), upper-tailed (ALT=1), or lower-tailed (ALT= −1) test is to be performed.

TWOSAMPLE WITH K C,C   (STAT: BASIC STATISTICS: 2-SAMPLE T)

> requests a $K\%$ confidence interval for the difference between two population means using the data in the two columns specified. If the subcommand

POOLED is used, the population variances are assumed equal. The results of a hypotheses test of $\mu_1 = \mu_2$ are also produced. The ALT=L subcommand can be used to specify the form of the hypotheses (L=0 for two-tailed, L=1 for upper-tailed, and L=-1 for lower-tailed).

```
TWOWAY DATA IN C SUBSCRIPTS IN C,C    (STAT: ANOVA: TWOWAY)
```

requests a two-way analysis of variance on the data listed in the first column. The second and third columns listed are used to indicate factor levels.

D. Arithmetic with Columns

Once a column (or several columns) of data has been read into MINITAB, arithmetic operations may be performed on it. This is accomplished through the use of the LET command. For example, to add two columns C1 and C2, the following command is used:

```
MTB > LET C3=C1+C2
```

This results in C3 containing the sums of the individual components in C1 and C2.

Examples of various operations available in MINITAB and the symbols used to denote them are:

Addition   +
Subtraction   −
Multiplication   *
Division   /
Exponentiation   **

The LET command can also be used with the following functions:

ABSOLUTE   Compute absolute value
SQRT   Compute square root
LOGE   Compute logarithm to base e
LOGTEN   Compute logarithm to base 10
SIN, COS, TAN   Compute sine, cosine, or tangent for an
                angle given in radians

These functions would be used in the following manner:

```
MTB > LET C5=SQRT(C2)
```

For many other functions available and uses of the LET command, see one of the MINITAB Handbooks.

In the MINITAB Windows version these operations can be performed by using the CALC menu, MATHEMATICAL EXPRESSIONS subheading, using the options available under this subheading. All functions available are listed as well as a number of other available operations.

E. Saving MINITAB Worksheets

During a MINITAB session there is a convenient way to save the data in a computer file for later use in MINITAB. For example, the command

```
MTB > SAVE 'FILENAME'
```

saves all of the data currently being used in the disk file named FILENAME.MTW. Not only will the data be saved but the names assigned to any columns will be saved also. The data saved includes any original columns read in plus any new columns created during the session (as well as constants and matrices if any have been used).

At any later time, either in the same session or another session, the data and names can be brought back into MINITAB's workspace by typing

```
MTB > RETRIEVE 'FILENAME'
```

This command serves the same function as the READ command but will also retrieve the names, if any, that were assigned to columns. The session may now proceed as usual.

In the Windows version use the FILE menu with SAVE WORKSHEET AS to save or OPEN WORKSHEET to retrieve.

F. Data Editing

After reading or setting data into columns in MINITAB there are commands to edit those columns to correct errors made when typing in the values or to see what would happen if certain values were changed. Some useful commands for editing in MINITAB are given here. Note that when using menus, these commands are available primarily under the MANIP heading.

```
DELETE K . . . K OF C . . . C
```

> where K . . . K indicate the row numbers to be deleted and C . . . C indicate from which columns these rows are to be deleted.
>
> Example: DELETE 4 5 C1 C2
> deletes rows 4 and 5 of columns 1 and 2.
>
> Example: DELETE 5:10 C1 C2
> deletes rows 5 through 10 (inclusive) of columns 1 and 2.

```
LET C(K)=L
```

> where K represents the row number of column C to be corrected and L represents a new value for that row. This form of the LET command is especially useful in correcting one wrong number in a column.
>
> Example: LET C1(5)=10
> puts the number 10 in row 5 of column 1.

```
INSERT C . . . C
```

inserts data to be typed in at the terminal at the end of columns C . . . C; you will be prompted for data as in the READ command.

Example: `INSERT C1 C2`
adds data to columns 1 and 2. Two data entries per line must be given. Type in END when all data have been entered.

```
COPY C . . . C INTO C . . . C;
OMIT ROWS K . . . K.
```

copies the first set of columns listed into the second set of columns listed (the number of columns in each group must be the same); the subcommand OMIT ROWS K . . . K, if used, prevents the listed rows from being copied.

Example: `COPY C1 C2 INTO C3 C4;`
        `OMIT ROWS 4 5 6.`
copies columns 1 and 2 into columns 3 and 4 but omits rows 4, 5, and 6 from columns 3 and 4.

Example: `COPY C1 C2 INTO C3 C4;`
        `OMIT ROWS 5:10.`
copies columns 1 and 2 into columns 3 and 4 but omits rows 5 through 10 (inclusive).

C.3
SAS

A. Data Input

SAS analyses consist of at least two steps: (1) a DATA step to input the data set and create any new variables and (2) a PROC step to conduct any analyses.

Consider the following measurements of height and weight taken of five people:

Height (in inches)	Weight (in pounds)
60	140
66	195
70	185
71	190
73	210

To input these data into SAS the following lines are used:

```
DATA SIZE;
INPUT HEIGHT WEIGHT;
CARDS;
60 140
66 195
70 185
71 190
73 210
```

The DATA command in the first line names the data set to be used, SIZE. The INPUT command in the second line specifies the names of the variables to be used, HEIGHT and WEIGHT. The names used can be at most eight characters long. The CARDS command indicates to SAS that the data are to follow. The data are then typed in with one entry for each variable per line with each entry on a line separated by at least one space. Note that each command in SAS is followed by a semicolon. The data values, however, are not.

When reading data from a disk file that has already been set up, the following commands might be used:

```
DATA COST;
INFILE COST4.DAT;
INPUT COST PAPER MACHINE OVERHEAD LABOR;
```

The DATA line indicates the name assigned to the data set in SAS. The INFILE command indicates the file name from which the data are to be read. The INPUT line names the variables to be read. This form of the DATA step assumes the data are arranged in the file COST4.DAT in five columns with the entries in each column separated by at least one space. These data were presented in Table 4.2 of the text. They represent the COST, PAPER production, MACHINE hours used, OVERHEAD cost, and LABOR hours used for a sample of 27 months. The disk file COST4.DAT was used to store the data and is available on the data disk provided with the text.

B. Arithmetic with SAS Variables

During the DATA step in SAS, other variables can also be created. The following example illustrates some of the possible variables that might be of use in a SAS analysis.

```
DATA EXAMPLE;
INFILE EXAMPLE.DAT;
INPUT Y X1 X2 X3 X4;
XISQR=X1**2;
X2INV=1/X2;
X3X4=X3*X4;
```

In this example, data on five variables were read in from a file called EXAMPLE.DAT (which is not one of the files on your data disk—this is just an example). The variables were named Y, X1, X2, X3, and X4. Several new variables were then created during the data input. The variable X1SQR is the square of X1; the variable X2INV is the inverse of X2, and the variable X3X4 is the product of the two variables X3 and X4.

Examples of various arithmetic operations available in SAS and the symbols used to denote them are

Addition	$+$
Subtraction	$-$
Multiplication	$*$
Division	$/$
Exponentiation	$**$

SAS can also be used to produce certain functions of variables. For example, to create a variable equal to the natural logarithm of X1 the following command could be used:

```
LOGX1=LOG(X1)
```

A variable named LOGX1 has been created by finding the natural logarithm of the values of the original variable.

Other functions available in SAS include:

ABS	Compute absolute value
SQRT	Compute square root
LOG10	Compute logarithm to base 10
SIN, COS, TAN	Compute sine, cosine, or tangent for an angle given in radians

These are used in the same manner as the LOG function.

C. Statistics Commands

Statistical analyses of all types in SAS are performed in the PROC steps. PROC stands for "procedure" and each PROC statement in SAS specifies a certain procedure to be performed with the data. The following PROCs may be useful in data analysis. Many are used throughout this text.

```
PROC ANOVA;
CLASSES X1;
MODEL Y = X1;
```

performs a one-way analysis of variance. The dependent variable is listed first in the MODEL statement and the variable used to specify the factor levels is indicated in the CLASSES statement and listed second in the MODEL statement.

```
PROC ANOVA;
CLASSES X1 X2;
MODEL Y = X1 X2 X1*X2;
```

> performs a two-way analysis of variance. The dependent variable is listed first in the MODEL statement and the variables used to specify the factor levels are indicated in the CLASSES statement and listed second in the MODEL statement. If an interaction term is desired, it is listed in the model statement as shown: X1*X2.

```
PROC CHART;
VBAR Y;
```

> produces a bar chart for the variable Y. It should be used with discrete data.

```
PROC CORR;
VAR Y X1;
```

> produces the pairwise correlation for the variables Y and X1 (as well as other statistics on Y and X1).

```
PROC FREQ;
TABLES Y;
```

> produces a frequency distribution for the variable Y. It should be used with discrete data.

```
PROC MEANS;
VAR Y;
```

> produces the following summary statistics for the variable Y: a count of the number of observations, the mean, standard deviation, minimum, maximum, and standard error of the mean.

```
PROC PLOT;
PLOT Y*X1 Y*X2 Y*X3 Y*X4;
```

> produces a scatterplot of each indicated pair of variables with the first variable of each pair plotted on the vertical axis and the second variable on the horizontal axis.

```
PROC REG;
MODEL Y = X1 X2 X3 X4/OPTIONS;
OUTPUT PREDICTED=FITS STUDENT=STRES;
```

> performs a regression analysis. The MODEL statement specifies the Y variable (listed first) and the explanatory variables (X1, X2, X3, and X4 in this example). In place of "OPTIONS" in the MODEL statement there are a variety of choices. These include:

DW to request the Durbin–Watson statistic

VIF to request variance inflation factors

INFLUENCE to request a variety of influence diagnostics

P to request that predicted values be printed

R to request that residuals be printed

CLM prints 95% upper and lower confidence interval limits for the estimate of the point on the regression line (the estimate of the conditional mean) for each observation.

CLI prints 95% upper and lower prediction interval limits for the prediction of an individual point for each observation.

SELECTION=RSQUARE if all possible regressions is to be used

SELECTION=FORWARD if forward selection is to be used

SELECTION=BACKWARD if backward elimination is to be used

SELECTION=STEPWISE if stepwise regression is to be used

SELECTION=MAXR if the maximum R^2 improvement technique is to be used

SLE= desired level of significance for entering a variable when using STEPWISE or FORWARD

SLS= desired level of significance for deleting a variable when using STEPWISE or BACKWARD

INCLUDE= variables to be included in all models when using variable-selection procedures

> The OUTPUT statement can be used to create a variety of new variables. As shown, the predicted or fitted values will be saved in a variable named FITS and the standardized residuals will be saved in a variable named STRES.

```
PROC TTEST;
CLASS X1;
VAR X2;
```

> produces a test for whether or not the difference between two population means is zero. The data from the two samples are in the variable X2. The variable X1 is used to indicate from which population the sample value was chosen. The test is performed twice, once assuming population variances are unequal and again assuming they are equal.

```
PROC UNIVARIATE PLOT NORMAL;
VAR Y2;
```

> produces a variety of descriptive statistics for the variable Y: the count of the number of observations; the mean; standard deviation; variance; standard error of the mean; coefficient of variation; measures of skewness and kurtosis; a t value for testing whether the population mean is zero; the minimum;

maximum; quartiles; median; range; interquartile range; mode; 1st, 5th, 10th, 90th, 95th, and 99th percentiles; and the five largest and smallest values.

PLOT and NORMAL are options. If PLOT is specified, a stem-and-leaf plot, box plot, and a normal probability plot will be produced. If NORMAL is specified, a test for whether the data came from a normal distribution will be conducted.

D

Matrices and Their Application to Regression Analysis

D.1
Introduction

In Chapter 3, the equations were provided to compute b_0 and b_1, the least-squares estimates of the simple regression coefficients. When multiple regression was discussed in Chapter 4, no equations were shown for the coefficient estimates because of the complexity involved. Instead, the computer was used to solve for the estimates of the multiple regression coefficients. There is, however, a very general way to represent the equations for the estimates of the regression coefficients (either simple or multiple). This involves the use of matrices.

A *matrix* is a rectangular array of numbers. For example, the following are matrices:

$$\mathbf{A} = \begin{bmatrix} 5 & 7 & 3 \\ 4 & 2 & 6 \end{bmatrix}, \mathbf{B} = \begin{bmatrix} 2 & 4 \\ 1 & 5 \end{bmatrix}, \mathbf{C} = \begin{bmatrix} 7 \\ 4 \\ 6 \end{bmatrix}$$

The dimensions of a matrix are the number of rows and columns. The matrix $\mathbf{A}$ has two rows and three columns, so $\mathbf{A}$ is referred to as a 2×3 matrix. Similarly, $\mathbf{B}$ is a 2×2 matrix, and $\mathbf{C}$ is a 3×1 matrix. $\mathbf{B}$ is called a *square matrix* because it has equal numbers of rows and columns. The *diagonal elements* of a square matrix are the elements that are located on the diagonal that runs from the upper left-hand corner of the matrix to the lower right-hand corner. In the case of matrix $\mathbf{B}$, the diagonal elements are 2 and 5. A matrix with only one column is usually referred to as a *vector*. In the previous example, the matrix $\mathbf{C}$ is a vector.

Certain arithmetic operations can be performed with matrices—addition, subtraction, and multiplication. Another operation of importance when working with matrices is determining the *transpose* of the matrix. Square matrices also can be inverted. In this appendix, each of these matrix operations will be defined, and then the use of matrices to represent a regression equation and the computations necessary to produce the estimates of the regression coefficients will be shown. This treatment is not intended to be complete by any means but it may serve as a brief introduction to the matrix approach to regression analysis. For a more complete treatment using the matrix approach, see, for example, *Classical and Modern Regression with Applications* by Raymond Myers.

D.2
Matrix Operations

D.2.1 Matrix Addition

Two matrices can be added together if their dimensions are the same. Consider the following matrices denoted **A** and **B**:

$$\mathbf{A} = \begin{bmatrix} 3 & 6 & 1 \\ 3 & 4 & 6 \end{bmatrix}, \mathbf{B} = \begin{bmatrix} 2 & 4 & 2 \\ 4 & 5 & 4 \end{bmatrix}$$

The sum of these two matrices is **A** + **B**:

$$\mathbf{A} + \mathbf{B} = \begin{bmatrix} 3+2 & 6+4 & 1+2 \\ 3+4 & 4+5 & 6+4 \end{bmatrix} = \begin{bmatrix} 5 & 10 & 3 \\ 7 & 9 & 10 \end{bmatrix}$$

Note that the corresponding elements of the original matrices **A** and **B** have simply been added together to obtain the sum of the two matrices.

D.2.2 Transpose of a Matrix

The *transpose* of a matrix is formed by exchanging the rows and columns of a matrix. For example, consider the matrix

$$\mathbf{A} = \begin{bmatrix} 3 & 6 & 1 \\ 3 & 4 & 6 \end{bmatrix}$$

The transpose of **A** (denoted $\mathbf{A}^T$) is

$$\mathbf{A}^T = \begin{bmatrix} 3 & 3 \\ 6 & 4 \\ 1 & 6 \end{bmatrix}$$

The rows of the matrix **A** have now become the columns of $\mathbf{A}^T$ and the columns of **A** have become the rows of $\mathbf{A}^T$.

D.2.3 Matrix Multiplication

Consider the following two matrices:

$$\mathbf{A} = \begin{bmatrix} 4 & 1 \\ 2 & 6 \end{bmatrix}, \mathbf{B} = \begin{bmatrix} 3 & 2 & 4 \\ 1 & 4 & 5 \end{bmatrix}$$

The product, **AB**, of the two matrices is found by multiplying the elements of each row of **A** by the corresponding elements of each column of **B** and then summing the individual products. In this example,

$$\mathbf{AB} = \begin{bmatrix} (4 \times 3 + 1 \times 1) \ (4 \times 2 + 1 \times 4) \ (4 \times 4 + 1 \times 5) \\ (2 \times 3 + 6 \times 1) \ (2 \times 2 + 6 \times 4) \ (2 \times 4 + 6 \times 5) \end{bmatrix}$$

$$= \begin{bmatrix} 13 & 12 & 21 \\ 12 & 28 & 38 \end{bmatrix}$$

To obtain the product matrix, **AB**, the first element in row 1 of **A** is multiplied by the first element in column 1 of **B**. Then the second element in row 1 of **A** is multiplied by the second element in column 1 of **B**. These two products then are added together to obtain the element in the first row and first column of **AB**. To obtain the element in the first row and *second* column of **AB**, the first element in row 1 of **A** is multiplied by the first element in column 2 of **B**. Then the second element in row 1 of **A** is multiplied by the second element in column 2 of **B**. This row-by-column multiplication process continues until all elements of the product matrix **AB** have been computed. For this process to work, the number of columns in **A** must equal the number of rows in **B**. In terms of the dimensions of the matrices, if **A** is an $m \times n$ matrix and **B** is a $p \times q$ matrix, n and p must be equal before the product matrix can be computed. The product matrix, **AB**, will be an $m \times q$ matrix. In the example used here, **A** is a 2×2 matrix, **B** is a 2×3 matrix, and the product matrix, **AB**, is a 2×3 matrix.

Consider another example. If

$$\mathbf{A} = \begin{bmatrix} 5 & 7 & 3 \\ 4 & 2 & 6 \end{bmatrix} \quad \text{and} \quad \mathbf{B} = \begin{bmatrix} 7 \\ 4 \\ 6 \end{bmatrix},$$

then

$$\mathbf{AB} = \begin{bmatrix} 5 \times 7 + 7 \times 4 + 3 \times 6 \\ 4 \times 7 + 2 \times 4 + 6 \times 6 \end{bmatrix} = \begin{bmatrix} 81 \\ 72 \end{bmatrix}$$

D.2.4 Matrix Inversion

A familiar property of multiplication is that any number multiplied by its multiplicative inverse will result in the answer "1." For example, $2 \times \frac{1}{2} = 1$, $3 \times \frac{1}{3} = 1$, and so on. Thus, $\frac{1}{2}$ is the multiplicative inverse of the number 2, and $\frac{1}{3}$ is the multiplicative inverse of the number 3. The inverse of a matrix **A**, denoted $\mathbf{A}^{-1}$, is defined as the matrix that produces an identity matrix when multiplied by the original matrix:

$$\mathbf{AA}^{-1} = \mathbf{I}$$

where **I** is the identity matrix. An identity matrix is a matrix with 1's as diagonal elements and 0's everywhere else. For example, consider the matrix

$$\mathbf{A} = \begin{bmatrix} 4 & 2 \\ 5 & 3 \end{bmatrix}$$

The inverse of **A** is

$$\mathbf{A}^{-1} = \begin{bmatrix} 1.5 & 1 \\ -2.5 & 2 \end{bmatrix}$$

Multiplication of **A** by $\mathbf{A}^{-1}$ will verify that these two matrices are inverses:

$$\mathbf{AA}^{-1} = \begin{bmatrix} (4 \times 1.5 + 2 \times (-2.5)) & (4 \times (-1) + 2 \times 2) \\ (5 \times (1.5) + 3 \times (-2.5)) & (5 \times (-1) + 3 \times 2) \end{bmatrix}$$
$$= \begin{bmatrix} 1 & 0 \\ 0 & 1 \end{bmatrix}$$

The resulting product is an identity matrix, denoted **I**. It has the property that any matrix multiplied by an identity matrix will result in the original matrix. For example, it is easy to verify that

$$\mathbf{AI} = \mathbf{A}$$

When working with numbers rather than matrices, the number 1 serves as the multiplicative identity. Thus, in matrix multiplication, the identity matrix serves the same purpose as the number 1.

Note that inverses can be computed only for square matrices. Any identity matrix **I** also must be a square matrix.

One method of finding the inverse of a matrix will be demonstrated through the following example. Consider the matrix **A**:

$$\mathbf{A} = \begin{bmatrix} 4 & 2 \\ 5 & 3 \end{bmatrix}, \mathbf{I} = \begin{bmatrix} 1 & 0 \\ 0 & 1 \end{bmatrix}$$

The identity matrix of the same dimension has been written next to **A**. A series of identical computations will now be performed on **A** and **I**. The intent of these computations is to transform **A** into an identity matrix. The same operations applied to **I** will transform this identity matrix into the inverse of **A**, $\mathbf{A}^{-1}$. Two types of computations will be allowed:

1   Any row of **A** can be multiplied or divided by a number.

2   One row of **A** can be added to or subtracted from another row of **A**.

The computations to produce $\mathbf{A}^{-1}$ are as follows:

Step 1: Because the goal is to transform $\mathbf{A}$ into an identity matrix, start by dividing the first row of $\mathbf{A}$ by the value of the element in the first row and first column (4). This will result in a 1 as the first diagonal element. Perform the identical computation on $\mathbf{I}$; that is, divide the elements in the first row by 4:

$$\mathbf{A} = \begin{bmatrix} 1 & 0.5 \\ 5 & 3 \end{bmatrix}, \mathbf{I} = \begin{bmatrix} 0.25 & 0 \\ 0 & 1 \end{bmatrix}$$

Step 2: Subtract 5 times row 1 from row 2; the result is a 0 in the first element of this row. As always, do the same to $\mathbf{I}$. Also, note that row 1 is not actually changed in this computation. A multiple of row 1 is subtracted from row 2, producing a new row 2, but row 1 remains as it was originally:

$$\mathbf{A} = \begin{bmatrix} 1 & 0.5 \\ 0 & 0.5 \end{bmatrix}, \mathbf{I} = \begin{bmatrix} 0.25 & 0 \\ -1.25 & 1 \end{bmatrix}$$

Step 3: Multiply row 2 by 2. The result is a 1 for the diagonal element in that row:

$$\mathbf{A} = \begin{bmatrix} 1 & 0.5 \\ 0 & 1 \end{bmatrix}, \mathbf{I} = \begin{bmatrix} 0.25 & 0 \\ -2.5 & 2 \end{bmatrix}$$

Step 4: Subtract 0.5 times row 2 from row 1 to eliminate the nondiagonal element:

$$\mathbf{A} = \begin{bmatrix} 1 & 0 \\ 0 & 1 \end{bmatrix}, \mathbf{I} = \begin{bmatrix} 1.5 & -1 \\ -2.5 & 2 \end{bmatrix}$$

The matrix $\mathbf{A}$ now has been transformed into an identity matrix. The inverse of $\mathbf{A}$ is

$$\mathbf{A}^{-1} = \begin{bmatrix} 1.5 & -1 \\ -2.5 & 2 \end{bmatrix}$$

D.3
Matrices and Regression Analysis

In Chapter 4, the multiple regression model was written as follows:

$$y_i = \beta_0 + \beta_1 x_{1i} + \beta_2 x_{2i} + \cdots + \beta_K x_{Ki} + e_i \tag{D.1}$$

In matrix notation the multiple regression model can be written:

$$\mathbf{Y} = \mathbf{X}\boldsymbol{\beta} + \mathbf{e}, \tag{D.2}$$

where $\mathbf{Y}$, $\mathbf{X}$, β, and $\mathbf{e}$ are matrices defined as follows:

$$\mathbf{Y} = \begin{bmatrix} y_1 \\ y_2 \\ \cdot \\ \cdot \\ \cdot \\ y_n \end{bmatrix}, \mathbf{X} = \begin{bmatrix} 1 & x_{11}, & x_{12}, & \dots, & x_{1K} \\ 1 & x_{21}, & x_{22}, & \dots, & x_{2K} \\ \cdot & \cdot & \cdot & & \cdot \\ \cdot & \cdot & \cdot & & \cdot \\ \cdot & \cdot & \cdot & & \cdot \\ 1 & x_{n1}, & x_{n2} & \dots, & x_{nK} \end{bmatrix},$$

$$\beta = \begin{bmatrix} \beta_0 \\ \beta_1 \\ \cdot \\ \cdot \\ \cdot \\ \beta_K \end{bmatrix}, \quad \text{and} \quad \mathbf{e} = \begin{bmatrix} e_1 \\ e_2 \\ \cdot \\ \cdot \\ \cdot \\ e_n \end{bmatrix}$$

The matrix $\mathbf{Y}$ is an $n \times 1$ matrix containing all n observations on the dependent variable. These observations are denoted y_1, y_2, and so on as in Chapter 4.

The matrix $\mathbf{X}$ is an $n \times (K + 1)$ matrix. The first column of the matrix $\mathbf{X}$ is a column of 1's. The second column of $\mathbf{X}$ consists of all n values of the first explanatory variable ($k = 1$), denoted $x_{11}, x_{21}, \dots, x_{n1}$. The third column of $\mathbf{X}$ consists of all n values of the second explanatory variable ($k = 2$), denoted $x_{12}, x_{22}, \dots, x_{n2}$, and so on. The initial column of 1's in the $\mathbf{X}$ matrix is necessary because there is a constant (or intercept) in the equation. These 1's can be thought of as multipliers of β_0, just as the appropriate x values can be thought of as multipliers of β_k.

The matrix β is a $(K + 1) \times 1$ matrix containing all of the population regression coefficients to be estimated. These are denoted $\beta_0, \beta_1, \dots, \beta_K$.

The matrix $\mathbf{e}$ is an $n \times 1$ matrix containing the disturbances $e_1, e_2, \dots, e_n$.

Equation (D.2) represents the same relationship as Equation (D.1) except in matrix form. This can be verified by actually performing the multiplication and addition of the matrices shown in Equation (D.2).

Equation (D.2) is the general representation of any multiple regression model. As a specific example, consider again the data from Example 3.1:

x	1	2	3	4	5	6
y	3	2	8	8	11	13

The $\mathbf{X}$ and $\mathbf{Y}$ matrices for this example are as follows:

$$\mathbf{Y} = \begin{bmatrix} 3 \\ 2 \\ 8 \\ 8 \\ 11 \\ 13 \end{bmatrix} \quad \text{and} \quad \mathbf{X} = \begin{bmatrix} 1 & 1 \\ 1 & 2 \\ 1 & 3 \\ 1 & 4 \\ 1 & 5 \\ 1 & 6 \end{bmatrix}$$

The matrix β is

$$\beta = \begin{bmatrix} \beta_0 \\ \beta_1 \end{bmatrix}$$

and the matrix **e** is

$$\mathbf{e} = \begin{bmatrix} e_1 \\ e_2 \\ e_3 \\ e_4 \\ e_5 \\ e_6 \end{bmatrix}$$

(There are no actual numbers in **e** because the disturbances are not observable.)

As least-squares estimates of β_0 and β_1 in Chapter 3, those values of b_0 and b_1 that minimized the error sum of squares (*SSE*) were used. *SSE* was written as

$$\sum_{i=1}^{n}(y_i - \hat{y}_i)^2,$$

where the $\hat{y}$ were the points on the regression line determined by b_0 and b_1. In matrix notation, the equation for the error sum of squares can be written as

$$(\mathbf{Y} - \mathbf{Xb})^T(\mathbf{Y} - \mathbf{Xb}),$$

where **b** is the matrix of estimated regression coefficients:

$$\mathbf{b} = \begin{bmatrix} b_0 \\ b_1 \end{bmatrix}$$

The equation representing the least-squares estimates of the regression coefficients is

$$\mathbf{b} = (\mathbf{X}^T\mathbf{X})^{-1}\mathbf{X}^T\mathbf{Y} \tag{D.3}$$

This equation represents the least-squares estimates of the regression coefficients in any simple or multiple regression. The matrices **b**, **X**, and **Y** just need to be defined appropriately. In the example used in this section, the least-squares estimates are found as follows:

$$\mathbf{X}^T = \begin{bmatrix} 1 & 1 & 1 & 1 & 1 & 1 \\ 1 & 2 & 3 & 4 & 5 & 6 \end{bmatrix}$$

$$\mathbf{X}^T\mathbf{X} = \begin{bmatrix} 1 & 1 & 1 & 1 & 1 & 1 \\ 1 & 2 & 3 & 4 & 5 & 6 \end{bmatrix} \begin{bmatrix} 1 & 1 \\ 1 & 2 \\ 1 & 3 \\ 1 & 4 \\ 1 & 5 \\ 1 & 6 \end{bmatrix}$$

$$= \begin{bmatrix} 6 & 21 \\ 21 & 91 \end{bmatrix}$$

$$(\mathbf{X}^T\mathbf{X})^{-1} = \begin{bmatrix} \dfrac{91}{105} & \dfrac{-21}{105} \\ \dfrac{-21}{105} & \dfrac{6}{105} \end{bmatrix}$$

$$\mathbf{X}^T\mathbf{Y} = \begin{bmatrix} 1 & 1 & 1 & 1 & 1 & 1 \\ 1 & 2 & 3 & 4 & 5 & 6 \end{bmatrix} \begin{bmatrix} 3 \\ 2 \\ 8 \\ 8 \\ 11 \\ 13 \end{bmatrix}$$

$$= \begin{bmatrix} 45 \\ 196 \end{bmatrix}$$

$$(\mathbf{X}^T\mathbf{X})^{-1}\mathbf{X}^T\mathbf{Y} = \begin{bmatrix} \dfrac{91}{105} & \dfrac{-21}{105} \\ \dfrac{-21}{105} & \dfrac{6}{105} \end{bmatrix} \begin{bmatrix} 45 \\ 196 \end{bmatrix}$$

$$= \begin{bmatrix} 39 - 39.2 \\ -9 + 11.2 \end{bmatrix} = \begin{bmatrix} -0.2 \\ 2.2 \end{bmatrix}$$

The least-squares estimate of β is

$$\mathbf{b} = \begin{bmatrix} -0.2 \\ 2.2 \end{bmatrix}$$

Because

$$\mathbf{b} = \begin{bmatrix} b_0 \\ b_1 \end{bmatrix},$$

it is clear that the regression equation can be written

$$\hat{y} = -0.2 + 2.2x$$

as in Chapter 3.

Many of the other relationships discussed throughout this text also can be expressed in matrix form. Some of these are listed but will not be discussed in detail.

1 $\hat{\mathbf{Y}} = \mathbf{X}\mathbf{b}$ is the vector of predicted or fitted values.

2 $\mathbf{Y} - \hat{\mathbf{Y}}$ is the vector of residuals.

3 $(\mathbf{Y} - \hat{\mathbf{Y}})^T(\mathbf{Y} - \hat{\mathbf{Y}})$ is the error sum of squares (*SSE*). *SSE* also can be written as $\mathbf{Y}^T\mathbf{Y} - \mathbf{b}^T\mathbf{X}^T\mathbf{Y}$.

4 $\mathbf{b}^T\mathbf{X}^T\mathbf{Y} - n\bar{\mathbf{Y}}^2$ is the regression sum of squares.

5 The variances of the regression coefficients are the diagonal elements of the matrix $s_e^2(\mathbf{X}^T\mathbf{X})^{-1}$.

6 The estimate of s_e^2 is $SSE/(n - K - 1)$ with *SSE* as given in 3.

7 The variance of the estimate of a point on the regression line, denoted in Chapters 3 and 4 as s_m^2, is given by $s_m^2 = s_e^2(x(\mathbf{X}^T\mathbf{X})^{-1}x^T)$, and the variance of the prediction for a single individual is $s_p^2 = s_e^2(1 + x(\mathbf{X}^T\mathbf{X})^{-1}x^T)$. The lowercased x's in these formulas represent the vectors of the values of the explanatory variables used to generate estimates or predictions.

Exercises

In Exercises 1 through 3, find the sum of the following matrices.

1 $A = \begin{bmatrix} 1 & 3 & 4 \\ 2 & 1 & 2 \\ 3 & 1 & 5 \end{bmatrix}, B = \begin{bmatrix} 4 & 1 & 6 \\ 2 & 1 & 5 \\ 1 & 4 & 3 \end{bmatrix}$

2 $A = \begin{bmatrix} 1 & 2 \\ 7 & 6 \end{bmatrix}, B = \begin{bmatrix} 4 & 5 \\ 1 & 9 \end{bmatrix}$

3 $A = \begin{bmatrix} 1 \\ 3 \\ 2 \end{bmatrix}, B = \begin{bmatrix} 6 \\ 1 \\ 5 \end{bmatrix}$

In Exercises 4 through 6, find the transpose of the following matrices.

4 $A = \begin{bmatrix} 1 & 3 & 4 \\ 2 & 1 & 2 \\ 3 & 1 & 5 \end{bmatrix}$

5 $B = \begin{bmatrix} 1 & 7 & 5 \\ 3 & 4 & 6 \end{bmatrix}$

6 $A = \begin{bmatrix} 1 \\ 3 \\ 2 \end{bmatrix}$

In Exercises 7 through 10, find the product of the following matrices.

7 $A = \begin{bmatrix} 1 & 2 \\ 7 & 6 \end{bmatrix}, B = \begin{bmatrix} 4 & 5 \\ 1 & 9 \end{bmatrix}$

8 $\mathbf{A} = \begin{bmatrix} 1 & 3 & 4 \\ 2 & 1 & 2 \\ 3 & 1 & 5 \end{bmatrix}, \mathbf{B} = \begin{bmatrix} 4 & 1 & 6 \\ 2 & 1 & 5 \\ 1 & 4 & 3 \end{bmatrix}$

9 $\mathbf{A} = \begin{bmatrix} 1 & 7 & 5 \\ 3 & 4 & 6 \end{bmatrix}$ and $\mathbf{A}^T$

10 $\mathbf{A} = \begin{bmatrix} 1 & 3 & 4 \\ 2 & 1 & 2 \\ 3 & 1 & 5 \end{bmatrix}, \mathbf{B} = \begin{bmatrix} 1 & 0 & 0 \\ 0 & 1 & 0 \\ 0 & 0 & 1 \end{bmatrix}$

In Exercises 11 and 12, compute the inverse of the following matrices.

11 $\mathbf{A} = \begin{bmatrix} 1 & 2 \\ 4 & 6 \end{bmatrix}$

12 $\mathbf{A} = \begin{bmatrix} 4 & 1 \\ 2 & 3 \end{bmatrix}$

In Exercises 13 through 16, use the following data to answer the questions.

y	5	6	9	10	14
x	1	2	4	5	6

13 Define the **X** and **Y** matrices that will be used to determine the least-squares estimates of β_0 and β_1.

14 Find the least-squares estimate

$$\mathbf{b} = (\mathbf{X}^T\mathbf{X})^{-1}\mathbf{X}^T\mathbf{Y}$$

15 Find the standard error of the regression s_e.

16 Find a 95% confidence interval estimate of β_1.

E

Solutions to Selected Odd-Numbered Exercises

E.1 Chapter 2

1   MTB > mean c1

           MEAN   =   28.815

       MTB > stan c1

              ST.DEV. =   5.3948

       MTB > medi c1

              MEDIAN =   28.000

3 $\mu = 3.5$

       $\sigma = 1.71$

       If the die was tossed a large number of times and the outcome recorded on each toss, the average of the numbers representing those outcomes would be close to 3.5.

5 $\mu = 7$

       $\sigma = 2.415$

7   **a**   1.10

       b $110

       c   0.2

9   **a**   0.8413

       b   0.0228

       c   2103.25 (approximately 2103)

11 **a** $z = 2.0$

       b $z = 1.65$

c $z = 2.33$

d $z = 2.58$

13 **a** 0.0228

b 0.3174

15 **a** 0.0228

b 0.0

17 0.5762

19 $(5.66, 6.34)$

21 $(27.932, 29.698)$

23 If a null hypothesis is rejected at the 5% level of significance, it would also be rejected at the 10% level of significance, since the 10% level requires less "evidence" to reject the hypothesis than does the 5% level. In other words, a test statistic that is more extreme than the 5% critical value is also more extreme than the 10% critical value.

25 Critical value: $t(0.05, 15) = 1.753$

Test statistic: $t = 0.5$

Decision: Accept H_0

27 Critical value: $t(0.05, 25) = -1.708$

Test statistic: $t = 6.45$

Decision: Accept H_0

29 $(2.55, 5.45)$

31 Since no information concerning the population variances is given, assume that the population variances are not equal. (Must also assume normal populations since the sample sizes are small.) The 95% confidence interval determined by MINITAB: $(-11.3, 2.6)$.

33 Critical value: $z(0.025) = 1.96$ (large samples)

Test statistic: $t = 1.76$

Decision: Accept H_0

35 Critical value: $t(0.025, 28) = 2.048$

Test statistic: $t = 3.97$

Decision: Reject H_0

37 Since no information concerning the population variances is given, we assume that the population variances are not equal.

Critical value: $t(0.05, 124) \approx 1.645$ (z value)

Test statistic: $t = 5.62$

Decision: Reject H_0

39 **a** Since no information concerning the population variances is given, we assume that the population variances are not equal. (Must also assume normal populations since the sample sizes are small.)

Critical value: $t(.025, \ 21) = 2.080$

Test statistic: $t = -0.09$

Decision: Accept H_0

b Conclusion: The population mean starting salaries for marketing and finance majors do not differ.

41 **a** Since no information concerning the population variances is given, we assume that the population variances are not equal.

Critical value: $t(0.05, 51) \approx 1.645$ (z value)

Test statistic: $t = -5.83$

Decision: Reject H_0

E.2 Chapter 3

1 **b** $b_1 = 0.9107$ $b_0 = 7.1001$

3 **a** Value $= -50035 + 72.8$ size

b Cost $= 16594 + 650$ numports

c Starts $= 1809 - 29.1$ rates

5 **a** Critical value: $t(0.025, 8) = 2.306$

Test statistic: $t = 41.92$

b Yes

c Critical value: $t(0.025, 8) = 2.306$

Test statistic: $t = -0.61$

Decision: Accept H_0

d The intercept of the line representing the relationship between number of items and labor is not significantly different from zero. (Note: This test does not suggest anything about whether there is or is not a relationship between number of items and labor.)

7 **a** Critical value: $t(0.025, 18) = 2.101$

Test statistic: $t = 10.70$

Decision: Reject H_0

b Sales and advertising appear to be linearly related. (Caution: see Section 3.7 in text. There may not be a *causal* relationship here.)

c $\hat{y} = -57 + 17.6x$

d $(-941.29, 826.69)$

e $(14.12, 21.02)$

f Critical value: $t(0.025, 18) = 2.101$

Test statistic: $t = -1.48$

Decision: Accept H_0

g The slope of the regression line is not significantly different from 20.

9 **a** $R^2 = 0.9955$

b 99.55%

    c   Critical value: $F(0.05; 1, 8) = 5.32$

        Test statistic: $F = 1762.7$

        Decision: Reject H_0

    d   Yes

11   **a**   86.4%

    b   Critical value: $F(0.05; 1, 18) = 4.41$

        Test statistic: $F = 114.54$

        Decision: Reject H_0

13   **a** $\hat{y}_m = -1.8353 + 2.0206(60) = 119.4007$

    b $119.4007 \pm 2.306(0.8871)$ or $(117.36, 121.45)$

    c $\hat{y}_p = -1.8353 + 2.0206(60) = 119.4007$

    d $119.4007 \pm 2.306(2.94)$ or $(112.62, 126.18)$

15   **a** $\hat{y}_m = 4335$ (in \$100) 95% confidence interval estimate: $(4007, 4663)$ (in \$100)

    b

x	Point Est.	95% Prediction Interval
20,000	3457	2130, 4783
25,000	4335	3043, 5627
30,000	5214	3933, 6494
35,000	6092	4800, 7385

        Note: Both point estimates and interval limits are in \$100.

17   **a** $\hat{y}_m = -57 + 17.6(600) = 10,503$ (\$1,050,300)

        Yes. The regression equation was developed using a range of values for the x variable (ADV) of 160 to 415. The value 600 is well outside this range. Caution should be exercised if this estimate is used because the relationship between SALES and ADV has been observed only over the range 160 to 415. It is not known whether the same relationship will serve as well outside this range.

    b   Disagree. The model was developed over the range of 160 to 415 for the x variable (ADV). Because ADV $= 0$ is outside this range, the resulting forecasts cannot be depended upon to make sense. Still, the least-squares method must choose a value as a y-intercept. In this case, the intercept value that minimized the error sum of squares was -5700.

19   **a**   Critical value: $t(0.025, 22) = 2.074$

        Test statistic: $t = 8$

        Decision: Reject H_0

    b   Critical value: $F(0.10; 1, 22) = 2.95$

        Test statistic: $F = 64$

        Decision: Reject H_0

    c $R^2 = 74.4\%$

21   **a**   Critical value: $t(0.05, 91) \approx 1.645$ (z value)

        Test statistic: $t = 4.31$

        Decision: Reject H_0

    b   17%

c $\hat{y}_p = 3819 + 128(12) = 5355$

d $\hat{y}_m = 3819 + 128(12) = 5355$

e As will be seen when this problem is continued later in this text, other factors might include experience and, unfortunately in this case, whether the employee is male or female. You can probably think of other factors that might be useful.

23　**a** $\hat{y} = 207 + 4.18x$ or COST $= 207 + 4.18$ MACHINE

　　b 99.5%

　　c Critical value: $t(0.025, 25) = 2.06$

　　　Test statistic: $t = 69.05$

　　　Decision: Reject H_0

　　d Point estimate of the conditional mean of y given $x = 350$: 1669.44

　　　95% confidence interval for the conditional mean of y given $x = 350$: (1659.40, 1679.49)

　　e Point estimate of the conditional mean of y given $x = 550$: 2505.20

　　　95% confidence interval for the conditional mean of y given $x = 550$: (2473.92, 2536.49)

25　The regression of wins on average salary suggests that there is a positive linear relationship between the two variables.

　　Critical value: $t(0.025, 26) = 1.706$

　　Test statistic: $t = 2.49$

　　Decision: Reject H_0

E.3　Chapter 4

1　**a** $\hat{y} = 51.7 + 0.948x_1 + 2.47x_2 + 0.048x_3 - 0.0506x_4$

　　　or COST $= 51.7 + 0.948$ PAPER $+ 2.47$ MACHINE $+ 0.048$ OVERHEAD $- 0.0506$ LABOR

　　b Critical value: $F(0.05; 4, 22) = 2.82$

　　　Test statistic: $F = 4629.17$

　　　Decision: Reject H_0

　　c $b_2 = 2.47$　　$2.47 \pm (2.074)(0.4656)$

　　d Critical value: $t(0.025, 22) = 2.074$

　　　Test statistic: $t = -0.43$

　　　Decision: Accept H_0

　　e 99.9%

　　f 99.9%

　　g The regression equation can be used to identify factors that are related to cost. After doing this these factors might be useful in reducing cost. For example, machine hours are related to cost. Obviously we cannot just start reducing machine hours since these hours are part of the manufacturing process. But there may be a way to use the hours more efficiently resulting in a reduction of overall hours without sacrificing production and a resulting decrease in cost. The regression equation shows the influence of a one-unit reduction of the variables included on cost.

3 Critical value: $F(0.05; 2, 22) = 3.44$

Test statistic: $F = 0.80$

Decision: Accept H_0

5 Critical value: $F(0.05; 2, 89) \approx 3.15$ (approximate)

Test statistic: $F = 8.4$

Decision: Reject H_0

7 **a** $\hat{y}_i = 0.297 + 0.941\,y_{i-1}$ or SILVER $= 0.297 + 0.941$ SILVERL1

   b Critical value: $t(0.025, 117) \approx 1.96$ (z value)

   Test statistic: $t = 41.27$

   Decision: Reject H_0

   c 93.6%

   d Using MINITAB the forecast of the price of silver in January 1993 is \$3.7996. Computed by hand, the forecast would be silver $= 0.297 + 0.941(3.72) = \$3.7975$. The difference is due to rounding.

9 **a** $\hat{y} = 4.49 + 0.231x_1 - 0.0540x_2$ or DIVIDEND $= 4.49 + 0.231$ EPS $- 0.0540$ PRICE

   b 9.8%

   c Critical value: $F(0.10; 2, 47) \approx 2.44$ (approximate)

   Test statistic: $F = 2.57$

   Decision: Reject H_0

   d The coefficients β_1 and β_2 are not both equal to zero. In other words, at least one of the variables x_1 or x_2 is explaining a significant amount of the variation in y. (Note, however, that a different conclusion would be reached if $\alpha = 0.05$).

E.4 Chapter 5

1 **a** Yes. It is not, however, a linear relationship.

   b $\hat{y} = 10.0$

   c Critical value: $t(0.005, 9) = 3.25$

   Test statistic: $t = 0.0$

   Decision: Accept H_0

   d There is a "strong" association. In fact, this is an exact relationship, but not a linear one. The equation expressing the relationship is

$$y = x^2$$

3   **a** $\hat{y} = 193 + 11.4t$ or PERCONS $= 193 + 11.4$ TREND

    b   99.3%

    c   The linearity assumption does appear to be violated. This is evident in the plot of the standardized residuals versus the fitted values (see Figure 5.53 [MINITAB] or Figure 5.55 [SAS]) and in the time series plot of the standardized residuals in Figure 5.54.

         This violation might be corrected by fitting a curvilinear trend. To determine an appropriate curvilinear trend model, refer to the time series plot of PERCONS in Figure 5.50. There may be more than one candidate for the curvilinear form. In this case a quadratic trend worked well. For the quadratic trend, the new equation would appear as:

$$y = \beta_0 + \beta_1 \text{ TREND } + \beta_2 \text{ TRENDSQR } + e$$

       where TREND represents the trend variable and TRENDSQR represents the square of the trend variable. The estimated equation is percons $= 234 + 7.64$ trend $+ 0.0577$ trendsqr. Examining new residual plots suggests that the quadratic trend regression is an improvement over the original linear trend regression model. [Actually, the residuals are not randomly distributed. There is still autocorrelation present but this problem has not been discussed yet. An alternate model (using lagged values of the dependent variable as an explanatory variable) for the personal consumption data which eliminates the autocorrelation may be better than the trend model presented here.]

5   The constant variance assumption appears to be violated. The time series plot of the standardized residuals (see Figure 5.74 in text) and the plot of the standardized residuals versus the fitted values (see Figure 5.75 in text) both exhibit the cone-shaped pattern that suggests a nonconstant variance. The log transformation would be the most likely candidate in this extrapolative time-series model.

$$\ln(y_i) = \beta_0 + \beta_1 \ln(y_{i-1}) + e$$

The residual plots from this regression appear much more randomly distributed than the original plots. The log transformation appears to be a reasonable correction. (The square root transformation is another alternative in this case, but it does not produce results as good as those of the log transformation.) The estimated equation is logexp $= 0.714 + 0.930$ logexp11.

7   Critical values: $d_L(0.05; 29, 1) = 1.34$ $d_U = (0.05; 29, 1) = 1.48$

    Test statistic: $d = 0.51$

    Decision: Reject H_0

11   **a**   .0606

    b   2.085

        2.063

        0.022

    c   4.6047

    d   The 95% prediction interval is (4.2354, 4.9741).

15 Critical values: $d_L(0.05; 27, 2) = 1.24$ $d_U = (0.05; 27, 2) = 1.56$

Test statistic: $d = 2.14$

Decision: Accept H_0

19 VOLUME is important in explaining the number of accidents although it explains only 16.4% of the variance. From MINITAB's table of unusual observations (as well as from the residual plots), two observations stand out as unusual in the y direction. These are observations 30 and 31. Both of these intersections have more accidents than would be expected given their volume of traffic. The city may want to investigate whether measures could be taken to make these intersections safer (install lights, remove obstructions, etc.). The estimated equation is accident $= 0.39 + 0.00200$ volume.

E.5 Chapter 6

1 **a** Critical value: $F(0.05; 4, 88) \approx 2.53$ (approximate)

Test statistic: $F = 22.98$

Decision: Reject H_0

b At least one of the coefficients $(\beta_1, \beta_2, \beta_3, \beta_4)$ is not equal to zero. At least one of the four explanatory variables (x_1, x_2, x_3, x_4) is important in explaining the variation in SALARY.

c Critical value: $t(0.025, 88) \approx 1.96$ (z value)

Test statistic: $t = 6.13$

Decision: Reject H_0

d There is a difference in salaries, on average, for male and female workers after accounting for the effects of the EDUC, EXPER, and MONTHS variables.

e Forecast of average salary for males with 12 years education, 10 years of experience and with months equal to 15:

$$\hat{y} = 3526 + 722 + 90(12) + 1.27(10) + 23.4(15) = 5691.7$$

Forecast of average salary for females with 12 years education, 10 years experience, and with months equal to 15:

$$\hat{y} = 3526 + 90(12) + 1.27(10) + 23.4(15) = 4969.7$$

3 **a** $R^2_{\text{ADJ}} = 49.4\%$ with interaction variable (see Figure 6.23 or 6.24 in text).

$R^2_{\text{ADJ}} = 48.9\%$ without interaction variable (see Figure 6.15 or 6.16 in text).

Although the full model has a higher adjusted R-square value, the difference is very small. It is unclear from the adjusted R-square alone whether the interaction variable is necessary. The hypothesis test in part b results in the conclusion that it is not.

b Critical value: $t(0.025, 87) \approx 1.96$ (z value)

Test statistic: $t = -1.42$

Decision: Accept H_0

c The interaction term is not important in this regression model. Choose the *reduced* model.

5 **a** Critical value: $F(0.05; 11, 153) \approx 1.91$ (approximate)

Test statistic: $F = \dfrac{(295052 - 8742)/11}{8742/153} = 455.54$

Decision: Reject H_0; there is seasonal variation in milk production.

b Critical value: $t(0.025, 153) \approx 1.96$ (z value)

Test statistic: $t = 2.89$

Decision: Reject H_0; the trend variable is important.

Critical value: $t(0.025, 153) \approx 1.96$ (z value)

Test statistic: $t = 23.53$

Decision: Reject H_0; the lagged variable is important.

E.6 Chapter 7

1A **a** $\hat{y} = 59.43 + 0.95x_1 + 2.39x_2$ OR COST $= 59.43 + 0.95$ PAPER $+2.39$ MACHINE

b 99.87%

c $R_{ADJ}^2 = 1 + \left(\dfrac{n-1}{n-K-1}\right)(R^2 - 1) = 1 + \left(\dfrac{26}{24}\right)(0.9987 - 1) = 0.9986$

d $s_e = 11.0$

e OVERHEAD and LABOR

Overhead and labor are related to COST. However, they add little to the ability of the equation to explain the variation in COST. The variables PAPER and MACHINE explain over 99% of the variation in COST. Due to the high correlation between these two variables and OVERHEAD and LABOR, the problem of multicollinearity discussed in Chapter 5 is present. The variables OVERHEAD and LABOR appear unrelated to COST in the equation since they are highly correlated with PAPER and MACHINE. OVERHEAD and LABOR are probably unnecessary since most of the variation in COST is explained by the other two variables.

1B **b** The two-variable set, PAPER and MACHINE, has a C_p value of 2.602 (and $p = 3$), so this is a very good possibility for our choice of best model. This is consistent with the backward elimination results discussed in part A.

c $R^2 = .9987$ (or 99.87%)

$R_{ADJ}^2 = .9986$ (see part A, c for computation)

$s_e = 11.0$

$C_p = 2.602$

E.7 Chapter 8

1 Critical value: $F(0.05; 8, 103) \approx 2.02$ (approximate)

Test statistic: $F = 14.82$

Decision: Reject H_0

3 *First test for interaction effects.*

Critical value: $F(0.05; 6, 12) = 3.00$

Test statistic: $F = 0.96/4.79 = 0.20$

Decision: Accept H_0

Test for main effects due to industry.

Critical value: $F(0.05; 3, 12) = 3.49$

Test statistic: $F = 238.71/4.79 = 49.8$

Decision: Reject H_0

Test for main effects due to contact.

Critical value: $F(0.05; 2, 12) = 3.89$

Test statistic: $F = 0.13/4.79 = 0.03$

Decision: Accept H_0

5 Critical value: $F(0.05; 2, 15) = 3.68$

Test statistic: $F = 102.32$

Decision: Reject H_0

7 Critical value: $F(0.05; 2, 4) = 6.94$

Test statistic: $F = 218.11/2.11 = 103.37$

Decision: Reject H_0

9 Critical value: $F(0.05; 6, 49) \approx 2.34$ (approximate)

Test statistic: $F = 29.21$

Decision: Reject H_0

E.8 Chapter 9

1 The proportion classified correctly by the discriminant model is 0.763. The model has correctly classified as male or female 76.3% of the employees on the basis of their salaries. This would suggest that salary contains information about gender and that Harris Bank may be paying males and females on a different scale.

The logistic regression output further supports the idea that Harris may be guilty of wage discrimination. The p value for the independent variable SALARY in the logistic regression is 0.0001 suggesting that SALARY is important in predicting the group (male or female) to which the individual belongs.

References

Belsley, D. A.; Kuh, E.; and Welsch, R. E. *Regression Diagnostics: Identifying Influential Data and Sources of Collinearity*. New York: John Wiley and Sons, 1980.

Bessler, D. A., and Babubla, R. A. "Forecasting Wheat Exports: Do Exchange Rates Really Matter?" *Journal of Business and Economic Statistics* 5 (1987): 397–406.

Bowerman, B. L., and O'Connell, R. T. *Time Series Forecasting: An Applied Approach*. 3d ed. Belmont, CA: Duxbury Press, 1993.

Conway, D. A., and Roberts, H. V. "Regression Analyses in Employment Discrimination Cases." In *Statistics and the Law*, edited by M. H. DeGroot, S. E. Fienberg, and J. B. Kadane, 107–168 (with comments and reply on pages 169–195). New York: John Wiley and Sons, 1986.

Cravens, D. W.; Woodruff, R. B.; and Stamper, J. C. "An Analytical Approach for Evaluating Sales Territory Performance." *Journal of Marketing* 36 (1972): 31–37.

Cryer, J. D. *Time Series Analysis*. Boston: Duxbury Press, 1986.

Farnum, N. R., and Stanton, L. W. *Quantitative Forecasting Methods*. Boston: PWS-Kent, 1989.

Graybill, F. A., and Iyer, H. K. *Regression Analysis: Concepts and Applications*. Belmont, CA: Duxbury Press, 1994.

Griffiths, W. E., and Surekha, K. "A Monte Carlo Evaluation of the Power of Some Tests for Heteroscedasticity." *Journal of Econometrics* 31 (1986): 219–231.

Groeneveld, R. A. *Introductory Statistical Methods: An Integrated Approach Using MINITAB*. Boston: PWS-Kent, 1988.

Hildebrand, D., and Ott, L. *Statistical Thinking for Managers*. 3d ed. Boston: Duxbury Press, 1991.

Judge, G. G.; Griffiths, W. E.; Hill, R. C.; Lutkepohl, H.; and Lee, T. *The Theory and Practice of Econometrics*. 2d ed. New York: John Wiley and Sons, 1985.

Kleinbaum, D. G.; Kupper, L. L.; and Muller, K. E. *Applied Regression Analysis and Other Multivariable Methods*. 2d ed. Boston: Duxbury Press, 1988.

Lawrence, K. D., and Marsh, L. C. "Robust Ridge Estimation Methods for Predicting U.S. Coal Mining Fatalities." *Communications in Statistics* 13 (1984): 139–149.

Lee, C. F., and Lynge, M. J. "Return, Risk, and Cost of Equity for Stock S&L Firms: Theory and Empirical Results." *Journal of the American Real Estate and Urban Economics Association* 13 (1985): 167–180.

Lunneborg, C. E. *Modeling Experimental and Observational Data*. Belmont, CA: Duxbury Press, 1994.

Mendenhall, W., and Beaver, R. J. *A Course in Business Statistics*. 3d ed. Boston: PWS-Kent, 1988.

Mendenhall, W.; Reinmuth, J. E.; and Beaver, R. J. *Statistics for Management and Economics*. 7th ed. Belmont, CA: Duxbury Press, 1993.

Miller, R. *MINITAB Handbook for Business and Economics*. Boston: PWS-Kent Publishing Co., 1988.

MINITAB Reference Manual, Release 10 for Windows. Minitab, Inc. July 1994.

MINITAB Reference Manual, Release 8, PC Version. Minitab, Inc. November 1991.

Moser, B. K., and Stevens, G. R. "Homogeneity of Variance in the Two-Sample Means Test." *The American Statistician* 46 (1992): 19–21.

Myers, R. H., *Classical and Modern Regression with Applications*. Boston: Duxbury Press, 1986.

Neter, J.; Wasserman, W.; and Kutner, M. H. *Applied Linear Statistical Models*. 2d ed. Homewood, IL: Richard D. Irwin, Inc., 1985.

Neter, J.; Wasserman, W.; and Kutner, M. H. *Applied Linear Regression Models*. 2d ed. Homewood, IL: Richard D. Irwin, Inc., 1989.

Ott, L. *An Introduction to Statistical Methods and Data Analysis*. 2d ed. Boston: Duxbury Press, 1984.

Peixoto, J. L. "A Property of Well-Formulated Polynomial Regression Models." *The American Statistician* 44 (1990): 26–30.

Ragsdale, C. T., and Stam, A. "Introducing Discriminant Analysis to the Business Statistics Curriculum." *Decision Sciences* 23 (1992): 724–745.

Ryan, B., and Joiner, B. *MINITAB Handbook*. 3d ed. Belmont, CA: Duxbury Press, 1994.

SAS/ETS User's Guide, Version 5. Cary, NC: SAS Institute Inc., 1985.

SAS Introductory Guide. 3d ed. Cary, NC: SAS Institute Inc., 1985.

SAS/STAT User's Guide: Vol. 1 and 2, Version 6. 4th ed. Cary, NC: SAS Institute, Inc., 1990.

Schafer, D. W. "Measurement-Error Diagnostics and the Sex Discrimination Problem." *Journal of Business and Economic Statistics* 5 (1987): 529–537.

Shapiro, S. S., and Wilk, M. B. "An Analysis of Variance Test for Normality (Complete Samples). *Biometrika* 52 (1965): 591–611.

Shiffler, R. E., and Adams, A. J. *Introductory Business Statistics with Computer Applications*. 2d ed. Belmont, CA: Duxbury Press, 1995.

Stack, S. "The Impact of Divorce on Suicide in Norway." *Journal of Marriage and the Family* 51 (1989): 229–238.

White, K. J.; Haun, S. A.; Horsman, N. G.; and Wong, S. D. *SHAZAM User's Reference Manual Version 6.1*. New York: McGraw-Hill, 1988.

Younger, M. S. *A First Course in Linear Regression*. 2d ed. Boston: Duxbury Press, 1985.

Index